ROUTLEDGE HANDBOOK
OF INDUSTRY AND DEVELOPMENT

The *Routledge Handbook of Industry and Development* is a global overview of industrialisation. Each chapter will provide readers with contemporary insights into this essential aspect of economic development.

Industrialisation has been at the forefront of discussion on economic development since the earliest days of development economics. But over the last fifty years, the manufacturing sectors of different countries and regions have grown at strikingly different rates. In 1960, developing countries took a very small share of global manufacturing production. Today the position has changed radically with fast growth of manufacturing in many parts of what was originally the developing world, particularly in China and the rest of East Asia. On the other hand, countries in Africa and parts of Latin America have been largely left behind by this process of industrialisation. This volume aims to illuminate this uneven development and takes stock of the current issues that hinder and support industrialisation in low and middle income economies.

This *Handbook* is a collection of chapters on different aspects of industrialisation experience in a range of countries. Key themes include: the role of manufacturing in growth, the nature of structural change at different stages of development, the role of manufacturing in employment creation, alternative options for trade and industrial policy, the key role of technology and technical change, and the impact of globalisation and the spread of global value chains and foreign direct investment on prospects for industrialisation. Several chapters discuss individual country experiences with examples from India, Mexico, South Africa and Tanzania, as well as an overview of African industrialisation.

This authoritative *Handbook* will be a key reference source for those studying or wishing to understand contemporary economic development. Offering inspiration and direction for future research, this landmark volume will be of crucial importance to all development economics scholars and researchers.

John Weiss is Emeritus Professor of Development Economics, University of Bradford, UK.

Michael Tribe is Honorary Lecturer, Department of Economics, University of Strathclyde, UK.

ROUTLEDGE HANDBOOK OF INDUSTRY AND DEVELOPMENT

Edited by John Weiss
and Michael Tribe

Routledge
Taylor & Francis Group

LONDON AND NEW YORK

First published 2016
by Routledge

2 Park Square, Milton Park, Abingdon, Oxfordshire OX14 4RN
52 Vanderbilt Avenue, New York, NY 10017

Routledge is an imprint of the Taylor & Francis Group, an informa business

First issued in paperback 2019

British Library Cataloging in Publication Data
A catalogue record for this book is available from the British Library

Library of Congress Cataloging in Publication Data
Routledge handbook of industry and development/edited by John Weiss
and Michael Tribe.
pages cm
Includes bibliographical references and index.
1. Industrialization. 2. Economic development. I. Weiss, John, 1948–
II. Tribe, Michael A., 1943–
HD2329.R68 2015
338—dc23
2015014784

ISBN: 978-0-415-81969-5 (hbk)
ISBN: 978-0-367-86797-3 (pbk)

Typeset in Bembo
by Book Now Ltd, London

CONTENTS

FIGURES

TABLES

CONTRIBUTORS

Prema-chandra Athukorala, Professor of Economics, Arndt-Corden Department of Economics, Australian National University, Australia

Ya-Shiou Chuang, Assistant Professor, Department of Marketing, Kainan University, Taiwan

Gaaitzen J. de Vries, Assistant Professor, Groningen Growth and Development Centre, Faculty of Economics and Business, University of Groningen, The Netherlands

Klaas de Vries, The Conference Board, Brussels, Belgium

Enrique Dussel Peters, Professor, Graduate School of Economics, National Autonomous University of Mexico (UNAM), Mexico City, Mexico

Nobuya Haraguchi, Industrial Research Officer, United Nations Industrial Development Organization, Vienna, Austria

Mozammel Huq, Professor of Economics, UttarBangla University College (National University), Bangladesh and Honorary Senior Lecturer, Department of Economics, University of Strathclyde, UK

Hossein Jalilian, Reader in Economic Development, Bradford Centre for International Development, University of Bradford, UK

Rhys Jenkins, Professor of Development Economics, School of International Development, University of East Anglia, UK

Uma Kambhampati, Professor of Economics, Department of Economics, University of Reading, UK

David Kaplan, Professor of Business Government Relations and Professor of Economics, University of Cape Town, South Africa

Raphael Kaplinsky, Honorary Professor, Science Policy Research Unit, University of Sussex, UK

Christian Kingombe, Economic Affairs Officer, Least Developed Countries Section, Research & Policy Analysis Branch, Division for Africa, Least Developed Countries and Special Programmes, UN Conference on Trade and Development, Geneva, Switzerland

Peter Lawrence, Emeritus Professor, Economics and Finance, Keele Management School, UK

Vincent Leyaro, Lecturer, Department of Economics, University of Dar-es-Salaam, Tanzania

Mike Morris, Director of PRISM (Policy Research on International Services and Manufacturing) and Professor, School of Economics, University of Cape Town, South Africa

Oliver Morrissey, Professor of Development Economics, School of Economics, Faculty of Social Sciences, University of Nottingham, UK

Khalid Nadvi, Reader, Institute for Development Policy and Management, University of Manchester, UK

Frederick Nixson, Emeritus Professor of Development Economics, University of Manchester, UK

Renee Prendergast, Reader in Economics, Queen's University Management School, Queen's University Belfast, UK

Kunal Sen, Professor of Development Economics and Policy, Institute for Development Policy and Management, University of Manchester, UK

Cornelia Staritz, Senior Researcher at the Austrian Foundation for Development Research (ÖFSE), Vienna, Austria

Dirk Willem te Velde, Head of Programme, International Economic Development Group, Overseas Development Institute, UK

Marcel Timmer, Professor of Economic Growth and Development, Groningen Growth and Development Centre, Faculty of Economics and Business, University of Groningen, The Netherlands

Fiona Tregenna, Professor, Department of Economics and Econometrics, University of Johannesburg, South Africa

Michael Tribe, Honorary Lecturer, Department of Economics, University of Strathclyde, UK

John Weiss, Emeritus Professor, Bradford Centre for International Development, University of Bradford, UK

Mo Yamin, Professor of International Business, Manchester Business School, UK

ACKNOWLEDGEMENTS

We wish to thank the contributors to this collection, who have produced original chapters which add substantially to the literature on global industrial development.

1

EDITORIAL INTRODUCTION

John Weiss and Michael Tribe

Introduction

Industrialisation is central to structural change. Historically, as most economies have evolved, workers have left the land to take up jobs in factories, mines or construction sites, attracted by the possibility of higher and more stable wages. Early theorists of development saw industry, most particularly its manufacturing branch, as critical to the transition of economies from low income to higher income status because of the higher productivity and technological dynamism associated with manufacturing.[1] When Arthur Lewis wrote of the possibility of a modern sector absorbing surplus labour at a constant real wage he had in mind that manufacturing would be the dominant 'modern' employer (Lewis, 1954). Similarly, when Ragnar Nurkse envisaged a group of new activities supporting each other in a pattern of balanced growth, these were to be principally new manufacturing activities (Nurkse, 1958). From the opposite perspective, when Albert Hirschman identified the key role of linkages in stimulating the new investment he pointed out that manufacturing creates more linkages than other branches of activity (Hirschman, 1958). Hence there is little doubt that from an early stage, industrialisation and economic development were seen as inextricably linked.

On the other hand, much of the early development literature stressed the serious obstacles to successful industrialisation. Having a large labour surplus clearly meant that low cost labour was available, but other preconditions in relation to funding for investment, and in particular the foreign currency needed to import the equipment needed for capital assets, were stressed. The perceived difficulty of generating export revenues in order to obtain this foreign currency was rationalised as a 'balance of payments constraint' on growth (Thirlwall, 1980). In addition, the unbalanced economic and political relations in the world economy were seen by some as posing major obstacles to the successful growth of poor countries. The interests of the rich centre and poor periphery were seen as in conflict, through an international trading system that kept the latter dependent on the export of primary commodities and through the activities of rich-country firms which dominated the domestic markets of manufactures of poor countries, either though imports or by displacing any nascent local capacity (Baran 1957).

From a contemporary perspective many of these arguments appear outdated and simplistic. Economic growth is now understood to be about a great deal more than the application of factors of production, with the role of technical change and the institutional base of an economy given prominence as key fundamentals. The role of economic policy in overcoming balance of payments difficulties and the potential for mutually beneficial trade are now better understood. Ownership of companies now appears to matter much less than other characteristics of their operations. However, this does not mean that all issues are resolved and that the most effective route to industrialisation has been mapped out. Progress in countries accepted as poor or 'developing' in 1960, for example, has been highly uneven with both success stories and disappointments, and it is important to address this difference in experience.[2]

This *Handbook* brings together a set of chapters on different aspects of industrialisation experience in these countries to give a contemporary perspective on industrialisation. These chapters focus on key issues from the academic and policy literature, combining a focus on general issues with a number of specific country experiences. This introductory chapter sets the scene by surveying the scope of the book. It begins with a discussion of why manufacturing has been seen as having a special role in initiating economic growth and structural change. A second section gives a broad comparison of the extent of industrialisation in 1960 and the present. A third section illustrates the unevenness of the industrial development of the past fifty years and the impact this has had on structural change in different economies. Given that in many poor or developing countries many manufacturing firms are small, a fourth section addresses the small-scale sector and its particular problems. The world economy has opened up considerably over this period in relation to trade and capital flows in a process now termed 'globalisation'. The important implications of this process for industrialisation are discussed in a fifth section. Of all the factors driving economic growth, technology and technical change are often considered the most critical. Poor or developing countries by definition are not technology innovators; however, as 'latecomers' they have the opportunity to draw on technology developed elsewhere. The role technology plays and has played in industrialisation is the focus of a sixth section. There is much evidence that policy towards industry matters and section seven discusses aspects of policy commencing with the wider debate on 'industrial policy' as a means of supporting and encouraging industrialisation and then moving to issues of regulation and competition policy. A final brief section concludes.

Why manufacturing?

A starting point for discussion of the theoretical approaches to 'industrialisation' can be provided by the observation that the process of economic growth and development is associated with significant increases in the level of labour productivity.[3] In turn, increases in labour productivity arise from the application of changes in production technology, from the introduction of adapted and new products, from the application of higher levels of investment to the production process, changes in the organisation of production, and from higher levels of skill embodied in the labour force. However, despite this focus on a contrast between traditional and modern segments of an economy there is a long tradition in economics, discussed in more detail in the chapter by Weiss and Jalilian, which argues that manufacturing industry is critical, particularly at relatively low levels of income per capita. This 'engine of growth argument' rests critically on the potential for technical change and productivity growth within manufacturing, arising from the scope for specialisation, learning and product diversification within the sector.

The normal historical pattern has been that in poor countries the share of manufacturing in total economic activity is very low, that as growth occurs and workers move out of agriculture it rises rapidly, but that once a threshold income level is passed the relative share of manufacturing starts to decline as demand shifts towards services. Recent experience has questioned some of these assumptions. As discussed in the chapter by Haraguchi, across all countries there is evidence that the relationship between a country's income per capita and the share of manufacturing in GDP has been weakening so that for a given level of income the manufacturing share predicted from cross-country analysis is lower than in earlier time periods. This is particularly the case where employment shares are concerned, with a weakening of the relationship between employment and manufacturing growth and absolute declines in manufacturing employment in some high income economies: the chapter by Tregenna in this volume discusses these issues. Furthermore, in recent decades rapid productivity growth has occurred outside manufacturing, in large part due to the application of computer-based technologies. The chapters by Timmer *et al.* and by Weiss and Jalilian in this volume produce detailed evidence on productivity levels and growth. Timmer *et al.* show that the level of manufacturing productivity remains higher than in services in all developing regions. The relative expansion of services has had a positive impact on overall productivity growth due to a static reallocation effect (as service productivity levels are above the economy-wide average) while the dynamic aspect of this reallocation is negative (as productivity growth in services is lower than in the declining sectors, principally manufacturing). However, there are regional differences and the net contribution of services to the growth of overall productivity exceeds that of manufacturing in Africa, whilst it is well below it in Latin America and roughly equal to it in Asia. Weiss and Jalilian disaggregate the productivity performance of services and show that it has been more rapid in some branches of services than in others. The implication is that the dynamic 'modern' branches of a low income economy need not all be concentrated within manufacturing and that parts of the service sector are showing the sort of dynamism associated in the past with manufacturing.

Nonetheless, recent empirical work has confirmed the importance of manufacturing to economic growth, particularly at lower income levels, where it can be an important source of employment at productivity levels well above those offered in the rest of the economy. At higher income levels it represents the key dynamic internationally traded activity. A shift in economic structure (whether in terms of share of value-added, employment or exports) in favour of manufacturing has been found to be associated with more rapid economic growth. This has been evidenced for growth accelerations (periods of sustained GDP growth). In part this may reflect a shift towards greater export activity driven by manufactured exports. Also shifts in economic structure in favour of manufacturing have been associated with higher aggregate productivity growth in Asia, and shifts against manufacturing have been associated with lower aggregate productivity growth in Africa and Latin America.[4] It should be noted that some empirical work also links the service sector share in GDP with growth accelerations, so the impact may not be unique to manufacturing (Timmer and de Vries, 2009).

Manufacturing post-1960 and uneven development

Countries that were identified as 'developing' in the 1950s accounted for only a very small share of global manufacturing. Precise statistics are unavailable, but one careful estimate suggests this was no more than 8 per cent in 1960, excluding China, where comparable data were unavailable (Table 1.1).[5] Unevenness was already present on a regional basis in 1960 with Latin American developing countries providing nearly 5 per cent of global manufacturing value-added, African countries 0.8 per cent and South and East Asian countries (excluding China) 1.8 per cent. By 2004 the picture was very different, with the same set of countries (excluding China) now providing just under 20 per cent of global manufacturing. The shares of Africa and Latin America were both slightly larger than in 1960, but the share for Asia was as much as 9 percentage points higher, driven by the rapid industrialisation in Korea, Singapore, Malaysia and Taiwan together with more modest growth, but a large absolute increase, in India.[6] The relatively recent impact of China on the world economy is reflected by the fact that it accounted for 8.5 per cent of global manufacturing in 2004.

Table 1.1 Estimates of percentage share of developing countries in world manufacturing value-added, 1960–2004 (constant 1990 prices)

	Africa	*South and East Asia*[a]	*China*	*Latin America*	*Developing countries*
1960	0.8	1.8		4.9	7.9
2004	1.1	10.8		5.3	19.6
2004[b]	1.0	10.0	8.5	4.9	26.6

Source: Szirmai *et al.* (2013: Table 1.4).

Notes
a Excluding China.
b Shares include China.

Alternative estimates distinguish between 'industrialised' and 'industrialising' economies, with the former higher income group now including Korea, Singapore, Taiwan and Malaysia as graduates from the developing-country classification due to their rapid growth and industrial development. With China still included in the group, the industrialising countries accounted for 18 per cent of global manufacturing value-added in 1992, whilst this share nearly doubled to 35 per cent in 2012. In 2012 the poorer, or least developed, countries in the industrialising group accounted for 9 per cent of the total value-added of this group or little more than 3 per cent of global value added.[7] This expansion of manufacturing was not only in simple low technology labour-intensive activity, since there are estimates to suggest that some developing countries also increased their share of world value-added in medium and high technology branches of manufacturing. In Latin America and sub-Saharan Africa where industrialisation has proceeded far more slowly, and has actually regressed in some countries, this was not the case as their share in these branches fell.[8]

A similar pattern occurs in relation to manufactured exports. The share of the developing-country group in world exports of manufactures was estimated at just below 6 per cent in 1963 and this rose rapidly to just below 31 per cent in 2005.[9] By region, Latin America's share rose by 3 percentage points over this period, whilst that of Africa fell by 0.5 percentage points from a low base. China is not included in the 1963 figures, but in 2005 its share in world manufactured exports was 9.4 per cent. Using the 'industrialised' and 'industrialising' classification, the share of the industrialising group in world manufactured exports rose from 14 per cent in 1997 to 30 per cent in 2011, although nearly half of the share in 2011 (or 13.5 per cent of world exports) was accounted for by China.[10]

The employment effects of manufacturing are an important source of income for the poor and their families in economies at relatively low levels of income, which is an issue discussed by Athukorala and Sen in this volume. However, given its relatively high productivity, the share of employment accounted for by manufacturing in most countries is well below its share of value-added. Data from the UNIDO database suggest that depending on an economy's income level the share of manufacturing in total employment lies between 10 per cent and 20 per cent, whereas the share in value-added can reach 30 per cent (UNIDO, 2013: Table 1.2).

In terms of broad shifts between regions, matching the relatively more rapid growth of value-added in the developing-country group, there has been a major relocation of manufacturing jobs with declines in formal employment in the old industrial centres of Europe, North America and Japan over the period 1970-2010. This was offset by substantial increases in manufacturing employment in the industrialising countries, particularly in China and other parts of East Asia, with China's share in global formal employment in manufacturing rising from 10 per cent in 1970 to 34 per cent in 2010 (Table 1.2). All industrialising regions showed a net growth in formal manufacturing employment over this period, although the increase and the absolute employment numbers are low for Africa. However, these employment figures exclude informal sector manufacturing, which is proportionately greater in lower income economies, and also manufacturing-related jobs in services which have become far more significant the in last two decades as manufacturing firms have out-sourced services to specialist providers. With these omissions included the total of manufacturing jobs would be much higher.

The general picture is therefore that from a low base in 1960 the group then known as 'developing countries' has, in the aggregate, experienced a significant expansion of manufacturing production and exports and this expansion has been one of the defining features of the recent history of the world economy. However, this process has been very uneven. The initial developing-country classification was income based and masked very considerable heterogeneity in population size, resources and income distribution. The increase in manufacturing output and exports since 1960 was, initially at least, concentrated heavily on a relatively small number of countries. For example, of the increase in manufacturing value-added in the developing-country group in the period 1973-80, over 70 per cent was provided by 10 countries which had 55 per cent of the population of the group. Four of these 10 – Brazil, Mexico, Korea and India – provided over 50 per cent of the incremental value added. Manufactured exports were even more concentrated in the 1970s with four South East Asian countries – Hong Kong, Taiwan, Korea and Singapore – accounting for 45 per cent of all manufactured exports from the group (Weiss, 1988: 14).

From the 1970s it became apparent that within the developing-country group some economies were proceeding much faster than others in the process of industrialisation. The first label to be attached to these was that of 'Newly Industrialising Countries' (NICs).The group was far from homogenous, but generally had the characteristic of a relatively large share

Table 1.2 Formal manufacturing employment: regions and selected countries, 1970–2010

Region	1970 numbers (millions)	Share of global manufacturing employment (%)	2010 numbers (millions)	Share of global manufacturing employment (%)
Europe	40	28.6	31	15.5
North America	20	14.3	14	6.9
East Asia and Pacific	31	22.2	97	48.4
South and Central Asia	6	4.3	20	10.0
Latin America and Caribbean	6	4.3	19	9.5
Individual countries				
USA	18.2	13.0	12.7	6.4
Japan	10.9	7.8	7.3	3.6
UK	8.0	5.69	2.3	1.1
Germany	8.2	5.9	6.2	3.1
China	14.2	10.1	68.8	34.3
India	4.7	3.4	11.8	5.9
Brazil	2.1	1.5	7.7	3.8
Korea	0.8	0.6	1.3	0.6
Indonesia	0.5	0.4	4.2	2.1
Vietnam	0.04	0.03	4.4	2.2
Bangladesh	0.2	0.2	5.1	2.5

Source: Calculated from UNIDO (2013) Table 2.1 and text. Data on Africa and Middle East are not reported.

of manufacturing in GDP. Table 1.3 includes data for countries most frequently associated with the group and shows a simple indicator of where each stood relative to the USA (taken as the frontier economy in terms of manufacturing technology) in 1980.[11] The position of each economy, using the same indicator, is shown for 2011 for comparison. As China only opened its economy in the 1980s it was not classed as an NIC at that time, but it is included here to show its speed of catch up. Taiwan was excluded from the original list due to lack of data. More recent categorisations of NICs would include Vietnam, Thailand and Indonesia as countries where manufacturing expansion has been rapid as evidenced by the employment data in Table 1.2.

The experience of countries in this original list is highly diverse. Singapore and Korea have now reached high income status with a higher manufacturing value-added per capita than the USA.[12] However, a number of the other NICs, including Argentina, Brazil (where resource-based activities have expanded in recent years) and the Philippines, have regressed relative to the USA. The case of Hong Kong is different, since manufacturing has declined dramatically with a focus on services and much manufacturing has migrated to mainland China where wages are considerably lower. The other NICs – Egypt, India, Malaysia, Mexico and Turkey – have experienced some catch-up relative to the USA, but only that of Malaysia can be said to be substantial. Egypt and India continue to have very low manufacturing value-added per capita. The experiences of India and Mexico are discussed in the chapters by Kambhampati and Dussel Peters respectively in this volume, while the case of China is discussed further below.

At the other extreme are economies with low incomes where industrialisation remains very modest. There are 78 economies in the UN classification of 'other industrialising economies' and 47 in the category 'least developed economies' (UNIDO, 2013: Table A8.2). For the former category, in 2011, average manufacturing value-added per capita at constant prices was only 4 per cent of the average for industrialised economies, and in the latter it was only 1 per cent (UNIDO, 2013: Table A6.1). Further, in a number of economies there was a process of de-industrialisation (using various definitions) where manufacturing regressed either in absolute or relative terms. Tregenna in this volume explores this issue in detail.

Table 1.3 Newly industrialising economies and catch-up, 1980–2011

Countries	Share of manufacturing in GDP, 1980 (%)	Relative to USA, 1980	Share of manufacturing in GDP, 2011 (%)	Relative to USA, 2011
Argentina	29.0	0.460	20.6	0.240
Brazil	27.0	0.250	13.6	0.130
Egypt	15.2	0.028	16.2	0.042
China	33.0	0.016	34.2	0.180
Hong Kong	21.5	0.480	1.8	0.100
India	14.2	0.010	14.9	0.030
Malaysia	19.4	0.096	26.7	0.290
Mexico	18.5	0.170	17.7	0.250
Philippines	26.9	0.059	22.4	0.056
Singapore	29.7	0.640	26.2	1.570
South Korea	22.8	0.180	27.7	1.060
Turkey	14.3	0.100	18.1	0.260

Source: Calculated from data in UNIDO (2013) and World Bank (2014).

Note: Original list also included Yugoslavia. Relative to USA is manufacturing value-added per capita divided by manufacturing value-added per capita in the USA.

Three chapters in this volume are devoted specifically to sub-Saharan Africa. Most commentators consider that in many aspects of development sub-Saharan Africa represent a special case. In relation to manufacturing development, shares in GDP are generally low and growth has been slow by standards elsewhere. Key problems highlighted in the literature relate to poor quality infrastructure, low productivity and in some countries governance issues.[13] However, the chapter by Lawrence in this volume demonstrates clearly that there is considerable diversity within the sub-Saharan African industrialisation experience – ranging between the comparatively advanced and substantial manufacturing sector of South Africa (the subject of Kaplan's chapter) and the small and undeveloped sectors of many other countries in the region (the chapter by Morrissey and Leyaro outlines Tanzanian experience in detail).

Structural change

Industrialisation has been linked closely with economic growth for theoretical reasons discussed in the chapter by Weiss and Jalilian. As already noted, economic growth generally involves a movement of labour off the land, out of agriculture and into either manufacturing or services. At relatively low income levels, productivity in manufacturing is generally above that in services and well above that in agriculture, so that the greater the shift of labour towards manufacturing the more there will be a 'structural change' bonus in the sense of a boost to the level of productivity in an economy,

Table 1.4 gives estimates for the average shares of manufacturing, agriculture and services in GDP for groups of developing and high income economies for the period from 1950. These figures mask regional differences between developing countries with Latin America being considerably more industrialised than other regions in 1950. The broad picture is of a drop in the share of agriculture in economic activity in the developing-country group, and a rise in the share of services and manufacturing.[14] In higher income economies there has been a very significant decline in the share of agriculture since 1950 and a substantial decline in that of manufacturing, consistent with the data presented in previous tables, with services taking a correspondingly more important role.

In general, across countries, there is a positive association between the growth of per capita income and the increase in the share of manufacturing value-added in an economy, or what can be interpreted as 'growth enhancing structural change'.[15] The recent experience of China, and earlier that of the East and South East Asian NICs, give the clearest examples of this process at work. On the other hand, several countries in Latin America have experienced a falling share of manufacturing in GDP and low growth of per capita income. However, generalisations about the association between income levels and the role of manufacturing need to be qualified carefully to allow for country circumstances. Analysis of the relationship between the

Table 1.4 Sectoral shares in GDP, 1950–2005 (percentage of GDP)

	1950			1980			2005		
	Agric.	*Manu.*	*Serv.*	*Agric.*	*Manu.*	*Serv.*	*Agric.*	*Manu.*	*Serv.*
Developing countries (68)	37	12	42	21	17	47	16	15	53
High income countries (21)	16	29	45	4	23	60	2	16	71

Source: Szirmai *et al.* (2013: Table 1.2); the original source is Szirmai (2009) which gives details of country composition of the groups.

Notes: Agric. = agriculture; Manu. = manufacturing; Serv. = services. The figures in brackets are number of countries in each group; the shares of mining and public utilities in GDP are not reported here.

level of income in an economy as measured by GDP per capita and the share of manufacturing in GDP has long recognised the existence of an inverted U-shaped relation with the share of manufacturing rising sharply at low income per capita, as labour moves out of agriculture, accelerating once a threshold income level has been passed and then stabilising at a peak before declining as income per capita rises further and high productivity services become more important in GDP.[16]

Work in UNIDO (2013) provides a helpful update of previous analyses by pooling data on 100 countries (industrialising and industrialised) and estimating the relation between the manufacturing share and income per capita for different periods; see Figure 1.1. For the period 1963-80 the manufacturing share peaks at around 24 per cent of GDP, an income per capita

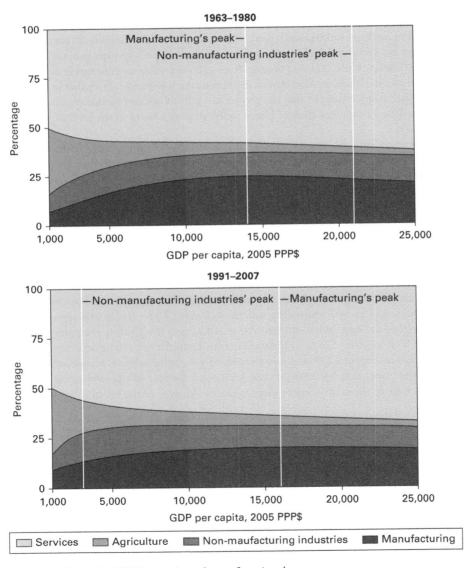

Figure 1.1 Relationship GDP/per capita and manufacturing share.

of US$14,000 in 2005 purchasing power parity prices.[17] At a very high income per capita of US$40,000 the manufacturing share falls to approximately that found at an income of around US$5,000, where industrialisation is starting to take off; hence the inverted U-shaped relation. However, the analysis confirms the results of earlier work, which found that this relationship has weakened over time (see for example Palma, 2005). The same analysis for a later period (1991-2007) finds that the manufacturing share peaks at a higher income per capita of $16,000 and at a lower share of GDP (20 per cent instead of 24 per cent), so that the curve has shifted downwards and to the right, suggesting that in the period of globalisation since the 1990s a given level of GDP is associated with a lower value of manufacturing activity.

These relationships are only averages across a diverse set of countries and it is recognised that factors like population size, resource endowments, institutions and policy decisions can all influence the relationship. Evidence for the importance of the first two of these is obtained where the sample of 100 countries is split into natural resource-rich and non-resource-rich, and into large and small economies, in relation to population size. As expected, in resource-rich economies the importance of manufacturing is lower at any given level of income and its share starts to decline at an income per capita of US$13,000. Again, as expected, population size creates the opposite effect. Large economies with large domestic markets can support a larger manufacturing sector and manufacturing takes a higher share of GDP at all levels of income in large, compared with small, economies. In large economies (defined as populations above 12 million) manufacturing reaches a peak at 24 per cent of GDP and at a per capita income of US$24,000.[18] The chapter by Haraguchi in this volume addresses structural change both at a macro level and within manufacturing in considerable detail, highlighting key empirical regularities and the extent of any change in these over time.

Given the diversity of experience noted above, we would not expect individual countries to adhere strictly to this relationship, and in general the faster growing countries have had higher than predicted levels of manufacturing in GDP. This is illustrated by an analysis for Asian countries for 2000. All the high growth countries in East and South East Asia (excluding Hong Kong) had higher than predicted shares of manufacturing in GDP with the difference particularly high for China, Korea and Singapore (around 7 percentage points). The Philippines, the outlier in the region in terms of its relatively modest growth, had a share in line with that predicted. However, India and several Central Asian economies had lower than predicted manufacturing shares, whilst the rest of South Asia – where growth had been relatively modest up to that point – had shares broadly in line with predictions.[19]

The general picture within manufacturing, as economies expand and incomes grow, is for low technology labour-intensive manufacturing activities (such as textiles, clothing, food, wood products and furniture) to dominate at low income levels. As GDP per capita rises their share in manufacturing declines and a combination of capital-intensive medium technology activities (such as metal products, basic metals and chemicals) and the labour-intensive elements of high technology activities (such as electronic goods) become more important. There are, of course, deviations from this general picture of structural change. However, a classification of manufacturing activities into 'early', 'middle' or 'late' depending upon the stage at which they become important in the sector as whole (Haraguchi and Rezonja, 2013: Tables 4.7 and 4.8) is possible. In general, of the early labour-intensive industries, the food and beverages sub-sector shows the most stability in value-added as income per capita of an economy increases. This contrasts with other labour-intensive activities such as clothing and textiles where value-added starts to decline at around US$15,000 per capita, and rising wages lead to production shifts to lower wage competitor economies (UNIDO, 2013: Figure 3.7). Medium technology capital-intensive activities show a decline in value-added at much higher levels of income per capita (at around US$35,000) in the case of basic metals, non-metallic minerals and fabricated metals (UNIDO, 2013: Figure 3.8). High technology activities generally continue to expand at higher levels of income (above US$ 40,000), although it is important to distinguish between labour-intensive simple assembly activities and more technologically complex product development and production, with value-added in the former clearly contracting as incomes and wages rise. As is to be expected, country size influences these patterns with large countries, as defined above, tending to be able to support a more diversified set of industries. For those industries where scale economies are important, such as motor vehicles and chemicals, and where technology is complex with high R and D content, such as electrical machinery, tend to be large in per capita terms in large economies.

How far governments can and should intervene to influence both the growth of manufacturing in the aggregate and its composition is an important policy issue, which is discussed in the chapter by Weiss on industrial policy. However, in development economics there is a long tradition which argues that both the composition and the size of manufacturing matter for growth. An early statement was the 'Mahalanobis model of growth', which stressed the need for a capital goods sector in which machines can make machines, replacing imported equipment and thus reducing the balance of payments constraint on investment.[20] The chapter on Indian industrial development by Kambhampati outlines the essentials of the Mahalanobis model, and it is also referred to in Nixson's chapter. This two-sector approach to industrial planning is closely related to the Harrod–Domar model and to basic input–output analysis. Current thinking on exchange rate management has undermined the logic of this policy, but the argument about production structure and growth has reappeared recently through a focus on the composition of exports. For example, analysis of export performance has argued that the composition in terms of sophistication or productivity of exports matters for GDP growth. The argument is that if industrialising countries can upgrade their export structure by increasing the share of higher technology goods similar to those exported by industrialised economies this will boost growth given the apparent strong demand and high productivity characteristics of these goods. Superficially at least, this explains Chinese experience from the 1990s onwards, and whilst not proved conclusively, the case is backed by econometric evidence (Hausmann *et al.*, 2007).

Small-scale industry

The chapters in this volume do not include discussion of the main contemporary characteristics and significance of the small-scale manufacturing (SSI) and small- and medium-scale manufacturing (SME) sub-sectors of developing countries (or for that matter of modern industrial economies). In part this was because a decision was taken to focus the small-scale aspect of industrial development on insights into the relationship between the SSI and SME sub-sectors and industrial clustering, largely because the literature in this area has been rich in recent years, and the chapter contributed by Nadvi represents the reflections of an authority on this issue.

The 'small industry' sub-sector ranges from micro-enterprises, which may be single proprietor entities, to medium-scale enterprises, which can be of quite considerable substance, the size criterion usually being based on number of workers. A World Bank/International Finance Corporation source contains the following basic definition, which tallies with conventional practice: "Where possible, MSMEs are defined as follows: micro enterprises: 1-9 employees; small: 10-49 employees; and medium: 50-249 employees" (Kushnir *et al.*, 2010: 2). Edusah (2013) has a comprehensive discussion of the definition of small-scale industry, including the 'informal sector', which is consistent with this quotation. Surprisingly, searching for definitions of small-scale industry and/or enterprises in the International Labour Organization and United

National Industrial Development Organization websites did not yield any generic results. It should be noted that reference to 'employees' in definitions of small-scale economic activity creates at least three methodological problems. First, many small industries are staffed by family, casual or part-time workers who may be self-employed or may not receive regular contractual remuneration and who are therefore not 'employees' as usually understood; second, many workers in small industries are likely to work irregular hours and so in order to achieve comparable 'employment' statistics it would be necessary to use a 'full-time equivalent' conversion factor; third, because of the part-time, and often seasonal, nature of work in small industries the use of 'full-time equivalent' conversion factors needs to allow for the fact that many workers will have multiple occupations, perhaps across a number of different sectors (e.g. working in each of clerical, teaching, agricultural and manufacturing activities within any one year). These issues make the assembly of small industry 'employment' statistics, and the estimation of comparable efficiency measures for small industry, exceptionally difficult (Tribe, 2005).

Two very valuable World Bank publications by Steel and Webster (1991, 1992) relating to small-scale enterprises in Ghana refer to a significant number of the key issues for this sub-sector of developing economies. For example, Steel and Webster (1991: 6) present data showing that in the mid-1980s in Ghana, as a best estimate, manufacturing in the small-scale sub-sector accounted for about 25 per cent of non-agricultural 'employment', compared with about 2.5 per cent accounted for by the large-scale sub-sector. On the other hand, small-scale manufacturing contributed about 25 per cent of manufacturing value added, compared with the 75 per cent contributed by the large-scale sub-sector. This comparison clearly demonstrates the labour productivity differential between the small- and large-scale manufacturing sub-sectors, productivity being defined as value-added per worker, even allowing for doubts about the accuracy of such data.

The literature on the small-scale enterprise sub-sector of the economy is exceptionally large and diverse, covering services (retail and maintenance activities as well as personal services such as hairdressing and laundry) in addition to agriculture and manufacturing. The development of the manufacturing sector has tended to include higher proportions of total product originating from large-scale establishments and it has been all too easy for this aspect of economic development to lead to the conclusion that the increasing size of large-scale manufacturing eclipses the small-scale sub-sector. However, there are several factors which lead to a continuing significance of the small-scale sub-sector in the process of economic growth and development.[21] These factors are: (a) locational, where markets for either raw materials or products are very localised; (b) process influences, with separable manufacturing operations, craft handiwork or simple assembly; and (c) market influences, relating to differentiated products with low-scale economies or industries serving small total markets. The implication of these factors is that market forces ensure the continuation of small-scale industries across all levels of industrial development, with the small-scale sub-sector being significant in both low income developing countries and high income industrially developed countries. Not least, small-scale operations have been important in what are now described as 'creative industries' (UNIDO, n.d.), including innovatory activity. Indeed, rather than small-scale firms growing into large-scale firms it is more likely that small-scale innovatory firms will be taken over by larger firms wishing to gain advantage from the ownership of the source of innovation. The rate of 'churning' or turnover (setting up and closing down) has been found to be rather high for small-scale enterprises (Mead and Liedholm, 1998: 64).

Finally, in considering issues around small-scale industry in economic development, it is important to consider whether this sub-sector is a source of dynamism or whether it simply acts as a 'sink' absorbing surplus labour in low productivity activities (Weiss, 2011: Chapter 6; Mensah *et al.*, 2007). In the recent literature on poverty reduction policies there has been some emphasis on the role of small enterprises (including those in the industrial sector) in employment creation (e.g. Green *et al.*, 2006). This involves, inter alia, a view of the extent to which small-scale industries generate profits, which are re-invested in expansion or replacement of capacity and in the adoption or adaptation of new technologies in a dynamic development process. The widely held view is that small-scale industries in developing countries are largely involved in a comparatively undynamic process of labour absorption so that even if a static employment creation function is fulfilled, this does not represent a continuing capacity to generate further employment and income generation through internally generated growth.

A factor in this context is the extent to which market segmentation is significant, and that limitations (particularly with respect to skilled labour) created a block on the development of the small-scale sector to the advantage of larger firms. Small firms owned and managed by people who have limited formal education, a modest amount of capital, and have skills which have largely been acquired informally are likely to experience difficulty in adopting more modern technology, so the 'leap' from the small-scale sector into the 'modern' sector requires knowledge and financial resources beyond their reach.[22]

Globalisation and manufacturing development

Manufactured products are internationally tradable, and policy towards trade has been linked inextricably with thinking on industrialisation, since the outset of what we think of as 'development economics'. The contribution of Arthur Lewis in terms of a model of development based on the transfer of labour from traditional low productivity to modern high productivity activities has been noted already as part of the early rationale for industrialisation. His contribution in the area of trade policy is equally interesting. Writing in relation to the development of the former 'Gold Coast' colony in West Africa – now the independent state of Ghana – in the *Report on the Industrialisation of the Gold Coast* (Lewis, 1953) he provided detailed policy guidance for the development of the manufacturing sub-sector. The Report is particularly notable because it was very influential across a wide range of sub-Saharan African countries, and indeed in developing countries more broadly. It came to measured, or even cautious, conclusions relating to the application of protective or promotional policies for industrial development.

> We may sum this up by recommending that the government should be prepared where necessary to give some assistance to any of the industries listed in Chapter II as 'favourable' or 'marginal'. The assistance should be for a short period only, say not exceeding five years, and should be limited in amount, say to the equivalent of a 20 percent tariff on imports. Industries which are not likely to be able to stand on their own feet without longer or greater assistance should not be supported.
>
> (Lewis, 1953: para 234)

This recommendation might be seen as supporting the 'infant industry' argument for protecting 'new starts', but Lewis's cautious and comprehensive analysis also includes discussion of 'economies of agglomeration', which he saw as potentially arising from the collective impact of a large number of 'new starts', which together could generate a kind of 'virtuous circle' and which links with the idea of clusters of similar and complementary firms familiar today and discussed in the chapter by Nadvi.

Within the same intellectual tradition as Lewis's contributions comes the 'model' of deteriorating terms of trade for the exports of developing countries' primary products developed independently by Prebisch and Singer, and which was also of considerable significance for industrialisation strategies from the early 1960s (Prebisch, 1950; Singer, 1950; Hadass and Williamson,

2001). The word 'model' has been used deliberately (despite the criticisms of Krugman (1997) in this respect) because the Prebisch–Singer argument depended upon the interaction of price and income elasticities within international market structures so that in the first instance the deteriorating terms of trade thesis was based upon logic – i.e. a 'model'. With this logical structure it was then possible to look for empirical evidence – and there is a significant and diverse literature relating to this evidence. The nub of the 'industrialisation' argument which is linked to the Prebisch–Singer thesis was that if developing countries were experiencing long-term deterioration of their terms of trade when economically dependent upon primary product exports, then the alternative was to develop manufacturing industry – i.e. to diversify their economies. If such industries were initially uncompetitive, the need to support them until they 'grew up' followed logically.

Subsequently the literature and the argument relating to the deteriorating terms of trade of developing countries took on a new direction, with attention being switched to the terms of trade between 'traditional' or 'low technology' manufactures and 'advanced' or 'high technology' manufactures (Sarkar and Singer, 1991; Sapsford *et al.*, 1992; Sapsford and Chen, 1999). Lall (2000) provided a widely used classification of internationally traded goods, which allowed a disaggregation of the structure of a country's export basket on the basis of technological characteristics. Similar market structures were identified for low technology exports of manufactures by developing countries to those which had earlier been identified for primary product exports. It perhaps seemed that developing countries could not 'win', so that deteriorating terms of trade for developing-country exports of these 'low technology' manufactures were the new focus of attention. This argument has been picked up in a slightly different context in studies noted above on the impact of export sophistication on economic growth (Hausmann *et al.*, 2007). In various ways these issues are raised in relation to industrial development in the chapters by Dussel Peters, Nixson, Jenkins and Lawrence.

Trade policy has provided a significant battleground between economists of diametrically opposed neo-classical and heterodox–structuralist allegiances. In his chapter Nixson provides a welcome contemporary overview of the controversies surrounding the 'import substitution' approach, arguing that in many respects the industrialisation perspective of development economists through the 1950s to the 1980s was largely eclipsed by the liberalisation and export orientation approach of trade policy protagonists in the 1990s. Nixson suggests that the perception that the trade policy emphasis needed to replace industrialisation strategies in development priorities was misplaced and that at least some of the policy approaches which have been regarded as mutually exclusive (such as import substitution and export orientation) can comfortably co-exist within a more holistic approach. Successful economies have both replaced imports with domestic production and exported to the world market and there is evidence that this process can be mutually supporting with success in one market leading to success in another.

The significance of trade issues has been heightened in the last two decades by the reduction in trade barriers and the substantial increase in trade and capital flows between nation states in the world economy. These flows are part of a wider process of globalisation creating an exchange of products, and a transfer not just of funds, but of ideas and values as well. The liberalisation of trade under the World Trade Organization (WTO) system and the removal of restrictions on capital flows and the integration of capital markets in a global financial system have been the policy drivers of this process. However, and critically, the economic potential of globalisation to raise incomes has been driven by technical change. One of the clearest areas is in transport and communications technology. The reduction in transport costs arising from containerisation, the increased size of ocean-going freight carriers, and harbour development have significantly affected international transactions costs. The influence of electronic communications, moving through telex and fax to internet technology over about three or four decades, has radically changed business practices and the methods of undertaking contractual and financial arrangements. Combined with the globalisation of financial and other business institutions the world has become very much more integrated – as evidenced, for example, by the speed of transmission of the 1997 Asian financial crisis and the more recent 'contagion' associated with the 2008 financial crisis.

Apart from explicit moves towards the establishment of 'single markets' – particularly within the European region – there has been a global tendency towards reducing barriers within product, service and financial markets, the main exception being labour markets. In the context of labour markets a limited degree of 'free movement' on a legitimate basis has been introduced within the European Union, while by way of contrast the extent of illegal 'human trafficking' has become a major international issue. Broadly the free movement of goods, services and capital has facilitated the business of transnational companies and has had a considerable impact on international industrial development as is clear from several of the chapters included in this collection. In particular, transnational corporations providing capital, technology and management skills through foreign direct investment (FDI) programmes have played a significant role in the manufacturing sector of a number of developing countries since the 1960's. Their contribution to development and industrialisation has been a hotly contested area and the role of these large international firms is discussed in the chapter by Yamin and Nixson. International product and safety standards have also been associated with the globalisation process, but these are by no means universal in their effective implementation. However, to some extent the wider application of international labour standards has been achieved through contracting systems. The application of such international standards can affect industrial production costs, but in the 'legitimate' (as opposed to the 'pirate') markets this impact is often regarded as an essential part of an international business culture. There is a significant literature on these issues, often within the context of corporate social responsibility (CSR) indicating that there is active attention paid to them (e.g. Jørgensen *et al.*, 2003; Andersen and Skjoett-Larsen, 2009).

For manufacturing development, globalisation offers great potential for lower and middle income countries to upgrade their industrial base and export to the world market. As discussed in the chapter by Kingombe and te Velde, many countries have established special economic zones operating under close to free trade conditions and with special tax and other incentives as a means of accessing the world market. However, globalisation also poses serious challenges, which are discussed in many of the chapters of this volume. In particular, two issues are highlighted here. First, trade liberalisation in terms of reduction of barriers to imports has historically been a process that countries have undertaken after they have achieved a minimum level of industrial capability and competitiveness. Examples include Great Britain in the nineteenth century, Japan in the 1960s and, more recently, China in the 1990s when it started its negotiations to enter the WTO. This liberalisation from a 'position of strength' is in contrast to the process in a number of countries in Latin America, Asia and Africa, where liberalisation was intended to improve efficiency through a competitive 'shock' to previously sheltered producers. The outcome of this policy experiment was not always negative, but it has been associated with a contraction of segments of manufacturing in a number of countries. The chapters by Tregenna on de-industrialisation and Lawrence on African experience address these issues.

The reduction in transport and communication costs combined with the lowering of trade barriers have made possible an increasing fragmentation of the process of production in many manufacturing activities. Global production networks, or global value chains, are terms used to describe this fragmentation, whereby parts and components are shipped across national boundaries, to take advantage of lower production costs in different sites, with value-added contributed in several different locations until they are combined into a final product. This process has been described as 'trade in tasks' as opposed to 'trade in products', with different tasks undertaken in different locations. In lower income and lower-middle income economies the tasks selected by the lead firms in their economies within the global network will be primarily labour-intensive because these countries' cost advantage will lie in their lower wage costs. The existence of these global networks at one level makes it easier for follower-economies to industrialise. Lead firms in high income economies in possession of the brand name and technology for the final product will sub-contract parts of the production process and typically the design and technology needed for a specific task. On the other hand, this process risks making the process of producing indus-trial goods less profound in the sense of creating few local linkages with suppliers or limiting the adaption and modification of the imported technology, since sub-contracting firms will have to meet strict standards and conditions set by the lead firm. There is also an issue of the extent to which activities set up in this context are 'footloose' and can be moved from one country to another very easily. However, the East Asian experience in Korea, Taiwan and Singapore, and to a lesser extent Thailand and Malaysia, shows that follower firms can evolve to develop their own designs and ultimately brands whilst starting out under this form of contracting arrangement, but the process is far from easy or automatic. The three chapters by Staritz and Morris, Kaplinsky and Chuang separately discuss aspects of the key issues associated with participation in global produc-tion networks. The chapter by Dussel Peters discusses the case of Mexico, a relatively industrialised upper middle income economy, whose manufacturing sector is very closely integrated into such networks and where manufacturing has developed on a highly import-intensive basis.

Innovation and technological change

The 'modern' theory of economic growth places technology change at the centre of its formulations (Romer, 1994; Pack, 1994; Weil, 2005: Chap. 8). In turn, the industrial sector provides the means by which new technology is embodied in production, distribution and other elements of the economy through the manufacture of capital goods and intermediate products. The way in which new technology is developed and adopted has been of great interest to economists for a very long time, and Prendergast's chapter in this volume discusses this aspect of industrialisation comprehensively. Over the years the literature on the role of technology in development has ranged widely. Also in this volume, Huq discusses the choice of technique issue, which exercised many authors in the past. The 'appropriate technology' movement always tended to focus particularly on 'traditional' small-scale technologies (for example the Indian cottage industry sub-sector mentioned by Kambhampati in her chapter), while technological 'appropriateness' from an economic viewpoint could equally point in the direction of large-scale technology or cutting edge modern technology (even at a small scale – e.g. solar or hydro power and computer-controlled production).

Lancaster's 'characteristics approach' to the analysis of consumption economics is particularly suggestive in this context (Lancaster, 1974: Chapter 7), and was used by Stewart in her influen-tial 1970s book on *Technology and Underdevelopment* (Stewart, 1977: Chapter 1). Over the years there have been considerable changes to the nature of consumption technology and to the char-acteristics of consumer products (one of the issues featured by Prendergast in her chapter), not only relating to the more obvious electrical goods but also to processed foodstuffs, both of which have been related to considerable changes to household technology, particularly in developed industrial countries but also for higher and middle income households in developing countries. These developments have been closely associated with changes in the characteristics of manu-factured products – and in the production technologies which produce them.

Broad international trends associated with globalisation have significantly changed the nature of the debate over technology and development. First, there has been a clear trend starting early

15

in the twentieth century for a bias in technological change in favour of skill-using technology. This is in direct contrast with nineteenth century technological change which was largely focused on skill-saving or deskilling as tasks previously undertaken by skilled artisans were replaced by repetitive factory-based operations. This demand for skills was accompanied by higher capital investment, so that skilled labour and capital became complements rather than substitutes. The trend towards this 'skills bias' present during most of the twentieth century was intensified from the late 1970s with the spread of computer-based production systems. It has been suggested that the spread of information and communications technology has been the equivalent of earlier key technological breakthroughs like the introduction of the printing press, steam power and electricity. The concept of a 'general purpose technology' with pervasive effects across the economy, a continual process of technological improvement leading to falling costs for users and a continual process of innovation associated with the new technology, has been put forward to characterise these breakthroughs (Bresnahan and Trajtenberg, 1995).

This skills bias has been explained by the rising supply of skilled workers in the technology-creating economies and may partly account for the fall in real wages of low-skilled workers. Across developed economies it is now fairly well established that technical change in a skills-biased direction has been a key factor in creating a falling labour share in GDP, as unskilled jobs are replaced by capital. The significance of this for low and middle income countries is that as technology importers, the technology transferred to them has been created in response to market conditions in the innovating economies. This technology bias effect has been put forward as one of the explanations as to why the one of the key predictions of standard trade theory, that the abundant factor – in this case unskilled labour – will see a rise in its relative price after barriers to trade are reduced, has rarely been fulfilled. If developing-country firms are forced by competition, which is induced by trade liberalisation, to import best-practice technology where there is little scope for factor substitution, this will raise the demand for skilled relative to unskilled labour and create a skills bias into the economy (see for example, Robbins, 2003; Arbache *et al.*, 2004). It also helps to explain the relatively weak employment effect from manufacturing growth in many countries.

Another strand of the literature on technological development has focused on 'technology transfer', including the commercialisation of technology and the role of transnational corporations in controlling technology and markets. A major contribution in the literature on the role of technology in industrial development was that of Vernon (1966, 1979) who developed a model of the 'product cycle', which included technological innovation, maturation and transfer between innovator and importer economies. Foreign direct investment is a means of accessing technology, which raises a distinct range of issues including how far technology brought to an economy by transnational corporations spills over as a knowledge externality to national producers. The three chapters by Yamin and Nixson, Nixson and Jenkins discuss aspects of the role of foreign direct investment, highlighting some of its limitations as a means of transforming the technological base of an economy.

The spread of global production networks has offered a new route for technology transfer which has been termed 'technology lending' as opposed to 'transfer', with international firms providing their technology to produce parts and components needed for other elements of their global operations. In this interpretation industrialisation has been made both 'easier and faster' but at the same time 'less meaningful' (Baldwin, 2011). Before the 1980s, export success required a deep industrial base, a network of domestic suppliers and technological mastery. In the new era of globalisation, developing-country firms can link with international production networks and draw on the technology and marketing links of the lead firms within these chains. This has the important implication that much of the technology which is lent/borrowed is firm-specific to the 'lead' firm and is closely protected in order to prevent imitation. Hence when developing-country firms are committed to global supply chains there is the risk that they will now find it considerably harder than their predecessors from East Asia did in moving through the various stages of 'own equipment manufacture', where they first work with the lead firm in design, then manufacture with their own designs, and finally break into world markets with their own brand. Chuang in this volume has examples of this process. Many observers have commented upon the risk that globalisation is creating a distinction between headquarter economies, where lead firms are based, where technology originates and manufacturing profits are high, and 'client' factory economies where there is little technical innovation, and wages and profits are low (see for example Kaplinsky, 2005).

Industrial policy: What can governments do?

Historical experience and economic theory indicate that governments have a role in supporting and influencing the process of industrialisation. Whether the evidence comes from Germany or the USA in the nineteenth century or from Japan and Korea in the twentieth there are well-documented cases of state intervention aiming to build up initially uncompetitive activities. Similarly, in the presence of real world 'market imperfections', economic theory implies that, where some activities have higher productivity potential and generate more externalities than others, there is a case for their promotion and special treatment. Attempts by governments to accelerate and guide the process of industrialisation by raising the relative profitability of manufacturing, and within it certain branches of manufacturing, are what we term 'industrial policy', which is central to the chapters by Weiss, Kaplan, Kambhampati and Morrissey and Leyaro in this volume. However, directly or indirectly, all of the chapters in this volume raise the issue of what governments can and should do.

The debate on the role of and scope for industrial policy is intense with widely differing views. The issue is clouded by the fact that good industrial policy, whilst important, is not easy to implement and the record in many parts of the developing world is at best mixed. Alongside the success stories from East Asia are well-documented failures from elsewhere, and there is always a risk of 'policy capture' where vested interests, not economic efficiency, drive decisions on where to subsidise or promote. The alternative view of what governments should do addresses the so-called 'investment climate' by reducing regulation, streamlining bureaucracy and improving infrastructure, leaving decisions on where to invest to the private sector. The chapter by Weiss points out that countries such as Singapore and Malaysia, which are generally perceived as having 'good' investment climates, have also pursued active industrial policies in the sense of having a vision for the sector and taking steps to implement this.

The profitability of economic activities can be boosted by industrial policy in a number of ways. As Nixson discusses in his chapter, in the past, trade policy was central to industrial policy, offering either a protected home market or export promotion through subsidies. The wave of trade liberalisation in most countries and the rules of WTO have changed this perspective over the last two decades, and have not excluded the possibility of further policy interventions. Import quota restrictions and export subsidies contravene WTO rules and member countries have to agree to set maximum tariffs that apply to imports from other WTO members.[23] However, in many low and lower middle income countries maximum (that is, 'bound') tariffs are well above actuals so that the discretion to use tariff protection still remains should a country wish to use it. The main restriction on freedom to do this comes from bilateral or multilateral free trade arrangements which countries negotiate with trading partners, and not from the

WTO rules per se. Similarly, policy tools such as local content agreements which force foreign firms to source a proportion of costs locally, and incentives offered on more favourable terms to individual firms or to priority 'strategic' sub-sectors, are clearly against WTO rules.[24] However, there are ways around these restrictions, which many governments have pursued. Government procurement contracts, for example, are subject to separate agreements, which few countries have signed up for, and thus provide a means of implementing an implicit local content policy. 'Specific' subsidies, which are defined as support which is not available to all producers who meet a specified objective criteria, are ruled out in principle by the WTO; however, many countries use packages of incentives in terms of tax rates, access to credit on favourable terms, infrastructure or training provisions which can be tailored either to individual sectors or to individual firms.[25] Such specific measures are actionable at the WTO, but the cases which have been brought are relatively few and usually involve high income economies.

As an illustration of the range of industrial policy measures that have been, and continue to be, applied we can consider the case of China, whose dramatic success in manufacturing has been highlighted earlier.[26] At a macro level capital controls have been used to support a policy of deliberately maintaining an undervalued exchange rate, in a form of 'exchange rate protection' in order to boost the traded goods sector, principally manufacturing. However, in addition a wide range of other measures have been pursued.[27] These measures have included:

- fiscal incentives offering tax reductions or exemptions for either general or specific (for example R and D) forms of manufacturing investment;
- research grants, either to individual companies or research institutes;
- financial support in the form of access to credit, often at subsidised rates and 'directed' through state-owned banks to priority areas;
- controls on FDI, for example with requirements for joint ventures in some sub-sectors as a means accessing the technology of multinational firms;
- use of government procurement to encourage national firms and to support innovation;
- creation of national technology standards in a wide range of manufacturing, which can act as an entry barrier to foreign products;
- infrastructure investment to serve the needs of industry.

A key area of industrial policy relates to technology and to the upgrading of the production structure. East Asian experience suggests clearly that technological upgrading and movement into more sophisticated product lines do not occur automatically but require a combination of risk-taking and learning strategies by companies, combined with support from public policy. Successful firms need their own R and D facilities but these need to be supplemented by access to external and foreign sources of knowledge.

Several routes for this type of access have been used in East Asian countries.[28] One form is the creation of public–private research consortia where firm capability is low and a public research agency will have to play a key role on the research side and transfer knowledge on findings and designs to the private partners. Successful examples of this collaboration include the development of indigenous digital telephone switch technology in Korea and technology for laptop computers in Taiwan in the 1980s. China's recent heavy public investment in solar energy technology also falls into this category. Another approach is the development of contracts with foreign technology partners in order to develop technology in collaboration with a national firm. A successful example is Hyundai's development of its own engine design in the 1970s in collaboration with a UK-based firm in order to free it from reliance on Mitsubishi technology. A third route is learning from FDI, with joint ventures with foreign firms used as a mechanism for technology transfer from the foreign firm to the local partner. As noted above, in several sectors the government of China has taken advantage of the size and importance of the domestic market to pressure foreign firms to transfer their technology to local partners, an example of which has led to the mastery of digital telephone switch technology by local producers. This route is open to only a limited number of countries, however, where domestic market access is of sufficient importance to create a strong incentive to share technology. A fourth approach is forward engineering, where an academic research institution, through the generation of scientific knowledge, sets up an enterprise with government support in order to apply this knowledge in a commercial context. Chinese universities and research institutes have been active in commercialising new technologies, although this route has been less common in Taiwan and Korea. Another route has been the acquisition of foreign technologies and brands through mergers and acquisitions. In China this has been part of an explicit technology strategy and it is viewed as a means of achieving rapid catch-up saving both the time and resources required in building up a firm's own brand and designs. Lenovo's acquisition of the personal computer division of IBM falls into this category. The chapters by Prendergast and by Chuang discuss many of these issues.

The success of some of these industrial policy initiatives in China is disputed. For example, it has been argued that whilst the imposition of joint ventures with local ownership requirements has allowed access to foreign technology, transnationals have been less prepared to transfer frontier technologies to national firms than they would be if the local production capacity were to be a wholly owned subsidiary. Similarly, whilst state-funded new initiatives, such as investment in wind and solar energy products, may give China 'first-mover' advantage in this area, some see this investment as speculative, and suggest that it will take a considerable time before yielding economic returns.[29] However, it may be necessary to take a broader view of these interventions. Like industrial policy in Japan, Korea and Taiwan 30 or 40 years earlier, policy in China has not been without mistakes and ineffective interventions. What matters is the overall impact of a series of policies. They have coincided in time with China's industrial transformation and it seems unlikely that their net impact has held back this transformation, rather than supporting it.[30]

Central to industrial policy is the question of how to maintain competition where governments are offering support to locally based producers. A remarkable feature of the literature on industrial economics is that for developed industrial countries the focus has been heavily on 'structure, conduct and performance' referring particularly to the nature of competition and to monopoly and merger policy, while for developing countries the focus has tended to be on industrial development, technology choice and international trade. This contrast has tended to decline in recent years, so that greater attention is now given to the issues of competition and regulation policy in the development context. Much of the change in emphasis for such countries has been contributed by the international donor community (for example Kitzmuller and Martinez Licetti, 2012; DFID, 2008) but there has been an increasing amount of independent research and writing on this issue (for example Ellis and Singh, 2010; Cook *et al.*, 2007). However, there appears to have been only limited recent research on the practice and effectiveness of competition policy in low and middle income countries. One of the key questions for competition policy in many low and lower middle income countries relates to their comparatively small market size, which makes the likelihood of monopolistic, or monopsonistic, power significant. Another question concerns the asymmetric power wielded by transnational corporations relative to the governments of these countries. A third important issue is the limited capacity of governments to investigate, assess and implement countervailing measures relating to restricted competition. India and South Africa, both of which feature in chapters in this volume, are examples of middle income countries which have well-established competition commissions – although the number of countries with competition regulation systems in place has been increasing.[31]

Another, associated, area which has been receiving more attention in recent years has been the impact of various types of regulation. Again, this is an issue which has been given much emphasis in developed countries, but less in a development context – no doubt in part because of the resource limitations relating to effective implementation of regulations in poorer countries.[32] Discussion of regulatory impact often takes an abstract form, without specifying any particular element of 'regulation'. This is true, for example, of much of the methodological approach to regulatory impact assessment. However, many areas within which regulations are common in developed countries have become more significant in low and middle income countries in the process of 'globalisation'. The WTO has played an active role in this area, in part because of the role of standards as non-tariff barriers to trade.[33] Another international body with interests in this area is the International Labour Organization. A number of international non-governmental organisations and other pressure groups have been very active in pursuing cases where it is suspected that international trade in manufactures involves breach of international standards and/or the exploitation of labour. Unfortunately it was not possible to arrange to include chapters in this book on these developing areas of interest, but they are of long-term significance for industrial development.

Conclusions

This introductory chapter has raised themes that are elaborated in subsequent chapters. There has been no attempt to summarise the chapters that follow as these are detailed works that merit reading in full. Given the very wide nature of the subject matter we have not managed to include chapters on all aspects of industrialisation and this introduction has highlighted what we see as a few important gaps. Some of the debates from the early development literature, for example on import substitution versus export promotion trade strategies and on the choice of techniques now seem rather dated. Others, for example on the role of transnational corporations, on routes for technology transfer and on the role of government in development, remain as active as ever. Consensus on policy towards industry remains elusive and the chapters that follow give a sense of this.

The broad messages we wish to convey from this Introduction are the following:

- Manufacturing, whilst perhaps not as special as once thought, remains an important source of income and employment, particularly in low and lower middle income economies.
- Over the last 55 years there has been a very uneven development of manufacturing in countries thought of as 'developing' in 1960, with some growing very rapidly and others stagnating.
- Technology and technological upgrading is critical to manufacturing development and all successful economies have gone through this process of upgrading, initially relying on technology from abroad.
- Trade policy has been linked with manufacturing development in the past in a protectionist way and more recently in the context of more open trading relationships.
- Globalisation has created both challenges and opportunities for low and middle income economies and the spread of global value chains has had important consequences for the way production is organised in many parts of manufacturing.
- Industrial policy is controversial, can be interpreted in different ways but remains important as mean of supporting the sector.

Notes

1 In international statistical compilations 'Industry' is composed of manufacturing, construction, mining and public utilities, although most discussions of industrialisation tend to focus on the manufacturing component and that is the sense in which the term is used in this volume.

2 Past overviews of industrialisation are in Sutcliffe (1971) and Weiss (2011, 2002, 1988).

3 The productivity issue is discussed in considerable detail in the chapter by Timmer, de Vries and de Vries in this volume.

4 See Hausmann *et al.* (2005), Rodrik (2007) and ADB (2007) for growth accelerations and McMillan and Rodrik (2011) for an analysis of productivity and structural change.

5 Including China is unlikely to add more than one percentage point as when the data are available for 1980 China took no more than 1.4 per cent of global manufacturing value-added.

6 Korea, Singapore, Taiwan and Malaysia are no longer classed as developing countries in UN publications such as UNIDO (2013) but they need to be included in the developing group in comparisons such as this.

7 Data from UNIDO (2013) Table S2.

8 Data refer to the period 1980-2000; see UNIDO (2004) Table A.4.

9 See Szirmai *et al.* (2013: Table 1.5); this group includes Korea, Singapore, Malaysia and Taiwan.

10 Calculated from UNIDO (2013) Table S3.

11 The list comes from Weiss (1988) Table 1.7.

12 Taiwan had a manufacturing value-added per capita approximately 80 per cent of the US level in 2011, so its pace of catch-up has also been rapid.

13 Dinh *et al.* (2012) examine the competitiveness of manufacturing in a number of African economies and compare production costs there with the cost of imports from China and Vietnam. Page (2013) and Collier (2000) discuss the future of manufacturing in Africa.

14 The authors suggest that their estimates will understate the importance of manufacturing due to the outsourcing of manufacturing-related activities to service suppliers and to the relative price effect created by higher inflation in service prices. These estimates are for shares at current prices and they suggest a constant price calculation would show a higher manufacturing share, although this estimate is not available.

15 See McMillan and Rodrik (2011) for evidence of this.

16 The classic early works on this were Kuznets (1957) and Chenery (1960).

17 All income per capita figures cited here are at 2005 purchasing power parity US dollars.

18 The analysis by resource endowment and population size covers the period 1963-2007.

19 The regression analysis used to derive the predictions made manufacturing share a function of income per capita, income per capita squared, trade share in GDP and population size; see ADB (2007: 294).

20 See Mahalanobis (1953) and a variant the 'basic industry strategy' of Thomas (1974).

21 These were identified by Staley and Morse (1965: Chapter 5) in a notable book about small-scale industry development – and were reiterated by Sutcliffe (1971: 236-237).

22 Two studies on tube-well development in Pakistan exemplify this process (Aftab and Rahim, 1986, 1989).

23 Quota restrictions are allowed exceptionally where significant market dislocation may result from a surge in imports and least-developed countries can still offer export subsidies.

24 Local content requirements contravene the Agreement on Trade and Industrial Measures (TRIMS) and specific subsidies are ruled out by the Agreement on Subsidies and Countervailing Measures.

25 Attracting high technology activities is now a priority for many countries and the experience of Costa Rica in attracting the semiconductor producer Intel is widely cited. As part of the negotiations the government, through its investment promotion agency, had to guarantee key infrastructure facilities – principally a renovation of the national airport earlier than planned, with special facilities for Intel freight, the building of a new power substation dedicated to the Intel plant and vocational training in which the national technological institute would design a training programme for IT workers, engineers and managers in collaboration with Intel. These were in addition to changes to the tax law to offer special tax treatment to Intel – see Moran (2015).

26 Surveys of Chinese manufacturing experience focusing on the role of the state from different perspectives are in Wu (2013) and Lo and Wu (2014). The discussion of industrial policy in China here draws on Poon (2014).

27 The issue of whether the Chinese currency (RMB) remains undervalued and by how much is still contentious.

28 This draws on Lee (2013: Chap. 7). Lee (2013) develops a theory to explain the success of Korea and Taiwan in terms of their focus on 'short cycle' technologies where technical change is rapid and therefore the advantage of established producer economies is less.

29 Long (2005) examines technology transfer in joint ventures versus wholly owned subsidiaries. Mazzucato (2013) discusses the support for the wind and solar power industry in China as one of the examples of a successful 'entrepreneurial state'.

30 Aghion *et al.* (2012) have a detailed econometric analysis of the impact of industrial policies in China (defined as tax holidays and subsidies) on manufacturing firms. They find such policies have a stronger positive impact on productivity when they are targeted at more competitive sectors.

31 Two publications which give some indication of the extent of competition policy in a development context are a substantial UNCTAD document edited by Qaqaya and Lipimile (2008) and a paper presented to an OECD Global Forum on International Investment meeting by Sengupta and Dube (2008).

32 Two significant publications are those by Kirkpatrick and Parker (2008) and Parker and Kirkpatrick (2012), the former being a major edited book and the latter a literature review undertaken for the OECD. In their 2012 OECD report, Parker and Kirkpatrick, inter alia, attempt to redress the balance between analysis of the costs and benefits of regulation, taking the view that there is often insufficient emphasis on the benefits (Parker and Kirkpatrick, 2012: 8).

33 International food safety standards, such as those developed by the joint WHO/FAO Codex Alimentarius Commission (WHO-FAO, 2015), are but one example of this. However, other issues relating to product safety standards (e.g. for electrical products, fireworks and toys) are also significant.

References

ADB. 2007. *Asian Development Outlook 2007*. Manila: Asian Development Bank.

Aftab, K. and Rahim, E. 1986. The Emergence of a Small-Scale Engineering Sector: The Case of Tubewell Production in the Pakistan Punjab. *Journal of Development Studies*. 23 (1): 60–76.

Aftab, K. And Rahim, E. 1989. 'Barriers' to the Growth of Informal Sector Firms: A Case Study. *Journal of Development Studies*. 25 (4): 490–507.

Aghion,P., Cai, J., Dewatripont, M., Harrison, A. and Legros, P. 2012. *Industrial Policy and Competition*. NBER Working Paper No. 18048. Cambridge MA: National Bureau of Economic Research.

Andersen, M. and Skjoett-Larsen, T. 2009. Corporate Social Responsibility in Global Supply Chains. *Supply Chain Management: An International Journal*. 14 (2): 75–86.

Arbache, J., Dickerson, A. and Green, F. 2004. Trade Liberalisation and Wages in Developing Countries. *Economic Journal*. 114 (493): F73–76.

Baldwin, R. 2011. *Trade and Industrialisation After Globalisation's Second Unbundling*. NBER Working Paper No. 17716. Cambridge MA: National Bureau of Economic Research.

Baran, P. 1957. *The Political Economy of Growth*. New York: Monthly Review Press.

Bresnahan, T. F. and Trajtenberg, M. 1995. General Purpose Technologies: Engines of Growth. *Journal of Econometrics*. 65 (1): 83–108.

Chenery, H. B. 1960. Patterns of Industrial Growth. *American Economic Review*. 50 (4): 624–654.

Collier, P. 2000. Africa's Comparative Advantage. In Jalilian, H., Tribe M. and Weiss, J. (eds.). *Industrial Development and Policy in Africa*. Cheltenham: Edward Elgar: 11–21.

Cook, P., Fabella, R. and Lee, C. (eds.). 2007. *Competitive Advantage and Competition Policy in Developing Countries*. Cheltenham: Edward Elgar.

DFID. 2008. *Competition Assessment Framework: An Operational Guide for Identifying Barriers to Competition in Developing Countries*. London: Department for International Development.

Dinh, H., Palmade, V., Chandra, V. and Cossar, F. 2012. *Light Manufacturing in Africa: Targeted Policies to Enhance Private Investment and Create Jobs*. Washington DC: World Bank.

Edusah, S.E. 2013. The Informal Sector, Micro-Enterprises and Small-Scale Industries: The Conceptual Quandary. *Journal of Economics and Sustainable Development*. 4 (20): 10 pages online at www.iiste.org

Ellis, K. and Singh, R. 2010. *Assessing the Economic Impact of Competition*. London: Overseas Development Institute.

Green, C. J., Kirkpatrick, C. H. and Murinde, V. 2006. Finance for Small Enterprise Growth and Poverty Reduction in Developing Countries. *Journal of International Development*. 18 (7): 1017–1030.

Hadass, Y. S. and Williamson, J. G. 2001. *Terms of Trade Shocks and Economic Performance 1870–1940: Prebisch and Singer Revisited*. NBER Working Paper 8188. Cambridge MA: National Bureau of Economic Research.

Haraguchi, N. and Rezonja, G. 2013. Emerging Patterns of Structural Change in Manufacturing. In Szirmai, A., Naude, W. and Alcorta, L. (eds.). *Pathways to Industrialization in the Twenty-First Century: New Challenges and Emerging Paradigms*. UNU-WIDER Studies in Development Economics. Oxford: Oxford University Press.

Hausmann, R., Hwang, J. and Rodrik, D. 2007. What You Export Matters. *Journal of Economic Growth*. 12 (1): 1–25.

Hausmann, R., Pritchett, L. and Rodrik, D. 2005. Growth Accelerations. *Journal of Economic Growth*. 10 (4): 303–329.

Hirschman, A. 1958. *Strategy of Economic Development*. New Haven, CT: Yale University Press.

Jørgensen, H. B., Pruzan-Jørgensen, P. M., Jungk, M. and Cramer, A. 2003. *Corporate Social Responsibility Practice: Strengthening Implementation of Corporate Social Responsibility in Global Supply Chain*. Washington DC: World Bank Group.

Kaplinsky, R. 2005. *Globalization, Poverty and Inequality*. Cambridge: Polity Press.

Kirkpatrick, C. H. and Parker, D. (eds.). 2008. *Regulatory Impact Assessment: Towards Better Regulation?* Cheltenham: Edward Elgar.

Kitzmuller, M. and Martinez Licetti, M. 2012. *Competition Policy: Encouraging Thriving Markets for Development*. Washington DC: World Bank.

Krugman P. 1997. The Fall and Rise of Development Economics. In *Development, Geography, and Economic Theory*. Krugman P. Cambridge, MA: The MIT Press.

Kushnir, K., Mirmulstein, M. L. and Ramalho, R. 2010. *Micro, Small, and Medium Enterprises Around the World: How Many are There, and What Affects the Count?* Washington DC: World Bank/International Finance Corporation – accessible from www.ifc.org

Kuznets, S. 1957. Quantitative Aspects of the Economic Growth of Nations: II. Industrial Distribution of National Product and Labour Force. *Economic Development and Cultural Change*. 5 (4) Supplement: 1–111.

Lall, S. 2000. The Technological Structure and Performance of Developing Country Manufactured Exports 1985–98. *Oxford Development Studies*. 28 (3): 337–369.

Lancaster, K. 1974. *Introduction to Modern Microeconomics* (2nd ed.). Chicago: Rand McNally College Publishing Company.

Lee, K. 2013. *Schumpeterian Analysis of Economic Catch-Up: Knowledge, Path-Creation, and the Middle-Income Trap*. Cambridge: Cambridge University Press.

Lewis, W. A. 1953. *Report on Industrialisation and the Gold Coast*. Accra: Government of the Gold Coast.

Lewis, W. A. 1954. Economic Development with Unlimited supplies of Labour. *Manchester School*. 22 (2): 139–91.

Lo, D. and Wu, M. 2014. The State and Industrial Development in Chinese Economic Development. In Salazar-Xitinachs, J., Nubler, I. and Kozul-Wright, R. (eds.). *Transforming Economies: Making Industrial Policy Work for Growth, Jobs and Development*. Geneva: UN Conference on Trade and Development and International Labour Organization.

Long, G. 2005. China's Policies on FDI: Review and Evaluation. In Moran, T., Graham, E. and Blomström, M. (eds.). *Does Foreign Investment Promote Development*. Washington DC: Institute of International Economics.

Mahalanobis, P. 1953. Some Observations on the Process of Growth of National Income. *Sankhya*. 12 (4): 307–312.

Mazzucato, M. 2013. *The Entrepreneurial State: Debunking Public vs. Private Sector Myths*. London: Anthem Press.

McMillan, M. S. and Rodrik, D. 2011. *Globalization, Structural Change and Productivity Growth*. NBER Working Paper 17143. Cambridge MA: National Bureau of Economic Research.

Mead, D. and Liedholm, C. 1998. The Dynamics of Micro and Small Enterprises in Developing Countries. *World Development*. 26 (1): 61–74.

Mensah, J. V., Tribe, M. and Weiss, J. 2007. The Small-Scale Manufacturing Sector in Ghana: A Source of Dynamism or of Subsistence Income? *Journal of International Development*. 19 (2): 253–273.

Moran, T. H. 2015. *Industrial Policy as a Tool of Development Strategy: Using FDI to Upgrade and Diversify the Production and Export Base of Host Economies in the Developing World*. Washington DC: International Center for Trade and Sustainable Development – downloadable from http://e15initiative.org/publications/

Nurkse, R. 1958. Some Aspects of the Problem of Economic Development. Reprinted in Agarwala, A. and Singh, S. (eds.). *The Economics of Underdevelopment*. Oxford: Oxford University Press.

Pack, H. 1994. Endogenous Growth Theory: Intellectual Appeal and Empirical Shortcomings. *Journal of Economic Perspectives*. 8 (1): 55–72.

Page, J. 2013. Should Africa Industrialise? In Szirmai, A., Naude, W. and Alcorta, L. (eds.). *Pathways to Industrialization in the Twenty-First Century: New Challenges and Emerging Paradigms*. UNU-WIDER Studies in Development Economics. Oxford: Oxford University Press.

Palma, G. 2005. Four Sources of Deindustrialisation and a New Concept of the Dutch Disease. In Ocampo, J. (ed.). *Beyond Reforms: Structural Dynamics and Macroeconomic Vulnerability*. Palo Alto, CA: Stanford University Press and Washington DC: World Bank.

Parker, D. and Kirkpatrick, C. H. 2012. *Measuring Regulatory Performance – The Economic Impact of Regulatory Policy: A Literature Review of Quantitative Evidence*. OECD Expert Paper No. 3. Paris: Organisation for Economic Cooperation and Development.

Poon, D. 2014. *China's Development Trajectory: A Strategic Opening for Industrial Policy in the South*. UNCTAD Discussion Paper 218. Geneva: UN Conference on Trade and Development.

Prebisch, R. 1950. *The Economic Development of Latin America and Its Principal Problems*. Lake Success, NY: United Nations Department of Economic Affairs – reprinted in the *Economic Bulletin for Latin America*. 1962. 7: 1–22.

Qaqaya, H. and Lipimile, G. 2008. *The Effects of Anti-Competitive Business Practices on Developing Countries and Their Development Prospects*. Geneva: United Nations Conference on Trade and Development – accessed from www.unctad.org

Robbins, D. 2003. *The Impact of Trade Liberalization upon Inequality in Developing Countries: Review of Theory and Evidence*. Working Paper 13. Geneva: International Labour Organization.

Rodrik, D. 2007. Industrial Development: Stylized Facts and Policies. In United Nations. *Industrial Development for the 21st Century*. New York: United Nations.

Romer, P. M. 1994. The Origins of Endogenous Growth. *Journal of Economic Perspectives*. 8 (1): 3–22.

Sapsford, D. and Chen, J.-R. (eds.). 1999. Policy Arena – The Prebisch–Singer Thesis: A Thesis for the New Millennium? *Journal of International Development*. 11 (6) September–October: 843–916.

Sapsford, D., Sarkar, P., and Singer, H. 1992. The Prebisch–Singer Terms of Trade Controversy Revisited. *Journal of International Development*. 4 (3) May–June: 315–332.

Sarkar, P. and Singer, H. 1991. Manufactured Exports of Developing Countries and Their Terms of Trade Since 1965. *World Development*. 19 (4) April: 333–340.

Sengupta, R. and Dube, C. 2008. *Competition Policy Enforcement Experiences from Developing Countries and Implications for Investment*. OECD Global Forum on International Investment VII March. Paris: Organisation for Economic Cooperation and Development – accessed from www.oecd.org/investment/globalforum

Singer, H. W. 1950. The Distribution of Gains Between Investing and Borrowing Countries. *American Economic Review*. 40 (2): 473–485.

Staley, E. and Morse, R. 1965. *Modern Small-Scale Industry for Developing Countries*. New York: McGraw-Hill.

Steel, W. F. and Webster, L. M. 1991. *Small Enterprises under Adjustment in Ghana*. World Bank Technical Paper 138 Industry and Finance Series. Washington DC: World Bank.

Steel, W. F. and Webster, L. M. 1992. How Small Enterprises Have Responded to Adjustment in Ghana. *World Bank Economic Review*. 6 (3): 423–438.

Stewart, F. 1977. *Technology and Underdevelopment*. London: Macmillan.

Sutcliffe, R. B. 1971. *Industry and Underdevelopment*. London: Addison-Wesley.

Szirmai, A. 2009. *Industrialization as an Engine of Growth in Developing Countries 1950–2005*. Working Paper 2009–10. Maastricht: UNU-MERIT.

Szirmai, A., Naude, W. and Alcorta, L. 2013. Introduction and Overview: The Past, Present and Future of Industrialization. In Szirmai, A., Naude, W. and Alcorta, L. (eds.). *Pathways to Industrialization in the Twenty-First Century: New Challenges and Emerging Paradigms*. UNU-WIDER Studies in Development Economics. Oxford: Oxford University Press.

Thirlwall, A. 1980 *Balance of Payments Theory*, London, Macmillan.

Thomas, C. 1974. *Dependence and Transformation*. New York: Monthly Review Press.

Timmer, M. and de Vries, G. 2009. Structural Change and Growth Accelerations in Asia and Latin America: A New Sectoral Dataset. *Cliometrica*. 3 (2): 165–190.

Tribe, M. 2005. Economic Efficiency Measures for Small-Scale Enterprises in Developing Countries. In Tribe, M., Thoburn, J. and Palmer-Jones, R. (eds.). *Development Economics and Social Justice: Essays in Honour of Ian Livingstone*. Aldershot: Ashgate.

UNIDO 2004 *Industrial Development Report 2004*. Vienna: United Nations Industrial Development Organization.

UNIDO. 2013. *Industrial Development Report 2013*. Vienna: United Nations Industrial Development Organization.

UNIDO. n.d. *Creative Industries and Micro & Small Scale Enterprise Development: A Contribution to Poverty Alleviation*. Private Sector Development Branch, Programme Development and Technical Cooperation

Division. Vienna: United Nations Industrial Development Organization – accessible from http://www. unido.org/fileadmin/user_media/Publications/Pub_free/69264_creative_industries.pdf

Vernon, R. 1966. International Investment and International Trade in the Product Cycle. *Quarterly Journal of Economics*. 80 (2) May: 190–207. Reprinted in Rosenberg N. (ed.). 1971. *The Economics of Technological Change*. Harmondsworth: Penguin Books: 440–460.

Vernon, R. 1979. The Product Cycle Hypothesis in the New International Environment. *Oxford Bulletin of Economics and Statistics*. 41 (4) November: 255–267.

Weil, D. N. 2005. *Economic Growth*. Boston: Pearson Addison Wesley.

Weiss, J. 1988. *Industry in Developing Countries*. London: Croom Helm (reprinted by Routledge 1990).

Weiss, J. 2002. *Industrialisation and Globalisation: Theory and Evidence from Developing Countries*. London: Routledge.

Weiss, J. 2011. *The Economics of Industrial Development*. London: Routledge.

WHO-FAO. 2015. *Codex Alimentarius Commission: International Food Standards* – accessible from http://www.codexalimentarius.org/

World Bank. 2014. *World Development Indicators 2014*. Washington DC: World Bank – accessible online at www.world.bank.org and through the UK Data Service at http://ukdataservice.ac.uk/

Wu, H. X. 2013. Rethinking China's path of industrialization. In Szirmai, A., Naudé, W. and Alcorta, L. (eds.). *Pathways to Industrialization in the Twenty-First Century: New Challenges and Emerging Paradigms*. United Nations University WIDER Studies in Development Economics. Oxford: Oxford University Press: 155–192.

2

MANUFACTURING AS AN ENGINE OF GROWTH

John Weiss and Hossein Jalilian

Introduction

There is a long tradition in economics which argues that manufacturing industry has a critical role in growth, particularly at relatively low income per capita. Several features of the sector have been highlighted to justify this focus:

- Output per worker (productivity) is normally considerably higher than in agriculture or services (although not in mining) so that structural change in favour of manufacturing raises the overall productivity of an economy.
- Productivity growth in manufacturing has historically been more rapid than in other sectors due to greater technical change and learning effects.
- Manufacturing is the sector where there is greater scope for specialisation as output grows.
- Its linkages with other parts of the economy are greater than for any other aggregate sector, thus offering the greatest scope for externalities.
- As a key tradable activity it offers the greatest potential for expansion via exports with considerable scope for transferability of skills, so that within manufacturing it is easier than in other sectors to branch out into the production of similar but differentiated products.

The normal historical pattern has been that in poor countries the share of manufacturing in total economic activity is very low, but that as growth occurs and workers move out of agriculture it rises rapidly. However, once a threshold income level is passed, the relative share of manufacturing starts to decline as demand shifts towards services.[1] Thus for example in 2005, manufacturing was 9 per cent of GDP in Ghana, 30 per cent of GDP in a middle income economy like Malaysia and averaged 16 per cent in the OECD economies (Szirmai, 2013: Table 2). It is at the transition from low to middle income status that the engine of growth effect can be expected to be greatest due to the greater scope for a productivity boost as workers shift out of agriculture.[2] If technical change and learning effects are stronger in manufacturing than elsewhere this structural shift will increase both the level and rate of growth of overall productivity. Clearly these features of manufacturing should not imply that an excessive anti-agriculture bias, for example through manipulation of the internal terms of trade, can be justified, particularly since at low income levels the agriculture sector provides a source of internal demand and a supply of wage goods for manufacturing. However, if these arguments hold they provide a rationale for a policy which eases the shift of resources out of agriculture and adjusts the balance of incentives towards manufacturing.

Is manufacturing still special?

Recent experience has questioned some of these assumptions. Across all countries there is evidence that the relationship between a country's income per capita and the share of manufacturing in GDP has been weakening, so that for a given level of income the manufacturing share predicted from cross-country analysis is lower than in earlier time periods. This is particularly the case where employment shares are concerned, with a weakening of the relationship between employment and manufacturing growth and absolute declines in manufacturing employment in some high income economies.[3] Some analyses of the relationship of sector share in GDP at the start of a period and subsequent economic growth show a much stronger relationship for manufacturing pre-1970 than more recently.[4] Furthermore there has been relatively rapid productivity growth in parts of the service sector and agriculture. Parts of services related to financial and professional services, retail and distribution have benefited from the application computer-based technologies to sustain higher productivity levels and growth. Agricultural productivity growth has also been relatively rapid in a number of countries as labour has left the sector and new agricultural technologies have allowed output per worker to rise for those remaining. On the world market in the last decade the price of manufactures has declined relative to that of many primary commodities.

This chapter considers some of the recent evidence on the role of manufacturing in economic growth and at the end presents data from the authors' own analysis on this question. It bases the discussion around the theoretical framework set out nearly 50 years ago by Nicholas Kaldor, the eminent Cambridge economist, which provides the most influential statement of the engine of growth case.

Kaldor's laws

Following the work of Kaldor (1966, 1967) the theoretical case for the special role for manufacturing involves not just the potential for greater externalities than in other sectors, but also a focus on dynamic increasing returns in the sense of declining unit costs as output grows over time. There is a long tradition in economics that contrasts increasing returns (that is productivity growth) in manufacturing with diminishing returns in agriculture and with services treated as an appendage of manufacturing. This is distinct from an argument about increasing returns in a static sense, where unit costs fall as plant scale is expanded. Static economies of scale are found in many lines of activity: for example, plantation agriculture may have lower cost per unit of crop output than small-holder agriculture and supermarkets are likely to have lower costs per product sold than small family shops. Furthermore, there will be a wide variation within manufacturing in the relation between higher output and decline in unit cost of production, with heavy capital-intensive activities showing the most scale effect.

The key focus here is on a dynamic rather than on a static relationship, with dynamic increasing returns referring to the tendency in manufacturing for the growth of output to be related systematically to the growth of productivity. Hence it is not the level of output that drives the decline in unit cost but its cumulative growth over time. The mechanisms underlying this process in manufacturing are learning by doing, technological imitation, adaptation and modification and the gains from increased specialisation as manufacturing is increasingly sub-divided into more specialised forms. Unlike static economies of scale, these dynamic gains should not be reversible if output subsequently declines, since they have created a higher skill and technological base for the sector.

The concept of dynamic increasing returns links with the discussion of externalities and linkages since they will be part of the process of productivity improvement. The complex set of linkages between firms found in manufacturing provides the mechanism for productivity gains in response to growing output. Historically it is well documented that as the scale of the national market for manufactures grows it allows the establishment of increasing specialisation and differentiation between firms (the increasing 'roundaboutness of production'), as newly specialised supplier firms are established through backward linkages from existing firms. Today, with the removal of many barriers to trade, this process has been heightened by the closer integration of most economies with the world market. The scale of the market is critical, since as it expands with growth, so will the opportunities for specialisation. Some of the resulting productivity gains will be internal to firms, but others will spill over as benefits to other firms.

Kaldor stressed dynamic increasing returns as the explanation for why manufacturing (as opposed to agriculture or services) was the only sector for which output growth and productivity growth were related. Productivity growth could occur in agriculture or in services, but in his view it was not related systematically to growth of output. For example, productivity growth in agriculture might be due to exogenous technical change in the form of new seed varieties or to the shift of workers off the land, not to the expansion of the sector itself and the increased specialisation and learning that this allows. As is discussed further below, more recent analyses have shown that increasing returns hold for a range of sectors, not just for manufacturing (Pieper, 2003; see also Timmer *et al.,* Chapter 4 this volume). However, the Kaldor argument goes further by asserting that manufacturing growth raises not just productivity in manufacturing, but through externality and spillover effects also raises overall productivity in the economy as labour is transferred from lower productivity activities into manufacturing and as manufacturing development stimulates improvements in the services that it uses. Kaldor's case was based on the relationship between output growth and productivity first established by the Dutch economist Jake Verdoorn (Verdoorn, 1949) and he put forward a simple empirical test (Kaldor, 1966; 1967). He estimated two equations for a number of sectors from a sample of developed countries.

$$p_i = a_1 + b_1 \cdot q_i \tag{1}$$

$$e_i = a_2 + b_2 \cdot q_i \tag{2}$$

where p, q and e are labour productivity growth, output growth and employment growth, respectively, for sector i.

Equation (1) is the relation established by Verdoorn, which has been found to hold for many branches of activity. Since, by definition, growth of output is the sum of growth of productivity and the growth of the number of workers ($q_i = p_i + e_i$) it is possible for spurious correlations to be found between q and p, when changes in e are small. Hence Kaldor's additional requirement to demonstrate the existence of dynamic increasing returns is that equation (2) should also be statistically significant with a coefficient b_2 of less than unity. This implies that the growth of employment is less than the growth of output, so by definition there will be a productivity gain.[5]

Kaldor's laws and empirical tests

The analysis in this tradition focuses on establishing empirical regularities or 'stylized facts' relating to the role of manufacturing in development. The empirical focus is on testing what have been termed Kaldor's laws (Felipe, 2010: 85). These can be summarised as follows:

1   Law 1 *The faster the growth of manufacturing output the faster the growth of GDP.*
2   Law 2 *There is a strong positive relation between the growth of manufacturing output and the growth of manufacturing productivity.*
3   Law 3 *The faster manufacturing grows the faster productivity outside manufacturing will increase.*

Evidence in support of these propositions for developed economies was found in Cripps and Tarling (1973) and in Kaldor's original analysis (Kaldor, 1966, 1967). More recent work has focused on how far these relationships still hold in the era of a more open global economy and how far their strength varies with stage of development or country income level.

The impact of growth in manufacturing on the rest of the economy (Law 1) can be tested simply by regressing growth of GDP on growth of manufacturing value-added and comparing the results with similar analyses for services and agriculture. For example, Dasgupta and Singh (2006) report this test for 50 developing countries for which data are available over the period 1990-2000. The coefficients on each sector's growth were found to be positive and statistically significant. However, whilst the equations for manufacturing and services are robust statistically, that for agriculture does not pass all the necessary diagnostic tests, so less confidence can be placed on the link between agriculture growth and GDP growth. It should be noted that the coefficient on the sector growth variable is higher in services (0.58) than in manufacturing (0.47), although the authors dispute the significance of this result, suggesting that for services reverse causation with a significant impact from GDP growth to services growth is likely to be operating.

This analysis may be misleading as by using growth of GDP as the dependent variable, part of GDP will be used to explain change in all GDP. Felipe *et al.* (2007) avoid this problem by setting GDP net of the sector whose impact is being tested as the dependent variable and also applying more sophisticated econometric techniques in a panel data analysis for 17 Asian economies over the period 1980-2004. Unlike the previous reported result they find that whilst each major sector has a significant impact on GDP growth (net of its own value-added) the impact of industry is greatest, followed by services and then manufacturing.[6] They stress that this test demonstrates that it is industry and services which have played the greatest engine of growth role over the period for the 17 countries covered.

These analyses are of limited value however, since they do not control fully for the influence of other variables on growth, for the development stage of an economy and for the difference between time periods. These problems are addressed more fully by Szirmai and Verspagen (2011) who create a model to explain growth in 89 countries (developed and developing) over different time periods from 1950 to 2005, where:

$$gGDPcap_t = f(\text{ManufShare, ServShare, RelGDP, } Z) \tag{3}$$

In equation (3) $gGDPcap_t$ is per capita GDP growth over period t, ManufShare is the share of manufacturing in GDP at the start of period t, ServShare is the same for services, RelGDP is country GDP per capita divided by the US figure at the start of the period to capture a convergence effect and Z is a vector of control variables for each country expected to explain growth. The term Z includes variables relating to education (Edu), population, climate and openness to trade. The differential impact of a change in sector share in GDP on growth depending on a country's stage of development is captured by including interaction terms that separately interact ManufShare with RelGDP and Edu. The expectation is that the sign on the former will be negative (so a growing manufacturing will have a greater GDP growth effect at lower income levels) and on the latter is positive (so GDP growth will respond more strongly the better educated is the workforce).

The initial results show manufacturing share in GDP to be statistically and positively significant implying higher growth over a five-year period the higher is the initial manufacturing share. The service sector share at the start of a period, however, is insignificant. The impact of the manufacturing share on growth is only modest (between 0.5 per cent and 1.0 per cent for a 10 per cent rise in manufacturing's share in GDP). This is a linear specification, however, so that the growth impact of a given rise in manufacturing share is the same for all levels of share. The interaction terms are designed to allow for non-linear effects. The coefficient on the interaction of ManufShare and RelGDP is negative and significant, implying that, as expected, manufacturing's growth impact is greater in lower income economies. Again, as expected, the sign on the interaction term between ManufShare and Edu is positive and significant, so that a better-educated workforce creates a bigger impact on growth for a given share of manufacturing in GDP. Hence the engine of growth case for manufacturing is strongest in countries with low incomes, but where a minimum threshold of human capital has been passed. After different time periods are controlled for, the picture changes. In the post-1990 period, a positive direct impact of manufacturing on growth is found only in the poorest economies.[7] For the early period (1950-70) when manufacturing's growth effect is stronger and unambiguous, the impact of services is also significant. However, the interaction of manufacturing with income and education remains significant in all periods. The authors conclude that "since 1990 manufacturing is becoming a somewhat more difficult route to growth than before" (Szirmai and Verspagen, 2011: 31). Hence a given marginal impact on growth from manufacturing requires more education attainment post-1990 and the growth impact through catching up at a given relative low income level becomes weaker. Nonetheless, despite these changing conditions there is support for what the authors term "an extended engine of growth hypothesis", where impact is conditional on relative income and human capital.

Law 2 relates to productivity growth within a sector. Many tests have been carried out on the Verdoorn relation between output growth and productivity growth. From recent experience there is evidence linking manufacturing with overall GDP and productivity growth. However, it appears that, unlike the earlier view of Kaldor, which saw services as a largely passive element in the economy, the modern service sector is also emerging as an engine of growth and is drawing workers into technologically dynamic activities with the potential for productivity growth. Kaldor (1975) himself found that whilst equation (1) generally holds for all sectors, equations (1) and (2) together only hold for manufacturing as a sector and not for the non-manufacturing sectors of the economy. His second law requires that (2) is significant with the coefficient $b_2 < 1$, which is the requirement for dynamic increasing returns in the sector. Unlike Kaldor's analysis for developed economies, in a detailed analysis across 30 developing countries, Pieper (2003) finds that there is clear regularity across sectors with the majority (not just manufacturing) showing evidence of increasing returns.

An alternative test highlighted in Rodrik (2011, 2013) relates to productivity convergence in a sector in order to assess whether there is a natural tendency within a sector for catch-up productivity growth either unconditionally (that is, regardless of country or sector characteristics) or conditional on specific features of the country or sector. Evidence of convergence can be interpreted as support for the learning mechanism in the engine of growth case.

Across countries, unconditional convergence is formulated as:

$$cg_{ij} = \alpha + \beta \ln y_{ij} + \varepsilon \tag{4}$$

where cg is the compound rate of growth of labour productivity for sector j in country i, y is the initial level of labour productivity for the sector and ε is the stochastic term. For unconditional convergence to hold, β should be negative and significant. Similarly, conditional convergence, controlling for features of an economy, is tested by an equation of the form:

$$cg_{ij} = \alpha + \beta_1 \ln y_{ij} + \mu \cdot Z_i + \varepsilon \tag{5}$$

where Z_i is a set of country-specific controls. Conditional convergence requires that β_1 be negative and significant.

Rodrik (2011, 2013) finds that manufacturing appears to be the only sector where there is a systematic tendency for productivity to catch up with international best practice independently of the policy environment in an economy. The implication is that once a manufacturing activity is established, through a process of learning producers move towards international best practice productivity levels. He conducts this analysis at a disaggregate level within manufacturing, showing considerable scope for both types of convergence with the conditional coefficient typically double that of the unconditional, as country-specific conditions play a large role. The implication is that within manufacturing catch-up and learning effects are strong. This 'convergence' test is not found to operate for non-manufacturing in the aggregate. However, this does not confirm how far these effects are unique to manufacturing and in the discussion below we extend the analysis by considering how far such effects operate in other sectors. Our focus is not on intra-manufacturing differences, but on whether manufacturing is different from other sectors in terms of convergence potential.

Law 3 relates to the impact of manufacturing on productivity elsewhere in the economy. The basic test here first used by Cripps and Tarling (1973) for developed economies uses a regression model to explain overall labour productivity growth in an economy by the growth of manufacturing value-added and the growth of employment outside manufacturing. If the Law holds, overall productivity growth in an economy is associated positively with the growth of manufacturing and negatively with the size of non-manufacturing employment. Thus:

$$g(VA/L)_t = a + b_1(g \cdot VA \cdot m) + b_2(g \cdot L \cdot n) + \varepsilon \tag{6}$$

where g is growth, VA is value-added, L is employment, m refers to manufacturing, n is non-manufacturing and t refers to the aggregate economy. Cripps and Tarling (1973) found b_1 to be positive and significant for manufacturing, with b_2 negative for non-manufacturing sectors.

Dasgupta and Singh (2006) repeated this analysis across a sample of 48 developing economies but re-specified (6) by replacing non-manufacturing employment with agricultural employment (L_{ag}). This is on the grounds that agriculture is the main decreasing-returns low productivity sector in low income countries and that its release of labour to manufacturing raises overall productivity. They found b_1 to be positive and significant for manufacturing, with b_2 negative for agricultural employment. However, when service value-added is included instead of manufacturing a similar result, with b_1 significant, is also obtained, casting doubt on the uniqueness of manufacturing.[8]

More disaggregate analysis

In this chapter we extend these earlier results by conducting more disaggregate tests on Laws 2 and 3. Our analysis is based principally on sector data on value-added and employment for a sample of 38 developed and developing countries drawn from the Groningen Growth and Development Centre database and extended by McMillan and Rodrik (2011). The dataset is further complemented by data from the World Development Indicators and the Penn World Tables (2011) with institutional variables taken from Kaufmann and Kraay (2011). The dataset gives a useful disaggregation of economic sectors and allows a focus on intra-sector productivity trends. It provides time series data on value-added and corresponding labour productivity for a number of sectors including agriculture, mining, manufacturing, public utilities, construction, wholesale and retail trade, transport and communication services, as well as finance and business services. It covers the following 38 countries over the period 1990-2005:

- *High income:* United States, France, Netherlands, Italy, Sweden, Japan, United Kingdom, Spain and Denmark;
- *Asia:* Hong Kong, Singapore, Taiwan, South Korea, Malaysia, Thailand, Indonesia, Philippines, China and India;
- *Middle East:* Turkey;
- *Latin America:* Argentina, Chile, Mexico, Venezuela, Costa Rica, Colombia, Peru, Brazil and Bolivia;
- *Africa:* South Africa, Mauritius, Nigeria, Senegal, Kenya, Ghana, Zambia, Ethiopia and Malawi.

Complementary data, such as purchasing power parity (PPP, constant 2000 US$) values of GDP per capita, GDP per capita growth and measures of openness, were added from the website of Penn World Tables (2011). Data for the institutional quality measures are taken from Kaufman and Kraay (2011). We test for regional effects with separate regional dummies. In common with most empirical research in this area, and in order to remove short term disturbances as well as business cycle effects from the data, we have converted the time series data on variables into five-year period averages covering 1991–95, 1996–2000 and 2001–05.

We first consider the evidence on convergence in labour productivity to check whether there is evidence of convergence within manufacturing from our dataset and second, how far this is replicated within other sectors. Table 2.1 presents the result of testing for productivity convergence in different sectors. The analysis applies both equations (4) and (5) to test for unconditional and conditional convergence, respectively.

Unconditional convergence is not confirmed for any of the productive sectors for the whole dataset, as there is no statistically significant relationship between the sectoral growth of labour productivity and its initial level and the signs of the parameter estimate for agriculture and manufacturing are positive, which is the opposite of convergence. Convergence is only confirmed for construction and weakly for transport and communications. If we exclude African countries on the grounds that their relatively weak economic performance in manufacturing makes them special cases, there is now some weak support with negative coefficients on initial productivity for manufacturing, as well as for mining and public utilities. There is no evidence that unconditional convergence is stronger in manufacturing than in the other two sectors, as might be expected from the engine of growth hypothesis, since the coefficient on the parameter initial productivity for manufacturing is lower than for mining and public utilities.

Once we apply a version of equation (4) the picture changes. We apply only one control variable, the composite institutional quality measure, on the grounds that this correlated with other plausible controls. For the full dataset the sign on initial labour productivity is now always negative and is significant in public utilities, construction and transport and communications and in the aggregate. However, when we exclude African countries, conditional convergence

Table 2.1 Testing for convergence

Independent variables:	Dependent variable: Cumulative sectoral growth								
	cgagr	cgmin	cgman	cgpu	cgcon	cgwrt	cgtcs	cgfin	cgsum
All countries included									
Initial level of sectoral labour productivity	0.14	−1.23	0.92	−2.43***	−2.20**	0.28	−1.21*	−0.75	0.07
All countries, adding institutional proxy									
Initial level of sectoral labour productivity	−0.06	−1.11	−0.89	−3.64***	−3.24***	−0.69	−2.30**	−0.76	−0.35
Institution	0.14	−0.22	0.93***	1.09*	0.61	0.5	0.56*	0.02	0.26
All countries excluding those in Africa									
Initial level of sectoral labour productivity	−0.27	−1.69*	−1.18*	−1.46*	−0.62	0.24	−0.23	−0.20	−0.81**
All countries excluding those in Africa, adding institutional proxy									
Initial level of sectoral labour productivity	−1.00	−1.2	−3.06***	−2.16*	−0.86	−1.17	−1.04	−0.19	−1.90***
Institution	0.44	−0.58	0.84***	0.41	0.11	0.62**	0.36	0.00	0.54***

Notes: cg in front of the variable stands for cumulative growth, agr = agriculture; min = mining; man = manufacturing; pu = public utilities; con=construction services; wrt = wholesale and retail trade; tsc = transport services and communication; and fin = financial services sector.

*, **, *** = parameter estimate is significant at 5%, 1% and 0.1% respectively.

is confirmed strongly for manufacturing and in the aggregate. It is also found in public utilities. In the non-African sample, once we control for institutional quality, convergence is faster and more significant in manufacturing than in public utilities. With the institutional control the relationship is insignificant for mining and agriculture, although the sign on the parameter estimate for initial productivity is negative. For services there is no evidence of convergence apart from transport and communications. Thus if we exclude African countries, where it is well known that in many places manufacturing has regressed in recent decades, catch-up productivity growth is found in manufacturing, but not in most of services.[9]

We also test for Law 3 by applying a version of equation (6) to our data with our results given in Table 2.2. We apply both an ordinary least squares (OLS) and a fixed panel approach across countries and following Dasgupta and Singh (2006) specify equation (6) using agricultural sector employment, but we also include non-manufacturing in the aggregate as an alternative. We find that sector growth in manufacturing is strongly and positively associated with total productivity growth and that agricultural employment growth is negatively associated with total productivity growth. However, we find that manufacturing is not unique in this respect. When we add a series of other sector variables separately to replace the manufacturing variable all three services branches included (financial services, transport and communications and wholesale and retail trade) appear to be performing similarly to manufacturing, as is construction. Mining and public utilities are the sectors where there is no significant, positive relation between their value-added growth and overall productivity growth. These results are consistent using both OLS and panel data.

Conclusions

Evidence on productivity growth, and some of the tests reported here, tend to suggest that the uniqueness of manufacturing as a source of learning and productivity dynamism is less strong than was once thought. Attention is now focused increasingly on services, particularly those with knowledge-intensive elements. This is likely to be due in part to the somewhat arbitrary distinction between a service and a manufacturing activity, and to the fact that some activities previously done in-house by manufacturers may now be outsourced to specialist suppliers who are recorded under services. However, it is clear that whilst some service activities in low and middle income countries, such as retail and wholesale trade and public bureaucracies, have low productivity, new dynamic elements of services are emerging, such as business and computer-based services, telecommunications and tourism. One interpretation of the results obtained from applying equation (6) is that these latter dynamic elements are starting to dominate within the sector and that the service sector as a whole is behaving in way similar to manufacturing, thus offering higher productivity employment to that available in agriculture. This argument is now particularly relevant in the context of India where service sector growth is seen as a key feature of recent development.[10]

However, our convergence analysis only finds evidence of convergence in labour productivity within one of the three service categories that we work with, transport and communications. Further, the fact that manufacturing is not unique in offering higher productivity employment to that available in agriculture should perhaps be unsurprising. What matters in terms of strategy is the growth and employment potential a sector offers and, in many lower income economies, shifting labour resources into manufacturing continues to produce greater growth potential than elsewhere in the economy. Our broad conclusion is that at a certain development level the engine of growth case remains valid, even if it is obvious that growth opportunities outside manufacturing should not be neglected.

Table 2.2 Testing Kaldor's laws

	Independent variables							
	gagr	cgmin	cgman	cgpu	cgcon	cgwrt	cgtsc	cgfin
Dependent variable is growth of total labour productivity								
Estimation technique: OLS								
1. Sectoral value-added growth	0.01***	0.00	0.01***	−0.00	0.00	0.01***	0.00*	0.00
Estimation technique: Fixed panel								
2. Sectoral value-added growth	0.01***	−0.00	0.01**	−0.00	0.00	0.01**	0.00	0.01*
Dependent variable is growth of total labour productivity								
Estimation technique: OLS								
3. Sectoral value-added growth	0.27***	−0.01	0.32***	0.02	0.13***	0.30***	0.22***	0.13**
4. Sectoral employment growth	−0.23**	0.04	−0.08	0.00	−0.03	−0.07	0.01	0.06
5. Sectoral value-added growth	0.25***	−0.02	0.31***	0.02	0.15***	0.31***	0.22***	0.14***
Growth of agricultural sector employment	−0.05	−0.25**	−0.15*	−0.23**	−0.28***	−0.26***	−0.23***	−0.25***
6. Sectoral value-added growth	0.21***	−0.03	0.31***	0.01	0.11***	0.28***	0.18***	0.12**
Growth of non-manufacturing employment	−0.48**	−0.73***	−0.57***	−0.67***	−0.61***	−0.54***	−0.49**	−0.64***
Estimation technique: Fixed panel								
7. Sectoral value-added growth	0.32***	−0.04	0.25***	0.01	0.13***	0.27***	0.18**	0.18***
8. Sectoral employment growth	−0.19*	0.05*	0.00	−0.02	0.00	−0.04	0.09	−0.01
9. Sectoral value-added growth	0.40***	−0.05*	0.25***	0.01	0.14***	0.28***	0.17**	0.18***
Growth of agricultural sector employment	0.16	−0.24**	−0.20*	−0.19*	−0.21*	−0.21**	−0.17*	−0.18*
10. Sectoral value-added growth	0.28***	−0.06**	0.25***	0.00	0.11***	0.25***	0.11	0.16***
Growth of non-manufacturing sector employment	−0.47**	−0.75***	−0.66***	−0.65***	−0.53**	−0.54***	−0.50***	−0.55***

Notes: *, **, *** = parameter estimate is significant at 5%, 1% and 0.1% respectively.

Notes

1 A report by the McKinsey Global Institute (2012) suggests that the downturn starts at a GDP of approximately US$10,000 per capita in 1990 prices at PPP exchange rates or approximately $21,000 at current prices.
2 See McMillan and Rodrik (2011) for an analysis of growth and structural change.
3 See Tregenna (Chapter 6, this volume) and Rodrik (2015).
4 See, for example, Fagerberg and Verspagen (2002), who use 1973 as a cut-off point.
5 Kaldor's original test was simplified in focusing only on labour productivity and can be modified by introducing a capital input and setting the analysis in a production function framework; see McCombie *et al.* (2002).
6 Industry here includes mining, public utilities and manufacturing.
7 These are defined as those where RelGDP is below 0.2 (that is, countries with less than 20 per cent of US GDP per capita).
8 Timmer *et al.* (Chapter 4, this volume) find that in the post-1990 period in low and middle income economies the expansion of the service sector has contributed to overall productivity growth both through intra-sector productivity growth and through a static reallocation effect, as the average level of productivity there is generally above the economy average due to low productivity in agriculture, However, as productivity growth has been slower in services than in some of the shrinking sectors the dynamic reallocation effect has weakened overall growth. The net contribution of services to total productivity growth exceeds that of manufacturing in Africa, but is well below it in Latin America.
9 This replicates the result of Rodrik (2011) who looked at convergence within branches of manufacturing.
10 Nonetheless, the evidence of Timmer *et al.* (Chapter 4, this volume) warns that this effect is far from universal and in Latin America in particular, productivity growth in services has been negative.

References

Cripps, T. and Tarling, R. 1973. *Growth in Advanced Capitalist Economies 1950–70*. Occasional Paper 40, Department of Applied Economics. Cambridge: University of Cambridge.

Dasgupta, S. and Singh, A. 2006. *Manufacturing, Services and Premature De-Industrialisation in Developing Countries*. UNU WIDER Research Paper 2006/49. Helsinki: United Nations University.

Fagerberg, J. and Verspagen, B. 2002. Technology Gaps, Innovation-Diffusion and Transformation: An Evolutionary Perspective. *Research Policy*. 31: 1291–1304.

Felipe, J. 2010. *Inclusive Growth, Full Employment and Structural Change*. Gurgaon and Manila: Anthem Press, India and Asian Development Bank.

Felipe, J., Leon-Ledesma, M., Lanzafame, M. and Estrada, G. 2007. *Sectoral Engines of Growth in Developing Asia: Stylized Facts and Implications*. ERD Working Paper 107. Manila: Asian Development Bank – accessible at www. adb.org

Kaldor, N. 1966. *Causes of the Slow Rate of Economic Growth of the United Kingdom: An Inaugural Lecture*. Cambridge: Cambridge University Press.

Kaldor, N. 1967. *Strategic Factors in Economic Development*. Ithaca, NY: Cornell University Press.

Kaldor, N. 1975. Economic Growth and the Verdoorn Law: A Comment on Mr Rowthorn's Article. *Economic Journal*. 85 (340): 891–896.

Kaufmann, D. and Kraay, A. 2011. *Worldwide Governance Indicators*. Washington, DC: World Bank – accessible at: http://info.worldbank.org/governance/wgi/index.asp

McCombie, J., Pugno, N. and Bruno, S. 2002. *Productivity Growth and Economic Performance: Essays on Verdoorn's Law*. Basingstoke: Palgrave Macmillan.

McKinsey Global Institute. 2012. *Manufacturing the Future: The Next Era of Global Growth and Innovation*. San Francisco: McKinsey Global Institute – accessible at http://www.mckinsey.com/

McMillan, M. and Rodrik, D. 2011. *Globalization, Structural Change, and Productivity Growth*. NBER Working Paper 17143. Cambridge, MA: National Bureau of Economic Research – accessible at http://www.nber.org/papers/w17143

Penn World Tables. 2011. *Penn World Table*. Center for International Comparisons of Production, Income and Prices. Philadelphia: University of Pennsylvania – accessible at https://pwt.sas.upenn. edu/ or http://pwt.econ.upenn.edu/php_site/pwt_index.php

Pieper, U. 2003. Sectoral Regularities of Productivity Growth in Developing Countries: A Kaldorian Interpretation. *Cambridge Journal of Economics*. 27 (6): 831–850.

Rodrik, D. 2011. *Unconditional Convergence*. NBER Working Paper No. 17546. Cambridge MA: National Bureau of Economic Research – accessible at http://www.hks.harvard.edu/fs/drodrik/research.html

Rodrik, D. 2013. Unconditional Convergence in Manufacturing. *Quarterly Journal of Economics*. 128 (1): 165–204.

Rodrik, D. 2015. Premature De-Industrialisation. *IAS School of Social Sciences, Economics Working Paper 107* – available at www.ias.edu

Szirmai, A. 2013. Manufacturing and Economic Development. In Szirmai, A., Naude, W. and Alcorta, A. (eds.). *Pathways to Industrialization in the Twenty-First Century*. UNU-WIDER Studies in Development Economics. Oxford: Oxford University Press.

Szirmai, A. and Verspagen, B. 2011. *Manufacturing and Economic Growth in Developing Countries 1950–2005*. Maastricht Economic and Social Research Institute on Innovation and Technology (MERIT) Working Paper Series 2011-69. Maastricht: United Nations University.

Verdoorn, P. J. 1949. Fattori che regolano lo sviluppo della produttivita del lavoro. *L'Industria*. 1: 45–53.

3

PATTERNS OF STRUCTURAL CHANGE AND MANUFACTURING DEVELOPMENT

Nobuya Haraguchi[1]

Introduction

Economic growth has been associated with changes in economic structure. Before the Industrial Revolution in the eighteenth century, the world economy grew very slowly and changed structure very little relative to the recent standard (Kuznets, 1966; Maddison, 2003). Modern economic growth has been characterised by an increase in population and an even faster increase in output, leading to higher growth in per capita income (Kuznets, 1966). This sustained income growth was not accompanied by the proportional increase in the outputs of different sectors but by continuous changes in the economic structure. A rapid increase in the share of industry with a decline of agricultural share, or industrialisation, initially plays a key role in catapulting the economy into a higher growth path (Ocampo *et al.*, 2009).[2] The importance of manufacturing relative to agriculture for economic growth has been attributed to the higher economies of scale of the former, higher income elasticity of demand for manufactured goods and higher potential of productivity catch-up of the manufacturing sector (Kaldor, 1967; Chenery *et al.*, 1986; Rodrik, 2011; Weiss, 2011). Manufacturing normally ceases being a dominant engine of growth when countries reach a high per capita income of roughly US$14,000 (in constant 2005 purchasing power parity, PPP).[3] Thereafter, the service sector's contribution to the economy carries an increasingly larger weight, and the manufacturing share tends to gradually decrease, although such a description based on official statistics tends to conceal an increasingly interdependent nature of the development of manufacturing and fast growing business-related services (Franke and Kalmbach, 2005; Tahara, 2009; Tomlinson, 2012). The development of an efficient and dynamic service sector depends especially on the kind of manufacturing structure that a country has established (Guerrieri and Meliciani, 2005).

The fact that the manufacturing sector plays a key role in a country's development makes us examine how the structure of manufacturing is associated with different stages of development. As modern economic growth has been accompanied by structural change at broadly aggregated levels of agriculture, industry and services, sustained economic growth entails structural change also at disaggregated levels within the manufacturing sector through technological upgrading and diversification and then possibly specialisation at a later stage (Imbs and Wacziarg, 2003).

As for the economy as a whole, structural change within manufacturing takes place due to: (1) demand and supply changes associated with the income level; (2) a country's given demographic and geographic conditions; and (3) a country's created conditions (Chenery and Syrquin, 1975). Based on a general formulation of Engel's law as per capita income increases incremental consumer demand for some groups of goods and services tends to increase faster than for other groups (Pasinetti, 1981). On the supply side, manufacturing production tends to evolve relative to changing factor endowments as per capita income increases (Lin, 2012). Lower income countries are therefore likely to focus on relatively labour-intensive or resource-intensive activities, and higher income countries are likely to specialise in capital-intensive or technology-intensive industries. While the relationship between income levels and manufacturing structure has some elements of universality (as countries follow a more or less similar path of structural change) as income increases, geographic and demographic conditions give countries natural advantages or disadvantages in the development of certain industries (Katz, 2000). For example, holding other conditions constant, abundant natural resources endowment would tend to work against manufacturing development (Haraguchi and Rezonja, 2010; UNIDO, 2012). Finally, the course of manufacturing structural change is not determined only by the universal effects of income levels and specific demographic and geographic conditions, but there is also space for individual countries to have an autonomously evolving structure. Therefore, country-created or specific conditions, such as history, culture and policy, are also significant (Lin and Chang, 2009).

In order to illustrate the respective universality and diversity highlighted in this discussion, the second section presents the patterns of structural change for the whole economy, giving particular attention to changes in the levels of manufacturing value added and employment in the economy. It illustrates how the relative importance of the manufacturing sector changes at different income levels as countries develop. In addition to the patterns of structural change by income level, the section discusses whether the patterns have been changing over time and evaluates the extent to which there has been any shift in the weight of manufacturing in the economy recently.

Following this discussion of economy-wide structural change, the third section focuses on the manufacturing sector and provides detailed analyses of structural change within the sector in order to illustrate patterns of manufacturing development. It discusses the effect of the three major factors of structural change proposed by Chenery and Syrquin (1975), namely the income level, geographic and demographic conditions, and other country-specific factors. In addition, this section discusses the emerging trends of manufacturing development based on changes in development patterns over the last 30 years.

The fourth section reviews the temporal aspects of manufacturing structural change, first shedding light on the development speeds of individual manufacturing industries, and then on the transformation of the manufacturing sector as a whole. The section also compares the performance of recently successful countries with that of earlier industrialised countries in order to assess how the speed of the industrialisation process has been changing.

The final section synthesises the analyses of different explanatory factors for manufacturing structural change discussed in the third and fourth sections and illustrates how they are individually related to the both the universal patterns and country specificities of manufacturing development as a whole, producing unique development paths for individual countries' manufacturing sectors.

Structural change and manufacturing sector in the economy

As countries' income levels increase, the share of agriculture tends to decline while the share of services gradually increases. However, the manufacturing sector does not continuously reduce or enlarge its weight in the economy throughout the course of country development, as it usually acts as an engine of growth only at certain stages of development. Figure 3.1 shows the estimated patterns of structural change across income levels based on panel data for 100 countries. As countries develop, the share of agriculture declines quite rapidly while other sectors increase their shares. Especially at low and lower middle income levels the share of manufacturing increases markedly, making a disproportionate contribution to economic development at a relatively early stage of development.[4] The increase in the manufacturing share of GDP slows down in the upper middle income stage, and its share reaches a peak (vertical line) before countries move into the high income level.

Figure 3.1 illustrates the patterns of structural change discussed above, representing the long-term period of more than 40 years from 1963 to 2007. During that period, international development discourse has changed, globalisation has progressed, and many advanced countries have started experiencing de-industrialisation. Figure 3.2 then splits the long period into earlier and later periods (1963–1980 and 1991–2007) as a basis for comparing the development patterns for these sub-periods.

In Figure 3.2, comparing the two sub-periods A and B, it can be seen that in the earlier period the manufacturing share varied more than it did in the later period, increasing from less than 10 per cent to more than 20 per cent, with this peak value not being achieved in the later period at all. This might lead us to think that the role of manufacturing in economic development has somewhat diminished in recent years. However, this view needs to be qualified, since as more countries reach high levels of income per capita there is a larger number of countries (most of the advanced countries) experiencing a reduction in manufacturing share because

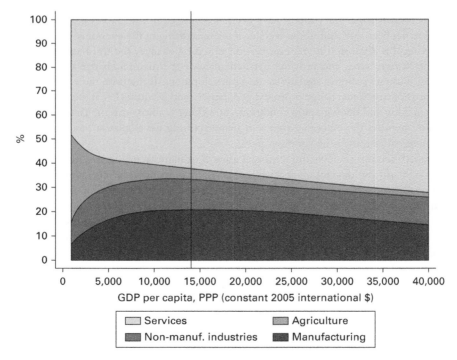

Figure 3.1 GDP composition by income and sector, 1963–2007. Pooled data for 100 countries.

Source: UNIDO's elaboration based on CIC (2009) and World Bank (2013).

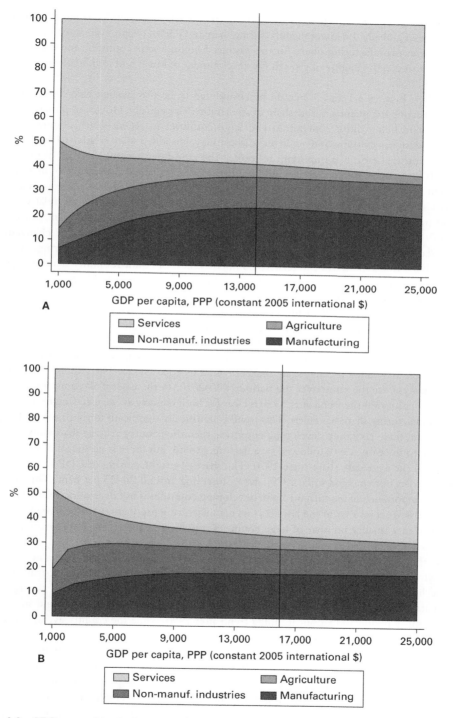

Figure 3.2 GDP composition by income and sector, (A) 1963–1980 and (B) 1991–2007. Pooled data for 100 countries.

Source: UNIDO's elaboration based on CIC (2009) and World Bank (2013).

they have lost their advantage in manufacturing and have become service-oriented economies. Therefore, if globally the lower manufacturing share in GDP in recent years is mainly attributed to the lower manufacturing shares for the advanced high income countries, the importance of manufacturing as the engine of growth for development of lower and middle income countries might still hold.

Further, Figures 3.1 and 3.2 could be considered to be the average patterns of structural change treating the manufacturing share of any country size equally. However, if manufacturing activities are being more concentrated in large countries in recent years, country averages might underestimate the world-wide manufacturing value added share relative to those of other sectors. In this regard, it is important to look at the world manufacturing share of total world GDP. If this share is decreasing it would confirm that the relative importance of manufacturing is in decline. However, if there is no evidence of such a global decline then manufacturing activities are just being concentrated in larger countries without changing the relative size of world manufacturing value added. If this is the case then the importance of manufacturing and of the development opportunities that it can offer to countries have not changed, but some (large) countries have been more successful in developing manufacturing industries than others. It is a matter of the relative competitiveness of countries rather than of a general shift in the world-wide economic structure, and there is a possibility of hitherto unsuccessful countries reversing the trend.

Changes in the shares of manufacturing value added are shown in Figure 3.3A and B for all countries for which the data are available (covering 182 countries including 112 developing countries) based on the two different methodologies – the first being based on the country average of manufacturing value added share and the second being total manufacturing value added (hereafter called the aggregate share) divided by total GDP.[5] The country samples used in this analysis are the same over the period 1970-2010. In the case of all countries (including advanced countries) the trend after 1990 is clear for both country average and aggregate shares – the manufacturing share has fallen. This trend is statistically significant for both methodologies. In contrast, if we take only developing countries, then the country average share shows a rising trend up to the early 1990s followed by a declining trend, but there is no statistically significant change in the aggregate share since 1970. The share of manufacturing in GDP for developing countries has not changed since 1970, always hovering around 20–23 per cent. This confirms that the importance of manufacturing in developing countries is not decreasing relative to other sectors. But it seems that in the last 20 years manufacturing production has become more concentrated in a smaller number of large countries, resulting in the recent lower manufacturing shares when calculated as country averages (rather than as aggregate shares).

On the basis of the manufacturing employment shares for all countries, as shown in Figure 3.4 for both the country average and the aggregate share methodologies, the trends for all countries are declining. However, if we limit our consideration to developing countries, the aggregate manufacturing employment share has had a statistically significant increasing trend since 1970 for the entire period and a non-declining trend after 1990, while the country average share has exhibited a declining trend since 1990.

Figures 3.3 and 3.4 show that the importance of the manufacturing sector in developing countries has not changed over the last 40 years. In 2010, manufacturing activities in developing countries added value to their economies in the same proportion as they did in 1970 and they also generated the same, if not a higher, proportion of employment. The difference between the results based on the country average and aggregate share methodologies, however, suggests that world manufacturing activities have become more concentrated in a smaller number of large countries, particularly in the last 20 years. This trend has probably reduced

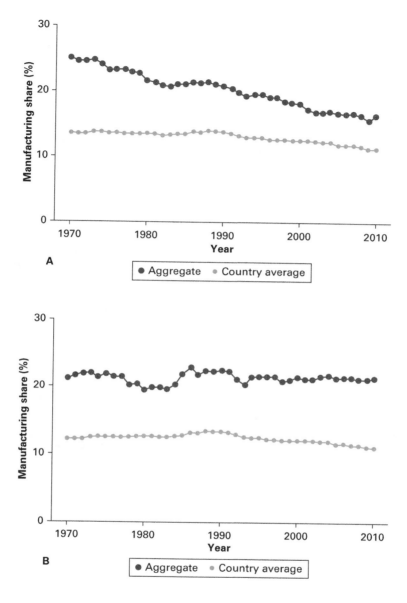

Figure 3.3 Manufacturing value added share, (A) all countries (182) and (B) developing countries (112). Excludes Soviet economies, includes island economies.

Source: United Nations (2014).

the manufacturing shares for a large number of countries, leading to lower world-wide manufacturing shares if calculated on the basis of country averages. However, if those countries which have experienced higher proportions of manufacturing production in recent years were to move to a mature stage of industrialisation in the future, they too are likely to start experiencing lower manufacturing value added shares as they follow the same development path as

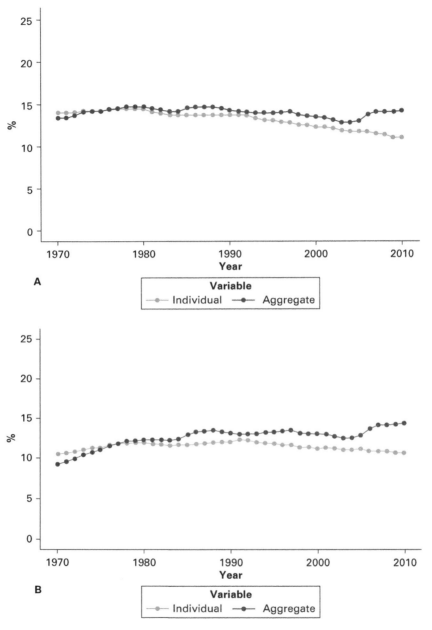

Figure 3.4 Manufacturing employment share, (A) all countries (106) and (B) developing countries (79). Excludes Soviet economies.

Sources: Groningen Growth and Development Centre (2014); ILO (2013, 2014).

Note: The country sample included in the database (79 developing and 27 developed countries) is the same over the period of the analysis from 1970 to 2010. The coherence of different data sources, if used, was maximised by calculating the share of manufacturing employment in each database first and multiplying that by the total employment numbers from the Total Economy Database of the Groningen Growth and Development Centre.

the current high income countries. When that happens there will be greater opportunities for manufacturing development in many 'follower' developing countries, so that industrialisation will be as relevant and important for these 'follower' countries as it has been for others in the process of economic development.

Structural change within manufacturing

As the Introduction illustrates, since 1970, manufacturing industry has been the source of 20–23 per cent of total value added in developing countries. Taking into account the stronger backward linkages from manufacturing to industries other than those which exist the other way around, the overall contribution of manufacturing to the economy is likely to be higher than its value added share might suggest.[6] Having observed manufacturing's position within the structure of the whole economy, this section discusses structural change within the manufacturing sector.

Chenery and Syrquin (1975) argue that a country's structural change depends on the following three factors: (i) the normal effect of universal factors that are related to the levels of income;[7] (ii) the effect of other general factors such as country size or natural resources over which the government has little or no control; (iii) the effects of the country's individual history, its political and social objectives, and the specific policies the government has followed to achieve these. Below, we illustrate factor (i), namely the relationships between structural changes within the manufacturing sector and income levels. We then examine the effects of geographic and demographic conditions, namely country size, population density and natural resource endowment. Finally, we review different countries' experiences with structural change within the manufacturing sector in order to shed some light on factor (iii). At the end of the chapter, the Appendix explains the regression analysis and the data used for the estimations of structural change.

Structural change in manufacturing along income levels
Value added

Figure 3.5 presents the estimated patterns of structural change within the manufacturing sector, illustrating how ten major manufacturing industries (based on the ISIC revision three at the two digit level) develop at different income stages. The vertical lines separate four development stages which exhibit distinct manufacturing structures. In the first stage, at very low income levels, there are commonly three industries which dominate the manufacturing sector: food and beverages, textiles and wearing apparel. These three industries are closely related to basic human needs, and usually exist before industrialisation 'takes off'. In this 'early' stage, labour-intensive industries[8] clearly have higher development potential in terms of value added, and their growth rates are also not much lower than those of emerging capital-intensive industries.

The ebb and flow of labour-intensive and capital-intensive industries become apparent in the second stage. The slowdown of the labour-intensive industries becomes increasingly noticeable as the manufacturing structure gradually shifts from labour-intensive to capital-intensive orientation. By the time that countries reach around $10,000 GDP per capita, many capital-intensive industries start surpassing the value added levels of textiles and wearing-apparel industries.

In the third stage, capital-intensive industries take a dominant position in terms of output. These industries, which include resource-processing industries such as basic and fabricated metals, as well as those which use such processed materials to produce final products including electrical machinery and motor vehicles, experience rapid growth. The difference between the growth rates of capital-intensive and labour intensive industries will be increasingly apparent in this stage.

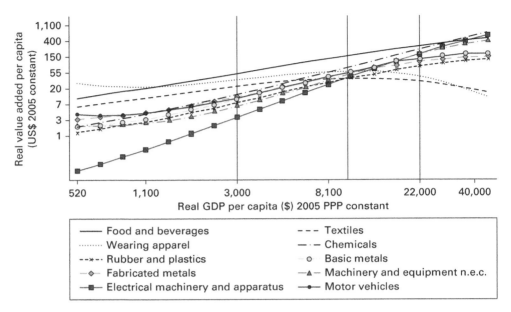

Figure 3.5 Patterns of structural change within manufacturing, all countries.

Source: UNIDO's elaboration based on Penn World Tables Version 7.0 and UNIDO (2014).

In the final stage at a very high income levels, labour-intensive industries, except for the food and beverage industry, decline and even some capital-intensive industries, such as resource-processing industries, start slowing down. Those which tend to sustain fast growth of value added are the chemicals, machinery and equipment, and electrical machinery and apparatus industries.

The development stages for all 18 manufacturing industries for which data are available are listed in Table 3.1. The early industries are mostly those which are relatively labour-intensive and/or are domestic-oriented industries. The middle industries include those which process natural resources to produce material inputs for other manufacturing industries. Finally, those that belong to the late industries tend to have a higher level of intensity in the application of technology and knowledge to production and, except for rubber and plastics, they produce capital or consumption goods for final use by firms or households.

Figure 3.5 contains clear estimated curves for the development patterns of manufacturing industries. However, this might give a false sense that the reliabilities of estimation are the same among industries and across income levels. Challenges and risks facing countries vary according to the characteristics of industries and stages of development, in addition to country-specific factors. Thus, there will be a tendency for countries to deviate from the estimated line, with greater variations for certain industries and at certain stages of development.

Figure 3.6 shows the estimated development patterns of industries with 95 per cent confidence intervals, indicating some important characteristics of manufacturing development. First of all, there are large differences between the performances of industries which play a crucial role in the relatively early stages of development. Textiles and wearing-apparel industries have wider confidence intervals around the estimated lines indicating a higher level of uncertainty with respect to the development of these industries. This suggests that risks facing countries are relatively high at early stages of development. The most difficult part of industrialisation can be to start it – that is, take-off of industrialisation.

Table 3.1 Development stages of manufacturing industries

Early	Food and beverages, tobacco, textiles, wearing apparel, wood products, publishing, furniture
	Non-metallic minerals
Middle	Coke and refined petroleum
	Paper
	Basic metals
	Fabricated metals
Late	Rubber and plastic
	Motor vehicles
	Chemicals, machinery and equipment, electrical machinery and apparatus, precision instruments

Notes: Manufacturing sub-sectors are classified into early, middle and late industries where sub-sector shares in GDP peak before $6,500 GDP per capita in PPP (constant 2005 price), between $6,500 and $15,000, and after $15,000, respectively. These income ranges correspond to our three income classifications – low and lower middle, upper middle and high incomes – in terms of GDP per capita PPP. In the table, industries are listed on the basis of those that peak at the lowest income level to those that peak the highest income level in terms of their value added shares in GDP. Industries that peak approximately at the same income level are listed horizontally.

A characteristic shared especially among middle and late industries is a high level of uncertainty in the early and mature stages of their development. As seen in Figure 3.6, their confidence intervals are wider at the lower and higher income ends, with a narrower interval for middle incomes. This suggests that at low incomes, when industrialisation is in its initial stages, country-specific conditions tend to have a significant influence over industrial development leading to a wider variance in performance between countries. However, after the industrial sector has taken off and has accumulated some experience the differences in performance between countries at the same income level become smaller. As countries come close to the end of the upper middle income stage (at around $15,000 GDP per capita in terms of PPP in 2005 constant prices) they again have wider differences in performance.

The greater uncertainty in manufacturing development from this stage onwards is attributed to the fact that countries are graduating from manufacturing development based on the acquisition of existing technologies from advanced countries and are moving to a stage where they have to take more risks in generating knowledge and technology themselves in order to directly compete with technology leaders (Lee 2013). At high incomes, countries which are successful in invention and innovation can sustain high growth of some manufacturing industries, such as the machinery and equipment and electrical machinery and apparatus industries, as indicated by the upper bound of their confidence intervals. Continued growth of these industries will be important to avoid premature de-industrialisation, to promote technological development and to generate employment in manufacturing, as well as related service industries, so that the manufacturing industry continues to contribute to a country's development.

Employment

The employment element of manufacturing structural change, as shown in Figure 3.7, is quite different from the value added element depicted in Figure 3.5. Food and beverages, textiles and wearing-apparel industries are the three major sources of manufacturing employment, with no other industries coming close to the peak employment levels of these industries at any income level. The food and beverages industry is a major and stable source of employment for all countries regardless of income levels. Textiles industries create jobs at earlier stages of development

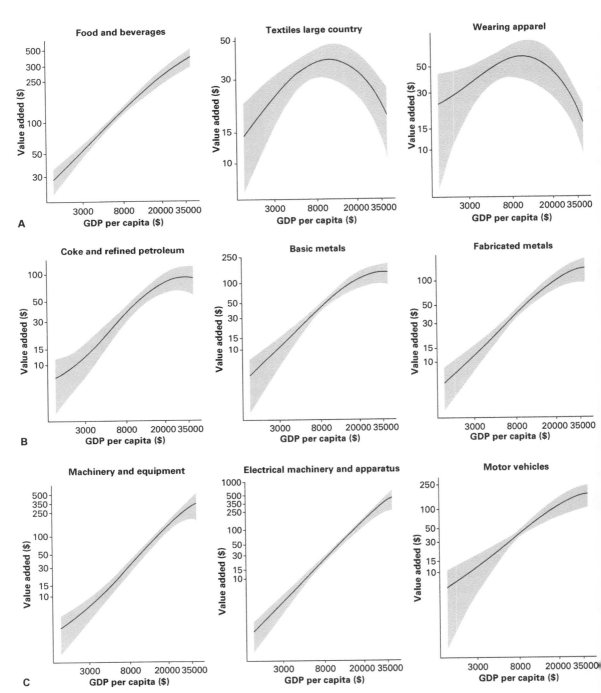

Figure 3.6 Confidence intervals for the estimated patterns, value added: (A) early industries; (B) middle industries; (C) late industries.

Source: UNIDO's elaboration based on Penn World Tables Version 8.0 and UNIDO (2014).

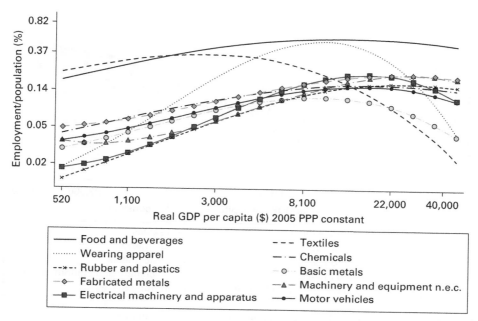

Figure 3.7 Patterns of employment change within manufacturing, all countries.

Source: UNIDO's elaboration based on Penn World Tables Version 8.0 and UNIDO (2014).

Note: The employment/population ratio is expressed as employment divided by population multiplied by 100.

than wearing-apparel industries. Unlike food and beverages and other industries, textiles and especially wearing-apparel industries reduce employment relatively fast once they reach their peak employment levels. The late industries steadily increase their employment and reach their peak employment levels, which are lower than those of the three labour-intensive industries discussed here, at a relatively high income level.

Impacts of demographic and geographic conditions on manufacturing structures

Country size

Past studies acknowledge that country size has an overarching influence on economic structural change (Chenery and Taylor, 1968; Haraguchi and Rezonja, 2011), with marked effects on both the intercepts and the slopes. This means that estimation of the industrial development patterns needs to use data samples classified according to country size.[9]

Some of the development patterns found in small countries (Figure 3.9) are similar to those for large countries (Figure 3.8). Labour-intensive industries develop at a relatively early stage, and capital-intensive industries only surpass the value added levels of labour-intensive industries at around $8,000–10,000 GDP per capita. The main difference between large and small countries is that labour-intensive industries tend to develop earlier in small countries, and after they reach their peak levels of output they decline relatively rapidly. The growth rates among industries at high income levels vary much more than those found in small countries. One particular industry which has a very different development path in small countries compared

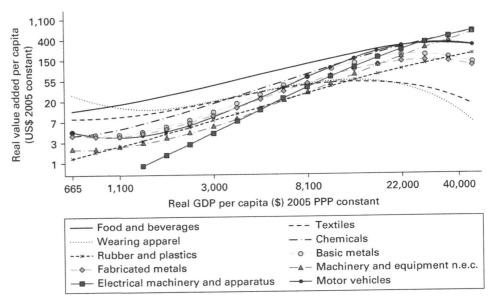

Figure 3.8 Patterns of structural change within manufacturing, large countries.

Source: UNIDO's elaboration based on Penn World Tables Version 7.0 and UNIDO (2014).

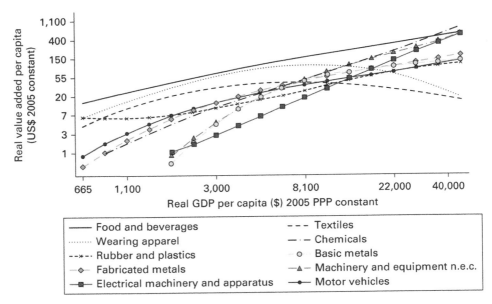

Figure 3.9 Patterns of structural change within manufacturing, small countries.

Source: UNIDO's elaboration based on Penn World Tables Version 7.0 and UNIDO (2014).

with large countries is the motor vehicle industry. The level of its development is much lower in small countries, and unlike the case of large countries, it does not sustain growth at high incomes, suggesting the importance of the domestic market for this industry.

Population density and natural resource endowment

Keesing and Sherk (1971) show that population density plays an important role in patterns of trade and development. Densely populated areas appear to have a greater impact, in particular, on the levels of exports of manufactured goods relative to primary products. This suggests that population density could affect the patterns of manufacturing development, with population density being determined by the simple division of a country's population size by the country's total area.

The negative impact of natural resource abundance on industrialisation is well documented. A country's natural resource base affects patterns of industrialisation in two related ways. First, orientation toward industrialisation occurs due to a lack of natural resources, which induces countries to find an alternative export base (Chenery and Syrquin, 1975). This is an explanation of why resource-poor countries are likely to specialise more in manufacturing than resource-rich countries. Second, as Sachs and Warner (2001) explain, the reasons why countries rich in natural resources tend to have a lower level of manufacturing development can be related to the 'natural resource curse' or 'Dutch disease' arguments, related to the cost disadvantage for tradable, typically manufacturing, sectors due to the rise in domestic prices, including input costs and wages, driven by the natural resource sector and its impact on the foreign exchange rate.

Figure 3.10 summarises the effects of high population density (left column) and high natural resource endowments[10] (right column) on manufacturing development. The industries in which these conditions have positive (or negative) effects are listed in the upper (or lower) cells. For both the population density and the natural resources columns, industries are listed from those which are most positively affected to those which are most negatively affected by the respective conditions.[11] A positive (or negative) effect means that the development pattern of the industries in Figure 3.5 shifts upward (or downward), so that value added per capita in that industry at a given income level is higher (or lower) than might be expected due to these effects.

Generally speaking, high population density tends to have positive effects on manufacturing development, especially for capital- and technology-intensive industries, while high natural resource endowment tends to have the opposite effect – a negative impact on manufacturing development in general and capital- and technology-intensive industries in particular. The result of the impact of high population density suggests that densely populated countries possess logistical and agglomeration advantages, which would be especially conducive to the development of industries that involve relatively complex and lengthy production processes and supply chains, such as the machinery and equipment and electrical machinery industries. As would be expected on the basis of the discussion in this section, high natural resource endowments have negative impacts on most manufacturing industries.

Country-specific conditions

Besides income levels and country-specific conditions, such as demographic and geographic conditions, country-created effects influence the patterns of manufacturing development. Country-created conditions are related to institutions, history and policies, which produce systematic and consistent differences in the potential levels of manufacturing development across countries over a long period of time. As seen in the examples of the Republic of Korea (KOR), Malaysia (MYS), and Sri Lanka (LKA) in Figure 3.11, countries can deviate from the estimated pattern positively (above) or negatively (below).[12] In terms of their development trajectories, however, these three countries tend to follow the general development patterns of industries, as seen in their more or less parallel movements along the estimated lines (solid lines). The similarity in development patterns also generally applies to other countries.

	High population density	**High resource endowments**
+	**Strongly positive** Machinery and equipment Electrical machinery Rubber and plastics Chemicals Precision instruments Non-metallic minerals Wood products Fabricated metals Motor vehicles	**Strongly positive** Basic metals
–	Wearing apparel Textiles Printing and publishing Tobacco **Strongly negative**	Food and beverages Wood products Printing and publishing Motor vehicles Fabricated metals Tobacco Chemicals Furniture, n.e.c. Non-metallic minerals Rubber and plastics Machinery and equipment Electrical machinery **Strongly negative**

Figure 3.10 Effects of high population density and high natural resource endowment.

Source: UNIDO's elaboration based on Penn World Tables Version 8.0 and UNIDO (2014).

Country-specific conditions can be estimated by a regression with country fixed effects as seen in the example of food and beverages in large countries. Figure 3.12 shows the relationship between per capita income and manufacturing value added per capita by country with deviations from the line explained by the country dummies. Some countries (A) have characteristics which give them distinct advantages over others, in relation to industry value added per capita for a given level of income, while others (B) have characteristics which give them a lower performance consistently over a long period of time.

If country-specific effects (indicated by the country fixed effects dummy in the regression analysis) have an influence on the potential level of manufacturing development, one needs to ask whether such effects are mostly related to the development of the manufacturing sector as a whole, or if they are specific to subsectors of manufacturing (such as food and beverages, wearing apparel, motor vehicles, etc.). Such country-specific effects provide useful evidence for the design and application of types of industrial policies, and the priorities between policies, that countries might consider. Table 3.2 classifies countries, which reported data for at least 12 out of 18 industries, into three groups based on whether their country-specific conditions across different manufacturing industries are consistently favourable or unfavourable. It is interesting to note that 60 per cent of the countries have a consistent condition, either favourable or

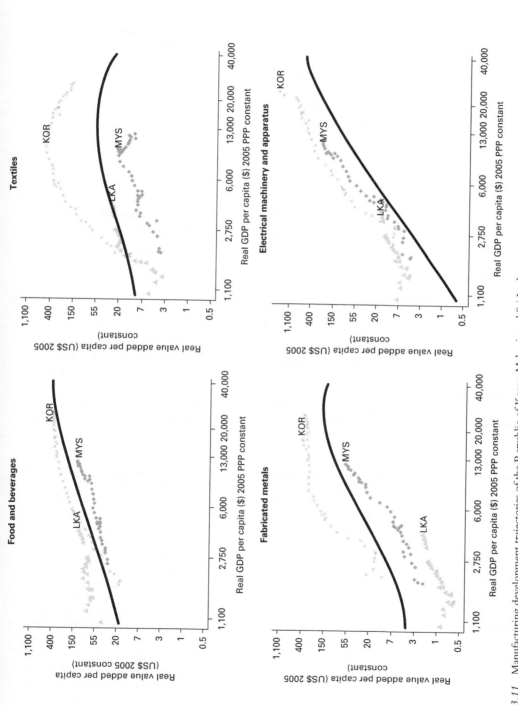

Figure 3.11 Manufacturing development trajectories of the Republic of Korea, Malaysia and Sri Lanka.

Source: UNIDO's elaboration based on Penn World Tables Version 8.0 and UNIDO (2014).

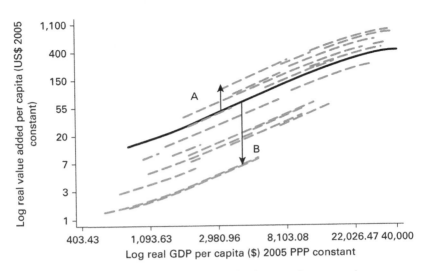

Figure 3.12 Country-specific effects on manufacturing development, large countries.

Source: UNIDO's elaboration based on UNIDO INDSTAT and Penn World Tables.

unfavourable, relative to their peers (defined by similar country size and income level) across most of the manufacturing industries covered. This is evidence that there are some specific country conditions which are important for the development of the manufacturing sector as a whole. These can include long-term conditions engendered by factors like political conditions, macroeconomic stability, quality of infrastructure, and factor prices, relative to other countries at a similar GDP per capita.

To understand further the relationships between general country conditions and the development potential of manufacturing industries, the size of the coefficient on country fixed effects

Table 3.2 Consistency of manufacturing performance

1 *Consistently high performance across most manufacturing industries*	Czech Republic, Brazil, Canada, Denmark, France, Finland, Germany, Iceland, Ireland, Israel, Italy, Japan, Republic of Korea, Netherlands, Norway, Singapore, Slovenia, Spain, Sweden, UK, USA
2 *Consistently low performance across most manufacturing industries*	Azerbaijan, Ethiopia, Georgia, India, Indonesia, Iran, Kenya, Kyrgyzstan, Mauritius, Mongolia, Oman, Philippines, Republic of Macedonia, Republic of Moldova, Senegal, Turkey, Egypt, Yemen
3 *Differences in performance depending on industries*	Australia, Bulgaria, China, Colombia, Costa Rica, Cyprus, Estonia, Greece, Hungary, Jordan, Kuwait, Latvia, Lithuania, Malaysia, Mexico, Morocco, Peru, Poland, Portugal, Qatar, Romania, Russian Federation, Serbia, Slovakia, South Africa, Sri Lanka, Trinidad and Tobago, Uruguay

Source: Produced by the author based on Penn World Tables version 8.0 and UNIDO INDSTAT (2014).

Notes: Countries having data which could be used to calculate impact of the selected characteristics for more than 12 industries are included. Those countries which had a higher level for the country fixed effects (reflecting country-specific effects) than the average for more than 80 per cent of their reported industries were placed in the first category in the table. Those countries with lower levels for the country fixed effects than the average for more than 80 per cent of their reported industries were placed in the second category. Countries falling in neither of the above categories were placed in the third category.

Table 3.3 Correlations between the size of country fixed effects and business conditions

Industry	Unit labour cost		Rule of law		Roads	
Food and beverages	−0.1083	(−0.3100)	0.2083	(6.6900)	0.0036	(2.6500)
Textiles	−0.4336	(−3.7500)	0.2082	(6.6800)	0.0036	(2.6500)
Wearing apparel	−0.5886	(−3.5400)	0.1977	(6.2700)	0.0037	(2.7800)
Chemicals	−0.5029	(−3.3300)	0.2048	(6.5700)	0.0034	(2.5400)
Basic metals	0.0524	(0.2000)	0.2609	(8.1300)	0.0035	(2.4700)
Fabricated metals	−0.1526	(−2.9500)	0.2090	(6.7200)	0.0035	(2.6000)
Electrical machinery and apparatus	−0.1095	(−0.4500)	0.3048	(9.3100)	0.0036	(2.3600)
Motor vehicles	−0.0743	(−0.3500)	0.2231	(6.8300)	0.0034	(2.3600)

Source: UNIDO's elaboration based on CIC (2009), UNIDO (2014) and the World Bank (2013).

Notes: The dependent variable used for the regression is the coefficient on country fixed effects. The numbers in parenthesis are *t*-values. Unit labour cost was calculated by nominal wages divided by real value added (ADB, 2005). The variables for the rule of law and road conditions are based on the Worldwide Governance Indicators and the World Development Indicators of the World Bank, respectively.

has been regressed against certain specific features of a country which can be expected to remain in place for a fairly long time and to affect the development potential of industrial development. The results reported in Table 3.3 confirm that higher unit labour cost and higher indicators for the rule of law and for infrastructure (proxied by the share of paved roads), which shape the general business climate, have negative and positive effects on the development potential of most manufacturing industries, respectively. These results provide support for the view that there would be significant benefits arising from improvements in the general business and institutional environment, which would raise the development potential across manufacturing industries in countries with a very low level of manufacturing development, before proceeding very far with ambitious industrial policies for specific manufacturing industries. Under a hostile business environment with limited development potential, industry-specific measures might not make much difference to the performance of industries, and any improved performance might not be sustainable without costly interventions.

Emerging trends of manufacturing industries

The development patterns of some industries have been changing over time as seen, for example, in the declining trend for value added in the textile industry in Figure 3.13. This declining trend is distinct from the decrease in the industry's value added related to increases in individual country income per capita. The clear downward shifts of the curves for each of the four time periods shown in Figure 3.13 show a steady change in consumer demand and technology, which leads to lower value added per capita for textile industries at all income levels. This change in industry characteristics is related to changing consumer preferences for its products over time (i.e. time series analysis), which are distinctly different to demand and supply changes related to different income levels across countries at a particular point in time (i.e. cross-section analysis).

Emerging trends within the manufacturing sub-sector, reflected in shifting patterns of value added and employment, are summarised in Table 3.4 (based on the criteria indicated in the note to the table). The tobacco and textiles industries have experienced reductions in both value added and employment levels over time. In contrast, the rubber and plastics industry

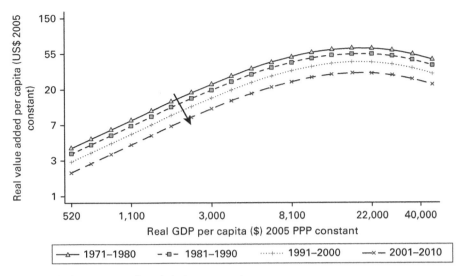

Figure 3.13 Shifting pattern of textile industry over time.

Source: UNIDO (2013).

has experienced increasing levels of value added and employment, making the industry relatively more important than before. Many middle and late industries have been changing their production technologies in such a way as to increase capital intensity, substituting capital for labour. Furniture is the only industry which has become more labour-intensive, while the technological characteristics of the food and beverage industry have been stable over time.

Table 3.4 Emerging characteristics of manufacturing industries since 1980

Emerging characteristics since 1980	Industry
Rising	Rubber and plastics
Declining	Tobacco
	Textiles
Intensifying capital use	Paper
	Chemicals
	Non-metallic minerals
	Basic metals
	Fabricated metals
	Electrical machinery and apparatus
	Motor vehicles
Intensifying labour use	Furniture
Stable	Food and beverages

Source: UNIDO (2013).

Notes: Where value added and employment have shown a statistically significant increase in all three decades since 1980 the industry has been classified as 'Rising'. Where an industry has shown consistent reductions in both variables it has been classified as 'Declining'. Where an industry has shown increased value added but decreased (or at least not increased) employment it has been classified as 'Intensifying capital use'. Where there is evidence of an increase in employment and a decrease, or no change, in value added it has been classified as 'Intensifying labour use'. If there has been no significant change in industry value added and employment it has been classified as 'Stable'.

Speed of manufacturing development and structural change

Our analysis thus far points to certain consistent patterns of manufacturing development which countries tend to follow, even though the exact levels for industry variables differ from country to country due to country-specific effects. The speed of an individual industry's development is therefore crucial for manufacturing upgrade, and structural change. As was seen in Table 3.1, different industries tend to emerge as leaders at different income levels. On the one hand, labour-intensive, low technology industries, such as food and beverages and wearing apparel, are major manufacturing industries for low income countries, while on the other hand, capital-intensive and technologically sophisticated industries, such as electrical machinery and apparatus and motor vehicles, are usually dominant industries in high income countries. If countries are to experience patterns of manufacturing development which are broadly associated with different income levels, it is very much in countries' interests to develop industries within existing comparative advantages as fast as possible so as to increase income along with such development (Figure 3.5) and move on to the next emerging industries.

The speed of manufacturing development in Malaysia, Republic of Korea and Sri Lanka is shown in Table 3.5, expressed in terms of increases in value added per capita per year. The Republic of Korea developed all eight manufacturing industries much faster than Malaysia and Sri Lanka over the same income range of between US$3,000 and US$4,500. Malaysia developed five out of the eight industries faster than Sri Lanka. However, the speed and level at which a country moves along the pattern (country-specific effects) are not necessarily associated with each other. For example, Sri Lanka developed textile and basic metals industries at a higher value added per capita level than Malaysia, even though the former moved slower than the latter. The preferred situation is the case of the Republic of Korea, which moved faster than Malaysia, Sri Lanka and most other countries, also at higher levels than those countries, allowing the Republic of Korea to generate greater value added from each industry while rapidly upgrading the industrial structure.

If a country climbs rapidly up a development curve of each industry, it is expected that the country will also move to emerging new industries quickly and thus accelerate the change in industrial structure. Figure 3.14 shows how countries have changed from one broad type of industry to another. The vertical axis shows the ratio of consumer goods to capital goods

Table 3.5 Speed of manufacturing development in Malaysia, Republic of Korea and Sri Lanka

Industry	Malaysia	Republic of Korea	Sri Lanka
Food and beverages	1.49	5.26	3.03
Textiles	0.70	21.47	0.43
Wearing apparel	1.40	42.97	1.81
Chemicals	1.69	4.05	3.04
Basic metals	0.53	6.33	0.34
Fabricated metals	0.29	11.51	0.04
Electrical machinery and apparatus	0.77	8.10	0.42
Motor vehicles	0.61	4.97	0.02

Source: UNIDO's elaboration based on CIC (2009) and UNIDO (2014).

Note: The speed is expressed as the percentage increase in value added per capita divided by the number of years taken over the range of GDP per capita from US$3,000 to US$4,500. The analysis focuses on this income range because different income ranges are associated with different growth rates and we need to use an income range where the observations of the three countries overlap.

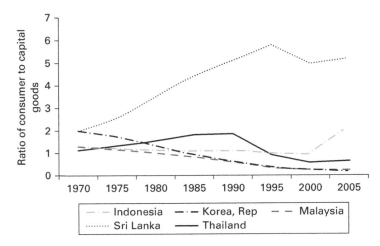

Figure 3.14   Speed of structural change within manufacturing.

Source: UNIDO (2014).

production. Food and beverages, tobacco, wearing apparel, footwear and leather goods, and furniture industries belong to the group of consumer-goods industries, while ferrous and non-ferrous metals, machinery, vehicle building and chemicals are included in the group of capital-goods industries. The consumer-goods industries roughly correspond to our early industries while capital-goods industries are found in our classification of middle and late industries (Table 3.1). Hence a reduction in the ratio means that the manufacturing structure is becoming more capital goods-intensive.

Figure 3.14, giving the ratio of consumer to capital goods, shows that even within a group of relatively successful Asian countries there are large differences. In 1970 the manufacturing structure of the Republic of Korea was dominated by the consumer-goods industries, or so-called early industries, which generated two-thirds of manufacturing value added at that time, even more so than other Asian countries such as Malaysia and Thailand. However, over the last 35 years the Republic of Korea has rapidly transformed the structure of its manufacturing production towards capital goods industries, so that its manufacturing structure is now comparable to that of mature industrialised countries, such as the UK, Germany and Japan.

Malaysia had a more capital-goods-intensive structure than the Republic of Korea in 1970, but from that structure the proportion of capital goods in Malaysian manufacturing production increased further. However, the speed of Malaysian structural transformation was slower than that of the Republic of Korea, so that the latter caught up and overtook Malaysia by 2000 in terms of the value added share of capital-goods industries in manufacturing. Sri Lanka, as a lower middle income country, still has a high and mostly increasing ratio of consumer goods (or early industries) perhaps strengthened by the country's economic liberalisation from the mid-1970s. In 1970 Thailand and Indonesia had a lower consumer/capital-goods ratio than the Republic of Korea and about the same level as Malaysia. However, in Thailand the ratio only started to fall from 1990, while in Indonesia it hardly changed for 30 years but has increased since 2000.

Figure 3.15 shows that a low consumer/capital-goods ratio is associated with the industrial structure of advanced countries whose manufacturing sectors are dominated by capital-goods

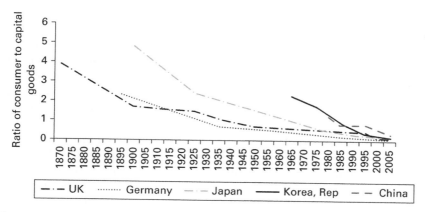

Figure 3.15 Long-term structural change in early industrialised countries.

Sources: UNIDO (2014) and Hoffmann (1958).

production and technology-intensive industries. The relatively recent case of the Republic of Korea's industrialisation is distinguished from the experiences of the earlier industrialisers by the much higher speed of its structural transformation. Reduction of the consumer/capital-goods ratio from 2 to the current levels of around 0.5 took approximately 105 years for the UK, 100 years for Germany, 70 years for Japan, but only 35 years for the Republic of Korea. China is now industrialising at a similar pace. These recent examples indicate how quickly countries can transform their industrial structure by climbing rapidly up the development curves of individual industries, which accelerates structural change in the manufacturing sector as a whole.

Conclusions

Following Chenery and Syrquin (1975) this chapter has discussed the three major factors which shape structural change. First, the stage of development is the most fundamental force of structural change as the differences in supply and demand capabilities associated with changing income levels drive the emergence of certain industries, as outlined in the third section. At an early stage of a country's development, low technology activities such as food and beverages, textiles and wearing-apparel production develop. These are labour-intensive industries and they are the major sources of manufacturing employment up to the upper middle income stage. As a country moves through the upper middle to the high income range, the dominant industries change from early to middle industries (such as basic metals) and then to late industries (such as electrical machinery and apparatus) with an increasingly capital and technology intensity in manufacturing production as a whole. This pattern of structural change is generally found across countries regardless of their country-specific conditions and the time periods considered.

In addition to the income level, which Chenery and Syrquin (1975) called a universal factor of structural change, country-specific factors shape manufacturing development and produce a unique path of structural change for individual countries. In the third section it was shown how a country's given conditions, such as demographic and geographic effects over which countries have no or very limited control, affect manufacturing development. Smaller countries tend to develop labour-intensive industries at an earlier stage of development than large countries and have a limited prospect for the sustained growth of the motor vehicle industry in particular. Abundant natural resource endowment has a negative impact on the development of almost all manufacturing industries, while a higher level of population density works especially positively for capital and technology intensive industries.

There are other country-specific conditions which raise or reduce an industry's level of development for a given income level. The importance of the general business environment was underscored, which can affect the development potential of manufacturing industries across the board. In countries where all or most of manufacturing industries have a lower than expected manufacturing value added per capita, an initial step for policy would be to improve the general business climate, such as unit labour costs, the condition of infrastructure services, and macroeconomic and political stability before resorting to industry-specific policy measures.

In addition to country conditions, different time periods have time-specific effects on manufacturing development, increasing or decreasing the development potential of industries for a certain period across all income levels. In the discussion of this issue, time-specific effects were traced over the last 30 years in order to identify emerging trends of manufacturing development. For example, the textiles industry has been experiencing falling value added and employment, at given income levels. The most common emerging characteristic is an increase in the capital intensity of the production process. Several industries have been increasing value added with disproportionately low additional inputs of labour, or in some cases with an absolute reduction of labour.

Finally, the fourth section discussed the speed of development as another dimension of both the level of manufacturing development and of structural change across countries. Even though their development patterns in relation to income per capita might be similar, some countries, such as the Republic of Korea, moved much faster than others along their income trajectory. Historically the speed of industrialisation and structural change in recent successful countries is much faster than that experienced by Western countries and Japan during their periods of industrialisation. This suggests that an increasingly globalised world might allow developing countries with decent human and institutional capabilities and business conditions to have greater opportunities for technical and policy learning, facilitated and incentivised by international assistance and competition.

The findings of this chapter are summarised in Figure 3.16. First of all, the development stage of a country is the most fundamental factor to shape its manufacturing development and its manufacturing structure, with comparative advantage associated broadly with income level. For example, Industry A can be considered a low-technology and labour intensive industry, which rapidly develops at a relatively early stage of development (say $3,000 GDP per capita), while Industry B is a capital- and technology-intensive industry, likely to emerge and grow rapidly at a higher income (say $10,000 GDP per capita). Although particular industries have generally followed similar development patterns across the range of countries, they do not take a single path but can deviate upwards or downwards due to their country-specific conditions, such as demographic and geographic conditions, other factors including history, institutions and policy and also time-specific effects. These country- and time-specific effects not only lead to different levels of manufacturing development but also generate different speeds of development for individual industries (C) and for structural change (D).

Different schools of thought have put forward a range of factors as the primary determinants of manufacturing development. However, as discussed in this chapter and as is seen in Figure 3.16, each determinant varies in terms of where and how it affects the development of different branches of manufacturing, and it is the combination of these effects that ultimately determine the level and path of manufacturing development at both the industry and the aggregate levels.

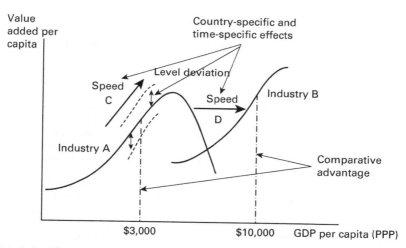

Figure 3.16   Schematic representation of the role of comparative advantage, and country-specific and time-specific effects in manufacturing development.

Source: Author's elaboration.

Appendix

The equation which appears below includes fixed effects and is used for the estimation of development patterns for 18 manufacturing industries at the two digit level of International Standard of Industrial Classification. For each industry the real value added, employment and labour productivity have been estimated. The panel dataset which is used consists of time series from 1963 to 2010 from 75 to 110 countries depending on the industries and variables estimated. In addition, we assessed the effects of population density, natural resource endowment and time periods on the three dependent variables.

Real value added per capita of each industry is calculated based on an industry-specific Index of Industrial Production. Similar analyses are carried out for employment and labour productivity.

$$\ln RVA_{ct}^i$$

$$\ln EMP_{ct}^i = \alpha_1 + \alpha_2 *\ln RDGP_{ct} + \alpha_3 *\ln RDGP_{ct}^2 + \alpha_4 *\ln RDGP_{ct}^3 + \alpha_c^i + e_{ct}^i$$

$$\ln LP_{ct}^i$$

RVA	real value added per capita
EMP	employment/population ratio
LP	labour productivity
$RGDP_2$	real GDP per capita (in constant PPP 2005 international dollars)
$RGDP_3$	real GDP per capita squared
$RGDP$	real GDP per capita cubed
α_c	country fixed effect
e	unexplained residual
i	manufacturing industry (ISIC 2 digit level – 18 industries)

Notes

1 The author is grateful to Mr. Charles Fang Chin Cheng and Ms. Eveline Smeets for their data processing and graphic support.
2 The relationship between growth and structural change is not of course without exceptions. A notable example is the key role that the services sector has played in India's economic growth.
3 The stage of development at which the share of manufacturing in total value added reaches its peak depends on geographic and demographic conditions as well as other country-specific factors besides income level (Chenery and Syrquin, 1975; Haraguchi and Rezonja, 2010).
4 The income levels are defined in terms of GDP per capita at constant 2005 PPP international dollar values. To make the income classifications of countries comparable with the World Bank classification, low and lower middle, upper middle income and high income have been defined as $6,500 or less, $6,500–$15,000 and more than $15,000 respectively.
5 The countries of the former Soviet Union have been excluded in the calculations for the entire period because their disintegration and economic restructuring did not necessarily represent the long-term general trend of structural change. Nevertheless, including the economies of the former Soviet Union in the calculations does not change the country average and aggregate trends after 1990.
6 For example, in the cases of BRICS countries see Haraguchi and Rezonja (2015).
7 The income effect includes both the supply and demand effects. The demand effect is usually associated with the fact that rising income leads to changes in the composition of demand, of which the decline in the share of food (Engel's law) is the most notable feature. The supply effect, on the other hand, entails two factors of general importance: (i) the overall increase in capital stock per worker, and (ii) the increase in education and skills of all kinds. Since the combination of labour, capital, and skills varies from industry to industry, a change in factor supplies causes a systematic shift in comparative advantage as per capita income rises (Chenery 1960).
8 In order to determine labour intensity, employment per unit of value added was estimated at $5,000 and $20,000 GDP per capita because the labour intensity changes with income levels. If an industry's labour intensity was higher than the median for 18 manufacturing industries at both income levels, it was considered labour-intensive. Among the industries presented here, the food and beverage, textiles and wearing-apparel industries are labour-intensive, while the others are relatively capital-intensive.
9 In order to classify countries into two groups of different sizes we applied thresholds to divide them into small and large countries. We then looked for the threshold level for which the development patterns for the maximum number of manufacturing industries differ statistically from one another. This was achieved by applying the Wald test. Based on our test results, we used a threshold per capita GDP of $12.5 million for the division of countries into the smaller and larger groups.
10 The natural resource proxy variable was calculated as the difference between exports and imports of crude natural resource commodities and was expressed in per capita terms. The commodities included are those categorised under SITC revision 1 in Codes 2 (crude materials, inedible, except fuels), 32 (coal, coke and briquettes), 331 (petroleum, crude and partly refined) and 3411 (gas, natural).
11 Of the 18 industries listed in Table 3.1, only industries for which population density or high natural resource endowment had statistically significant impacts are included.
12 The Republic of Korea, Malaysia and Sri Lanka were selected as examples because these three countries are within the group of large countries and have relatively long data time-series which can be used to observe their development trajectories. Also, because they are within same development stage (from approximately $3,000 to $4,500 GDP per capita) we could compare the speed of their development as discussed in Section 3.4.

References

ADB. 2005. *Key Indicators 2005: Labor Markets in Asia: Promoting Full, Productive, and Decent Employment.* Manila: Asian Development Bank.

Chenery, H. B. 1960. Patterns of Industrial Growth. *American Economic Review.* 50(4): 624–654.

Chenery, H. B. and Syrquin, M. 1975. Accumulation and Allocation Processes. In Chenery, H. B. and Syrquin, M. (eds.). *Patterns of Development: 1950–1970.* Oxford: Oxford University Press for the World Bank.

Chenery, H. B. and Taylor, L. J. 1968. Development Patterns: Among Countries and Over Time. *Review of Economics and Statistics.* 50(4): 391–416.

Chenery, H. B., Robinson, S. and Syrquin, M. 1986. Structural Transformation. In Chenery, H. B., Robinson, S. and Syrquin, M. (eds.). *Industrialization and Growth: A Comparative Study*. Oxford: Oxford University Press: 11–12.

CIC. 2009. *Penn World Table 6.3 and 8.0 Database*. Philadelphia, PA: Center for International Comparisons – accessible at www.pwt.sas.upenn.edu – last Accessed September 2013.

Franke, R. and Kalmbach, P. 2005. Structural Change in the Manufacturing Sector and Its Impact on Business-Related Services: An Input–Output Study for Germany. *Structural Change and Economic Dynamics*. 16 (4): 467–488.

Groningen Growth and Development Centre. 2014. *10-Sector Database and Africa Sector Database*. Groningen: University of Groningen – accessible from www.rug.nl/research/ggdc/data/10-sector-database – last Accessed October 2014.

Guerrieri, P. and Meliciani, V. 2005. Technology and International Competitiveness: The Interdependence Between Manufacturing and Producer Services. *Structural Change and Economic Dynamics*. 16(4): 489–502.

Haraguchi, N. and Rezonja, G. 2010. *In Search of General Patterns of Manufacturing Development*. Development Policy and Strategic Research Branch Working Paper 02/2010. Vienna: United Nations Industrial Development Organization.

Haraguchi, N. and Rezonja, G. 2011. *Emerging Patterns of Manufacturing Structural Change*. UNU-WIDER Working Paper 2011/43. Helsinki: United Nations University World Institute for Development Economics Research.

Haraguchi, N. and Rezonja, G. 2015. Structural Change in the BRICS Manufacturing Industries. In Naudé, W. Szirmai, A. and Haraguchi, N. (eds.). *Structural Change and Industrial Development in the BRICS*. Oxford: Oxford University Press, forthcoming.

Hoffmann, W. G. 1958. *The Growth of Industrial Economies*. Manchester: University of Manchester Press (translated from the German by Henderson, W. O. and Chaloner, W. H.).

ILO. 2013. *Key Indicators of the Labour Market (KILM)*. Geneva: International Labour Organization – accessible from http://www.ilo.org/empelm/what/WCMS_114240/lang–en/index.htm – last accessed October 2014.

ILO. 2014. *ILOSTAT Database*. Geneva: International Labour Organization – accessible from www.ilo.org/ilostat – last accessed October 2014.

Imbs, J. and Wacziarg, R. 2003. Stages of Diversification. *American Economic Review*. 93(1): 63–86.

Kaldor, N. 1967. *Strategic Factors in Economic Development*. Ithaca, NY: Cornell University.

Katz, J.2000. Structural Change and Labour Productivity Growth in Latin American Manufacturing Industries 1970–96. *World Development*. 28(9): 1583–1596.

Keesing, D. B. and Sherk, D. R. 1971. Population Density in Patterns of Trade and Development. *American Economic Review*. 61(5): 956–961.

Kuznets, S.1966. *Modern Economic Growth: Rate, Structure and Spread*. New Haven, CT, and London: Yale University Press.

Lee, K. 2013. *Schumpeterian Analysis of Economic Catch-Up: Knowledge, Path-Creation, and the Middle-Income Trap?* New York: Cambridge University Press.

Lin, J. 2012. *New Structural Economics: A Framework for Rethinking Development and Policy*. Washington DC: World Bank.

Lin, J. and Chang, H-J. 2009. Should Industrial Policy in Developing Countries Conform to Comparative Advantage or Defy It? A Debate between Justin Lin and Ha-Joon Chang. *Development Policy Review*. 27(5): 483–502.

Maddison, A. 2003. *The World Economy: Historical Statistics*. Paris: Organisation for Economic Cooperation and Development.

Ocampo, J. A., Rada, C. and Taylor, L. 2009. Economic Structure, Policy, and Growth. In Ocampo, J. A., Rada, C. and Taylor, L. (eds.). *Growth and Policy in Developing Countries: A Structuralist Approach*. New York: Columbia University Press: 1–24.

Pasinetti, L. L. 1981. Introduction. In Pasinetti, L. L. (ed.). *Structural Change and Economic Growth*. Cambridge: Cambridge University Press: 1–25.

Rodrik, D. (2011), The Future of Economic Convergence. *NBER Working Paper Series*, No. 17400. National Bureau of Economic Research.

Sachs, J. and Warner, A. W. 2001. The Curse of Natural Resources. *European Economic Review*. 45 (4–6): 827–838.

Tahara, S. 2009. Seizougyo to Saabisugyo no Sougorenkan to Kouzouhenka (Linkage Between Manufacturing and Service Sectors and Structural Change). *Yokohama International Social Science Research*. 14(3): 111–130.

Tomlinson, M. 2012. *Industrialization and Employment: Long-Term Perspective*. Background paper prepared for the 2013 Industrial Development Report. Vienna: United Nations Industrial Development Organization.

UNIDO. 2012. *Promoting Industrial Diversification in Resource Intensive Economies: The Experiences of Sub-Saharan Africa and Central Asia Regions*. Vienna: United Nations Industrial Development Organization.

UNIDO. 2013. *Industrial Development Report 2013. Sustaining Employment Growth: The Role of Manufacturing and Structural Change*. Vienna: United Nations Industrial Development Organization.

UNIDO. 2014. *Industrial Statistics Database 2-Digit Level, ISIC Revision 3 (INDSTAT2)*, 2014. Vienna: United Nations Industrial Development Organization – accessible from www.unido.org/en/resources/statistics/statistical-databases/indstat2-2014-edition.html

United Nations. 2014. *National Accounts Main Aggregate Database*. New York: United Nations Statistics Division – accessible from www.unstats.un.org/unsd/snaama/ – last accessed in October 2014.

Weiss, J. 2011. *The Economics of Industrial Development*. New York: Routledge.

World Bank. 2013. *World Development Indicators Database*. Washington, DC: World Bank – accessible from data.worldbank.org/indicator – last accessed September 2013.

4

PATTERNS OF STRUCTURAL CHANGE IN DEVELOPING COUNTRIES

Marcel Timmer, Gaaitzen J. de Vries and Klaas de Vries

Introduction

A central concept in development economics is the notion of structural change. Structural change, which we narrowly define in this chapter as the reallocation of labour across sectors with different productivity levels, featured prominently in the early literature on economic development by Kuznets (1966). Technological change typically takes place at the detailed industry level and thereby induces differential patterns of sector productivity growth. At the same time, changes in demand and international trade drive a process of structural transformation in which production factors such as capital, labour and intermediate inputs are continuously relocated across locations and economic activities (Kuznets, 1966; Chenery *et al.*, 1986; Harberger, 1998; Hsieh and Klenow, 2009; Herrendorf *et al.*, 2014).

The long-run pattern of structural transformation has been carefully documented for advanced economies (see e.g. Jorgenson and Timmer, 2011). One of the best known patterns of structural change for this set of currently mature economies is the shift of capital and labour away from the production of primary goods and towards manufacturing and services. This development pattern featured prominently in explanations of divergent growth across Europe, Japan and the United States in the post-World War II period (Denison, 1967; Maddison, 1987). More recently, differential productivity growth rates in market services sectors such as retail trade, distribution, and financial services between the United States and Europe have been emphasised (Timmer *et al.*, 2010; Jorgenson and Timmer, 2011). While the process of structural change in advanced economies is well documented, we know much less about the nature of structural transformation in today's developing economies. The absence of long-term and detailed sector data for developing economies since the seminal work by Chenery *et al.* (1986) has obscured a proper quantitative assessment of the role of structural transformation in accounting for aggregate productivity growth.

In this chapter we aim to partially fill that gap by describing similarities and differences in the patterns of structural change across developing countries in Asia, Africa and Latin America since the 1950s. To this end, we introduce the updated and extended Groningen Growth and Development Centre (GGDC) sector database in the second section. The database includes annual time series of value added and persons employed for ten broad sectors of the economy. It now includes eleven countries in Asia (China has been added since the previous release), nine in Latin America and eleven in Sub-Saharan Africa (referred to as Africa in the remainder of this chapter). Data on the number of workers is based on the broadest employment concept, including self-employed, family workers and other informal workers. The dataset is based on a critical assessment of the coverage and consistency of concepts and definitions used in various primary data sources. Data and documentation are freely and publicly available online.[1]

The third section uses the GGDC sector database to document patterns of structural change. We show that the expansion of manufacturing activities during the early post-World War II period led to a growth-enhancing reallocation of resources in Asia, Africa and Latin America. This process of structural change stalled in Africa and Latin America during the mid-1970s and 1980s. When growth rebounded in the 1990s, workers mainly relocated to market services industries, such as retail trade and distribution. Though such services have higher productivity than much of agriculture, they are not technologically dynamic and have been falling behind the world frontier.

This development pattern has important ramifications for the role of structural change in accounting for productivity growth in developing countries currently. In the third section we use a method that splits structural change into the contribution from the reallocation of workers to above-average productivity *level* sectors (static reallocation effect) and the contribution from the reallocation to above-average productivity *growth* sectors (dynamic reallocation effect). A key finding is that in Africa and Latin America, workers moved from below-average productivity to above-average productivity sectors (static gains). However, sectors with above-average productivity levels that expanded in terms of employment shares experienced below-average productivity growth (dynamic losses). This development pattern in Africa and Latin America contrasts to that observed in Asia where dynamic losses are hardly observed. A key role for these static gains and dynamic losses is the missing contribution from manufacturing nowadays in Africa and Latin America. In the fourth section we provide concluding remarks and outline promising areas for future research.

The GGDC sector database

Comparative studies of growth have been hampered by the lack of a large-scale international database on output and productivity trends by sector in developing countries. In this section we present the updated and extended GGDC sector database, which is the first database to provide long-term series on sectoral developments.[2] The database is constructed on the basis of an in-depth study of available statistical sources on a country-by-country basis. This section discusses the contents of the database, the selection procedure of the sources used, as well as the methods employed to ensure intertemporal, international and internal consistency. Compliance with consistency requirements is important to ensure the usefulness of the database in long-term analyses of growth and productivity. Readers more interested in the patterns of structural change across developing countries can skip this section and continue reading in the third section.

Contents of the dataset

Table 4.1 gives an overview of the contents of the GGDC sector database. The dataset currently includes eleven Asian, nine Latin American and eleven African countries. It includes annual data on gross value added at current, constant and international prices from 1950 onwards. In addition, annual data on persons employed is available, which allows the derivation of labour productivity (value added per worker) trends. The database covers the ten

Table 4.1 Overview of the GGDC sector database

Economic activities distinguished (*ISIC rev. 3.1 code*)	1 Agriculture, hunting, forestry and fishing (AtB)
	2 Mining and quarrying (C)
	3 Manufacturing (D)
	4 Electricity, gas and water supply (E)
	5 Construction (F)
	6 Wholesale and retail trade, hotels and restaurants (GtH)
	7 Transport, storage and communication (I)
	8 Finance, insurance, real estate and business services (JtK)
	9 Government services (LtN)
	10 Community, social and personal services (OtP)
Variables included	Persons engaged
	Gross value added at current national prices
	Gross value added at constant 2005 national prices
	Gross value added at international 2005 prices (PPPs)
Countries included	*Africa:*
	Botswana, Ethiopia, Ghana, Kenya, Malawi, Mauritius, Nigeria, Senegal, South Africa, Tanzania, Zambia
	Asia:
	China, Hong Kong (China), India, Indonesia, Japan, Korea (Rep. of), Malaysia, Philippines, Singapore, Taiwan, Thailand
	Latin America:
	Argentina, Bolivia, Brazil, Chile, Colombia, Costa Rica, Mexico, Peru, Venezuela
Time period	1950–2010

Notes: Starting date of time series varies across variables and countries depending on data availability. Typically, for Latin American countries the series start in 1950, for Africa in the 1960s, while for many Asian countries series start in the 1970s.

main sectors of the economy as defined in the International Standard Industrial Classification, Revision 3.1 (ISIC rev. 3.1). These ten sectors cover the total economy. The dataset has been updated to 2010 and now includes China.

Construction of variables

Gross value added in current and constant prices is taken from the national accounts of the various countries. As these have all been compiled according to the UN System of National Accounts (SNA), international comparability is high, in principle. However, national statistical institutes frequently change their methodologies. Within the national accounts, GDP series are periodically revised, which includes changes in the coverage of activities (for example after a full economic census has been carried out and 'new' activities have been discovered), changes in the methods of calculation (for example the inclusion of software expenditures as investment rather than intermediate consumption) and changes in base year of the prices used for calculating volume growth rates.[3] For sectoral GDP our general approach is to start with GDP levels for the most recent available benchmark year, expressed in that year's prices, from the national accounts provided by the National Statistical Institute or Central Bank. Historical national accounts series were subsequently linked to this benchmark year.[4] This linking procedure ensures that growth rates of individual series are retained although absolute levels are adjusted according to the most recent information and methods.

Employment in our dataset is defined as 'all persons employed', thus including all paid employees, but also self-employed and family workers. Labour input is normally not available from a country's national accounts as they are not part of the System of National Accounts. Two different primary sources of employment data exist, namely labour force surveys (LFS) with data collected at the household level, and business surveys which are based on firm-level questionnaires. Both have their advantages and disadvantages as a source for annual sectoral employment trends.

The LFS are a comprehensive and well-established source with substantive international harmonisation of concepts because they use definitions set out by the International Labour Organization (ILO), although sampling size and techniques may still differ substantially between countries. The LFS cover employees as well as self-employed and family labour. The main problem with LFS is the limited consistency with output data from the national accounts, especially at the sectoral level due the relatively small sample size. In addition, the sample is sometimes restricted to particular regional areas, such as urban areas.

Information from business surveys is often more consistent with value added measures in the national accounts, because output series for the national accounts are also based on this source. However, while the coverage by business surveys is reasonably accurate for goods producing industries, this is not always the case for services. Moreover, business surveys typically only cover firms who surpass a certain threshold (for example, >20 employees or above a certain turnover level). This excludes smaller firms, which are especially abundant in developing countries. Another limitation is that data on self-employed and unpaid family members are usually not collected. This is problematic for sectors like agriculture and informal parts of the economy, where these categories make up a significant share of total employment. Business surveys are therefore not well suited to provide employment statistics by sectors that cover the total economy.

Therefore we often use an alternative source based on household questionnaires but with a much larger coverage than the samples of the LFS: the population census. This ensures full coverage of the working population and a much more reliable sectoral breakdown than from the LFS.[5] However, population censuses are typically quinquennial or decennial and cannot be used to derive annual trends. Therefore we use the population census to indicate absolute levels of employment, and use LFS and business surveys to indicate trends in between. This is the general strategy followed for most countries, but not for all.[6]

Consistency

In constructing the database, we paid careful attention to three checks on consistency, namely intertemporal consistency, international consistency and internal consistency. Our time series of gross value added and employment are consistent over time (that is, intertemporal consistency). Through the linking procedure described above, major breaks in the series have been repaired. International consistency of the cross-country sectoral data is ensured through the system of national accounts for value added, the employment concept of persons engaged and the use of a harmonised sectoral classification. We classify activities into ten sectors, using the International Standard Industrial Classification (ISIC), Revision 3.1 (United Nations, 2002). The industrial classification used in the national primary data sources is based on this classification or is directly related to it.

Finally, for the derivation of meaningful productivity measures, the labour input and output measures should cover the same activities (i.e. being internally consistent). As we use persons employed as our employment concept rather than employees, and base our employment numbers on large-scale surveys, overlap in coverage of the employment statistics and value added from the national accounts is maximised. However, a notable exception is the own-account production of housing services by owner-occupiers. For this an imputation of rent is made and added to GDP in many countries, according to the System of National Accounts. This imputed production does not have an employment equivalent and should preferably not be included in output for the purposes of labour productivity comparisons.[7] Therefore, the GGDC sector database presents separate series for imputed rents. In our decomposition analysis we exclude imputed rents.

Reliability

A note of caution on the data is warranted. Recently, scholars have pointed out that the statistical foundations underlying GDP and employment estimates in many developing countries, notably but not exclusively Africa and China, are subject to substantial measurement error (Devarajan, 2013; Jerven, 2013). The low quality of statistics is related to a weak capacity to collect, manage and disseminate data; inadequate funding of statistical offices; diffuse responsibilities on who is collecting what; and fragmentation in surveys and gathering exercises. Young (2012) argues that many African countries do not have a well-established statistical system, not even reporting national accounts data on a consistent basis. He therefore explores alternative sources of information on national income using demographic and health survey data. Likewise, GDP and employment estimates in large developing countries such as India and China might have substantial measurement errors (de Vries *et al.*, 2012). However, most countries included in the sector database do have a considerable history of collecting national accounts data and in conducting labour and household surveys. The quantity and quality of the data varies between countries, reflected in the list of countries included in the Appendix tables.

Patterns of structural change in developing countries

In this section we first document the main shifts in value added and employment across sectors and countries using the GGDC sector database. We document the declining manufacturing employment share in Africa and Latin America since the mid 1970s. Production and employment increasingly originates in services activities. In particular, the share of trade and distribution services in developing economies has expanded to levels observed in OECD economies. However, productivity levels in market services have been falling behind the technology frontier, implying that the sector lacks technological dynamism. Next, we briefly outline a methodology to decompose aggregate productivity growth into growth at the sector level (the within-effect) and a reallocation effect. A key finding is that the expansion of trade and distribution services after 1990 resulted in static reallocation gains, but with productivity growth in market services that was below average. This pattern of static gains but dynamic losses from resource reallocation holds for most African and Latin American countries, but not for Asia.

Sector shares of GDP and employment

Tables 4.2 and 4.3 show value added and employment shares by sector for Africa, Asia and Latin America for the years 1960, 1975, 1990 and 2010.[8] The shares are computed as unweighted regional averages. Typically most attention is paid to the size of the manufacturing sector as economic development is often thought to be closely associated with industrialisation (Lewis, 1954). Two important trends emerge from Tables 4.2 and 4.3 in this respect. First, manufacturing expanded during the 1960s and early 1970s. After 1975 the share of manufacturing in aggregate

GDP started to decline in most African and Latin American countries. This contrasts to the pattern observed in Asia, where the manufacturing share in value added has held up at about 25 per cent of GDP, although shares have also fallen back somewhat since the 1990s. Individual country experiences differ. For example, manufacturing employment shares increased in Botswana and Tanzania during the past decades (McMillan *et al.* 2013). However, most African and Latin American countries have de-industrialised in terms of a falling share in GDP since the mid 1970s. Second, for most African countries, the share of manufacturing in GDP and the labour force has never reached levels observed in either Asia or Latin America. Together, these trends suggest that de-industrialisation sets in at earlier development stages and at lower employment levels in developing countries (Rodrik, 2015).

In employment terms, the pattern is even more striking. In 2010, only 7 per cent of the African workforce was employed in manufacturing, in comparison with 15 per cent in Asia and 12 per cent in Latin America. Workers who moved out of agriculture were mainly absorbed in the (formal and informal) services sector. This employment reallocation has been strongest in Latin America, where the agricultural employment share fell from 47 per cent in 1960 to 14 percent in 2010. At the same time, services expanded from 32 to 64 per cent of the total workforce. Disaggregating the services sector suggests that the biggest employment expansion occurs in trade and distribution services, although other community, personal and household services expanded rapidly as well.

Trade and distribution services expanded to levels observed in OECD countries. Its share increased from 8 per cent of the African workforce in 1960 to 20 per cent in 2010 and in Latin

Table 4.2 Value added shares (current prices), 1960–2010

	Africa				Asia				Latin America			
	1960	*1975*	*1990*	*2010*	*1960*	*1975*	*1990*	*2010*	*1960*	*1975*	*1990*	*2010*
Agriculture	38	29	25	22	26	21	13	8	19	14	10	7
Industry	24	30	33	28	30	35	38	36	33	38	39	37
Mining	8	6	11	9	3	4	3	3	6	7	8	12
Manufacturing	9	15	14	10	22	24	27	24	19	22	23	16
Other industry	7	9	7	9	6	7	8	8	8	9	8	9
Services	38	41	43	50	43	44	49	56	48	48	54	56
Market services	24	25	28	34	31	31	36	40	33	32	37	36
Trade and distribution	*21*	*21*	*23*	*25*	*24*	*24*	*26*	*27*	*26*	*24*	*26*	*24*
Financial services	*3*	*5*	*5*	*9*	*7*	*7*	*10*	*14*	*7*	*8*	*11*	*11*
Non-market services	14	15	14	16	13	13	13	16	14	16	17	20
Governmental services	*11*	*12*	*12*	*12*	*7*	*7*	*7*	*8*	*4*	*5*	*7*	*8*
Other services	*3*	*3*	*3*	*4*	*6*	*6*	*6*	*8*	*11*	*11*	*10*	*12*
Total economy	**100**	**100**	**100**	**100**	**100**	**100**	**100**	**100**	**100**	**100**	**103**	**100**

Source: Authors' calculations using the GGDC sector database.

Notes: For some countries time series start later (BWA: 1964; ETH: 1961; KEN: 1969; MWI: 1966; MUS: 1970; SEN: 1970; TZA: 1961; ZMB: 1965; CHN: 1952; HKG: 1974; IDN: 1971; KOR: 1963; MYS: 1975; PHL: 71; SGP: 1970; TWN: 1963). For these countries we took the share from the most nearby year. Figures are unweighted averages across regions. 'Other industry' includes construction and public utilities. 'Trade and distribution' includes transport services and distributive trade as well as hotels and restaurants. 'Finance and business services' excludes real estate activities. 'Other services' includes other community, personal and household services. Numbers may not sum due to rounding. The countries distinguished are shown in Appendix Tables 4.A1–4.A3.

Table 4.3 Employment shares, 1960–2010

	Africa				Asia				Latin America			
	1960	*1975*	*1990*	*2010*	*1960*	*1975*	*1990*	*2010*	*1960*	*1975*	*1990*	*2010*
Agriculture	73	66	62	51	48	43	32	21	47	34	25	14
Industry	9	13	14	13	19	23	26	23	21	24	24	22
Mining	2	1	2	1	1	1	1	0	2	1	1	1
Manufacturing	5	8	9	7	15	18	19	15	14	15	15	12
Other industry	3	4	4	4	4	5	6	8	5	7	7	9
Services	18	21	24	37	33	34	42	56	32	42	51	64
Market services	9	10	13	23	20	21	28	37	16	21	27	40
Trade and distribution	*8*	*9*	*11*	*20*	*18*	*18*	*23*	*28*	*13*	*17*	*22*	*31*
Financial services	*1*	*1*	*1*	*3*	*2*	*3*	*5*	*9*	*3*	*4*	*5*	*9*
Non-market services	9	10	11	13	13	13	15	18	17	21	24	25
Governmental services	*4*	*4*	*6*	*8*	*6*	*6*	*7*	*8*	*4*	*6*	*7*	*7*
Other services	*5*	*6*	*5*	*5*	*7*	*7*	*8*	*10*	*12*	*15*	*17*	*17*
Total economy	**100**	**100**	**100**	**100**	**100**	**100**	**100**	**100**	**100**	**100**	**100**	**100**

Source: Authors' calculations using the GGDC sector database.

Notes: For some countries time series start later (BWA: 1964; ETH: 1961; KEN: 1969; MWI: 1966; MUS: 1970; SEN: 1970; TZA: 1961; ZMB:1965; CHN: 1952; HKG: 1974; IDN: 1971; KOR: 1963; MYS: 1975; PHL: 71; SGP: 1970; TWN: 1963). For these countries we took the share from the most nearby year. Figures are unweighted averages across regions. 'Other industry' includes construction and public utilities. 'Trade and distribution' includes transport services and distributive trade as well as hotels and restaurants. 'Finance and business services' excludes real estate activities. 'Other services' includes other community, personal and household services. Numbers may not sum due to rounding. Employment in our data set is defined as 'all persons employed', thus including all paid employees, but also self-employed and family workers.

America from 13 to 31 per cent. This employment expansion is not matched by an expansion in output as the value added share remained roughly constant between 21 and 27 per cent of GDP (see Table 4.2). For comparison, the employment share of trade and distribution services is between 19 and 21 per cent in Europe, Japan and the United States (Jorgenson and Timmer, 2011).[9]

A comparison of sector shares in Tables 4.2 and 4.3 gives an indication of relative productivity differences across sectors. Labour productivity in agriculture is much lower compared to services and even lower in relation to manufacturing. In 2010, for example, the agricultural value added share in Africa was 22 per cent, while the employment share was 51 per cent. This suggests agricultural labour productivity is about half that of the total economy average. In contrast, the services value added share is 50 per cent, while the employment share is 37 per cent, whilst the same shares for manufacturing are 10 and 7 per cent respectively. Therefore, labour productivity in services is above the economy average, although still below that in manufacturing. Also, note that the productivity gap between manufacturing and services is considerably higher in Asia than in Africa. Below we outline a methodology to quantify the contribution of these sector differences and reallocation effects in accounting for productivity growth.

An international perspective on sector performance

First we extend the national perspective on the performance of sectors by comparing with the world technology frontier. In principle the use of the SNA framework allows us to compare output across countries. Yet, to compare productivity across countries and sectors, a key issue is how to convert real value added into common currency units. Conceptually, the appropriate rate of exchange is to use a Purchasing Power Parity exchange rate (PPP). In addition, by now it is well known that relative prices vary substantially across tradable and non-tradable sectors, such that the use of aggregate PPPs is not appropriate for productivity comparisons of disaggregated data. Therefore, we use sector-specific PPPs provided by Inklaar and Timmer (2014). Relative prices across sectors are based on price data collected by the World Bank in the 2005 International Comparison Program (ICP) round except for agriculture, which is based on unit value information from the Food and Agriculture Organization (FAO). Basic headings from the ICP round are matched to sectors that are the main producers of the good or service and PPPs are estimated using the EKS method (see Inklaar and Timmer, 2014 for details).

We define the United States as the frontier country and measure labour productivity relative to the frontier using sector-specific PPPs. This approach is followed for each sector and country at different points in time. Figure 4.1A shows the average productivity level across Africa, Asia and Latin America for manufacturing. Values of the mean closer to the frontier correspond to a higher level of relative labour productivity.

Nowadays, the mean productivity level in Africa and Latin America lies substantially below the US productivity level. For manufacturing the sample mean is about 7 per cent in Africa, taking 2010 for comparison. This implies labour productivity of an average African manufacturing worker is about one-fourteenth that of an average American worker. For manufacturing, we observe productivity divergence, not convergence, in Africa and Latin America during the past fifty years.[10] However, during the 1960s and 1970s, in these regions on average productivity trends were in line with growth at the US frontier as manufacturing productivity was not falling behind. This suggests that during the period 1960–75 the expansion of manufacturing activity in Africa and Latin America was also a positive development when viewed from an international efficiency perspective.

Figure 4.1B shows average productivity in market services. In the previous subsection we observed that market services expanded rapidly after 1990. Productivity growth was below the average of the total economy during that period. When viewed from an international perspective, the productivity performance of African and Latin American market services sectors since the 1990s was also not matching growth at the frontier.[11] Figure 4.1B suggests that productivity in market services fell further behind the frontier during a period in which its employment expanded rapidly. In the next subsection we will seek to quantify the contribution of structural change in accounting for productivity growth in developing countries.

Patterns of structural change: Decomposition results

To measure the contribution to growth from the reallocation of workers across sectors of the economy, researchers typically use a variant of the canonical decomposition originating from Fabricant (1942), which we follow. The decomposition method we use here has base periods for both employment shares and productivity levels. The change in aggregate productivity can be decomposed as follows:

$$\Delta P = \sum_i (P_i^T - P_i^0) S_i^0 + \sum_i \left(S_i^T - S_i^0 \right) P_i^0 + \sum_i (P_i^T - P_i^0) \star (S_i^T - S_i^0), \tag{1}$$

where S_i is the share of sector i in overall employment, P_i the labour productivity level of sector i, and superscripts 0 and T refer to initial and final period. In equation (1), the change in aggregate productivity is decomposed into within-sector productivity changes (the first term

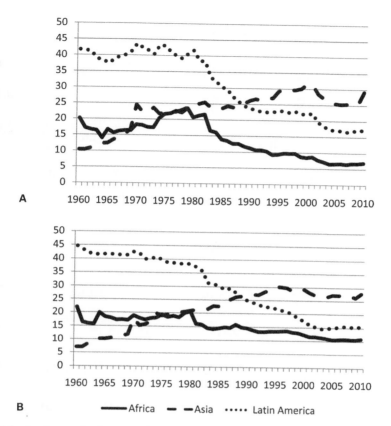

Figure 4.1 An international perspective on productivity (USA = 100), unweighted averages across regions. (A) manufacturing; (B) market services.

Sources: Authors' calculations using GGDC sector database, as well as sector-specific PPPs from Inklaar and Timmer (2014).

on the right-hand side which we call the 'within-effect' also known as 'intra-effect') and two other effects. The within-effect is positive (negative) when the weighted change in labour productivity levels in sectors is positive (negative). The second term measures the contribution of labour reallocation across sectors, being positive (negative) when labour moves from less (more) to more (less) productive sectors. The third term in equation (1) is known as the cross term or interaction term. It represents the joint effect of changes in employment shares and sectoral productivity growth. It is positive (negative) if workers are moving to sectors that are experiencing positive (negative) productivity growth. Hence, the second term in equation (1) measures whether workers move to above-average productivity level sectors (static reallocation effect) whereas the third term measures whether productivity growth is higher in sectors that expand in terms of employment shares (dynamic reallocation effect).

Decomposition results are shown in Figure 4.2. We have used a periodisation that has become common in the literature on structural change (e.g. IADB, 2010; McMillan and Rodrik, 2011), namely 1960–75, 1975–90 and 1990–2010. The first period roughly coincides with a world-wide economic boom. Productivity growth was high across most developing countries, and the decomposition results suggest that a large part is accounted for by within-productivity growth.

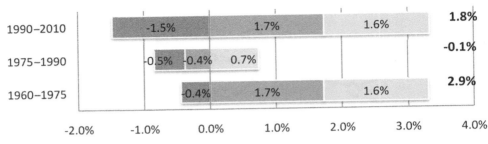

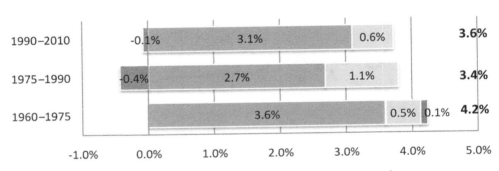

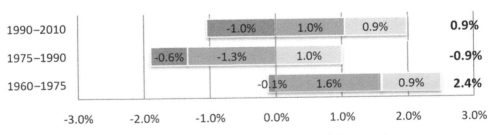

■ Within   ▨ Between – static   ■ Between – dynamic

Figure 4.2   Decomposition results for 1960–1975, 1975–1990 and 1990–2010, using equation (1).

Sources: Authors' calculations using the GGDC sector database. Detailed country results are available in the Appendix tables.

However, the reallocation of workers to above average productivity sectors also positively contributed to growth. The period from 1975 to 1990 is associated with a radical change in economic prospects for many African and Latin American countries. Indeed, average productivity growth during this period is close to zero. Decomposition results suggest that within-sector productivity growth accounts for a large share of the decline, but workers continued to move to above-average productivity *level* sectors. That is, the between effect is positive in both Africa and Latin America, despite low productivity growth.

In the period 1990–2010, productivity growth resumed. Our decomposition results suggest that the within-effect is positive, and also the static reallocation effect is positive. The latter suggests that, on average, in developing countries positive static reallocation gains were achieved. What is striking, however, is the contribution from the cross term. The cross term is substantially negative in Africa and Latin America suggesting dynamic losses. This suggests the marginal productivity of additional workers in expanding sectors was below that of existing activities. In Asia the interaction term is small, in line with findings by Timmer (2000) and earlier findings for Europe by Maddison (1987) and van Ark (1996), which may relate to a greater dynamism in manufacturing in Asia and Europe.

Overall, it seems that changes in the importance of manufacturing and market services for GDP and employment are relevant for explaining divergent patterns of growth and structural change across developing countries. However, to what extent is the expansion of trade and distribution services, discussed above, accountable for the lack of productivity dynamics in Africa and Latin America? To properly measure the role of sectors in accounting for growth, we first have to adjust the decomposition presented in equation (1). The rationale for this adjustment is as follows. In the decomposition method presented above, all expanding sectors contribute positively to aggregate productivity, even when they have below-average productivity levels. Consider, for example, the expansion of employment in trade and distribution services at the expense of manufacturing. And assume that the productivity growth rate in distribution services is below average, while manufacturing labour productivity growth is above average. As a result of the shift in employment shares, aggregate productivity growth will become lower. Nevertheless, as measured in the traditional method, the contribution from the expansion of trade and distribution services is positive (if productivity growth is positive). In the modified method we therefore adjust the between and the cross term of an expanding sector to take into account its relative productivity level and its growth rate. To this end, we will divide sectors into expanding and shrinking based on their changes in employment shares and calculate the between-effect relative to the average productivity level of the shrinking sectors and the cross term relative to the average productivity change of the shrinking sectors. The decomposition in equation (1) is modified as follows:

$$P^T - P^0 = \sum_i^I \left(P_i^T - P_i^0\right)S_i^0 + \sum_j^J \left(S_j^T - S_j^0\right)\left(P_j^0 - P^{0\star}\right)$$
$$+ \sum_j^J \left(\left(P_j^T - P_j^0\right) - \left(P^{T\star} - P^{0\star}\right)\right)\left(S_j^T - S_j^0\right) \tag{2}$$

where J is the set of expanding sectors, and K is the set of shrinking sectors, and average labour productivity of shrinking sectors at time T and 0 is given by:

$$P^{0\star} = \left.\sum_k^K \left(S_k^T - S_k^0\right)P_k^0 \middle/ \sum_k^K \left(S_k^T - S_k^0\right)\right.$$

$$P^{T\star} = \left. \Sigma_k^K \left(S_k^T - S_k^0 \right) P_k^T \middle/ \Sigma_k^K \left(S_k^T - S_k^0 \right) \right.$$

Table 4.4 shows the decomposition results from using equation (2). We decompose labour productivity growth for each country included in the GGDC sector database, and report the unweighted average by region for the period from 1960 to 2010. This adjusted decomposition does not affect the contributions coming from the various terms in the aggregate. Total economy results are therefore equal to those shown in Figure 4.2. However, using equation (2) we are better able to examine the contribution of sectors in accounting for productivity growth. Table 4.4 suggests that the productivity growth is to an important extent accounted for by the shift of workers to above-average productivity level sectors. Across Africa, Asia and Latin America the most important sector was services, in particular, trade and distribution services, which accounted for 0.73 percentage points of labour productivity growth in Africa.

Positive static reallocation gains are put into perspective in the light of the cross term in the decomposition method. Table 4.4 suggests that sectors that expanded employment shares had productivity growth rates below those of shrinking sectors, suggesting a shift away from manufacturing. Again, in particular the distribution services sector appears to account for a large part of these dynamics. The negative cross term for distribution services (−0.74 percentage points for Africa) suggests that its productivity growth was well below that observed in shrinking sectors. This finding also holds for other financial and business services in the case of Latin America.

Table 4.4 Decomposition results by region, 1990–2010

(A) Africa

	Labour productivity growth	Component due to:		
		Within	*Between*	*Cross*
Total economy	**1.85**	1.73	1.59	−1.48
Contribution of:				
Agriculture		**0.65**	**0.00**	**0.00**
Industry		**0.76**	**0.53**	**−0.43**
Mining		0.17	0.04	−0.03
Manufacturing		0.15	0.19	−0.17
Other industry		0.44	0.31	−0.23
Services		**0.32**	**1.06**	**−1.05**
Market services		0.12	0.91	−0.86
Trade and distribution		*0.03*	*0.73*	*−0.74*
Financial services		*0.09*	*0.18*	*−0.12*
Non-market services		0.20	0.15	−0.19
Governmental services		*0.03*	*0.15*	*−0.15*
Other services		*0.17*	*0.01*	*−0.04*

(B) Asia

Total economy	**3.64**	**3.08**	**0.62**	**−0.06**
Contribution of:				
Agriculture		**0.43**	**0.00**	**0.00**
Industry		**1.59**	**0.11**	**0.09**
Mining		0.17	0.00	0.00

Manufacturing		1.27	0.04	0.12
Other industry		0.14	0.07	−0.03
Services		**1.06**	**0.51**	**−0.15**
Market services		0.76	0.42	−0.07
Trade and distribution		0.65	0.14	0.03
Financial services		*0.11*	*0.28*	*−0.10*
Non-market services		0.30	0.09	−0.08
Governmental services		*0.12*	*0.06*	*−0.07*
Other services		*0.18*	*0.03*	*−0.02*

(C) Latin America

Total economy	**0.93**	**1.05**	**0.93**	**−1.04**
Contribution of:				
Agriculture		**0.34**	**0.00**	**0.00**
Industry		**0.74**	**0.33**	**−0.30**
Mining		0.19	0.26	−0.17
Manufacturing		0.46	0.03	−0.05
Other industry		0.09	0.04	−0.08
Services		**−0.04**	**0.59**	**−0.75**
Market services		−0.11	0.60	−0.71
Trade and distribution		*0.02*	*0.17*	*−0.31*
Financial services		*−0.13*	*0.43*	*−0.40*
Non-market services		0.07	−0.01	−0.04
Governmental services		*0.11*	*−0.01*	*−0.01*
Other services		*−0.04*	*0.00*	*−0.02*

Source: Authors' calculations using the GGDC sector database.

Notes: Figures are unweighted averages across countries. 'Other industry' includes construction and public utilities. 'Trade and distribution' includes transport services and distributive trade as well as hotels and restaurants. 'Finance and business services' excludes real estate activities. 'Other services' includes other community, personal and household services. Numbers may not sum due to rounding.

Concluding remarks and directions for future research

This chapter has documented development patterns across Asia, Africa and Latin America since the 1950s. We have taken a very narrow perspective on structural change, studying changes in the sector structure over time. This parsimonious approach ignores other structural changes taking place in the economy, such as changes in savings and investment rates, urbanisation, demographic transitions, changes in income inequality and changes in culture and institutions. At the same time the narrow focus allows us to study several salient characteristics of many developing countries in detail. We have shown that current employment reallocation patterns in Africa and Latin America strikingly differs from that in earlier periods. In particular, during the 1960s and early 1970s, many developing countries took a step forward by expanding their manufacturing activities. This was related to growth-enhancing structural change. In contrast, after 1990 market services activities such as retail trade and distribution services expanded. Although productivity levels in market services were above the average for the rest of the economy, productivity growth was not. Therefore, we observe static reallocation gains but dynamic losses. The overall effect was a limited role for structural change post 1990, which compares unfavourably to Africa's and Latin America's earlier period of high growth.

The analysis in this chapter is based on the updated and extended GGDC sector database. In comparison to an earlier version presented in Timmer and de Vries (2009), the dataset has been updated to 2010. It has been extended by including China and eleven Sub-Saharan African countries. Our aim is to further extend the time and country coverage in the coming years. In particular, we would like to add countries from the Levantine. Also, more detailed survey data could be used to distinguish between formal and informal activities within sectors. De Vries *et al.* (2012) distinguish unregistered activities by sector in Brazil and India and show that it matters for the relative role of structural change. For example, formalisation of economic activities in Brazil were related to positive structural change post 2000. In addition, we would like to add to the diversity of countries included in the dataset. Earlier work by Hollis Chenery and others have emphasised differences in patterns of structural change (Chenery *et al.*, 1986) For example, resource-rich countries may experience a delay in the shift away from agriculture and mining, and because of higher wages may choose more capital-intensive resource-processing manufacturing activities. Small countries may specialise in producing a more select set of industrial products, whereas larger developing countries could have more diversified industrialisation patterns. In addition, the nature of industrial policies may affect industrialisation. Instead, in this chapter we have closely followed the recent literature by studying averages across continents instead of accounting for much of the country heterogeneity.

Changes in the nature of economic globalisation, in particular the emergence of international production networks call forth new empirical and methodological approaches to analyse structural change. Increased integration and fragmentation of production across national borders implies that a closed economy view on structural change is less relevant compared to an integrative view of structural change and comparative economic development (Matsuyama, 2009). For example, South Korea's manufacturing share in GDP has been stable, partly because it has been exploiting its comparative advantage in manufacturing activities, deeply integrating in 'factory Asia' (Sposi, 2011). Something similar might apply for other Asian countries which would explain the constant share of manufacturing in Asia observed in this chapter. In particular, recent research that integrates a supply and demand perspective on structural change using input–output data is promising (Herrendorf *et al.*, 2014). Another benefit of this approach is that it allows one to decompose gross output per worker, which is more consistent compared to current decompositions that mix a net measure (GDP) with gross flows (employment). Indeed, the analysis by Herrendorf *et al.* (2014) could be extended to an international setting by using world input-output tables, which might help to explain stable manufacturing shares in many Asian countries and falling shares in Africa and Latin America.

We have provided a quantitative account of structural transformation in developing countries. Our analysis suggests multi-sector models of economic growth should aim to include differential sectoral development within services activities. Indeed, an important explanation of differential productivity growth between African and Latin American countries on the one hand and Asian and OECD countries on the other lies in the nature and expansion of market services activities such as retail trade and distribution. Future research should aim to explain why these patterns occur. In addition, analysis of the role of resource reallocation for aggregate growth should be built up from the micro-level. Crucially, that would allow one to observe the marginal productivity of workers that reallocate across firms. Indeed, the increasing availability of firm-level data and international input–output data opens up a promising research agenda.

Notes

1 The Groningen Growth and Development Centre 10 sector database (release June 2014). Available from: http://www.ggdc.net/dseries/10-sector.html
2 Various international organisations, such as the World Bank, the United Nations, the Asian Development Bank and also the Oxford Latin American Economic History Database, collect sectoral

data for developing countries and make it publicly available. But series are often short (starting only in the 1980s or 90s), not consistent over time and across countries, and the series sometimes lack sectoral detail. Timmer and de Vries (2009) compare the GGDC sector database with other publicly available sectoral datasets.

3 In most developing countries a fixed-base Laspeyres volume index is used and this base is usually updated every 5 or 10 years.

4 Because of the application of fixed-base Laspeyres volume indexes by most statistical offices, linked sectoral GDP does not add up to total GDP for earlier periods. We aggregate sectoral GDP data.

5 Official population censuses data for 1950, 1960 and 1970 appear to be unreliable in Latin America. In order to remedy this problem we used the harmonised population census results published by PREALC (1982). This study makes adjustments in order for the population censuses to be reliable and comparable within and between countries (for example correcting for age limitations, reference periods, ISIC revisions, workers entering the labour market, unspecified workers and on the under-estimation of agricultural workers).

6 The sources and methods document available at http://www.ggdc.net/dseries/10-sector.html provides a detailed discussion of the construction of the employment and value added series on a country-by-country basis.

7 Typically, imputed rents are included in the output of the financial and business services sector and frequently increase output in this sector by 50 per cent or more without any labour input equivalent. Worse, this percentage varies over time and across countries.

8 This periodisation has become common in the recent literature on structural change (see e.g. IADB, 2010; McMillan and Rodrik, 2011). See the decomposition results below for further discussion of these periods. See Appendix Tables 4.A1–4.A3 for the countries distinguished. These countries were selected to have a relatively geographically representative sample of countries by continent. In addition, they account for the major part of the continents' GDP.

9 Jorgenson and Timmer (2011) use hours worked instead of employment to compute shares. In addition, they exclude hotels and restaurants. The shares reported by Jorgenson and Timmer (2011) will be higher if hotel and restaurant services are included and employment shares are used.

10 This finding is in contrast to that in Rodrik (2013) whose finding of unconditional convergence applies only for formal manufacturing activities.

11 Faster productivity growth in US market services is partly related to differences in accounting for price changes in retail output (Inklaar and Timmer, 2008). The US statistical office uses a quality-adjusted price deflator, especially for the consumption of information and communication technology goods. Measured sales volumes are smaller in many developing countries, partly because they do not make use of hedonic price deflators.

References

Chenery, H., Robinson. S. and Syrquin, M. 1986. *Industrialization and Growth: A Comparative Study*. Oxford: Oxford University Press.

de Vries, G. J., Erumban, A. A., Timmer, M. P., Voskoboynikov, I. and Wu, H. 2012. Deconstructing the BRICs: Structural Transformation and Aggregate Productivity Growth. *Journal of Comparative Economics*. 40 (2): 211–227.

Denison, E. F. 1967. *Why Growth Rates Differ*. Washington, DC: Brookings Institution.

Devarajan, S. 2013. Africa's Statistical Tragedy. *Review of Income and Wealth*. 59 (2): 1–7.

Fabricant, S. 1942. *Employment in Manufacturing 1899–1939*. New York: National Bureau of Economic Research.

Harberger, A. 1998. A Vision of the Growth Process. *American Economic Review*. 88 (1): 1–32.

Herrendorf, B., Valentinyi, A. and Rogerson, R. 2014. Growth and Structural Transformation. Chapter 6 in Aghion, P. and Durlauf, S. (eds.). *Handbook of Economic Growth*, Vol. 2B. Amsterdam: North Holland: 855–941.

Hsieh, C. T. and Klenow, P. J. 2009. Misallocation and Manufacturing TFP in China and India. *Quarterly Journal of Economics*. 124 (4): 1403–1448.

IADB. 2010. *The Age of Productivity: Transforming Economies from the Bottom Up*. New York: Palgrave Macmillan for the Inter-American Development Bank.

Inklaar, R. C. and Timmer, M. P. 2008. *GGDC Productivity Level Database: International Comparisons of Output, Inputs and Productivity at the Industry Level*. GGDC Research Memorandum GD-104, Groningen Growth and Development Centre. Groningen: University of Groningen.

Inklaar, R. C. and Timmer M. P. 2014. The Relative Price of Services. *Review of Income and Wealth.* 60 (4): 727–746.

Jerven, M. 2013. *Poor Numbers: How We are Misled by African Development Statistics and What to Do About It.* Ithaca, NY: Cornell University Press.

Jorgenson, D.W. and Timmer, M. P. 2011. Structural Change in Advanced Nations: A New Set of Stylised Facts. *Scandinavian Journal of Economics.* 113 (1): 1–29.

Kuznets, S. 1966. *Modern Economic Growth: Rate, Structure and Spread.* London: Yale University Press.

Lewis, W. A. 1954. Economic Development With Unlimited Supplies of Labour. *Manchester School of Economic and Social Studies.* 22 (2): 139–191.

Maddison, A. 1987. Growth and Slowdown in Advanced Capitalist Economies: Techniques of Quantitative Assessment. *Journal of Economic Literature.* 25 (2): 649–698.

Matsuyama, K. 2009. Structural Change in an Interdependent World: A Global View of Manufacturing Decline. *Journal of the European Economic Association.* 7 (2–3): 478–486.

McMillan, M. and Rodrik, D. 2011. *Globalization, Structural Change, and Productivity Growth.* NBER Working Paper 17143. Cambridge, MA: National Bureau of Economic Research.

McMillan, M., Rodrik, D. and Verduzco-Gallo, I. 2014. Globalization, Structural Change, and Productivity Growth: With an Update for Africa. *World Development.* 63: 11–32.

PREALC. 1982. *Mercado de trabajo en cifras.* Santiago: ILO – Programa Regional del Empleo para América Latina y el Caribe.

Rodrik, D. 2013. Unconditional Convergence. *Quarterly Journal of Economics.* 128 (1): 165–204.

Rodrik, D. 2015. *Premature Deindustrialization.* NBER Working Paper 20935. Cambridge, MA.: National Bureau of Economic Research – accessible at www.nber.org/papers.html

Sposi, M. 2011. Evolving Comparative Advantage, Structural Change, and the Composition of Trade. Iowa City IA: University of Iowa – accessible at http://tippie.uiowa.edu/economics/tow/papers/sposi-fall2011.pdf

Timmer, M. P. 2000. *The Dynamics of Asian Manufacturing: A Comparison in the late Twentieth Century.* Cheltenham: Edward Elgar.

Timmer, M. P. and de Vries, G. J. 2009. Structural Change and Growth Accelerations in Asia and Latin America: A New Sectoral Data Set. *Cliometrica.* 3 (2): 165–190.

Timmer, M. P., O'Mahony, M., van Ark, B. and Inklaar, R. 2010. *Economic Growth in Europe.* Cambridge: Cambridge University Press.

United Nations. 2002. *International Standard Industrial Classification of All Economic Activities (ISIC) Revision 3.1.* New York: United Nations – accessible at www.unstats.un.org/unsd/cr/registry/

van Ark, B. 1996. Sectoral Growth Accounting and Structural Change in Post-War Europe. Chapter 3 in van Ark, B. and Crafts, N. (eds.). *Quantitative Aspects of Post-War European Economic Growth.* Cambridge: Cambridge University Press.

Young, A. 2012. The African Growth Miracle. *Journal of Political Economy.* 120 (4): 696–739.

Appendix

Table 4.A1 Decomposition results by country, 1960–1975

Region	Time period	Component due to:			Labour productivity growth (%)
		Within (%)	Between, static (%)	Between, dynamic (%)	
Sub-Saharan Africa					
Botswana	1964–75	3.2	6.0	−0.6	8.6
Ethiopia	1961–75	−0.6	1.5	−0.6	0.3
Ghana	1960–75	−0.7	−0.1	−0.2	−1.0
Kenya	1969–75	0.6	0.8	−0.2	1.2
Malawi	1966–75	1.2	0.5	−0.2	1.5
Mauritius	1970–75	11.0	2.6	−1.8	11.8
Nigeria	1960–75	4.1	−0.2	1.7	5.6

Senegal	1970–75	−2.9	0.9	−0.2	−2.2
South Africa	1960–75	2.1	1.3	0.6	4.0
Tanzania	1961–75	1.2	4.8	−3.4	2.6
Zambia	1965–75	−0.4	−0.6	0.1	−1.0
Asia					
India	1960–75	2.0	0.2	−0.3	2.0
Japan	1960–75	4.9	0.7	0.7	6.3
South Korea	1963–75	2.6	0.6	0.5	3.6
Taiwan	1963–75	4.7	0.4	0.6	5.7
Thailand	1960–75	2.5	1.7	0.4	4.6
China	1960–75	5.0	−0.4	−1.3	3.2
Latin America					
Argentina	1960–75	2.6	0.3	−0.5	2.4
Bolivia	1960–75	1.0	2.6	0.1	3.6
Brazil	1960–75	1.9	2.0	0.3	4.2
Chile	1960–75	2.0	0.1	−0.5	1.6
Colombia	1960–75	1.5	1.1	−0.4	2.2
Costa Rica	1960–75	0.9	1.4	−0.1	2.2
Mexico	1960–75	0.9	1.5	0.1	2.5
Peru	1960–75	2.1	0.9	0.3	3.3
Venezuela	1960–75	1.3	−1.6	−0.4	−0.6

Table 4.A2 Decomposition results by country, 1975–1990

Region	Time period	Component due to:			Labour productivity growth (%)
		Within (%)	Between, static (%)	Between, dynamic (%)	
Sub-Saharan Africa					
Botswana	1975–90	4.3	4.2	−1.4	7.1
Ethiopia	1975–90	−1.9	0.2	−0.1	−1.7
Ghana	1975–90	−1.2	0.0	−0.1	−1.3
Kenya	1975–90	−0.6	1.5	−0.6	0.3
Malawi	1975–90	−1.0	0.2	−0.3	−1.1
Mauritius	1975–90	0.3	1.2	−0.6	0.9
Nigeria	1975–90	0.7	−0.7	−0.4	−0.3
Senegal	1975–90	−3.2	1.1	−0.7	−2.8
South Africa	1975–90	−1.0	1.3	−0.3	−0.1
Tanzania	1975–90	−0.9	0.9	−0.5	−0.5
Zambia	1975–90	0.3	−1.7	−0.3	−1.6
Asia					
Hong Kong	1975–90	2.9	2.0	−0.1	4.8
India	1975–90	1.2	0.7	0.1	1.9
Indonesia	1975–90	0.1	2.9	−1.2	1.9
Japan	1975–90	3.1	0.3	0.1	3.5
Korea	1975–90	2.2	2.3	−0.2	4.3
Malaysia	1975–90	7.5	−0.3	−4.0	3.2
Philippines	1975–90	0.4	0.3	−0.4	0.4
Singapore	1975–90	2.9	0.4	−0.1	3.2

(Continued)

Table 4.A2 (Continued)

Region	Time period	Within (%)	Between, static (%)	Between, dynamic (%)	Labour productivity growth (%)
		Component due to:			
Taiwan	1975–90	4.5	0.7	0.1	5.3
Thailand	1975–90	2.6	1.2	0.8	4.6
China	1975–90	2.1	1.6	0.1	3.8
Latin America					
Argentina	1975–90	−1.4	−0.2	−0.2	−1.8
Bolivia	1975–90	−1.9	1.2	−1.0	−1.6
Brazil	1975–90	−0.5	1.4	−0.5	0.5
Chile	1975–90	0.2	1.2	−0.5	0.8
Colombia	1975–90	0.6	0.9	−0.4	1.1
Costa Rica	1975–90	−1.0	0.6	−0.3	−0.6
Mexico	1975–90	−1.1	1.1	−0.4	−0.3
Peru	1975–90	−3.6	1.9	−1.4	−3.1
Venezuela	1975–90	−3.4	0.7	−0.4	−3.1

Table 4.A3 Decomposition results by country, 1990–2010

Region	Time period	Within (%)	Between, static (%)	Between, dynamic (%)	Labour productivity growth (%)
		Component due to:			
Sub-Saharan Africa					
Botswana	1990–2010	4.1	0.1	−2.3	1.9
Ethiopia	1990–2010	1.2	2.5	−1.1	2.6
Ghana	1990–2010	2.3	0.7	−0.1	2.9
Kenya	1990–2010	−1.3	2.4	−1.6	−0.5
Malawi	1990–2010	−0.1	4.7	−3.1	1.5
Mauritius	1990–2010	3.1	0.9	−0.5	3.6
Nigeria	1990–2010	2.8	−0.2	−0.7	1.8
Senegal	1990–2010	2.1	1.7	−2.7	1.0
South Africa	1990–2010	2.0	0.4	−0.9	1.5
Tanzania	1990–2010	0.6	2.8	−1.4	2.0
Zambia	1990–2010	2.3	1.6	−1.7	2.2
Asia					
Hong Kong	1990–2010	2.5	0.9	−0.2	3.2
India	1990–2010	3.4	1.4	−0.1	4.6
Indonesia	1990–2010	2.0	0.7	0.1	2.7
Japan	1990–2010	1.4	0.2	−0.3	1.3
Korea	1990–2010	3.8	0.8	−1.4	3.2
Malaysia	1990–2010	2.7	0.1	0.2	3.0
Philippines	1990–2010	1.1	0.4	0.0	1.5
Singapore	1990–2010	2.5	0.3	−0.7	2.1
Taiwan	1990–2010	3.2	0.2	−0.1	3.3
Thailand	1990–2010	4.3	1.5	0.1	5.9
China	1990–2010	7.4	0.3	1.5	9.3

Latin America					
Argentina	1990–2010	2.5	−0.1	−0.5	1.9
Bolivia	1990–2010	2.1	1.5	−2.9	0.7
Brazil	1990–2010	0.7	0.4	−0.4	0.7
Chile	1990–2010	3.0	0.6	−0.8	2.8
Colombia	1990–2010	0.0	0.6	−0.3	0.3
Costa Rica	1990–2010	0.9	1.3	−1.1	1.1
Mexico	1990–2010	−0.2	1.6	−1.7	−0.3
Peru	1990–2010	1.4	0.5	−0.2	1.7
Venezuela	1990–2010	−1.0	2.0	−1.5	−0.6

Notes: Authors' calculation based on the GGDC sector database, using equation (1).

5

INDUSTRIALISATION, EMPLOYMENT AND POVERTY

Prema-chandra Athukorala and Kunal Sen

Introduction

Industrialisation[1] is an important driver of employment growth and poverty reduction in developing countries. At the early stage of transition from an agrarian economy to a modern economy, the manufacturing sector in the typical developing economy has greater potential to absorb surplus labour compared to the services sector, which in the typical low-income country is dominated by informal services. While it is feasible to move unskilled workers from agriculture into better-paid jobs in manufacturing activities, it is not feasible to move them into the formal services sector. Formal services sectors such as banking, insurance, finance, communications, and information technology are characterised by relatively low employment elasticity and also employment in these sectors requires education to at least upper secondary school level. Unskilled workers can find employment only in informal services such as retail trade and distribution, passenger transport and construction, where wages and productivity are often low. By contrast, employment in manufacturing, particularly in traditional labour-intensive industries such as clothing and footwear, require mostly on-the-job training.

As countries industrialise, workers are pulled out of low productivity agriculture to manufacturing, leading to both an increase in overall productivity in the economy as well as an increase in the share of workers employed in better paid jobs in manufacturing compared to the subsistence income they may obtain in agriculture. The wage gains associated with industrialisation can play an important role in pulling significant proportions of the population out of poverty because, in the typical low-income country, labour is the only asset owned by the poor. In addition to these direct effects, industrialisation can also be crucial in reducing poverty indirectly through the economy-wide positive employment effect of economic growth (Lavopa and Szirmai, 2012; UNIDO. 2013; Weiss, 2013).

While it is generally recognised that industrialisation can potentially be a powerful force for employment generation and poverty reduction, the magnitude of the employment and poverty impact may differ by stage of economic development. At an early stage of economic development, countries are more likely to specialise in labour-intensive industries, so that for low income countries, industrialisation can potentially have a strong positive effect on job creation and consequently, poverty reduction, under the appropriate policy environment. At higher levels of income, as countries start moving out of labour-intensive industries and into capital and technology-intensive industries, the direct effect of industrialisation on employment and poverty reduction will be weaker, though there may be strong indirect effects of industrialisation on poverty reduction, as the profits obtained from the growth of capital-intensive industries are re-invested in the economy, leading to further economic growth and poverty reduction.

Although low income countries have a natural advantage in labour-intensive manufacturing because of the lower costs of labour, we observe that relatively few developing countries have had success in producing and exporting labour-intensive manufacturing products. It is mostly in the East Asia and South East Asian region, that we observe the success of countries in labour-intensive industrialisation. Several countries in these two regions, starting sequentially with Japan, then Korea, Singapore, and Taiwan, and more recently, China and Vietnam, have moved from the import-substituting phases of their economic development to an export-oriented development strategy that involved a strong growth in the labour-intensive segment of the manufacturing sector in the initial years (Riedel, 1988; Haggard, 1996; Krueger, 1997; Perkins, 2013). In all these countries, as their economies integrated more closely into world markets, economic growth and structural transformation (that is, a shift of employment from agriculture to manufacturing) went hand in hand, and surplus labour was pulled from less productive agriculture to the more productive manufacturing sector.

What explains the success of some countries in labour-intensive industrialisation and not of others? The relationship between industrialisation on one hand and employment and poverty on the other has been a matter of great interest both in the scholarly literature as well as in policy debates. In this chapter, we first survey the literature relating to the debate on the relationship between industrialisation, employment and poverty reduction. We then present some stylised facts of industrialisation and its employment and poverty reduction impacts. The final section makes some policy inferences.

Industrialisation, employment and poverty reduction: The state of the debate

The overall level of manufacturing employment in an economy is by definition equal to the level of manufacturing output times the weighted average employment coefficient for the manufacturing sector:

$$L = Q \sum w_i (L/Q)_i \tag{1}$$

where L is total manufacturing employment; Q is total manufacturing output; $w_i = Q_i/Q$; and i refers to branches of manufacturing.

The relationship between industrialisation and employment can therefore be decomposed into these three elements.[2] First, there is the direct effect of industrialisation on employment operating through the increase in the total output of the manufacturing sector (Q). Second, in the process of industrialisation, there may be changes in the shares of different industries in overall manufacturing output (w_i), increasing the output of labour-intensive sectors and reducing output of capital-intensive sectors. Finally, employment can increase by an increase in the labour coefficients, which is an increase in labour intensity of production, within industries $(L/Q)_i$.

Thus, achieving high manufacturing growth rates is not a sufficient condition for employment generation; employment impact of a given rate of output expansion depends on capital deepening in the production process at the individual industry level and a shift in the product mix from relatively more labour-intensive product lines to capital-intensive product lines (Krueger, 1981; Gutierrez *et al.*, 2007). As we will discuss below, the relative importance of these three components of industrialisation-employment nexus is determined not only by the nature of the resource endowment of a given country but also by its policy regime choice.

In the 1950s and 1960s there was a broad consensus in the economics profession that the primary-commodity-dependent status inherited from the colonial era was the main cause of economic backwardness of developing countries. It was also believed that the gap in living standards between developed and developing countries would continue to widen because of both an inexorable deterioration in the terms of trade against primary commodities and the slower growth of world demand for these commodities. Industrialisation was therefore considered the key to economic development.[3] Apart from economic considerations, two important historical phenomena greatly influenced policy makers' thinking in favour of import-substituting industrialisation. The first was the strong nationalistic and anti-colonial sentiments that accompanied the attainment of independence; domestic manufacturing was of symbolic importance as a sign of national economic independence. The second inspiration came from the apparently successful rapid industrialisation in the Soviet Union under a command economy (central planning).

Since the domestic demand for most manufactured goods in these countries was historically met through imports, it seemed to follow logically that domestic production of manufactured goods, by taking over the 'ready-made' markets of imports, was the main avenue for industrialisation. Consequently, controls over import trade became the main policy instrument of planning for industrialisation. Industrialisation through export-orientation was however not considered as a viable option. The consensus at the time was that given the 'weakness' of domestic economic activities in these countries and their inability to compete with established industries abroad, industrialisation could not be undertaken without insulating the domestic economy from competition from established foreign industries (Myint, 1965: 127-28). In most developing countries protection and other incentives were, therefore, automatic for any new import-substitution industry, without provision for reduction or removal of them after an initial period.

In the ISI policy advocacy during this period, the prime focus was on the expansion of manufacturing output; employment generation and poverty reduction was rarely mentioned as 'specific' objectives. This was because the widely held view at the time was that manufacturing growth would automatically absorb surplus labour and this 'pull-up' force would help eradicating poverty[4] (Bhagwati, 1988a).

The case for import-substitution industrialisation (ISI) was so widely accepted at the time that 'developing-country exemptions' were even incorporated into the General Agreement on Tariff and Trade (GATT). The Article XVIII(B) of GATT exempted the developing countries from the 'obligations' of industrial countries, explicitly permitting them to adopt tariffs and quantitative restrictions as policy tools. The Bretton Woods institutions (the International Monetary Fund [IMF] and the World Bank) and other international organisations with commitment to economic development in developing countries also generally supported the basic thrust of the import-substitution policy (Krueger, 1995; 1997).

The period from about the late 1960s has witnessed a decisive shift in development thinking and policy away from the entrenched import-substituting views and in favour of export-oriented (outward-oriented) industrialisation strategy. This policy shift was brought about by a combination and interaction of two factors; the contrasting experiences of those developing countries that rigidly followed import-substituting policies and those that took the advantage of trade opportunities, and a substantial neo-classical revival in the trade and development literature based on these experiences and theoretical advances.

Many developing countries experienced rapid growth at the early stage of substituting domestic production for imports of consumer goods and other light manufactures. But, as these 'easy' import-substitution opportunities dried up, further growth was naturally limited to the rate of growth of domestic demand, and that was not generally high in most developing countries. In almost every country, and particularly in small countries, import-substitution policies encouraged high-cost, inefficient activities that showed little productivity gains over time, partly due to their sheltered position in the domestic market. Import substitution, which was rationalised as a means of reducing dependence on the international economy, in fact increased import dependence. Most of the newly established industries relied heavily on imported capital goods intermediate goods. To make matters worse, the protectionist policies pulled resources into high-cost import competing industries and discouraged export production. As a result, periodic foreign exchange shortages and 'stop-go-macroeconomic cycles' usually emerged with deleterious effects on output and employment (Baer and Hervé, 1966; Morawetz, 1974).

Relating to equity considerations, manufacturing growth yielded the perverse outcome of regressive shifts in the distribution of income and disappointing performance in terms of employment generation. In most countries the manufacturing sectors' rate of labour absorption fell behind the growth rate of labour force and in some cases manufacturing employment even declined in absolute terms as the balance of payments constraint put a limit on output expansion. Ironically, some countries began to face a 'new' problem of massive urban unemployment because of the failure of new industries to absorb the surplus labour streaming into urban centres (Diaz-Alejandro, 1975; Krueger 1997).

Against the dismal overall performance of import-substitution-addicted developing countries, a number of countries in East Asia, in particular Hong Kong, South Korea, Taiwan and Singapore, which shifted early to export-oriented industrialisation (which involved removing bias in the incentive structure in favour of domestic-market-oriented production so that firms produce for exports as well as for the domestic market) moved dramatically upward on the income scale, with substantial improvement in their overall economic performance.[5] More importantly, rapid and sustained growth in these countries was accompanied by a remarkable equity outcome, more equal distribution of income and rapid reduction in poverty through impressive employment growth (Fei, Ranis and Kuo, 1979; Perkins, 2013).

From the mid-1960s, a number of comparative multi-country research projects around the world probed the contrasting industrialisation and development experiences of export-oriented import-substituting countries.[6] Empirical evidence of these studies created greater awareness of the economic inefficiency and capital-intensity bias of ISI, and of the inherent growth-conducive traits of export-oriented regimes. It was revealed that most of the explanation for low labour absorption countries which followed ISI was underpinned by capital-intensive production rather than by increase in the efficiency of workers (increase in labour productivity). An increase in capital intensity was observable even in some traditional industries which presumably were more labour intensive. At the same time there was a structural shift in the overall manufacturing product mix towards relatively more capital-intensive industries. By contrast there was convincing incidence that the country which achieved an early transition from ISI to EOI recorded an impressive rate of labour absorption as the cumulative outcome of faster output expansion and structural adjustment in manufacturing in line with the countries' comparative advantage in labour-intensive production. The latter reflected both a shift in the industry composition towards new labour-intensive product lines and an increase in labour intensity of the existing industries.

Hand in hand with the appearance of these multi-country studies were considerable advances in the theoretical literature that scrutinised various aspects of the way in which protection actually works and the economic costs involved.[7] These theoretical advances not only provided more powerful tools for the anatomy of the consequences of controlled trade regimes but also gave credibility to the emerging empirical evidence on economic costs of such regimes.

Based on experience and research, export-oriented industrialisation (EOI) became the new orthodoxy of development policy from about the late 1970s. This policy advocacy soon became an integral part of aid conditionality of the World Bank and the IMF and the major bilateral donors. This new ideological orientation, which became the cornerstone of the so-called 'Washington Consensus' *à la* Williamson (1994), coupled with the influence of aid conditionality, produced a palpable shift in industrial policies of many countries (including that of China and many countries in the former Soviet Bloc) towards greater reliance on export orientation. During the late 1980s and early 1990s, most of the Latin American countries that had favoured ISI since the 1930s, went through unilateral liberalisation reforms. Similar processes took place in Asia, where countries that have pursued highly protectionist policies for decades, including India, are implementing major trade liberalisation efforts (Sachs and Warner, 1995; Wacziarg and Welch, 2008).[8]

After more than four decades of experience and research, the range of the debate over trade and industry policies in developing countries has undoubtedly been narrowed. It is now widely accepted that import substitution has outlived its usefulness and openness to foreign trade is "a friend of economic development and growth, not an enemy, as many policy makers and economists had feared in the immediate post-war period" (Rodrik, 1995: 101).

With this broader consensus, the debate is now centred upon the question of how to tackle the challenges associated with a policy regime shift from inward-oriented to outward-oriented trade regimes. The mainstream case for 'letting factor endowment speak' by getting product and factor prices right has come under attack from a strong revisionist school of thought, based on re-interpretations of economic transformations in the East Asia high-performing economics. These economists argue that market imperfection in the typical developing economy and 'dynamic externalities' associated with infant industry protection really call for the 'right kind' of intervention, and government intervention in the form of selective credit and other forms of promotion was an essential element in the success of Taiwan, Korea, Singapore and Japan (Amsden, 1989; Wade, 1990; Taylor, 1991; Rodrik, 1992, 1995). The revisionist view has gained added impetus from the lack-lustre outcome of market-oriented policy reforms undertaken in many countries in Latin America and the Sub-Saharan Africa over the past two decades (Edwards, 2010).[9]

In a clear departure from the conventional wisdom, the World Bank (1991), in its *World Development Report 1991*, acknowledged that 'market friendly' intervention undoubtedly played a role in dramatic economic transformations in these countries. Then, in the context of the East Asian Miracle study, the Bank specifically mentioned that directed credit, an important instrument of industrial policy, may have made a substantial contribution to successful industrialisation efforts in both Korea and Taiwan (World Bank, 1993).[10]

The mainstream economists, however, continue to stress that it was the firm commitment to outward orientation and relatively less reliance (by the developing-country standards) on restrictive trade policies (rather than some isolated attempts to promote specific industries through selective incentives) that played the critical role in successful industrial transition in East Asian countries (Pack and Saggi, 2006). In particular, they argue that the outstanding success of these countries was based on a phenomenal growth of labour-intensive manufactures (including light electrical and electronics machinery, largely consisting of consumer goods), not the typical 'heavy' sectors (chemicals, non-metallic minerals and base metals), which received favoured treatment (Krueger, 1997; Little, 1994). Various selective interventions, so the argument goes, were important only to the extent that they "played an important role in making the export promotion strategy work successfully by ensuring credibility of commitment on the part of governments" (Bhagwati, 1988b: 260).

Industrialisation, employment and poverty: Stylised facts

In this section, we review the stylised facts of the outcomes of industrialisation, and in particular, its links with poverty and other development outcomes.

The available data on manufacturing employment and its *direct* contribution to total employment in 32 countries are summarised in Table 5.1. In most developing countries manufacturing employment is increasing in absolute terms, but manufacturing share in total employment has continuously increased only in a handful of countries. In 2005 (the latest year for which comparable data are available), the share of manufacturing in total employment varied between 10 and 20 per cent for the bulk of the countries listed in the table; manufacturing accounted for more than 20 per cent in only four countries (Singapore, Malaysia, Italy and Taiwan).

Table 5.1 Direct employment in manufacturing across the world: number of workers and share in total employment, 1985–2005

	Manufacturing workers (thousands)			Manufacturing share in total employment (%)		
	1985	*1995*	*2005*	*1985*	*1995*	*2005*
All listed countries	219,598	254,026	279,762	19	17	15
Advanced countries	61,413	56,309	49,163	23	19	15
Australia	1,129	1,112	1,054	16	13	11
France	4,714	3,815	3,538	21	17	14
Germany	9,768	8,441	7,515	29	22	19
Italy	5,818	5,169	5,072	27	23	21
Japan	14,390	13,830	10,979	24	21	17
Netherlands	1,035	1,067	975	19	15	12
UK	5,372	4,212	3,632	22	17	13
USA	19,187	18,663	16,399	18	14	11
Latin America	17,051	19,318	21,205	16	15	12
Argentina	2,094	1,907	1,635	18	15	12
Brazil	7,852	8,292	9,619	15	14	13
Chile	507	810	723	14	16	11
Colombia	1,024	1,678	1,774	11	13	11
Mexico	4,742	5,618	6,622	19	18	17
Venezuela	832	1,018	832	17	14	10
Africa	2,897	4,924	7,230	—	8	9
Ethiopia	—	577	1,529	—	2	5
Ghana	—	613	1,013	—	9	12
Kenya	—	822	1,686	—	8	11
Nigeria	1,292	1,004	908	4	3	2
Senegal	—	360	388	—	12	9
South Africa	1,605	1,548	1,706	15	15	14
East Asia	111,429	133,722	155,645	19	18	17
China	93,275	102,486	120,409	16	15	16
Hong Kong	919	535	228	36	18	7
Indonesia	6,025	11,505	12,406	10	14	14
Malaysia	855	2,052	2,271	15	26	23
Philippines	1,927	2,578	3,049	10	10	9
Singapore	313	385	485	25	23	21

(Continued)

89

Table 5.1 (Continued)

	Manufacturing workers (thousands)			Manufacturing share in total employment (%)		
	1985	*1995*	*2005*	*1985*	*1995*	*2005*
South Korea	3,504	4,797	4,234	24	24	19
Thailand	2,109	4,293	5,588	9	14	16
Taiwan	2,502	2,449	2,726	34	27	27
Vietnam	—	2,642	4,250	—	8	10
South Asia	26,808	39,753	46,519	10	11	12
India	26,160	38,965	45,134	10	11	12
Sri Lanka	648	788	1,385	13	15	16

Sources: for Sri Lanka, Athukorala and Rajapatirana (2000) and Athukorala (2005); for Vietnam, Nguyen (2014); for other countries, Lapova and Szirmai (2012, Table 2).

Note: — = data not available.

For a meaningful discussion of the role of manufacturing in employment creation (and poverty alleviation), it is important to distinguish between the direct creation of jobs in manufacturing and the jobs created in other sectors as an outcome of the expansion of manufacturing production (indirect employment). For instance, in many countries a growing number of jobs are created in manufacturing-related services such as warehousing, transport, and human resource management and information technology. In recent years, the rapid expansion of global production sharing has been a key driver of the expansion of these manufacturing-related services jobs. The growing importance of processed foods in world trade has contributed to strengthening the linkages between manufacturing and the agricultural sector. There is convincing evidence that employment multipliers in manufacturing are usually much higher than in the other sectors and one job in manufacturing generally creates two or three jobs in the other sectors (Lavopa and Szirmai, 2012).

There are notable variations in labour productivity in manufacturing across developing countries (Table 5.2). For instance, labour productivity in Korea is by far the highest among countries for which we have data for 2010, and labour productivity levels in Cambodia, Estonia and Lao PDR are less than 5 per cent of Korea's. The labour productivity of Azerbaijan, the Czech Republic and Chile in the secondary sector is the closest to Korea's, yet the levels of labour productivity in these countries are less than half that of Korea's.

As already noted, different countries, even at similar levels of economic development, show very different rates of employment generation for a given rate of manufacturing growth. The employment intensity of manufacturing – the ratio of the percentage change in manufacturing employment to the percentage change in manufacturing real output – provides a useful summary indicator of these inter-country differences. Table 5.3 reports this indicator both by major region and by five year periods, starting in 1965-69 and ending in 2000-04. The employment intensity of manufacturing is the lowest in Africa (in fact, negative) and the highest in East/ South East Asia and Central/Eastern Europe.

As part of our on-going research, we have examined the patterns and determinants of employment intensity of industrialisation using a new panel data set covering 42 developing countries over the period 1970-2010 (Athukorala and Sen, 2014). The preliminary findings point to a strong positive relationship between the openness of trade policy regimes

Table 5.2 Labour productivity in manufacturing in developing countries, 2005–2010 (annual averages)

	Labour productivity[a]	Ratio of country labour productivity to Korea's labour productivity (%)
Albania	8,110	8.8
Argentina	24,822	27.0
Armenia	28,403	30.9
Azerbaijan	44,847	48.8
Bhutan	25,363	27.6
Brazil	18,599	20.3
Bulgaria	13,748	15.0
Cambodia	3,359	3.7
Chile	39,481	43.0
China	10,799	11.8
Colombia	23,951	26.1
Costa Rica	16,232	17.7
Croatia	34,397	37.5
Cuba	12,553	13.7
Czech Republic	38,029	41.4
Dominican Republic	17,142	18.7
Ecuador	14,885	16.2
Egypt, Arab Rep. of	10,894	11.9
El Salvador	10,641	11.6
Estonia	1,992	2.2
Hungary	31,452	34.3
India	4,089	4.5
Indonesia	15,500	16.9
Jamaica	13,113	14.3
Jordan	26,114	28.4
Kazakhstan	28,778	31.3
Korea, Rep. of	91,830	100.0
Kyrgyz Republic	2,183	2.4

Source: World Bank (2013a).

Note

a Value added per worker in constant (2005) US dollars.

Table 5.3 Employment elasticity in manufacturing by region and period

Region	1965–2004	Various sub-periods	
Developed countries	0.34	1965–1969	0.62
Africa	−0.69	1970–1974	0.52
Latin America and Caribbean	0.03	1975–1979	0.66
Central and Eastern Europe	0.40	1980–1984	−0.23
East and South-East Asia	0.42	1985–1989	0.19
South Asia	−0.87	1990–1994	−8.77
Other Asia and the Pacific	0.19	1995–1999	−0.09

Source: Computed from *UNIDO Industrial Statistics*, various years.

(as measured by the Sachs–Warner index) and the degree of employment intensity across countries: on average the degree of employment intensity is 20 per cent higher in countries with open trade policy regimes compared to the other countries. The degree of employment intensity, however, seems to correlate negatively with levels of income, suggesting that countries shift away from labour-intensive towards capital-intensive sectors in manufacturing in the process of economic development. We also find that employment intensity declines with higher levels of schooling, suggesting that with greater levels of human capital, countries tend to move to more capital-intensive methods of production. Interestingly, so far we have not uncovered a clear relationship between employment intensity and the restrictiveness of labour regulations.

Finally, what is the relationship between industrialisation, economic growth and poverty? There is a weak positive relationship between industrialisation and the level of per capita income (Figure 5.1). However, as can be seen in Figure 5.2, there is a much stronger negative relationship between industrialisation and income poverty, with countries that are more industrialised having lower poverty. This may be because industrialisation contributes to poverty reduction both directly (through increase in industrial output and employment) but also though economy-wide spread effects on the other sectors in the economy (as discussed before). Also, as we have already noted, the poverty-reduction effect of industrialisation is likely to be greater in poorer countries. In contrast to the strong negative relationship between industrialisation and poverty, there is no clear relationship between industrialisation and income inequality as measured by the standard Gini coefficient (Figure 5.3).

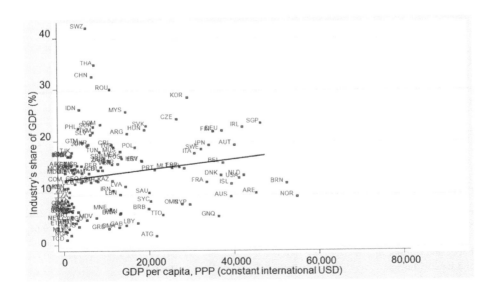

Figure 5.1   Industrialisation and per capita income, 2010.

Source: Based on data extracted from World Bank, World Development Indicators database (World Bank, 2013b).

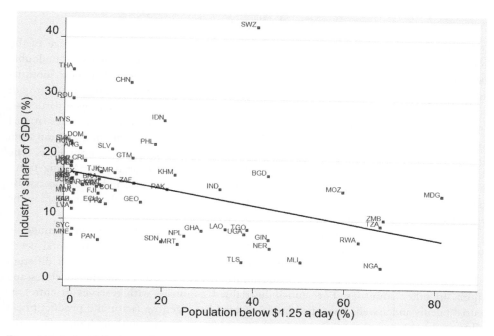

Figure 5.2 Industrialisation and poverty, 2010.

Source: Authors' calculations, data from Teorell *et al.* (2013), accessed 1 February 2014.

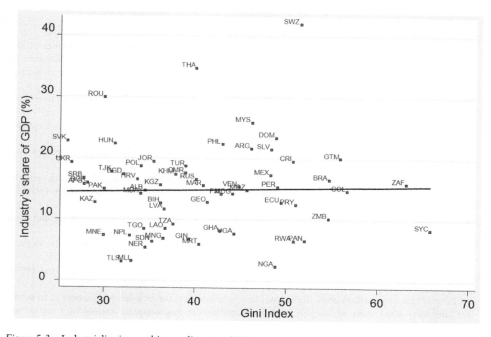

Figure 5.3 Industrialisation and inequality, *circa* 2010.

Source: Authors' calculations, data from Teorell *et al.* (2013), accessed 1 February 2014.

Concluding remarks

After more than four decades of development experience and research, the range of the debate over the appropriate policy for industrialisation in developing countries has undoubtedly narrowed. There is a consensus that the early emphasis on 'forced' import substitution through trade protection and state intervention has outlived its usefulness and growth prospects in general, and poverty alleviation though employment generation in particular, are greatly enhanced by industrialisation through greater integration into the international economy. Despite this broader consensus, the debate on how to manage the transition from import-substitution to export-oriented industrialisation remains a contentious issue. The neo-classical (mainstream) economists by and large continue to argue that letting factor endowment 'speak' through neutral incentives is the way to achieve industrial success. By contrast the revisionist, or heterodox, economists argue for an activist role for the state in the form of selective incentives.

The changes for improved outcomes in policy reforms in the future seem to hinge on policy makers' ability to craft policies by carefully taking into account structural peculiarities and the policy history of individual countries while drawing on both different economic schools of thought and the accumulated evidence of economic successes and failures in other countries. For semi-industrialised countries with reserves of entrepreneurial talents and a well-developed human capital base, getting factor and product prices right may be the appropriate recipe for achieving labour absorption though manufacturing expansion. For low-income countries which do not enjoy these preconditions, there may be a case for some government intervention in the form of providing well-targeted and time-bound incentives.

Notes

1 In the standard national accounts terminology the term 'industry' encompasses mining, manufacturing, construction, and utilities (electricity, water and gas). Following the general practice in the literature on development economics we used this term specifically to refer to 'manufacturing'; and the two terms are used interchangeably in the rest of the paper (United Nations, 2009).

2 There is also the indirect, economy-wide, effect of industrialisation on employment via input–output linkages, which we ignore for the time being.

3 For surveys of the relevant literature see Baer and Hervé (1966), Morawetz (1974), Diaz-Alejandro (1975), Krueger (1997), Bruton (1998) and Pack and Saggi (2006).

4 Theoretical underpinning for this view was provided by the celebrated surplus-labour model of Arthur Lewis (1954).

5 These four countries were subsequently joined by Malaysia, Thailand, Indonesia and China to form the country grouping of 'East Asian Miracle Economies' or High Performing Asian Economies' (HPAEs) (World Bank 1993).

6 The main publications arising from these multicounty research projects are Little, Scitovsky and Scott (1970), Balassa (1982), Bhagwati (1978), Krueger (1978) and Donges (1976).

7 For a comprehensive survey of these theoretical advances with extensive references to the relevant literature see Corden (1997).

8 For details on policy shifts in various countries see Chenery and Keesing (1981), Michaely *et al.* (1991, Chapter 2), Thomas and Nash (1991), Edwards (1995) and Sachs and Warner (1995).

9 As Edwards has vividly illustrated, the revisionists often interpret the lack-lustre outcome as an inherent limitation of the main-stream policy advocacy, without paying adequate attention (or completely overlooking) the half-hearted nature of the actual reform process.

10 See also Stiglitz (1996). Lall (1997) argues that there may be important limitations in the effective use of such selective policies in the low income country context.

References

Amsden, A. H. 1989. *Asia's Next Giant: South Korea and Late Industrialization*. New York: Oxford University Press.

Athukorala, P. 2005. Outward-Oriented Policy Reforms and Industrialization in Sri Lanka. *Economic Papers*. 26 (4): 372–391.

Athukorala, P. and Rajapatirana, S. 2000. Liberalization and Industrial Transformation: Lessons from the Sri Lankan Experience. *Economic Development and Cultural Change*. 48 (3): 542–572.

Athukorala, P. and Sen, K. 2014. The Determinants of the Employment Intensity of Manufacturing in Developing Countries. Mimeo.

Baer, W. and Hervé, M. 1966. Employment and Industrialization in Developing Countries. *Quarterly Journal of Economics*. 80 (1): 88–107.

Balassa, B. 1982. *Development Strategies in Semi-Industrial Economies*. Baltimore, MD: Johns Hopkins University Press.

Bhagwati, J. N. 1978. *Anatomy and Consequences of Exchange Control Regimes*. Cambridge, MA: Ballinger Publishing Company.

Bhagwati, J. N. 1988a. Poverty and Public Policy. *World Development*. 16 (5): 539–555.

Bhagwati, J. N. 1988b. Export Promoting Trade Strategy: Issues and Evidence. *World Bank Research Observer*. 3 (1): 27–52.

Bruton, H. T. 1998. A Reconsideration of Import Substitution. *Journal of Economic Literature*. 35 (2): 903–936.

Chenery, H. B. and Keesing, D. B. 1981. The changing composition of developing country exports. In Grassman, S. and Lundberg, E. (eds.). *The World Economic Order: Past and Prospects*. London: Macmillan: 234–263.

Corden, W. M. 1997. *Trade Policy and Economic Welfare* (2nd ed.). Oxford: Clarendon Press.

Diaz-Alejandro, C.F. 1975. Trade Policy and Economic Development. In Kenen, P. B. (ed.). *International Trade and Finance: Frontiers for Research*. Cambridge: Cambridge University Press: 93–150.

Donges, J. 1976. A Comparative Study of Industrialisation Policies in Fifteen Semi-Industrial Countries. *Weltwirtschaftliches Archiv*. 12 (4): 626–659.

Edwards, S. 1995. *Crisis and reform in Latin America: From Despair to Hope*. New York: Oxford University Press.

Edwards, S. 2010. *Left Behind: Latin America and the False Promise of Populism*. Chicago: University of Chicago Press.

Fei, J., Ranis, G. and Kuo, S. 1979. *Growth with Equity: The Taiwan Case*. New York: Oxford University Press.

Gutierrez, C., Orecchia, C., Paci, P. and Serneels, P. 2007. *Does Employment Generation Really Matter for Poverty Reduction?* Policy Research Working Paper 4432. Washington DC: World Bank.

Haggard, S. 1996. Lessons from Successful Reformers: Korea and Taiwan. *Economic Reform Today*, 2(1): 15–22.

Krueger, A. O. 1978. *Foreign Trade Regimes and Economic Development: Liberalization Attempts and Consequences*. Cambridge, MA: Ballinger Publishing Company.

Krueger, A. O. 1981. *Trade and Employment in Developing Countries: Synthesis and Conclusion*. Chicago: University of Chicago Press.

Krueger, A. O. 1995. *Trade Policies and Developing Nations*. Washington, DC: Brookings Institution.

Krueger, A. O. 1997. Trade Policy and Economic Development: What have We Learned? *American Economic Review*. 87 (1): 1–22.

Lall, S. 1997. *Selective Policies for Export Promotion: Lessons from the Asian Tigers*. WIDER Research for Action No. 43. Helsinki: UN University, World Institute for Development Economics Research.

Lavopa, A. and Szirmai, A. 2012. *Industrialisation, Employment and Poverty*. UNU-MERIT Working Paper No. 81. Maastricht: Maastricht Economic and Social Research institute on Innovation and Technology.

Lewis, W. A. 1954. Economic Development with Unlimited Supplies of Labour. *The Manchester School*. 22 (2): 139–191.

Little, I. M. D. 1994. Trade Liberalization Revisited. *Pakistan Development Review*. 33 (4): 359–89. (Reprinted as Chapter 9 in Little, I. M. D. 1999. *Collection and Recollections*. Oxford: Clarendon Press: 155–161).

Little, I. M. D., Scitovsky, T. and Scott, M. 1970. *Industry and Trade in Some Developing Countries: A Comparative Study*. Oxford: Oxford University Press.

Michaely, M., Papageorgiou, D. and Choksi, A. M. (eds.). 1991. *Liberalising Foreign Trade: Lessons of Experience in the Developing World*. Oxford: Basil Blackwell.

Morawetz, D. 1974. Employment Implications of Industrialisation in Developing Countries: A Survey. *Economic Journal.* 84 (335): 491–542.

Myint, H. 1965. *The Economics of the Developing Countries.* London: Hutchinson University Library.

Nguyen, K. T. 2014. *Economic Reforms, Manufacturing Employment and Wages in Vietnam.* PhD Dissertation, Australian National University.

Pack, H. and Saggi, K. 2006. Is There a Case for Industrial Policy? A Critical Survey. *World Bank Research Observer.* 21 (2): 267–297.

Perkins, D. H.(2013. *East Asian Development: Foundations and Strategies.* Cambridge, MA: Harvard University Press.

Riedel, J. 1988. Economic Development in East Asia: Doing What Comes Naturally? In Hughes, H. (ed.). *Achieving Industrialisation in East Asia.* Cambridge: Cambridge University Press.

Rodrik, D. 1992. The Limits of Trade Policy Reform in Developing Countries. *Journal of Economic Perspectives.* 6 (1): 87–105.

Rodrik, D. 1995. Trade and Industrial Policy Reforms. In Berman, J. R. and Srinivasan, T. N. (eds.). *Handbook of Development Economics* Vol. III. Amsterdam: North Holland.

Sachs, J. D. and Warner, A. 1995. Economic Reform and the Process of Global Integration. *Brookings Papers on Economic Activity.* 26 (1): 1–118.

Stiglitz, J. E. 1996. Some Lessons from the East Asian Miracle. *World Bank Research Observer.* 11 (2): 151–177.

Taylor, L. 1991. Economic Openness: Problems to the Century's End. In Baruni, T. (ed.). *Economic Liberalisation: No Panacea: The Experience of Latin America and Asia.* Oxford: Clarendon Press: 99–147.

Teorell, J., Charron, N., Dahlberg, S., Holmberg, S., Rothstein, B., Sundin, P. and Svensson, R. 2013. *The Quality of Government Dataset,* version 20 December 2013. University of Gothenburg: The Quality of Government Institute – accessible from www.qog.pol.gu.se

Thomas, V. and Nash, J. 1991. *Best Practices in Trade Policy Reforms.* New York: Oxford University Press.

UNIDO. 2013. *Sustaining Employment Growth – The Role of Manufacturing and Structural Change: Industrial Development Report 2013.* Geneva: United Nations Industrial Development Organization.

United Nations. 2009. *System of National Accounts 2008.* Geneva: United Nations.

Wacziarg, R. and Welch, K. H. 2008. Trade Liberalization and Growth: New Evidence. *World Bank Economic Review.* 22 (2): 187–231.

Wade, R. 1990. *Governing the Market: Economic Theory and the Role of the Government in East Asian Industrialization.* Princeton, NJ: Princeton University Press.

Weiss, J. 2013. Industrial Policy for the Twenty-First Century: Challenges for the Future. In Szirmai, A., Naude, A. and Alcorta, L. (eds.). *Pathways to Industrialisation in the Twenty-First Century: New Challenges and Emerging Paradigms.* Oxford: Oxford University Press.

Williamson, J. 1994. In Search of a Manual for Technopols. In Williamson, J. (ed.). *The Political Economy of Policy Reforms.* Washington, DC: Institute for International Economics: 9-24.

World Bank. 1991. *World Development Report 1991.* New York: Oxford University Press for the World Bank.

World Bank. 1993. *The East Asian Miracle: Economic Growth and Public Policy.* Oxford: Oxford University Press for the World Bank.

World Bank. 2013a. *World Development Report 2013: Jobs.* Washington, DC: World Bank.

World Bank. 2013b. *World Development Indicators.* Washington, DC: World Bank – accessible from http://data.worldbank.org

6

DEINDUSTRIALISATION

An issue for both developed and developing countries

Fiona Tregenna

Introduction

Industrialisation has been seen as central to the development process since the earliest days of Development Economics as a field. In the policy sphere, this recognition was reflected in the prioritisation of industrialisation in developing countries' drives to modernise and 'catch up', especially in the decades of the 1950s to 1970s.

However, with the notable exception of East Asia, many developing countries began to *deindustrialise* at relatively low levels of industrial development. Deindustrialisation is generally taken to refer to a fall in the share of manufacturing in a country's GDP and/or employment. Deindustrialisation in many developing countries began before they even reached the levels of industrialisation that had been typical in advanced economies before those countries began deindustrialising around the 1970s. This is one of the key differences between the typical patterns of deindustrialisation in developing and advanced economies.[1]

There have arguably been five central debates in the literature on deindustrialisation. The first of these concerns the *causes* of deindustrialisation. Most importantly, about the extent to which deindustrialisation is driven by domestic or international factors. A second key debate in the literature has been around the most appropriate way of *defining* deindustrialisation. Third, there is an issue about how much of apparent deindustrialisation is a genuine structure shift and how much is a 'statistical illusion' arising from the reclassification of jobs due to outsourcing. A fourth area of debate centres on the *effects* of deindustrialisation, particularly on economic growth. The question here is basically whether or not a decline in manufacturing is a pathological phenomenon which is likely to depress economic growth, due to special properties of manufacturing for growth. A related set of issues concerns the social and political effects of deindustrialisation. Fifth, there has been discussion in the literature about *premature* deindustrialisation in developing countries, including around whether and how this differs from deindustrialisation in advanced economies.

These debates, along with other relevant issues from the literature on deindustrialisation, are reviewed in this chapter. The existing literature on deindustrialisation focuses primarily on developed countries, for obvious reasons, but special attention is paid here to issues of deindustrialisation in developing countries as well. This chapter begins with an overview of the different definitions and typologies of deindustrialisation and then in the third section considers the heterogeneity of deindustrialisation experiences internationally. the fourth section discusses the sources of deindustrialisation, and the fifth focuses on the specificity of deindustrialisation in developing countries. The sixth section explores the debate around the extent to which deindustrialisation is a 'statistical illusion'. The economic effects of deindustrialisation are reviewed in the seventh section and the social and political effects of deindustrialisation in the eighth. This is followed by a brief consideration of the spatial dimensions of deindustrialisation, in the ninth section. The tenth section concludes.

Definitions and typologies of deindustrialisation

While deindustrialisation always refers to some sort of problems or shrinkage in the manufacturing sector, there are different ways in which deindustrialisation has been defined. Different definitions would give rise to different judgements as to whether particular experiences should be characterised as deindustrialisation.

An early study of deindustrialisation was by Bluestone and Harrison (1982) for the USA. They defined deindustrialisation as "systematic disinvestment in a nation's core manufacturing industries" (p. 6). Another prominent early contribution to the conceptualisation of deindustrialisation was that of Singh (1977). He conceptualises deindustrialisation in terms of an 'efficient' manufacturing sector, in terms of whether or not manufacturing can generate sufficient net exports to meet a country's import requirements at acceptable levels of output, employment and the exchange rate. Singh considers deindustrialisation to be an outcome, instead of a cause, of this 'inefficiency' or of disequilibrium. He sees deindustrialisation as problematic insofar as it is indicative of structural disequilibrium.

Cairncross (1979) supports Singh's approach to deindustrialisation and labels this the 'Cambridge' view of deindustrialisation. In a different perspective, Bacon and Eltis (1976) attribute deindustrialisation in the United Kingdom to excessive public spending crowding out manufacturing by starving it of resources.

Rowthorn and Wells (1987) introduced an important distinction between what they term 'positive' and 'negative' deindustrialisation. This distinction rests on both the causes and effects of deindustrialisation. In terms of causes, positive deindustrialisation is seen as a normal product of growth and development in mature economies, resulting from rapid productivity growth in the manufacturing sector. Because this rapid productivity growth is accompanied by even faster output growth, and extensive job creation in the services sector, there is no resultant increase in employment. While Rowthorn and Wells do not foresee negative economic effects of deindustrialisation, their focus is on employment. If the manufacturing sector does indeed have special properties that are important for growth, then even 'positive' deindustrialisation could arguably have negative effects for growth. Still, what they see as deindustrialisation, that is, a symptom of economic success, is in contrast to the pathological phenomenon of negative deindustrialisation. This results from economic failure, more specifically serious problems in industry. Negative deindustrialisation causes unemployment to rise because labour shed from the manufacturing sector is not absorbed into the service sector. Rowthorn and Wells also identify a third type of deindustrialisation, in which the composition of net exports shifts from manufactures towards other goods and services, bringing about a reallocation of labour and other resources from manufacturing to other sectors.

More recently, drawing on an empirical analysis of deindustrialisation in developing countries, Pieper (2000) puts forward a taxonomy distinguishing between three types of deindustrialisation. She defines productivity deindustrialisation as a negative contribution of the industrial sector to overall productivity growth in an economy, and employment deindustrialisation and output deindustrialisation as decreases in the contribution of the industrial sector to overall output and employment respectively.

Jalilian and Weiss (2000) develop a novel test for deindustrialisation, based on an analysis of countries' manufacturing level and share of GDP relative to what would be econometrically predicted based on cross-country regressions that include relevant country characteristics. A country is considered to have deindustrialised in absolute terms if the size of its manufacturing sector is lower than predicted and if this deviation has grown over time; similarly for relative deindustrialisation measured in the share of manufacturing.

One important issue in defining and measuring deindustrialisation is whether it should be understood as a fall in the share of manufacturing in total *employment*, or in *value added* (/GDP), or both. Deindustrialisation is most commonly defined in the literature as a fall in the share of manufacturing in total employment (see, for example, Palma, 2008; Rowthorn and Coutts, 2004; Rowthorn and Ramaswamy, 1997; Saeger, 1997; Alderson, 1999; Dasgupta and Singh, 2005).

The fact that the declines in manufacturing employment share have generally exceeded those in manufacturing output might partly explain the emphasis on the fall in the share of manufacturing *employment* in the deindustrialisation literature. This emphasis on manufacturing employment specifically probably also derives in part from a perspective that the special properties of manufacturing operate through the employment channel in particular, and in part from the social and political dimensions of falling manufacturing employment. Furthermore, apparent changes in manufacturing output share are complicated by concurrent changes in relative prices. The fall in the relative price of manufactures might make it difficult to pin down the real decline in manufacturing output, given the limitations of sectoral deflators, and this could be part of the reason for the focus in the literature on changes in manufacturing employment share rather than output share. In addition, in advanced capitalist economies in the 1980s, the decline in manufacturing employment was arguably more acutely felt socially and politically than was the decline in manufacturing output. The shedding of manufacturing jobs, and the apparent inability of the rest of the economy to absorb those who lost their jobs, made this an important political and social issue. The relative visibility and 'political' nature of manufacturing job losses may have contributed to the focus on this dimension of deindustrialisation (Tregenna, 2009). Conversely, the fact that sectoral employment is not as readily available as value added data could also be a factor leading empirical analyses to focus more on output than on employment, especially in developing countries.

Tregenna (2009, 2013) suggests that deindustrialisation should be defined in terms of a sustained decline in *both* the share of manufacturing in total employment and the share of manufacturing in GDP. This is based in part on an argument that manufacturing may act as an engine of growth through both output and employment channels. The growth-pulling effects of manufacturing through backward and forward linkages with the rest of the domestic economy are related more to the share of manufacturing in GDP and the growth of manufacturing output, than to its share of employment or growth in manufacturing employment. Manufacturing might also pull growth through Keynesian-type demand multiplier effects, through wages paid. In this respect it would clearly be manufacturing employment, rather than output per se, that would be relevant. However, this can be considered a 'special property' of manufacturing only insofar as manufacturing wages are higher than those in other sectors of the economy. A positive differential between manufacturing wages and average wages in the domestic economy can give manufacturing special growth-pulling properties, especially in an (effective) demand-constrained economy. The share of manufacturing in total employment is thus central in this particular regard.

Tregenna's proposition that deindustrialisation should be defined as the share of manufacturing in both output and employment is also based on an empirical analysis suggesting that not all episodes in which the employment share of manufacturing falls should appropriately be classified as deindustrialisation, as discussed in the next section.

Heterogeneity of deindustrialisation experiences

Figure 6.1 decomposes changes in the level of manufacturing employment into changes in the value added of manufacturing and changes in the labour-intensity of manufacturing.[2] The coordinates of each point show the contribution of changes in manufacturing labour-intensity (that is, the inverse of labour productivity) (*x*-axis) and changes in manufacturing growth (*y*-axis), to the percentage change in manufacturing employment for a country.

Developing Asian countries are grouped towards the top left of the chart, with large and positive sector growth effects and large and negative labour-intensity effects. This is indicative of their strong manufacturing performance, both in value added and in productivity. The only developing Asian country that is an exception to this pattern is the 'honorary Latin American' case of the Philippines. Compared to developing Asian countries, Latin American countries have relatively low sector growth effects and the labour-intensity effects are either positive or less negative than in the case of Asian countries. The difference between the results for Asia and

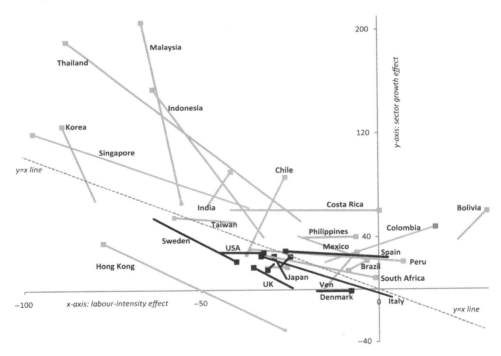

Figure 6.1 Decomposition of change in the level of manufacturing employment.

Source: Figure taken from Tregenna (2013).

Notes: Square marker refers to 1985–1995; end of line refers to 1995–2005. Venezuela, Argentina, France and Netherlands are included in the chart but are not labelled for reasons of space; these are the short lines located nearby the UK and Japan. Developed countries are shown in black and developing countries in grey.

Latin America fits in with the fact that the former generally had higher growth in both value added and productivity in manufacturing than the latter. The contrast between Latin American and Asian countries can be illustrated with a comparison of manufacturing performance in Korea and Venezuela. These two countries experienced roughly similar trends in the level of manufacturing employment between the two periods. However, the performance is vastly different when it comes to manufacturing value added and productivity, with growth of these variables multiple times higher in Korea than in Venezuela.

Unlike most developing countries, almost all developed countries fall below the dashed diagonal line in both periods, indicating absolute falls in manufacturing employment. The positive sector growth effects were outweighed by larger negative labour-intensity effects. This shows a different pattern of deindustrialisation in advanced economies.

In Figure 6.2, changes in the *share* of manufacturing in total employment are decomposed into three components. The labour-intensity effect measures the contribution of changes in the labour-intensity of manufacturing. The sector share effect measures the contribution of changes in the share of manufacturing in total value added. The aggregate labour productivity effect measures the contribution of changes in aggregate labour productivity; this component is not shown here. Each point in Figure 6.2 shows the combination of the labour-intensity effect (*x*-coordinate) and sector share effect (*y*-coordinate) for a country. For each country, the initial point (square marker) is for 1985–95 and the second point is for 1995–2005.

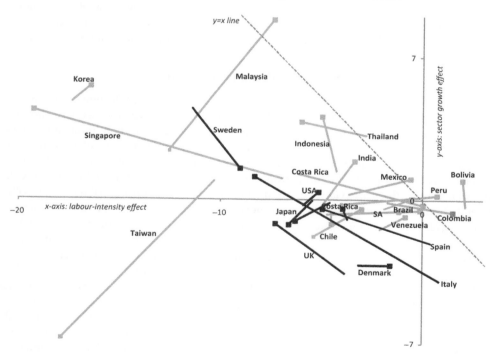

Figure 6.2 Partial results from decomposition of changes in the share of manufacturing employment.

Source: Figure taken from Tregenna (2013).

Notes: Only the labour-intensity and sector share effects are shown here, not the aggregate labour productivity effect. Square marker refers to 1985–1995; end of line refers to 1995–2005. Italy and the Philippines are included in the chart but are not labelled for reasons of space. Developed countries are shown in black and developing countries in grey.

The paucity of points in the North-East quadrant points to the unlikelihood of a country's manufacturing sector simultaneously becoming more labour-intensive and growing as a share of total value added, especially at higher levels of income per capita. The overwhelming majority of points are located either in the South-West quadrant, where manufacturing became less labour-intensive while shrinking as a share of total value added, or in the North-West quadrant below the $y = x$ line, where manufacturing became less labour-intensive but grew as a share of total value added.

There is again an interesting difference between Asian and Latin American countries. Almost all the Asian Newly Industrialised Countries (NICs) in both periods are in the North-West quadrant, with manufacturing becoming less labour-intensive (i.e. more productive) and growing as a share of value added. In most middle-income Latin American countries, by contrast, both the labour-intensity and sector share effects were negative in both periods. Even though manufacturing constituted a lower share of GDP in Latin America than in the Asian NICs at the beginning of the period, the share of manufacturing in GDP shrank further in the Latin American countries while growing further in the Asian NICs.

Where falling manufacturing employment share is mostly accounted for by falling labour-intensity of manufacturing, and in particular where manufacturing output is growing (in level and as a percentage of GDP), this should arguably not be regarded as deindustrialisation. Such a phenomenon would not necessarily negatively affect growth. This differs from cases where the fall in the share of manufacturing employment is accounted for primarily by a decline of the manufacturing sector as a share of GDP. In such a scenario, an economy would be particularly at risk of losing out on the growth-pulling effects of manufacturing. This difference underscores the need to recognise the heterogeneity of 'deindustrialisations' and for nuanced analysis of any specific country experience.

Sources of deindustrialisation

Various factors causing or contributing to deindustrialisation have been discussed in the literature. Rowthorn and Coutts (2004) identify five key explanations of deindustrialisation. First, the reclassification of jobs from manufacturing to services due to 'specialisation' through the outsourcing of activities to domestic service providers. Second, decline in the share of manufacturing in total consumer expenditure due to a fall in the relative prices of manufactures. Third, slower employment growth in manufacturing than in services because of higher productivity growth in manufacturing than in services. Fourth, the negative effects of international trade (especially imports from lower-cost producers) on manufacturing employment in developed countries. Fifth, negative effects of lower rates of investment on the share of manufacturing (in both GDP and employment), since investment expenditure goes disproportionately into manufacturing.[3]

The relationship between the share of manufacturing in total employment and income per capita is described in Rowthorn's well-known inverted-U curve (Rowthorn, 1995). This relationship between income per capita and the share of manufacturing in total employment is depicted in Figure 6.3 (based on a cross-country regression using 1990 data). As countries' income per capita grows over time, industrialisation sees the share of manufacturing in total employment initially growing and the share of agriculture declining concomitantly. At a turning point (which Rowthorn estimates to be around $12,000), the share of manufacturing in total employment levels off and declines. With deindustrialisation defined as a fall in the share of manufacturing in total employment, this turning point marks the onset of deindustrialisation.

Palma (2005, 2008) conceptualises deindustrialisation through the framework of Rowthorn's inverted-U curve. He starts with Rowthorn's influential approach in which deindustrialisation occurs through a transition into the downwards part of the curve – the fall in the share of manufacturing in total employment as economies mature. This is the 'classical' form of deindustrialisation

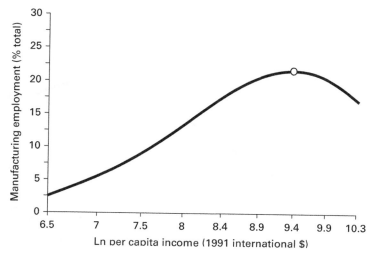

Figure 6.3 Replicating Rowthorn's regression: manufacturing employment and income per capita, 1990.

Source: Figure taken from Palma (2008), with permission.

Note: ln = natural logarithm.

in the literature, with deindustrialisation understood as being part of the stylised facts of a transition from the secondary to tertiary sectors. However, Palma argues that there are more complex dynamics at work than those identified by Rowthorn and the 'classical' school.

First, he shows empirically that the curve itself has shifted over time. This means that whether or not countries reached the turning-point, there was a declining level of manufacturing employment associated with each level of income per capita. Graphically, this is represented by a series of downward shifts in the inverted-U curve over time, as shown in Figure 6.4.

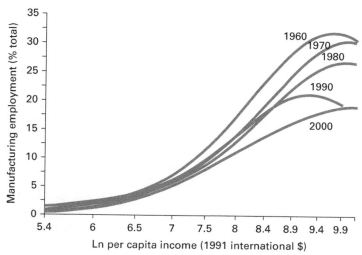

Figure 6.4 Second source of de-industrialisation: a declining relationship, 1960–2000.

Source: Figure taken from Palma (2008), with permission.

Note: ln = natural logarithm.

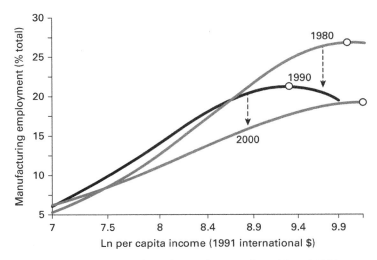

Figure 6.5 The changing nature of de-industrialisation between the 1980s and 1990s.

Source: Figure taken from Palma (2008), with permission.

Note: ln = natural logarithm.

Second, he also shows that there is a decline in the level of income per capita at which the share of manufacturing in total employment begins to decline, in particular during the 1980s. This is understood as a leftwards shift in the turning-point of the curve, as can be seen in Figure 6.5. Between 1980 and 1990 the income per capita turning-point of the regression halved, from approximately $21,000 in 1980 to just over $10,000 in 1990 (1985 international US$). The reversal of this shift between 1990 and 2000 is indicative of the fact that deindustrialisation affected mainly advanced economies during the 1980s but primarily middle-income developing countries during the 1990s.

Together, these two phenomena mean that since the 1960s, deindustrialisation has begun at lower levels of income per capita and lower shares of manufacturing in total employment than was previously the case. This is of particular importance for developing countries, as will be discussed further later.

Third, Palma (2008) defines Dutch Disease as a specific form of deindustrialisation, resulting from the fact that commodity-rich countries have a different (i.e., lower) path of industrialisation than commodity-poor ones. As some of the latter countries have become commodity-rich, these countries have experienced an 'extra' degree of deindustrialisation. This is due to switching from one (higher) path of industrialisation to the other (lower) one. In this context, Dutch Disease should only be regarded as the *additional* level of deindustrialisation associated with the latter movement. Palma demonstrates that this 'excess' degree of deindustrialisation is not only found in cases where a country discovered significant natural resources, but also when countries have developed significant export finance or tourism. Additionally, he shows that it can also happen as a result of policy shifts (notably trade or financial 'liberalisation') in middle-income countries – as has happened in Latin America since economic reform.

Figure 6.6 illustrates Palma's conception of Dutch Disease as a form of deindustrialisation, with reference to four Latin American countries and the classical case of the Netherlands. Here, countries are divided into two groups: those that show a trade surplus in manufacturing ('mf') and those that show a trade surplus in primary commodities or services ('pc'). The 'pc' countries have a lower level of industrialisation than do the 'mf' countries at any point in time, as

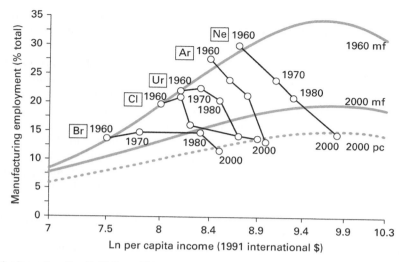

Figure 6.6   Argentina, Brazil, Chile and Uruguay: catching the Dutch Disease, 1960–2000.
Ar = Argentina; Br = Brazil; Cl = Chile; Ur = Uruguay; and Ne = the Netherlands.

Source: Figure taken from Palma (2008), with permission.

Note: ln = natural logarithm.

can be seen here by the '2000 pc' line lying below the '2000 mf' line (an intercept dummy differentiates the two groups of countries). For both groups, the level of industrialisation fell over time, evident here in the downwards shift of '1960 mf' to '2000 mf'. However, countries that experienced an additional degree of deindustrialisation associated with the Dutch Disease actually jumped from the 'mf' line to the 'pc' line by 2000. As can be seen in Figure 6.6, these five countries began on the 'mf' line in 1960, but by 2000 had switched to the 'pc' line.

The specificity of deindustrialisation in developing countries

Palma (2005, 2008) has argued that, in general, deindustrialisation in developing countries is policy-induced to a greater extent than was the case in deindustrialisation in advanced economies. In particular, trade and financial liberalisation has instigated or accelerated dein-dustrialisation among developing countries.

In the case of Latin America specifically, these liberalisations and other aspects of economic reforms have shifted economies from paths of industrialisation similar to countries that are commodity-poor (due to the 'forced-industrialisation' from import-substituting industrialisation), to their Ricardian 'commodity-rich' path. This can be understood as a form of Dutch Disease, as discussed in the previous section. In Latin America the share of manufacturing in total employment has been falling for at least the past two decades, while the share of manufacturing in GDP started falling even earlier.

In many African countries, the share of manufacturing in employment and GDP began falling at even lower levels of income per capita than in Latin America. The shares of manu-facturing in employment and output began to fall before reaching levels anywhere close to the typical turning points marking the onset of deindustrialisation internationally. There have been prominent debates around deindustrialisation in Africa. These debates have centred on whether or not there has actually been deindustrialisation in Africa and, if so, what has caused it and in particular whether there is a link to Structural Adjustment Programmes (SAPs).

Using the novel test mentioned earlier, Jalilian and Weiss (2000) find no evidence that Africa as a whole experienced deindustrialisation beyond that experienced elsewhere (over the period 1975–1993), although deindustrialisation is identified in certain African countries. The empirical analysis of Noorbakhsh and Paloni (1999) through to 1994 shows that manufacturing output and employment in Africa contracted, labour productivity in manufacturing fell, there was little technological transfer or advancement, investment and the productivity of investment in manufacturing were stagnant, and industrial non-diversification continually worsened. Their empirical analysis indicates that SAPs in Africa have contributed to deindustrialisation. Stein (1992) believes that there has been deindustrialisation in Africa and criticises SAPs for causing or contributing to this. He critiques the World Bank/IMF approach for neglecting the structural nature of Africa's industrial crisis and argues that SAPs reduce import-substituting public sector manufacturing, but without promoting other manufacturing, leading to deindustrialisation. The World Bank itself (1994) disputes the hypothesis of deindustrialisation in Africa and argues that adjustment programmes that led to successful macroeconomic reforms were also associated with industrial growth, thus rejecting a link between SAPs and deindustrialisation. Tribe (2002) finds that there is no evidence for strong deindustrialisation having occurred in Africa in the late 1990s, and not much empirical support for liberalisation either having caused deindustrialisation or strengthened manufacturing. While there was an initial contraction of manufacturing after liberalisation, there was subsequently some recovery, albeit based largely on increased capacity utilisation and followed by a slowdown, at least in some African countries. This points to the need for a focus on long-term trends in evaluating whether deindustrialisation has occurred, and the importance of measuring deindustrialisation as a *sustained* decline in manufacturing, as discussed in the second section of this chapter.

There are important differences in the causes of deindustrialisation in developed and developing countries. In particular, international trade would affect manufacturing in developing countries in dissimilar ways from developed countries. As discussed above, trade with the global South has been identified in the literature as one of the causes of deindustrialisation in developed countries, with debates about its importance in explaining deindustrialisation. A different analysis is thus needed for analysing deindustrialisation in the global South.

The manufacturing power of China and other relatively low unit cost producers from Asia is important in understanding industrialisation and deindustrialisation among developing countries. Developing countries with levels of income per capita both above and below that of China struggle in competing with the unit costs of Chinese manufacturing. This relates not just to unit labour costs but to the entire cost structure of manufacturing in China, including the competitive advantages afforded by the state of infrastructure. The challenge for lower-income countries is particularly sharp and is very different from earlier deindustrialisation in advanced economies that was associated in part with cheaper manufacturing from countries at lower levels of income per capita. The situation faced by low-income countries is that economies (notably China) at *higher* levels of income per capita than they are able to manufacture goods at *lower* unit costs.

In these developing countries the issue is thus not deindustrialisation in existing 'grandfather industries' due to the emergence of lower-cost production in lower-income countries. Rather than the displacement of existing mature industries, it is industrialisation itself that is being stymied as many low-income countries are unable to break into manufacturing markets and into the 'globalisation club'. This is even the case for labour-intensive manufactures such as clothing, which have traditionally been amongst the important stepping stones in countries' industrialisation paths. There is thus a failure for nascent industries to develop, or for industries that may have emerged to do so. Given the importance of economies of scale, positive externalities, cumulative causation and industry networks in manufacturing, this also hampers the emergence of a dynamic manufacturing sector in low-income countries.

In earlier deindustrialisation in advanced economies, manufacturing was squeezed by lower-cost imports from less developed countries, due primarily to lower labour costs in the latter countries. Nonetheless, advanced economies had technological and other advantages over developed economies. Hence, even as advanced economies underwent deindustrialisation (especially in relatively labour-intensive industries), they retained comparative advantages in other parts of manufacturing. To put it simply, even as advanced economies were deindustrialising, there were some things that they could still manufacture better and/or cheaper than their developing-country competitors. By contrast, many developing countries today are uncompetitive relative to a country such as China, with respect to *both* unit labour costs and technology, and with respect to both simple labour-intensive manufactures and more technologically advanced manufactures. With a few exceptions, countries at lower levels of income per capita than China are almost universally behind in technology and cannot currently compete in manufacturing electronics, cars and other relatively advanced manufactures. However, they commonly *also* cannot currently compete with China on unit labour costs, and so import goods such as clothing instead of developing their own labour-intensive manufacturing industries.

Negative effects of deindustrialisation on economic growth are likely to be particularly pronounced in developing countries, especially low-income developing countries. There are three main reasons for this, all related to the point of development at which deindustrialisation commences. First, compared to deindustrialisation in advanced economies, deindustrialisation in developing countries will typically commence not only at lower levels of income per capita but also at a lower turning point of manufacturing's share in the economy. This suggests that a country will have obtained less of the benefits of manufacturing for broader economic growth by the time deindustrialisation begins. Second, the sustainability of a dynamic services sector is questionable under such circumstances. The services that develop are unlikely to be technologically advanced services with strong growth-pulling properties. The types of services that 'replace' manufacturing in a low-income deindustrialising country may be for example low value added consumer services. In an advanced economy, at least some of the types of services that are 'replacing' manufacturing may be relatively high-technology, high-skills, tradable, increasing-returns producer services with strong linkages with the rest of the economy. Third, the usual causes of deindustrialisation differ in developing and developed countries. In developing countries, deindustrialisation is typically brought on by policy shifts, especially trade liberalisation and/or tight monetary policy. This is not the sort of incremental 'maturation' found in advanced economies (which may well still have negative effects on growth but of a different form and magnitude).

The 'statistical illusion' aspect of deindustrialisation

How much of deindustrialisation can be attributed merely to a reclassification of jobs instead of structural change in the economy? To illustrate: information technology (IT) personnel within a factory would be classified as manufacturing workers, but if the IT function is then outsourced to a specialised IT company, those personnel would be classified as service workers. This change would show up in the national employment statistics as a relative decline in manufacturing employment, suggesting deindustrialisation. This would occur despite the same personnel being employed in the IT activity as were previously employed at the factory, with their sector merely being reclassified. This has been referred to in the literature as the 'statistical illusion' or 'statistical artefact' component of deindustrialisation.

Rowthorn and Coutts (2004) drew attention to this as one of the sources of apparent deindustrialisation. They characterise this as a reclassification of activities as opposed to a genuine shrinkage in the manufacturing sector. It is suggested that a broad definition of the manufacturing sector would include all of the service inputs embodied in the final output of the sector. Using such a definition, broadly defined manufacturing employment would have fallen less than is evident from official statistics. Rowthorn and Coutts did not undertake any empirical analysis to quantify the extent of outsourcing and its contribution to apparent deindustrialisation. However, they argue that "it seems implausible that this accounts for more than a modest fraction of the huge recorded fall in the share of manufacturing employment in advanced economies over the past thirty years" (Rowthorn and Coutts, 2004: 5).

From the perspective of *The Economist*, by contrast, much of (apparent) deindustrialisation can be attributed to domestic outsourcing of services:

> a small part of the fall in manufacturing jobs is a statistical illusion caused by manufacturers contracting out services. If a carmaker stops employing its own office cleaning services and instead buys cleaning services from a specialist company, then output and employment in the service sector appear to grow overnight, and those in manufacturing to shrink, even though nothing has changed.
>
> (*The Economist*, 2005: 82)

Along similar lines to Rowthorn and Coutts (2004), Karaomerlioglu and Carlsson (1999) argue that manufacturing and producer services should be grouped together as they are complementary and interdependent and the boundaries between them have become increasingly blurred. Empirically analysing changes in sectoral structure in the USA using input–output tables, the study finds that the 'unbundling' of producer services (such as legal or data processing services) from manufacturing explains most of the apparent growth in producer services between 1987 and 1994. This result goes against the expectations of Rowthorn and Coutts. With a concomitant broader definition of manufacturing including producer services, Karaomerlioglu and Carlsson argue that total manufacturing employment in the USA declined only slightly.

Tregenna (2010) developed a methodology for estimating the extent to which intersectoral outsourcing might account for apparent changes in the sectoral composition of employment using employment survey microdata. For the case of South Africa, the relatively high growth in services employment in the 2000s was based in part on the outsourcing-type reallocation of services such as cleaning and security from manufacturing and from the public sector towards private services. An increasing share of the total employment of these occupations was thus classified in private services. Had there not been intersectoral outsourcing, it is projected that manufacturing employment would actually have grown slightly faster than employment in private services over that period. This suggests a strong 'statistical illusion' aspect to deindustrialisation in this case.

There is as yet no comprehensive evidence about the extent to which domestic outsourcing might account for deindustrialisation in different countries. This is likely to vary considerably between countries. Taking account of how much of deindustrialisation is a 'statistical artefact' is important to understanding the degree to which there is a real shift in the underlying structures of production and employment. This is particularly germane where deindustrialisation is defined in terms of employment (as opposed to output or other measures).

A similar source of apparent deindustrialisation could arise from the privatisation and restructuring of state-owned manufacturing enterprises, especially in developing countries, where welfare and other services previously provided by the enterprise to employees and the surrounding community are either outsourced or closed down. These services would have been classified in manufacturing, and their closure would reflect as a decline in manufacturing. The underlying dynamic is, however, actually the closure of service activities. Identifying and quantifying the closure or outsourcing of service activities previously classified as part of manufacturing is important for ascertaining the extent to which apparent deindustrialisation is a genuine structural shift.

Economic effects of deindustrialisation

One of the important debates around deindustrialisation concerns its effects on economic growth. From an international econometric analysis, Dasgupta and Singh (2005) conclude that the manufacturing sector plays a critical role in economic growth. Although a similar econometric result is found for services, Dasgupta and Singh argue that in terms of causal interpretation of the model, services does not necessarily play a similar role as manufacturing as an engine of growth.

Thirlwall (1982) and Bazen and Thirlwall (1986) analyse the negative effects of deindustrialisation in the UK on growth. They attribute deindustrialisation especially to falling demand for manufactured exports from the UK, and emphasise a concern with the effects of the resulting balance of payments constraint on growth.

Most studies of the effects of deindustrialisation on growth are for advanced economies. A study of deindustrialisation in developing countries (Pieper, 2000) finds industrial performance to be correlated with overall economic performance. Industry has a strong influence on aggregate productivity and employment outputs. Pieper's results show 'productivity deindustrialisation' to be associated with negative aggregate productivity growth. Slow industrial growth seems to lead to 'low road development' in which there is a trade-off between productivity growth and employment growth.

Several studies analyse the effects of deindustrialisation on growth at the sub-national level. Friedhoff *et al.* (2010) studied 114 metropolitan areas of the USA that had been specialised in manufacturing in 1980 and which deindustrialised between then and 2005. They found that two-thirds of these areas performed worse that the national averages in job and wage growth over that period. Interestingly, emergent services jobs appear to be complementary to, rather than competitive to or substitutes for, manufacturing jobs. The areas that lost the fewest manufacturing jobs gained the most non-manufacturing and advanced service jobs (although no causal relationship is established). Friedhoff *et al.* also conclude that the loss of manufacturing jobs reduced wages in the deindustrialised areas.

Kottis (1972) studied the relationship between employment and non-manufacturing employment in urban areas of Michigan, USA. His results show that changes in manufacturing employment cause changes in non-manufacturing employment (in the same direction). Although not proving causality, these findings point to complementarity between manufacturing and non-manufacturing employment and suggest that a decline in manufacturing employment may negatively affect non-manufacturing employment as well.

Dasgupta and Singh (2005) econometrically analyse the effects of manufacturing on aggregate economic growth across the states of India. The results suggest that manufacturing, as well as the formal and informal manufacturing sectors when analysed separately, play an important role in growth.

In a perspective different from much of the literature, Crafts (1996) warns against what he views as exaggerated dire predictions about the economic effects of deindustrialisation. Focusing on the economic performance of the UK during the 1980s, he argues that deindustrialisation of the labour force was actually necessary for raising growth, in order to make the returns to innovation better able to be appropriated and to liberalise the economy. Crafts views deindustrialisation as a distraction, rather than as a cause of unsatisfactory economic performance. He advocates greater policy attention to human capital formation and technological advancement, rather than physical investment and the balance of payments.

Perhaps surprisingly, there is not yet a solid body of empirical evidence that comprehensively analyses the effects of deindustrialisation on economic growth. This could provide a fruitful avenue for future research. Clear evidence in this regard would be helpful in shedding light on the extent to which deindustrialisation should be considered a problem, and concomitantly whether policymakers should be concerned with it. Research in this direction could be enriched by taking into account any relevant differences in the effects of deindustrialisation on growth by type of country (such as by region and level of development), as well as by type of deindustrialisation.[4] The economic effects of deindustrialisation will certainly be strongly contingent on the level of development at which a country begins to deindustrialise, as well as the nature of that deindustrialisation.

Social and political effects of deindustrialisation

Beyond the possible effects of deindustrialisation on growth, as discussed above, loss of manufacturing jobs may have welfare effects. In aggregate, these effects depend partly on whether there is simply a change in the sectoral *composition* of employment, or a *net loss* in manufacturing jobs without these being replaced by new jobs in other sectors.

We can identify several factors determining the welfare effects on those losing jobs in the manufacturing sector: first, the probability of obtaining alternative employment; second, the differential in wages and non-wage benefits between the lost manufacturing job and an alternative job; third, other differences or changes between a lost manufacturing job and an alternative job, such as spatial relocation that may be required; fourth, in the case of people displaced from the manufacturing sector but unable to find alternative employment, the change in their income and other circumstances. This difference between manufacturing employment and an unemployed 'fall-back position' would in turn depend on the level of social security and other factors.

There is an interdisciplinary literature, including several sociological studies, concerning the broader effects of deindustrialisation. Case studies of specific geographic areas have attempted to track the social effects of deindustrialisation on communities.

In an early study of deindustrialisation, Bluestone (1983) draws attention to the devastating effects of deindustrialisation in the USA on workers and communities. He points to evidence that displaced workers are put at a long-term earnings disadvantage, and experience prolonged unemployment and deleterious effects to health and wellbeing. He also notes that job losses associated with deindustrialisation in the USA affected black workers proportionately more than whites.

Manufacturing is a major source of employment for skilled and semi-skilled workers. According to Armah (1992), this means that manufacturing contributes to an egalitarian income distribution to a greater extent than do other industries. Deindustrialisation is thus likely to lead to higher poverty and earnings inequality. Furthermore, since the median wage in manufacturing is higher than in other sectors, deindustrialisation is likely to depress the overall median wage. Armah also argues that, given the demographics of industrial employment in the USA, deindustrialisation particularly affects minorities.

Rowthorn and Webster (2008) econometrically analyse the effects of male worklessness on lone parenthood in Great Britain over the period 1971–2001. They argue that deindustrialisation has eliminated many traditionally male jobs, especially in certain regions of Great Britain, and that this has contributed to lone parenthood as a social problem. Their regression results suggest that the fall in male employment explains between 38 per cent and 59 per cent of the increase in lone parent families over the period of analysis. The effects were greatest in the areas that suffered most from deindustrialisation. Rowthorn and Webster also draw attention to associated high rates of child poverty, especially in the old industrial areas of Great Britain.

Brady and Wallace (2001) analyse the effects of deindustrialisation on poverty in Lake County, Indiana, United States from 1964 to 1993. Using time series econometric analysis, they find that deindustrialisation (especially the loss of steel jobs) contributed significantly to impoverishment in the area. The growth in services jobs did little to mitigate the negative effects of deindustrialisation.

A 20–year case study tracked the effects of deindustrialisation in the sawmill industry in British Columbia on the health and wellbeing of workers who were employed there immediately prior to the onset of deindustrialisation (Ostry *et al.*, 2001). High unemployment followed deindustrialisation. Even workers who were subsequently employed commonly experienced protracted periods of unemployment. However, the physical and psychosocial conditions of workers who were re-employed outside the sawmill sector were found to be superior to those of workers from the original cohort who remained employed in the sawmill sector, particularly unskilled workers.

The literature on the social effects of deindustrialisation focuses on advanced economies. This is probably in part because their longer experience of deindustrialisation allows for an analysis of the longer-term social effects thereof. There is certainly a gap in the literature pertaining to the social effects of deindustrialisation in low- and middle-income countries. Compared to most advanced economies, low- and middle-income countries tend to have poorer social security systems and less well-developed services sectors in which alternative employment may be found. Both of these factors may exacerbate the social effects of deindustrialisation. Conversely, factors such as dynamic informal sectors and well-developed family networks may somewhat cushion the effects of deindustrialisation in low- and middle-income countries. Overall, differences between developed and developing countries regarding the social effects of deindustrialisation will depend on differences in the four factors suggested earlier in this section.

There is a separate debate in the literature, especially in political science, regarding the effects of deindustrialisation on the welfare state. One line of argument is that deindustrialisation erodes the political support for the welfare state, with the channel being the decline of the organised blue-collar working class (see for example Piven, 1991). A contrary view, which Iversen (2001) advances through an international empirical study, is that deindustrialisation has actually been a key driver of the expansion of the welfare state since the 1960s. The mechanism postulated is the need to support the displaced blue-collar working class, particularly in the context of limited transferability of skills between the manufacturing and services sectors (see also Iversen and Cusack (2000).) In an empirical study of the effects of deindustrialisation in Latin America, Carnes and Mares (2010) find little evidence of a positive relationship between deindustrialisation and social spending, but they do find a positive relationship between deindustrialisation and the introduction of non-contributory health and old-age insurance policies. They surmise that deindustrialisation brings about labour market changes, specifically changes in employment status from more stable contractual relationships with employers to forms of 'independent employment', which influences preferences towards non-contributory programmes.

Spatial dimensions of deindustrialisation

Several studies take a spatial angle to the analysis of deindustrialisation, focusing on regional differences in the changes in manufacturing employment. Hanham and Banasick's (2000) study analyses spatial aspects of structural change, for the case of Japan, using shift-share analysis. The results show that local spatial structure had an important influence on changes in regional manufacturing employment in Japan from 1981 to 1995.

Fotopoulos *et al.* (2009) also use shift-share analysis to analyse spatial differences in the growth of manufacturing employment, in the case of Greece. Important determinants of regional employment in manufacturing which they identify include the degree of specialisation, imports, and domestic demand.

Green and Sanchez (2007) draw attention to the spatial aspects of changes in manufacturing employment in the US Midwest. They find significant differences in the effects of manufacturing employment between localised labour markets. Graham and Spence (2000) study the decline in manufacturing employment in Britain, quantifying this as a loss of 20 per cent of manufacturing employment, or just over 900,000 jobs, between 1987 and 1994. They emphasise the pronounced regional character of this decline. Over 40 per cent of the losses affected just one region, the South East (a 31 per cent loss for that region). These job losses occurred despite growth in manufacturing GDP over this period, including in the South East. Significant regional differences can thus be observed in manufacturing output, employment, and labour productivity. Graham and Spence find that technological growth and changes in the price of capital and in the wage rate are crucial in explaining spatial differences in the growth of labour productivity.

There is very little evidence on the spatial aspect of deindustrialisation in developing countries. This presents as a fruitful avenue for future research. It would be expected that there would a pronounced spatial dimension to deindustrialisation in developing countries, as appears to be the case in developed countries. The composition of manufacturing invariably varies between the regions of a country, and deindustrialisation itself is uneven between the various sectors of manufacturing. The combination of these two factors implies that deindustrialisation has uneven effects on different regions of a country. This spatial unevenness will be especially pronounced where there is a lack of diversification of manufacturing within regions, which could well be the case in developing countries in particular. Manufacturing in a region could have strong backward linkages to primary sectors such as agro-processing. For example, a decline in the production of certain agricultural commodities would induce deindustrialisation in the sectors of manufacturing based on those. This would hit hardest in those regions of a country most dependent on that agriculture and associated agro-processing.

Conclusion

Reindustrialisation is arguably especially necessary in developing countries that have deindustrialised compared to advanced economies. It may be more necessary in developing countries for the same reasons advanced above for why deindustrialisation is likely to be especially harmful in these countries.

Reindustrialisation may also potentially be more feasible, compared to advanced economies. This is in the sense that policy-induced deindustrialisation could be at least partially reversible with alternative policies, where an economy was not yet 'ready' for the original policy-induced deindustrialisation.

This is not to suggest that reindustrialisation is easy anywhere. It takes 'effort' to rebuild manufacturing production capacity, even where this capacity was lost over a short time period due to policy changes. When manufacturing firms downsize or close, there is generally a loss in firm and/or country share in international manufacturing markets, depreciation of skills, tacit knowledge and fixed capital, and loss of production and marketing networks. Where manufacturing production capacity has dissipated and linkages and spillovers have been lost, it is unlikely that capacity will be regained without active policy interventions. Furthermore, what is needed for a country to reindustrialise is not just the regaining of the same manufacturing capacity that was previously lost, but different manufacturing capacity that is competitive and sustainable.

This underscores the need for active industrial policies. Industrial policy is crucial both for avoiding or mitigating deindustrialisation, and for reindustrialisation. Developing countries are likely to face particular challenges of resource and state capacity constraints in implementing comprehensive industrial policies. Yet these constraints need not prevent developing countries from undertaking effective industrial policy. This is demonstrated by the experiences of East Asian countries in implementing successful industrial policies whilst they were still at low levels of economic development.

There seems to be a fresh appreciation of the need for industrialisation and for industrial policies in recent years. In Africa for example, various continental, regional and national initiatives seek to advance new industrial policy measures for African countries, in an effort to promote rapid industrialisation.[5] Such measures will also need to halt deindustrialisation, where this has already taken place, while advancing sustainable reindustrialisation.

Notes

1 See Tregenna (2015) for an empirical overview of changes in sectoral structure in different country groupings.
2 This analysis is based on Tregenna (2013), which contains further technical details and discussion of results.
3 See Tregenna (2015) for a broader discussion of the causes of deindustrialisation.
4 See Tregenna (2014) for a theoretical typology of different forms of deindustrialisation using Marxian tools of analysis, and a conceptualisation of how these different forms of deindustrialisation may affect growth.
5 See for instance the African Union/NEPAD the African Productive Capacity Initiative (APCI), the African Union Plan of Action for Accelerated Industrial Development (PAAID), the West African Common Industrial Policy (WACIP) of the Economic Community of West African States (Ecowas) (United Nations Economic Commission for Africa, 2011).

References

Alderson, A.S. 1999. Explaining deindustrialization: globalization, failure, or success? *American Sociological Review*. 64 (5): 701–721.

Armah, B. 1992. Trade sensitive manufacturing employment: some new insights. *The Review of Black Political Economy*. 21 (2): 37–54.

Bacon, R.W. and Eltis, W.A. 1976. *Britain's Economic Problem: Too Few Producers*. London: Macmillan.

Bazen, S. and Thirlwall, A.P. 1986. De-industrialization in the UK. In Atkinson, B. (ed.). *Developments in Economics No. 2*. Ormskirk: Causeway Press.

Bluestone, B. 1983. Deindustrialization and unemployment in America. *The Review of Black Political Economy*. 12 (3): 27–42.

Bluestone, B. and Harrison, B. 1982. *The Deindustrialization of America*. New York: Basic Books.

Brady, D. and Wallace, M. 2001. Deindustrialization and poverty: manufacturing decline and AFDC recipiency in Lake County, Indiana 1964–93. *Sociological Forum* 16 (2): 321–358.

Cairncross, A. 1979. What is deindustrialisation? In Blackaby, F. (ed.). *De-Industrialisation*. London: Heinemann for the National Institute of Economic and Social Research.

Carnes, M. and Mares, I. 2010. *Deindustrialization and the rise of non-contributory social programs in Latin America*. Paper presented at a Workshop on Social Policy in Developing Countries, Duke University May 2010 – accessible from www.googlegroups.com

Crafts, N. 1996. Deindustrialisation and economic growth. *Economic Journal.* 106 (434): 172–183.

Dasgupta, S. and Singh, A. 2005. Will services be the new engine of Indian economic growth? *Development and Change.* 36(6), 1035–1057.

The Economist (no individual author) 2005. Industrial metamorphosis. *The Economist,* 1 October: 81–82.

Fotopoulos, G., Kallioras, D. and Petrakos, G. 2010. Spatial variation of Greek manufacturing employment growth: the effects of specialization and international trade. *Papers in Regional Science.* 89 (1): 109–133.

Friedhoff, A., Wial, H. and Wolman, H. 2010. *The Consequences of Metropolitan Manufacturing Decline: Testing Conventional Wisdom.* Washington, DC: Brookings Institution.

Graham, D.J. and Spence, N. 2000. Manufacturing employment, change, output demand and labor productivity in the regions of Britain. *International Regional Science Review.* 23 (2): 172–200.

Green, G.P. and Sanchez, L. 2007. Does manufacturing still matter? *Population Research and Policy Review.* 26 (5): 529–551.

Hanham, R.Q. and Banasick, S. 2000. Shift-share analysis and changes in Japanese manufacturing employment. *Growth and Change.* 31 (1): 108–123.

Iversen, T. 2001. The dynamics of welfare state expansion: trade openness, deindustrialization, and partisan politics. In Pierson, P. (ed.). *The New Politics of the Welfare State.* Oxford: Oxford University Press.

Iversen, T. and Cusack, T.R. 2000. The causes of welfare state expansion: deindustrialization or globalization? *World Politics.* 52 (3): 313–349.

Jalilian, H. and Weiss, J. 2000. De-industrialisation in Sub-Saharan Africa: myth or crisis? *Journal of African Economies.* 9 (1): 24–43; also in Jalilian, H., Tribe, M. and Weiss, J. (eds.). 2000. *Industrial Development and Policy in Africa.* Cheltenham: Edward Elgar: 137–158.

Karaomerlioglu, D.C. and Carlsson, B. 1999. Manufacturing in decline? A matter of definition. *Economics of Innovation and New Technology.* 8 (3): 175–196.

Kottis, G.C. 1972. Short-term relationship between manufacturing and non-manufacturing employment in the nine urban areas. *Annals of Regional Science.* 6 (2): 96–107.

Noorbakhsh, F. and Paloni, A. 1999. Structural adjustment programs and industry in Sub-Saharan Africa: restructuring or de-industrialization? *Journal of Developing Areas.* 33 (4): 549–580; also in Jalilian, H., Tribe, M. and Weiss, J. (eds.). 2000. *Industrial Development and Policy in Africa.* Cheltenham: Edward Elgar: 107–136.

Ostry, A.S., Hershler, R., Kelly, S., Demers, P., Teschke, K. and Hertzman, C. 2001. Effects of de-industrialization on unemployment, re-employment and work conditions in a manufacturing workforce. *BMC Public Health.* 1 (1): 1–11.

Palma. J.G. 2005. Four sources of "de-Industrialisation" and a new concept of the "Dutch disease". In *Beyond Reforms: Structural Dynamics and Macroeconomic Vulnerability.* Ocampo, J.A. (ed.). Palo Alto, CA and Washington, DC: Stanford University Press and World Bank.

Palma, J.G. 2008. Deindustrialisation, premature deindustrialisation, and the Dutch disease. In Blume, L.E. and Durlauf, S.N. (eds.). *The New Palgrave: A Dictionary of Economics* (2nd ed.). Basingstoke: Palgrave Macmillan: 401–410.

Pieper, U. 2000. Deindustrialisation and the social and economic sustainability nexus in developing countries: Cross-country evidence on productivity and employment. *Journal of Development Studies.* 36 (4): 66–99.

Piven, F. 1991. *Labor Parties in Postindustrial Societies.* New York: Oxford University Press.

Rowthorn, R. 1995. *Korea at the Cross-roads.* Working Paper No. 11, Centre for Business Research. Cambridge: Cambridge University.

Rowthorn, R. and Wells, J.R. 1987. *De-Industrialization and Foreign Trade.* Cambridge: Cambridge University Press.

Rowthorn, R. and Ramaswamy, R. 1997. *Deindustrialisation: causes and implications.* IMF Working Paper no. 97/42. Washington, DC: International Monetary Fund.

Rowthorn, R. and Coutts, K. 2004. Deindustrialisation and the balance of payments in advanced economies. *Cambridge Journal of Economics.* 28 (5): 767–790.

Rowthorn, R. and Webster, D. 2008. Male worklessness and the rise of lone parenthood in Great Britain. *Cambridge Journal of Regions, Economy and Society.* 1 (1): 69–88.

Saeger, S.S. 1997. Globalization and deindustrialization: myth and reality in the OECD. *Weltwirtschaftliches Archiv.* 133 (4): 579–608.

Singh, A. 1977. UK industry and the world economy: a case of de-industrialisation? *Cambridge Journal of Economics.* 1 (2): 113–136.

Stein, H. 1992. Deindustrialization, adjustment, the World Bank and the IMF in Africa. *World Development.* 20 (1): 83–95.

Thirlwall, A.P. 1982. Deindustrialisation in the UK. *Lloyd's Bank Review*. 144: 22–37.

Tregenna, F. 2009. Characterising deindustrialisation: an analysis of changes in manufacturing employment and output internationally. *Cambridge Journal of Economics*. 33 (3): 433–466.

Tregenna, F. 2010. How significant is the intersectoral outsourcing of employment in South Africa? *Industrial and Corporate Change*. 19 (5): 1427–1457.

Tregenna, F. 2013. Manufacturing productivity, deindustrialization and reindustrialisation. In Szirmai, A., Naudé, W. and Alcorta, L. (eds.). *Pathways to Industrialization in the 21st Century: New Challenges and Emerging Paradigms*. Oxford: Oxford University Press.

Tregenna, F. 2014. A new theoretical analysis of deindustrialisation. *Cambridge Journal of Economics* 38 (6): 1373–1390.

Tregenna, F. 2015. Deindustrialisation and premature deindustrialisation. In Ghosh, J., Kattel, R. and Reinert, E. (eds.). *Elgar Handbook of Alternative Theories of Economic Development*. Cheltenham: Edward Elgar.

Tribe, M. 2002. An overview of manufacturing development. In Belshaw, D.G.R. and Livingstone, I. (eds.). *Renewing Development in Sub-Saharan Africa: Policy, Performance and Prospects*. London: Routledge.

United Nations Economic Commission for Africa. 2011. Industrial policies for the structural transformation of African economies: options and best practices. *Policy Research Paper no. 2*. Addis Ababa: United Nations Economic Commission for Africa.

World Bank. 1994. *Adjustment in Africa: Reforms, Results, and the Road Ahead*. New York: Oxford University Press.

7

WHAT ROLE FOR SMALL ENTERPRISES?

Industrial clusters, industrial policy and poverty reduction

Khalid Nadvi[1]

Introduction

Small and medium enterprises (SMEs) have long been recognised as key to economic development (Anderson, 1982; Mead, 1984; Schmitz, 1995). They are the backbone of all economies, constituting the biggest segment of manufacturing sector firms and employment, and their predominance is seen in both developed and developing economies. In the latter, SMEs are particularly significant in that they provide employment and incomes for the poor, especially where SMEs merge into informalised, or non-regulated, forms of production and service delivery (Tendler, 2002), and they help promote local and regional economic development (Parrilli *et al.*, 2013). The aim of this chapter is to assess the role SMEs can play in industrial development and poverty reduction. SMEs are usually constrained by their very size in terms of access to technical, financial and managerial resources and capabilities. On the other hand, there is a substantial body of conceptual argument and empirical evidence that illustrates how SMEs can and do enhance their competitiveness when they build on their inherent flexibilities and where they are a part of clusters, or agglomerations, of similar producers. The next section outlines the potential benefits that can arise from clusters. The third section considers the links between clusters and pro-poor outcomes, drawing both on the conceptual connections between, and empirical evidence on, cluster processes and dynamics and poverty reduction. The fourth section illustrates how clustering has become a key area for industrial strategy in many countries and discusses how cluster development policies have evolved in specific developing country contexts. The fifth section concludes.

Clusters and the potential gains for SMES

The concept of clustering, and the agglomeration economies that it can generate for co-located SMEs, is now well understood (Porter, 1990, 1998; Schmitz and Nadvi, 1999; Gordon and McCann, 2000; Martin and Sunley, 2003; Ketels, 2013). Clustering owes it origins to the work of Alfred Marshall, who illustrated how during the late nineteenth century small firms in the industrial heartlands of UK and Europe acquired agglomeration economies by locating within geographically defined areas. The concomitant division of labour between firms, and the rise of specialisation and flexibility enhanced the competitiveness of such clustered regions (Marshall, 1920). In the context of post-Fordist manufacturing this phenomenon is now observed extensively across Europe, the United States and, most notably for our purposes, in developing country contexts. There is now substantial case evidence from the developing world illustrating how clustering helps SMEs, often working in precarious and informal settings, to produce for, and effectively compete in, highly demanding local and global markets (see for example the collections in Nadvi and Schmitz, 1999; van Dijk and Rabellotti, 1999; Pietrobelli and Rabellotti, 2006; Holmstrom and Cadene, 1998; Das, 2005; Dinh *et al.*, 2013).

Clusters are geographical agglomerations of firms and ancillary units engaged in various activities that fall within the ambit of the same industrial sector. This generates both the presence of agglomeration economies – including the presence within the cluster of specialised markets for inputs, labour and skills, as well as a specialised division of labour between producers and service providers. This enhances efficiency and reduces costs, but also facilitates the ability of firms with limited endowments to specialise and to spread risks. In most cases, individual firms within clustered SMEs face various constraints as a consequence of their size, including access to resources, and to human and financial capital. SMEs are also heavily disadvantaged in their ability to compete alongside larger, better endowed and more capable, firms. Clusters can help offset such constraints and address some of the capability deficits that small producers and workers potentially suffer from. In addition, clusters offer the opportunity for collective action by local firms. Such forms of joint action can include joint marketing – whereby firms reduce costs through joint purchasing or share costs around marketing – as well as firms coming together to address collective problems and to seek out common solutions, including those relating to technical innovations and to research and development. The concept of 'collective efficiency', defined as the economic gains arising from agglomeration economies and joint action, has been put forward as the capturing of benefits arising from SME clustering (Schmitz, 1995; Schmitz and Nadvi, 1999: 1504). It is also noted that the potentially contradictory characteristics of local co-operation and local competition that mark out the cluster environment need effective forms of local governance. This includes a strong sense of common social identity. Thus many clusters have shared norms, or common notions of community ties, that lie in ethnic, religious, regional or cultural identities. This can result in local social capital that strengthens the relationship between clustered firms, fosters trust between local actors and promotes local forms of co-operation.

Research on clusters has shown that in addition to agglomeration economies, clustered firms can engage in various forms of co-operation and collective action. This can lead to significant competitive advantages, through the setting up of marketing consortia, research and development and the upgrading of local skills and technological capabilities. But ensuring the success of collective action in an environment where clustered SMEs are also in close competition with each other requires complex mechanisms of institutional support as well as socially embedded norms of trust (Humphrey and Schmitz, 1998; Nadvi, 1999c). Local clustered institutions, such as formal business associations as well as informal social practices, can – alongside public agencies – help clustered firms to effectively and simultaneously compete and co-operate (Nadvi, 1999d).

Clusters are far from homogenous. Gulati (1997), in the context of Indian examples, distinguishes between 'modern' urban and 'artisanal' rural clusters. Schmitz and Nadvi (1999) speak of 'incipient' clusters, those at an early stage of industrial development, located in poor areas and producing for local markets with simple technologies and labour skills, and 'mature' clusters, relatively more advanced in terms of technology and skills, and often producing for global markets and thus vulnerable to global competitive pressures. Altenburg and Meyer-Stamer (1999) distinguish between 'survival' clusters, 'advanced mass production' clusters and 'clusters of trans-national corporations'. Their notion of 'survival' clusters (similar to the 'incipient' clusters) have low barriers to entry, with large numbers of small and micro-enterprises manufacturing for local markets, often under informal conditions, with low wages and low productivity. Mass production clusters are more advanced, often an outcome of import substitution trade strategies, where firms produce for local markets but increasingly face global competitive pressures. Finally, 'clusters of transnational corporations' are technically advanced foreign firms that locate in particular areas to draw on regional agglomeration economies but maintain limited links with local firms and institutions. Markusen (1996) underlined the presence of 'hub and spoke' clusters where large firms are surrounded by smaller suppliers who operate in close proximity. Hub and spoke clusters are especially pronounced in sectors such as car and electronics manufacturing where low inventory just-in-time production systems require effective logistics and close access to first tier suppliers.

The presence of an agglomeration of producers and suppliers engaged in the same sector promotes knowledge spillovers and can enhance innovative activities. Much of the interest in clusters, especially in the developed world has focused on the ways in which clustering potentially facilitates innovation (Malmberg, 1996; Malmberg and Maskell, 2002). This can be seen in both the most celebrated of clusters – Silicon Valley – as well as in a number of clusters across Europe (Saxenian and Hsu, 2001; Bathelt *et al.*, 2004). Innovation, knowledge spillovers and technological upgrading have also been central to much of the policy discussion on clusters in the developing world (UNIDO, 2001; World Bank, 2001).

While the focus on the cluster framework is on local inter-linkages between SMEs, clusters do not operate in isolation. Local clusters connect to global markets in a variety of ways, including through intermediary traders, global buyers as well as global lead firms who ensure access to global markets (Schmitz and Knorringa, 2000). The literature on clusters and global value chain (GVC) linkages provide extensive illustrations of this (Schmitz, 2004; Nadvi and Halder, 2005).

The GVC framework generates a heuristic model for the understanding of how global production is undertaken by various independent and geographically dispersed actors who collectively turn raw materials into finished goods and services that can be traded in distant markets. Central to the GVC model is the role of 'lead firms' which organise and structure the market and therefore effectively govern the ties within the value chain: determining who does what, where and at what price. Much of the GVC literature has been concerned with two inter-connected issues. First, how do firms within the chain upgrade, take on higher value added activities, and capture the resultant rents (Humphrey and Schmitz, 2002; Kaplinsky, 2005)? Second, what determines the governance of the chain itself (Gereffi *et al.*, 2005; Ponte and Sturgeon, 2014)? Gereffi *et al.* (2005) have argued that GVC governance is rooted in attempts by lead firms to minimise transaction costs incurred in their supplier linkages. These governance costs incurred through supplier ties are determined by the capabilities of the supplier, the complexity of the transaction and the extent to which the transaction can be easily codified. This framework has been used to show how local clustered producers can be integrated into global value chains with differing levels of power asymmetry between clustered suppliers and global lead firms. The framework has been critiqued as being static and failing to recognise that in the multi-scalar contexts in which most GVC ties are organised there may be more than one governance arrangement in place (Coe *et al.*, 2008). Recent work by Ponte and Sturgeon (2014) builds on this gap by considering a multi-polar governance agenda.

These recent interventions are significant for considering the ways in which local clusters interact with global markets through global value chain linkages. Such interactions, as well as the tensions between local, cluster-based, governance and different levels of global governance are the key to understanding how local clusters engage, upgrade and compete in global and local markets.

In the clusters to GVC literature (see, for example, Humphrey and Schmitz, 2004; Bair and Gereffi, 2001; Nadvi and Halder, 2005) there is a tendency to view two distinct aspects of governance. The 'global' governance within the GVC is exercised and orchestrated by the global lead firms that co-ordinate the chains, and by virtue of this also extract the most significant rents within the chain. One aspect of global governance is the increasing importance of the 'new trade rules' that pertain to quality assurance, health and safety, environmental, labour and social compliance concerns (Bartley, 2007; Nadvi and Waltring, 2004; Nadvi, 2008). The other aspect is 'local' governance exercised within the cluster and cluster-based institutions including representative business associations, as well technical institutions and local government agencies. Local and global governance can at times co-exist, but can also become conflictual. Messner (2004) notes how the nature of such governance conflicts between local and global actors can effectively shape the ways in which particular patterns of regional economic development take place. Knorringa and Nadvi (2014), drawing on secondary evidence from clusters in Brazil, China and India, have argued that there needs to be a greater focus on the national and regional institutional frameworks within which local clusters are embedded. This defines not only the regulatory environment for local clusters but also, critically, the nature of the 'local social contract' between the state, civil society and local clustered actors. This can help explain how, and to what extent, clusters are able to engage effectively with concerns around social and environmental norms encapsulated within corporate social responsibility.

Finally, clusters are far from static agglomerations. They evolve as firms attempt to upgrade to face new competitive challenges. Much of the policy focus on clustering has tended to be concentrated on the issue of upgrading, what forms it takes and how it can be promoted. Upgrading, whether it is of products, processes or functions that clustered firms are engaged in, have differentiated consequences. Not all firms and, for that matter, workers have the ability to upgrade, and the dynamic growth trajectories of clusters lead to some firms and workers gaining and others losing out. It is also argued that, as clusters are inserted into global value chains, external linkages may begin to gain prominence over internal linkages as local firms seek to access new technologies and know-how from outside the cluster.

To conclude, clustering can generate a number of significant agglomeration economies for SMEs as well as providing a basis for local collective action by small producers. This can potentially enhance the competitiveness of SMEs and promote innovation through local knowledge spillover effects. However, there are potential limitations to this. Local competition can often undermine co-operative behaviour. To offset this there is often the need for socially embedded trust ties between firms and other agents within clusters. Local clusters are also linked to global markets through various forms of engagement. This can both strengthen, and potentially weaken, intra-cluster ties. This requires a more careful consideration of local and global governance arrangements that link clusters to global markets. Finally, clusters are dynamic. They evolve over time with distinct winners and losers in terms of competitive outcomes within and between clusters. The discussion now turns to a more specific consideration of the relationship between SME clusters and poverty reduction.

Clusters and poverty reduction

There is general acknowledgement that clusters can play an important role in fostering incipient industrial development, especially in poor regions (Schmitz and Nadvi, 1999). The very presence of a cluster changes the context in which the poor live, by enhancing the ability of individual cluster actors, be they workers or producers, to potentially raise their capabilities and functioning. The process of clustering can also generate other benefits such as agglomeration gains to clustered firms in the markets for labour, inputs, know-how and information. Clustering opens up possibilities for economies of scale and scope, as individual small firms take on specialised tasks through a division of labour. In resource-poor regions, or at early stages of industrial development, this can be especially significant, promoting specialisation by way of 'small riskable steps' (Schmitz and Nadvi, 1999). Small producers do not have to invest in the entire production process. They can focus in specific areas allowing others to develop complementary functions. Easy access to inputs lowers the need for extensive working capital to hold stocks, while the ready availability of skilled labour reduces costs of training to individual firms.

There are numerous examples of clusters at early stages of industrialisation, engaged in labour intensive sectors and operating within or on the boundaries of the urban informal economy. Such clusters generate employment and incomes for the working poor, and in many cases for the very poor. From Latin America, Altenburg and Meyer-Stamer (1999) cite cases of shoe, garment, furniture, and metal working clusters in Honduras, Mexico, Costa Rica and Peru. From Ghana and Kenya McCormick (1999) describes incipient clusters producing garments, furniture, vehicle repair and agricultural products. The evidence of incipient clusters in Asia is equally strong. The Indian cluster observatory reports over 6000 rural and urban micro enterprise clusters in India (Cluster Observatory, 2014). Weijland (1999) suggests some 10,000 rural cottage industry clusters in Indonesia. Brautigam (1997) and McCormick (1999) describe similar small-scale vehicle repair and metalworking clusters in Nigeria and Kenya respectively. Knorringa (1999: 1590) found that the shoe cluster of Agra, India, employing 60,000 workers, consisted of "5000, mostly informal small scale units". According to Visser (1999) the Gamarra garment cluster of Lima, Peru included over 6,000 small enterprises as well as large numbers of informal micro-enterprises and street traders.

Clusters of often informalised SMEs are thus a significant element of the urban and rural landscape in most developing countries. What impacts do such clusters have, or might they have, on poverty reduction? In analysing the relationship between clusters and poverty, we consider: First, clustering's impact on employment and wages; second, cluster processes including agglomeration gains, joint action, cluster institutions and local social capital and their implications for poverty reduction; and third, cluster dynamics including cluster growth, cluster upgrading, cluster and value chain governance, and cluster differentiation and their consequences for pro-poor growth.

Employment and incomes

With regard to employment growth, Bair and Gereffi (2001) report employment levels rising by 300 per cent in the 1990s in the blue jeans cluster of Torreon, Mexico, a cluster that has rapidly expanded as a 'full package' garment exporter to the USA. Employment levels in Torreon rose from 12,000 in 1993 to 75,000 in 2000. There was, however, only limited growth in wages, and while women accounted for almost 50 per cent of the workforce, men tended to take on the more skilled and higher paid functions. Also within the garments sub-sector, Tewari (1999) reported that the woollen knitwear cluster of Ludhiana in India employed some 64,000 persons, or 32 per cent of Ludhiana's labour force. More recent evidence on garment sub-sector employment in the Tirupur cluster shows that it is now well over 200,000 (Singh, 2003). Much of this growth, according to Carswell and de Neve (2013), has come about through migration initially from nearby villages and more recently from poorer rural districts further afield.

While there is some evidence on employment growth in clusters of small firms in the developing world, data on income growth for workers and small entrepreneurs in clusters is extremely sparse. Bair and Gereffi's (2001) study of the Torreon jeans cluster shows that minimum wages rose from 182 pesos a week in 1998 to around 650 pesos a week in 2000. However, much of these gains were a reflection of the Mexican peso devaluation with real wages only just returning to their pre-1994 devaluation levels. In the Tirupur cluster, Singh (2003) reports daily wages for male workers at Rs 85, but for female workers wages were much lower, ranging between Rs 40 and 50 a day, which was below the Tamil Nadu legal minimum wage. But the issues are not just of wage levels and growth. There is extensive evidence from various cluster studies that point to substantial growth at the level of the cluster and of the firm. Much of this growth is found in the more mature, export-oriented, clusters. In most cases, such growth has also resulted in an expansion in employment levels if not in incomes. Even if wage levels are not rising clearly in clusters, what is more critical is whether they are falling behind wage levels in non-clustered alternative employment that such wage workers could take on. Thus, the key issue is relative wages. Both Schmitz (1999) and Nadvi (1999a) argue that while wage levels were low within the respective clusters which they studied (the Brazilian Sinos Valley shoe cluster and the Pakistani Sialkot surgical instrument cluster), they were nevertheless better than the regional average wage levels. Visser (1999), in his assessment of the counterfactual for the Gamarra garment cluster in Peru, suggests that wage levels in the cluster were above those in 'similar' non-clustered firms. Visser (1999: 1559) reports that average monthly pay per worker was "30 per cent higher in the cluster than elsewhere in the city" of Lima, although he also noted that workers in the cluster tended to work longer hours.

Cluster processes and poverty

We know that clusters can generate employment for the poor, but *how* does clustering help small producers and poor workers improve their economic positions, reduce their vulnerability to exogenous and external shocks and enhance their capabilities? We will focus on the processes associated with clustering, namely agglomeration economies, local joint action, local institutions and the role of social capital in fostering local co-operation.

Clustering can allow small firms to access markets in ways that would be infeasible were they operating in isolation. Moreover, the presence of specialised markets for raw materials, inputs and labour reduces costs to individual firms, while the easy flow of information and know-how within clusters can be critical for small producers.

As Weijland states, clusters generate critical 'search and reach economies'. This attracts traders and lowers costs. Among many of the rural Indonesian cottage industry clusters, Weijland (1999: 1519) found that clustering "reduced the transaction costs of purchasing inputs and marketing outputs ... [and] ... eased information flows and facilitated order-sharing, labour sharing and sub-contracting". But, as Weijland further noted, while rural clusters performed better (in terms of higher productivity for example) than dispersed rural enterprises, there was wide variation by sectors. In certain sectors (such as textiles, garments, roof tiles and wood products) there were stronger tendencies to cluster and more significant agglomeration gains for clustered producers. These differences across sectors were largely determined by technological factors – the extent to which the production process could be sub-divided, thus promoting specialisation and sub-contracting, as well as by markets.

In her review of African clusters, McCormick found the reduction in 'search and reach costs' to be a critical advantage that clustering generated for small, often informal, firms: "Location in clusters gave firms access to such traders and, through them, to customers" (McCormick,

1999: 1539). Scale economies were also key, especially in the (informal) garment manufacturing cluster in Nairobi where there was some division of labour and the presence of suppliers of fabrics, buttons and other inputs. In other cases, such as the Kumasi auto-parts cluster, in addition to better market access, labour market pooling and extensive sub-contracting, clustered producers benefited from local technological spillovers and knowledge flows. Similarly, Visser (1999) found that agglomeration gains were important in the Gamarra garment cluster. They lowered transaction costs to clustered small firms through their ability to easily access inputs, through the sub-contracting of specific and specialised finishing tasks which generated scale and scope economies, and through knowledge spillovers within the cluster. The easy and cheap availability of information promoted innovation and product development, and the costs savings to firms as a consequence of clustering were, according to Visser (1996: 1562), "largely responsible for the … performance gap between clustered and dispersed producers". Moreover, the performance gap was most acute amongst smaller firms which found that clustering gains were especially critical.

Agglomeration economies are also significant in the more mature clusters in the developing world which generate employment for the poor. Nadvi (1999a) illustrates these gains in the Sialkot surgical instruments cluster, where the labour force is skilled but largely illiterate and poor. Schmitz (1999), Knorringa (1999) and Rabellotti (1999) provide similar evidence from the shoe clusters of Sinos Valley, Agra and Guadalajara respectively. In each case, the cluster has a predominance of small, often (as in Agra) with a large number of informal, firms employing relatively poor labour. In each cluster agglomeration economies were critical for such small firms to compete in both local and increasingly global markets, to grow and to generate further employment.

In addition to agglomeration economies, clusters can foster local collaboration. This can be between individual enterprises which join together to take on combined tasks, such as joint marketing or product development, or take place at a cluster-wide level through local business associations, collective service centres and other bodies that provide a range of producer services within the cluster. Local collaboration is not an obvious outcome of clustering, it requires active intent on the part of local actors. Where it does develop, it can lead to significant gains, enhancing the collective capabilities of local entrepreneurs, as well as workers, and raise the overall competitiveness and growth prospects of the cluster. To what extent can such joint action address poverty concerns? There are two aspects to this. First, is there evidence that joint action through local institutions can raise the capability of small enterprises, even within incipient clusters, to engage markets and overcome constraints? Second, is there evidence that joint action can limit the vulnerability of clustered firms and workers in the face of external threats?

In most of the incipient clusters, signs of joint action are often limited. McCormick (1999) found very little evidence of local co-operation, either between firms or at the level of the cluster, in her review of African clusters. In Nairobi's garment cluster, joint action was not evident. In the Kumakunji metalworking cluster, however, some local producers were able to come together to jointly market their products – wheelbarrows. Collective associations, such as *jua kali* (informal sector) associations in Kenya, provide a channel between local enterprises and the state but exhibit no signs of being a basis for helping local clusters to develop. Similarly, despite the existence of a local co-operative society with wide membership, the Lake Victoria fishing cluster was unable to address common problems such as over-fishing or the need to raise quality standards (McCormick, 1999). In many other examples of such incipient clusters, from the Gamarra garment cluster in Lima to the vehicle repair cluster in Kumasi, we find at best only limited signs of active local co-operation. There are, however, a few exceptions. Sandee (1995), for example, cites the case of a rural roof tiles sector in Indonesia where producers came together to collectively acquire new technologies, and thereby access scale economies through the collective investment, raise productivity and improve quality. Weijland (1999) reports, again from rural Indonesia, the attempts by state policy to encourage cluster-based business groups to act as co-operatives, take on joint tasks such as training and marketing and to become the focal points for policy interventions. Weijland also describes some rural clusters, such as in textiles, making collective initiatives which resulted in positive outcomes by accessing markets and thus bringing about higher rates of employment and output growth (Weijland, 1999: 1526). But this impact was far from uniform.

The evidence on joint action in mature clusters is much stronger. More importantly, in many cases of relatively mature clusters, many of them only in the recent past having been incipient clusters, such forms of joint action are often pronounced in the face of external threats. Clusters that compete in global markets are particularly vulnerable to the exigencies of global competition. Liberalisation, new competition, demands from global buyers to meet global standards (on environmental, labour and quality issues for example) and new technologies can force co-operation as clusters seek collective paths to enhancing collective capabilities.

Thus, in Mexico, Rabellotti (1999) found that trade liberalisation had a significant impact on the footwear cluster of Guadalajara, a cluster that employed 25,000 persons in over 1,000, predominantly small, enterprises. Reductions in import tariffs led to a sharp rise in footwear imports, especially from China, severely threatening small domestic producers. Thus, in Guadalajara alone – accounting for some 27 per cent of Mexican shoe production – membership of the local footwear trade association fell from 500 to 315 as many firms closed down (Rabellotti, 1999: 1574). In response to such pressures, local co-operation within the cluster increased. Firms began to build networks with other local producers to increasingly share information. Some firms came together to jointly develop products and to source components. Cluster-wide institutional initiatives, particularly through the trade association, were especially significant in terms of promoting technological development and technical assistance to firms, training, information gathering on external buyers and the development of promotional trade fairs. Rabellotti found that greater local co-operation by firms had a statistically significant and positive impact on firm performance.

Knorringa (1999), in his study of the Agra shoe clusters, also found increased joint action in the face of new competitive challenges as producers, in both export and the premium domestic markets, were faced with rising demands for improved quality and lower price. Joint action through the local trade association did increase and this had positive consequences for performance, although Knorringa noted that such co-operation was skewed towards the larger producers. Schmitz's (1999) study of the Brazilian shoe cluster of the Sinos Valley also pointed to increased local co-operation as small firms faced up to global challenges, especially from competition with low-priced Chinese shoe production. Joint action was particularly strong in backward ties with local suppliers of leather and other key components, as well as sub-contractors. Multilateral joint action initiatives did take place but, as Schmitz noted, with the expansion of the cluster there was a growing differentiation in the competing interests of shoe producers (between large firms which had strong ties with external buyers and smaller enterprises), and between the shoe sector and the components sectors within the cluster.

Stronger evidence on cluster-wide institutional joint action was observed by Nadvi (1999b), in the context of the Sialkot surgical instrument cluster in Pakistan, by Kennedy (1999) for the tanning cluster of the Palar Valley in Tamil Nadu, India, and by Almeida (2008) for the jeans laundries of the Toritama cluster in Brazil. Compliance with global quality assurance standards, a necessary requirement for exports to leading global markets by the Sialkot cluster, came about through the catalytic role of the local trade association in channelling new know-how on quality management practices to the cluster. Had the association not taken on this function, most small firms would have closed given that the USA and the EU accounted for over 90 per cent of the cluster's sales. Similarly, in the Palar Valley, pressures to meet environmental standards in leather processing called for the setting up of common effluent treatment plants. As Kennedy (1999) notes, local tanneries had to co-operate to survive, forming common effluent treatment plants through collaborative arrangements, and monitoring problems of free riding. As a result, numbers of tanneries expanded, while the common treatment plants emerged as key local institutions for collective organisation. A further example of how clusters can promote collective responses to external threats comes from the response of export-oriented sports goods clusters in Sialkot, Pakistan, and Jallandhar, India, regarding the presence of child labour in manufacturing units within the cluster. Local joint action resulted in direct gains for the cluster, employment and cluster exports rose, while immediate poverty concerns for many of the more vulnerable members of the sports goods labour force began to be addressed (Lund-Thomsen and Nadvi, 2010).

Joint action can thus be a key potential advantage arising from clusters. But, it is neither an obvious outcome of clusters, nor is it easy to achieve. The evidence that emerges from cluster studies suggests that joint action is less common in incipient clusters than it is in more mature clusters. Even in mature clusters, joint action is far from uniform. The fast-growing jeans cluster of Torreon, where exports to the USA have expanded with NAFTA (the North American Free Trade Association), has seen local firms building closer ties with their external buyers than with other local producers (Bair and Gereffi, 2001). In many other cases, we see similar patterns where, in the face of global pressures, ties with external actors begin to supersede local linkages (Brazil's Sinos Valley is another example – see Bazan and Navas-Alemán, 2004; Schmitz, 1999). Nevertheless, in a number of cases, local co-operation can assist local small enterprises access markets, overcome constraints and confront vulnerabilities that they face in local and global markets. Often where such co-operation does take place it is strengthened by local social capital, common ties of community and identity that can foster co-operation and generate trust.

Social capital is often cited as a key feature of small-firm clusters. Social capital can assist local trust ties. It can also contribute to the provisioning of local social protection, providing an informal basis to cover risk and insurance as well as support for weaker members of the local community. There is a danger, however, that social capital is viewed in either an idealised fashion, or that it is seen as acting uniformly. Fostering trust, even with strong community ties can be difficult especially when enterprises are in direct and stiff competition with each other, where barriers to entry are low and where conditions of poverty are high. Moreover, differentiation within communities can mean that local social ties effectively marginalise particular groups, on the basis of caste, ethnicity, religion, migration and gender. What evidence is there on the links between social capital, one of the process outcomes of clustering, and poverty?

The presence of strong social networks is a feature in many incipient clusters. Weijland (1999: 1518) suggests that Indonesia's rural clusters have strong social networks that generate "a substantial stock of social capital." This serves to lower transaction costs through "traditions that seemed to safeguard social control and stability" and that promote trust within communities. Actual evidence of such social capital in practice is, however, limited. Furthermore, as Weijland notes, social networks usually uphold dominant local norms. Thus, in much of rural Indonesia, social networks are encapsulated within local patron–client relationships based on "socio-political hierarchy, land ownership and traditional family bonds" (Weijland, 1999) that allow key players within rural clusters, such as wealthy landowners and village elders (always men), to exercise a degree of power over other members of the community, and their families.

However, Altenburg and Meyer-Stamer (1999: 1697) argue that, for many of the survivalist clusters, it is "low trust and poor contract enforcement mechanisms [that] compromise the potential to reap benefits of clustering". Thus, instead of collaboration, opportunistic behaviour is often the norm in such clusters.

The evidence on social networks is somewhat stronger in parts of South Asia. Kennedy (1999: 1676–7) argues that a key element in promoting local co-operation amongst tanneries in the Palar Valley is their strong Muslim community identity. She mentions a 'Muslim ethic' and the presence of important religious and charitable institutions. This sense of community identity, enhanced by Muslims being a minority community within the wider region, provides a basis for local self-regulation and 'social control' that "ensure compliance to rules and norms." This religious identity has been central, states Kennedy, to promoting local co-operation amongst tanneries in forming and managing collective treatment plants. Strong religious hierarchies and norms provide the basis for an effective regulatory framework. But this only extends to tannery owners. Most tannery workers are low caste Hindus, and here religious identities serve to strengthen the divide between labour and capital. In the Agra footwear cluster, Knorringa (1999) also observes strong community ties, based on caste identities. As in Palar, there is differentiation by caste (and religious) groups within the cluster. Footwear workers tend to be poorer, low caste Jatavs (Hindus), while traders are usually high caste Hindus, Sikhs and Muslims. This differentiation, cemented by social and religious differences, further fuels obvious tensions between enterprise owners and workers. In the Tirupur knitwear garment cluster, Chari (2000) argues that the agricultural caste of Goundars became dominant in the industry largely through kin and caste networks as poor rural labourers, including landless peasants, moved to Tirupur in search of jobs. A similar story on the importance, and the shifting basis, of social identities is cited by Nadvi (1999b) in the context of the Sialkot surgical instrument cluster. Social networks were found to be critical to business ties but with their dominant forms shifting over time from *baradari* (quasi caste) ties to a strong sense of local social identity, based on location and family ties.

From the review of cluster processes, of agglomeration gains, joint action and social capital, we turn now to the evidence on cluster dynamics and poverty. As clusters develop what consequences emerge for poverty concerns? In particular, given that clusters are themselves heterogeneous in the composition of firms, producers and workers, who gains and who loses as clusters evolve?

Cluster dynamics and poverty

A number of cluster studies focus on cluster growth and upgrading, and the role of internal and external linkages in bringing this about. This has increasingly led to an emphasis on the ways in which local clusters are inserted into global value chains. Ties within the global chain can often determine the autonomy of local actors in terms of their power and ability to adopt particular growth trajectories. That is not to say that local networks and local linkages do not matter. Local institutions, local technological capacity, and local government policies can play a significant function. Nevertheless, cluster studies have begun to pay greater attention to the interface between what is termed local and global governance (Humphrey and Schmitz, 2004; Nadvi and Halder, 2005; Bathelt et al., 2004). Furthermore, identification of growth trajectories also point to the differentiated gains within clusters. As clusters develop, particular categories of local entrepreneurs and local workers gain while others lose. Here we assess the evidence on such differentiated outcomes for producers and workers, and its consequences for a broader poverty reduction agenda.

As with joint action, there is a clear distinction in patterns of upgrading between incipient and mature clusters. It is in the more mature clusters where we see substantial development as clustered firms upgrade their products, processes and functions within GVCs and in some cases enhance their ability to compete in global markets. The Torreon blue jeans cluster in Mexico is one example. As the cluster expanded, a number of jeans manufacturers moved from simple, assembly only, functions to 'full package' production. This involved undertaking new tasks such as fabric sourcing, trims and labels, fabric cutting, finishing and distribution. The highest value added functions of design, marketing and retail remain firmly in the hands of US lead firms. Nevertheless, as Bair and Gereffi (2001) show, the cluster's producers have upgraded significantly, enhancing their skills and capabilities, obtaining a three-fold increase in unit prices for garment assembly between 1993 and 2000, and rapidly increasing employment in the cluster. In the process, vertical ties with US lead firms have become stronger for local producers. In addition, such upgrading at the cluster level does not translate to upgrading by all firms. Large firms have been at the forefront of this process, with the necessary capital, links with the US buyers to access the know-how, and the buyer pressures, which allowed upgrading in order to undertake full package production. As a result concentration within the cluster increased. Of the 360 garment producers within Torreon, the ten largest firms account for over 40 per cent of total cluster production. Many of these large firms, as Bair and Gereffi (2001) point out, increasingly rely on large numbers of smaller sub-contractors, although ties with sub-contractors are organised through hierarchical vertical production networks. The pressures that large firms face from their US buyers to lower prices, raise quality and speed delivery, are transferred to local sub-contractors, squeezing the latter's profits and wages. According to Bair and Gereffi (2001: 1896) "the development of full package networks in Torreon is primarily benefiting a wealthy domestic elite whose control over the local industry is being further strengthened by its exclusive access to the US customers".

This pattern of differentiation between large and small firms as clusters develop is observed in a number of other cases, from the Sinos Valley shoe cluster, the Sialkot surgical instruments cluster, the Guadalajara shoe cluster to even the Gamarra garment cluster. Firm size can be a critical dimension to success, and this can have poverty consequences. Visser's (1999) study shows that clustered firms outperform Lima's dispersed garment producers, but that clustered firms tend to be larger than dispersed producers. Thus, most dispersed firms were smaller and poorer micro-enterprises. They were more reliant on unpaid family labour, were often more recent migrants to the city, and aspired to locate in the Gamarra cluster in order to access its advantages. Gamarra's producers were an 'elite' amongst the poor, with the high rents in Gamarra cluster acting as a barrier to entry for poorer entrepreneurs and newer migrants.

In many cases, the relative expansion of large firms within clusters often takes place alongside more hierarchical ties that such large firms have with local sub-contractors, or second- and third-tier suppliers. Sub-contractors are more vulnerable to demand shifts, and less able to directly access markets. This, for example, is seen in the Tirupur cluster where sub-contractors have no direct market access, work in poorer conditions and have limited skills and capital. Here 'job workers', who are effectively micro-enterprises or own account worker that specialise in particular tasks, are "because of the seasonal nature of demand for job workers, [the] most vulnerable group [within the cluster] and experience huge income variations" (Singh, 2003: 11).

Thus, cluster growth can lead to sharply differentiated gains at the firm level, with smaller producers often being squeezed or having less autonomy in their ties with larger producers within the cluster. Furthermore, growth trajectories within clusters, especially for those that produce for global markets, often involve a shift in the weights attached to local and external linkages, as was seen in Torreon and Sialkot. In Sinos Valley, Schmitz (1999) reports a similar pattern so that as the cluster expands and upgrades ties with external buyers become increasingly more important and external linkages are unevenly distributed within the cluster. Moreover, increasingly closer ties with external buyers, especially among the cluster's leading large producers, effectively undermined efforts at cluster-wide joint action. Growing dependency on external buyers through global value chain ties also implies, as Navas-Alemán (2011) notes from the highly clustered Brazilian shoe and furniture sectors, that when firms seek to upgrade they may run into conflicts with buyers over competing core competencies. In a similar context Tewari (1999) noted from the Ludhiana knitwear cluster that, for some producers, being able to turn down high volume but low priced orders from leading global buyers in preference for low volume, high quality orders from smaller international buyers was a better strategy for firms wishing to systematically learn and upgrade. Both Knorringa and Tewari, from their respective reviews of the Agra shoe and Ludhiana knitwear clusters, argue that producing for demanding domestic buyers can be valuable to the growth and learning trajectories of clustered enterprises.

Managing local and global governance is, therefore, key to a sustained cluster growth trajectory. Local know-how and demanding local buyers can matter. At the same time, external know-how is often essential for firms to innovate and develop, raise productivity and thus wages, and adopt a high road growth strategy. This can require a change in mind sets. One of the limits of the Gamarra garment cluster, according to Visser (1999), is likely to be the inability of local clustered producers to take on board best practices from outside the cluster especially at a time of growing liberalisation. The risk in such situations is thus of what Visser (1999: 1567) refers to as 'entropic death'. These points are echoed by Bathelt *et al.* (2004) and Nadvi and Halder (2005) indicating that innovation within clusters often requires access to complementary knowledge from outside the cluster.

Evidence of upgrading within incipient clusters is less apparent, in part because such clusters appear to advance more slowly, and because in many cases such clusters are constrained by various factors from taking discontinuous leaps in their growth trajectories. Nevertheless, in both types of clusters, we observe that dynamic trajectories also result in uneven gains. Particular groups of firms and of workers lose out with substantial poverty consequences.

While the cluster literature has paid attention to the issue of differentiated gains at the firm level, it has been far less informative on the effects that cluster dynamics can have on labour. As we have noted, the nature of employment, and of the labour contract, can be critical to poverty concerns. Many clusters generate employment for the poor in labour intensive sectors where skill requirements are low. To what extent do cluster dynamics, however, have differentiated impacts on different categories of labour? Take the case of Torreon, a cluster where upgrading has been substantial, generating a demand for new jobs and new skills. Bair and Gereffi (2001) report that women accounted for a substantial component of the labour force, especially in the labour intensive, but relatively lower paid, assembly and sewing tasks. However, as firms acquired new functions, such as the cutting of fabrics and the laundering of finished garments, the new, more skilled and better paid jobs were allocated predominantly, if not uniformly, to men. There was, they state, "a reluctance of companies to invest in enhancing the skills of female employees" as women were seen as transient within the labour force, prone to leaving work as they married and raised families.

In Tirupur, we see further evidence that cluster dynamics not only imply that women, who constitute some 65 per cent of the cluster's labour force, are squeezed into the lower paid tasks of sewing and packing, but that the nature of the labour contract also changes. Tiripur has had a history of labour unrest and of union activism. Yet, Tiripur's development in recent years is marked by a growth of contract labour, an increasing emphasis on piece-rated payments, a decline in trade unionism (Singh, 2003 reports that only 10 per cent of the labour force is represented in trade unions) and the erosion of collective bargaining rights (Carswell and De Neve, 2013).

In the Agra footwear cluster, Knorringa (1999) also found that despite cluster growth, employment as a whole shrank and particular segments of the cluster's labour force were especially squeezed. Thus, while employment in the export and premium domestic market segments of the Agra cluster rose, in the more traditional parts of the local industry it fell sharply. "Thousands of home-based women workers lost piece rate work on upper making" (Knorringa, 1999: 1594), while poorer *Jatav* artisans, engaged in direct sales, were also severely affected. The arrival of newer rural migrants, the closure of many firms with the subsequent expansion of the artisanal labour force, and the limited employment options available to low-caste *Jatavs* (whose work with leather was seen as 'polluting' by higher caste Hindus) led to growing evidence of poverty within Agra's shoe-making *Jatav* community.

What we see quite clearly from the evidence on cluster dynamics is that cluster upgrading does not necessarily translate into universal gains within the cluster. Particular types of firms are squeezed, and where there is limited evidence on labour, particular elements of the labour force are also at risk. Thus, the notion that clusters can bring about a 'high road' growth trajectory needs to be refined: a high road for some, but not for all. Clearly, enumerating the gains for labour, and discerning how these gains, in a dynamic context, vary by types of labour is a critical area for further research in cluster studies. It has direct consequences for a cluster and poverty agenda as well as for the broader understanding of cluster dynamics.

Cluster policy frameworks

Cluster promotion has become a mainstream aspect of both national government policy in many countries as well as part of the toolkit on SME and private enterprise development promotion undertaken by a range of international donors. This section provides a brief summary of some of the ways in which such policy frameworks have evolved. The discussion focuses in particular on two developing countries where there has been some of the most active engagement of national policy towards cluster development – India and Brazil.

India

The Abid Hussain Committee in 1997 provided the first official documentation on the extent of clustering and the need for a focused policy framework targeted at clustered enterprises (Hussain, 1997). The leading cluster development programme within India at the time was that initiated by the United Nations Industrial Development Organisation (UNIDO) in 1995 (Ceglie *et al.*, 1999). This programme, which ran until 2007, initially focused its efforts on identifying and intervening in a small number of pilot industrial clusters with the aim of promoting networking and collaboration between clustered firms to encourage technological upgrading and improved marketing that could effectively strengthen the national and international competitiveness of these clusters (Russo *et al.*, 2000). By 2003, the UNIDO programme broadened its scope to include interventions that aimed primarily to promote poverty alleviation in rural, peri-urban and artisanal clusters. A cluster development strategy was designed and implemented by UNIDO for the state of Orissa, one of the poorest states in the country, and targeted at low-income artisanal clusters. Towards the end of its programme the UNIDO initiative focused on two specific aims: first, to mainstream the cluster development strategy within Indian industrial and SME development programmes, and second, to initiate an agenda on clusters and corporate social responsibility (FMC, 2007).

On mainstreaming, the UNIDO programme was incredibly successful. It was able to convince key government agencies on the potential benefits in terms of economic, export, employment and incomes growth to be had from targeted cluster development programmes (CDP). The national Ministry of Micro, Small and Medium Enterprises (formerly the Ministry of Small Scale Industry) started with a budget of INR 7 billion (approximately US$ 130 million) allocated to 24 CDPs to be completed by 2006, with cluster promotion interventions taking place in over 1,300 clusters (FMC, 2007). The primary objective in these programmes was to strengthen infrastructure within clusters, and a variety of national and state level public and private bodies were identified through which CDPs were to be administered. The Government of India's subsequent 11th Five Year Plan (2007–12) earmarked INR 45 billion (approximately US$ 830 million) to cluster development during the plan period while the 12th Plan (2012–17) raised the overall budget for cluster development strategies to US$ 2.5 billion (Planning Commission Government of India, 2013).

Cluster promotion strategies have involved a number of federal level ministries (Ministry of MSMEs, Ministry of Textiles, and Ministry of Commerce and Industry), state level governments (including the state governments of Orissa, Gujarat, Kerala, Rajasthan, Madhya Pradesh and West Bengal) and various parastatal agencies (including the State Bank of India, the Small Industries Development Bank of India, and the National Bank for Agricultural and Rural Development) (FMC, 2007). Cluster promotion activities have focused on a range of areas, including the development of networks to undertake bulk purchasing of inputs (such as in the Bangalore machine tools cluster, the Alleppy coir cluster, the Chanderi silk weaving cluster, the Rajkot engineering cluster), the development of market linkages through bulk tendering (such as in the Rajkot engineering cluster), common market outlets (as in the Ludhiana garment cluster) and the promotion of trade fairs (as in the Jaipur handblock textiles cluster). A number of CDPs have targeted technological upgrading and knowledge dissemination, such as design development (in the Jaipur handblock textiles and Chanderi handloom silk textiles cluster), promotion of quality systems (as in the Pune food cluster, the Tirupur garment cluster) and common training facilities (for example in the Jalandhar cluster). Finally, infrastructure development and infrastructure facilities have been central to CDPs focusing on the tannery clusters in Tamil Nadu (through the development of common effluent treatment plants), the Pune food cluster (through the building of research and development facilities) and the Bangalore machine tools cluster (through the common design facility) (FMC, 2007).

In 'pro-poor' interventions aimed primarily at rural and artisanal clusters there has been a focus on the use of micro-credit interventions, targeting of poor and vulnerable workers and communities, the linking of health and education to local entrepreneurship, the promotion of local self-help groups (SHGs), and the training of women workers (as seen, for example, in the UNIDO cluster development programmes implemented in the Chanderi silk handloom cluster, and in the Orissa cluster programmes) (Ray and Sarkar, 2007). Finally, a few initiatives have sought to focus on the promotion of corporate social responsibility concerns, especially with respect to labour and environmental considerations. One of the most significant of these have been the interventions undertaken in the Jalandhar football cluster (see Lund-Thomsen and Nadvi, 2010; Ray and Sarkar, 2007).

Brazil

While there are no accurate measures of the numbers of clusters in Brazil, the phenomenon of clustering, known locally within Brazilian policy circles as *arranjos productivos locais*

(APLs – or local productive arrangements) is widespread. One recent study suggests over 2000 potential cluster regions within the country (Pires *et al.*, 2013) while there are over 260 officially recognised APLs. These include a number of cases that have been documented in the cluster literature, such as the well-known shoe cluster of Sinos Valley (Schmitz, 1999; Bazan and Navas-Alemán, 2004; Navas-Alemán, 2011), the ceramics cluster of Santa Catarina (Meyer-Stamer, 1998), the fruit clusters of Northeast Brazil (Gomes, 2006), the furniture clusters in Rio Grande de Sol and Santa Catarina (Puppim de Oliviera, 2008; Navas-Alemán, 2011), the jeans cluster of Toritama (Almeida, 2008), the auto and auto components cluster of the Sao Paulo ABC region (Quadros, 2004), to name a few. Examples of Brazilian clusters extend from agro-processing activities to labour intensive manufacture, capital intensive and knowledge intensive industries as well as in the services sector. Moreover, clustered firms are engaged in developing products and services for export and domestic markets.

The promotion of industrial clusters has been a key plank of Brazil's industrial strategy, with a primary objective of raising employment and incomes especially in poorer regions in the country. As the strategy unfolded, enhancing competitiveness of clustered firms also led to a growing emphasis on firm and cluster upgrading. Thus, in more recent years cluster promotion policies have in large measure addressed firm-level technological upgrading, cluster-level research and development activities, including building linkages with universities and research centres, and improving the capabilities of clustered firms and workers through training programmes. The key agencies implementing these cluster development activities are the Brazilian Support Service for Micro and Small Enterprises (better known as SEBRAE) and the National Service for Industrial Training (SENAI). SEBRAE employs more than 5,000 employees and over 8,000 consultants distributed between the headquarters and 27 state-level centres who deliver services to SMEs through 750 points of service delivery.[2] SENAI runs a large network of vocational training, technical education, and innovation of industrial technologies initiatives. These institutional interventions have a long history. SENAI, for example, was founded in 1942. It has over 780 operations unit, including 323 mobile units, with many located in and undertaking specific training functions for designated clusters.[3]

Brazil is known for its relatively strong labour and environmental regulations (Coslovsky, 2014). Yet the Brazilian experience on the engagement of local clusters with national social and environmental considerations is mixed. Tendler (2002) made a very powerful observation when she noted that in order to 'protect' relatively weak and under-resourced SMEs Brazilian politicians and government regulators would take a more lax approach on the enforcement of labour, environmental and social regulations for clustered firms. This "devil's deal" as she coined it was seen as one way to promote small producers in relatively backward regions.

Cluster promotion policy continues to remain a core plank of industrial development policy in a number of developing economies. Having said that, evidence on the actual impacts of cluster promotion remain unclear. Individual case studies suggest that a number of distinct activities in cluster development, such as the provisioning of business services and the technical assistance that helps firms to collectively upgrade can promote competitiveness (World Bank, 2001). But to what extent can individual cases be mainstreamed into the wider policy framework remains challenging. India provides possibly the most ambitious agenda on mainstreaming cluster promotion but the danger is that given the scale of the programme, the volumes being invested into it, and the diverse range of actors involved can result in a devolution of core cluster promotion objectives built around fostering networking between SMEs and addressing collective challenges especially for poorly endowed firms and workers, and instead become a platform to promote infrastructure development. In this regard, Brazil, with a longer institutional history on SME development policies and more recently around the APL agenda, may offer a more hopeful strategy. This, however, requires careful empirical evaluation before clear cut policy outcomes and strategies can be defined.

Conclusion

This chapter seeks to assess how clustering can help SMEs to address their size limitations, become more competitive in local and global markets, and more particularly the consequences of this for poverty reduction agendas. It outlines the core conceptual arguments for clustering set out in the now extensive literature from the distinct business studies, development studies and economic geography disciplines. The conceptual case for, and the empirical evidence on, agglomeration economies, knowledge spillovers and technological upgrading to be found within clusters is strong. This has in large measure driven much of the national and international policy interest on clusters and local and regional economic development (Parrilli *et al.*, 2013). It is also apparent that clusters are not only highly heterogeneous but that they can directly generate employment and incomes for the poor, often the very poor both in urban and rural setting. The evidence on incipient, informalised, clusters is extensive. Yet, many of these clusters are directly linked into global value chains that feed into the most demanding international markets (Mezzadri, 2014). Moreover, cluster processes have direct pro-poor consequences. Agglomeration economies and joint action can assist poor producers overcome their financial, technical and managerial constraints, reduce their risks and vulnerability to external shocks and face various local and global challenges. At the same time, cluster dynamics clearly point to differentiated outcomes. This can have seriously detrimental implications for particularly categories of local firms and workers. While policy frameworks have begun to engage with aspects of this agenda, and in some countries and in key international institutions this engagement has been pronounced, there still remains a need for more in-depth and rigorous analysis of not only the impacts on cluster competitiveness but also the pro-poor and sustainability outcomes of cluster policies.

Notes

1 Parts of the arguments presented in this chapter were first developed in Nadvi and Barrientos (2004). My thanks to Mike Tribe for his very helpful suggestions on an earlier draft of the chapter.
2 http://www.sebrae.com.br/sites/PortalSebrae/canais_adicionais/conheca_quemsomos
3 http://www.senai.br/portal/br/home/index.aspx

References

Almeida, M. 2008. Understanding Incentives for Clustered Firms to Control Pollution: The Case of the Jeans Laundries in Toritama, Pernambuco, Brazil. In Puppim de Oliviera, J. A. (ed.). *Upgrading Clusters and Small Enterprises in Developing Countries: Environmental, Labor, Innovation and Social Issues.* Aldershot: Ashgate: 107–134.
Altenburg, T. and Meyer-Stamer, J. 1999. How to Promote Clusters: Policy Experiences from Latin America. *World Development.* 27 (9): 1693–1714.
Anderson, D. 1982. Small Industry in Developing Countries: A Discussion of Issues. *World Development.* 10 (11): 913–948.
Bair, J. and Gereffi, G. 2001. Local Clusters in Global Value Chains: The Causes and Consequences of Export Dynamism in Torreon's Blue Jeans Industry. *World Development.* 29 (11): 1885–1903.
Bartley, T. 2007. Institutional Emergence in an Era of Globalization: The Rise of Transnational Private Regulation in Labor and Environmental Conditions. *American Journal of Sociology.* 113 (2): 297–351.
Bathelt, H., Malmberg, A. and Maskell, P. 2004. Clusters and Knowledge: Local Buzz, Global Pipelines and the Process of Knowledge Creation. *Progress in Human Geography.* 28 (1): 31–56.

Bazan, L. and Navas-Alemán, L. 2004. The Underground Revolution in the Sinos Valley: Upgrading in Global and National Value Chains. In Schmitz, H. (ed.). *Local Enterprises in the Global Economy: Issues of Governance and Upgrading*. Cheltenham: Edward Elgar: 110–139.

Brautigam, D. 1997. Substituting for the State: Institutions and Industrial Development in Eastern Nigeria. *World Development*. 25 (7): 1063–1080.

Carswell, G. and De Neve, G. 2013. Labouring for Global Markets: Conceptualising Labour Agency in Global Production Networks. *Geoforum*. 44 (1): 62–70.

Ceglie, G., Clara, M. and Dini, M. 1999. Cluster and Network Development Projects in Developing Countries: Lessons Learned Through the UNIDO Experience. In Organization for Economic Cooperation and Development. *Boosting Innovation: The Cluster Approach*. Paris: OECD: 269–292.

Chari, S. 2000. The Agrarian Origins of the Knitwear Industrial Cluster in Tirupur, India. *World Development*. 28 (3): 579–599.

Cluster Observatory. 2014. *Cluster Observatory: Compendium of Cluster Resources for Undertaking Cluster Initiatives*. New Delhi – accessible from www.clusterobservatory.in

Coe, N. M., Dicken, P. and Hess, M. 2008. Global Production Networks: Realizing the Potential. *Journal of Economic Geography*. 8 (3): 271–295.

Coslovsky, S. 2014. Flying Under the Radar? The State and the Enforcement of Labour Laws in Brazil. *Oxford Development Studies*. 42 (2): 190–216.

Das, K. (ed.). 2005. *Indian Industrial Clusters*. Aldershot: Ashgate.

Dinh, H. T., Rawski, T. G., Zafar, A., Wang, L. and Mavroeidi, E. with Tong, X. and Li, P. 2013. *Tales from the Development Frontier: How China and Other Countries Harness Light Manufacturing to Create Jobs and Prosperity*. Washington, DC: World Bank.

Foundation for MSME Clusters (FMC). 2007. Policy and Status Paper on Cluster Development in India. New Delhi: FMC. Accessed from: http://msmefoundation.org/folder/Publication/48.pdf

Gereffi, G., Humphrey, J. and Sturgeon, T. 2005. The Governance of Global Value Chains. *Review of International Political Economy*. 12 (1): 78–104.

Gomes, R. 2006 Upgrading Without Exclusions: Lessons from SMEs in Fresh Fruit Clusters in Brazil. In Pietrobelli, C. and Rabellotti, R., (eds.). *Upgrading to Compete: Global Value Chains, Clusters and SMEs in Latin America*. Washington: IADB & David Rockefeller Foundation.

Gordon, I. R. and McCann, P. 2000. Industrial Clusters: Complexes, Agglomeration and/or Social Networks? *Urban Studies*. 37 (3): 513–532.

Gulati, M., 1997. *Restructuring and Modernisation of Small and Medium Enterprise Clusters in India*. Small and Medium Enterprise Programme Report. Vienna: United Nations Industrial Development Organization.

Holmstrom, M. and Cadene, P. 1998. *Decentralised Production in India. Industrial Districts, Flexible Specialization and Employment*. Delhi: Sage Publications.

Humphrey, J. and Schmitz, H. 1998. Trust and Inter-Firm Relations in Developing and Transition Economies. *Journal of Development Studies*. 34 (4): 32–61.

Humphrey, J. and Schmitz, H. 2002. How does Insertion in Global Value Chains Affect Upgrading in Industrial Clusters? *Regional Studies*. 36 (9): 1017–1027.

Humphrey, J. and Schmitz, H. 2004. Governance in Global Value Chains. In Schmitz, H. (ed.). *Local Enterprises in the Global Economy: Issues of Governance and Upgrading*. Cheltenham: Edward Elgar: 95–109.

Hussain, A. 1997. *Report of the Expert Committee on Small Enterprises*. New Delhi: Government of India, Jan 27, 1997. Accessed from: www.isedonline.org/uploads/userfiles/file/file/Report%20of%20the%20Expert%20Committee%20on%20Small%20Enterprises%20Shri%20Abid%20Hussain.pdf

Kaplinsky, R. 2005. *Globalization, Poverty and Inequality: Between a Rock and a Hard Place*. Cambridge: Polity Press.

Kennedy L. 1999. Co-Operating for Survival: Tannery Pollution and Joint Action in the Palar Valley. *World Development*. 27 (9): 1673–1691.

Ketels, C. 2013. Recent Research on Competitiveness and Clusters: What are the Implications for Regional Policy? *Cambridge Journal of Regions, Economy and Society*. 6 (2): 269–284.

Knorringa, P. 1999. Agra: An Old Cluster Facing the New Competition. *World Development*. 27 (9): 1587–1604.

Knorringa, P. and Nadvi, K. 2014. Rising Power Clusters and the Challenges of Local and Global Standards. *Journal of Business Ethics*. published online September 2014.

Lund-Thomsen, P. and Nadvi, K. 2010. Clusters, Chains and Compliance: Corporate Social Responsibility and Governance in South Asia. *Journal of Business Ethics.* 93 (2 Supplement): 201–222.

Malmberg, A. 1996. Industrial Geography: Agglomeration and Local Milieu. *Progress in Human Geography.* 20 (3): 392–403.

Malmberg, A. and Maskell, P. 2002. The Elusive Concept of Localisation Economies: Towards a Knowledge-Based Theory of Spatial Clustering. *Environment and Planning A.* 34 (3): 429–449.

Markusen, A. 1996. Sticky Places in Slippery Space: A Typology of Industrial Districts. *Economic Geography.* 72 (3) 293–313.

Marshall, A. 1920. *Principles of Economics* (8th ed.). London: Macmillan.

Martin, R. and Sunley, P. 2003. Deconstructing 'Clusters': Chaotic Concept or Policy Panacea? *Journal of Economic Geography.* 3 (1): 5–35.

McCormick, D. 1999. African Enterprise Clusters and Industrialisation: Theory and Reality. *World Development.* 27 (9): 1531–1552.

Mead, D. 1984. Of Contracts and Subcontracts: Small Firms in Vertically Disintegrated Production/Distribution Systems in LDCs. *World Development.* 12 (11–12): 1095–1106.

Messner, D. 2004. Regions in the 'World Economic Triangle'. In Schmitz, H. (ed.). *Local Enterprises in the Global Economy.* Cheltenham: Edward Elgar: 20–52.

Meyer-Stamer, J. 1998. Path Dependence in Regional Development: Persistence and Change in Three Industrial Clusters in Santa Catarina, Brazil. *World Development.* 26 (8): 1495–1511.

Mezzadri, A. 2014. Indian Garment Clusters and CSR Norms: Incompatible Agendas at the Bottom of the Garment Commodity Chain. *Oxford Development Studies.* 42 (2): 238–258.

Nadvi, K. 1999a. The Cutting Edge: Collective Efficiency and International Competitiveness in Pakistan. *Oxford Development Studies.* 27 (1): 81–107.

Nadvi, K. 1999b. Collective Efficiency and Collective Failure: The Response of the Sialkot Surgical Instrument Cluster to Global Quality Pressures. *World Development.* 27 (9): 1605–1626.

Nadvi, K. 1999c. Shifting Ties: Social Networks in the Surgical Instrument Cluster of Sialkot, Pakistan. *Development and Change.* 30 (1): 141–175.

Nadvi, K. 1999d. *Facing the New Competition: Business Associations in Developing Country Industrial Clusters.* Working Paper 103 – International Institute for Labour Studies. Geneva: International Labour Organization (ILS).

Nadvi, K. 2008. Global Standards, Global Governance and the Organisation of Global Value Chains. *Journal of Economic Geography.* 8 (3): 323–343.

Nadvi, K. and Barrientos, S. 2004. *Industrial Clusters and Poverty Reduction: Towards a Methodology for Poverty and Social Impact Assessment of Cluster Development Initiatives.* Report for UNIDO. Vienna: United Nations Industrial Development Organization.

Nadvi, K. and Halder, G. 2005. Local Clusters in Global Value Chains: Exploring Dynamic Linkages Between Germany and Pakistan. *Entrepreneurship and Regional Development.* 17 (5): 339–363.

Nadvi, K. and Schmitz, H. 1999. Special Issue: Industrial Clusters in Developing Countries. *World Development.* 27 (9).

Nadvi, K. and Waltring, F. 2004. Making Sense of Global Standards. In Schmitz, H. (ed.). *Local Enterprises in the Global Economy: Issues of Governance and Upgrading.* Cheltenham: Edward Elgar: 53–94.

Navas-Alemán, L. 2011. The Impact of Operating in Multiple Value Chain for Upgrading: The Case of the Brazilian Furniture and Footwear Industries. *World Development.* 39 (8): 1386–1397.

Parrilli, M. D., Nadvi, K. and Yeung, H. W.-C. 2013. Local and Regional Development in Global Value Chains, Production Networks and Innovation Networks: A Comparative Review and the Challenges for Future Research. *European Planning Studies.* 21 (7): 967–988.

Pietrobelli, C. and Rabellotti, R. (eds.). 2006. *Upgrading to Compete: Global Value Chains, Clusters and SMEs in Latin America.* Washington: Inter-American Development Bank and the David Rockefeller Foundation.

Pires, J. C., Cravo, T., Lodato, S. and Piza, C. 2013. *Industrial Clusters and Economic Performance in Brazil.* IDB Working Paper Series WP 475. Washington, DC: Inter-American Development Bank.

Planning Commission Government of India. 2013. *Twelfth Five Year Plan (2012–2017): Faster, More Inclusive and Sustainable Growth, Volume 1.* New Delhi: Sage.

Ponte, S. and Sturgeon, T. 2014. Explaining Governance in Global Value Chains: A Modular Theory-Building Effort. *Review of International Political Economy.* 21 (1): 195–223.

Porter, M. 1990. *The Competitive Advantage of Nations.* London: Macmillan.

Porter, M. E. 1998. Clusters and the New Economics of Competition. *Harvard Business Review.* November: 77–90.

Puppim de Oliviera, J. A. 2008. Environmental upgrading of industrial clusters: Understanding Their Connections with Global Chains in Brazilian Furniture Sector. In Puppim de Oliviera, J. A. (ed.). *Upgrading Clusters and Small Enterprises in Developing Countries: Environmental, Labor, Innovation and Social Issues.* Aldershot: Ashgate: 45–64.

Quadros, R., 2004. Global Quality Standards and Technological Upgrading in the Brazilian Auto-Components Industry. In Schmitz, H. (ed.). *Local Enterprises in the Global Economy: Issues of Governance and Upgrading.* Cheltenham: Edward Elgar: 265–296.

Rabellotti, R. 1999. Recovery of Mexican Cluster: Devaluation Bonanza or Collective Efficiency? *World Development.* 27 (9): 1571–1586.

Ray, S. and Sarkar, T. 2007. *Cluster Development and Poverty Alleviation: Policy suggestions. May.* New Delhi: Foundation for MSME Clusters. Accessed from: http://www.msmefoundation.org/folder/Publication/49.pdf

Russo, F., Clara, M. and Gulati, M. 2000. *Cluster Development and Promotion of Business Development Services (BDS): UNIDO's Experience in India.* Private Sector Development (PDS – SME) Technical Working Papers 6. Vienna: United Nations Industrial Development Organization.

Sandee, H.M. 1995. *Innovation Adoption in Rural Industry: Technological Change in Roof Tiles Clusters in Central Java, Indonesia.* PhD dissertation, Free University: Amsterdam.

Saxenian, A. and Hsu, J-Y. 2001. The Silicon Valley-Hsinchu Connection: Technical Communities and Industrial Upgrading. *Industrial and Corporate Change.* 10 (4): 893–920.

Schmitz, H. 1995. Collective Efficiency: Growth Path for Small-scale Industry. *Journal of Development Studies.* 31 (4): 529–566.

Schmitz, H. 1999. Global Competition and Local Cooperation: Success and Failure in the Sinos Valley, Brazil. *World Development.* 27 (9): 1627–1650.

Schmitz, H. (ed.). 2004. *Local Enterprises in the Global Economy: Issues of Governance and Upgrading.* Cheltenham: Edward Elgar.

Schmitz, H. and Nadvi, K. 1999. Clustering and Industrialization: Introduction. *World Development.* 27 (9): 1503–1514.

Schmitz, H. and Knorringa, P. 2000. Learning from Global Buyers. *Journal of Development Studies.* 37 (2): 177–205.

Singh, N. 2003. Readymade Garment Industry in Tirupur. Mimeo. New Delhi: National Council for Applied Economic Research.

Tendler, J. 2002. Small Firms, the Informal Sector and the Devil's Deal. *IDS Bulletin.* 33 (3): 1–15.

Tewari, M. 1999. Successful Adjustment in Indian Industry: The Case of Ludhiana's Woolen Knitwear Cluster. *World Development.* 27 (9): 1651–1672.

UNIDO. 2001. *Development of Clusters and Networks of SMEs: The UNIDO Programme.* Vienna: United Nations Industrial Development Organization.

Van Dijk, M. P. and Rabellotti, R. 1999. *Enterprise Clusters and Networks in Developing Countries.* Routledge Research EADI Studies in Development. London: Routledge.

Visser, E-J. 1999. A Comparison of Clustered and Dispersed Firms in the Small Scale Clothing Industry of Lima. *World Development.* 27 (9): 1553–1570.

Weijland, H. 1999. Microenterprise Clusters in Rural Indonesia: Industrial Seedbed and Policy Target. *World Development.* 27 (9): 1515–1530.

World Bank. 2001. Business Development Strategies for Small Enterprises: Guiding Principles for Donor Intervention. Committee of Donor Agencies for Small Enterprise Development, SME Dept. Washington, DC: World Bank.

8

INDUSTRIAL POLICY

Back on the agenda

John Weiss

Industrial policy (IP) is back on the policy agenda of many countries with concerns over national competitiveness in a globalised world.[1] In academic circles, debates over the role of IP never ceased, despite from the 1980s onwards the prevailing policy consensus on the need for a dominant role for markets in determining resource allocation. This chapter commences with a discussion of different versions of IP. It then considers the role these envisage for governments, since the newer version of IP has far greater focus on the role of the private sector. A third section has a classification of IP and a fourth links IP with economic theory. A fifth section considers examples of IP in recent years and a sixth looks at several country cases. A final section concludes.

Different versions of industrial policy

Two separate strands in the literature on IP in a development context can be separated, since they imply distinct interpretations of how such a policy might be implemented. First, there is what we can term an historical tradition that draws on experience from today's rich countries where in the nineteenth century 'infant industry' protection was used effectively to create new industries in 'latecomer' or follower countries, such as the USA and Germany. In addition, there are the twentieth century examples of state intervention to foster industrial development starting with Japan and followed by most notably Korea and Taiwan, but also by other countries in East Asia.[2] These policies were geared predominantly at supporting industrialisation as a means of raising productivity levels and rates of economic growth and hence IP in this sense implies a bias towards industrialisation.

The impact of the policies pursued in these country cases has been the subject of very extensive debate but many believe that, despite the empirical difficulty of establishing the argument precisely, state intervention did help transform the structure of the economies concerned and allowed the emergence of a globally competitive industrial sector. The types of policies pursued varied, but focused principally on developing particular sub-sectors or branches of industry with the potential for both high levels of productivity relative to the average for the economy concerned and for high rates of productivity growth. Trade policy at this time was relatively protectionist, with periods of import protection combined with export promotion measures. Trade liberalisation generally followed rather than preceded the emergence of competitive activities. Industrial policy was state-driven, with key government bodies like the Ministry of International Trade and Industry (MITI) in Japan and the Economic Planning Board in Korea setting the agenda in terms of priority areas. However, there was extensive interaction with the private sector, for example through industry associations and deliberation councils, an active dialogue on the implications of policy for producers and at times the setting of quantitative targets for private firms. Significantly, industrial policy was defined in terms of interventions to shift the allocation of resources in favour of the manufacturing sector and within manufacturing towards high productivity, dynamic sub-sectors.[3]

This strand of the literature is in contrast with the more recent discussion of 'strategic industrial policy', which has emerged largely from the work of the Harvard economists Dani Rodrik and Ricardo Hausmann (Rodrik, 2008; Hausmann *et al.*, 2008). The authors have built on the standard argument from micro economics that where markets fail to meet the restrictive conditions of the abstract model of perfect competition (due to lack of information, monopoly, external effects and so forth), or where markets are incomplete or missing (so there are goods which can only be supplied by a public provider), that there is a theoretical case for government intervention. However, they have added the important insight that the driver of development is innovation, and thus it is important to do things in different ways and create new products (or products new to an economy). The role of policy is therefore not just to correct for market failure in a static sense, but critically to encourage the innovation that will foster long-term productivity growth. In their interpretation IP is an intervention that alters the allocation of resources towards new, dynamic activities in any sector of the economy, not just in industry. Thus despite its name under their definition IP can promote services or agriculture, for example, as well as manufacturing industry. Their focus is on types of activity – new and dynamic – rather than sectors or sub-sectors. Hence manufacturing industry is not given a special role despite the fact that Rodrik himself has provided empirical evidence in support of the thesis has manufacturing industry has a special role in the process of economic growth due to its potential for productivity increases.[4]

The focus of strategic IP is also on process, rather than on either the precise branches or sub-sectors to be promoted, or the policy instruments to be used (whether subsidies, tax concessions, import tariff protection, credit allocations and so forth). This is because the dialogue between the government and the relevant private sector stakeholders is meant to draw out areas for growth and identify obstacles to this growth, which the government can intervene to remove. At its least ambitious (what the authors term 'in the small') strategic IP should remove constraints to growth in existing activities as identified through this dialogue. Co-funding by private partners to remove bottlenecks can help to reinforce the public–private partnership element.

The more ambitious side to this policy (what the authors term 'in the large') involves moving into genuinely new activities – although how far away these should be from the existing types of goods produced by an economy remains a point of considerable dispute and will be a major point to which we will return. Here policy requires taking 'strategic bets' on new activities (or sub-sectors) and providing the risk capital – for example through development banks or venture capital funds – to allow them to be established. Because innovation – through both the scope for copying and its demonstration effect by highlighting new markets – is a key externality, this policy amounts to compensation for the externalities arising from innovation. Interventions which compensate for external benefits created for others are wholly compatible with standard micro economics, so this recommendation is uncontroversial in a theoretical sense. Dialogue with the private sector appears to be less central to this aspect of IP and, in the way the argument is phrased, ideas could be identified either from the side of the government or the private investor. The focus on innovation in the newer IP literature links it with an earlier tradition in development economics which has focused on the way in which successful

economies have organised the creation of technical change and the development of the capabilities needed for industrialisation.[5]

The contrast between strategic policy and what we have termed the historical tradition
(or what has been termed 'old style') IP is not as great as might be imagined. One major difference is that strategic policy is intended for an open trading world, so unlike the historical
version, trade protection is unlikely to figure prominently in the policy instruments applied.
However, as noted, discussion and dialogue with the private sector was present in the East
Asian version of earlier industrial policy and, as practised in some contexts, for example
in Taiwan, interventions were in the form of modest assistance rather than major support
through either subsidised funding or high levels of protection.[6] Further, the more ambitious
version of strategic policy leaves open the possibility that it will be the government through
either a development bank or a venture capital fund which selects new activities on which to
place a strategic bet and these bets may be on broadly defined sub-sectors.[7]

What is the role of government?

The question of how far governments should take the initiative in driving the direction of change
is an ambiguity central to IP. From the foregoing analysis, two stylised versions emerge with
actual practice likely to be a combination of the two. One is where the full model envisaged by
strategic policy can apply. There is a regular and effective dialogue with the private sector and the
government plays the role of promoting competition, reducing transaction costs and facilitating
private sector innovation. In this version the government invests in infrastructure, promotes risk
taking through strategic bets of public venture capital or development bank lending and arranges
contests whereby the private sector can bid for public resources. It may promote foreign direct
investment in selected areas or technologies through fiscal incentives and an attractive investment
climate. This requires an effective public sector bureaucracy and a dynamic private sector capable
of responding to the opportunities offered by industrial policy. Strategic IP recommends that the
private sector be engaged through not just a regular dialogue but also through contests through
which consortia of firms – for example organised by business associations – can bid for government support through the provision of public goods (whether physical infrastructure, skills training or joint R and D funding). Similarly, governments can invite bids to fund feasibility studies
for products or processes new to an economy. These contests would involve modest state support
for ideas developed by the private sector and are a means of reinforcing the dialogue side of IP.

The second version is closer to the older historical tradition in that it is public sector-driven
with the government identifying sub-sectors or technologies it wishes to promote, whilst
engaging in a dialogue with the private sector on how best to do this. Expert advice through
commissioned consultancy studies may be required to complement the evidence provided by
the private sector itself, and donors will have a role in providing both funding and technical
assistance. Central to this will be identification of the key constraints to growth in strategic sub-
sectors and the devising of policy interventions to overcome these. To demarcate these alternative versions by a country's income level is an over-simplification, but broadly we can think
of the former as relevant to middle or lower-middle income economies and the latter to lower
income economies where the private sector is relatively weak and needs considerable public
sector support. The latter version would apply in most of sub-Saharan Africa, for example.

In relation to how far governments should intervene to change industrial structure the
debate between Justin Lin and H.-J. Chang provides a helpful insight into alternative visions
on technological upgrading and structural transformation in industrialising economies (Lin and
Chang, 2009). While both agree on the need for government support, they disagree on how

far and how fast it is wise for countries to move, for example into 'distant' products in the sense of goods that are far removed from current comparative advantage. Lin writes of the importance of a facilitating state that will support innovation and correct for short-term market failures, but which will not make the mistake of pursuing activities that require skills and capabilities that the economy does not yet possess – what he terms *comparative advantage defying* policies. Chang, on the other hand, argues for the importance of policies that aim to transform production structures in an economy by sharing risks and funding between public and private sectors, with the government channelling support selectively to sub-sectors with the greatest perceived potential.

The significance of this debate for the discussion of IP is that, drawing on different readings of both historical experience in Asia and economic theory, both authors construct a case for differential incentives between activities. They differ principally over how far countries should try to depart from their existing specialisation and how far they should aim to move into products that require significantly new skill sets. Probably the balance of professional opinion would agree with Lin rather than Chang and would caution against too radical a shift away from current production, but this does not rule out the possibility of a limited number of strategic bets on new or 'distant' activities.

Classification of industrial policy

IP – in either its historical or strategic variant – can be defined as a set of interventions to alter resource allocation in favour of what are perceived as high productivity, dynamic activities. IP interventions can be categorised in different ways, but a schematic 2-by-2 matrix is a helpful way of clarifying the concepts. Interventions to can be either through the provision of public inputs – activities or services which the private sector would not supply in the necessary amounts – or through market-based incentives – subsidies, tax holidays, funding, import protection.[8] Similarly they can be available to all who meet the specified criteria regardless of sub-sector – horizontal incentives – or only to specified sub-sectors – vertical incentives.[9] Table 8.1 illustrates this approach to classification with examples of the different policies.

Table 8.1 Classification of policy interventions

	Horizontal	*Vertical*
Public inputs	Broad-based skills training	Sector-specific skills training
	Infrastructure regulatory reform	Targeted infrastructure investment
	Banking sector regulatory reform	Business plans for selected sectors
	Standard setting bodies	Public–private research consortia
Market-based provision	Corporation tax reform	Specific tax holidays
	General labour subsidy	Sector-specific labour subsidy
	Export promotion – credit availability, duty-drawbacks, tax treatment	Sector-specific export promotion
	Export processing zones	Selective import protection
	General venture capital funding	Sector-specific venture capital funding
	General credit guarantees for SMEs[a]	Selective credit guarantees
	Subsidised credit to all SMEs	Directed credit
	Tax incentives for R and D	Selective R and D incentives
		Price support schemes

Note: a Small and medium enterprises.

Horizontal measures by definition are open to all producers and households who wish to take advantage of them. However, ex post there is no such thing as genuinely horizontal measures, since in practice any measure will impact differentially depending on the nature of firms or activities. Investment in road or power improvements will have a different impact on firms depending on the extent to which they use roads or are power-intensive in terms of cost structure. Even general as opposed to skill-specific labour training will benefit labour-intensive firms disproportionately and, conversely, tax credits related to depreciation will benefit capital-intensive firms more than others. Special support for SMEs differentiates by scale of production and employment, and export processing zones and other export promotion schemes benefit exporters as opposed to domestically oriented firms. Thus perfect neutrality of outcome is impossible even if all IP is based ex ante on neutral, horizontal interventions.

Industrial policy and economic theory

In terms of the underlying economic rationale for IP, horizontal interventions are clearly linked with 'market failures' as they are designed to make markets work more effectively by compensating for 'distortions' such as lack of information and external effects, or by removing monopoly or monopsony structures and by offering incentives or public goods equally to all firms.

For example, publicly funded skills training is designed to compensate for the fact that firms acting independently will under-invest because newly trained workers can leave and take their skills elsewhere, creating an external benefit for competitors. Regulatory reform in the power sector is usually designed to create a quasi-competitive market to avoid the creation of a monopoly position.[10] Similarly, banking sector reform is often designed to induce commercial banks to enter the long-term credit market by helping to overcome the basic information asymmetry that hinders long-term lending. Funding for venture capital initiatives can be rationalised as a compensation for the external benefit created by innovation as followers can learn and copy from the example of innovators. Similarly, tax incentives or direct subsidies for R and D reflect the fact that not all knowledge can be patented and that the knowledge and example created by R and D-active firms can spill over as benefits to others. Labour subsidies – for example through reduced social security payments or tax liability deductions – can be rationalised as a compensation for labour markets that fail to reduce under-employment due to structural frictions and which thereby allow wages to exceed the opportunity cost of labour.[11]

Credit market imperfections have received a lot of attention because poorly functioning financial systems are recognised as a key constraint in many countries. Credit guarantees are a horizontal measure usually used to ease access to credit for smaller firms on the grounds that due to their lack of collateral they are unable to access long-term funding. They are a form of market correction in that they compensate for the lack of information on the potential returns to investment by small borrowers. Where a state guarantee is offered it allows commercial banks to avoid the problem of adverse selection – where only risky projects are put forward at high interest rates – and lowering the overall risk level of their portfolio allows them to hold lower reserves. State partial guarantees are thus a form of risk sharing between three parties: banks, borrowers and government. Theoretically they are a means of overcoming a co-ordination failure in the credit market, since without the government's guarantee neither the banks nor the borrowers would be able to organise a sharing of risk.

Support for innovation has become one of the central planks of recent policy discussion rationalised on the basis of the externality created by innovators. Innovation can operate at different levels in terms of both product and process innovation. Hence support can be targeted at R and D, for example through tax allowances for R and D expenditure or through upfront cash grants. Investment to create output embodying new products or processes can be supported through the provision of credit through a development bank or state venture capital fund. At middle income levels, where technological innovation becomes a key policy objective, a key plank of IP will be to stimulate domestic research through links between industry and domestic research institutes.

The case of vertical or selective IP measures is more controversial because these aim to alter market incentives and to anticipate future market development rather than compensate for the imperfections in the current market environment. Micro economic theory provides a rationale for differentiated vertical measures based on the propositions that:

- As externalities in both a positive or negative sense will vary as a proportion of a firms' sales revenue, so compensation or taxation for these external effects should vary as a proportion of revenue.
- The potential for productivity growth and the learning period in terms of technology mastery will vary between technologies and thus between activities.
- The capacity to generate future productivity growth and technical change will also vary between firms using a given technology.

Since in theory there is no reason to expect uniformity between types of activity or firms, there is a case for selective or differentiated intervention. The most convincing objection to this is on practical grounds in terms of the difficulty of assessing the extent of current externalities or of forecasting where there is dynamic potential for the future. The strategic IP literature is ambivalent on the balance between horizontal and vertical measures with, for example, Hausmann and Rodrik (2005: 79) suggesting that "in principle, interventions should be as horizontal as possible and as sectoral as necessary". Their key point is that horizontal measures that enhance growth can span a range of sectors and therefore access to these should not be restricted selectively. However, they acknowledge that in some circumstances it may be easier to support specific sectors, both as a way of co-ordinating firms and of organising the provision of key public goods.

Vertical measures can be classed broadly into four groups:

- support for any firm operating a specific 'frontier' technology, deemed likely to create productivity growth and product innovation, as well as wider external spillovers, such as ICT, biotechnology, nanotechnology and so forth;
- support for any firm in specific sectors or sub-sectors with the potential for significant productivity growth and spillovers, where it is judged the economy can become internationally competitive;
- support for individual firms either as key foreign investors or 'national champions' operating in an area with significant potential for growth and competitiveness;
- support for sectors, sub-sectors or individual firms in need of rehabilitation and restructuring.

Past applications of IP have used all four approaches, and examples of such interventions can still be found. In the strategic IP literature the discussion on vertical incentives focuses on where to place 'strategic bets' on technologies, activities or firms that with support in the short term can become competitive in the longer term. As the bulk of these will be internationally traded, this discussion highlights the strategic choice of how far to invest to try to change an economy's comparative advantage more rapidly than the 'natural' change that the market itself would create. This is a problem of identifying where a country's long-term comparative advantage lies. Recent policy work has revived the application of the Domestic Resource Cost measure as an efficiency indicator to assess short-run comparative advantage with projected values of the indicator used to assess the longer-term position.[12]

What have governments done?

Formal industrial policy was out of favour with most governments during most of the period from the early 1980s to relatively recently, in part because it was associated with what were widely perceived to be failed policies of import substitution industrialisation behind relatively high barriers to imports. Nonetheless, whilst it was not described as IP, during this time the majority of governments continued to intervene in markets often in ways that affected the industrial sector in a highly selective manner. These forms of intervention were in the context of a much more open trade and investment policy, often involving Special Economic Zones and incentives to foreign investors, as well as differential credit and tax policies for domestic investors. In more recent years these interventions have been described as 'competitiveness policy' instead of IP and many countries have established programmes to raise competitiveness, usually focusing on incentives for R and D and innovation.

For example, for Latin America and the Caribbean, Peres (2006) surveys the competitiveness policies employed from the early 1980s to around 2005, a time when industrial policy per se was clearly not an acceptable policy topic. He reports that in seven countries public sector development banks carried out lending oriented towards specific targeted sectors and in 18 countries fiscal incentives differentiated by sector were on offer. Of note, however, is the fact that most countries did not give priority treatment to manufacturing, favouring instead parts of agriculture, tourism and various forms of services. He also reports that in the 1990s there were several instances of the active engagement of the private sector in pushing for policy reform through their industry associations, so the various measures applied were not necessarily government-driven. The Brazilian industrial policy launched in 2008 included seven programmes targeted at leading sectors (aeronautics, oil, natural gas and petrochemicals, bioethanol, mining, steel, pulp and paper and meat) with credit supplied by the key development bank (BNDES) (Peres and Primi, 2009: 38).

Similarly, in a survey of seven low and lower-middle income countries, Altenberg (2011: 71–72) identifies the relatively frequent use of IP, often on a selective basis. Modest success is identified for investments that built on existing specialisms – for example Tunisia's garments exports to the EU, Vietnam's exports of coffee, fish and shrimps, Ethiopia's cut-flower industry and Namibia's move into the export of inputs for cosmetics and pharmaceuticals. In these cases most of the policy initiatives appeared to be top-down from government bodies rather than through the type of participatory dialogue envisaged in the new strategic policy. For sub-Saharan Africa, South African experience with IP is discussed by Kaplan in this volume (Chapter 22). South Africa is an upper-middle income economy with a relatively large manufacturing sector and is thus quite different from the rest of the region. The use of IP in a low income African economy Ethiopia is discussed below.

The original authors of strategic IP have been used as consultants in a number of countries, including amongst others South Africa, Colombia and El Salvador. Evidence of the influence of the ideas of strategic policy can be found most clearly in Colombia. A high level national competitiveness commission composed of senior public and private sector members was created in 2007 and a private sector equivalent was also created in the same year, with Ricardo Hausmann as its main adviser. To develop a national competitiveness strategy, potential new export growth sectors were identified and bids for support were invited from the private sector through their industry associations based on detailed business plans. Subsequently this was matched by requests for innovative bids from mature export sectors. The government would fund 50 per cent of the cost of the best bids. The plans contained in the successful bids formed the basis of industry programmes of 'productive transformation' launched in 2008. The government stressed the difference between this approach operating through the private sector via industry associations and traditional IP as practised in Latin America, since the new policy was based on competitive bidding from the private sector and involved no tariff or tax concessions or subsidies, but rather an upfront commitment by the state to provide various public inputs in support of the sub-sectors concerned. However, other aspects of IP in Colombia less obviously follow the precepts of strategic policy with, it is suggested, continued differential support unrelated to any discernible economic rationale and largely driven by cronyism, particularly through profits tax concessions (Melendez and Perry, 2010).

Country cases

Empirical tests to establish the impact of any policy, let alone one as pervasive as IP, are always subject to empirical concerns regarding the counterfactual and difficulties in isolating the impact of the specific interventions of interest. In the case of the high growth East Asian economies typically seen as the star performers of IP – Korea and Taiwan – empirical tests have proved largely inconclusive.[13] Even where empirical analysis reveals a positive effect on growth this is modest.[14] Part of the problem is that many of the empirical tests focus on the broad impact of policy rather than on the effect of specific policy interventions, although in the last few years, rigorous impact evaluation methodology has been applied to specific measures in several Latin American countries with mixed results.[15]

Nonetheless, despite the ambiguity of empirical tests in East Asia, the fact that Korea and Taiwan had an active policy and also grew rapidly suggests an association. The ability of policy to stimulate high private investment in manufacturing, which subsequently led to productivity improvement and to export, is the key. Industrial policy interventions were not optimal *first best* policies (in the theoretical sense of minimising any negative or distortionary side effects). Individual policies may have led to resource misuse and high cost production and not all supported firms were profitable (for example, not all of the investment in the Korean Heavy and Chemical Industry Drive was successful). However, collectively these interventions raised the profitability of manufacturing, and the export incentives on offer ensured that the bias against exporting found in many other countries was largely absent in East Asia. Thus industrial policy (even when it was not well targeted in efficiency terms) succeeded in stimulating industrial investment.[16] In addition, IP also had a strong technology component in supporting product and process innovation though links between public research institutes and firms which assisted greatly the rapid catch-up of national firms.[17]

Other country examples are available which suggest (even if they do not prove rigorously) that measures applied flexibly to shift private investment into high productivity activities can impact significantly on growth. Below we discuss four country cases, which are less well known than other East Asian examples, where IP was not used to implement an import substitution strategy but an alternative approach engaging fully with the world market and which made support for, and a dialogue with, the private sector a key aspect of policy. In addition, as a contrast we also discuss the case of Ethiopia, a low income African economy which has explicitly pursued an industrialisation strategy modelled on aspects of the East Asian experience.

Singapore

IP in Singapore was driven from the highest level of government with a clear view of the need to upgrade and diversify the economy. Singapore was one of the first countries to set up Competitiveness Reports and to engage in detailed dialogue between government officials and the private sector on the obstacles to business.[18] The investment promotion agency, the Economic Development Board (EDB), pioneered the concept of the 'one-stop shop' and foreign company executives served as Board members of the EDB. At several points over the last 50 years strategic decisions were taken to develop new priority areas, based principally on foreign direct investment. In the late 1960s, Singapore was one of the first countries to develop export platforms for labour-intensive manufacturing in electronics. This was followed in the 1970s and 1980s by moves into higher skill activities within electronics and more capital-intensive activities like petro-chemicals. During the 1990s the focus was on upgrading value-chains (as in the Manufacturing 2000 Programme), particularly in electronics, chemicals and biomedical sciences. In more recent years the major focus has been on building a knowledge-based economy with R and D and innovation at the centre of the economy.

As an illustration, the Manufacturing 2000 Programme was based around industrial clusters in sub-sectors like chemicals, electronics and bio-medical sciences. The intention was to strengthen capacity at different points in the value-chain whether related to production, purchased inputs or supporting services. The Programme was based on detailed analysis across the value-chain for the various clusters to identify gaps that needed to be filled, with co-funding provided by the EDB for an equity stake in joint ventures and strategic activities.[19]

As well as offering foreign investors high standard infrastructure, a stable and welcoming investment climate and access to regional markets through free-trade agreements, these shifting priorities were backed by a series of IP interventions that aimed to steer private investment into priority areas. Firm-specific packages with differential rates of tax holidays, grants for new investment and support in terms of factory space were offered in the early years to encourage key firms to locate in Singapore. In addition the EDB played the role of venture capitalist in key start-ups. Critically important is the point that through fiscal incentives and the provision of a high standard infrastructure and human capital base, IP in Singapore encouraged multinational firms to reconfigure their operations on a regional basis by relocating production parts of the value-chain in lower wage economies of the region and concentrating activities at the higher end of the chain, in distribution, services and R and D in Singapore. The fact that many international firms have made Singapore their regional hub and have located their R and D development activity in the country is put down to the high standard research infrastructure facilities developed with public funding, as well as the fiscal incentives offer to encourage R and D within the country (Amsden *et al.*, 2001). Significantly there has been a turnover of foreign firms, as those in declining sub-sectors for Singapore have left as those in expanding sub-sectors have grown. The government implicitly has encouraged this process of entry and exit, since all incentives are for fixed periods.

Ireland

Success in Ireland in transforming the production structure through foreign investment has been less dramatic than in Singapore, and the reputation of the Celtic Tiger has been badly damaged by the recent economic crisis there, although this was due to problems in the financial sector, not in manufacturing.[20] The Irish government, like that of Singapore, had a clear view that it wished to upgrade the production structure, and since the 1970s the Industrial Development

Authority (IDA) has operated an aggressive promotional policy aimed at attracting foreign direct investment into new sub-sectors, principally electronics, software and pharmaceuticals. The fiscal incentives on offer combined automatic and discretionary incentives. The automatic feature was a low rate of profits tax, initially at 10 per cent and now at 12.5 per cent, which is the lowest rate in the EU and has been found to have been highly influential in international firms' location decision (Ruane and Görg, 1997). This low tax rate was combined with a series of double-taxation agreements to maximise the benefits to investing firms. However, in addition, as in Singapore, particular firms were targeted and offered discretionary packages. The IDA could negotiate upfront grants to cover a variable proportion of the planned investment with the grant conditional on the firm creating an agreed number of jobs. Ceilings on levels of grant per job were applied but within that range IDA had discretion in negotiations. All grant payments to firms were put in the public domain to ensure transparency. This heavy focus on foreign direct investment in the IP of both countries has been more controversial in Ireland in part because of the concern that unlike Singapore there has been much less technological depth − as measured by R and D expenditure to sales − in foreign investor operations in Ireland. This is an issue both for future productivity levels, but also critically because if the focus is on relatively low skill operations the investments become considerably more footloose, with a higher risk that they may move to lower wage or lower tax locations.

Malaysia

Malaysia shares some of the experience of the other two cases. It was also one of the countries that saw relatively early the potential for using foreign direct investment to develop an export-oriented manufacturing sector, particularly in electronics. Low wages and tax incentives rather than upfront grants were the principal incentive offered to foreign investors. There were also efforts in the 1980s to develop heavy and chemical industries, involving tax incentives and import protection, although these are generally regarded as being less successful, with the Proton car project being the best known failure. As in the other two cases, major efforts were made to develop more knowledge-intensive activities. In Malaysia the Multimedia Super Corridor project had the ambitious objective of making the country a regional and global leader in information technology-based services. Incentives on offer within the 75 kilometre corridor included hard infrastructure, transportation and fibre-optic telecommunications, as well as soft infrastructure in the form of both tax incentives and a supportive legal and regulatory environment, with legislative changes introduced to protect new investors.[21] Firms supported under the project were required to meet employment targets and to specify how they would transfer technology or knowledge or otherwise contribute to the development of the corridor. Eligible products and services could come from anywhere in the value-chain for multimedia activity − whether from content, distribution or the user environment. National and foreign firms were given equal treatment and in 2005 a majority of firms were locally owned.

IP in Malaysia was driven at the very highest political level with then Prime Minister Mahathir showing strong personal commitment to several of the modernisation schemes including the Multimedia Super Corridor. Strategic shifts were typically based on detailed Master Plans with the private sector closely involved in discussions over detailed implementation.[22] Development agencies in different regions were given the responsibility of not only promoting inward foreign investment, but also of linking these investors with local suppliers. In electronics, in some regions, such agencies have been credited with playing a key co-ordinating role in linking local suppliers with foreign investors and in this way deepening linkages within the economy (Oyelaran-Oyeyinka and Rasiah, 2009: Chap. 4). Significantly the government was willing to put public funds into strategic bets on new activities. These major initiatives started with support for palm oil production in the 1960s, which became highly successful but was perceived as highly risky at the time and was followed by support for electronics, automobiles, petrochemicals and more recently ICT and multimedia. As noted, not all of these efforts have been deemed successful but the willingness to take risks as part of a programme for structural change was one of the key characteristics of policy in Malaysia.

Chile

Despite its strong tradition of neoliberal economic policy since the Pinochet years, there has also been a modest and increasing use of interventionist measures to alter the allocation of resources. An early use of a strong vertical intervention was a policy package introduced by the military regime in the early 1970s to develop the forestry sector to exploit pine timber. This involved legal changes protecting land purchased under the scheme from subsequent expropriation, cash payments to developers of 75 per cent of the initial cost of planting and subsidised credit lines to forestry companies. The potential for pine forestry in Chile had been under discussion for a long time, but this nonetheless represented a strategic bet which most observers conclude was highly successful, as wood remains one of the country's major exports. Recent horizontal measures have included a range of innovation subsidies, largely grants but also tax incentives available across sub-sectors, borrowing guarantees for small enterprises with size of borrower the criterion for inclusion and a subsidy to new exports of up to 10 per cent of sales revenue (in lieu of a duty-drawback), which was dropped in 2003 as it did not comply with World Trade Organization rules.

In the period since 2005, vertical measures have become increasingly significant, although their overall scale relative to size of the economy is still modest. The National Council on Innovation and Competitiveness set up by the President in 2006 issued a report in 2007 highlighting priority sub-sectors that showed good prospects in world markets and were close to the country's current specialisation. In terms of incentives on offer, risk capital is available through Fundacion Chile, whose success in sponsoring the application of Norwegian technology to develop salmon exports was one of the key examples cited by Rodrik (2008) in his discussion of strategic bets. Fundacion Chile has focused on the application of foreign technology in six sub-sectors, mostly related to natural resources – principally marine, forestry and agribusiness.[23] In addition the main initiative sponsoring innovation Innova Chile has partly shifted to a sub-sectoral basis with a set of priority clusters. The other main vertical programme has been to attract foreign investment in ICT-related activities, covering software, hardware, multimedia, biotechnology and pharmaceuticals , through assistance in dealing with the bureaucracy and upfront cash grants for feasibility studies and, if the investment goes ahead, grants for land and buildings purchase, training and first year wage costs. These are negotiated on a case by case basis. The programme was launched originally in response to Intel's decision to locate in Costa Rica rather than Chile. It has clear similarities with the approach followed in Ireland but the funds available to the Ireland Development Agency have far exceeded those for the Chilean programme.

Ethiopia

The 2003 Industrial Development Strategy identified a wide range of priority areas – initially textiles and garments, meat processing, leather products, sugar processing, construction and micro and small enterprises. Following its success through private sector initiatives the cut-flower industry was added later along with some import substitution activities, so the approach was de facto almost horizontal. To meet the targets set for the priority sectors, support programmes included both market-based economic incentives and, as well as the provision of public inputs through capacity building, cluster development programmes and direct public investment in selected areas, where private investment was deemed inadequate (details of the strategy are in Gebreeyesus, 2013).

The incentives included credit on favourable terms (for example, long repayment periods and sub-market-clearing interest rates) and export credit guarantee loans. Funds were provided through the Development Bank of Ethiopia, and government-owned land was made available to firms in the selected sectors. In relation to capacity building a number of industry-specific institutions were created such as the Textile Industry Development Institute and the Leather Industry Development Institute to support and co-ordinate the private sector. These institutes have been implementing capacity building programmes to enhance competitiveness. In 2009 a 'benchmarking' initiative was launched in which selected enterprises in these sectors were to receive direct support and technical advice from relevant international firms under a government-funded programme. The respective sector Institutes were also to be twinned with an appropriate international institute to learn best-practice. The Leather Industry Development Institute has been twinned with the Indian Leather and Leather Products Institute, for example.

Support for the cut-flower cluster came after its initial success. Early entrants to the sector faced difficulties relating to logistics, and access to land and finance. In 2002 they formed an industry association to negotiate with the government and in 2003 the sector was added to the list of priorities and started to receive support. Important was access to government land at a low rental, which allowed the establishment of a location-based cluster, funding through the Development Bank of Ethiopia and government intervention to resolve the co-ordination problem in providing air freight facilities by initiating collaboration between exporters and Ethiopian Airlines, which reserved space for shipments of flowers to Europe. Manpower needs for specialists were partially addressed by one of the public universities being upgraded to offer specialist degree and diploma courses in floriculture. The industry association is seen as having an important role in the development of the sector by initiating industry standards, linking producers and assisting in export marketing, and the experience is now cited widely a successful state–business partnership.

Success in some of the other priority areas has been more difficult to achieve and economic efficiency in manufacturing remains low, with production costs high relative to competition from imports.[24] Thus despite an active IP the manufacturing sector remains small and uncompetitive, highlighting the difficulties of transforming some economies.

Conclusions

IP has seen a revival in recent years with concerns over globalisation and disappointment with the outcomes of market-oriented policy solutions. Most governments intervene in some way although how successful they have been has varied very considerably. However whilst there are many examples internationally of governments intervening to support individual sectors or sub-sectors through industrial or competitiveness policies there are relatively few examples of interventions that correspond precisely to the recommendations of the newer strategic policy. This is despite its theoretical base in the established precepts of micro economics and the influence of the key authors both as academics and advisers.

The four successful country cases noted above reveal several broad similarities:

- a committed government with a long-run vision on diversification and innovation and policy continuity in the operation of incentives;

- an awareness of the need to attract foreign investment and foreign technology to develop new activities;
- a willingness to offer a range of incentives, often as firm-specific packages;
- an outward-looking rather inward-looking trade policy which exposes recipient firms to competition in export markets.

These countries are relatively small, with high levels of education attainment and political stability, conditions that make them atypical, particularly in comparison with some of the poorer economies of sub-Saharan Africa. However, these examples reveal that IP has been operated successfully in countries with what most observers would judge to be a relatively good business environment, so that the two approaches of IP and business environment reform are not incompatible, even in economies where vertical interventions have been used, in some cases very extensively. Naturally, where inefficient or corrupt bureaucracies misuse interventions or are captured by sectional interests the outcomes are unlikely to be positive. IP, defined broadly, has a far better track record than popular financial discourse might suggest. Nonetheless, as the Ethiopian case reveals, in low income contexts there can be limits on its success.

Parts of this chapter are based on a Working Paper written for the Donor Committee for Enterprise Development (DCED) and available at www.enterprise-development.org. They are included here with the permission of the DCED, but reflect the views of the author and should not be regarded as representing the views of the DCED.

Notes

1 A fuller version of the arguments here is in Weiss (2013a), a paper written for the Donor Committee on Enterprise Development (DCED). The author acknowledges the support of DCED and is very grateful for their permission to reproduce the material here.
2 Examples of this tradition include Chang (2002), Amsden (1989, 2001), Wade (1990) and Johnson (1982). For analyses of the different dimensions of industrial policy, see Warwick (2013) and Weiss (2013b).
3 Y. Ojimi, the ex-Vice Minister for International Trade and Industry, in a speech before the OECD Industry Committee rationalised the approach as follows:

> MITI *decided to* establish in Japan industries which require intensive employment of capital and technology, industries that in consideration of comparative costs of production should be most inappropriate for Japan …. But from a long-range viewpoint these are precisely those industries where income elasticity of demand is high, technological progress is rapid and labour productivity rises fast.
>
> (OECD 1972: 15, emphasis added)

4 See Rodrik (2008) and McMillan and Rodrik (2011). The argument that manufacturing has a special role in growth is summarised in Weiss (2011). In two papers (Hausmann and Rodrik, 2005; Hausmann *et al.,* 2008) the authors restrict the attention of strategic IP to internationally tradable goods; a justification for this focus might be that productivity growth tends to be higher in traded than in non-traded sectors.
5 See for example the discussion of national systems of innovation in Nelson (1993) and the work of Lall (1992) on industrial capabilities.
6 Wade (2009) makes this point in arguing for the continued relevance of industrial policy in a low income economy context. As an illustration of how the system of guiding the market ('administrative guidance') worked in Taiwan Wade (1990: 207) describes how the Industrial Development Bureau the key body for IP would make frequent visits to individual firms in priority areas. If they judged a particular activity was one the country should develop (he cites dot matrix printers) they would initiate talks with a selected number of local firms to encourage them to look for joint venture partners, whilst indicating the sort of fiscal and other incentives the government could provide.

7　For example, Hausmann *et al.* (2008: 11) admit that development banks may need to be "instruments of strategic bets … as sources of ideas about high return activities … as the relevant actors will not come knocking on your door".

8　In economic theory the need for public inputs can arise because they are non-marketed or because they create external effects which benefit others, but not the original provider.

9　Horizontal incentives are sometimes referred to as 'functional' and vertical incentives as 'selective'. The horizontal/vertical and public input/market distinction has been used frequently in discussions on policy in Latin America; see Peres (2006) for example.

10　The overlap in this case is so great that it is possible to classify regulatory reform under either industrial policy or the business environment.

11　Note this is a separate argument from the case for labour subsidies based on the social effects of job creation.

12　Two of the early analyses of the domestic resource cost indicator are Krueger (1966) and Bruno (1972). Weiss (2013a) develops the argument on its use in the application of industrial policy.

13　See for example the analysis in World Bank (1993). Weiss (2011) Chapter 7 gives more details of the East Asian cases.

14　Analysis using an input–output framework suggests a positive but modest impact of an additional 0.5 percentage points to the annual growth rate of Korea in the 1970s and 1980s; for Taiwan the result is similar but slightly lower; see Noland and Pack (2003).

15　See Crespi *et al.* (2014).The perspective adopted is that where 'markets fail' the issue is not whether to intervene with a form of IP but how to intervene most effectively.

16　Weiss (2005) develops this argument.

17　Lee (2013) develops a theory of economic catch-up and links it with the technology policy pursued in East Asia.

18　The report of the Committee on Singapore's Competitiveness 1998 was written by a main committee with the support of five sub-committees and involved over 100 persons from the government, business and academic sectors. Similarly the Economic Review Committee Report 2003 on the restructuring of the economy involved consultation with over 1000 persons (Chia 2005).

19　See Chia (2005) and Lall (2003). Lall (2003) argues that the strategy allowed Singapore "to become the leading centre for hard disk production in the world with local considerable local linkages with advanced suppliers and R and D institutions".

20　In January 2008, Dani Rodrik wrote that the Irish economy "has become the envy of many others ever since it took off in the 1990's. Behind the miracle lies sensible fiscal policies, a wage accord with labour and − surprise, surprise − a range of industrial policies" − see Dani Rodrik's weblog (Rodrik, 2014). Apart from showing how even highly eminent observers can fail to spot problems the quote reveals the respect with which Irish industrial policy was held by one of the key authors of the new strategic industrial policy.

21　Aznam Yusof and Bhattasali (2008:21) describe this as a cluster approach to reform which they see as more realistic and effective than focusing on a single binding constraint.

22　How far the private sector initiated, as opposed to participated in, this process is less clear. Aznam Yusof and Bhattasali (2008) imply that key measures like the privatisation programme and the Multimedia Super Corridor were driven by government with the private sector only involved at the implementation not broad design stage.

23　Not all of the investments of Fundacion Chile have been profitable in social terms; see Agosin *et al.* (2010).

24　Dinh *et al.* (2012) includes an analysis of costs in a range of sectors relative to import prices from China.

Bibliography

Agosin, M. R., Larrain, C. and Grau, N. 2010. *Industrial Policy in Chile*. IDB Working Paper Series WP-170. Washington, DC: Inter-American Development Bank.

Altenburg, T. 2011. *Industrial Policy in Developing Countries: Overview and Lessons from Seven Country Cases*. GDI Discussion Paper 4/2011. Berlin: German Development Institute − downloaded from http://www.die-gdi.de/en/discussion-paper/article/industrial-policy-in-developing-countries-overview-and-lessons-from-seven-country-cases/

Amsden, A. 1989. *Asia's Next Giant: South Korea and Late Industrialization.* Oxford: Oxford University Press.

Amsden, A. 2001. *The Rise of "The Rest": Challenges to the West from Late Industrializing Economies.* Oxford: Oxford University Press.

Amsden, A., Chang, T. and Goto, A. 2001. *Do Foreign Companies Conduct R and D in Developing Countries?* ADB Institute Working Paper 14. Tokyo: Asian Development Bank Institute – downloaded from www.adbi.org

Aznam Yusof, Z. and Bhattasali, D. 2008. *Economic Growth and Development in Malaysia: Policy Making and Leadership.* Commission on Growth and Development Working Paper No. 27. Washington, DC: World Bank – downloaded from http://documents.worldbank.org/curated/en/2008/01/13186231/economic-growth-development-malaysia-policy-making-leadership

Bruno, M. 1972. Domestic Resource Cost and Effective Protection: Clarification and Synthesis. *Journal of Political Economy.* 80 (1): 16–33.

Chang, H-J. 2002. *Kicking Away the Ladder: Development Strategy in Historical Perspective.* London: Anthem Press.

Chia, S. Y. 2005. *The Singapore Model of Industrial Policy: Past Evolution and Current Thinking.* Paper presented at the Second LAEBA Annual Conference Buenos Aires 28–29 November 2005 Tokyo: Asian Development Bank Institute – downloaded from www.adbi.org

Crespi, G., Fernández-Arias, E. and Stein, E. (eds.). 2014. *Rethinking Productive Development: Sound Policies and Institutions for Economic Transformation.* Inter-American Development Bank, Palgrave Macmillan.

Dinh, H., Palmade, V., Chandra, V. and Cossar, F. 2012. *Light Manufacturing in Africa: Targeted Policies to Enhance Private Investment and Create Jobs.* Washington, DC: World Bank.

Gebreeyesus, M. 2013. *Industrial Policy and Development in Ethiopia: Evolution and Present Experimentation.* WIDER Working Paper 2013/125. Helsinki: United Nations University – World Institute for Development Economics Research.

Hausmann, R. and Rodrik, D. 2005. Self-Discovery in Development Strategy in El Salvador. *Economia* 6 (1) Fall: 43–101.

Hausmann, R., Rodrik, D. and Sabel, C. 2008. *Reconfiguring Industrial Policy: A Framework with an Application to South Africa.* CID Working Paper 168. Cambridge, MA: Harvard Kennedy School – Centre for International Development.

Johnson, C. 1982. *MITI and the Japanese Miracle: The Growth of Industrial Policy 1925–1975.* Stanford, CA: Stanford University Press.

Krueger, A. 1966. Some Economic Costs of Exchange Control: The Turkish Case. *Journal of Political Economy.* 74 (5) October: 466–480.

Lall, S. 1992. Technological Capabilities and Industrialisation. *World Development.* 20 (2): 165–186.

Lall, S. 2003. *Reinventing Industrial Strategy: The Role of Government Policy in Building Competitiveness.* QEH Working Paper 111, October. Oxford: Oxford University – Queen Elizabeth House – downloaded from http://www3.qeh.ox.ac.uk/pdf/qehwp/qehwps111.pdf

Lee, K. 2013. *Schumpeterian Analysis of Economic Catch-up.* Cambridge: Cambridge University Press.

Lin, J. and Chang, H-J. 2009. DPR Debate – Should Industrial Policy in Developing Countries Conform to Comparative Advantage of Defy It? A Debate Between Justin Lin and Ha-Joon Chang. *Development Policy Review.* 27 (5): 483–502.

McMillan, M. and Rodrik, D. 2011. *Globalization, Structural Change and Productivity Growth.* NBER Working Paper No. 17143. Cambridge, MA: National Bureau of Economic Research.

Melendez, M. and Perry, G. 2010. *Industrial Policies in Colombia.* IDB Working Paper WP-126, June. Washington, DC: Inter-American Development Bank.

Nelson, R. (ed.). 1993. *National Innovation Systems: A Comparative Analysis.* New York: Oxford University Press.

Noland, M. and Pack, H. 2003. *Industrial Policy in an Era of Globalization: Lessons from Asia.* Washington, DC: Institute for International Economics.

OECD. 1972. *The Industrial Policy of Japan.* Paris: Organisation for Economic Co-operation and Development.

Oyelaran-Oyeyinka, B. and Rasiah, R. 2009. *Uneven Paths to Development: Innovation and Learning in Asia and Africa.* Cheltenham: Edward Elgar.

Peres, W. 2006. The Slow Comeback of Industrial Policies in Latin America and the Caribbean. *CEPAL Review.* 88 April: 67–83 – downloadable from www.cepal.org

Peres, W. and Primi, A. 2009. Theory and Practice of Industrial Policy: Evidence from Latin American Experience. *Serie Desarrollo Productivo.* 187. Santiago, United Nations Economic Commission for Latin America and the Caribbean.

Rodrik, D. 2008. *Normalizing Industrial Policy*. Working Paper No. 3, Commission on Growth and Development. Washington, DC: World Bank.

Rodrik, D. 2014. How Ireland does It – January 17 2008. *Dani Rodrik's Weblog: Unconventional Thoughts on Economic Development and Globalization* – accessible at http://rodrik.typepad.com/dani_rodriks_weblog/2008/01/how-ireland-doe.html

Ruane, F. and Görg, H. 1997. *Reflections on Irish Industrial Policy Towards Foreign Investment*. Trinity Economic Paper Series Policy Paper 97/3. Dublin: Trinity College.

Wade, R. 1990. *Governing the Market: Economic Theory and the Role of Government in East Asian Industrialisation*. Princeton, NJ: Princeton University Press.

Wade, R. 2009. Rethinking Industrial Policy for Low Income Countries. *African Development Review*. 21 (2): 352–366.

Warwick, K. 2013. *Beyond Industrial Policy: Emerging Issues and New Trends*. OECD Science, Technology and Industry Policy Papers 2. Paris: Organisation for Economic Cooperation and Development.

Weiss, J. 2005. *Export Growth and Industrial Policy*. ADB Institute Discussion Paper 26. Tokyo: Asian Development Bank Institute – downloaded from www.adbi.org

Weiss, J. 2011. *The Economics of Industrial Development*. London: Routledge.

Weiss, J. 2013a. *Strategic Industrial Policy and Business Environment Reform: Are They Compatible?* DCED Working Paper. Donor Committee for Enterprise Development – downloadable from www.dced.org

Weiss, J. 2013b. Industrial Policy for the Twenty-First Century: Challenges for the Future. In Szirmai, A., Naude, W. and Alcorta, L. (eds.). *Pathways to Industrialisation in the Twenty-First Century: New Challenges and Emerging Paradigms*. WIDER Studies in Development Economics. Oxford: Oxford University Press.

World Bank. 1993. *The East Asian Miracle: Economic Growth and Public Policy*. Washington, DC: World Bank.

9

IMPORT SUBSTITUTING INDUSTRIALISATION (ISI)

Can or should we divorce industrialisation and trade strategies?

Frederick Nixson

Introduction

Import substituting industrialisation (hereafter ISI) was the dominant strategy of industrialisation over the period from the early twentieth century until the late 1970s in a large number of less developed countries (LDCs). However, there was no one single 'model' of ISI and it varied over time and place with respect to the role of the state, the role of foreign capital via direct foreign investment (DFI), the variety and type of incentives offered to investors, the sectors accorded priority in investment and the political circumstances reigning at the time. Nevertheless, there are sufficient similarities in the variety of experiences of ISI to allow key characteristics and common problems to be identified and a 'model' of ISI to be described. The loss of momentum in, and the not uncommon collapse of, the strategy often in conditions of dramatic economic, social and political turbulence, allow a close examination of the dynamics of the ISI process and the identification of alternative schools of thought that have been advanced to explain the apparent failure of ISI.

The establishment of import substituting industries was not always the result of a deliberate strategy. New market opportunities might emerge and investors, both local and foreign, might take advantage of them, with or without investment incentives. Some manufacturing activities, producing heavy, bulky low value commodities (for example building materials, furniture) would have a 'comparative advantage' – in part the result of poorly developed transport systems and consequent high transport costs – without the need for subsidies or protection (noted by Lewis, 1953).

In other cases the imposition of import duties, intended to generate revenue for the government, might have the unintended consequence of providing protection to domestic producers. In the 1960s and early-1970s, import duties were a significant proportion of total tax revenue in both East and West African economies (Livingstone and Ord, 1968; Livingstone *et al.,* 1987), with duties on food, beverages, tobacco, mineral fuels and manufactured goods contributing the major share of the total. It was noted by Ghai (1966: 46) that fiscal problems would arise in the future "as ambitious programmes of import substitution are launched and successfully carried through".

But the more typical experience or strategy of ISI was of the development of a highly protected domestic market within which infant import substituting industries would be protected from competing imports via tariff barriers, various quantitative restrictions and other measures. In the absence of the infants maturing into efficient, competitive 'adults', this led to the development of an inefficient, uncompetitive, import dependent, often capital-intensive, low value added manufacturing sector, the criticism of which led to a resurgent neo-classical economics school in the early-1970s. It is often forgotten, however, that many structuralist economists, especially in Latin America, were early critics of the outcomes of the ISI strategy and provided a powerful alternative critique to the orthodox neo-classical approach. We examine both these schools of thought below.

Three points which are complementary to, and sometimes overlap with, the two schools of thought identified above, need to be emphasised here:

1   Many development economists (and Lewis, 1953, 1984, was a leading exemplar) emphasised the need for ISI to be accompanied by the transformation of the agricultural sector and rising agricultural sector productivity, both to create new markets for the import substituting industries and to release resources to the manufacturing sector. Successful industrialisation depended on agricultural sector transformation.

2   Economic performance in general, and the performance of the manufacturing sector in particular, depended on the maintenance of macro-economic stability in the face of turbulent external conditions (Rodrik, 1992, 1996, 1999). Not only did this mean being able to react positively to instability in global commodity prices, to sudden changes in international capital flows and rising real interest rates, but also with respect to issues relating to problems of global indebtedness and exchange rate regimes. It also meant maintaining domestic macro-economic stability even in a 'stable' international environment, with respect to, for example, the management of monetary and fiscal policy, dealing with both monetary and structural factors fuelling inflationary pressures and maintaining some flexibility in exchange rate regimes.

3   Some economists developed longer-run stagnationist models of ISI. For example, Merhav (1969) argued that the reliance on large-scale imported technologies created monopolistic structures at low levels of development, which in turn forced diversification into increasingly suboptimal products (suboptimal relative to the size of the domestic market for these products) but which could not assure sustained growth because of the absence of a domestic capital goods sector.

The chapter is structured as follows. The second section provides a brief overview of the origins of ISI; the third discusses the measurement of the extent of actual and estimated ISI; the fourth describes the actual outcome of reliance on an ISI strategy, outlines alternative critiques and considers their implications for the balance of payments impact of ISI in particular; the fifth considers the impact of the ISI strategy on issues of longer-run growth and development and discusses the attempt to identify a 'post-ISI' model; the sixth enquires as to what lessons can be learned from the re-examination of the ISI experience. The seventh section draws a number of conclusions from the discussion.

The origins of ISI

ISI was initiated in many Latin American countries (for example, Brazil, Argentina, Mexico) as a response to the disruption caused by World War I (1914–18), the economic depression of the 1930s and World War II (1939–45), when imports were either not generally available or there was insufficient foreign exchange to pay for them. Domestically produced goods thus had to be substituted for those previously imported. The United Nations Economic Commission for Latin America (UNECLA) emphasised the need to accelerate industrialisation via ISI to promote employment, alleviate the balance of payments constraint and secure the benefits of technological progress (Colman and Nixson, 1994: Chap. 9, 294).

ISI became more widespread as an industrialisation strategy in the post-1945 world. In some cases it was stimulated by balance of payments difficulties ('saving' foreign exchange through import substitution was seen as an easier option than 'earning' foreign exchange through export promotion); in other cases, newly independent governments wishing to stimulate industrial development would impose protective tariffs and quantitative restrictions on imports of manufactured goods and force transnational corporations, or domestic enterprises previously engaged in the import of manufactured goods to establish domestic production facilities if they wished to protect their domestic market position (Kilby, 1969 provides support for this market protection hypothesis in his study of Nigerian industrialisation) (Colman and Nixson, 1994: Chap. 9).

India implemented the ISI strategy post-1947 (the year of Independence) and it became part of a planned development strategy from 1951 (the year of the first Five Year Plan) (Kiely, 2007: Chap. 3). Most North African and sub-Saharan economies incorporated ISI programmes into their development plans in the immediate post-Independence period (for example, Ghana, Nigeria, Uganda, Kenya, Zambia, Algeria) as did the South East Asian economies on the achievement of Independence (for example, Malaysia, Indonesia, Thailand, the Philippines) and a variety of other countries including Iran and Turkey. In some cases the imposition of international sanctions led to enforced ISI for essential commodities: for example in 1965 in the then Southern Rhodesia (later Zimbabwe) with the declaration of UDI (Unilateral Declaration of Independence), and in the apartheid-era South Africa.

There was also a theoretical rationale for ISI arising from the work of the Soviet economist G.A. Fel'dman, who in the 1920s (his work was published in Russian in 1928) focused attention on the relationship between the consumer goods and the producer goods industries in the plan for rapid economic growth (Ellman, 1979: Chap. 5; Post and Wright, 1989: Chap. 3; Jones, 1975: Chap. 5). This approach was further elaborated in the work of the Indian statistician, economist and planner P.C. Mahalanobis (1953) whose model developed in the 1950s provided part of the rationale for the Indian Planning Commission's draft Second Five-Year Plan (1956–60) (Colman and Nixson, 1994: Chap. 2; see also Bronfenbrenner, 1960/61; Nurkse, 1957).

The model developed by Raj and Sen (1961) highlights the issue of choice of sector and also illustrates that, at least in principle, the strategy of ISI has a number of options open to it. In the foreign exchange constrained economy, assumed by Raj and Sen, a number of options are open to the economic planners:

1   Foreign exchange can be used to import investment goods (for example, looms), raw materials, fuel, etc. to manufacture consumer goods (cloth, clothing).
2   Foreign exchange can be used to import capital goods (machine tools) to make both investment goods (looms), which in turn produce consumer goods (cloth, clothing) and to make intermediate goods (leather, rubber, steel, aluminium, etc.) and to develop domestic raw material supplies.
3   Foreign exchange can be used to import capital goods (machine tools) to make capital goods, which in turn can reproduce themselves and make investment goods, which in turn lead to the development of intermediate and consumer goods industries.

One advantage of the Raj and Sen (1961) approach is that it allows us to see ISI as a series of 'options' or 'stages'. In principle, any one of the three options can be selected and/or they can be seen as stages between which a transition must be achieved for an integrated industrial sector to be established.

It is option 3 above that demands high levels of saving and investment in order to produce the most rapid economic growth but also demands the greatest short-term sacrifices from the population. Smaller LDCs would presumably require some form of regional co-operation or integration for the successful implementation of this approach. Option 3, often referred to as a 'heavy industry' strategy, has been selected and implemented by very few countries: the Former Soviet Union in the 1920s–30s; India in its Second Five-Year Plan; the People's Republic of China in the 1950s, and with lip service paid to the strategy by one or two other countries which had 'socialist' development pretensions. The great majority of LDCs however, selected and implemented option 1, the implications of which we discuss below in the fourth section.

The measurement of ISI

ISI is relatively easy to define but very difficult to measure. Definitions vary from the substitution of domestically produced goods for those previously imported (Colman and Nixson, 1994: 293) to "a rise in the share of domestic products in a growing market for manufactured goods from all sources" (Clark, 1965: 87). Sutcliffe (1971: 255) argued that the term 'import substitution' should be used to cover "only the direct substitution of domestic production for the import of the same product". This definition is intuitively appealing; both to public sector planners and policy makers who need to identify new opportunities for investment and to the private sector on the look-out for new and profitable market opportunities. But the newly domestically produced good will generate a demand for intermediate inputs (steel, leather, textiles, chemicals, etc.) which in turn must either be imported or obtained from domestic sources if such exist. These newly required intermediate outputs were previously 'supplied' by the import of the final product and thus a definition of import substitution focusing only on the domestic production of the final product will lead to the underestimation of actual ISI, depending upon the level of development of the intermediate good sectors (Morley and Smith, 1970).

One of the earliest attempts to measure the extent of ISI was provided by Chenery (1960) who saw ISI as a 'cause' of economic growth which recommended itself as a development strategy. Historically, ISI had accompanied economic growth (Maizels, 1963), with the import content of supplies falling with the progress of industrialisation until it had reached a fairly mature level. But ISI could equally be a cause or a consequence of economic growth. Chenery's influential study of 1960 seemed to indicate that ISI was responsible for perhaps 50 per cent of industrial growth in a large number of countries. The analysis was based on a cross-section regression equation in which per capita value added in each industrial sector was regressed on per capita income and the population of the economy concerned. As income grew it was found that the industrial sector grew more rapidly than the rest of the economy and Chenery (1960) established the existence of a fairly uniform pattern of change in the production and import of industrial products.

For each industry, the positive deviation from proportional or 'normal' growth was calculated and Chenery (1960) estimated that ISI was responsible for 50 per cent of this positive deviation from proportionality. He also argued that import substitution arose largely out of changes in supply conditions, that is, from changes in comparative advantage, rather than from changes in demand.

Chenery's work was undoubtedly influential and was followed by more sophisticated and disaggregated analyses of patterns of structural change (summarized in Kirkpatrick *et al.*, 1984: Chap. 2). But it was also subject to criticism, and later estimates of the quantitative importance of ISI were significantly below the 1960 estimates.

The appeal of ISI as an industrialisation strategy becomes obvious when we consider the estimation of its potential. In principle, a product can be considered suitable for domestic production if the domestic market, as given by the value or volume of imports of that product, is equal to or greater than the minimum economic output of a manufacturing unit. Protection will be given to the domestic market so that the price of the imported product is equal to or greater than the price of the domestic product. Early examples of this approach in the context of East African industrialisation can be found in Brown (1961) and Newlyn (1965).

Actual outcomes and alternative critiques

We noted above in the second section that the great majority of LDCs commenced their ISI strategies with the 'easiest' option of using foreign exchange earnings to import investment goods (machines that make consumer or intermediate goods), raw materials and manufactured inputs to produce domestically the consumer goods previously imported (Nixson, 2005). Although most economies established some intermediate activities (iron and steel, cement, leather, etc.), these were often on a small scale, and very few economies moved on to the more complex stage of using foreign exchange to import capital goods (machines that make machines) as a basis for the establishment of large-scale, technologically sophisticated investment and intermediate goods sectors, which in turn would produce the intermediate and final goods to serve the domestic market and provide opportunities for the development of export-oriented industries. Exceptions to this generalisation included Brazil, Mexico, Republic of Korea, India and the People's Republic of China.

At one level, it is relatively straightforward to explain the failure to make this transition between 'stages' of the ISI process (Nixson, 2005). Many of the 'first stage' import substituting consumer goods industries used readily available or accessible technologies, did not require large investments, were not characterised by significant economies of scale and were often able to utilise locally available raw materials and other inputs and indigenous semi-skilled labour. Where transnational corporations (TNCs) were involved in this so-called 'tariff hopping' industrial development, capital, technology and skilled personnel were included in the DFI 'package'. As noted above, the domestic market was relatively easy to protect (encouraged no doubt by pressure both from local producers wishing to minimise competition in the domestic market and from TNCs wanting to protect their market position against rivals).

These early stage import substituting activities included a wide range of largely consumer together with some intermediate goods – basic foodstuffs, cigarettes and tobacco, soft drinks, beer and spirits, household durable goods, simple footwear and clothing, cosmetics, leather products, basic furniture, basic chemicals, some iron and steel products and building materials (cement, bricks, roofing materials, window frames, doors, etc.). In the 1970s, the larger and more advanced economies had moved into automobile assembly, the assembly of household electrical products and the larger-scale production of a wider range of intermediate goods. With due regard for individual country characteristics and variations in geography and climate however, the manufacturing sectors of the majority of LDCs would have closely resembled one another by the early-1970s.

In reality, it proved very difficult to move on to the next 'stage' of ISI. TNCs were less willing to shoulder the increased risks, economies of scale became more important, investment requirements increased, technology became more complex and sophisticated (and more closely guarded by its 'owners') and there was greater political uncertainty and social instability. The tendency noted by Felix (1964) was for a 'premature widening' of the consumer goods sector (automobile assembly being an obvious example), rather than a major move into 'second stage' activities. A wider range of more sophisticated consumer goods was produced which were in turn more dependent on the establishment or expansion of middle and upper income market demands, with implications for the national distribution of income.

The first 'stage' of ISI thus in reality gave rise to a timid and conservative industrialisation strategy that by its very nature was not sustainable in the longer run and would not lead to the structural transformation of the low income economy. There was general agreement in the literature that ISI had given rise to relatively small, inefficient, uncompetitive manufacturing sectors, highly protected, over-diversified, with substantial excess capacity, often utilising complex, capital-intensive technologies with low employment creation potential, and not surprisingly with limited export potential.

It appeared that the ISI strategy could stimulate economic growth for perhaps 8–12 years or thereabouts but then appeared to lose momentum (Nixson, 2005). In addition, in a number of high profile cases, the ISI strategy appeared to come to an end or collapse in conditions of economic collapse and social and political upheavals, of an often violent nature. Military coups (often several in fairly close succession) took place in major import substituters – Brazil, Argentina, Chile, Pakistan, Indonesia, the Philippines, Turkey, Thailand, Nigeria and Ghana – but notably not in Mexico, India or Malaysia, which nevertheless had their own internal upheavals. This is not of course to suggest that it was the apparent failure of ISI that was responsible for these upheavals, but there were clearly complex inter-relationships between the failure of development and industrialisation strategies to lead to sustained growth, structural transformation and significant employment opportunities, and the growing political instability and social unrest in many of these countries (Nixson, 2005).

Why did the strategy of ISI appear to fail so comprehensively? The dominant critique has been the neo-classical school which drew on mainstream, orthodox analysis. Heterodox economists can be grouped under the 'structuralist' umbrella and come from a variety of different (and often contradictory) perspectives – Latin American structuralism, dependency theory and Neo-Marxist. Although there are some similarities at the level of description of the various schools, they differ fundamentally in terms of their analytical perspectives and policy prescriptions.

The neo-classical school

What Toye (1987) has called the "Neo-Classical Counter-Revolution" in development economics can be linked to and dated with the critique of ISI provided by the study of Little *et al.* (1970). The essence of the neo-classical argument is that underdevelopment persists largely as a result of distorted and inefficient product and factor markets in low income economies. The main source of market imperfections is government intervention in the economy aimed in part at the rapid promotion of industrialisation (taken to mean ISI). Excessive protection of the domestic market, permitting or encouraging the overdevelopment of ISI, violates the principle of comparative advantage and gives rise to domestic market distortions and the misallocation of scarce resources. In domestic factor markets, labour is allegedly overvalued, capital is undervalued, thus encouraging the adoption of capital-intensive technologies and exacerbating problems of unemployment. The exchange rate is overvalued, favouring production for the domestic market (employing imported intermediate and investment goods for the import substituting sector) and creating a bias against exports (Colman and Nixson, 1994: Chap. 9).

The protection of the domestic industrial sector turns the domestic terms of trade against the agricultural sector, thus discouraging agricultural production and exports. The urban bias of ISI activities exacerbates rural–urban migration, and the use of capital-intensive technologies and the failure to generate adequate employment opportunities worsens existing inequalities in the distribution of income. Little *et al.* (1970) argue for the promotion, rather than the protection of industry.

The focus of the neo-classical critique on *exchange* rather than on *production* helps explain why in so many textbooks ISI is categorised as a trade strategy rather than as an industrialisation strategy (for example in Thirlwall, 2006: Chap. 16; Todaro and Smith, 2006: Chap. 13; Meier and Rauch, 2005: Chap. 3). The exception to this among the major texts is Szirmai (2005), but the widespread textbook approach explains why so much attention is paid to the balance of payments impact (see below).

The structuralist/dependency schools

Writers within the analytical frameworks provided by the structuralist or dependency schools locate their analyses, to a greater or lesser extent, within a broad historical, political economy framework. They are concerned with the 'distorted' structure of production and trade inherited from the colonial period, the penetration of the economy by foreign capital, its dependence on foreign technology, foreign indebtedness and the more general issues arising out of the ownership and control of the means of production and the social relations arising out of different ownership patterns (especially in the agricultural sector). Many structuralist critiques of the ISI process are avowedly reformist (rather than the more explicitly revolutionary Marxist critiques) but they nevertheless have virtually nothing in common with the neo-classical school. We return to the contributions of individual writers under this broad heading in the fifth section below.

ISI and the balance of payments

Two key assumptions appear to have been made by the early advocates of the ISI strategy. First, that the strategy would save foreign exchange and hence alleviate the balance of payments constraint (the domestic production of goods previously imported would 'capture' value added, and thus reduce the import bill). Second, that the ISI strategy would reduce the relative importance of foreign trade to the import substituting economy and thus make the economy less susceptible to external fluctuations.

Neither of these two assumptions held in practice. With respect to the first, there is no evidence that convincingly shows that foreign exchange savings result from ISI strategies Colman and Nixson, 1994: Chap. 9), although it is not clear that there is a single, unambiguous explanation for this perhaps surprising finding. Among a number of possible explanations are the following:

- Leff and Netto (1966) developed a model to illustrate the national income and balance of payments effects of an ISI programme in Brazil. Despite ISI policies and massive capital inflows, the balance of payments deficit was larger at the end of the model run than at the beginning. The dynamic income creating effects of ISI created additional demand for new imports and thus the imports stimulated by growing national income were greater than the foreign exchange saved by the domestic production of the goods previously imported.

- A second explanation focuses on the import intensity (the import content) of IS industries. Some categories of IS industries will have relatively high import contents (for example electrical consumer durable goods demanded by upper income groups) while basic consumer goods (for example lower value clothing, footwear, furniture) will have much lower import contents. The choice of industries in an ISI programme will thus in part determine the balance of payments effect (it will not explain the deficit worsening but it does help explain the less than expected improvement).
- Where foreign capital via DFI by TNCs is heavily involved in the ISI process, there will be outward flows of profit remittances and interest payments, royalty payments and the negative effects of transfer pricing in TNCs with significant amounts of intra-corporate trade (Vaitsos, 1974).
- From the neo-classical perspective, the development of the concept of the effective rate of protection (ERP) was an important analytical innovation (Corden, 1971). The ERP is defined as the percentage excess of domestic value added obtained through the imposition of tariffs and other protective devices on the product and its imported inputs, over what value added would have been at world prices (Little *et al.*, 1970). A tariff on an imported input will act as a tax, rather than as a protective device and will reduce the ERP of any individual product. In certain cases, protection is so high that domestic value added, measured at world prices, is negative (meaning that the value of the domestic industry's output at world prices is less than the cost of its imported inputs and so the activity costs the economy foreign exchange and is deemed fundamentally inefficient). In other cases protective tariffs on imports of the final product are less than the tariffs on imported inputs so that the final product receives 'negative protection' (for a detailed discussion see Greenaway and Milner, 1993: Chap. 5).
- Empirical estimates for a range of countries show large variations in ERPs (Soligo and Stern, 1965; Greenaway and Milner, 1993). Although there are conceptual and measurement problems in their estimation, ERP estimates are also useful from a non-neo-classical point of view in that they might indicate that tariffs are having perverse effects, that is, having the opposite effect from what is intended and either giving high levels of protection to low priority activities or taxing high priority ISI activities.
- The domestic resource cost (DRC) measure was also widely used by the neo-classical school as an indicator of the efficiency of resource allocation and utilisation. The DRC attempts to take "all distortions in a particular sector or production process into account when calculating the social opportunity cost of a given activity" (Greenaway and Milner, 1993: 98). The DRC can also be thought of "as indicating the comparative advantages of competing activities … the cost of saving foreign exchange (through import substitution) or acquiring foreign exchange (through exporting)" (Greenaway and Milner, 1993: 100). Estimated DRC ratios for the manufacturing sector in Madagascar indicate "considerable resource misallocation associated with commercial and industrial policy" (Greenaway and Milner, 1993: 106).
- We noted above (under 'The neo-classical school') that Little *et al.* (1970) argued that the process of ISI led to a redistribution of income from agriculture to industry and within industry from wages to profits. Income is thus redistributed towards those groups (the urban sector in general and middle and upper income groups in particular) that are likely, other things being equal, to have a higher marginal propensity to consume imported goods (and services) or domestically produced import-intensive products. We return to this point in the fifth section below.

The second major issue referred to above concerns the impact of ISI on the import ratio or coefficient (the ratio of total imports to GDP) and the changing composition of imports under the ISI regime. In general, as would be expected, the import ratio fell at least during the early stages of ISI, although this did not necessarily imply either a reduction in the absolute value or quantity of imports. A falling import ratio and, other things being equal, a stagnant or falling export ratio (given the alleged bias against exports referred to above) would imply that, adopting a conventional measure, the ISI economy was becoming less 'open', one of the reasons why the neo-classical school was advocating, *inter alia,* trade liberalisation measures to encourage the development of a less 'inward looking', more 'open', trade-oriented economy. However, it is likely that some minimum limit on imports will exist determined, *inter alia,* by the country's size and resource endowments, technological capabilities, level of development and rate of growth (Robock, 1970).

It can be argued, however, that of greater importance than the behaviour of the import ratio is the changing composition of imports as ISI proceeds. As noted above, ISI typically starts with the domestic production of previously imported consumer goods. The highest tariffs are imposed on the 'less essential' consumer goods imports and there is a perverse outcome that the least 'essential' imports are given the greatest incentive for domestic production (Colman and Nixson, 1994: Chap. 9). One result of this is that as ISI proceeds, the commodity composition of imports changes. Other things being equal, consumer goods imports become less important and imports of machinery, raw materials, intermediate goods and fuels become of greater importance. In other words, 'non-essential' consumer goods imports are replaced by 'essential' imports necessary to maintain domestic output and employment. ISI increases the proportion of domestic value added supported by imports and in these circumstances, any decline in foreign exchange availability (a decline in export receipts, reduced capital inflows, lower aid receipts) will lead to unplanned import curtailments and industrial recession. ISI, originally conceived as giving low income economies greater autonomy and flexibility, ironically had the opposite effect. As the eminent scholar of Brazil's development noted (Baer, 1972: 108) "the net result of ISI has been to place Latin American countries in a new and more dangerous dependency relationship with the more advanced industrial countries than ever before".

It is of course the case that consumer goods imports never disappear and ISI can never be complete (a point made by Weisskoff, 1980, in the context of Brazil). Technological developments lead to product innovation and the demand for new, sophisticated, higher technology products quickly spreads to middle and upper income groups in all countries – what has been referred to as the importation of substitutes, not just the substitution of imports. Personal computers and mobile phones are obvious examples – neither existed when the debates on ISI were taking place in the 1960s and 1970s. We return to these issues in sixth section below.

ISI and long-run growth and development

The issue that preoccupied many development economists in the 1960s and early-1970s was how to explain the apparent inability of the ISI process in the long run to continue to reduce the import ratio and thus sustain a rate of growth of GDP in excess of the growth of the capacity to import (remembering that many economists at this time were 'export pessimists'). As noted above, ISI appeared to be able to sustain high rates of growth in the short run, but with the economy experiencing stagnation at low levels of development once ISI opportunities appeared to have become exhausted and the foreign exchange constraints once again become dominant.

As indicated in the fourth section above, we can broadly distinguish between the neo-classical school and a variety of structuralist/dependency perspectives. Bruton (1970), a prominent neo-classical economist, argued that ISI distorted the economy, created activities alien to the economic and social environment of the community and created conditions which dampened productivity growth. Along with Little *et al.* (1970) he recommended the promotion rather than the protection of industry – uniform tariffs, currency realignments, subsidies to enterprises doing research, tax advantages or subsidies aimed at correcting market imperfections, provision of market information and so on. The neo-classical critique focused on the implementation of ISI, rather than the strategy itself (that is, there was nothing wrong as such with ISI as long as it was directed by market forces and led to a competitive, efficient manufacturing sector). In some respects, these early neo-classical critiques look remarkably similar to contemporary industrial policy strategies. As Ha-Joon Chang (2003) has noted, neo-classical development economists up to the early- to mid-1970s were not necessarily the neo-liberal, free market fundamentalists many of them later became.

The various structuralist/dependency schools tended to focus on the characteristics and dynamics of ISI itself, rather than on its implementation. Hirschman (1968) described the ISI process as "industrialisation by tightly separated stages" and as a "highly sequential affair". We have already noted ('ISI and the balance of payments' in the fourth section) that ISI typically began with the domestic production of consumer goods and then in principle moved on to the production of intermediate and capital goods. The United Nations Economic Commission for Latin America (UNECLA, 1964) in its major study of Brazil, had already argued that this process was virtually impossible to achieve. The substitution process might rather be "regarded as a building of which every storey must be erected simultaneously, although the degree of concentration on each varies from one period to another" (UNECLA, 1964: 5–6).

It is not generally appreciated or indeed acknowledged, that (mainly) Latin American structuralist economists produced critiques of ISI long before the neo-classical school (UNCTAD, 1964). UNECLA (1964) focused attention on the economic and social characteristics of the ISI model of development and argued that stagnation was the result of specific imbalances or disequilibria that occurred during ISI. These took the form of: sectoral imbalances (between the industrial and other sectors of the economy, and within the industrial sector, between consumer and capital goods); regional imbalances; social imbalances (unequal distribution of income and increasing social inequalities); and financial imbalances (the generation of inflationary pressures). The UNECLA argued for policies to reduce the duality of the system and expand the domestic market, improve infrastructural facilities, encourage investment in intermediate industries, the primary sector and underdeveloped areas and regions in order to achieve a 'fairer' distribution of income.

We have already discussed the balance of payments impact of ISI in the fourth section but we must briefly return to the issue. Felix (1968) noted that many Latin American economies had exhausted their capacity to lower the import coefficient and that insufficient attention had been paid to the changing composition of final demand under ISI. He argued that only by postulating a persistent import bias in the final demand mix could a levelling off of the import ratio be adequately explained. Rising incomes shifted demand towards products with high income elasticities of demand and higher import intensities than products with slow growing demand, but he argued further that import-biased demand shifts occurred independently of income changes, through an international demonstration effect:

> The import bias of consumer demand is positively related not merely to rising income but also to the rate of product innovation in advanced countries, to factors reducing information lags concerning such products in borrowing countries, and to the trend towards greater technological complexity of these products and their components.
>
> (Felix, 1968: 67)

Felix (1968) found empirical evidence from Argentina for the period 1953–60 to support this hypothesis and as noted above (under 'ISI and the balance of payments'), there appeared to be a shift in demand over time to 'dynamic' industries (with an income elasticity of demand greater than 1) with above-average import coefficients.

The 'post-ISI' model

The late-1960s and early-1970s saw the major Latin American economies attempt to re-orientate the direction of their development effort, from the so-called 'inward-looking' model of ISI to the so-called 'outward-looking' export-oriented industrialisation (EOI). In Mexico, for example, efforts were made from the early-1960s onwards to promote manufactured exports, via financial assistance to exporters; export duty reductions and other tax concessions; and in the border area with the USA, attempts were made to attract assembly activities for re-export back to the USA (Aspra, 1977). In Brazil, from the mid-1960s onwards, efforts were made to diversify and expand exports, the tax system was modernised to stimulate investment in priority sectors, the financial system was reformed, DFI was encouraged and large-scale government investment programmes were implemented to eliminate structural bottlenecks (in the power, transport and communications sectors, for example) (Bacha, 1977).

Whether 'post-ISI' should be seen as a strategy in its own right or simply a transitional stage between ISI and EOI remains an open, and perhaps no longer an important question, given the issues we raise briefly in the following section. But the 'post-ISI' model had a number of characteristics which make it worth considering:

- The state continued to play a key role in the development process, not to supplant but to encourage and sustain the process of capitalist development.
- DFI continued to be of critical importance, especially in the manufacturing sector.
- Efforts were made to diversify and expand exports (in contrast to the preceding market-based ISI focus on the domestic market).
- Greater reliance was placed on the market as the main allocator of resources, with emphasis placed on efficiency and growth, rather than equity.
- Reform and modernisation of the tax system, of capital markets and of exchange rate systems (to prevent the re-emergence of over-valued exchange rates) was adopted.

What can we learn from the experience of ISI?

The analysis of the historical experience of ISI is more than just an exercise in economic history. In part as a consequence of the 2008 global financial crisis, industrial policy has returned to the development agenda and there is no reason why import substitution will not be a part of that agenda in the future. It had long been recognised in the development literature (Robock, 1970) that ISI and EOI strategies were not mutually exclusive (a "false dichotomy" to use Robock's 1970 terminology) and Singer and Alizadeh (1988) had emphasised the need for an industrial strategy that combined the best elements of both ISI and EOI recognising, however, that the precise balance between the two would vary over time and that in the longer run, *ceteris paribus*, EOI would become relatively more important than ISI as the manufacturing sector became more competitive. Almost by definition, successful EOI gives rise to new opportunities for import substituting activities (Nixson, 2005).

We have emphasised that ISI should be seen as an industrialisation strategy rather than as a trade strategy (see fourth section). All economic activities, directly or indirectly, have implications for trade (creating new demands for imports, substituting for existing imports, creating new export opportunities, etc.) and of course trade policy is an important element in the ISI strategy. We cannot in reality separate industrial and trade policies but the former should not be made subservient to the latter (as is the case in the neo-classical perspective). What we can learn from the historical experience of ISI is that the indiscriminate blanket protection of the domestic market by an often irrational structure of tariffs and quantitative restrictions, and unfocused incentives may well encourage inefficiency, lack of competitiveness and complacency and corruption. From a political economy perspective, the strategy of ISI was clearly engineered to encourage or accelerate the emergence of an 'infant' capitalist class and/or to protect existing vested interests. In part to address these issues, Lall (1991) emphasised the need for selectivity in policy actions to encourage both static and dynamic efficiency in the manufacturing sector, although the capacity to design and implement an effective 'market friendly' industrial policy may well be absent in many low-income economies (Weiss, 2002).

Of course, many would argue that the global economy has undergone such profound changes in the past three decades as to make the so-called 'lessons' learnt from the experience of ISI irrelevant. The rise of China and other emerging economies, continued rapid technological change, the continued dominance of orthodox, neo-liberal economic policies, especially the liberalisation of trade and capital flows, and the apparent triumph of EOI, have all contributed to an often ill-defined notion of 'globalisation' that dominates the development discourse (Nixson, 2012). The emergence of so-called global value chains (GVCs) or global production networks (GPNs) in particular has led many to question the validity of state-centred development models (Henderson *et al.*, 2002) and to challenge the concept of 'late development' (Whittaker *et al.*, 2010).

It is clear that participation in GVCs/GPNs has led to rapid economic growth and structural change, rapid employment growth (especially for women) and the development of globally competitive activities in the manufacturing and other sectors of many emerging economies. But at least in the early stages of their evolution, GVCs/GPNs generate limited domestic value added (owing to the import intensity of these activities). Economies thus have to import substitute (raise the domestic content of exports) in order to raise their share of manufacturing value added. It is also the case that participation in GVCs/GPNs reduces the autonomy of the state in pursuing its own development goals, for example, in the creation of linkages with domestic enterprises, the introduction and absorption of new skills and technologies and the more general pursuit of poverty alleviation strategies. A third and more speculative point to bear in mind is the possibility of the 'reshoring' of assembly and processing activities back to their countries of origin with possible negative effects on the economies which they are leaving. There is some evidence that 'reshoring' is occurring, albeit on a limited scale at present (Nixson, 2012).

Participation in GVCs/GPNs should thus be seen as one part of an industrial strategy, in other words as a complement to other strategic initiatives, one of which might well require an increased focus on ISI and a reconsideration of infant industry arguments for the promotion of industry (Tribe, 2000, 2002). Given global economic and political uncertainties, it would be ill-advised to rule out revitalised ISI strategies at any time in the future and ignore the lessons that can in principle be learned from the experience of the twentieth century.

Conclusions

Rather than attempt to summarise the chapter, we focus on three major issues in this concluding section, namely: was the import substituting sector actually as inefficient and costly as has been argued by neo-classical economists? Did the focus on ISI prevent or delay the development of export-oriented manufacturing activities? In the absence of the neo-classical counter-revolution of the 1970s, could the continued development of the ISI sector have led to the emergence of industrial capitalism more widely in the LDCs?

It has always been recognised that the manufacturing sector displays the characteristics of an 'engine of growth', namely rapid productivity growth, dynamic increasing returns to scale, rapid technological change and dynamic externalities (Weiss, 1988). These effects are not captured by the static welfare analysis of the neo-classical paradigm and we are thus in danger of writing off the whole experience of ISI without recognising the likely economic benefits – limited but still important technology transfer and employment generation, limited although still important training of labour in both specific skills and the routine of factory work, the development of linkages with other sectors (especially agriculture), the development of the capacity to exploit potential export opportunities, both regionally and globally, the development of small- and medium-scale enterprises (SMEs) and the stimulation of entrepreneurship more generally. A more realistic and pragmatic appreciation of the importance and variety of infant industry development (Tribe, 2000) may well have led to the realisation of many of these benefits to offset the neo-classical charge of inefficiency.

The second issue follows from the above. Could and should these potential economic benefits have been better exploited and realised by an 'outward'-oriented, export-led industrialisation strategy? We have noted above that there was, or is, no necessary conflict between ISI and EOI (although superficially there appears to be). There are examples of economies that successfully made the transition between the two strategies – the Republic of Korea, Malaysia, Thailand, Brazil, Chile, Mexico, for example (Amann, 2000; Rodrik, 2007; Lee, 1997) – with the capabilities gained during the period of ISI leading, with appropriate and effective government policies, to the development in turn of export capabilities. It is a difficult, but not an impossible, transition to make.

This leads to the third issue. To what extent can it be argued that ISI, if it had survived the neo-liberal assault of the 1970s–80s, could have led to the establishment of the foundations of industrial capitalism in a larger number of the low-income economies than has actually occurred? Without wishing in any way to weaken or undermine structuralist and dependency critiques of ISI, and recognising that this is an impossible question to answer definitely, we can nevertheless speculate that the LDCs may have been better able to survive the global economic shocks of the mid- to late-1970s, and the recession of the early-1980s, with their industrial sectors still largely intact. With active and dynamic industrial policies (necessarily revised to take into account both the structuralist critiques of the 1960s–70s and the later work of Lall (1991) and Chang (1994), for example), sustained economic growth could have led to structural transformations not yet witnessed in the majority of these countries. The missing factor was the failure of developmental states to emerge and consolidate their power in this crucial period of global change.

References

Amann, E. 2000. *Economic Liberalization and Industrial Performance in Brazil*. Oxford: Oxford University Press.

Aspra, L.A. 1977. Import Substitution in Mexico: Past and Present. *World Development*. 5 (1/2): 111–123.

Bacha, E. 1977. Issues and Evidence on Recent Brazilian Economic Growth. *World Development*. 5 (1/2): 47–67.

Baer, W. 1972. Import Substitution and Industrialization in Latin America: Experiences and Interpretations. *Latin America Research Review*. 7 (1) Spring: 95–122.

Bronfenbrenner, M. 1960/61. A Simple Mahalanobis Development Model. *Economic Development and Cultural Change*. 9 (1): 45–51.

Brown, A.J. 1961. Economic Separatism Versus a Common Market in Developing Countries. *Yorkshire Bulletin of Economic and Social Research*. Part I – 13 (1): May: 33–40; Part II – 13 (2): November: 88–96.

Bruton, H.J. 1970. The Import-Substitution Strategy of Economic Development: A Survey. *Pakistan Development Review*. 10 (2) Summer: 123–146.

Chang, H-J. 1994. *The Political Economy of Industrial Policy*. London: Macmillan.

Chang, H-J. (ed.). 2003. *Rethinking Development Economics*. London: Anthem Press.

Chenery, H.B. 1960. Patterns of Industrial Growth. *American Economic Review*. 50 (4): 624–654.

Clark, P.G. 1965. *Development Planning in East Africa*. Nairobi: East African Publishing House.

Colman, D. and Nixson, F. 1994. *Economics of Change in Less Developed Countries* (3rd ed.). London: Harvester Wheatsheaf.

Corden, W.M. 1971. *The Theory of Protection*. Oxford: Clarendon Press.

Ellman, M. 1979. *Socialist Planning*. Cambridge: Cambridge University Press.

Felix, D. 1964. Monetarists, Structuralists and Import-Substituting Industrialisation: A Critical Appraisal. In Baer, W. and Kerstenetzky, I. (eds.). *Inflation and Growth in Latin America*. Homewood, IL: R. D. Irwin.

Felix, D. 1968. The dilemma of import substitution – Argentina. In Papanek, G.F. (ed.). *Development Policy: Theory and Practice*. Cambridge, MA: Harvard University Press.

Ghai, D.P. 1966. *Taxation for Development: A Case Study of Uganda*. Nairobi: East African Publishing House.

Greenaway, D. and Milner, C. 1993. *Trade and Industrial Policy in Developing Countries*. London: Macmillan.

Henderson, J., Dicken, P., Hess, M., Coe, N. and Wai-Chung Yeung, H. 2002. Global Production Networks and the Analysis of Economic Development. *Review of International Political Economy*. 9 (3) August: 436–464.

Hirschman, A.O. 1968. The Political Economy of Import-Substituting Industrialisation in Latin America. *Quarterly Journal of Economics*. 82 (1): 1–32.

Jones, H. 1975. *An Introduction to Modern Theories of Economic Growth*. London: Nelson.

Kilby, P. 1969. *Industrialisation in an Open Economy: Nigeria 1945–1966*. Cambridge: Cambridge University Press.

Kiely, R. 2007. *The New Political Economy of Development*. Basingstoke: Palgrave Macmillan.

Kirkpatrick, C.H., Lee, N. and Nixson, F.I. 1984. *Industrial Structure and Policy in Less Developed Countries*. London: George Allen and Unwin.

Lall, S. 1991. Explaining Industrial Success in the Developing World. In Balasubramanyam, V.N. and Lall, S. (eds.). *Current Issues in Development Economics*. London: Macmillan: 118–155.

Lee, J. 1997. The Maturation and Growth of Infant Industries: The Case of Korea. *World Development*. 25 (8) August: 1271–1281.

Leff, N.H. and Netto, A.D. 1966. Import Substitution, Foreign Investment and International Disequilibrium in Brazil. *Journal of Development Studies*. 2 (3): 218–233.

Lewis, W.A. 1953. *Report on Industrialisation and the Gold Coast*. Accra: Government Printing Department.

Lewis, W.A. 1984. Development Economics in the 1950s. In Meier, G.M. and Seers, D. (eds.). *Pioneers in Development*. New York: Oxford University Press for the World Bank.

Little, I., Scitovsky, T. and Scott, M. 1970. *Industry and Trade in Some Developing Countries*. Oxford: Oxford University Press.

Livingstone, I. and Ord, H.W. 1968. *An Introduction to Economics for East Africa*. Nairobi: Heinemann.

Livingstone, I., Teriba, O. and Diejomoah, V.P. 1987. *Economics for West Africa*, 2nd ed. Ibadan: Heinemann.

Mahalanobis, P.C. 1953. Some Observations on the Process of Growth of National Income. *Sankya*. 12. September: 307–312.

Maizels, A. 1963. *Industrial Growth and World Trade*. Cambridge: Cambridge University Press.

Meier, G. M. and Rauch, J. E. 2005. *Leading Issues in Economic Development*, 8th ed. Oxford: Oxford University Press.

Merhav, M. 1969. *Technological Dependence, Monopoly and Growth*. Oxford: Pergamon.

Morley, S.A. and Smith, G.W. 1970. On the Measurement of Import Substitution. *American Economic Review*. 60 (4): 728–735.

Newlyn W.T. 1965. Gains and Losses in the East African Common Market. *Yorkshire Bulletin of Economic and Social Research*. 17 (2) November: 130–138.

Nixson, F.I. 2005. Reflections on Industrialisation Strategies and Experiences in Sub-Saharan Africa. In Tribe, M., Thoburn, J. and Palmer-Jones, R. (eds.). *Development Economics and Social Justice: Essays in Honour of Ian Livingstone*. Aldershot: Ashgate: 235–249.

Nixson, F.I. 2012. The Dynamics of Global Value Chain Development: A BRICS Perspective. Paper prepared for the UNIDO project *The Untold Story: Structural Change for Poverty Reduction: The Case of the BRICs*. Vienna: UNIDO. August.

Nurkse, R. 1957. Reflections on India's Development Plan. *Quarterly Journal of Economics*. 71 (2): 188–204.

Post, K. and Wright, P. 1989. *Socialism and Underdevelopment*. London: Routledge.

Raj, K.N. and Sen, A.K. 1961. Alternative Patterns of Growth Under Conditions of Stagnant Export Earnings. *Oxford Economic Papers*. 13 (1): 43–52.

Robock, S.H. 1970. Industrialisation Through Import-Substitution or Export Industries: A False Dichotomy. In Markham, J.W. and Papanek, G.F. (eds.). *Industrial Organisation and Economic Development: In Honor of E.S. Mason*. Boston, MA: Houghton Mifflin.

Rodrik, D. 1992. Conceptual Issues in the Design of Trade Policy for Industrialization. *World Development*. 20 (3): 309–320.

Rodrik, D. 1996. Understanding Economic Policy Reform. *Journal of Economic Literature*. XXIV, March: 9–41.

Rodrik, D. 1999. *The New Global Economy and Developing Countries: Making Openness Work*. Policy Essay No. 24. Washington, DC: Overseas Development Council.

Rodrik, D. 2007. *One Economics: Many Recipes; Globalization, Institutions and Economic Growth*. Cambridge, MA: Princeton University Press.

Singer, H.W. and Alizadeh, P. 1988. Import Substitution Revisited in a Darkening External Environment. In Dell, S. (ed.). *Policies for Economic Development*. London: Macmillan.

Soligo, R. and Stern, J.J. 1965. Tariff Protection, Import Substitution and Investment Efficiency. *Pakistan Development Review*. 5 (2): 249–270.

Sutcliffe, R.B. 1971. *Industry and Underdevelopment*. London: Addison-Wesley.

Szirmai, A. 2005. *The Dynamics of Socio-Economic Development: An Introduction*. Cambridge: Cambridge University Press.

Thirlwall, A.P. 2006. *Growth and Development, with Special Reference to Developing Countries*, 8th ed. Basingstoke: Palgrave Macmillan.

Todaro, M. and Smith, S. 2006. *Economic Development*, 9th ed. Harlow: Pearson Addison Wesley.

Toye, J. 1987. *Dilemmas of Development*. Oxford: Basil Blackwell.

Tribe, M. 2000. The Concept of 'Infant Industry' in a Sub-Saharan African Context. In Jalilian, H., Tribe, M. and Weiss, J. (eds.). *Industrial Development and Policy in Africa: Issues of Deindustrialisation and Development Strategy*. Cheltenham: Edward Elgar: 30–57.

Tribe, M. 2002. An Overview of Manufacturing Development in Sub-Saharan Africa. In Belshaw, D. and Livingstone, I. (eds.). *Renewing Development in Sub-Saharan Africa: Policy, Performance and Prospects*. London: Routledge: 263–284.

UNCTAD (United Nations Conference on Trade and Development). 1964. *Towards a New Trade Policy for Development*. (The Prebisch Report). New York: United Nations.

UNECLA (United Nations Economic Commission for Latin America). 1964. The Growth and Decline of Import Substitution in Brazil. *Economic Bulletin for Latin America*. 9 (1).

Vaitsos, C. 1974. *Intercountry Income Distribution and Transnational Enterprises*. Oxford: Clarendon Press.

Weiss, J. 1988. *Industry in Developing Countries: Theory, Policy and Evidence*. London: Routledge.

Weiss, J. 2002. *Industrialisation and Globalisation: Theory and Evidence from Developing Countries*. London: Routledge.

Weisskoff, R. 1980. The Growth and Decline of Import Substitution in Brazil – Revisited. *World Development*. 8 (9): 647–675.

Whittaker, D.H., Zhu, T., Sturgeon, T., Tsai, M.H. and Okita, T. 2010. Compressed Development. *Studies in Comparative International Development*. 45 (4): 439–467.

10

NEW DIRECTIONS OF FOREIGN DIRECT INVESTMENT AND INDUSTRIAL DEVELOPMENT

Mo Yamin and Frederick Nixson

Introduction

Although they appear to be separate bodies of literature, and indeed are usually treated as such, there are in fact strong continuities and synergies between the largely critical heterogeneous literature of the 1960s and 1970s on foreign direct investment (FDI), multinational corporations (MNCs) and economic development, and the contemporary international business (IB) literature. In this context, this chapter has two basic objectives.

First, it presents a brief historical overview of how economists have attempted to deal with and understand the complex relationships between FDI and economic development, within a global economy which is itself undergoing fundamental transformations. Within this context, it attempts to identify issues that remain of importance for economic development within the contemporary global economy but which are in danger of not getting the attention that they deserve. The issues that remain on the 'development agenda' are: linkage creation (largely but not only within the context of global value chains (GVCs) (Kaplinsky, 2005 and Chapter 11, this volume); tax minimisation strategies, involving, *inter alia,* the manipulation of intra-corporate transfer prices (as identified by Vaitsos, 1974); conflicts of interest both within GVCs (given much emphasis in the relevant literature) and between MNCs more generally and the interests of host country governments or economic development broadly defined; technological development (no longer a discussion of 'appropriate technology' but often described as 'green technology'). Almost totally forgotten or ignored is the discussion of FDI as one dimension of oligopolistic competition (Knickerbocker, 1973; Yamin, 1983). Finally, the importance of industrial policy is returning to the development agenda, admittedly having been kept alive by, among others, Lall (1992, 2003); Chang (2003); Lin and Chang (2009); and Weiss (Chapter 8, this volume).

Second, the chapter presents an overview of the contemporary IB literature on the foreign investment activities of MNCs, highlighting a number of implications for the process and nature of economic development. The discipline of IB has naturally focused on the firm or the business as the focal unit of analysis and for a long time, inquiries beyond the firm as the unit of analysis, including its potential developmental impacts, were not in the core domain of IB. Nevertheless, since the 1970s, many writers have assumed that MNCs, by utilising their superior technological and other ownership advantages would in most cases impart significant economic benefits to host developing countries (a view challenged by heterodox, structuralist, neo-Marxist and dependency theorists, discussed in the following section). The orthodox view sees MNCs as 'engines of growth' (UNCTAD, 1992 for example).

This view has more recently become more qualified and the earlier optimism has tended to be replaced with a general realisation that the positive developmental impacts of FDI are not automatic, and that a reassessment of the impact must start with the recognition that the direction, purpose and impact of FDI is largely dependent on the strategy of the MNCs. In this chapter we argue that MNC strategies have undergone major changes and are currently not so much 'market seeking', but are rather mainly 'efficiency seeking', where access to cheap labour and other assets is a major driver of the investment. The large literature on linkage creation and assumed spill-over effects is directly relevant to any assessment of the impact of FDI on economic development (discussed in the fourth section). Although the notion of spill-overs has had a rather seductive appeal for advocates of FDI as a key input in the development process, the experience of most host developing economies has not been unambiguously positive in this respect.

The above discussion has so far implicitly focused on the more developed country MNCs (henceforth DMNCs), and on developing rather than 'emerging' host economies (see the third section below for a broad definition). The latter category of countries complicates the situation for at least two reasons. As hosts for DMNCs the situation in emerging economies increasingly demands that DMNCs must become 'strategic insiders' and correspondingly commit themselves to a longer-term engagement with these economies (Luo, 2007).

But it must also be recognised that 'emerging economies' are increasingly the home economies of MNCs (henceforth referred to as EMNCs). EMNCs possess distinctive capabilities and follow distinctive strategies of internationalisation (Ramamurti and Singh, 2009; Amsden, 2009; Williamson *et al.*, 2013). Recent data also confirm that EMNCs have begun significantly to challenge the previously dominant position of DMNCs in terms of their share of outward FDI (including flows to developing and emerging economies (see the third section).

The chapter is structured as follows: the following section reviews the literature from the 1960s through to the early-1980s and draws out what are considered to be the salient issues still relevant at the present time. The third section considers the more recent literature, including the IB literature and discusses the implications of that perspective for economic development. The focus in this section is on a selected number of issues, including the impact of FDI on economic growth, linkage creation and technological development. We argue that the need for selective and effective industrial policies in both 'emerging' and 'developing' economies is as great as it has ever been and we re-introduce and re-emphasise the importance of oligopoly and the nature of oligopolistic competition into the discussion.

A brief historical overview

At the outset it is useful to point out that contributors to the 'old' literature, irrespective of their differing standpoints, implicitly regarded MNCs and FDI outflows to be almost exclusively a developed economy phenomenon. There was a small literature that looked at the 'third world multinationals' (Lall, 1982) but these were small players and did not seriously challenge DMNCs. Thus in practical terms, the literature relating to the impact of FDI and development was overwhelmingly about the investment activities of DMNCs.

The impact of the DMNCs on economic development through FDI and technology transfer has always excited controversy and passionately held opposing views. The seminal work of Hymer (1976) argued that the ability to undertake FDI and other forms of 'international operations' were rooted in oligopolistic market power and that the key driver for international expansion was the retention of control over markets. Although Hymer's views have remained influential (Yamin, 2000), the dominant, orthodox, view has been that DMNCs were a response to 'natural' market imperfections largely rooted in transactions costs (Buckley and Casson, 1976). From this orthodox perspective, many writers (for example, Hood and Young, 1979) argued that the rise of DMNCs made possible the optimal use of global resources, and that the contribution that they could make was vital for the rapid growth and development of all economies. The rise of the DMNC was seen as a consequence of imperfections in both goods and factor markets, especially in the market for knowledge, and that the overcoming of such imperfections through the creation of internal markets *within* MNCs through FDI would permit the more efficient exploitation of global comparative advantage, allowing greater international specialisation and an increase in world economic welfare.

On the other hand, development economists of a largely heterodox outlook (including under this heading structuralists, dependency theorists and neo-Marxists) over a period covering approximately the late-1960s to the early-1990s, raised a number of key issues which remain of some concern in the 'age of globalisation'. At the radical end of this spectrum were those who argued that MNCs were the most important aspect of the imperialist penetration of the less developed countries (LDCs), heightening their dependency on the developed capitalist economies and deepening the process of dependent development. There was little unanimity among the more radical critics, however, and MNCs were variously alleged to underdevelop, to distort or block the development of the host less developed economy (Colman and Nixson, 1994: 342). We return to these arguments below.

Between these competing schools of thought were those economists who emphasised the potential contribution of DMNCs to development, but also recognised the impact of actual or potential conflict of interests on the distribution of the benefits and costs of FDI between the parent DMNC and the host economy. It was argued that within a modified global framework (an internationally negotiated Code of Conduct agreed to by DMNCs) and working within an agreed set of guidelines and rules, the MNC, through its ownership and control over technology, capital and marketing and managerial skills *could* make a unique contribution to the development effort. In other words, FDI was not a zero sum game – both sides could benefit but the distribution of the benefits (and costs) depended on the bargaining strength of the two sides.

From the huge literature that these competing theoretical perspectives and empirical studies generated, we can list what we consider to be the main issues and focal points of dispute:

- Why do LDCs want FDI? What does FDI provide that they lack or have an inadequate supply of?
- What effect does FDI have on the market structures (especially the manufacturing sector) of LDCs? Why is this important?
- Do DMNCs create linkages with other companies within the host LDC? Are those linkages with the subsidiaries of other DMNCs or with locally owned companies? If linkage creation is not adequate, what policies can LDC governments pursue to rectify the situation?
- How much net employment does FDI create? Does FDI have a positive or negative effect on other enterprises/sectors of the host economy? How can host country governments increase employment creation by DMNCs?
- Do DMNCs utilise or transfer labour- or capital-intensive technologies to host LDCs? What factors influence the types of technologies actually transferred by DMNCs? What is the real cost of those technologies and how are they paid for? Will the use of DMNC

technologies lead to 'technological dependence' and if so, what are the implications of this situation for sustained economic development and industrialisation?

- Should LDCs attempt to develop their own labour-intensive, 'appropriate' or 'intermediate' technologies?
- What is the impact on the host economies' balance of payments (BoPs) of FDI over time? How import-intensive is FDI in general? Do DMNCs encourage the export of manu-factured goods? If not, why not? What impact, over time, does FDI have on the capital account of the host economies' BoPs? That is, does FDI actually increase the capital available for investment in the host economies, does it utilise local capital already avail-able or does FDI lead to a drain of capital from the host economy (the de-capitalisation of the economy or a drain of surplus in neo-Marxist terminology)? What are the channels through which capital is 'drained' from the host economy? How important is the manipu-lation of transfer (intra-corporate) prices within the DMNC, used to avoid controls on the repatriation of profits, or as part of a global tax minimisation strategy?
- How profitable are DMNC activities in LDCs? Are they net contributors to government revenue or are the incentives/subsidies that governments might offer worth more than offset taxes paid?
- Does import substituting (or domestic market oriented) FDI lead to a transfer of tastes, creating a demand for luxury or 'inappropriate' products, with implications for patterns of consumption and income distribution in the host economy? Who is to decide what an 'inappropriate' product is?
- What are the implications for economic development of the emergence of MNCs from LDCs (highlighted for example, by Lall, 1982)? Would FDI by LDC MNCs have a more beneficial impact on the development process? This is an issue of special importance in the contemporary global economy (see the fourth section).
- What are the main conflicts of interest between DMNC parent companies and host LDC governments? Who will benefit most from the eventual resolution of such conflicts? What role might global codes of conduct play in conflict resolution and would such codes alter the balance of power between the two sides in favour of the LDCs?

The answers given to these questions were rarely definitive, unambiguous and acceptable to the majority of economists working in development. The questions posed, and the answers given, were largely influenced by the schools of thought and ideological perspectives within which they were framed. The orthodox, mainly neo-classical school of thought, from the mid-1970s onwards, emphasised the economic benefits of free markets (both for the factors of production and commodities) and minimum 'interference' by governments in those markets. Increasingly as the 1980s progressed, this view led to policies of trade liberalisation, privatisa-tion, liberalisation of capital flows and other supply-side measures aimed at freeing 'market forces'. Less attention was paid to the developmental impact of FDI, and DMNCs were unambiguously regarded as a 'good thing'.

As noted above, on the opposite side of the ideological barricades, structuralists, dependency theorists and neo-Marxists challenged many of these received ideas. From approximately the mid-1950s onwards, into the early-1990s, as we noted above, the various radical/heterodox schools of thought questioned the impact of FDI and were critical of the nature of the develop-ment process emerging. From Baran (1957) onwards, through the work of such writers as Frank (1967), Sunkel (1969, 1973), (Dos Santos (1973), Palma (1978) and Cardoso and Faletto (1979), there emerged a variety of critiques of 'dependent development' or 'underdevelopment' , par-ticularly associated with the work of Frank (1967) in which FDI/the DMNC played a leading role. Much of this work has been marginalised (or forgotten) by the continuing transformation of the global economy (see the fourth section), but some of the issues raised have re-emerged often under a different guise ('globalisation') or rediscovered in their original role.

From this perspective, we identify four areas of current concern:

- linkage creation (largely but not solely within the context of GVCs);
- issues related to the taxation of MNCs' profits and transfer pricing;
- conflicts of interest and changing bargaining powers and strategies;
- technological development.

The discussion of these issues raises the question of the role of industrial policy which we address below.

Global transformations: Changing strategies of DMNCs and the rise of EMNCs

The 'old' literature on the FDI-development nexus was largely informed by the debates and analytical frameworks of development studies: the strategies and structures of the organisations that undertook FDI – namely MNCs – were not a focal point of interest and did not receive detailed attention. By contrast, the IB perspective has a narrative that is mainly focused on the strategy and structural attributes of the MNC. As already noted, initially this literature largely ignored issues relating to host country impact and development, although there has been a partial change in this respect. In any case, it is our belief that understanding MNC strategy is necessary in terms of evaluating the impacts of FDI inflows. In particular, it is clearly important to consider the main changes in the global economic landscape since the last decades of the twentieth century. In part this is because 'globalisation', arguably the key aspect of global transformation in the last two to three decades, has complex and 'non-linear' impact effects vis-à-vis FDI flows. Broadly, it is necessary to differentiate between different groups of 'non-advanced' economies – namely less developed and 'emerging' countries (see below). Even more important, the emergence of EMNCs is a new element in any assessment of the impact of FDI flows on recipient countries, even though there is as yet little systematic empirical evidence on the impact of EMNC FDI flows on other emerging and less developed countries.

Accordingly, in this section we first consider the impact of globalisation on the strategies and structure of incumbent DMNCs. We follow this by broadly considering the impact of FDI flows to LDCs. We then consider the emergence and growth of a 'new breed' of MNCs based in emerging economies – the EMNCs.

Globalisation and the DMNCs

International business theory has argued that established or mature MNCs (DMNCs) confront a strategic tension between the need to adapt to the economic and institutional specificities of individual countries on the one hand, and benefiting from global integration on the other (Bartlett and Ghoshal, 1987). The need for national responsiveness, in part, has reflected an environment in which national governments, especially in less developed economies, had significantly more bargaining power in their dealings with DMNCs than they generally do today. The degree of bargaining power that national governments could exert was mainly dependent on how attractive their market was to potential incoming FDI, which in turn was a function of the size and the growth rate of their economies. However, compared to the present situation, all national governments had more policy scope to regulate access to the national economy and, in particular their markets.

Multinational expansion frequently took the form of establishing 'miniature replicas', i.e. subsidiaries which performed several value chain activities in an integrated way and whose main function was to adopt or adapt the products and technologies of the DMNC to the market and customer environment of the host countries. In the context of LDCs, 'miniature replicas' constituted a significant component of import substituting industrialisation (ISI) often behind protectionist barriers erected by governments. From the perspective of economic development, this 'old model' of (DMNC) expansion had a positive quality (Hirschman 1968 and Nixson Chapter 9 in this volume) – compared to what has replaced it – in encouraging linkages in the domestic economy and the development of industrialisation, although in practice the model's implementation was often mired in excessively protectionist policies.

Globalisation has brought a shift in the strategy and structure of multinationals. Two key drivers of globalisation have been the extensive liberalisation of trade and investment policies which have lowered the barriers to cross-border operations, and technological developments, particularly in the realm of information and communication technologies (ICT).

Since the early-1990s there has been a more or less uninterrupted process of lowering restrictions on FDI flows, especially the adoption of policies that promote FDI inflows. The change in policy stance has been particularly dramatic for less developed and emerging countries (see Table 10.1 and Figure 10.1).

Second, advances in technology, primarily through the application of ICT, have increased the scope for production modularity and facilitated a more effective management of the supply chain, wherein the imperatives for vertical integration via direct ownership have been significantly reduced. Leading DMNCs in many sectors have taken on the role of 'system integrators' whereby they increasingly focus on planning *and* coordinating the supply chain, rather than direct manufacture. The traditional ownership-based structures have been replaced with a complex and variegated web of relationships (UNCTAD, 2013: 143; Gereffi *et al.*, 2005). However, the relationships with core suppliers are far from being 'arms- length'. Nolan and co-authors (2002, 2008) show that in industries as diverse as aerospace, automobiles, telecom services and equipment, and beverages, the leading DMNCs ('system integrators') put intense pressure on leading (first tier) suppliers to invest large amounts in R&D to meet the assemblers' needs. The leading suppliers are invariably also large MNCs in their own right and transmit cost-reduction pressures further down the value chain. Thus contrary to suggestions that globalisation has led to a weakening of the 'visible hand' of corporate integration and control (Langlois, 2003), the advances in ICT and production modularity do not necessarily or unambiguously favour

Table 10.1 The dominance of pro-FDI policies in emerging and developing countries, 1991–2000

	1991	1992	1993	1994	1994	1996	1997	1998	1999	2000
Number of countries that introduced changes in their investment regimes	35	43	57	49	64	65	76	60	63	69
Number of regulatory changes	82	79	102	110	112	114	151	145	140	150
Of which:										
More favourable to FDI	80	79	101	108	106	98	135	136	131	147
Less favourable to FDI	2	0	1	2	6	16	16	9	9	3

Source: UNCTAD (2001: 6).

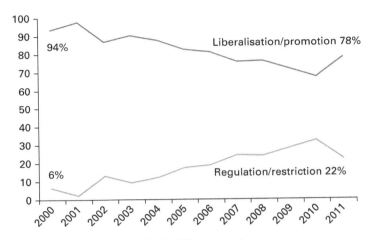

Figure 10.1　National regulatory changes, 2000–2011 (per cent).

Source: UNCTAD (2012: 76).

markets or relational contracting (Perrow, 2009); they can and do also enhance the ability of the visible hand, wielded by the system integrators to effectively coordinate a chain or network of independent but captive suppliers and service providers across many national borders. Other important recent contributions have also noted the growing control capabilities of leading DMNCs, pointing out that planning by the lead firms rather than ownership is the key criterion for delineation of firm boundaries (Buckley, 2009; Yamin, 2011).

Overall, the most important consequence of globalisation for DMNC strategy is that it has significantly enhanced strategic flexibility in terms of much greater locational choices as well as ownership policies. In the 'old', vertically integrated, structures much of the HQ's resources and energy was taken up by the organisational tussle with powerful and entrenched subsidiaries (Buckley and Ghauri, 2004; Yamin and Forsgren, 2006). The new structure has enhanced the power of the centre vis-à-vis subsidiaries and has, as a consequence, given the HQ greater scope and ability to effectively pursue 'asset seeking' strategies in addition to the 'efficiency seeking' (cost minimisation) strategies. In particular, DMNCs monitor and access strategic assets from 'dynamic' locations. Emerging markets are perceived as 'hard' to understand and yet they generate 'unconventional' innovative capabilities (Bhattacharya *et al.*, 2013) and have induced DMNCs to seek 'insider' positions in key business and policy/political networks within emerging markets (Luo, 2007).

FDI impacts on less developed countries

The current and somewhat variegated patterns of MNC involvements in emerging and less developed countries, whether through FDI or other 'non-equity' modalities, can only be understood in the context of the broader changes, indicated briefly above, in the strategy and structure of leading DMNCs. Consistent with this, the pattern of FDI flows to less developed countries is influenced by the fact that host countries fit into the strategic calculation of DMNCs as sites for resources rather than markets. This does not mean that DMNCs are not interested in markets but that, owing to low trade barriers, market access is no longer a major issue. Most LDCs have attracted FDI that entails the transfer of low technology and low value activities to be combined with the main location-bound advantages of these countries – cheap and unskilled labour, often with additional incentives offered by host governments such as tax exemptions (UNCTAD, 2003). FDI flows to LDCs are associated with LDC participation in DMNC-controlled production networks. LDCs usually enter these networks as 'junior' partners, as second and more frequently third tier suppliers, and therefore as sites for the production of a highly specified and narrow range of low value-adding activities.

Recent studies, focusing on the impact of FDI flows on economic growth in recipient LDCs, suggest at best ambiguous results with a weak or zero effect on economic growth (Narula and Driffield, 2012; Beugelsdijk *et al.*, 2008). One solid, consistent finding is the relevance of domestic absorptive capacity in recipient countries in the generation of positive productivity or growth effects (for example Xu, 2000; Crespo and Fontura, 2007). This in turn highlights the relevance of a strong infra-structure, especially in terms of cumulative investment in education and training (Yamin and Sinkovics, 2009).

The literature on spill-over effects of FDI in LDCs is consistent with the weak or ambiguous growth effects of FDI. Spill-overs are the 'external economy' associated with FDI: they can generate benefits that are not fully captured by the DMNC undertaking the investment. Thus in theory LDC firms gain productivity and knowledge advantages that they do not pay for in full (Zanfei, 2005). The mechanisms through which spill-overs can occur have been discussed at length in the literature (see for example Bloomström *et al.*, 2000; Kokko *et al.*, 2001) and include learning by doing and knowledge transfer to domestic firms and enhanced productivity growth through greater competition induced by the entry of the DMNC. The focus on the extent and depth of DMNC linkages in the host economy reflects an expectation of the enhanced possibility of knowledge and productivity benefits accruing to the DMNCs' local partners at a lower cost than would otherwise be the case. However, such an outcome is not automatic (Meyer and Sinani, 2009). The literature suggests only a positive correlation rather than a definite causal relationship between linkages and spill-overs. Generally, the greater the degree of an DMNCs' resource commitment to the host economy, through linkages and sourcing of intermediate inputs (Rodriquez-Clare, 1996), the greater the degree of positive spill-overs likely to occur in LDCs.

Only a few studies have examined DMNC affiliates in LDCs for the pattern of their linkages in host countries (UNCTAD, 2001). Available aggregate data on FDI flows relating to the last decades of the twentieth century provide clear indications that, although there was a very large influx by DMNCs into LDCs, these typically resulted in extremely 'shallow' levels and types of investment in these countries with a low or absent potential for positive spill-overs. Thus there is a sharp disparity between the shares of LDCs in inward FDI stocks/ flows by DMNCs on the one hand and their share of the number of foreign affiliates on the other. According to the World Investment Report (UNCTAD, 2001), 51.5 per cent of all DMNC affiliates were located in LDCs in the year 2000, accounting for only 24 per cent of FDI inflows. The developed countries by comparison accounted for 14 per cent of all affiliates but 73 per cent of FDI inflows (UNCTAD, 2001). The magnitude of the disparity is partly due to a change in the structure of DMNC activity in many LDCs, away from a focus on local markets (which would entail greater investment in support of integrated local production) and towards their incorporation into the rationalised global production networks that they control.

Studies focusing on individual LDCs conform to the above picture. A study by Edwards, Ahmad and Moss (2002) on DMNC subsidiaries in Malaysia shows that subsidiaries have low levels of decision-making autonomy and low integration into the Malaysian economy. Mirza and Giroud (2004), focusing on Vietnam, report very similar findings. Studies specifically focusing on linkages have generally observed that indigenous local firms are usually second or third, rather than first, tier suppliers vis-à-vis DMNCs (e.g. Sanchez-Ancochea, 2006). Luo's (2004) study of the determinants of resource commitments in emerging economies shows that resource commitment is lower when DMNC strategies stress cost rather than demand-side gains. A more recent study (Morrissey, 2012) provides strong confirmation of this in that where FDI is motivated by cost or efficiency motives rather than by market development, the linkage and spill-over effects are weak or non-existent. We will return to this issue of linkages in the next main section.

The rise of multinationals from emerging markets (EMNCs)

As we have already noted, an important feature of the contemporary global economic environment is that 'non-advanced' economies constitute more heterogeneous categories than has hitherto been the case, although lumping all non-advanced countries as 'the third world' or even as 'less developed' was never very accurate. However, it is probably the case that globalisation has accentuated such heterogeneities. The main distinction between 'emerging' and 'less developed' countries is that, compared to 'less developed countries', emerging countries benefit from a relatively long history of (import substituting) industrialisation and have gained greater technological skills – production and project execution capabilities as well as a modicum of innovation capabilities (Amsden, 2001; 2009). They also have more capable governments with a more assertive stance with respect to negotiating with DMNCs, and have for long followed mixed economy policies significantly at odds with the prescriptions of the 'Washington Consensus' (Fourcade, 2013). Broadly, emerging economies are considered to be 'catching up' with advanced economies while the rest ('less developed') are either not catching up or are even 'falling behind' (Dunning and Narula, 2004). As noted already, emerging economies have been a major destination for FDI flows and are considered as important not only as offshoring sites but also as strategic locations in terms of future market growth. According to the World Investment Report (UNCTAD, 2014) emerging economies occupy top positions as prospective markets for DMNCs' future investments (see Figure 10.2). It is also noteworthy that 'south–south' FDI flows have increased at a rapid pace over the last two decades, now accounting for 45 per cent of all FDI inflows into developing countries (see Figure 10.3). For the BRICS (Brazil, Russia, India, China and South Africa) the percentage of FDI flows to LDCs is 50 per cent (UNCTAD, 2013: 5).

The IB literature has paid growing attention to the rise and to the rapid growth of EMNCs, particularly those based in the larger emerging economies and notably the BRICS (Ramamurti and Singh, 2009; Williamson *et al.*, 2013).

Much of this discussion focuses on whether EMNCs are really 'different' from DMNCs, and thus whether new theories or concepts are needed to understand them. However, their development impact has not been a focal part of these discussions. Nevertheless a growing number of case studies have suggested that a significant portion of EMNCs may have capabilities and are relatively development 'friendly'. In fact recent research is suggestive of 'transformative' capabilities for some EMNCs in terms of upsetting the dominant 'rules of the global competition game' (Sinkovics *et al.*, 2014).

Specifically, it has been argued that EMNCs have capabilities that better "match the requirements of the new global environment" (Gao, 2011: 541). An important aspect of the new global economic environment is indeed the very rapidly growing domestic markets of emerging economies where the vast majority of the population is poor by developed country standards but who nevertheless constitute important markets – this being particularly true of China and India. The growing size of the low and middle income segments in the emerging economies

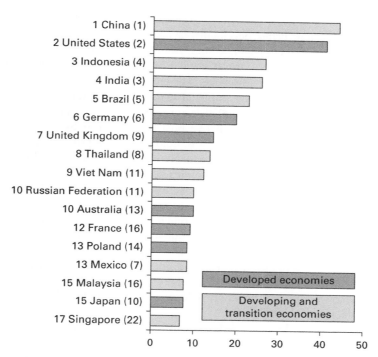

Figure 10.2 MNCs top prospective markets for 2014–2016 (% of respondents selecting market as top destination). (X) = 2013 ranking.

Source: UNCTAD (2014: 28).

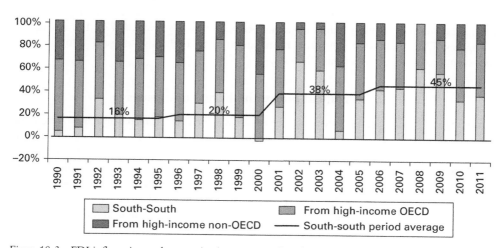

Figure 10.3 FDI inflows in south countries (percentage of total, 1990–2011).

Note: South–South FDI is calculated here as a residual after accounting for North inflows and North–South flows. See methodological notes in the original source for more detail.

Source: IADB (2013: 27), citing IADB Integration and Trade Sector based on UNCTAD, WDI and OECD FDI statistics.

has enabled EMNCs to generate distinctive capabilities that both challenge the dominance of DMNCs and have arguably 'better' developmental impacts.

In an important study focusing on China, Brandt and Thun (2010) demonstrate that the crucial battleground between DMNCs and EMNCs is increasingly the 'fight for the middle'. EMNCs have a decided advantage over DMNCs in this battle because they have brought forth innovations specifically "targeted at the middle or the base of the economic pyramid" (Williamson *et al.*, 2013: 296) that are perceived by consumers as being 'good enough' (Gadiesh *et al.*, 2007). The distinctive aspect of innovation by EMNCs, particularly for Chinese EMNCs, is cost innovation, that is, innovations that provide advanced technology and good quality products at low cost which are affordable by low and middle income segments in emerging and less developed countries (Williamson *et al.*, 2013: 67–69). The cost innovation and 'good enough' phenomena are not only about consumer goods. For example, in the medical diagnostics devices industry cost innovation has created a greater range of Chinese 'alternative' products priced much more cheaply than those of established foreign competitors (Little, 2008). As a consequence, a vastly expanded market has been developed among second tier hospitals and clinics (typically located in small towns in the hinterland) which were formerly unable to consider this class of equipment due to high costs. As Little (2008: 6) has noted: "The delivery of state-of-the-art-technology to the health system [as a whole] rather than only to leading research and teaching hospitals echoes the bottom of the pyramid sensibility".

The cost innovation capabilities of EMNCs have important implications for LDCs. EMNCs have developed expertise in mass production which they utilise to manufacture technologically standardised products in other emerging and developing markets where the demand for such items is huge. As noted by Luo and Tung (2007), their low-cost advantage enables EMNCs to offer a price that is very attractive to local consumers, thus enabling them to increase their market share vis-à-vis DMNCs that have been there for a long time. This echoes a much earlier debate in the development literature about 'appropriate' products and technologies and the potential benefits of 'south–south' trade and investment flows (Stewart, 1977). The emergence of the new EMNCs may be generating more 'appropriate' FDI flows to less developed countries compared to FDI flows from DMNCs.

Government policy and bargaining issues

In the second section we identified four broad areas which had attracted much attention and debate in the earlier literature on the developmental impact of FDI: (a) bargaining issues in general, with particular reference to (b) the taxation and transfer pricing strategies of MNCs which have implications both for the generation of government revenue and reinvestment strategies by the MNCs themselves, as well as of course having an impact on the BoPs of host economies; (c) linkage creation; and (d) technological development. We argue that these issues are at least as important today in the contemporary world as they were earlier. We address these issues under two headings: bargaining and taxation issues, and linkages and technological development.

Bargaining and taxation

The overall impact of globalisation on the bargaining power of LDC governments vis-à-vis MNCs has been complex and somewhat contradictory, in some respects enhancing bargaining power while in other respects undermining it. The complexity arises partly because unlike the earlier periods, bargaining is not necessarily always a dyadic interaction between host governments and incoming MNCs. As noted in the previous section, DMNCs have been instrumental in the disaggregation and dispersal of value activities and the formation of global production networks. Given the transnational scope of such networks, each LDC is hosting only a small portion of the overall production chain. Consequently, individual LDC governments' influence in the shaping of the governance of the network is relatively minor. Levy (2008) has argued that global production networks should be conceptualised as politically contested fields within which a number of stakeholders, in addition to governments, seek to exert influence. Non-governmental players, such as NGOs which also possess transnational perspectives, can be effective in capturing limited gains for disadvantaged groups, although fundamental asymmetries are bound to favour the nodal DMNCs (Levy, 2008: 957). Another relevant issue is that DMNCs have shown more ability (compared with LDC governments) to act collectively and to shape the macro-institutional environment in the global economy in their favour. The Uruguay round of the General Agreement on Trade and Tariffs (GATT) and the formation of the World Trade Organisation (WTO) are prime examples (Sell, 2003; Wade, 2003).

On the other hand, the emergence of EMNCs, with their distinctive capabilities and rapidly growing investment, should arguably enhance the bargaining power of governments in recipient LDCs. As we noted in the previous section, EMNCs are actively investing in other emerging and less developed countries with nearly half of all FDI inflows currently (i.e. 2014) being carried out by EMNCs. Thus in a quantitative sense, EMNCs are certainly a significant economic presence in many LDCs. Furthermore, although not all EMNCs' investments in LDCs are necessarily market seeking (Azmeh and Nadvi, 2014), it is at least plausible that, compared to DMNCs, EMNCs' investments in LDCs are, at least in principle, likely to be more market seeking, implying relatively more resource commitment to the local economy. This, per se, will improve the bargaining power of host governments as the investments are likely to be less 'foot-loose'. More obviously, however, the very emergence of EMNCs in various sectors simply enhances the level of competition and hence increases the options available to LDC governments. This echoes an earlier discussion relating to the positive effect of (oligopolistic) competition on the bargaining power of host economies vis-à-vis MNCs (Knickerbocker, 1973; Yamin, 1983).

Nevertheless, even though globalisation may intensify competition, thus enhancing the bargaining power of LDCs, we must take note of the fact that it also makes it easier for MNCs to avoid or 'wriggle out' of regulation. The key change is that enforcement costs with respect to regulation are now arguably higher than before and this imposes greater constraints on countries with weaker public administration infrastructures (Yamin and Sinkovics, 2009). A clear and very important illustration of this is the issue of taxation and transfer pricing. While tax avoidance by MNCs has a very long history (Shaxson, 2011), globalisation has arguably increased the opportunities for it while at the same time making its detection and regulation more demanding. Tax avoidance and transfer pricing practices are now more institutionalised than during the 1970s and 1980s. There are two related reasons for this. First, MNCs (and particularly the mature DMNCs) have greater experience and expertise with managing intra-firm resource transfers and more extensive financial planning capabilities. Arguably, these capabilities are the foundation for 'flexibility', which, as was argued earlier, is now the key plank in the strategy of DMNCs. Second, multinational accounting firms (notably the 'Big Four': Price Waterhouse Cooper, Ernst and Young, Deloitte & Touche and KPMG) have perfected a large array of complex and opaque 'tax planning' mechanisms for their MNC clients which challenge even the tax authorities of the USA and the UK (Sikka and Willmott, 2013; Palan *et al.*, 2010). The latest aggregate data strongly suggest that tax avoidance or 'planning' is a significant factor influencing the level and the direction of flows of company funds. Offshore finance mechanisms in FDI include mainly offshore financial centres or tax-havens and 'Special Purpose Entities' (SPEs). SPEs have been defined as: "Foreign affiliates that are established for a specific purpose (e.g. administration, management of foreign exchange risk, facilitation of financing of investment). ... They tend to be established in low tax countries. They have few employees and few non-financial assets" (UNCTAD, 2013: 15).

The 2013 World Investment Report (UNCTAD, 2013: 17) reports very high levels of fund movements during 2012 to and from offshore financial centres ($90bn) and SPEs ($600bn). One study estimates the annual revenue loss (during 2006–07) to LDC governments as a consequence of tax avoidance at around $500bn of which some $365bn is attributed to transfer pricing practices that shift profits from developing to developed countries (Sikka and Willmott, 2013 – citing Kar and Cartwright-Smith, 2008).

IB scholarship recognises, and some contributors even strongly emphasise, that globalisation actually reinforces the role of governments in generating positive impacts from incoming FDI. Thus Dunning and Narula (2004) argue that, rather paradoxically, even though globalisation is associated with greater mobility of knowledge-based 'ownership' advantages of MNCs, the competitive advantages of countries (and firms) increasingly depend on combining mobile assets with 'sticky' locational assets and capabilities. Government policy and support for the development of domestic absorptive capacity is crucial in ensuring positive impacts. Narula and Driffield (2012: 6) imply that governments in many LDCs have been unnecessarily lax in their approach towards incoming FDI, observing that "countries that have taken a 'generic' approach to FDI as a determinant of development have largely been disappointed". This implies that many governments have been slow in recognising that FDI cannot be considered as an automatic 'engine' of development. They have focused more on attracting FDI than on ensuring that benefits actually flow from it.

Linkages and technological development

Development economists have stressed the important link between technological learning and industrialisation (for example, Amsden, 1989). Technological learning is an evolutionary and incremental process always beset, to varying degrees, by market failure in that it is subject to significant risk, uncertainty, and externalities. These characteristics imply that, especially in the context of developing countries, technological learning processes cannot be left to market forces (Wade, 1990). The experience of the newly industrialised countries in East Asia confirmed the importance of industrial policy in supporting industrialisation and the development of technology capabilities. In particular, Korea and Taiwan followed a set of policies which allowed FDI only in selected sectors and exerted pressures for raising local content, technology diffusion and local subcontracting. Technological development was promoted not only by a set of 'functional' industrial policies (policies that benefit all economic activity) such as investment in education and the infrastructure, but also *selective* policies that promoted particular dynamic activities and industries (Lall and Teubal, 1998). The basis of such selectivity was the degree of difficulty of the learning and knowledge acquisition process, which reflected the premise that market forces would provide insufficient support for such activities. Reliance on market forces tends to encourage development along the existing structure of comparative advantage (typically promoting labour-intensive activities).

In the current context, in order to increase domestic value added (especially as part of GVCs), LDCs need to encourage linkage creation with domestic enterprises. Linkage creation is difficult (Lall, 1982) and requires effective government support and some measure of selective industrial policy which are however, more difficult in the context of WTO regulations, especially for smaller LDCs with weaker bargaining power.

The recent experience of most LDCs is that, in the absence of government pressure or the lure of capturing and securing greater market share in rapidly growing markets, DMNCs are unlikely to encourage linkage formation. LDC involvement in narrow-scope activities as a part of the global production networks has generated few local linkages (Miozzo and Yamin, 2012). The work of Amsden (1989, 2009; Amsden and Hikino, 1994) provides a useful benchmark for evaluating the impact of FDI and other types of involvement on technological progress in LDCs. This work has highlighted three levels of technological learning: production capability, project execution capability and innovative capability. Linkages with DMNCs often result in only limited technological learning, limited to production capability, and have been characterised as 'passive' learning (Nam and Li, 2013). Learning beyond production capability (project execution and innovative capability) requires 'active' learning by local firms and suppliers and is unlikely to be generated through knowledge transfer from global buyers (Nam and Li, 2013; Gentile-Ludeke and Giroud, 2012). Given the uncertainty and risk associated with technological learning, most suppliers are likely to avoid going along such a path unless there is a degree of sustained government support.

As noted above, WTO regulations restrict or prohibit the kinds of selective government support that technological development and effective linkage formation would require. In this connection, it is a useful reminder that WTO rules are somewhat more tolerant of government support for science and technology development than of 'industrial policy' in general. However, in the context of the 'catch-up' process this seems an artificial distinction. LDC learning necessarily requires a large degree of government support for what are now mature or 'traditional' industries or for activities in advanced capitalist countries. Ironically the very governments which are ardent advocates of liberal market policies have been very active in support of their own emerging science-based industries. The development of sectors such as biotechnology, microelectronics, information technology, new materials and nanotechnology has been strongly promoted and subsidised by the EU and US governments (Weiss, 2010). In effect this is industrial policy providing 'infant' industry protection and/or promotion for science-based industries (but which is labelled and legitimised as promoting science and technology, and which is therefore permitted by the WTO). Government regulations and industrial policy incentivising/compelling meaningful ('deep') linkage formation are also necessary to support the development of technological capabilities and learning through the development of industries that are infant or adolescent in the LDCs. Restricting this sort of industrial policy in LDCs is an aspect of "kicking away the ladder" (Chang, 2002; see also Weiss, Chapter 8 this volume).

Conclusions

In this chapter, we have focused on the changing role of the multinational corporation (MNC), and of foreign direct investment (FDI), in the transformation of both individual economies and of the global economy as a whole. 'Globalisation' is viewed as a process of economic change that is both a product of, and in turn has led to, significant transformations and non-linearities in the global economy. The 'non-advanced' economies of the so-called 'Third World' have become more heterogeneous and diversified in structure and character. Economic growth has led to significant structural change, and the accelerated acquisition of capabilities in a number of these countries which, combined with effective and targeted state interventions, have led to the development of what are now termed the 'emerging economies'. These economies, in turn, have in many cases developed their own MNCs which many commentators predict are already having, or are likely to have in the future, a more beneficial impact on the development process in host less developed countries (LDCs) than more 'traditional' advanced country MNC FDI.

It is now more difficult, and is potentially more misleading, to make broad generalisations about the process and nature of economic development and the specific impact of FDI on those processes. In many cases the broad 'meta theories' of the 1960s and 1970s, briefly referred to in the second section, now look rather dated if not plain 'wrong' in their predictions. However, we argue that there are key continuities between issues highlighted in the earlier literature and perceived real world problems in the contemporary global economy. A number of separable issues can be identified: the urgent need to create economic linkages between sectors and enterprises in host economies (in order to raise domestic value added and increase employment opportunities) and related issues of technological development, and issues relating to the tax avoidance or tax minimisation strategies pursued by many MNCs in part through the extensive use of tax-havens and the role played by, and the importance of, transfer price manipulation, in the achievement of those corporate objectives. We argue that the creation of an effective regulatory framework to deal with these problems requires a state structure with the political will, political power and competence to bargain effectively with MNCs, a set of conditions long recognised as essential but rarely achieved in practice. Although it has been out of fashion under the dictates of 'Washington Consensus' economic policies, industrial policy becomes even more important as the boundaries of the nation state are eroded by continued 'globalisation' and the autonomy of the state to pursue explicit development objectives is weakened.

The chapter briefly touched on the emergence of EMNCs, particularly Chinese enterprises which have distinct characteristics within the category of EMNCs and FDI. It is increasingly recognised that they have emerged in part as a result of strong government policies, and have developed innovative capabilities focused on the needs of low and middle income markets in the LDCs, in contradistinction to advanced country MNCs whose target tended to be higher income sectors. Whether or not the promise of EMNCs continuing to develop and serve these markets through innovative product innovation will be fulfilled remains to be seen. In the shorter run, these developments may continue as such enterprises develop and protect new markets, but this is a development which may not survive in the longer run. Future research will need to focus on the actual impact of emerging economy FDI on the development process in order to ascertain to what extent the 'promise' has been realised.

This chapter has focused mostly on FDI issues in the manufacturing sector in line with the theme of the present volume. However, we recognise that this focus has a number of unavoidable limitations. It does not discuss FDI in the extractive sectors of LDCs, which is of increasing importance to many sub-Saharan African economies where Chinese FDI has, in a relatively short space of time, established a commanding presence. It has also not dealt directly with the question of increased FDI flows into the service sectors of host economies and the impact of this on development (including so-called 'non-equity modes' of international production – refer to UNCTAD, 2011).

References

Amsden, A. H. 1989. *Asia's Next Giant: South Korea and Late Industrialization*. Oxford: Oxford University Press.

Amsden, A. H. 2001. *The Rise of 'the Rest': Challenges to the West from Late Industrialising Countries*. Oxford: Oxford University Press.

Amsden, A. H. 2009. Does Firm Ownership Matter? POEs vs. FOEs in the Developing World. In Ramamurti, R. and Singh, V. (eds.). *Emerging Multinationals from Emerging Markets*. Cambridge: Cambridge University Press.

Amsden, A. H. and Hikino, T. 1994. Project Execution Capability, Organizational Know-How and Conglomerate Corporate Growth in Late Industrialization. *Industrial and Corporate Change*. 3 (1): 111–147.

Azmeh, S. and Nadvi, K. 2014. Asian Firms and the Restructuring of Global Value Chains. *International Business Review*. 23 (4): 708–717.

Baran, P. 1957. *The Political Economy of Growth*. New York: Monthly Review Press.

Bartlett, C. A. and Ghoshal, S. 1987. Managing Across Borders: New Strategic Requirements. *Sloan Management Review*. 28 (4): 7–17.

Beugelsdijk, S., Smeets, R. and Zwinkels, R. 2008. The Impact of Horizontal and Vertical FDI on Host Country Economic Growth. *International Business Review*. 17 (4): 452–472.

Bhattacharya, A., Bradtke, T., Ermias, T., Haring-Smith, W., Lee, D., Leon, E., Meyer, M., Michael, D., Tratz, A., Ukon, M. and Waltermann, B. 2013. *Allies and Adversaries: 2013 Global Challengers*. Boston, MA: Boston Consulting Group.

Bloomström, M., Kokko, A. and Zejan, M. 2000. Host Country Competition, Labor Skills, and Technology Transfer by Multinationals. *Weltwirtschaftliches Archiv*. 130 (3): 521–533.

Brandt, L and Thun, E. 2010. The Fight for the Middle: Upgrading, Competition, and Industrial Development in China. *World Development*. 38 (11): 1555–1574.

Buckley, P. 2009. The Impact of the Global Factory on Economic Development. *Journal of World Business*. 44 (2): 131–143.

Buckley, P. and Casson, M. 1976. *The Future of the Multinational Firm*. London: Macmillan.

Buckley, P. and Ghauri, P. N. 2004. Globalisation, Economic Geography and the Strategy of Multinational Enterprises. *Journal of International Business Studies*. 35 (2): 81–98.

Cardoso, F. H. and Faletto, E. 1979. *Dependency and Development in Latin America*. Oakland: University of California Press.

Chang, H-J. 2002. *Kicking Away the Ladder: Development Strategy in Historical Perspective*. London: Anthem Press.

Chang, H-J. 2003. Trade and Industrial Policy Issues. In Chang, H-J. (ed.). *Rethinking Development Economics*. London: Anthem Press.

Colman, D. and Nixson, F. 1994. *Economics of Change in Less Developed Countries*, 3rd ed. Hemel Hempstead: Harvester Wheatsheaf.

Crespo, N. and Fontoura, M. 2007. Determinant Factors of FDI Spillovers – What do We Really Know? *World Development*. 35 (3): 410–425.

Dos Santos, T. 1973. The Crisis of Development Theory and the Problem of Dependence in Latin America. In Bernstein, H. (ed.). *Underdevelopment and Development*. Harmondsworth: Penguin.

Dunning, J. and Narula, R. 2004. *Multinationals and Industrial Competitiveness: A New Agenda*. Cheltenham: Edward Elgar.

Edwards, R., Ahmad, A. and Moss, S. 2002. Subsidiary Autonomy: The Case of Multinational Subsidiaries in Malaysia. *Journal of International Business Studies*. 33(1): 183–192.

Fourcade, M. 2013. The Material and Symbolic Construction of the BRICs: Reflections Inspired by the RIPE Special Issue. *Review of International Political Economy*. 20 (2): 256–267.

Frank, A. G. 1967. *Capitalism and Underdevelopment in Latin America*. New York: Monthly Review Press.

Gadiesh, O., Leung, P., and Vestring, T. 2007. The Battle for China's Good-Enough Market. *Harvard Business Review*. 85 (9): 71–94.

Gao, H. 2011. Changing the Rules of the Game in the New Era of Global Competition the Chinese Way. *Thunderbird International Business Review*. 53 (4): 539–542.

Gentile-Ludeke, S. and Giroud, A. 2012. Knowledge Transfer from TNCs and Upgrading of Domestic Firms: The Polish Automotive Sector. *World Development*. 40 (4): 796–807.

Gereffi, G., Humphrey, J. and Sturgeon, T. 2005. The Governance of Global Value Chains. *Review of International Political Economy*.12 (1): 78–104.

Hirschman, A. O. 1968. The Political Economy of Import-Substituting Industrialization in Latin America. *Quarterly Journal of Economics*. 82 (1): 1–32.

Hood, N. and Young, S. 1979. *The Economics of Multinational Enterprise*. London: Longman.

Hymer, S. 1976. *The International Operations of National Firms: A Study of Direct Foreign Investment*. Cambridge, MA: MIT Press.

IADB. 2013. *Trade and Integration Monitor*. Washington, DC: Inter-American Development Bank.

Kaplinsky, R. 2005. *Globalization, Poverty and Inequality: Between a Rock and a Hard Place*. Cambridge: Polity Press.

Kar, D. and Cartwright-Smith, D. 2008. *Illicit Financial Flows from Developing Countries: 2002–2006*. Washington, DC: Global Financial Integrity – accessible from www.gfintegrity.org

Knickerbocker, F. 1973. *Oligopolistic Reaction and Multinational Enterprise*. Boston, MA: Harvard School of Business Administration.

Kokko, A., Zejan, M. and Tansini, R. 2001. Trade Regimes and Spillover Effects of FDI: Evidence from Uruguay. *Weltwirtschaftliches Archiv*. 137 (1): 124–149.

Lall, S. 1982. The Emergence of Third World Multinationals: Indian Joint Ventures Overseas. *World Development*. 10 (2): 127–146.

Lall, S. 1992. Explaining Industrial Success in the Developing World. In Balasubramanyam, V. N. and Lall, S. (eds.). *Current Issues in Development Economics*. London: Macmillan.

Lall, S. 2003. Technology and Industrial Development in an Era of Globalization. In Chang, H-J. (ed.). *Rethinking Development Economics*. London: Anthem Press.

Lall, S. and Teubal, M. 1998. 'Market Stimulating' Technology Policies in Developing Countries: A Framework with Examples from East Asia. *World Development*. 26 (8): 1369–1385.

Langlois, R. N. 2003. The Vanishing Hand: The Changing Dynamics of Industrial Capitalism. *Industrial and Corporate Change*. 12 (2): 351–385.

Levy, D. L. 2008. Political Contestation in Global Production Networks. *Academy of Management Review*. 33 (4): 943–963.

Lin, J. and Chang, H-J. 2009. Should Industrial Policy in Developing Countries Conform to Comparative Advantage or Defy It? A Debate Between Justin Lin and Ha-Joon Chang. *Development Policy Review*. 27 (5): 483–502.

Little, S. 2008. Disruptive Dragons: Can China Change the Rules of Globalization's Game? *Prometheus*. 26 (4): 1–15.

Luo, Y. 2004. Building a Strong Foothold in an Emerging Market: A Link Between Resource Commitment and Environment Conditions. *Journal of Management Studies*. 41 (5): 749–773.

Luo, Y. 2007. From Foreign Investors to Strategic Insiders: Shifting Parameters, Prescriptions and Paradigms for MNCs in China. *Journal of World Business*. 42: 14–34.

Luo, Y. and Tung, R. L. 2007. International Expansion of Emerging Market Enterprises: A Springboard Perspective. *Journal of International Business Studies*. 38 (4): 481–498.

Meyer, K. E., and Sinani, E. 2009. When and Where Does Foreign Direct Investment Generate Positive Spillovers? A Meta-Analysis. *Journal of International Business Studies*. 40 (7): 1075–1094.

Miozzo, M. and Yamin, M. 2012. Institutional and Sectoral Determinants of Headquarters–Subsidiary Relationships: A Study of UK Service Multinationals in China, Korea, Brazil and Argentina. *Long Range Planning*. 45 (1): 16–40.

Mirza, H. and Giroud, A. 2004. Regionalization, Foreign Direct Investment and Poverty Reduction. *Journal of the Asia Pacific Economy*. 9 (2): 223–248.

Morrissey, O. 2012. FDI in Sub-Saharan Africa: Few Linkages, Fewer Spillovers. *European Journal of Development Research*. 24 (1): 26–31.

Nam, K-M. and Li, X. 2013. Out of Passivity: Potential Role of OFDI in IFDI-Based Learning Trajectory. *Industrial and Corporate Change*. 22(3): 711–743.

Narula, R. and Driffield, N. 2012. Does FDI Cause Development? The Ambiguity of the Evidence and Why it Matters. *European Journal of Development Research*. 24 (1): 1–7.

Nolan, P., Sutherland, D., and Zhang, J. 2002. The Challenge of the Global Business Revolution. *Contributions to Political Economy*. 21 (1): 91–110.

Nolan, P., Zhang, J. and Liu, C. 2008. The Global Business Revolution, the Cascade Effect, and the Challenge for Firms from Developing Countries. *Cambridge Journal of Economics*. 32 (1): 29–47.

Palan, R., Murphy, R. and Chavagneux, C. 2010. *Tax Havens: How Globalization Really Works*. Ithaca, NY: Cornell University Press.

Palma, G. 1978. Dependency: A Formal Theory of Underdevelopment or a Methodology for the Analysis of Concrete Situations of Underdevelopment? *World Development*. 6 (7/8) July/August: 881–924.

Perrow, C. 2009. Modeling Firms in the Global Economy. *Theory and Society*. 38 (3): 217–243.

Ramamurti, R., and Singh, J. V. (eds.). 2009. *Emerging Multinationals in Emerging Markets*. Cambridge: Cambridge University Press.

Rodriguez-Clare, A. 1996. Multinationals, Linkages, and Economic Development. *American Economic Review*. 86 (4): 852–873.

Sanchez-Ancochea, D. 2006. Development Trajectories and New Comparative Advantages: Costa Rica and the Dominican Republic Under Globalization. *World Development*. 34 (6): 996–1015.

Sell, S. K. 2003. *Private Power, Public Law: The Globalization of Intellectual Property Rights*. Cambridge: Cambridge University Press.

Shaxson, N. 2011. *Treasure Islands: Tax Havens and the Men Who Stole the World*. London: Bodley Head.

Sikka, P. and Willmott, H. 2013. The Tax Avoidance Industry: Accountancy Firms on the Make. *Critical Perspectives on International Business*. 9 (4): 415–443.

Sinkovics, R., Yamin, M., Nadvi, K. and Zhang, Y. 2014. Rising Powers from Emerging Markets – The Changing Face of International Business. *International Business Review*. 23 (4): 675–679.

Stewart, F. 1977. *Technology and Underdevelopment*. London: Macmillan.

Sunkel, O. 1969. National Development Policy and External Dependence in Latin America. *Journal of Development Studies*. 6 (1): 23–48.

Sunkel, O. 1973. The Pattern of Latin American Dependence. In Urquidi, V. and Thorp, R. (eds.). *Latin America in the International Economy*. London: Macmillan.

UNCTAD. 1992. *World Investment Report: Transnational Corporations as Engines of Growth*. New York: United Nations.

UNCTAD. 2001. *World Investment Report: Promoting Linkages*. New York: United Nations.

UNCTAD. 2003. *World Investment Report: FDI Policies for Development: National and International Perspectives*. New York: United Nations.

UNCTAD. 2011. *World Investment Report: Non-Equity Modes of International Production and Development*. New York: United Nations.

UNCTAD. 2012. *World Investment Report: Towards a New Generation of Investment Policies*. New York: United Nations.

UNCTAD. 2013. *World Investment Report: Global Value Chains and Trade for Development*. New York: United Nations.

UNCTAD. 2014. *World Investment Report: Investment in the Sustainable Development Goals*. New York: United Nations.

Vaitsos, C. 1974. *Intercountry Income Distribution and Transnational Enterprises*. Oxford: Clarendon Press.

Wade, R. 1990. *Governing the Market: Economic Theory and the Role of Government in East Asian Industrialization*. Princeton, NJ: Princeton University Press.

Wade, R. 2003. What Strategies are Viable for Developing Countries Today? The World Trade Organization and the Shrinking of 'Development Space'. *Review of International Political Economy*. 10 (4): 621–644.

Weiss, L. 2010. The State in the Economy: Neoliberal or Neo-Activist? In Morgan, G., Campbell, J., Crouch, C., Pedersen, O. K. and Whitley, R. (eds.). *The Oxford Handbook of Comparative Institutional Analysis*. Oxford: Oxford University Press.

Williamson, P., Ramamurti, R., Fleury, A. C. C. and Fleury, M. T. L. 2013. *The Competitive Advantage of Emerging Market Multinationals*. Cambridge: Cambridge University Press.

Xu, B. 2000. Multinational Enterprises, Technology Diffusion, and Host Country Productivity Growth. *Journal of Development Economics*. 62 (2): 477–493.

Yamin, M. 1983. Direct Foreign Investment as an Instrument of Corporate Rivalry: Theory and Evidence from the LDCs. In Kirkpatrick, C. H. and Nixson, F. I. (eds.). *The Industrialization of Less Developed Countries*. Manchester: Manchester University Press.

Yamin, M. 2000. A Critical Re-Evaluation of Hymer's Contribution to the Theory of International Operations. In Pitelis, C. and Sugden, R. (eds.). *The Nature of the Transnational Firm*. London: Routledge: 57–71.

Yamin, M. 2011. A Commentary on Peter Buckley's Writings on the Global Factory. *Management International Review*. 51 (2): 285–293.

Yamin, M. and Forsgren, M. 2006. Hymer's Analysis of the Multinational Organization: Power Retention and the Demise of the Federative MNE. *International Business Review*. 15 (2): 166–179.

Yamin, M. and Sinkovics, R. R. 2009. Infrastructure or Foreign Direct Investment? An Examination of the Implications of MNE Strategy for Economic Development. *Journal of World Business*. 44 (2): 144–157.

Zanfei, A. 2005. Globalization at Bay? Multinational Growth and Technology Spillover. *Critical Perspectives on International Business*. 1 (1): 5–17.

11

GLOBAL VALUE CHAINS IN MANUFACTURING INDUSTRY

Where they came from, where they are going and why this is important

Raphael Kaplinsky

Introduction

This chapter focuses on the origins and trajectories of global value chains (GVCs). It charts their growing significance in global trade and identifies a series of literatures which have documented their global extension. The early documentation of dispersed global production chains was often largely heuristic. By contrast, the contemporary GVC literature is rich in theory and provides important insights into the dynamics of the global economy and the distributional outcomes of growth. The transformation of a heuristic framework into an analytical framework draws on a series of theoretical constructs, namely on changing market dynamics, core competences and rent, chain governance, upgrading, embeddedness and the subordination of labour. The chapter concludes with a discussion of possible future dynamics in GVCs, and in particular the potential impact of the emergence of low and middle income rising powers.

Simple and complex definitions

In its simplest form the value chain (VC) describes the full range of activities which are required to bring a product or service from conception, through the different phases of production (involving a combination of physical transformation and the input of various producer services), delivery to final consumers, and final disposal after use. However, contemporary VCs are considerably richer and more complex than this simple description. The purpose of this chapter is to explore these complexities to show the analytical strengths of VC analysis and to show their dynamics.

The simple definition of a VC provided above is a heuristic device which recognises that the life cycle of production, distribution, consumption and recycling of a product (a physical good or a service) involves a series of discrete and linked activities. It enables us to identify and plot each of these discrete links in the chain. What it does not do is tell us anything about the coordination and governance of these diverse activities, the geography in which these activities are located, their consequences for the distribution of incomes in the chain, or their impact on the environment and their sustainability. Contemporary VC literature therefore seeks to move beyond heuristic description and to provide an analytical framework which helps us to understand the economic, social, political and environmental dynamics of the evolving global economy.

In this introductory discussion we briefly outline the significance of VCs in the global economy. Because many chains have become increasingly global in their geographical spread, we will therefore refer to these chains as global value chains. This is followed by a discussion of the diverse origins of the GVC. This helps us to understand the multiple ways in which the GVC concept is used in much of contemporary analytical and policy discourse. In the second section we focus on the analytical underpinnings of the GVC framework. The chapter concludes by focusing on the dynamics of contemporary GVCs.

The growth of GVCs

For reasons which will be elaborated in the second section below, two central features of VCs are that they have become increasingly fractured (a growing number of links in the chain) and that chains have become increasingly dispersed globally.

The depth of integration of the global economy has grown in recent decades. The ratio of global exports to global GDP more than doubled from 11.4 per cent in 1970 to 26.1 per cent in 2009 (falling back to 16 per cent in 2012 as a consequence of the global financial crisis).[1] A similar process of global integration occurred in the second half of the nineteenth century. This earlier phase of integration (which Baldwin refers to as the 'first great unbundling') involved trade in primary products and in final products driven by improvements in transport infrastructure (Baldwin, 2013). By contrast, the 'second great unbundling' after the 1950s saw a dramatic growth in the share of semi-processed intermediate products in global trade, increasingly driven in recent decades by advances in information and communications technology (for both IT and transportation systems). By 2012, more than half of total global merchandise exports and more than half of traded services comprised intermediate products and services (Miroudot *et al.*, 2009).

Behind these trends in global macro aggregates lies the restructuring of production in GVCs. The well-known example of the Apple iPhone4 illustrates this well. Each device retailed at just under $500 in the USA. The phones were exported from China – 'made in China' – at a unit price of $179. But the value added in China was only $6.50, with the balance made up of imported components (for example, valued at $80 from Korea, $25 from the US and $16 from Germany), and service payments to Apple in the USA (Xing and Detert, 2010).[2] This reflects a production chain in which parts are sourced from all over the world, are assembled under Apple's design in China and then branded and marketed in the USA and other final markets. A similar process of fragmented production can be observed in the aerospace sector (Figure 11.1).

This structure of production involving the fragmentation of production across national borders is evidenced in an increasing number of sectors, in both physical goods and services. So great is the resultant trade in intermediates, that according to the World Trade Organisation, 28 per cent ($5tr out of $19tr) of global trade in 2010 involved double-counting, that is the value of intermediate products traded directly across national borders and indirectly as subsequently incorporated in final products (UNCTAD, 2013a). Reflecting the pervasiveness of these GVCs, particularly in manufacturing, most of the world's exporting firms thus combine imported inputs into final products. In the USA in 2011, firms that both exported and imported accounted for 92.5 per cent of all US exports and 84.4 per cent of all imports (US Census Bureau News, 2013).

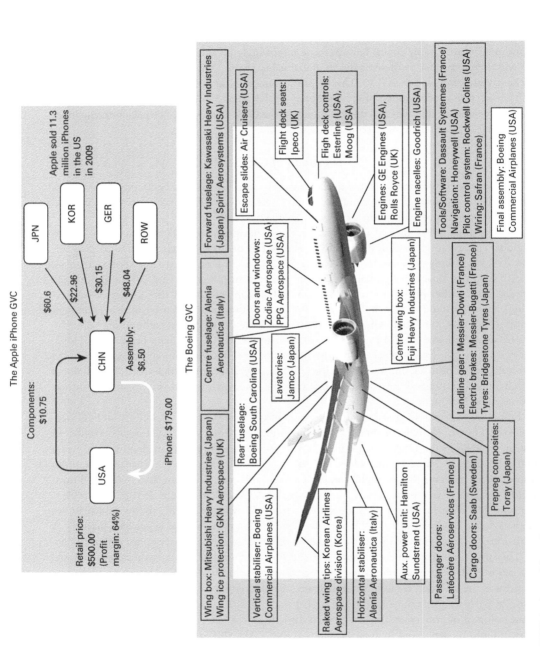

Figure 11.1 GVCs in the mobile and aerospace sectors.

The origins of the GVC framework[3]

There are multiple origins to the GVC framework, some of which developed independently and others which reflect a process of explicit cross-referencing. It is possible to identify six loosely clustered families of literature. The boundaries between these families are porous and some of the contributions span more than one category. The taxonomy is, however, useful since it helps to explain why it is that the GVC concept often means different things to different people and why GVC analysis is sometimes pursued under different labels.

The division of labour

A key component of the GVC framework is the decision between in-house versus outsourced production. The roots of this discussion can be traced back to Adam Smith. His discussion of the division of labour transcended the enterprise and identified the growing role of a specialised capital goods sector (Smith, 1776). Moving on a couple of centuries, Williamson's analysis of why large firms may wish to internalise production – a reduction in transaction costs, the asset-specificity of some inputs and the inability to trust suppliers – provides important insights into equity-based GVCs (Williamson, 1985). But not long after Williamson's contribution, it became increasingly clear that large firms were bent on outsourcing non-core-competences (Hamel and Prahalad, 1994). To protect themselves from the costs identified by Williamson they were required to engage in structured processes of supply chain management (Park *et al.*, 2013). The experience of Toyota in the management of suppliers in the 1970s and 1980s (Cusumano, 1985) was critical in the extension of supply chain management across a swathe of industries.

The filiere, the value stream and beneficiation

French scholars focused on the structure of value added in US agricultural research to analyse the processes of vertical integration and contract manufacturing in French agriculture during the 1960s (Raikes *et al.*, 2000). It was then applied in French colonial agricultural policy and, during the 1980s, to French industrial policy, particularly in electronics and telecommunications. Although there is no conceptual reason why this should have been the case, in general filiere analysis was confined to domestic value chains, thus stopping at national boundaries.

Although not linked in any explicit manner to the thinking on filieres, Porter's analysis of value streams after the mid 1980s (Porter, 1985, 1990) similarly identifies the significance of different links in the chain, but without any analysis of the power relations which this involves. His analysis of the value stream distinguished two important elements of modern value chain analysis.

First, he decomposed the different activities which occurred within particular links in the chain. Porter made the distinction between different *stages in the process of supply* (inbound logistics, operations, outbound logistics, marketing and sales, and after sales service), the *transformation of these inputs into outputs* (production, logistics, quality and continuous improvement processes) and the *support services the firm marshals to accomplish this task* (strategic planning, human resource management, technology development and procurement). Second, Porter observed that these functions need not be performed within a single link in the chain, but may be provided by other links (for example, by outsourcing). Confusingly, Porter refers to these essentially *intra-link* activities as the value chain and what is now referred to as the value chain (that is, all links in the chain), as the *value system*. Analysis which built on this tradition further confused nomenclature by characterising Porter's 'value system' (which we call the 'value chain') as the 'value stream' (Womack and Jones, 1996).

A complementary stream of analysis on the structure of value chains is the literature on the distribution of rents along primary commodity value chains. During the 1970s and 1980s, in part responding to the growing recognition of the significance of transfer pricing, UNCTAD produced a number of reports charting the successive links in a series of commodity chains (Girvan, 1987). The relevance to the GVC framework was the fact that VCs crossed national borders and that the chain analysis could be used to understand comparative income growth, industrial diversification and employment creation. More recently, there has been a growing clamour for downstream linkages to be deepened in Africa's primary commodity sectors (UNECA, 2013), flying under the banner of 'beneficiation', a phrase coined in South Africa around the time of majority rule in 1994 to reflect the desire to deepen the downstream processing of minerals.

World Systems Analysis and the New International Division of Labour

In many respects, World Systems Analysis (Hopkins and Wallerstein, 1986; Wallerstein, 2000; Arrighi and Drangel, 1986) closely resembles the UNCTAD programme with its focus on sequential stages of value accretion in global chains and a concern with the global distribution of incomes (Bair, 2009). But it goes beyond this largely filiere-based framework to extend the discussion to long term dynamics in the global economy. It traces back the global division of labour in the primary sector to the origins of capitalist-driven trade in the seventeenth century. Referring to these as 'global commodity chains', it draws on this division of labour and the associated income returns to identify a world of an unchanging hierarchy of core and peripheral economies.

Putting flesh to the World Systems Analysis and similarly influenced by a radical critique of contemporary capitalism, the New International Division of Labour literature led the way in documenting the global fragmentation of production in the apparel VC (Frobel *et al.*, 1980). It focused on the German clothing sector, describing how labour-intensive stages of the production process had been outsourced to low wage economies.

From global commodity chains to global value chains

Drawing explicitly on the World Systems literature, in 1994 Gereffi made the decisive contribution which transformed the heuristic and descriptive analysis of Porter and others into an analytical framework (Gereffi *et al.*, 1994). As such he can be anointed as 'parent' of modern GVC theory. His key contribution was to move the discussion from a description of *what is* to an explanation of *why it is* and *how it is*. Observing the increasingly rapid fracturing of value chains, and the cross-national nature of the consequent outsourcing, his central insight was to place power and governance at the centre of these trends. Gereffi argued that these chains – invariably involving complex relationships between independent firms – required coordination, and that this coordination had embedded power relations in which lead firms controlled the dynamics of the chain.

Gereffi characterised these governed chains as 'global commodity chains' and this remained the primary lexicon until 1999, when he and colleagues joined up with a group of British researchers working on globalisation (Gereffi *et al.*, 2001). This collaboration advanced the GVC analytical and research agenda in three important respects. First, recognising the ambiguity of the word 'commodities' (used both to describe primary commodities and undifferentiated factors, products and services), the nomenclature was altered from global *commodity* chains to global *value* chains. In so doing, it also sharpened the focus of the GVC framework on value creation, rents and their impact on distribution. Second, recognising the intensity of global competition and the danger that insertion in GVCs might in some cases lead to a race to the bottom, upgrading was placed at the centre of GVC analysis (Humphrey and Schmitz, 2000; Kaplinsky and Morris, 2001). Third, as the unfolding research focused increasingly on the role of labour in GVCs and the environmental and social sustainability of GVCs, a global consortium of researchers, working with large buyers in Europe, the International Labour Organization and non-government organisations, adopted a more synoptic and normatively driven approach addressing the extent of trade-offs between economic and social upgrading (Barrientos *et al.*, 2011; Capturing the Gains, 2014).

Global production networks and embeddedness

Once the analytical framework moved beyond the push-factors driving outsourcing and the extension of GVCs, more attention was given to the determinants of successful incorporation in economies where outsourced production was located. Why were some low income economies more gainfully inserted in value chains than others, and why did production often occur in locations involving agglomerated clusters of producers? Thus, it was argued, 'place' and 'agency' belong more centrally to the analysis of the dispersion of GVCs, as does an analysis of industrial districts and industrial regions (Schmitz and Nadvi, 1999). In so doing, the networks associated with GVCs have to be taken account. This led to a family of research on global production networks (GPNs) (Henderson *et al.*, 2002: Coe *et al.*, 2008; Rainnie *et al.*, 2011). More recently, the analysis of embeddedness has been explicitly linked to the International Business literature on FDI, and has focused on the extent to which the embeddedness of subcontracting firms contributes to the sustainability of subcontracted production in footloose GVCs (Morris and Staritz, 2014 – refer to 'Embeddedness' below). Although often describing itself as presenting an independent perspective, in reality, good GPN research focuses also on vertical chain relationships, and good GVC research also addresses the embeddedness of local actors and the importance of national and regional systems of innovation (Parrilli *et al.*, 2013).

Economists[4]

Arriving relatively late on the stage (and around the turn of the millennium), economists began to take note of the significance of GVCs. Their concern was driven by the recognition that the aggregates which they were using for measuring production and trade were increasingly meaningless in a world of fragmentation. Moreover, they had come to recognise that world trade was increasingly dominated by trade in intermediate rather than finished products and that firms and countries were specialising in capabilities rather than products. This trend towards capability-specialisation poses a particular challenge to the Heckscher–Ohlin framework which has long dominated trade theory and which assumes that international competitiveness is explained by factor endowments.

There have been a variety of attempts to measure the importance of intermediates in trade (Miroudot *et al.*, 2009: Sturgeon and Memedovic, 2010),[5] and the difference between 'gross' and 'net' aggregates in measures of 'vertical specialization' (Hummels *et al.*, 2001). Extensive use is made of input–output analysis in the literature charting the complex flows of intermediate products in GVCs, albeit hindered by the fact that the sector classifications used in even the most disaggregated input–output tables are too blunt to capture the sorts of flows evidenced in the detailed analysis of the iPhone described above. Drawing on these input–output tables, the World Trade Organisation and the OECD are together developing methodologies to capture these trends.[6] At the time of writing these are early attempts at cleaning up trade data, but they do hold potential and are crucial to a better understanding of the evolving nature of global trade and production for trade, particularly in relation to manufacturing (refer to UNCTAD, 2013b).

The analytical underpinning of GVC analysis

As observed earlier, the heuristic family of GVC analysis is strong on description and light on analysis. It tells us little of the why, the where and the how of GVCs, and does not provide substantive insights into policy. *Per contra*, by being analytically rooted, contemporary GVC literature is more useful in helping us to understand the dynamics of the global economy. In this section we consider six of these analytical underpinnings – the nature of final markets; core competences, outsourcing and rents, chain governance; the complexity of upgrading, embeddedness in production, and the subordination of labour as a determinant of location.

Market dynamics

The textbooks driving mainstream economic theory begin with an analysis of markets made up of arms-length transactions between anonymous partners. They also assume homogeneity and substitutability of undifferentiated output. Taken together these two assumptions were helpful in explaining industrial structure in the global economy until the late 1960s. This reflected a supply-pushed world in which producers sold into price-sensitive, predictable and relatively unchanging final markets generally characterised (in the post World War Two environment) by a shortage of supply.

This final market structure in the now high income markets began to change radically from the 1970s. It reflected the end of relative scarcity and the emergence of customers seeking for branded and individualised products. It also reflected a world of intensifying competition as trade barriers were lowered and global producers began to emerge. At the same time, new structures of production allowed producers to tailor their final products to these increasingly differentiating markets. In their path-breaking book, *The Second Industrial Divide* (the first divide being the transition to mass production in the first half of the twentieth century) Piore and Sabel (1984) characterised this as a process of flexible specialisation. The title of the book captures the increasingly niched basis of dynamic markets. But this fragmented market structure was subject also to increasing volatility and time to market became an imperative for profitable production (Stalk and Hout, 1990).

These changing market requirements placed enormous pressure on firms which had been accustomed to a world of stable and predictable markets which largely accepted their product offerings. They consequently had to find a way of adapting to this new competition, and one path to this was to refine and specialise their roles in their value chains. They did this in part by focusing on their core competences.

Core competences, outsourcing and rents

Core competences describe a series of capabilities which satisfy three basic conditions – they are unique to the firm, they are difficult to copy and they have a value in the marketplace (Hamel and Prahalad, 1994). In a world of growing knowledge-intensity in production, there is increasing space for unique capabilities. But at the same time, in a world of intensifying competition, there is increasing pressure on what is unique to the firm. Unless firms can identify and protect these core competences they will find themselves subject to increasing competition and diminishing returns.

The logical outcome of the need to identify and exploit core competences is to give up on those parts of the chain which are not unique to the firm and/or which are easily copied. These non-core competences can then be outsourced to other parties in the value chain, subject of course to the firms capacity to manage this outsourcing structure (see below). In a world of falling trade barriers, declining transport costs (Kaplinsky and Morris, 2008) and the growing capabilities of information processing and communicating technologies, this outsourcing was increasingly global in nature. For many of the world's largest producers who had previously offshored parts of their internal operations to foreign subsidiaries to reduce production costs, this global outsourcing was a natural development of trajectories which they already had in place. For other key actors in global final markets – particularly in the increasingly concentrated retail sector in the USA and Europe (Hamilton and Gereffi, 2009; Kaplinsky, 2005) – global outsourcing had to be learned. But it was a lesson rapidly learned in highly competitive final markets.

Underlying these linked processes of core competences and outsourcing is the concept of rent. A rent is an attribute which is protected from competition. In Ricardo's original conception, rents were natural endowments, gifts of nature reflected in the differential productivity of parcels of land (Ricardo, 1817). But developments of the theory of rent see it as an outcome of agency – rents can be created or augmented. In the Schumpeterian and Marxian frameworks it is the pursuit of rent which drives innovation (Kaplinsky, 2005). But the capacity to generate rents through purposeful activity needs to complemented by the capacity to protect and appropriate rents, and it is here that intellectual property rights (patents, copyright and brand names) play such an important role in a world of intensive global competition.

A final characteristic of rents which helps to understand the extension of GVCs is that they are inherently dynamic. A special attribute today, despite intensive attempts to protect rents, may become a commodity tomorrow, that is, a product or service which has few barriers to entry. This understanding of commodities as activities and products without barriers to entry can be applied to factors as well as products. For example, labour and skills are inherently subject to rents. Some years ago, countries with developed primary education systems were able to generate rents from their labour forces. Nowadays it is vocational and tertiary skills, and the capacity of firm to develop internal routines and management practices (Teece *et al.*, 1994) which provide sustainable human resource rents.

Thus, rents are distributed through the chain and the core imperative is to focus on areas of high rent protected from competition. The balance of chain activities is outsourced. But this outsourcing has to be managed to both ensure systemic chain efficiency and to institute processes which ensure that the chain as a whole responds to changing market conditions. The management of these chain relations is characterised in the GVC literature as governance.

Governance in GVCs

During the 1970s and the 1980s, the Japanese auto firms rapidly penetrated the US motor industry. The initial reaction of the three major corporations was that this was a consequence of more rapid rates of automation in Japan and a subsidised yen. However, once they began to unpick the source of Japanese competitiveness, they came to understand that it arose largely from a series of organisational competences. These were both within the firm (for example, just-in-time production and total quality control) and in the management of the supply chain (Cusumano, 1985; Hoffman and Kaplinsky, 1988; Womack *et al.*, 1990). Whereas the American firms were buying-in less than 30 per cent of their components and services, their Japanese competitors were outsourcing more than 40 per cent of these purchases. This enabled the Japanese industry to innovate more quickly, to respond more flexibly to final market volatility and to lower production costs. But to work effectively, it required tight control of supply chains, that is, a process of chain governance.

Governance is central to the GVC framework, but there is some confusion in the literature. Whilst it is generally taken to include the governance of offshored operations within globally dispersed firms, most of the discussion of governance is focused on the management of chains involving relations between firms with little or no equity links.

Initially, in his seminal contribution in 1994, Gereffi distinguished two major types of governance. The first was buyer-driven chains, where the lead firms were final buyers such as retail chains and branded product producers. These mostly characterised non-durable final consumer products such as clothing, footwear and food. The second governance type identified by Gereffi was producer-driven chains. Here the technological competences of the lead firms (generally upstream in the chain) defined the chain's competitiveness. Subsequently, Gereffi identified the emergence of 'triangular' chains in which the lead firm specified product requirements, and a systems coordinator took control of the outsourcing function and the management of the supply chain (Gereffi, 1999). Typically, in these triangular chains, the lead firms were based in final northern markets, much of the chain produced in dispersed locations in low income economies, and the network coordinators were based in Hong Kong (for example, Li and Fung in garments) and Taiwan (for example, Foxconn in mobile telephony).

However, since the buyer- and producer-driven archetypes were posed, GVCs have evolved in multiple directions, and it is now widely acknowledged that individual chains can be subject to multiple forms of governance. The most widely used framework for characterising governance types is that contributed by Gereffi and colleagues in 2005 (Gereffi *et al.*, 2005) (Figure 11.2). This identifies five different sets of relationships between firms in the chain. At the one extreme are the classic arms-length relationships in commodity markets; at the other extreme are the fully internalised operations of vertically integrated firms. Between these two extremes are various degrees of networked governance. Modular governance (for example in triangular governance) involves durable relations between lead firms and their suppliers and customers in the chain, but with low levels of chain governance. This is because characteristically, the key suppliers in the chain possess their own unique competences and this means that they are able to operate reasonably independently of the lead firm. Relational chains are chains with somewhat higher levels of governance, but where suppliers and/or intermediate suppliers possess competences of their own. They require less 'hand-holding' from lead firms than in modular chains. Finally, captive chains, involve suppliers or intermediate customers with low levels of capabilities, who require high levels of support and are the subject of well-developed supply chain management from lead firms.

In the early years of the extension of GVCs, outside of arms-length and internalised operations, chain governance more often than not involved captive suppliers and intermediate customers. But as capabilities have grown in many low and middle income economies, chain governance has tended to veer more towards the modular type. In many respects lead firms prefer this form of governance. It reduces the costs of supply chain management and allows lead firms to promote competition in their supply chains. The flip side, though is that many of the key chain intermediaries have begun to develop considerable competences of their own, and are emerging as competitors to the lead firms who have historically driven these chains.

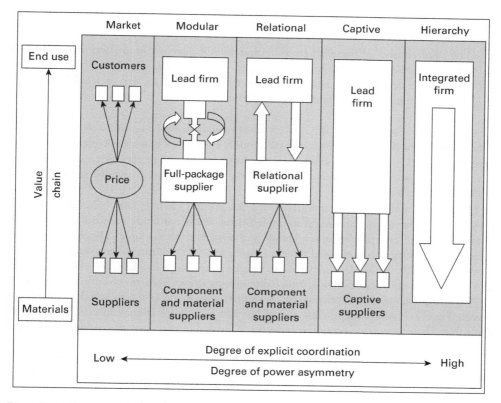

Figure 11.2 Five types of value chain governance.

Source: Gereffi *et al.* (2005: 89).

Whatever the pros and cons of modular chains, the result has been a growing global concentration of both buying and supplying functions. Both involve a considerable increase in size which acts as a barrier to entry for new producers, for small producers and for technologically weak producers (Gereffi and Lee, 2012). China may have found it easy to enter GVCs in the 1980s and 1990s; the same can probably not be said to be the case for emergent potential suppliers in Africa and elsewhere in the early decades of the twenty-first century (Gereffi, 2013).

Standards are a central component of governance in virtually all chains. These standards play a critical role in deciding who is incorporated in the chain, what they do in the chain and how they perform their allotted tasks. There are four sets of standards which perform these allocative functions (Kaplinsky, 2010):

- The first is corporate standards which are internal to the chain. Typically they address quality, cost and delivery (QCD), and increasingly also environmental processes. These are used to specify the requirements of the lead firm for supplier firms to ensure systemic chain competitiveness. An ability to innovate is another critical component of supplier performance, but is typically not measured in the same way as quality (parts per million defects), 'cost-down' (a specified annual decrease in unit prices) and delivery (percentage on time delivery, agreed batch-sizes). Some of these standards may be firm specific.
- The second set of standards is generic, and may be industry specific or relevant across a range of sectors such as ISO9000 standards on quality and ISO14000 on the environment.

The two other sets of standards are defined externally from the chain:

- The third consists of those set by governments (for example food safety standards) and international bodies (for example, EU farm-to-fork standards).
- The fourth category of standards is those emerging from civil society, such as labour standards, organic standards and fairtrade certification.

As a general rule, corporate, industry and regulatory standards are non-negotiable – the supplier either performs or does not perform, and the product either does or does not qualify for market entry. By contrast, civil society standards are seldom mandatory but affect the market niche in which the VC inserts itself. Typically, civil society standards tend to involve participation in higher margin niche markets.

However, whether optional or mandatory, a common characteristic of standards is that they involve upfront expenditure (even though many of the corporate standards do ultimately reduce costs) and generally require a literate and numerate labour force. These requirements often act to exclude small scale and informal producers, who are further disadvantaged by the costs of (generally renewable) accreditation. On the other hand, standards are often an important conduit for capability-building, hence diminishing the learning involved in exporting.

A recent phenomenon of potentially high significance is the extent to which standards are involved in GVCs which sell into low and middle income markets (Kaplinsky *et al.*, 2011). Lead firms from these importing economies may have fewer and less exacting corporate standards; the regulations affecting entry into these markets (for example, those governing food safety) may be less well developed, and the pressure exerted by civil society groups in low and middle income economies tends to be lower. One consequence of the lower standards-intensity of southern markets is that it reduces the barriers to entry for small scale suppliers in these chains.

The complexity of upgrading

As observed above, in the context of intense global competition, rents are inherently dynamic. The degree of dynamism is a function of the depth of rents (that is, the margins which they provide) and the strength of barriers to entry. Even within intellectual property rights the relative strength of different barriers may vary – brand names, for example, effectively exist in perpetuity, whereas patents are time-bound. But even brand names are subject to erosion without heavy investments in promotion and in the development and consolidation of product attributes.

The continuous pressure on rents therefore means that throughout the GVC there is a continuous drive towards upgrading. In the past, innovation theory and the economics of innovation have focused on two major components of upgrading. The first of these is improvements in process, which may take an embodied form or reflect changes to organisation, within specific links in the chain or in the chain as a whole. The second of these more established forms of upgrading is improvements in products, which as in the case of process, may be in tangible products or services.

GVC theory adds two additional dimensions to this upgrading agenda (Humphrey and Schmitz, 2000; Kaplinsky and Morris, 2001). The first of these is functional upgrading, that is, changing position in the chain. This may mean engaging in links which are new to the firm – for example, moving beyond assembly to the manufacture of components, or developing capabilities in design or marketing. But it may also involve the vacating of existing links so that the firm moves out of manufacturing into design, rather than engaging in both manufacturing and

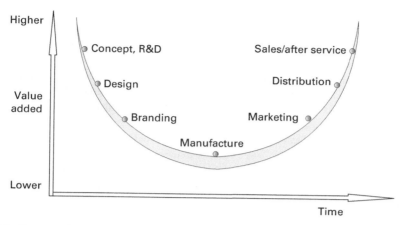

Figure 11.3 Functional upgrading and the Smile Curve.

Source: Park *et al.* (2013).

design. The final component of upgrading in the GVC framework is to move from one chain to another, in the way that Nokia progressed from rubber boots, through timber machinery to mobile telephony.

A widely used graphic which illustrates the nature of functional upgrading in GVCs is that developed by Stan Shih, the founder of the Taiwanese electronics and computer company Acer (Figure 11.3). This points to a strategy in which the firm moves from manufacturing (seen as 'low value added') to related services in the VC.[7] As a general rule though and as a direct consequence of the growth of manufacturing competences in China and other low and middle income countries, there has been a distinct trend across GVCs in very many manufacturing, agricultural and services sectors for the rents to shift from the embodied manufacturing processes to the knowledge-intensive disembodied links in the chain.

Embeddedness

GVC analysis takes a vertical slice of production and distribution and, as we have seen, addresses chains where these different activities cross national boundaries. At about the same time as the GVC framework was emerging, there was a complementary set of literature on the significance of industrial districts (sometimes referred to as clusters) (Best, 1990). Initially the focus was on the clusters in high income economies (the Emilia Romania region in Italy, Hollywood, Silicon Valley), but increasingly it became apparent that clusters were an important phenomenon in low income economies as well (Schmitz and Nadvi, 1999). These clusters described environments in which producers gain from their interaction with each other, from the proximity of buyers and sellers and from the local and national systems of innovation.

Thus whilst the GVC framework focuses on the 'stickiness' of vertical relations in the chain the cluster literature highlights the importance of horizontal 'stickiness'. The empirical literature suggests that, often, insertion into GVCs weakens the 'glue' in horizontal relations (Nadvi and Halder, 2005). Nevertheless, the importance of clusters in capability-building remains, and their significance has grown as lead firms increasingly search for dynamic suppliers which allows them to move from relational to modular governance. It not only removes the imperative for supplier development for the lead firms, but enables them to play suppliers off against each other. Hence, gainful insertion into GVCs increasingly requires the attributes which clustering supports and it is for this reason that rigorous GVC analysis necessarily incorporates a focus on embeddedness.

Another reason why embeddedness is a core component of GVC dynamics is because it sharpens the focus on ownership. This is a neglected topic in much of the GVC literature, perhaps reflecting the transition from the dirigisme of the 1970s to the neoliberal orthodoxy of the 1980s and 1990s. Neoliberalism abjures nationalism and identity, viewing firms as homogenous entities driven by market parameters. But in fact, the location and sustainability of production in many GVCs, and its volatility, is crucially affected by the embeddedness of the key local actors. This, for example, has clearly been the case in Madagascar in recent years where the export-oriented garments industry, after years of dynamism, was heavily affected by the loss of market preferences after a military coup in 2012. The upshot was that many foreign investors withdrew from the sector. In contrast, locally embedded firms, made up of second and third generation non-citizen residents, continued to export by developing new markets. Regionally embedded firms, centred in Mauritius and offshoring labour-intensive activities to Madagascar, were also much less footloose than the Asian foreign investors (Morris and Staritz, 2014). A similar story can be told for Jordanian and Egyptian garment exports after the 2008 financial crisis. The Egyptian industry was dominated by embedded local actors and sustained exports. By contrast, the Jordanian industry comprised footloose Asian investors, producing with thin levels of value added, and this resulted in a more than 30 per cent fall in exports between 2008 and 2010 (Azmeh, 2013).

The subordination of labour as a determinant of location[8]

The mobility of capital is central to the GVC framework. The outsourcing of non-core tasks is partly about the division of labour between different knowledge-intensive firms and is thus a story of maximising innovative potential in the chain. But it is also a story about cost-minimisation. The ability to outsource production to sites of low labour costs is evidenced within the core economies (for example, the migration of industry from the 'rustbelt' to new sites with low levels of labour organisation in the USA – Storper and Walker, 1989). Export processing zones are a manifestation of this (global) flight of capital to sites of low wages and weak labour organisation.

However, the location of production is not only determined by the mobility of capital; labour mobility is also a crucial determinant of place. At the national level, much of the production in export processing zones occurs through the shift of labour from rural to urban areas. This is particularly prominent in the case of China (where until very recently, residence in urban areas was denied to rural residents unless they were employed in export-oriented processing zones). But the mobility is also an important determinant of global location within GVCs. Outsourced production in many chains depends heavily on skilled labour which is mobile and which can readily cross national boundaries. In this context, skilled labour includes not only high level skills from the core northern economies but also, and perhaps more importantly, intermediate and artisanal skills from low and middle income economies. The triangular systems which coordinate production in many GVCs are particularly prominent in marshalling these mobile skills. However, it is not only skilled labour which is mobile so that, in the most extreme form, the large export-oriented Jordanian garments industry is almost wholly staffed by unskilled Asian contract workers.

Bringing labour into the equation as a determinant of location necessarily requires the analysis to focus on the social construction of the labour force. In this sense, the discussion is analogous to the incorporation of embeddedness in the understanding of the stickiness of offshored production in times of economic, political and industry turmoil. Migrant labour – particularly unskilled migrant labour – invariably involves the 'push' of 'surplus labour' from the rural areas, and their ghetto-isation in hostels in export processing zones. The working conditions and the low levels of end-of-contract pay in many of these export processing zones is less a matter of supply-and-demand than one of the subordination of labour. For whilst supply-and-demand may be a necessary condition for the flow of migrant labour, the effective harnessing of this labour force requires close collaboration between capital and the state.

The dynamics of contemporary GVCs

As we observed in the Introduction, GVCs are a phenomenon of the last four decades. They represent a new stage in globalisation – the 'second great unbundling' – involving the fracturing, decomposition and global dispersion of chain activities, driven by advances in information technology and the lowering of transport and coordination costs. The question is where this second great unbundling is going – what are the dominant trajectories which currently frame the global division of labour? Given the length-limitations for this chapter, this discussion will focus briefly on three dynamic characteristics involving GVCs – the thinning of value added at the firm and national level; the trajectory of functional upgrading; and the potential impact on GVCs in a world in which the increase in global demand is driven by middle and lower income economies. It goes without saying that this paints a broad-brush picture, and there will be many chains which will not reflect these trends.

The thinning of value added

Economies and firms on a growth path have historically sought to deepen their presence along the chain. In the clothing and textile sector, firms have targeted 'full package production' and governments have promoted industrial policies designed to foster production within the whole textiles and clothing VC. Their individual and collective ambition has been to deepen their share of the value added in final product value. We might refer to this as a 'classic' industrial policy designed to build full production capabilities (Figure 11.4).

However, entry into GVCs turns this classic strategy on its head. Instead of seeking full production capabilities with a deep share of chain value added, individual producers (and the economy) specialise in discrete outsourced segments of these value chains. At the extreme this may involve the mere assembly of shoes (yielding a value added per shoe of $0.23 in the Dominican Republic in the early 1990s – Kaplinsky, 1993) or the $6.50 share of the iPhone4 accruing to China in 2010 (Xing and Detert, 2010). But as time goes by, firms and countries which had begun by severely thinning their presence in GVCs deepen their participation beyond simple assembly, and seek to augment their share of final product value added. But, however great, this augmented share seldom reaches the levels sought (and sometimes realised) in the classic pre-GVC full production package strategy.

Linked to this shallowing, and subsequent deepening, of participation in the value chain and drawing on the insights which GVC analysis offers on upgrading (see 'The complexity of upgrading' in the second section above), it is possible to identify an upgrading trajectory which has been pursued in many successful Asian economies (Kaplinsky and Morris, 2008). This suggests a hierarchy of upgrading which is illustrated in Figure 11.5 through the example of the manufacturing sector. The firm enters the GVC by merely assembling to the designs of

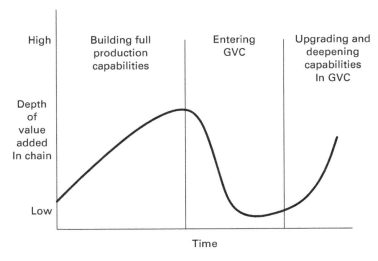

Figure 11.4 Shallowing and deepening in the global value chain.

Source: I am grateful to Wil Milberg for the central idea underlying this figure (Milberg and Winkler, 2013).

the lead firm (for example, the iPhone4 in China). Its upgrading trajectory in this early stage is one of process improvement. Subsequently, as capabilities increase, the firm moves from assembly to manufacturing, that is the transforming of materials and incorporating a greater degree of local components.[9] As capabilities deepen, the firm develops the capacity to design its own products (for example, laptop computers in Taiwan and China sold under the brand names of global firms). After a while, the firm then builds its own brand-presence, either in its own right (Samsung) or by acquiring the brand name of a recognised firm (Lenovo purchasing IBM computers and marketing the Thinkpad). Finally, once chain capabilities are mastered by

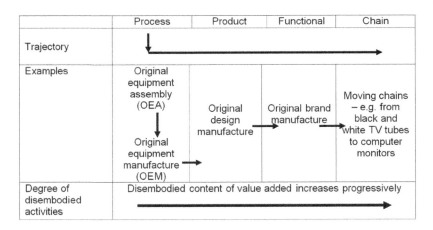

Figure 11.5 Is there a hierarchy of upgrading?

Source: Kaplinsky and Morris (2001).

competitors, the firm moves to a new chain. An underlying trend along this trajectory is one of growing knowledge-intensity and an increase in the share of disembodied activities.

When demand shifts to the south

The world economy as we came to know it in the late twentieth century was cast in the image of the northern OECD economies. They dominated global production and consumption. Their high income markets were the target of innovating firms, and their factor prices moulded technological change. Their civil society organisations played an important role in the rolling out of global standards governing labour, the environment and products (for example, in the promotion of organic standards in many GVCs). Their lead firms either dominated global buying or set the standards which were to be met by triangular systems integrators and their dispersed global suppliers.

Even before the 2008 global financial crisis began to have an impact on the trajectory of the global economy, this hegemonic dominance of the north was being eroded. Until the early nineteenth century, China and India had together accounted for more than half of global output (Figure 11.6). Their combined share sank to a nadir of less than 7 per cent in 1969, but thereafter grew sharply. By 2006 their share had grown to more than 20 per cent and there is every expectation that it will expand further to more than 30 per cent by 2030. If we add to this the contribution of other large rapidly growing rising powers such as Brazil, Mexico, Indonesia, Vietnam, Nigeria and South Africa, it is clear that within a very short time the major share of global consumption will take place in low and middle income economies. We are also likely to observe the growing presence of low and middle income firms such as Lenovo and Haier (from China), Tata (India), Vale (Brazil) and MTN (South Africa), each of whom will be playing a lead role in the extension of their own GVCs.

It is less clear whether this shift in the centre of gravity of global production will be reflected in the structure of GVCs. As observed above, there is evidence that markets in the south are less demanding of environmental and labour standards than markets in the north (Kaplinsky *et al.*, 2011). But at the same time, there are pockets of high income demand in these southern countries which are largely indistinguishable from those in the north. There is also evidence that when markets shift to the south, the degree of value added in commodity exporting southern economies falls (Kaplinsky *et al.*, 2011).

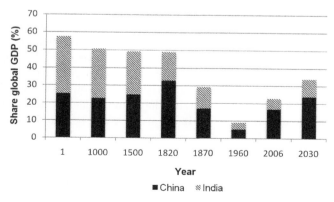

Figure 11.6   The combined share of China and India in global GDP, years 1–2030.

Source: Drawn from Maddison (2007).

Moreover, we are also uncertain whether lead firms which originate in low and middle income economies will fracture their value chains to the same extent and engage in global sourcing in the same way and to the same degree as do the lead firms from the north. On the one hand, triangular systems integrators such as Foxconn in electronics and Li and Fung in garments appear to be following in the footsteps of their northern buyers. But on the other hand the pressures promoting the hollowing out of manufacturing which have gutted much of the manufacturing sector in northern economies may not apply in low and middle income economies. Their lead firms in these sectors may therefore behave rather differently to northern lead firms. Therefore, whilst we can hypothesise that GVCs governed by lead firms from southern economies and selling into low and middle income markets may in many respects differ from those which currently dominate the global economy and sell into high income markets, it is too early to determine whether this hypothesis will be sustained.

Re-shoring and near-shoring

Whilst the competitive strategies promoting the outsourcing of non-core competences are likely to remain in place for some time, there is less certainty about the future location of these outsourced chain links. As we have seen, over the past four decades, in both manufacturing and services, an increasing share of global production shifted to low and middle income economies. This was in order to take advantage of low wage costs, the relative neglect of environmental and social considerations and the capacity to make physical capital 'sweat' (that is, to be used intensively) in the south. The question is whether this locational trajectory will be sustained. This does not mean that the positioning of particular economies in this global division of labour will be frozen (for example, China as a low wage economy), but rather whether outsourcing as a phenomenon will continue to gravitate globally. In other words, under what circumstances might *global* value chains become *local*, or perhaps *regional* value chains?

Three sets of factors might affect this locational trajectory. The first is that new technologies, and particularly 3D additive manufacturing, provide the potential for capital- and labour-saving decentralised production (Livesey and Thompson, 2013). This will reduce the need to ship components in large volumes over long distances and to incur large inventory costs. The second is that rising energy prices (Dobbs *et al.*, 2011; Farooki and Kaplinsky, 2012) reduce the cost incentive to locate outsourced activities far from consuming markets. And the third is that global social and political insecurity creates uncertainties and pecuniary costs which undermine the attractiveness of dispersed production systems (Kaplinsky, 2005).

Whilst none of these three factors reduces the incentive for firms to outsource, they do affect the optimal location of these outsourced activities. If they hold, a premium will be placed on proximity to consumption, and hence to nearsourcing. In some cases, this might lead to the re-shoring of previously offshored activities. This occurred in 2012 when General Electric, America's largest industrial firm, brought back production of some white goods to the USA, even though it had committed itself to shifting the locus of much of its innovation activities to China and India (Immelt *et al.*, 2009). In 2013, Apple also brought back some previously offshored assembly to the USA. Beyond the re-shoring of previously offshored activities lies the potentially reduced likelihood of offshoring outsourced activities in the future.

In summary, whilst the global trade–GDP ratio at the end of the nineteenth century was not dissimilar from that at the end of the twentieth century, it had a distinctly different structural form. The recent globalisation era – the 'second great unbundling' – was driven by the fracturing and global dispersion of value chains, particularly in manufacturing. In so doing these chains contributed to the hollowing out of manufacturing in the previously industrialised north and the very rapid rise of manufacturing capabilities and value added in the south, particularly in north- and south-east Asia. In the process of this unbundling, the centre of gravity of global growth and manufacturing production has begun to shift from the north to the south. Although it is still too early to determine their significance, a series of recent developments – notably the vibrancy of middle income economy markets, technological change, rising energy costs and growing global insecurity – suggest that the nature of GVCs and their impact on global manufacturing in the future may be rather different to that of the past.

Notes

1 Calculated from statistics accessed at UNCTAD (2013a).
2 This widely cited example does not tell the full story of the complexity of GVCs, since many of the intermediates and capital goods involved in the production of components imported into China for assembly into the iPhone were in part also processed in China. The headline $6.50 figure consequently underestimates the real value added in China.
3 Histories of the GVC framework can also be obtained from Bair (2009) and Park *et al.* (2013).
4 For a rigorous critique of mainstream economics neglect and misunderstanding of the fracturing of GVCs, see Milberg and Winkler (2013).
5 See, also, from outside of the economists ghetto, Sturgeon and Memodovic (2010).
6 Measuring Trade in Value Added: An OECD-WTO Joint Initiative, http://www.oecd.org/industry/ind/measuringtradeinvalue-addedanoecd-wtojointinitiative.htm, accessed 16 October 2013.
7 In fact, the vertical axis in this widely cited Smile Curve is unhelpful, since strategic positioning in the chain is not driven by a share of overall chain value added, but by the rents which accrue, that is, the incomes which the activity support. For example, if manufacturing is highly specialised and employs very few people, it would not be at the base of this Smile Curve.
8 The discussion in informed by the PhD dissertation of Shameh Azmeh (Azmeh, 2013).
9 For example, between 2011 and 2013, the number of firms supplying batteries for the iPhone in China doubled from 8 to 16, and local firms began to produce formerly imported inputs such as acoustic components (Mishkin, 2013). Although undocumented, the value added in China in the production of the iPhone5 almost certainly is much greater than the $6.50 incorporated in the early versions of the iPhone4.

References

Arrighi, G. and Drangel, J. 1986. The Stratification of the World Economy: An Exploration of the Semiperipheral Zone. *Review.* 10 (1): 9–74.

Azmeh, C. 2013. *Asian Capital and Labour Flows into the Apparel Industry of Jordan and Egypt: The Integration of the Qualifying Industrial Zones (QIZs) of Egypt and Jordan into Apparel Global Production Networks.* PhD Dissertation. Manchester: University of Manchester.

Bair, J. 2009. Global Commodity Chains: Genealogy and Review. In Bair, J. (ed.). *Frontiers of Commodity Chain Research.* Stanford, CA: Stanford University Press: 1–34.

Baldwin, R. 2013. Global Supply Chains: Why They Emerged, Why They Matter, and Where They are Going. In Elms, D. K. and Low, P. (eds.). *Global Value Chains in a Changing World.* Geneva: World Trade Organisation: 13–60.

Barrientos, S. C., Gereffi, G. and Rossi, A. 2011. Economic and Social Upgrading in Global Production Networks: A New Paradigm for a Changing World. *International Labour Review* 150 (3–4): 319–340.

Best, M. 1990. *The New Competition.* Oxford: Polity Press.

Capturing the Gains. 2014. *Capturing the Gains: Economic and Social Upgrading in Global Production Networks and Trade* – accessible from http://www.capturingthegains.org/

Coe, N., Dicken, P. and Hess, M. 2008. Global Production Networks: Realizing the Potential. *Journal of Economic Geography.* 8 (3): 271–295.

Cusumano M. A. 1985. *The Japanese Automobile Industry: Technology and Management at Nissan and Toyota.* Cambridge, MA: Harvard University Press.

Dobbs, R., Oppenheim, J., Thompson, F., Brinkman, M. and Zornes, M. 2011. *Resource Revolution: Meeting the World's Energy, Materials, Food and Water Needs.* No location: McKinsey Global Institute – accessible from http://www.mckinsey.com/insights

Farooki, M. and Kaplinsky, R. 2012. *The Impact of China on Global Commodity Prices: The Global Reshaping of the Commodity Sector.* London: Routledge.

Frobel, F., Heinrichs, J. and Kreye, O. 1980. *The New International Division of Labour.* Cambridge: Cambridge University Press.

Gereffi, G. 1999. International Trade and Industrial Upgrading in the Apparel Commodity Chain. *Journal of International Economics.* 48 (1): 37–70.

Gereffi, G. 2013. Global Value Chains in a Post-Washington Consensus World: Shifting Governance Structures, Trade Patterns and Development. *Review of International Political Economy.* 20 (4): 1–29.

Gereffi, G. and Lee, J. 2012. Why the World Suddenly Cares About Global Supply Chains. *Journal of Supply Chain Management.* 48 (3): 24–42.

Gereffi, G., Korzeniewicz, M. and Korzeniewicz, R. P. 1994. Introduction. In Gereffi, G. and Korzeniewicz, M. (eds.). *Commodity Chains and Global Capitalism.* London: Praeger: 1–14.

Gereffi, G., Humphrey, J., Kaplinsky, R. and Sturgeon, T. 2001. Globalisation, Value Chains and Development. *IDS Bulletin.* 32 (3): 1–8.

Gereffi G., Humphrey, J. and Sturgeon, T. 2005. The Governance of Global Value Chains. *Review of International Political Economy.* 12 (1): 78–104.

Girvan, N. P. 1987. Transnational Corporations and Non-Fuel Primary Commodities in Developing Countries. *World Development.* 15 (5): 713–140.

Hamel, G. and Prahalad, C. K. 1994. *Competing for the Future.* Cambridge, MA: Harvard Business School Press.

Hamilton, G. and Gereffi, G. 2009. Global Commodity Chains, Market Makers, and the Rise of Demand-Responsive Economies. In Bair, J. (ed.). *Frontiers of Commodity Chain Research.* Stanford, CA: Stanford University Press: 136–161.

Henderson, J., Dicken, P., Hess, M., Coe, N. and Yeung, H. W-C. 2002. Global production networks and the analysis of economic development. *Review of International Political Economy.* 9 (3): 436–464.

Hoffman K. and Kaplinsky, R. 1988. *Driving Force: The Global Restructuring of Technology, Labor and Investment in the Automobile and Components Industries.* Boulder, CO: Westview Press.

Hopkins, T. K. and Wallerstein, I. 1986. Commodity Chains in the World Economy Prior to 1800. *Review.* 10 (1): 150–170.

Hummels, D., Ishii, J., Yi, K-M. 2001. The nature and growth of vertical specialization in world trade. *Journal of International Economics.* 54: 75–96.

Humphrey, J. and Schmitz, H. 2000. *Global Governance and Upgrading: Linking Industrial Cluster and Global Value Chain Research.* IDS Working Paper 120, Brighton: Institute of Development Studies.

Immelt, J. R., Govindarajan, V. and Trimble, C. 2009. How GE is Disrupting Itself. *Harvard Business Review.* 21 September.

Kaplinsky, R. 1993. Export Processing Zones in the Dominican Republic: Transforming Manufactures into Commodities. *WorlPd Development.* 21 (11): 1851–1865.

Kaplinsky, R. 2005. *Globalization, Poverty and Inequality: Between a Rock and a Hard Place.* Cambridge: Polity Press.

Kaplinsky, R. 2010. *The Role of Standards in Global Value Chains and Their Impact on Economic and Social Upgrading.* Policy Research Working Paper 5396. Washington, DC: World Bank.

Kaplinsky, R. and Morris, M. 2001. *A Handbook for Value Chain Research* – accessible from: http://asiandrivers.open.ac.uk/documents/Value_chain_Handbook_RKMM_Nov_2001.pdf

Kaplinsky, R. and Morris, M. 2008. Value Chain Analysis: A Tool for Enhancing Export Supply Policies. *International Journal of Technology of Technological Learning.* 1 (3): 283–308.

Kaplinsky, R., Terheggen, A. and Tijaja, J. P. 2011. China as a Final Market: The Gabon Timber and Thai Cassava Value Chains. *World Development.* 39 (7): 1177–1190.

Livesey, F. and Thompson, J. 2013. *Making at Home, Owning Abroad: A Strategic Outlook for the UK's Mid-Sized Manufacturers.* London: Royal Society for the encouragement of Arts, Manufactures and Commerce – accessible from www.thersa.org

Maddison, A. 2007. *Chinese Economic Performance in the Long Run.* Paris, OECD Development Centre.

Milberg, W. and Winkler, D. 2013. *Outsourcing Economics: Global Value Chains in Capitalist Development.* Cambridge: Cambridge University Press.

Miroudot, S., Lanz, R. and Ragoussis, A. 2009. *Working Party of the Trade Committee Trade in Intermediate Goods and Services.* OECD Trade Policy Working Paper No. 93. Paris: Organization for Economic Co-operation and Development.

Mishkin, S. 2013. Chinese Companies Moving into Supply Chain for Apple Components. *Financial Times* 29 September – http://www.ft.com

Morris, M. and Staritz, C. 2014. Industrialisation Trajectories in Madagascar's Export Apparel Industry: Ownership, Embeddedness, Markets, and Upgrading. *World Development.* 56: 243–257.

Nadvi, K. and Halder, G. 2005. Local Clusters in Global Value Chains: Exploring Dynamic Linkages Between Germany and Pakistan. *Entrepreneurship and Regional Development.* 17 (5): 339–363.

Park, A., Nayyar, G. and Low, P. 2013. *Supply Chain Perspectives and Issues: A Literature Survey.* Hong Kong and Geneva: Fung Global Institute and World Trade Organisation.

Parrilli, D., Nadvi, K. and Yeung, H. W-C. 2013. Local and Regional Development in Global Value Chains, Production Networks and Innovation Networks: A Comparative Review and the Challenges for Future Research. *European Planning Studies.* 21 (7): 967–988.

Piore, M. J. and Sabel, C. 1984. *The Second Industrial Divide: Possibilities for Prosperity.* New York: Basic Books.

Porter, M. E. 1985. *Competitive Advantage: Creating and Sustaining Superior Performance.* New York: The Free Press.

Porter, M. E. 1990. *The Competitive Advantage of Nations.* London: Macmillan.

Raikes P., Friis-Jensen, M. and Ponte, S. 2000. Global Commodity Chain Analysis and the French *Filière* Approach. *Economy and Society.* 29 (3): 390–417.

Rainnie, A., Herod, A. and McGrath-Champ, S. 2011. Review and Positions: Global Production Networks and Labour. *Competition and Change.* 15 (2): 155–169.

Ricardo, D. 1817. *The Principles of Political Economy and Taxation.* London: Dent (Reprinted 1973).

Schmitz, H. and Nadvi, K. 1999. Clustering and Industrialization: Introduction. Special Issue on Industrial Clusters in Developing Countries. *World Development.* 27 (9): 1503–1514.

Smith, A. 1776. *An Enquiry into the Nature and Cause of the Wealth of Nations* (4th ed.). Oxford: Oxford University Press. (Republished 1976. Edited by R. H. Campbell and A. S. Skinner.)

Stalk, G. (Jnr) and Hout T. M. 1990. *Competing Against Time: How Time-Based Competition is Reshaping Global Markets.* New York: The Free Press.

Storper, M. and Walker, R. 1989. *The Capitalist Imperative: Territory, Technology and Industrial Growth.* Oxford: Basil Blackwell.

Sturgeon, T. and Memedovic, O. 2010. *Mapping Global Value Chains: Intermediate Goods Trade and Structural Development.* Working Paper 05/2010, Policy and Strategic Research Branch. Vienna: United Nations Industrial Development Organization.

Teece, D., Pisano, G. and Shuen, A. 1994. *Dynamic Capabilities and Strategic Management.* Berkeley, CA: University of California Press.

UNCTAD. 2013a. *World Investment Report.* Geneva: United Nations.

UNCTAD. 2013b. UNCTAD Statistics accessed from http://unctad.org/en/Pages/Statistics.aspx

UNECA. 2013. *Economic Report on Africa 2013: Making the Most of Africa's Commodities: Industrializing for Growth, Jobs and Economic Transformation.* Addis Ababa: Economic Commission for Africa.

US Census Bureau News. 2013. *Census Bureau Tip Sheet.* 5 April – accessible from http://www.census.gov/newsroom/releases/archives/tip_sheets/tp13-07.html

Wallerstein, I. 2000. Introduction Special Issue on Commodity Chains in the World Economy 1950 to 1970. *Review.* 23 (1): 1–13.

Williamson, O. E. 1985. *The Economic Institutions of Capitalism: Firms, Markets and Relational Contracting.* New York: Praeger.

Womack, J. and Jones, D. T. 1996. *Lean Thinking: Banish Waste and Create Wealth in Your Corporation.* New York: Simon & Schuster.

Womack, J., Jones, D. and Roos, D. 1990. *The Machine That Changed the World.* New York: Rawson Associates.

Xing, Y. and Detert, N. 2010. *How the iPhone Widens the United States Trade Deficit with the People's Republic of China.* ADBI Working Paper 257. Tokyo: Asian Development Bank Institute.

12

ELECTRONICS AND GLOBAL VALUE CHAINS

Ya-Shiou Chuang

Introduction

In the past decade or two, research on technology and industrial development in developing countries has revealed the role of global value chains (GVCs) in pulling their export forward and helping them climb the technology ladder – moving from assembly, to manufacturing, to engineering, to design and, increasingly, research and development (Gereffi *et al.*, 2005; Ernst and Kim, 2002; Evans *et al.*, 2006; Imai and Shiu, 2011; Kawakami, 2011; Oikawa, 2011; Sturgeon and Kawakami, 2011; Yeung, 2009). In particular, the rise of the Asian electronics industry has attracted a great deal of research interest, highlighting the inter-connection with lead firms (e.g. global brand buyers or transnational corporations, TNCs) via GVCs which has contributed to the fostering of export-led growth in Asia (Ernst and Kim, 2002; Gereffi, 1998; OECD, 2012).

It appears that the rate and direction of economic growth have been quite different in the countries choosing to participate in GVCs. Over a sustained period of time some engaged in rather simple, mature products and struggled to catch up with others, while others have begun to move into new functional and sectoral areas on the basis of their accumulated technological capabilities. Explanations for this difference range from the geography perspective (Hsu and Chiang, 2001; Saxenian and Hsu, 2001; Yeung and Lin, 2003), to government industrial policies (Amsden, 2001; Lall, 1995; Mathews, 1997; Wade, 1990), to institutional structures and strategies (Mathews, 2002; Hobday, 2001; Ernst and Kim, 2002; Yeung, 2007), and to the role of coordination between actors (Gereffi *et al.*, 2005; Gereffi and Lee, 2012; Sturgeon and Kawakami, 2011).

Most studies credit the roles of export-led demand in particular value chains in specific groups of countries, specifying that local suppliers' ongoing engagement in GVCs with global firms is the key to their economic growth (Gereffi, 1999; Gereffi *et al.*, 2001; Ernst and Kim, 2002; Sturgeon, 2002; Gereffi *et al.*, 2005; Evans *et al.*, 2006; Yeung, 2007). However, the significance of the rise in the domestic market in host countries has been largely neglected from most GVC perspectives. As firms accumulate experience and knowledge from export-oriented production, they might begin to consider their domestic market demand and connect with the emergence of their home-based key supplier network to create a new GVC network (Whang and Hobday, 2011; Yang, 2013; Imai and Shiu, 2011). As firms increase their knowledge base, they may also begin to move towards functional and inter-sectoral industrial upgrading. In general, little empirical evidence or theoretical reflection exists on the characteristics, problems and strategies of functional and inter-sectoral industrial upgrading in either export or demand-led GVCs in developing countries.

Moreover, although the above studies have all made important contributions to the field of GVCs, by explaining the industrial development in developing countries, few have yet examined in any depth the processes by which firms acquired and generated the knowledge base required for their growth in the host countries. In order to climb up the technology ladder and catch up with market leaders, firms in developing countries need to exploit the emerging opportunities available to them because of the changing industrial structure of GVCs. In fact, the majority of these studies have not examined the endogenous capabilities inherent in bringing about industrial development in developing countries. This chapter aims to provide a coherent theoretical framework that incorporates the dynamics of GVCs for understanding the following issues: (a) the changing economic geography of electronics in developing countries; (b) to what extent the experience of developing country firms explains the fragmentation of production in the electronics sector; (c) why some countries advance or fail to advance in the global value chains; and (d) to bring the lessons of this experience for industrial policy.

This chapter aims to shed light on the apparent new form of GVCs – local demand-led GVCs – in a manner which is different from that of previous studies, in order to provide a new tool to examine industrial upgrading and economic development in developing countries that aim to catch up with international market leaders. There are thought to be many differences between export-led and domestic demand-led GVCs in the ways of growing a country's economy. The chapter draws upon both the export-led GVC literature and local demand-led GVC literature which is concerned with the importance of industrial upgrading and strategic capability building within firms in their transition to global leading firms. However, these parts of the literature have been largely disconnected and appear to offer different and only partial perspectives on the issue of functional and inter-sectoral upgrading in latecomer firms. The second section reviews export-led GVCs with regard to industrial upgrading. The third section reviews local demand-led GVCs, a potential new source of building capability which stimulates technological upgrading in developing countries. This is followed by a presentation of a framework for the analysis of the transition to global leading firms via GVCs in developing countries.

Export-led demand GVCs in developing countries

This section provides definitions of the main terms used in the chapter and develops the categories relevant to export-led GVCs, with the aim of identifying the types, determinants and sources of technology upgrade in GVC contexts. One of the key purposes of this section is to identify the attributes and motivations for upgrading in export-led GVCs in order to develop an appropriate framework that can help illustrate the local demand-led industrial upgrading in GVCs for developing countries.

The concept of the GVC

The concept of the GVC was introduced in the early 2000s (Gereffi *et al.*, 2001; Humphrey and Schmitz, 2001, 2002; Gereffi *et al.*, 2005). Gereffi *et al.* (2005) cite Kogut (1985: 15) in defining a value-added chain as "the process by which technology is combined with material and labour inputs, and then processed inputs are assembled, marketed, and distributed." That is to say, a value chain identifies the full range of activities that firms undertake to bring a product or a service from its conception to its end use by final consumers, which is associated with the fragmentation of production across national borders. GVCs not only involve a series of input–output relationships, but more importantly, are subject to chain-coordination and governance (Gereffi *et al.*, 2005).[1] Linkage and GVC governance studies can contribute to this issue by examining incipient interactions between TNCs and local firms in developing countries (Gereffi *et al.*, 2005; Morrison *et al.*, 2008; Kaplinsky *et al.*, 2011). Later studies investigate how globalisation (based on export performance) was organised in relation to the concept of GVCs (Chesbrough and Kusunoki, 2001; Dedrick *et al.*, 2009; Ernst and Kim, 2002; Evans *et al.*, 2006; Gereffi and Lee, 2012; Kawakami, 2011; Sturgeon and Kawakami, 2011) and how local industrial development is linked to the nature of ties developed through GVCs (Humphrey and Schmitz, 2002; Giuliani and Pietrobelli, 2005; Iammarino and McCann, 2006; Yeung, 2007, 2009).[2]

Types of governance in GVCs

Gereffi *et al.* (2005) examine five types of GVC – market, relational, modular, captive and hierarchical chains– ranging from low to high levels of explicit coordination and power asymmetry. Market chains represent the classic arms-length relationships found in many commodity markets. Relational and modular chain governance exhibits closer relations between lead firms and their suppliers and customers in the chain. The main suppliers in the chain possess their own unique competences and can operate independently on behalf of customers. Quasi-hierarchical (or captive) chains involve suppliers or intermediate customers with low levels of capability, who require high levels of support and are the subject of well-developed supply chain management from a lead firm (often called the chain governor). Hierarchical chains represent the fully internalised operations of vertically integrated firms.

For the electronics industry the research focus has been related to the coordination and integration of inter-firm networks; quasi-hierarchical relationships between lead firms and those which are independent but subordinate in the GVCs (Hobday, 2001; Oikawa, 2011; Sturgeon and Kawakami, 2011; Kadarusman and Nadvi, 2012; Shin *et al.*, 2012). The shifting governance structures in sectors producing for global markets, or the evolution of global scale industrial organisation, affects not only the fortunes of firms and the structure of industries, but also how and why some countries are more advanced and some are far behind others in the global economy. Enhancing capabilities in firms may help them to push the architecture of GVCs away from hierarchy and captive networks and toward the relational, modular and market types (Gereffi *et al.*, 2005).

Key players in electronics GVCs

Value chains in the electronics industry are increasingly global and firms are moving towards a business model of increasing specialisation in value chain activities (Gereffi *et al.*, 2005). Sturgeon and Kawakami (2011) identify three principal actors in the electronics industry – lead firms, contract manufacturers, and platform leaders – showing how these three interact, and providing a useful portrait of the changing industrial organisation in the global electronics sector.

Sturgeon and Kawakami (2011) emphasise that lead firms capture most value in GVCs, so that firms such as Apple initiate or lead GVC activities by placing orders with suppliers which gives them market power over those suppliers. Lead firms globally outsource non-core activities, and specialise in their core competences (e.g. product development and marketing).

Most lead firms in the electronics industry are located in developed economies, especially Europe, Japan and the United States. Korea's achievement has been remarkable since firms such as Samsung and LG became lead firms in the 2000s. Taiwanese companies such as Acer and HTC successfully followed in Korea's footsteps.[3] In contrast, emerging countries such as China are characterised more by contract manufacturers although emerging multinational firms such as Huawei, Lenovo, Haier and more recently Xiaomi have successfully moved up through the GVC from OEM to ODM to OBM.[4] It can be seen that in the past 20 years, the participation of East Asia in GVCs has contributed to industrial development, particularly in electronics (both as production locations and final markets). From a strategic point of view, lead firms' advantages come not only from innovation in the form of R&D, but also from capabilities such as product design, branding and market development.

Platform leaders are companies that have been successful in implanting their technology in the products of other companies (e.g. IBM, Microsoft, and Intel). In some extreme cases, platform leaders can capture the bulk of industry profits and retain tight control over the innovative trajectory of the industry. For example, Qualcomm and Apple USA control almost 90 per cent of the mobile phone chipset market. However, MediaTek, a Taiwan-based company, has challenged the dominance of Qualcomm and Apple in American smartphones with nearly 13 per cent of the global market and over 50 per cent of the Chinese market (discussed below).

While contract manufacturers produce goods for lead firms and sometimes provide design services as well, the popularity of contract manufacturing in the electronics industry is a direct result of value chain modularity, which enables a clear technical division of labour between design and manufacturing at multiple points in the value chain. Originating in the USA, contract manufacturers have worked within industry-defined standards and have established facilities throughout the world. They purchase huge volumes of electronic components on behalf of their customers. They have usually located in developing countries such as Korea, Taiwan, Indonesia, China, Malaysia, the Philippines, Thailand, Vietnam and Mexico. In the 1990s, some firms emerged to become large global suppliers and managed to upgrade their functional activities in logistics, inventory management, and the day-to-day management of factories (Sturgeon and Kawakami, 2011). The growth of contract manufacturers in the East Asian region is notable. In recent years, some of them have grown to begin marketing of their own brands in their home countries and in emerging countries; for example, Foxconn (a Taiwan-based electronics manufacturing service) has recently launched its *Infous* smartphones, first in Taiwan in 2013, and later targeting its market in China.[5] Similarly, TSMC exploits its distinctive position in the semiconductor industry and acts as an open innovation platform in providing comprehensive support for its customers' major operational tasks, ranging from prototyping, design and engineering, to logistics. In so doing, both organisations have found that their essential value lies in their position within their GVCs, going beyond manufacturing (Chen, 2002).

The geographic distribution of the electronics industry

In the electronics industry, even the largest firms today must coordinate to varying degrees with widely distributed alliance networks to bring new ideas to the global market. Thus, their GVCs are more geographically extensive and dynamic than in any other capital goods producing sector. In general, it is relatively easy for electronics firms to engage in outsourcing and offshore operation. Nevertheless, the electronics industry is characterised by the intensity of international competition, the high rate of technological change, and the ongoing dispersion and interpenetration of productive activity. Participators in electronics GVCs must be capable of recognising and responding to changing market characteristics (Teece *et al.*, 1997).

Japanese companies were some of the earliest sources of low cost consumer electronics goods for large retailers in the USA and they produced for branded lead firms such as RCA and Philips in the 1980s. However, when wages began to rise, Japanese companies then relocated their manufacturing to other Asian countries, and then directly exported products to Western countries. Eventually, as firms in the West learned how to buy directly from factories in Asian countries, they began to narrow their focus to product development and marketing while outsourcing production and production-related functions to suppliers in Asia (Gereffi, 1999). As a result, Asian firms have emerged with a distinct role in the world economy with respect to their integration into regional and global markets (Evans *et al.*, 2006). In some product areas, Taiwan and Korea overtook Japan to become the world's number one producer. Over a sustained period of time firms in Korea and Taiwan learned and acquired technologies from firms in developed countries and they also began to supply more technology-intensive products in electronics.

During the 1980s, Korean *Chaebols* emerged as large, diversified business groups with a vertically integrated approach toward product development, manufacturing and marketing. With government support, Korean firms began to increase production volumes and reduce manufacturing costs, and then progressed to the development of capital- and technology-intensive products. Today, using their own brand names, Samsung, LG and Hyundai Motors have developed as suppliers of components, contract manufacturing and design services and now compete head-to-head with firms based in the USA, Japan and Europe in global markets.

In Taiwan, local manufacturers began by supplying components and (re)assemblies, rather than finished products for lead firms. Some firms began to improve their capabilities by assisting with the design process for lead firms and taking full responsibility for component purchasing, final assembly and the organisation of GVCs in East Asia. On one hand, as Taiwanese suppliers improved their capabilities, they were also forced to undertake more production functions, such as component purchasing, final assembly and testing, and to deal with the logistics due to the rising costs associated with brand development, increasing product diversity in lead firms, ever decreasing product life-cycles and intensified international competition. On the other hand, this functional upgrading triggered the merging of small and medium-sized suppliers to form larger consolidated suppliers to provide more services for multiple lead firms. For example, in recent years, Foxconn, based in Taiwan but with very large production facilities in China, Vietnam and the Czech Republic, has emerged as the industry's largest electronics manufacturing service (EMS). In addition, some firms were able to proceed with their efforts to become original brand manufacturers (OBMs), selling their own branded products in global markets (Hobday, 1995).

In many developing countries, governments have been motivated to provide incentives to attract TNC affiliates (known as inward foreign direct investments, FDIs) in the hope of facilitating industrial development and economic growth. In Southeast Asia, the cooperation between TNCs and local firms has been described by ASEAN[6] as 'TNC-led industrialisation' (Hobday, 2001). Such developmental strategies have been particularly welcomed in Southeast Asia. In Thailand and Malaysia a relatively high rate of local TNC affiliate procurements concentrated in the manufacturing sector, especially in the electrical and electronics industries, was reported by Oikawa (2011). TNCs' degree of embeddedness in local contexts, together with the development of the local skill endowment and the ability to handle knowledge are stressed as important pre-conditions, making it possible for foreign firms to engage in knowledge transfer, and for domestic firms to gain access to foreign knowledge (Saliola and Zanfei, 2009; Hobday and Rush, 2007).

China's electronics industry has overtaken that of the United States as the largest in the world, with production at US$413.1 billion in 2008 (Chen and Wen, 2013). In contrast to other newly industrialising economies in East Asia the industry's growth in China has been driven, to a significant degree, by lead firms' decisions to locate production in East Asia through TNC affiliate production, joint venture production, component sourcing, or contract manufacturing. In the following section we will discuss the emergence of local firms in China's mobile phone handset industry and how their development has co-evolved with the larger GVCs that make up the worldwide industry (Imai and Shiu, 2011).

The changing geographic concentration of GVCs in electronics during the past two decades has significantly reshaped the global economy. GVCs in electronics, therefore, were expected to generate substantial impacts on national economies. However, not many participants were able to enjoy the benefits generated by GVCs. How does insertion in GVCs affect industrial upgrading? Industrial upgrading is the key to economic growth. Gereffi (1999) observes that producers entering a quasi-hierarchical chain have good prospects for upgrading their processes and products, while others have stated that insertion in a quasi-hierarchical chain may offer very favourable conditions for process and product upgrades, but may hinder functional upgrades (Dallas, 2014; Yang, 2013; Kadarusman and Nadvi, 2012). Taiwanese contract manufacturers and Korean *Chaebols* were able to leverage this learning opportunity from lead firms. Whether the outsourcing strategies of TNCs' local affiliates are sufficiently beneficial to local suppliers to help them upgrade to a higher level of product and process technology and to stimulate national economic growth remains unclear.

Upgrading in GVCs

To upgrade, or to change to another governance structure, firms need to be able to move up to higher value-added activities, to build up their capabilities, and to improve their competitive position in the global market. In other words, upgrading refers to the ability to build innovative capabilities in order to increase value in products and processes. Humphrey and Schmitz (2002) identify four types of upgrading in GVCs. *First*, process upgrading is transforming inputs into outputs more efficiently by reorganising the production system or introducing superior technology. *Second*, product upgrading is moving into more sophisticated product lines in terms of increased unit values. According to Sturgeon (2002) modularity in electronics GVCs not only implies a lower degree of power asymmetry between lead firms and their suppliers, but also greater interaction between suppliers and lead firms in areas of product development and process innovation. *Third*, functional upgrading is acquiring new, superior functions in the chain, such as design or marketing or abandoning existing low value-added functions to focus on higher value-added activities. *Finally*, inter-sectoral upgrading involves applying competencies acquired in a particular function within one sector in order to move into another sector.

Researchers looking at the 'Learning by Exporting via GVCs' model suggest that, for developing countries, GVCs improve the potential for upgrades (Hobday, 1995; Kim, 1997; Mathews, 2002; Ernst and Kim, 2002; Gereffi *et al.*, 2005; Kawakami, 2011). This might be true for product and process upgrades, but it may not be easy or might hinder firms pursuing functional (design, marketing and branding) and inter-sectoral upgrading (moving into another sector). Firms may also begin to lock-in to the chains governed by lead firms or platform technology providers. Hobday *et al.* (2004) for example, point out that, as leading South Korean firms approach the innovation frontier and begin to compete on the basis of new products supported by in-house R&D, they appear to be confronting a new and difficult 'strategic dilemma' on whether they should continue with their low cost catch-up competitiveness, relying on the global leaders to generate new products and new markets, or should try to compete as leaders on the international stage by deploying in-house R&D to develop their own leading edge products and systems. Becoming an OBM would bring them into direct competition with their buyers (usually brand leaders). Another study, conducted by Dallas (2014), shows that Chinese exports may have caused weaknesses in its domestic firms which were within the governance of value chains. The Chinese government encouraged FDIs in industries they sought to promote, that is, the higher technology sectors, and therefore ignored low tech, labour-intensive industries. Similarly, Kadarusman and Nadvi (2012) suggest that export firms in Indonesia were trapped by their insertion into captive (garments) and hierarchical (TNC-led electronics) governance relationships with their global lead firms. In Mexico, the rise of contract manufacturers in China caused the Guadalajara electronics cluster in Mexico to change to produce higher value, lower volume products previously manufactured in the USA and Western Europe. However, the Guadalajara electronics cluster is deeply embedded within electronics GVCs. With few exceptions, electronic goods produced in Guadalajara are designed and sold by US-based lead firms. Most are produced by affiliates of US-based global EMS contract manufacturers using imported components and equipment, especially from East Asia (Sturgeon and Kawakami, 2011).

Local suppliers might face technology uncertainty that is initiated by lead firms in GVCs. Being locked-in to TNC-led GVCs might cause rigidity and inflexibility with regard to technological change, as happened with Singapore's Hard Disk Drive TNC-led GVCs (Cooke, 2013). Singapore was a global hub for HDDs in the 1990s but now it has lost its competitive advantage due to the rise of the USB flash drive and cloud computing. In fact, none of the TNC-led local suppliers was able to engage in the new GVCs created by Apple or Google Android. While it is true that most firms which are stuck in captive electronics value chains only pursue their production capabilities, failing to build up innovative capabilities to generate and manage new functions or other areas of product and process technology (Bell, 2009; Bell and Pavitt, 1995), only a few firms have persistently pursued competitive strategies that give rise to low cost advantages and production capabilities (Hobday, 1995; Imai and Shiu, 2011).

Sturgeon and Kawakami (2011) examine four strategies for overcoming the limitations to industrial upgrading in the electronics industry: global expansion through acquisition of declining brands, separation of branded product divisions from contract manufacturing (ODM spin-offs), leveraging modularity to define new (low end) product categories, and the founding of factory-less product firms. In general, studies attempt to define the upgrading and moving patterns with respect to how firms respond to their upgrading limitations, but rarely to provide new understanding of how they accumulate the capabilities to do so. Lenovo can be seen as an example of a small but dynamic set of 'emerging multinationals' – in Lenovo's case upgrading and expanding through the acquisition of IBM's notebook department. In many cases, such firms can fairly be characterised as updated, globalised manifestations of traditional national champions.

However, in response to the lock-in to TNC-led GVCs syndrome, some firms have chosen not to insert themselves into the GVCs. These firms have not only managed to enhance their competitive edge through functional upgrading into areas of own design and own brand manufacturing, but have also engaged in domestic and emerging export markets. Explicitly, local suppliers might apply capabilities gained from one chain governed by global firms to apply to their local conditions (e.g. to create new chains, as in the case of Korean and Chinese mobile handsets). A few of them may have particular knowledge, allowing them to employ continuous innovation in manufacturing technologies or to leverage their 'supplier capabilities' and increase their functional and inter-sectoral industrial upgrading. That is, local suppliers can choose to be competitive in both domestic and emerging export markets, but only if they can adopt specific strategies for the development, acquisition and utilisation of knowledge (Whang and Hobday, 2011).

The review of export-led demand GVCs suggests the following four conclusions:

1   Most studies have attempted to examine the relative merits of export-led growth GVCs in specific groups of countries and overstate the role of lead firms in facilitating economic growth. Firm-specific strategies and practices towards the technology frontier do matter. More attention should be paid to the indigenous factors of firms in developing countries that may or may not facilitate economic development, particularly the purposeful efforts embodied in the strategies of local firms in developing countries (Yeung, 2007, 2009).

2   So far, studies have tended to emphasise the ways in which developing country firms have acquired information and knowledge from firms in advanced countries through their participation in GVCs. However, most studies have defined knowledge at an abstract level, without reference to the micro-detail of how firms are able to learn and assimilate foreign technologies via GVCs in order to upgrade from simple to complex technological levels.

3   While most literature comes from a traditional viewpoint which places emphasis on production capability building for product and process industrial upgrading, more attention should be paid to GVCs and their strategic capability building for functional and intersectoral industrial upgrading.

4   Despite the fact that industrial upgrading is an important feature of economic growth, it requires further elaboration if it is to function as a core notion in an evolutionary economic geography. Also, this understanding of upgrading is relatively weak in its conceptualisation of how technological progress, learning and capabilities are acquired.

From an export-led to a local demand-led GVC approach

So far, little is known about why it is that some regional economies become locked into development paths that lose dynamism (such as TNC-led GVCs), whilst other regional economies seem able to avoid this danger and in effect are able to create new GVCs which are suited to them. The rise of the domestic market of 'host countries' for intermediate and finished goods has been largely neglected in conceptual constructs and empirical analyses of regional development from the GVC perspective. In fact, local demand and regional assets can become an advantage for regional development only if they fit the strategic needs of global production networks (Yang, 2013). There is little empirical literature on local demand-led GVCs. Some representative studies are briefly reviewed in this section.

Traditionally, local demand in latecomer economies has been considered too small and unsophisticated to stimulate innovation and to enable catch-up. Asian catch-up study models pay little attention to the role of domestic demand as a distinctive feature or force for technological development (Whang and Hobday, 2011). However, as advanced latecomer firms have progressed, the growth in domestic demand has, in some cases, become larger and more sophisticated, providing a potential new source of demand pull on the technological capabilities of latecomer firms. Therefore, it is interesting to explore the role of local demand in stimulating not only technological catch-up but the transition process towards becoming a leading firm.

Hobday (1995) defines the concept of the 'latecomer firm' as being distinct from follower and leader firms. According to Hobday (1995), latecomer firms are typically manufacturing companies in developing countries. They face two sets of competitive disadvantages when they attempt to enter and compete in world markets. The first is that they are located far from the leading sources of technology and they operate in isolation from the world's most advanced technologies. The second is that they are dislocated from international markets and from demanding users in advanced countries. They usually face undeveloped, small local markets and unsophisticated users in developing countries. Similarly, unlike firms in advanced countries, latecomers in developing countries do not benefit so directly from being located within the advanced markets which they serve and, therefore find it more difficult to benefit from user-producer links, the understanding of market trends which this imparts, and the close connections with capital goods and component suppliers, which together are often essential for developing new vintages of technology (von Hippel, 1986).

Chuang (2010) examines how Taiwanese firms acquired their technology base and moved from other electronics sectors (e.g. semiconductors and computers) to the TFT-LCD sector. Initially, Taiwan's TFT-LCD development was driven by the strong demand for screens used for monitors and notebook computers. Local sources of demand became critical for the backward vertical integration of firms into TFT-LCDs as components used for screens. Taiwanese TFT-LCD producers had large local downstream markets for their products within Taiwan, mainly from local OEM contractors. Thus, TFT-LCDs became both an export-led industry as well as an industry oriented toward the domestic market. As a strategic move to replace imported components, this reflects a deepening of Taiwan's industrialisation into key components or intermediate goods. In comparison with other export-led industries, Taiwan's TFT-LCD strategy has been to supply its domestic notebook and personal computer markets and then to generate exports on the basis of the capabilities developed in the local market. As firms began to increase their knowledge base, they then developed an advanced technology position becoming both an export-led and domestic-oriented industry.

Mobile handsets are important and renowned cases of industries where platform and brand leaders dominate. The cases of the Korean and Chinese mobile industry are interesting as very few platform and brand leaders have as yet emerged from the developing countries. Whang and Hobday (2011) examine the role of local demand in shaping latecomer firms' innovation in the example of the South Korean mobile phone industry. Their study shows that in Korea, intermediate demand (via the network operators) played a crucial role. In the Korean case, networks act as an intermediary, consolidating demand from end consumers. They adopted proactive strategies as though they were end-users of mobile handsets, pulling forward the technological capabilities of local suppliers to very advanced levels. Manufacturers launched new products with different features and product designs to suit each segment to attract the attention of networks (intermediate demand) and end-users (final customers). In this respect, firms went beyond the traditional manufacturing-focused subcontracting (e.g. OEM) catch-up model prevalent in Asian innovation studies, to one of leadership based on a combination of locally developed and foreign technology (Motorola, AT&T and Qualcomm) which was absorbed and integrated into Korean products.

However, not all markets possessed the characteristics shown in Korea and Taiwan. Companies may directly supply the local market (e.g. as in the case of consumer goods, computers or cars) removing the function of a service operator (as in the case of the Korean mobile phone industry or other kinds of intermediary, for example, Taiwan's TFT-LCD industry). Also, the Taiwanese and Korean economies are small and medium sized respectively. For other larger economies (e.g. Brazil, India and China), local demand-led economic growth may tell a different story.

In the case of the Chinese mobile industry, after three decades of rapid development relying on exports, there has been a dramatic transition from TNC-led to local demand-led growth. Some recent studies have begun to draw attention to the role of domestic demand (Chen and Wen, 2013; Imai and Shiu, 2011; Kaplinsky *et al.*, 2011; Yang, 2013; Brandt and Thun, 2010) in China's economic and industrial development. China has also increased its emphasis on open economic policies to attract investment from all over the world, particularly in high tech industries. On the other hand, although export-oriented industrial development has been successful, it has been for the first time criticised by central government in its regional planning scheme as "unsustainable development, low value added, low technology input, labour- and resource-intensive, over dependent on exports and TNCs, and environmentally and socially unsound" (Yang, 2013: 1054 quoting NDRC, 2008).

Technological spillover from TNCs to their Chinese partners, for example in the area of product development, was very limited because local joint ventures were only responsible for assembling mostly imported components. Yang (2013) examines the transformation of the cross-border production networks driven by Hong Kong and Taiwan-based TNCs during the period mid-2008 to early 2012 and regional trajectories moving from the Pearl River Delta to the inland provinces, such as Sichuan and Hubei. Particular attention is paid to the changing power relations away from the TNC-led export market and towards East Asian contract manufacturer-driven production networks in China. In the Chinese domestic market TNCs from Taiwan and Hong Kong have developed advantages (e.g. through a common culture and language) over other (traditional non-Chinese) TNCs (Evans *et al.*, 2006). Traditional non-Chinese TNCs may be unwilling to lead market re-orientation from exports to lower tiers of domestic markets, particularly those TNCs aiming to export their products to the higher tiers of the global market during regional transformation in China.[7]

For national security reasons, foreign firms have not been allowed to participate in some Internet Content Services (ICPs), such as online sales, according to the Chinese Foreign Investment Industrial Guidance Catalogue (Chen and Wen, 2013). Also, in the context of its rapid pace of economic development, China has been characterised by high income inequity, market diversity, and high price elasticity of demand compared to mature markets in developed economies (Chen and Wen, 2013). As developing country markets grow, the space for these 'less than cutting edge' product categories is expanding rapidly, providing openings for developing country lead firms relying on highly modular design solutions. The Chinese government announced an aggressive 12th Five-Year Plan (2011–15) (KPMG, 2011) to ease the economic focus based on TNC exports through stimulation of domestic demand and consumption (Yang, 2013). As a result, not only have nearly all major mobile phone TNCs entered, or sought to enter, China's domestic market, but also, many local firms have emerged and acted as suppliers and contract manufacturers, as competitors to TNCs. In addition, Western TNCs may not be interested in investing in low and medium income consumers (domestic sales) in China. Their main target is the global markets, particularly in Western countries. Because the market in question is domestic, local firms can potentially exploit their knowledge of local consumers' preferences and local clients' needs as an advantage over TNCs. Therefore, we address not only technological capabilities but also the capability to sense and capture market opportunities. Thus, when it came to migration towards smartphones and broadband mobile communications services in 2012 in the Chinese market, strong local demand in the lower tiers of the market created an opportunity for local firms (such as Coolpad, Huawei, Lenovo, ZTE and Xiaomi) to engage in the Chinese mobile phone industry and become leading players in the Chinese market.

According to Sturgeon and Kawakami (2011), without capital and intellectual resources, emerging factory-less start-ups may be unable to develop in depth design, system integration and markets. However, firms with specific knowledge and expertise may be able to compete at the vanguard of growing and fast moving markets. For example in 2011 Xiaomi, a Chinese-based smartphone maker, began to sell high end phones at low prices. The company hired a top Google executive and launched the 'Xiaomi model' to contribute towards its branding, marketing and sales strategy. When it came to marketing, to cut down its costs, Xiaomi deployed some unique and innovative strategies. The company ran festivals, engaged with fans on the MIUI mobile phone forum gaining over 1 million registered users which it called Mi fans. To generate revenue, the phone maker focused on selling apps, special Android themes and Internet services to meet the diverse demands in the Chinese market and the growing popularity of mobile internet services with Chinese versions and flavours. For this, Xiaomi offered a customised version of Android, called MIUI, featuring additional functionality not found in stock Android mobile phones, including a fully customisable user-interface, gallery, camera apps, new music, and an alarm clock that rings even if the device is turned off. In order to keep its customers involved, the company planned to release a new version of the operating system every Friday. By 2014, Xiaomi had overtaken market-leader Samsung to become the leading smartphone vendor in China (NASDAQ, 2014).

The emergence of these Chinese home-grown brands has benefited from the emergence of the rise of the domestic market. However, it has also had much to do with the trend for platform-based development in the migration towards smartphones and mobile digital services. As Chinese mobile telephone producers began to take advantage of the growing domestic market an important force behind their success was MediaTek, a Taiwanese chip maker whose products have greatly reduced what it costs manufacturers to bring new phones to market.[8] MediaTek entered the smartphone business late, introducing its first chipset in 2011 in a Lenovo phone, but within 18 months it took nearly 50 per cent of China's market for smartphone chips. Rather than simply provide a chip the company offers a turnkey total solution – instructions for building a phone, the software architecture to run it and dedicated consultants to advise phone makers during the production process – saving new mobile telephone producers the high cost of R&D. The company has proved widely popular among Chinese mobile telephone producers (such as Huawei, Lenovo, TCL and ZTE, and other lesser-known manufacturers). With MediaTek's help, phone makers in China were able to reach their market twice as fast as other solutions (Taipei Times, 2013). It seems that firms like MediaTek have employed their strong influence in reshaping the value chain, and extracting a large share of the value created.

Taiwanese contract manufacturers have found it difficult to become OBMs (Hobday, 1995), however, the rise of the Chinese market may create a window of opportunity for them to overcome these barriers. They have been doing so by taking advantage of the large size of the low and medium end segments and the strong pre-existing capabilities built as specialised manufacturers. Despite the modularity or OEM trap (Chesbrough and Kusunoki, 2001; Ernst, 2000), the original equipment manufacturers which were the leading first tier suppliers in the electronics industry are now well known.[9] Due to the increasing competition with local suppliers, some Taiwanese companies have actively tapped into non-manufacturing businesses, such as distribution and retail, based on their accumulated experience in the Chinese market. According to Yang's (2013) study, the proportion represented by manufacturing of total investment by Taiwanese companies in China decreased from 91.6 per cent in the 1990s to 74.2 per cent in 2010, while that of non-manufacturing increased from 3.4 per cent to 18.8 per cent in 2010.

In the case of the Chinese mobile industry, modularisation most notably exists in the evolution of the technology platform, which encapsulates the increasingly comprehensive and complex core functions of the handset system.[10] This has opened up opportunities for local firms with lower technological capabilities to enter the industry. Some firms are now successfully marketing their mobile phones in emerging markets (such as Southeast Asia, India and Latin America). Although global brand leaders such as Samsung and Apple still dominate the global smartphone market, we do not know whether these Chinese local brand leaders are able to compete head-to-head with global market leaders. According to Shin's smiling curve, most of the value is assumed to be captured in upstream (e.g. R&D, design) and downstream (e.g. marketing, branding, logistics) activities. However, in the case of China, a few domestic firms (mostly private ones) are able to compete with well-established foreign firms, leading to local industrial upgrading. The most interesting subject in GVCs is not how firms like those in East Asia repeatedly succeed, but what roles might be available in electronics GVCs in the future (Sturgeon and Kawakami, 2011). This suggests that in the case of the mobile industry, Taiwanese (MediaTek, TSMC and HTC) and Korean (Samsung) firms have become dynamic innovators, displacing Western component suppliers (e.g. Qualcomm) and brand leaders (Nokia, Blackberry) in the smartphone and recent tablet product markets previously dominated technologically by advanced countries.

The review of local demand-led GVCs suggests the following three conclusions:

1   Most studies attempt to examine how local firms have tried to leverage their ability to sense and act on business opportunities arising from the domestic market. Because of their proximity to the market, local firms have better knowledge of domestic consumers' preferences and the needs of their clients (local branded handset firms). They can be more flexible and responsive. However, so far, little is known about how local firms acquire and accumulate knowledge to take part in the market previously led by global leaders. It appears that quasi-hierarchical GVCs, dominated by buyers or TNCs, have also facilitated a process of learning in local firms, which has allowed them to functionally upgrade over time.

2   The demand in lower income countries for less sophisticated products with regard to quality and variety can have major implications for upgrading (Kaplinsky *et al.*, 2011). The emergence of key suppliers, platform leaders and local brand leaders in domestic market-oriented production networks has challenged the prevalent Western-led, firm-dominated GVCs. This requires further investigation and the completion of comparative studies in the future. Examples such as the Chinese mobile phone handset industry reveal the opportunities, but also the challenges and limitations, of electronics GVC industrial upgrading. On one hand, they have challenged the governance of GVCs controlled by global lead firms. On the other hand, studies suggest that new models of learning through close engagement with GVCs could be emerging, with broader lessons for developing countries (Yeung, 2009). It is notable that most of the emerging local lead firms were engaged in extremely mature product areas where the competition is intense. Very limited value (or profit) can be captured by contract manufacturers. Also, in a way, China's industrial development path has relied very heavily on TNCs (e.g. firms from advanced countries and overseas Chinese companies). A crucial point is that the future of Chinese local firms has become increasingly dependent on patterns of change at the level of components and technology platforms.

3   So far, similarly to studies of export-led GVCs, functional upgrading is only emerging in a few case studies, and inter-sectoral upgrading appears almost never to have occurred in the new form of GVCs created by domestic markets. Researchers may find it is important to assess whether and how local firms with prior related knowledge adapted and improved it in order to provide more products and technologies that were previously dominated by TNCs, as in the case of Taiwan's TFT-LCD development.

Transition towards a global leading firm

The ability to build capabilities in catching-up economies and the transition to leadership depends on the quality and dynamics of the local market, domestic users, local suppliers, favourable government policies, and strong producer-user links (Whang and Hobday, 2011).

Research shows that some firms in Korea, Taiwan and China have begun to engage in more complex, high technology products close to or at the technology frontier moving from user to producer of technology (Chuang and Hobday, 2013; Hobday *et al.*, 2004; Lee and Lim, 2001; Park and Lee, 2006; Whang and Hobday, 2011). Previous 'latecomer firm' research has shown that the capability building of companies has formed an important part of competitive and strategic advancement, showing how some have managed to transform themselves from a low technology and labour-intensive focus to an advanced, high technology and complex industrial focus. Thus, based on transition studies, this section hopes to provide a new understanding of how latecomer firms accumulate supplier capabilities in response to their growing domestic markets, going beyond the development of more narrowly defined capabilities and producing mature products and processes.

Based on the literature of export-led and local demand-led GVCs the intention is to build a framework for identifying the capabilities required for a firm to become a global leading firm. In line with Whang and Hobday (2011), Korea's success in its domestic telecommunications resulted from a long experience in international export markets which enabled the accumulation of a base of strong export-led capabilities (as shown in Figure 12.1–❶). The literature on firm capabilities and learning argues that the learning required to effectively develop the capability to engage in certain value chain activities may be difficult and time-consuming to achieve. However, it is essential that firms intensify the knowledge base that they have accumulated from prior experience so that they make use of required knowledge when upgrading to functional and inter-sectoral activities in the later stages of industrial development. Researchers have shown the importance of local firms' capabilities and absorptive capacities as necessary conditions for knowledge spillover to other functional and inter-sectoral activities in the host economies (Cohen and Levinthal, 1990; Criscuolo and Narula, 2008; Lane and Koka, 2006). In contrast to firm experience in advanced countries latecomer absorptive capacity tends to focus on the capabilities accumulated over long periods of time in specific product-technology fields, mostly from export-led industrial experience (Chuang and Hobday, 2013). However, building absorptive capacity requires a firm to engage in R&D (Cohen and Levinthal, 1990). With deeper and wider knowledge bases (e.g. absorptive capacity), firms have been able to assimilate foreign technology that was available as a result of GVC engagement and to apply R&D to develop new products and technologies.

Local demand-led GVCs have created a window of opportunity for local firms, but only if they work effectively with others can they enjoy the value generated from GVCs. Capability building, learning and capacity acquisition do not necessarily come from GVC ties with global lead firms and their agents: much of the learning comes from local suppliers and customers. As

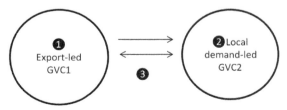

❶ Accumulating knowledge base from export-led GVC
❷ Coordinating with external firms within local demand-led GVC network
❸ Moving toward becoming global leading firm (both an export-led and
  domestic-oriented industry)

Figure 12.1   Latecomer transition and industrial upgrading in GVCs.

shown in the previous section, the consequence of value chain evolution during the last decade is a large and dynamic indigenous industrial base that is associated with large actors which have emerged from global markets and the domestic market, as shown in the East Asian case studies (see Figure 12.1–❷). Tacit knowledge is difficult to transfer from others due to its location within informal processes: the social context in which it exists is costly to imitate and hard to trade (Simonin, 1999; Szulanski, 1996) and must be understood as socially constructed (Kogut and Zander, 1992). Much of knowledge accumulation comes not only from the efforts firms make themselves but also from learning with others, in building technical ties with suppliers and component manufacturers and lead firms, as we have seen from the Korean, Taiwanese and Chinese electronics firms.

It has been established that some firms are now moving from domestic markets to global markets (as shown in Figure 12.1–❸). While this chapter argues that working with firms from advanced countries is very important for developing country companies wishing to become leading firms in global markets, simply because most innovative and advanced technologies are located in firms in advanced countries, most lead firms were willing to collaborate with local suppliers to bring new products to market through co-development. In this way, the prior growth of knowledge allowed local firms to aspire to an equal status with foreign firms (Chuang, 2014). This experience also enabled the local firms to continue to acquire the necessary foreign inputs and components which have not been available in the local market. Clearly, aggressive technological and managerial efforts by local suppliers can work to alter inter-firm dynamics in GVCs, especially over time.

Conclusions

This chapter has developed a framework for understanding industrial upgrading in GVCs from export-led situations to local demand-led situations and for understanding the transition from being contract manufacturers to becoming leading firms. Further theoretical work is needed to integrate the concept of GVCs more fully with the existing literature to provide a framework to show how firms in developing countries build upon their experience in GVCs and successfully move towards other functional or inter-sectoral upgrading, or the processes of becoming global leading firms. Also, the GVC concept needs to be more closely linked to the level of local industrial infrastructure and local technology institutions as industrial upgrading requires levels of infrastructure, including transport and communications, that facilitate the emergence of production segmentation, value chains, and associated increases in productivity (Evans *et al.*, 2006).

There is no doubt that the deployment of resources from GVCs has helped developing countries with their economic growth and industrial development. This chapter has focused on firms in developing countries, particularly Asian countries, and it makes some suggestions for the study of the electronics industry and GVCs in other developing countries, whilst recognising that it may not be appropriate to draw direct lessons for others. Recently, latecomer firms in China began to follow Taiwan in the area of semiconductors and TFT-LCDs in the hope of becoming major players. However, in the immediate future they face challenges different from those in Taiwan, as TNC investments and joint ventures play a far greater role in the transition process in China and their current technological focus is more on a par with their low cost advantage. By contrast, firms in advanced developing countries such as South Korea have made similar strides forward to those identified in Taiwan and may face similar challenges; some Korean leaders (for example Samsung) are much further ahead of Taiwan in some specific products and technologies. This suggests that it is important to understand the context with regard to GVCs, the level of governance, the level of knowledge base and opportunities facing any particular country before a specific strategy can be developed.

In the earliest phase of the industry's growth, policy interventions played an important role in supporting the entry of local firms. Policy makers may consider shifting the traditional emphasis away from export-led policies towards the domestic market and the long term technological development of, for example, capital goods and materials, to further deepen and strengthen the local industrial infrastructure and to support local sources of knowledge and skill across a range of advanced and diverse technology fields. Policies might focus on high value added fields, such as equipment, materials and components, to help support industrial development and upgrading. However, it is important to note that GVC patterns change and policies should consequently be ready to adjust, allowing local firms to exploit the opportunities and pressures that result from network participation (Ernst and Kim, 2002).

What remains to be seen is whether the examples provided in this chapter are exceptions which prove that the vanguard of local demand-led GVCs has become a new form of GVC prevailing in the developing world. However, the implications of the ongoing GVC restructuring in developing countries lack comprehensive investigation. More research is needed to investigate the role of local demand-led industrial upgrading in the GVC context. However, going forward, new sectors in the electronics industry and value chain combinations will inevitably include more firms – lead firms, contract manufacturers, component suppliers, and even platform leaders – based in newly developed and developing countries. We can expect that a few new leading firms born in developing countries will emerge. However, research is needed to establish whether firms in developing countries will follow the processes shown in Figure 12.1. No doubt, whilst the framework proposed in this chapter takes us part of the way toward a more systematic understanding of global value chains, much still remains to be done.

Notes

1 Gereffi (1994: 97) introduced the notion of 'governance' of value chains. He defined governance as "authority and power relationships that determine how financial, material, and human resources are allocated and flow within a chain".

2 The fact that they are increasingly spread over several countries explains why the value chain is regarded as global.

3 HTC is a Taiwanese manufacturer of smartphones and tablets. Founded in 1997, HTC began as an original design manufacturer and original equipment manufacturer, designing and manufacturing devices such as mobile phones, touchscreen phones and PDAs based on Windows Mobile OS and Brew MP to market to mobile network operators. HTC released and marketed its smartphones under the HTC brand in 2009.

4 Xiaomi is a privately owned Chinese electronics company. It is one of China's biggest, and designs, develops and sells smartphones, mobile apps and consumer electronics. Since the release of its first smartphone in August 2011, Xiaomi has gained market share in mainland China and expanded to develop a wider range of consumer electronics. In the text OEM stands for original equipment manufacturer, ODM for original design manufacturer and OBM for original brand manufacturer.

5 In recent years, Foxconn, based in Taiwan but with very large production facilities in China, Vietnam, and the Czech Republic, has emerged as the industry's largest player, in part on the basis of huge orders received from Apple for the production of the iPod and iPhone product lines. To avoid direct competition with its buyers Foxconn entered a joint venture with InFocus, an American brand which had been based on selling projectors but which was not operating in the mobile phone business. However, after the establishment of the joint venture Foxconn became the actual controller of InFocus and aimed to re-shape its future business interests including launching in the US market.

6 The Association of Southeast Asian Nations (ASEAN) is a political and economic organisation of ten countries located in Southeast Asia, which was formed on 8 August 1967 by Indonesia, Malaysia, the Philippines, Singapore and Thailand. Since then, membership has expanded to include Brunei, Cambodia, Laos, Myanmar (Burma) and Vietnam. The aim of ASEAN is to promote political and economic cooperation and regional stability.

7 The lower tier of smartphones is the key driver of market growth in China.

8 MediaTek was founded in 1997. It made chips for home entertainment electronics like DVD players and televisions before moving into components for CD and DVD-ROM devices. In 2004, it began making chips for small mobile phones.

9 Ernst (2000) argues that OEM suppliers became locked into OEM in relationships, which hinder independent brand name recognition and marketing channels. According to Ernst OEM is a vehicle for upgrading a firm's internal knowledge base but it is not necessary for firms to follow the stages of OEM–ODM–OBM technology development (Chuang, 2010).

10 Modularisation can both decrease the requirements for interaction between product development and production (which usually results in shorter lead times and fewer mistakes in the process) and facilitate capability building by allowing participants to concentrate on those activities where they have a comparative advantage (Baldwin and Clark, 2000).

References

Amsden, A. 2001. *The Rise of the Rest: Challenges to the West from Late-Industrializing Economies.* Oxford Scholarship Online. New York: Oxford University Press.

Baldwin, C. Y. and Clark, K. B. 2000. *Design Rules: The Power of Modularity.* Cambridge, MA: The MIT Press.

Bell, M. 2009. *Innovation Capabilities and Directions of Development.* STEPS Working Paper 33. Brighton: Institute of Development Studies.

Bell, M. and Pavitt, K. 1995. The Development of Technological Capabilities. In Haque, ul-H. (ed.). *Trade, Technology, and International Competitiveness.* Washington, DC: World Bank: 69–101.

Brandt, L. and Thun, E. 2010. The Fight for the Middle: Upgrading, Competition, and Industrial Development in China. *World Development.* 38 (11): 1555–1574.

Chen, S-H. 2002. Global Production Networks and Information Technology: The Case of Taiwan. *Industry and Innovation.* 9 (3): 249–265.

Chen, S-H. and Wen, P-C. 2013. *The Evolution of China's Mobile Phone Industry and Good-Enough Innovation.* Taipei City: Chung-Hua Institution for Economic Research.

Chesbrough, H. and Kusunoki, K. 2001. The Modularity Trap: Innovation, Technology Phase Shifts, and the Resulting Limits of Virtual Organizations. In Nonaka, I. and Teece, D. (eds.). *Managing Industrial Knowledge: Creation, Transfer and Utilization.* London: Sage: 202–230.

Chuang, Y-S. 2010. *The Development of Absorptive Capacity in Latecomer Firms: Case Studies from the Taiwanese TFT-LCD Industry.* Brighton: School of Business, Management and Economics. SPRU, University of Sussex.

Chuang, Y-S. 2014. Learning and International Knowledge Transfer in Latecomer Firms: The Case of Taiwan's Flat Panel Display Industry. *IEEE Transactions on Engineering Management.* 61 (2): 261–274.

Chuang, Y-S. and Hobday, M. 2013. Technological Upgrading in Taiwan's TFT–LCD Industry: Signs of a Deeper Absorptive Capacity. *Technology Analysis and Strategic Management.* 25 (9): 1045–1066.

Cohen, W. M. and Levinthal, D. A. 1990. Absorptive Capacity: A New Perspective on Learning and Innovation. *Administrative Science Quarterly.* 35 (1): 128–152.

Cooke, P. 2013. Global Production Networks and Global Innovation Networks: Stability Versus Growth. *European Planning Studies.* 21 (7): 1081–1094.

Criscuolo, P. and Narula, R. 2008. A Novel Approach to National Technological Accumulation and Absorptive Capacity: Aggregating Cohen and Levinthal. *European Journal of Development Research.* 20 (1): 56–73.

Dallas, M. P. 2014. Manufacturing Paradoxes: Foreign Ownership, Governance, and Value Chains in China's Light Industries. *World Development.* 57: 47–62.

Dedrick, J., Kraemer, K. L. and Linden, G. 2009. Who Profits from Innovation in Global Value Chains? A Study of the iPod and Notebook PCs. *Industrial and Corporate Change.* 19 (1): 81–116.

Ernst, D. 2000. Inter-Organizational Knowledge Outsourcing: What Permits Small Taiwanese Firms to Compete in the Computer Industry? *Asia Pacific Journal of Management.* 17 (2): 223–255.

Ernst, D. and Kim, L. 2002. Global Production Networks, Knowledge Diffusion, and Local Capability Formation. *Research Policy.* 31 (8–9): 1417–1429.

Evans, D., Kaplinsky, R. and Robinson, S. 2006. Deep and Shallow Integration in Asia: Towards a Holistic Account. *IDS Bulletin.* 37 (1): 12–22.

Gereffi, G. 1994. The Organisation of Buyer-Driven Global Commodity Chains: How U.S. Retailers Shape Overseas Production Networks. In Gereffi, G. and Korzeniewicz, M. (eds.). *Commodity Chains and Global Capitalism.* Westport, CT: Praeger: 95–122.

Gereffi, G. 1998. Commodity Chains and Regional Divisions of Labor in East Asia. In Kim E. M. (ed.). *The Four Asian Tigers: Economic Development and the Global Political Economy.* Bingley: Emerald Group Publishing: 93–124.

Gereffi, G. 1999. International Trade and Industrial Upgrading in the Apparel Commodity Chain. *Journal of International Economics.* 48 (1): 37–70.

Gereffi, G. and Lee, J. 2012. Why the World Suddenly Cares About Global Supply Chains. *Journal of Supply Chain Management.* 48 (3): 24–32.

Gereffi, G., Humphrey, J., Kaplinsky, R. and Sturgeon, T. 2001. Introduction: Globalisation, Value Chains and Development. *IDS Bulletin.* 32 (3): 1–8.

Gereffi, G., Humphrey, J. and Sturgeon, T. 2005. The Governance of Global Value Chains. *Review of International Political Economy.* 12 (1): 78–104.

Giuliani, E. and Pietrobelli, C. 2005. Upgrading in Global Value Chains: Lessons from Latin American Clusters. *World Development.* 33 (4): 549–573.

Hobday, M. 1995. *Innovation in East Asia: The Challenge to Japan.* Cheltenham: Edward Elgar.

Hobday, M. 2001. Governance of Technology in the Electronics Industries of East and South-East Asia. *Technovation.* 21 (4): 209–226.

Hobday, M. and Rush, H. 2007. Upgrading the Technological Capabilities of Foreign Transnational Subsidiaries in Developing Countries: The Case of Electronics in Thailand. *Research Policy.* 36 (9): 1335–1356.

Hobday, M., Rush, H. and Bessant, J. 2004. Approaching the Innovation Frontier in Korea: The Transition Phase to Leadership. *Research Policy.* 33: 1433–1457.

Hsu, C-W. and Chiang, H-C. 2001. The Government Strategy for the Upgrading of Industrial Technology in Taiwan. *Technovation.* 21: 123–132.

Humphrey, J. and Schmitz, H. 2001. Governance in Global Value Chains. *IDS Bulletin.* 32 (3): 19–29.

Humphrey, J. and Schmitz, H. 2002. How Does Insertion in Global Value Chains Affect Upgrading in Industrial Clusters? *Regional Studies.* 36 (9): 1017–1027.

Iammarino, S. and McCann, P. 2006. The Structure and Evolution of Industrial Clusters: Transactions, Technology and Knowledge Spillovers. *Research Policy.* 35 (7): 1018–1036.

Imai, K. and Shiu, J. M. 2011. Value Chain Creation and Reorganization: The Growth Path of China's Mobile Phone Handset Industry. In Kawakami, M. and Sturgeon, T. (eds.). *The Dynamics of Local Learning in Global Value Chains: Experiences from East Asia.* Basingstoke: Palgrave Macmillan: 43–67.

Kadarusman, Y. and Nadvi, K. 2012. Competitiveness and Technological Upgrading in Global Value Chains: Evidence from the Indonesian Electronics and Garment Sectors. *European Planning Studies.* (7): 1007–1028.

Kaplinsky, R., Terheggen, A. and Tijaja, J. 2011. China as a Final Market: The Gabon Timber and Thai Cassava Value Chains. *World Development.* 39 (7): 1177–1190.

Kawakami, M. 2011. Inter-Firm Dynamics in Notebook PC Value Chains and the Rise of Taiwanese Original Design Manufacturing Firms. In Kawakami, M. and Sturgeon, T. (eds.). *The Dynamics of Local Learning in Global Value Chains: Experiences from East Asia.* Basingstoke: Palgrave Macmillan: 16–42.

Kim, L. 1997. *Imitation to Innovation: The Dynamics of Korea's Technological Learning.* Boston, MA: Harvard Business School Press.

Kogut, B. 1985. Designing Global Strategies: Comparative and Competitive Value-Added Chains. *Sloan Management Review.* 26 (4): 15–28.

Kogut, B. and Zander, U. 1992. Knowledge of the Firm, Combinative Capabilities, and the Replication of Technology. *Organization Science.* 3 (3): 383–397.

KPMG. 2011. *China's Twelfth Five-Year Plan – Overview.* Beijing: KPMG Advisory (China) Limited – Accessible from http://www.kpmg.com/CN/en/

Lall, S. 1995. The Creation of Comparative Advantage: The Role of Industrial Policy. In ul Haque, L., Bell, M., Dahlman, C., Lall, S. and Pavitt, K. *Trade, Technology, and International Competitiveness.* Washington, DC: Economic Development Institute of the World Bank: 103–133 – Accessible from www.worldbank.org

Lane, P. J. and Koka, B. R. 2006. The Reification of Absorptive Capacity: A Critical Review and Rejuvenation of the Construct. *Academy of Management Review.* 31 (4): 833–863.

Lee, K. and Lim, C. 2001. Technological Regimes, Catching-Up and Leapfrogging Findings from Korean Industries. *Research Policy.* 30 (3): 459–483.

Mathews, J. 1997. A Silicon Valley of the East: Creating Taiwan's Semiconductor Industry. *California Management Review.* 39 (4): 26–53.

Mathews, J. 2002. Competitive Dynamics and Economic Learning: An Extended Resource-Based View. *Asian Pacific Journal of Management.* 19 (4): 467–488.

Morrison, A., Pietrobelli, C. and Rabellotti, R. 2008. Global Value Chains and Technological Capabilities: A Framework to Study Learning and Innovation in Developing Countries. *Oxford Development Studies.* 36 (1): 39–58.

NASDAQ. 2014. *Samsung, Apple Lose to China Smartphone Makers.* 30 October – Accessible from http://www.nasdaq.com/article/samsung-apple-lose-to-china-smartphone-makers-20141030-00101

NDRC. 2008. *The Outline of the Plan for the Reform and Development of the Pearl River Delta (2008–2020).* Beijing: National Development and Reform Commission.

OECD. 2012. *Mapping Global Value Chains.* Document produced by the Working Party of the Trade Committee. Paris: Organisation for Economic Cooperation and Development – Accessible from www.oecd.org

Oikawa, H. 2011. To be or Not to be a Supplier to TNCs? An Entrepreneurial Approach to Linkage Formation in the Malaysian Electronics Industry. In Kawakami, M. and Sturgeon, T. (eds.). *The Dynamics of Local Learning in Global Value Chains: Experiences from East Asia.* Basingstoke: Palgrave Macmillan: 136–166.

Park, K-H. and Lee, K. 2006. Linking the Technological Regime to the Technological Catch-Up: Analyzing Korea and Taiwan Using the US Patent Data. *Industrial and Corporate Change.* 15 (4): 715–753.

Saliola, F. and Zanfei, A. 2009. Multinational Firms, Global Value Chains and the Organization of Knowledge Transfer. *Research Policy.* 38 (2): 2369–2381.

Saxenian, A. and Hsu, J-Y. 2001. The Silicon Valley and Hsinchu Connection: Technical Communities and Industrial Upgrading. *Industrial and Corporate Change.* 10 (4): 893–920.

Shin, N., Kraemer, K. L. and Dedrick, J. 2012. Value Capture in the Global Electronics Industry: Empirical Evidence for the 'Smiling Curve' Concept. *Industry and Innovation.* 19 (2): 87–109.

Simonin, B. L. 1999. Ambiguity and the Process of Knowledge Transfer in Strategic Alliances. *Strategic Management Journal.* 20 (7): 595–623.

Sturgeon, T. 2002. Modular Production Network: A New American Model of Industrial Organization. *Industrial and Corporate Change.* 11 (3): 1451–496.

Sturgeon, T. and Kawakami, M. 2011. Global Value Chains in the Electronics Industry: Characteristics, Crisis, and Upgrading Opportunities for Firms from Developing Countries. *International Journal of Technological Learning, Innovation and Development.* 4 (1/2/3): 102–147.

Szulanski, G. 1996. Exploring Internal Stickiness: Impediments to the Transfer of Best Practice Within the Firm. *Strategic Management Journal.* 17 (S2): 27–43.

Taipei Times. 2013. *MediaTek's Chips Transforming China's Smartphone Market.* 13 January – Accessible from http://www.taipeitimes.com/News/biz/archives/2013/01/13/2003552387

Teece, D., Pisano, G. and Shuen, A. 1997. Dynamic Capabilities and Strategic Management. *Strategic Management Journal.* 18 (7): 509–533.

von Hippel, E. 1986. Lead Users: A Source of Novel Product Concepts. *Management Science.* 32 (7): 791–805.

Wade, R. 1990. *Governing the Market: Economic Theory and the Role of Government in East Asian Industrialisation.* Princeton, NJ: Princeton University Press.

Whang, Y-K. and Hobday, M. 2011. Local 'Test Bed' Market Demand in the Transition to Leadership: The Case of the Korean Mobile Handset Industry. *World Development.* 39 (8): 1358–1371.

Yang, C. 2013. From Strategic Coupling to Recoupling and Decoupling: Restructuring Global Production Networks and Regional Evolution in China. *European Planning Studies.* 21 (7): 1046–1063.

Yeung, H. W-C. 2007. From Followers to Market Leaders: Asian Electronics Firms in the Global Economy. *Asia Pacific Viewpoint.* 48 (1): 1–25.

Yeung, H. W-C. 2009. Regional Development and the Competitive Dynamics of Global Production Networks: An East Asian Perspective. *Regional Studies.* 43 (3): 325–351.

Yeung, H. W-C. and Lin, G. 2003. Theorizing Economic Geographies of Asia. *Economic Geography.* 79 (2): 1107–1128.

13

GLOBAL VALUE CHAINS IN APPAREL

Still a path for industrial development?

Cornelia Staritz and Mike Morris

Introduction

Industrial development and export diversification into higher value added products and away from primary commodities remains a major development objective for low-income countries (LICs). Several industries have played an important role in this process. This chapter discusses the specific case of the apparel sector (often also referred to as garment or clothing sector) in the contemporary context of global value chains (GVCs).[1] The apparel sector has traditionally been a gateway to export diversification for LICs and is generally regarded as a first step for developing countries embarking on an export-oriented industrialisation process (Gereffi, 1999). In most developed countries and newly industrialised economies (NIEs), it was central in the industrialisation process (Dickerson, 1999). Historically, this was the case in the UK, the USA, Germany, Japan, and in the NIEs of Hong Kong, Taiwan and South Korea. More recent cases are Malaysia, Thailand, Indonesia, Sri Lanka, China, Vietnam, Bangladesh, Cambodia and Mauritius. Given its low entry barriers (low fixed costs and relatively simple technology) and its labour-intensive nature, the apparel sector absorbed large numbers of unskilled, mostly female, workers and provided upgrading opportunities into higher value added activities within and across sectors, most importantly textiles. Hence, apparel sector development can have important short-term effects by providing employment, incomes and foreign exchange and long-term effects by furthering export diversification, industrial development and linkages to other sectors.

In this context, many LICs have tried to enter into apparel production and exporting. In 2013, global apparel exports accounted for US$378 billion, making apparel one of the most traded manufactured products. Developing countries have accounted for a rising share of apparel exports and the apparel sector constituted the first manufacturing sector where exports became dominated by developing countries. Global apparel exports are dominated by Asian developing countries but, over the past two decades, also LICs from other regions have developed export-oriented apparel sectors.[2] For many LICs, apparel exports are the main manufacturing export and the largest share of formal manufacturing employment – for example in Lesotho it accounts for around 80 per cent of formal manufacturing employment and 72 per cent of merchandise exports, in Honduras for 79 per cent and 51 per cent, in Bangladesh for 40 per cent and 82 per cent, and in Cambodia for 30 per cent and 61 per cent respectively (Frederick and Staritz, 2012).

However, the defining characteristics of the apparel industry also mean that it is very competitive with problematic labour issues. It is easy to enter and relatively footloose as production and trade patterns can be adjusted quickly to changing market conditions. This can be also seen in the important role of export processing zones (EPZs) or special economic zones (SEZs) which generally offer tax, duty and infrastructure incentives to attract particularly foreign direct investment (FDI) in the apparel industry in many developing countries (Singa Boyenge, 2007; see also Kingombe and te Velde, Chapter 14 this volume). The environment for global apparel trade has further changed significantly in the 2000s which may also condition the role of the sector in promoting export diversification and industrial development in LICs (Staritz, 2011, 2012). This chapter assesses the extent to which the apparel sector can still provide a gateway to export diversification and industrial development for LICs focusing on the key question: Is there still a labour-intensive manufacturing path through apparel exports for LICs today?[3]

The following section assesses main developments in the global apparel sector, while the third section discusses the implications of these developments for LICs that aim to develop through apparel exports. The concluding section identifies main policy areas to ensure that the apparel sector still provides opportunities for industrial development.

Dynamics in apparel global value chains

Main actors in apparel global value chains

As in many other sectors, production and trade in the apparel sector are organised into GVCs where production of components and assembly into final products is carried out in inter-firm networks on a global scale. The apparel sector is particularly suited for these global production arrangements as most (intermediate) products can be exported at each stage of the chain (Morris and Barnes, 2009). The apparel GVC can be roughly divided into four stages that are intertwined with the textile sector (Figure 13.1): (i) raw material supply, including natural and synthetic fibres; (ii) yarn, fabric and finished textile goods; (iii) apparel production; and (iv) wholesale and retail distribution and sales. Natural and synthetic fibres are produced from raw materials such as cotton, wool, silk, flax and chemicals. These fibres are spun into yarn which is used to produce woven or knitted fabric. The fabrics are then finished, dyed or printed and cut into pieces to produce apparel, home furnishings and industrial and technical textile products for a variety of end-use markets.

A large part of apparel production remains labour intensive, has low start-up and fixed costs and requires simple technology. These characteristics have encouraged the move to low-cost locations, mainly in developing countries. In contrast, textile production is more capital and scale intensive, demands higher worker skills and has partly remained in developed countries or shifted towards middle-income countries. In addition to the tangible, production-related steps in this value chain there are also 'intangible' activities that add value. They include product development, design, textile input sourcing, logistics and distribution, branding and retail. These activities are controlled by a combination of lead firms, intermediaries and supplier firms.

Lead firms

Apparel represents a classic example of a buyer-driven value chain. These value chains, common in labour-intensive consumer goods industries, are characterised by decentralised, globally dispersed production networks, coordinated by lead firms that control activities that add 'value' to products (e.g., design, branding), but often outsource all or most of the manufacturing

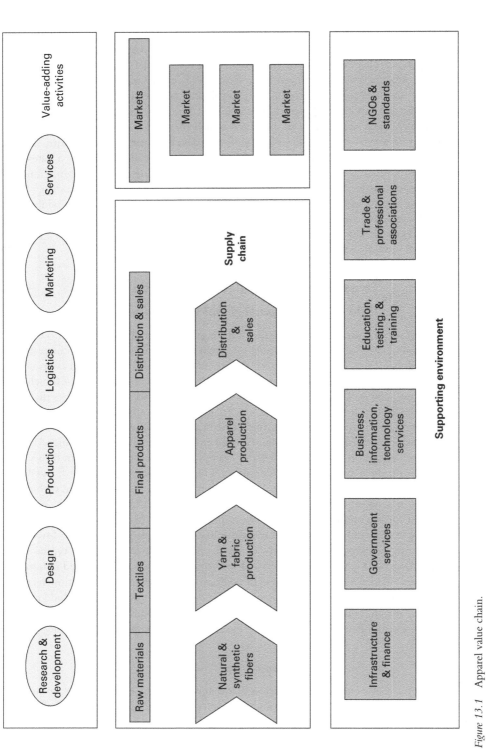

Figure 13.1 Apparel value chain.

Source: Frederick (2010).

process to a global network of suppliers (Gereffi, 1994, 1999; Gereffi and Memedovic, 2003). In the context of heightened competition at the production level, rents derive less from relatively standardised and commodified production-related activities which are globally available than from activities that differentiate the product in the eyes of the consumer. The latter are protected by entry barriers and are the core competencies of lead firms. Although buyers are not directly involved in production, through detailed product and production specifications they significantly control manufacturers.

In apparel the strategies of lead firms, in particular their global sourcing policies, shape production and trade patterns. Sourcing decisions are importantly motivated by labour cost differentials given the labour-intensive nature of apparel production. But in addition to the classic criteria of costs, quality and reliability, other criteria are increasingly shaping sourcing decisions (Gereffi and Frederick, 2010; Staritz, 2011). These are:

- *Lead times and flexibility.* The importance of 'time' in sourcing decisions is related to the shift to lean retailing and quick response production where buyers defray the inventory risks associated with supplying apparel to fast-changing, volatile and uncertain consumer markets by replenishing items on their shelves in very short cycles and minimising inventories (Abernathy *et al.*, 2006). Lead times have declined from several months to several weeks which requires more efficient and flexible supply chains, production processes, and work arrangements (Plank *et al.*, 2012).

- *Non-manufacturing capabilities.* Buyer concentration on their core competencies (i.e., branding and design) to reduce costs and increase flexibility has multiplied the functions demanded from suppliers. Buyers desire capabilities such as input sourcing, product development, inventory management and stock holding, logistics and financing. Fulfilling these new minimum requirements does not, however, necessarily lead to better contracts or higher prices for supplier firms.

- *Consolidation of supply base.* Buyers have focused on the most competitive suppliers that offer consistent quality, reliable delivery, large-scale and flexible production, competitive prices, and broader non-manufacturing capabilities. The objective is to ensure more cost-effective forms of supply chain management and reduce the complexity of their supply chains. This has led to a consolidation of the supply base, reducing the number of supplier countries and firms within countries.

- *Compliance.* Compliance with labour and environmental standards has assumed prominence in buyers' sourcing decisions due to civil society pressures. Many buyers have developed codes of conduct (CoC) that include labour and environmental standards. Compliance with these codes is a minimum criterion for entering and remaining in supply chains, but buyers often do not support firms to improve standards or reward them. These standards are essentially in the private and civil society domain. There have also been discussions of bringing labour issues into the World Trade Organization with contrasting positions where largely developing countries argue that in the current global trade context this would undermine their 'competitive' advantage, or strengthening the role of the International Labour Organization.

Intermediaries

Intermediaries (importers, exporters, agents and trading houses) play a central role in apparel GVCs. They are generally responsible for coordinating production, including input sourcing and logistics, but increasingly also for providing services in areas such as product development, design and marketing (Gereffi and Frederick, 2010). In the 1990s, large manufacturers, in particular in East Asia, developed into intermediaries organising far-flung transnational production and sourcing networks (Gereffi, 1999; Appelbaum, 2008). Faced with high demands on price, quality and lead time, high and changing volume demands, and demands for broader non-manufacturing capabilities from global buyers, more capable suppliers tried to position themselves as transnational producers that coordinate networks with a global supply base. Asian producers headquartered in the 'Big Three' (Hong Kong, Taiwan, South Korea) are the prototypes in this respect (Appelbaum, 2005). In the 1990s, they extended their networks to Latin America, the Caribbean and Sub-Saharan Africa (SSA). These transnational producers have become an important source of FDI in LICs' apparel export sectors. More recently, other large manufacturers in Asian countries such as Singapore, Malaysia, China, India and Sri Lanka as well as the Middle East have also developed transnational and regional manufacturing networks.

Suppliers

Apparel manufacturing is highly competitive and is becoming more consolidated. Developing countries are in constant competition for FDI and contracts with lead firms or intermediaries, leaving many suppliers with little leverage in the chain. Given this intense competition and the commodity nature of manufacturing activities, strategies of upgrading are extremely important for suppliers to sustain and improve their positions in apparel value chains. Upgrading in GVCs is defined as moving to higher value activities to increase the benefits from participating in global production (Bair and Gereffi, 2003). Supplier countries and firms can pursue several strategies to upgrade in apparel value chains. Five are identified in the literature (Kaplinsky and Morris, 2001; Gereffi *et al.*, 2001, 2005; Humphrey and Schmitz, 2002; Frederick and Staritz, 2012):

- *Process upgrading* – improving technology or production systems to gain efficiency and flexibility;
- *Product upgrading* – shifting to more sophisticated and complex products ;
- *Functional upgrading* – increasing the range of functions or changing the mix of activities to higher value tasks (e.g. moving beyond production-related activities to design, input sourcing or distribution and logistics);
- *Supply chain upgrading* – establishing backward manufacturing linkages within the supply chain, in particular to the textile sector;
- *End market upgrading* – diversifying to new buyers or new geographic or product markets.

Functional upgrading is of specific importance for apparel suppliers, and the other upgrading strategies can be viewed as 'steps along the way' to achieve functional upgrading (Gereffi, 1999; Frederick, 2010). These are encompassed within the following types: An assembly or cut-make-trim (CMT) manufacturer is responsible for sewing apparel and may be responsible for cutting the fabric and providing simple trim (buttons, zippers). The buyer provides product specifications and the fabric. The apparel factory is paid a processing fee rather than a price for the product. A full package manufacturer purchases (or produces) the textile inputs and provides all production services, finishing and packaging for delivery to the retail outlet. The customer provides the design and often specifies textile suppliers. An original design manufacturer (ODM) is involved in the design and product development process, including the approval of samples and the selection, purchase and production of required materials. Original brand manufacturing (OBM) is where suppliers develop their own brands and are in charge of branding and marketing (Gereffi, 1999).

Regulatory context of apparel trade

The apparel (and textile) industry has been one of the most trade-regulated manufacturing activities in the global economy. Until 2005, textile and apparel trades had been governed by a system of quantitative restrictions (i.e. import quotas) under the Multi Fibre Arrangement (MFA) which was signed in 1974. The objective of the MFA was to protect the major import markets (Europe, USA, Canada) by imposing quotas on the volume of textile and apparel imports for most countries. Important textile and apparel exporter countries were thus restricted by these quotas, whilst other countries had available quotas. The quota restrictions hence led to global spreading of production from quota-restricted countries to countries with free quotas or no quota limitations, allowing many developing countries to establish an apparel industry (Gereffi, 1999). When manufacturers, mostly from Japan, South Korea, Hong Kong, Taiwan and later China, reached quota limits in their home countries, they searched for producer countries with under-utilised quotas or for countries with no quota to set up apparel plants or source from existing apparel firms. Many of these countries previously had no important apparel exporting industry, which is why they initially faced no quota restrictions under the MFA.

The Uruguay Round of the General Agreement on Trade and Tariffs (GATT) brought the apparel and textile trade under the purview of the newly founded World Trade Organization (WTO). The 1994 Agreement on Textiles and Clothing (ATC) aimed to phase out the MFA by end 2004. In 2005 this allowed buyers to freely source apparel globally (with the exception of some temporary restrictions of Chinese imports until the end of 2008). This had adverse implications for LICs relying heavily on apparel exports or seeking to diversify into apparel production as large exporters were no longer restricted by quotas, hence increasing global competition and consolidation trends.

While quotas have been eliminated, tariffs still play a central role in the global apparel trade. Most Favoured Nation (MFN) tariffs on apparel imports are on average around 11 per cent for the EU and the USA with considerable variations for product categories – US tariffs varying between 0 and 32 per cent. In this context preferential market access has a substantial impact on global apparel trade patterns. Major preferential market access schemes can be divided into two types of agreements – regional or bilateral trade agreements, and the Generalised System of Preferences (GSP) (Frederick and Staritz, 2012).

- Developed countries, in particular the EU, Japan and the USA, have negotiated regional trade agreements to advance regional production networks. Developing countries have also increasingly negotiated a variety of regional trade agreements. However, negotiations and implementation have been slow, and apparel and textile products are often excluded. In addition to regional agreements, countries have increasingly negotiated bilateral trade agreements, with the EU and the USA being most active in this regard.
- Twenty-seven developed countries have provided tariff preferences to over 100 beneficiary countries through the GSP. However, tariffs for apparel products are only marginally reduced in the standard EU and US GSP. Within the GSP, some countries have negotiated preferential access for least developed countries (LDCs) – e.g. the EU's Everything But Arms (EBA) and the Lomé Convention and its successors, the Cotonou Agreement and the Economic Partnership Agreements (EPAs), as well as the US's Africa Growth and Opportunity Act (AGOA).[4]

Preferential market access in these agreements is governed by more or less restrictive rules of origin (ROOs), which ensure that the actual products of trading partners receive preferential market access and that exporters from third countries do not use transhipment and 'light' process-ing to circumvent external tariffs (Brenton and Oezden, 2009).[5] A motivation behind restrictive ROOs is to support backward integration and also regional integration as cumulation provisions often allow for the use of regionally produced inputs. Restrictive ROOs may, however, hinder market access, in particular for LICs, given the capital- and scale-intensive nature of textile production that makes establishing competitive textile sectors challenging.

The crucial impact of preferential market access and ROOs on trade and production patterns can be shown by the following two examples from SSA:

- Until 2000, nearly three-quarters of SSA apparel exports were directed to the EU market where SSA countries enjoyed duty- and quota-free access under the Lomé Convention. However, only South Africa and Mauritius were important exporters to the EU as prefer-ential market access required fulfilling double transformation ROOs which other countries could not fulfil due to limited textile capacities. These export patterns changed dramatically from 2000/01 when the USA signed AGOA and the Third Country Fabric (TCF) deroga-tion that allowed for single transformation for lesser developed countries. US exports more than doubled while EU exports stagnated. Lesotho, Kenya, Madagascar and Swaziland became large apparel exporters to the USA as they (as lesser developed countries) only had to fulfil single transformation ROOs (Kaplinsky and Morris, 2006; Staritz, 2011).
- SSA also provides an example that ROOs can encourage investment in textile production in certain contexts. In Mauritius, double transformation ROOs requirements in the EU market encouraged building up a vertically integrated sector in the knit segment, whilst in Lesotho the expected phase-out of the TCF derogation resulted in Taiwanese investment in a denim fabric mill in 2004.[6] Both examples illustrate the importance of combining ROOs requirements with industrial policies to support local backward linkages; other-wise restrictive ROOs may constrain access to markets for apparel producers without any positive impact on local linkages and input suppliers.

Although trade preferences are crucial in the apparel sector, they are eroding due to generally decreasing tariffs through trade negotiations at different levels and access to tariff preferences for more countries. In particular, at the bilateral level the USA and the EU are negotiating preferential trade agreements with an increasing number of countries.

Global trade patterns

The MFA phase-out together with the related shifts in competitive dynamics and sourcing policies of global buyers have had crucial implications on apparel export patterns. China is the largest exporter of apparel, increasing its world export share after the MFA phase-out (from 28 per cent in 2004 to 40 per cent in 2013) (Table 13.1). Excluding the second largest exporter – the EU-15 (which includes intra-EU trade) – the other top exporter countries, Bangladesh, Vietnam, Turkey, India and Indonesia, accounted together for a bit more than half (23 per cent of world export share) of China's total exports in 2013. Generally the top 15 export countries increased their market share from 81 per cent to 87 per cent from 2005 to 2013. Within the top 15 global apparel exporter countries, Asian exporter countries such as China, Bangladesh, India and Vietnam and to a lesser extent Indonesia and Cambodia have increased their export shares since 2004. Most other apparel producing countries have lost global market share since 2004, including higher cost Asian apparel exporter countries (Hong Kong, Taiwan, South Korea), US and EU regional suppliers (Mexico, North Africa and Eastern Europe), as well as SSA countries (Gereffi and Frederick, 2010; Staritz, 2011).

Table 13.1 Top 15 apparel exporting countries

Country/region	Value ($ million)						World share (%)					
	2000	2005	2007	2009	2011	2013	2000	2005	2007	2009	2011	2013
World	**193,669**	**268,431**	**318,533**	**299,415**	**375,113**	**377,619**						
China	48,019	89,890	118,362	123,988	155,478	149,585	24.8	33.5	37.2	41.4	41.4	39.6
EU-15	33,980	47,598	56,470	51,405	61,069	56,792	17.5	17.7	17.7	17.2	16.3	15.0
Bangladesh	4,862	8,038	11,208	14,241	21,938	26,450	2.5	3.0	3.5	4.8	5.8	7.0
Vietnam	–	4,739	7,708	9,410	14,077	18,667	–	1.8	2.4	3.1	3.8	4.9
Turkey	6,711	12,942	15,568	13,160	16,289	17,341	3.5	4.8	4.9	4.4	4.3	4.6
India	5,131	9,476	11,458	11,931	14,346	13,563	2.6	3.5	3.6	4.0	3.8	3.6
Indonesia	4,675	5,679	7,386	7,169	9,574	10,073	2.4	2.1	2.3	2.4	2.6	2.7
Cambodia	–	–	3,770	3,482	5,601	7,404	–	–	1.2	1.2	1.5	2.0
Sri Lanka	–	3,083	3,602	3,537	4,274	4,682	–	1.1	1.1	1.2	1.1	1.2
Pakistan	–	–	–	3,222	4,477	4,550	–	–	–	1.1	1.2	1.2
Mexico	8,924	6,683	5,131	3,927	4,541	4,447	4.6	2.5	1.6	1.3	1.2	1.2
Romania	2,737	5,177	4,394	3,219	4,177	4,333	1.4	1.9	1.4	1.1	1.1	1.1
Morocco	–	3,331	4,239	3,598	4,095	4,290	–	1.2	1.3	1.2	1.1	1.1
Tunisia	2,645	3,478	4,121	3,788	4,110	3,665	1.4	1.3	1.3	1.2	1.1	1.0
Thailand	3,672	3,862	4,098	3,509	3,788	3,355	1.9	1.4	1.3	1.2	1.0	0.9
Top 15	**147,007**	**216,185**	**265,407**	**259,586**	**327,834**	**329,199**	**75.9**	**80.5**	**83.3**	**86.7**	**87.4**	**87.2**

Source: UN COMTRADE (2015).

Notes: Apparel represented by harmonised system (HS) codes 61 and 62; '–' indicates country not in top 15 in given year; EU-15 values include intra-EU trade.

Table 13.2 Top 15 apparel importing countries

Country/region	Value ($ million)						Share (%)					
	2000	2005	2007	2009	2010	2011	2000	2005	2007	2009	2010	2011
World	**193,669**	**268,431**	**318,533**	**299,415**	**326,254**	**375,125**						
EU-15	69,556	110,711	136,578	133,218	138,692	160,686	35.9	41.2	42.9	44.5	42.5	42.8
USA	61,741	74,155	78,920	66,795	75,647	81,514	31.9	27.6	24.8	22.3	23.2	21.7
Japan	18,613	21,167	22,598	24,070	25,262	31,110	9.6	7.9	7.1	8.0	7.7	8.3
Hong Kong	14,953	17,255	18,137	14,706	15,709	16,091	7.7	6.4	5.7	4.9	4.8	4.3
Canada	3,261	5,374	6,908	6,859	7,543	8,654	1.7	2.0	2.2	2.3	2.3	2.3
Russia	–	–	2,841	3,674	5,551	6,747	–	–	0.9	1.2	1.7	1.8
Rep. of Korea	1,239	2,719	4,085	3,162	4,124	5,722	0.6	1.0	1.3	1.1	1.3	1.5
Switzerland	2,983	4,143	4,794	4,860	4,908	5,697	1.5	1.5	1.5	1.6	1.5	1.5
Australia	1,604	2,840	3,379	3,714	4,440	5,354	0.8	1.1	1.1	1.2	1.4	1.4
Poland	–	–	1,898	3,165	3,496	4,184	–	–	0.6	1.1	1.1	1.1
China	1,135	1,510	1,812	1,652	2,238	3,572	0.6	0.6	0.6	0.6	0.7	1.0
Turkey	–	–	–	1,910	2,557	2,959	–	–	–	0.6	0.8	0.8
Saudi Arabia	745	1,350	–	–	2,116	2,730	0.4	0.5	–	–	0.6	0.7
Norway	1,206	1,709	2,126	2,123	2,319	2,684	0.6	0.6	0.7	0.7	0.7	0.7
Mexico	–	–	–	–	–	2,497	–	–	–	–	–	0.7
Top 15	**183,654**	**249,999**	**290,877**	**274,251**	**297,033**	**340,196**	**94.8**	**93.1**	**91.3**	**91.6**	**91.0**	**90.7**
Top 3	**149,911**	**206,032**	**238,096**	**224,083**	**239,601**	**273,311**	**77.4**	**76.8**	**74.7**	**74.8**	**73.4**	**72.9**

Source: UN COMTRADE (2015).

Notes: Apparel represented by HS codes 61 and 62; '–' indicates country not in top 15 in given year; EU-15 values include intra-EU trade; Top 3 includes EU-15, USA and Japan.

The EU-15 and the USA have been by far the largest apparel importing markets accounting for 62 per cent of global apparel imports in 2013 (Table 13.2). Between 2000 and 2007 the EU-15 market nearly doubled, whilst US imports of apparel increased by 28 per cent. However the 2008 economic crisis resulted in a sharp decline in global demand for apparel in 2009.[7] Imports recovered in 2010. In 2012, however, global imports declined again with the largest reduction in the EU-15 due to the Eurozone crisis. In 2013, imports increased again – globally, in the USA and the EU-15. The US and the EU markets will remain major apparel import markets, but emerging country markets such as Russia, China, Turkey, Saudi Arabia and Mexico are gaining in importance, accelerated by the global economic crisis.

Implications for low-income apparel exporters
Increasing entry barriers and global consolidation

The main arguments for the apparel sector as a springboard for export diversification and industrial development in LICs are twofold: First, entry barriers are low and LICs with large supplies of unskilled labour can quickly participate in apparel manufacturing. Second, apparel manufacturing can be a launching pad for upgrading into higher value added and more skill- and technology-intensive activities within and across sectors. But are these still valid for the apparel sector under current global conditions?

The changes in global regulatory and competitive conditions discussed above have accelerated changes in large US and EU buyers' sourcing policies which can be described as supply chain rationalisation. This involves consolidation of sourcing countries, concentration on core suppliers, higher demands on suppliers with regard to manufacturing but also other capabilities, detailed performance monitoring, and stringent selection principles for new suppliers (Palpacuer *et al.*, 2005; Gereffi and Frederick, 2010). However, crucial differences in sourcing practices still exist between large global and smaller buyers (Staritz, 2011).

At the country level, low-cost Asian apparel exporter countries are increasing their market share in the USA and the EU, primarily at the expense of regional supplier countries, SSA apparel suppliers and smaller LICs. At the firm level, the increasing adoption of supply chain rationalisation sourcing strategies has benefited larger and more capable suppliers at the expense of smaller, lesser developed and marginal suppliers in all countries. Global consolidation has increased entry barriers at the country and firm level. Preferential market access is still central and provides windows of opportunities for LIC apparel exporters but preferences are eroding in the medium term. Global buyers demand more capabilities and higher standards from suppliers with firms only being able to enter supply chains if they can meet these manufacturing and other capabilities. These developments mean that low labour costs and preferential market access are not enough for supplier firms in LICs to be competitive in the apparel sector today.

Whilst it has become more difficult for firms in LICs to enter apparel GVCs, suppliers which only offer basic manufacturing functions may still be able to enter supply chains as second-tier suppliers through intermediaries. In particular, in triangular manufacturing networks of transnational producers, entry barriers are substantially lower. However, upgrading opportunities, in particular for functional upgrading, are also limited by the intermediaries' control over key decision-making and high-value functions (Staritz and Morris, 2012). A main motivation for intermediaries to source from LICs has been preferential market access (and earlier also MFA quota-hopping). The competitiveness of certain LICs, in particular in SSA, still heavily depends on these preferences.

Furthermore, there are two underlying structural challenges which condition the role of the apparel sector in the industrial development process of LICs today: (i) changing global supply and demand structures and (ii) asymmetric market and power structures within GVCs. These structural challenges are related to and have been accelerated by supply chain rationalisation strategies of global buyers.

The previous period of export growth by newly industrialised economies particularly from East Asia was primarily at the cost of domestic producers in developed countries. Today, however, there is substantial competition between developing countries wishing to expand their low-cost apparel production and export and hence growth of exports is largely at the expense of other developing countries (Kaplinsky, 2005; Morris, 2006). The heightened competition between developing countries has been reinforced by overcapacity in the global apparel industry, due to the MFA phase-out, and the entry of large developing countries such as China and India, as well as new apparel exporting regions such as Southeast Asia (Kaplinsky and Morris, 2008). This has constrained space for other participants in apparel exporting (Kaplinsky and Messner, 2008; Kaplinsky and Morris, 2008).

Price pressures are also related to asymmetric market and power structures in GVCs. In the context of heightened competition at the supplier level, rents do not derive from relatively standardised manufacturing activities which are globally available. Rather, rents are associated with design, branding, marketing, R&D and retailing (Gereffi, 1994) which are the core competencies of buyers and these parts of the GVC are protected by high entry barriers. By controlling these high-rent activities, buyers wield significant power over other actors in the chain. Power at the buyers' level has further increased due to consolidation among retailers resulting from mergers and acquisitions and the emergence of large discount chains and speciality apparel stores (Morris and Barnes, 2009). These asymmetric market and power structures further impede the capture of margins and upgrading of suppliers to higher value and rent activities (Gibbon and Ponte, 2005).

However, some developments may signal a partial shift in competitive and power structures in apparel GVCs. First, some intermediaries and first-tier suppliers, in particular global trading houses and transnational producers such as Li & Fung and the Esquel Group, have captured high value added activities and control far-flung manufacturing networks. These large global suppliers have reached powerful positions in apparel GVCs which potentially signal a shift in the governance structure of these chains and a reduction of power of global buyers vis-à-vis some actors (Appelbaum, 2008). Further, in the context of shifting demand structures, the role of buyers from emerging and developing countries is increasing in importance. Second, there is insecurity about China's future as a competitor to LIC apparel exporters. In the early 2000s, China upgraded its apparel production to include a higher proportion of higher value products, but this was at least partly reversed during the global economic crisis. It is not clear how fast China is moving into higher value added products. Furthermore, labour costs are rising in China and the exchange rate has gradually appreciated (Economist, 2012). Such developments could change supply structures and increase the space for LICs in apparel exporting, at least in the low-value market segment.

Importance of end market diversification

New global developments, including the emergence of powerful intermediaries and first-tier suppliers in developing countries, shifting end markets to large developing countries, regional and domestic markets, and the increasing importance of developing countries' buyers, could lead to new opportunities for LIC apparel exporters.

Global demand structures are changing as import demand for apparel in the USA and the EU, as well as in Japan, might stagnate, while demand will increase in fast growing emerging and developing countries. Currently, the large majority of apparel exports are geared towards the EU, the USA and Japan. Yet these markets only represent about 10 per cent of the world's population. The wealth of their population, and therefore the ability to buy apparel, is growing at a much slower pace than that of emerging and developing countries where demand for apparel increases at an even higher rate than economic growth (Morris and Barnes, 2009). The Economic Intelligence Unit found that the fastest growth in apparel retail demand for the period 2008–13 was located in China, Eastern Europe (including Russia), India, Turkey and Brazil (Textiles Intelligence, 2009). For large emerging economies, including China, India and Brazil, this has translated into a greater focus on domestic markets. For smaller economies, an increasing focus might be put on exporting to regional or large emerging or developing country markets (Cattaneo *et al.*, 2010; Staritz *et al.*, 2011). China, for instance, has increasingly diversified its export markets to emerging countries, including Russia and countries from the former Soviet bloc (for finished goods) and India, Brazil and Turkey (for intermediate goods such as textiles). In addition to new export markets, China has increased production for the domestic market. Estimates indicate that already in 2007 more than half of China's apparel production went already to local consumers (Clothesource, 2008) with total revenues in the domestic market continuing to rise significantly faster than exports (Butollo, forthcoming). This mirrors efforts to extend production for the local market by apparel firms in India and Turkey (Just Style, 2010).

These shifts in end markets may also lead to changing governance structures because the role of developed country-based buyers may be complemented by buyers from developing countries. Buyers from the USA and the EU have increased sales outlets and stores in fast growing emerging markets and have gained market share. While large markets in Latin America are largely dominated by foreign retailers, in China, India and South Africa local or regional retailers play an important role. Buyers in China, India, Brazil, Turkey or Russia, as well as in regional and domestic markets, may have different requirements and they may source differently compared with US or EU buyers. On the one hand, these markets may be less demanding with regard to design and product development, lead time and fashion content than markets in the USA and the EU, and they may also offer more opportunities to upgrade to higher value adding functions, in particular in regional and domestic markets (Gereffi and Frederick, 2010). But on the other hand, they may demand different capabilities such as smaller runs, different design and quality requirements as well as different sales, marketing and communication channels. Understanding these new markets and the sourcing policies of buyers selling in these markets will be essential for entry to, and upgrading within, these chains.

For instance in SSA, the US, EU and South African end markets have distinct requirements with different entry and upgrading possibilities which results in highly differentiated strategies for firms supplying them in Lesotho, Swaziland, Kenya, Mauritius and Madagascar (Gibbon, 2008; Morris and Sedowski, 2009; Staritz, 2011; Kaplinsky and Wamae, 2010; Morris *et al.*, 2011; Staritz and Morris, 2012; Morris and Staritz, 2014). US buyers demand high volumes of largely basic products. They emphasise the ability to produce to buyer specifications, nominate fabric and other input suppliers, and are generally not interested in suppliers' contributions to design. Lesotho, Swaziland, and Kenyan exporters to the USA follow these requirements, are owned by Asian large producers and have become locked into a low upgrading trajectory. EU buyers on the other hand require smaller orders, higher fashion content, more complex apparel products, and are open to more design–intensive products. South African buyers follow the EU market in many respects (but often demand smaller orders). Firms in Madagascar and

Mauritius supplying the EU market (and the smaller South African market) are hence more flexible, exhibit greater upgrading trajectories, and are more locally and regionally embedded. Likewise South African owned firms recently located to Lesotho and Swaziland supplying the South African market with products with a higher fashion content where lead times and volume flexibility are central in addition to pricing. In all these SSA countries, production for the EU and South African markets tends to bring a firm set-up and an overhead structure that is uncompetitive for the US market, and vice versa.

Role of ownership and local embeddedness for upgrading

Many LICs are integrated into apparel GVCs through FDI (Gereffi, 1999; Staritz, 2011; Staritz and Morris, 2012; Morris and Staritz, 2014; see also Kingombe and te Velde, Chapter 14 this volume). In these cases, it is not only crucial to analyse buyers' strategies and related value chain dynamics but also the strategic interest of foreign investors. 'Ownership' of supplier firms specifies how these firms are linked to global production and distribution networks and is an important criterion for the understanding of, and the differentiation between, their behaviour and activities. It reveals the extent to which firms are locally embedded, i.e. have roots in the social and economic fabric of the host country, and captures different strategies of investors and how they play out in terms of local decision-making power, value added and linkages to the local economy. These strategies are determined not only by the nationality of the investor but by the drivers and governance structures of different value chains and end markets in which differently owned firms are integrated (Morris *et al.*, 2011; Staritz and Morris, 2012; Morris and Staritz, 2014).

Three main groups of foreign investors can be identified in apparel GVCs with different entry and upgrading potential (Staritz and Frederick, 2012b). First, brand manufacturers, largely from the USA and Europe, have established regional and global production networks largely via FDI. This group of lead firms has, however, declined in importance and many have shifted to marketers or retailers and sourcing networks based on contract manufacturing. Second, faced with quota restrictions, rising labour costs and high demands from global buyers, transnational producers in Asian countries have developed manufacturing networks in Asia, Latin America, the Caribbean and SSA (Appelbaum, 2008; Gereffi, 1999). These firms generally own or source from production units in several countries and follow a global strategy. Head offices are generally in charge of input sourcing (often drawing on their own textile mills or sourcing networks based in Asia), product development and design, merchandising and marketing, and have direct relationships with buyers. A third group of foreign investors is more diverse – regionally embedded investors that organise production networks within a region, e.g. Indian and Sri Lankan investors in South Asia, Malaysian and Thai investors in Southeast Asia, and South African and Mauritian investors in SSA.

Integration through FDI on the one hand has promoted access to global sourcing and merchandising networks and, hence, facilitated entry to apparel exporting for LICs with no established local apparel producers. On the other hand, it has limited upgrading possibilities as critical decision-making and certain higher value functions are located at the head offices and are not transferred to supplier firms. Unlike locally owned plants, foreign-owned plants in LICs have limited leverage and autonomy in terms of strategic decision making and in attracting orders as relations and negotiations with buyers are generally located at the head offices (Natsuda *et al.*, 2009). Which functions are located in host countries and which production methods are used is determined by the strategic choice of foreign investors in terms of which functions, skills, inputs and expertise they are able to leverage from their head offices and global networks, which limits the need for capacity-building, investment and upgrading in LIC supplier firms (Paus and Gallagher, 2008).

Many LICs face challenges in how to use the presence of FDI as a basis for building locally embedded apparel industries. FDI has been central in the development of export apparel sectors in many LICs. But in particular, the integration via triangular manufacturing networks of transnational producers has locked LIC suppliers into second-tier positions and has often resulted in limited development of local skills, value added and linkages (Staritz and Frederick, 2012b). Building a locally embedded apparel sector is a precondition for sustainability and industrial development. However, local ownership is largely absent in many LICs, particularly in SSA (Morris *et al.*, 2011; Staritz and Morris, 2012; Morris and Staritz, 2014). But some countries such as Sri Lanka, Bangladesh and Mauritius have been successful in developing locally embedded industries based on FDI.

Increasing entry barriers have, however, raised the bar for local firms in LICs such as in SSA where the export apparel sector only started on a larger scale in the late 1990s and early 2000s. Industrial policies and industry associations have also played crucial roles in increasing local involvement in the apparel sector in LICs; where such policies have been absent, development of local firms and suppliers has been difficult. In Lesotho and Swaziland the focus has been on employment and foreign revenue generation. In Madagascar, the government has focused on rural development rather than manufacturing. Hence, governments and industry associations have not established explicit policies and programmes supporting the establishment and development of local firms, and existing policy incentives have catered to foreign investors that are involved in larger and export-oriented investments. Therefore policies have largely not taken into account local management and business skill shortages, access to credit, existence of local inputs and service providers, and access to foreign buyers (Morris *et al.*, 2011; Staritz and Morris, 2012; Morris and Staritz, 2014).

Conclusions and policy issues

The apparel sector still provides opportunities for export diversification and industrial development in LICs today. But the apparel GVC and associated entry and upgrading possibilities look different from a decade ago. Policy challenges to enter and upgrade in apparel GVCs relate to: (i) regulatory contexts; (ii) GVC dynamics, in particular asymmetric market structures and sourcing policies of buyers; (iii) the nature of FDI and the strategic interest of foreign investors in LICs; and (iv) local conditions, institutions and policies which also fundamentally shape upgrading opportunities.

Poor physical, bureaucratic and institutional infrastructure, limited local capabilities and skills, and non-existing or non-effective industrial policies constrain the use of the existing entry, upgrading and broader industrial development potential. Tackling these requires proactive policies. In conclusion, we emphasise four broad policy areas which require further specific articulation in any particular industry and country context:

- *Upgrading*. Policies have to focus on improving competitiveness and initiating upgrading in LIC's apparel sectors, especially in the context of supply chain rationalisation strategies. Competitiveness increasingly involves fulfilling high performance requirements with regard to quality, lead times and flexibility, complexity of products and different types of product, social and environmental standards, and broader non-manufacturing functions. This requires industrial policies focusing on expanding the skilled labour and management pool, fostering a culture to raise the operational competitive levels of manufacturing operations, and improving the institutional fabric related to training, as well as physical and bureaucratic infrastructure (Morris *et al.*, 2011). Furthermore, it requires the involvement of a multiplicity of actors in the process. Cooperation between industry associations and public actors have played critical roles to further upgrading of apparel industries in Turkey, Sri Lanka, Bangladesh and Mauritius (Staritz, 2011; Staritz and Frederick, 2012a, 2012b).

- *Market diversification and regional integration.* Most LIC apparel exports are still concentrated in a few end markets in high-income countries. End market diversification and shifting demand structures reduces the dependency on specific markets and buyers and may assist upgrading opportunities and increase bargaining power in value chains. Moreover, given increasing opportunities in emerging and large developing country markets, as well as in regional and domestic markets, these markets might exhibit better growth and upgrading potential and hence more beneficial outcomes (Pickles and Smith, 2010). Given the size, capacities and capabilities of many LIC's apparel sectors, a regional perspective, both with regard to end markets and production networks, is crucial for sustainable competitiveness and upgrading in the apparel industry. Regional integration could play a central role in reducing lead times and costs, capturing more value added and linkages in the region, and diversifying end markets. In this context, different complementary advantages in the region could be leveraged and economies of scale, vertical integration and horizontal specialisation could be promoted by policies aimed at regional coordination and integration.

- *Locally embedded apparel industries.* Focusing on locally embedded firms and increasing local involvement at the management and entrepreneur level to build locally embedded apparel industries is crucial to extend the impact of the apparel industry beyond its direct employment creation effect. Governments and industry associations have, however, not focused on supporting the establishment and development of local firms, suppliers and linkages. There are no straightforward policy recommendations for developing local entrepreneurship. However, certain internal conditions and policies are at least preconditions for local entrepreneurial activities: (i) access to low-cost and long-term finance for productive investment; (ii) access to industry-specific skill training in areas such as management and higher value and technical functions; (iii) support in establishing relationships with foreign investors, buyers and input suppliers; (iv) access to at least the same (or preferably higher) incentives as foreign investors; and (v) use of public procurement to further the development of local apparel firms and input suppliers (Staritz and Frederick, 2012b).

- *Preferential market access.* For many LICs preferential market access remains essential in sustaining a position in apparel GVCs. Preferences even have to be combined with single transformation ROOs for several LICs, in particular in SSA, to be able to take advantage of preferential market access. However, as more countries receive preferences and as tariff rates are generally declining, preferences will become eroded. In the short run, however, preferential market access will remain crucial for SSA LICs to sustain apparel exports. The effects of preference erosion on LIC apparel exporters have to be taken into account in trade negotiations at the international, regional and bilateral level.

LIC governments have often supported the apparel sector. However, most policies have focused on investment and particularly FDI attraction and incentives, and not on furthering upgrading, local involvement, value added and skills, and linkages to the local economy. To ensure the potential of apparel exports for industrial development, industries and countries need to improve their productive and institutional capacities but they also need to make sure that they 'capture the gains' of integration into and upgrading in apparel GVCs in terms of increased and sustained incomes, decent working conditions, local and regional linkages, and broader industrial and national development (Kaplinsky, 2005; Kaplinsky and Morris, 2001).

Notes

1 Although the apparel sector has its own specific characteristics, many of the industrialisation principles discussed apply also to other low- and medium-technology industries (footwear, furniture, parts of electronics and automotives, etc.).

2 The Asian-12 (Bangladesh, Cambodia, China, India, Indonesia, Laos, Nepal, Pakistan, Philippines, Sri Lanka, Thailand and Vietnam) increased their global market share from 33 per cent in 1995 to 64 per cent in 2013 (UN COMTRADE, 2015).

3 The chapter is based on a diverse set of primary and secondary data. It utilises trade and national sector data, and draws on a number of firm-level surveys and interviews conducted between 2008 and 2012 in Bangladesh, Cambodia, Sri Lanka, Kenya, Lesotho, Swaziland, Madagascar, and information from experts and industry informants. It also draws on buyer interviews in Europe, the United States and South Africa conducted in 2008. Field work was carried out partly in the context of research projects conducted for the African Clothing and Footwear Research Network (ACFRN), the Capturing the Gains (CtG) research network, the World Bank and the African Development Bank (AfDB).

4 From 2000 onwards, AGOA has provided quota- and duty-free market access for apparel products from SSA countries to the US market coupled with non-restrictive rules of origins (ROOs) as the Third Country Fabric (TCF) derogation allowed for single transformation for lesser developed countries. This led to a strong increase in apparel exports from few SSA countries, most importantly Lesotho, Kenya, Swaziland, Madagascar and Mauritius, to the USA (Kaplinsky and Morris, 2006; Staritz, 2011; Staritz and Morris, 2012; Morris and Staritz, 2014; Phelps *et al.*, 2009).

5 They are either stipulated as a certain percentage of the total value of products or certain production steps that have to take place in the beneficiary country. For apparel it is common to differentiate single transformation (involving only the sewing stage), double transformation (involving an additional production step – knitting or weaving) and triple transformation (adding spinning).

6 The TCF provision was, however, extended to 2007, 2012 and 2015.

7 Estimates for job losses attributable to the global economic crisis in different developing countries include: 10 million in China, 1 million in India, 200,000 in Pakistan, 100,000 in Indonesia, 80,000 in Mexico, 75,000 in Cambodia and 30,000 in Vietnam (Gereffi and Frederick, 2010).

References

Abernathy, F. H., Volpe, A. and Weil, D. 2006. The Future of the Apparel and Textile Industries: Prospects and Choices for Public and Private Actors. *Environment and Planning.* A 38 (12): 2207–2232.

Appelbaum, R. P. 2005. *TNCs and the Removal of Textiles and Clothing Quotas.* Center for Global Studies, University of California, Santa Barbara. Geneva: UNCTAD – accessible from http://unctad.org/en/Docs/iteiia20051_en.pdf

Appelbaum, R. 2008. Giant Transnational Contractors in East Asia: Emergent Trends in Global Supply Chains. *Competition & Change.* 12 (1): 69–87.

Bair, J. and Gereffi, G. 2003. Upgrading, Uneven Development, and Jobs in the North American Apparel Industry. *Global Networks.* 3 (2): 143–169.

Brenton, P. and Oezden, C. 2009. Trade Preferences for Apparel and the Role of Rules of Origin: The Case of Africa. In Hoekman, B., Martin, W., Braga, C. and Primo, A. (eds.). *Trade Preference Erosion: Measurement and Policy Response.* Basingstoke: Palgrave Macmillan.

Butollo, F. forthcoming. Growing Against the Odds. Industrial Upgrading in the Textile and Garment Industry in the Pearl River Delta. *Cambridge Journal of Regions, Economy and Society.* Published online July 2015.

Cattaneo, O., Gereffi, G. and Staritz, C. 2010. Global Value Chains in a Post-Crisis World: Resilience, Consolidation, and Shifting End Markets. In Cattaneo, O., Gereffi, G. and Staritz, C. (eds.). *Global Value Chains in a Post-Crisis World. A Development Perspective.* Trade and Development Series. Washington, DC: World Bank.

Clothesource. 2008. *The Great Apparel Sourcing Issues of 2008 – and How to Deal with Them.* March Management Briefing. Bromsgrove, UK: Aroq Limited.

Dickerson, K. G. 1999. *Textiles and Apparel in the Global Economy* (3rd ed.). Englewood Cliffs, NJ: Prentice Hall.

Economist. 2012 . The End of Cheap China: What do Soaring Chinese Wages Mean for Global Manufacturing? 10 March 2012 – Accessible from http://www.economist.com/printedition/2012–03–10

Frederick, S. 2010. *Development and Application of a Value Chain Research Approach to Understand and Evaluate Internal and External Factors and Relationships Affecting Economic Competitiveness in the Textile Value Chain.* Doctoral dissertation. Raleigh NC: North Carolina State University.

Frederick, S. and Staritz, C. 2012. Apparel Industry Developments After the MFA Phase-out. In Lopez-Acevedo, G. and Robertson, R. (eds.). *Sewing Success? Employment and Wage Effects Following the End of the Multi-Fibre Arrangement.* Washington, DC: The World Bank.

Gereffi, G. 1994. The Organization of Buyer-Driven Global Commodity Chains: How US Retailers Shape Overseas Production Networks. In Gereffi, G. and Korzeniewicz, M. (eds.). *Commodity Chains and Global Capitalism.* Westport, CT: Praeger.

Gereffi, G. 1999. International Trade and Industrial Upgrading in the Apparel Commodity Chain. *Journal of International Economics.* 48 (1): 37–70.

Gereffi, G. and Memedovic. O. 2003. *The Global Apparel Value Chain: What Prospects for Upgrading for Developing Countries.* Sectoral Studies Series. Vienna: UNIDO.

Gereffi, G. and Frederick, S. 2010. The Global Apparel Value Chain, Trade and the Crisis: Challenges and Opportunities for Developing Countries. In Cattaneo, O., Gereffi, G. and Staritz, C. (eds.). *Global Value Chains in a Post-Crisis World.* Washington, DC: The World Bank: 157–208.

Gereffi, G., Humphrey, J., Kaplinsky, R. and Sturgeon, T. J. 2001. Introduction: Globalisation, Value Chains and Development. *IDS Bulletin.* 32 (3): 1–8.

Gereffi, G., Humphrey, J. and Sturgeon, T. J. 2005. The Governance of Global Value Chains. *Review of International Political Economy.* 12 (1): 78–104.

Gibbon, P. 2008. Governance, Entry Barriers, Upgrading: A Re-Interpretation of Some GVC Concepts from the Experience of African Clothing Exports. *Competition and Change.* 12 (1): 29–48.

Gibbon, P. and Ponte, S. 2005. *Trading Down: Africa, Value Chains and the Global Economy.* Philadelphia, PA: Temple University Press.

Humphrey, J. and Schmitz, H. 2002. How does Insertion in Global Value Chains Affect Upgrading in Industrial Clusters? *Regional Studies.* 36 (9): 1017–1027.

Just Style. 2010. *August 2010 Management Brief: Part I – The Role of Location in Global Sourcing.* 26 March – accessed from just-style.com

Kaplinsky, R. 2005. *Globalization, Poverty and Inequality: Between a Rock and a Hard Place.* Cambridge: Polity Press.

Kaplinsky, R. and Morris, M. 2001. *A Handbook for Value Chain Research.* Prepared for the IDRC. Milton Keynes: The Open University – accessible from http://asiandrivers.open.ac.uk/documents/

Kaplinsky, R., and Morris, M. 2006. *Dangling by a Thread: How Sharp are the Chinese Scissors?* Prepared for the Africa Policy Division, DFID. Brighton: Institute for Development Studies – accessible from http://asiandrivers.open.ac.uk/documents/

Kaplinsky, R. and Messner, D. 2008. Introduction: The Impact of Asian Drivers on the Developing World. *World Development.* 36 (2): 197–209.

Kaplinsky, R. and Morris, M. 2008. Do the Asian Drivers Undermine Export-Oriented Industrialization in SSA? *World Development.* 36 (2): 254–273.

Kaplinsky, R. and Wamae, W. 2010. *The Determinants of Upgrading and Value Added in the African Clothing Sector: The Contrasting Experiences of Kenya and Madagascar.* Working Paper 59 – Innovation, Knowledge, Development series. Milton Keynes: The Open University.

Morris, M. 2006. China's Dominance of Global Clothing and Textiles: Is Preferential Trade Access an Answer for Sub-Saharan Africa? *IDS Bulletin* 37 (1): 89–97.

Morris, M. and Barnes, J. 2009. *Globalization, the Changed Global Dynamics of the Clothing and Textile Value Chains and the Impact on Sub-Saharan Africa.* UNIDO Research and Statistics Branch Working Paper 10. Vienna: United Nations Industrial Development Organization.

Morris, M. and Sedowski, L. 2009. The Competitive Dynamics of the Clothing Industry in Madagascar in the Post-MFA Environment. In McCormick, D., Kuzilwa, J. A. and Gebre Egziabher, T. (eds.). *Industrialising Africa in the Era of Globalisation: Challenges to Clothing and Footwear.* Nairobi: University of Nairobi Press.

Morris, M. and Staritz, C. 2014. Industrialization Trajectories in Madagascar's Export Apparel Industry: Ownership, Embeddedness, Markets, and Upgrading. *World Development.* 56 (April): 243–257.

Morris, M., Staritz, C. and Barnes, J. 2011. Value Chain Dynamics, Local Embeddedness, and Upgrading in the Clothing Sectors of Lesotho and Swaziland. *International Journal of Technological Learning, Innovation and Development.* 4 (1–3): 96–119.

Natsuda, K., Goto, K. and Thoburn, J. 2009. *Challenges to the Cambodian Garment Industry in the Global Garment Value Chain*. Ritsumeikan Center for Asia Pacific Studies (RCAPS).Working Paper No. 09–3, July. Ōita, Japan: Ritsumeikan Asia Pacific University.

Palpacuer, F., Gibbon, P. and Thomsen, L. 2005. New Challenges for Developing Country Suppliers in Global Clothing Chains: A Comparative European Perspective. *World Development*. 33 (3): 409–430.

Paus, E. A. and Gallagher, K. P. 2008. Missing Links: Foreign Investment and Industrial Development in Costa Rica and Mexico. *Studies in Comparative International Development*. 43 (1): 53–80.

Phelps, N. A., Stillwell, J. C. H. and Wanjiru, R. 2009. Broken Chain? AGOA and Foreign Direct Investment in the Kenyan Clothing Industry. *World Development*. 37 (2): 314–325. Pickles, J. and Smith, A. 2010. Clothing Workers After Worker States: The Consequences for Work and Labour of Outsourcing, Nearshoring and Delocalization in Postsocialist Europe. In McGrath-Champ, S., Herod, A. and Rainnie, A. (eds.). *Handbook of Employment and Society*. Edward Elgar: Cheltenham: 106–123.

Plank, L., Rossi, A. and Staritz, C. 2012. *Workers and Social Upgrading in 'Fast Fashion': The Case of the Apparel Industry in Morocco and Romania*. ÖFSE Working Paper 33. Vienna: Austrian Research Foundation for International Development (ÖFSE).

Singa Boyenge, J.-P. 2007. *ILO Database on Export-Processing Zones (Revised). Sectoral Activities Programme.* Working Paper 251. Geneva: International Labour Office.

Staritz, C. 2011. *Making the Cut? Low-Income Countries and the Global Clothing Value Chain in a Post-Quota and Post-Crisis World*. Washington DC: The World Bank.

Staritz, C. 2012. *Apparel Exports – Still a Path for Industrial Development? Dynamics in Apparel Global Value Chains and Implications for Low-Income Countries*. ÖFSE Working Paper 34, Vienna: Austrian Research Foundation for International Development (ÖFSE).

Staritz, C. and Frederick, S. 2012a. Summaries of the Country Case Studies on Apparel Industry Development, Structure, and Policies. In Lopez-Acevedo, G. and Robertson, R. (eds.). *Sewing Success? Employment, Wages, and Poverty Following the End of the Multi-Fibre Arrangement*. Washington, DC: The World Bank.

Staritz, C. and Frederick, S. 2012b. *Sector Background Paper: Apparel*. FDI and Global Value Chains in Sub-Saharan Africa: Understanding the Factors that Contribute to Integration and Spillovers. Unpublished draft. The World Bank, Washington, DC.

Staritz, C. and Morris, M. 2012. *Local Embeddedness, Upgrading and Skill Development: Global Value Chains and Foreign Direct Investment in Lesotho's Apparel Industry*. ÖFSE Working Paper 32. Vienna: Austrian Research Foundation for International Development (ÖFSE).

Staritz, C., Gereffi, G. and Cattaneo, O. 2011. Editorial. In: Shifting End Markets and Upgrading Prospects in Global Value Chains. Special Issue of the *International Journal of Technological Learning, Innovation and Development*. 4 (1/2/3).

Textiles Intelligence. 2009. World Trade in Textiles and Clothing. Presentation by Sam Anson at the World Free Zones Conference in Hyderabad, India, December.

UN COMTRADE. 2015. *International Merchandise Trade Statistics*. New York: United Nations Statistics Division – accessed from http://unstats.un.org/unsd/trade/imts/ in April 2015.

14

THE ROLE OF SPECIAL ECONOMIC ZONES IN MANUFACTURING DEVELOPMENT IN SUB-SAHARAN AFRICA

Structural transformation and employment creation[1]

Christian Kingombe and Dirk Willem te Velde

Introduction

This chapter examines the role of special economic zones (SEZs) in promoting employment growth, raising productivity and generating spill-over and linkage effects which benefit the rest of the economy. There is a well-established debate on the role of the state in steering development and governing the market (e.g. Wade, 1990). Recent developments in the theory and practice of growth identification and facilitation suggest there is an important role for the state in supporting growth.[2] The main growth policy tool considered in this debate is the creation of SEZs (and export processing zones – EPZs) as a means of attracting foreign direct investment (FDI) (Madani, 1999; ILO, 2008; Farole, 2011; Farole and Akinci, 2011). The recent emphasis on the success of SEZs in middle income countries, and on the new SEZs being built by emerging markets in Africa, is leading to a reassessment of whether SEZs can help to facilitate development transformations (Draper *et al.*, 2011).

There has been much interest in the performance of SEZs, and of EPZs in particular, and of their potential for stimulating manufacturing exports from developing countries. Contributions by Warr have been especially valuable in providing insights into this area of development policy based on country case studies (1987a, 1987b, 1989), and through an important review chapter (Warr, 1990). Other overall reviews of experience with SEZs/EPZs have been those by Wall (1976), Spinanger (1984), Tsuchiya (1987) and Balasubramanyam (1988). Other country case studies have been provided by Alter (1991), Chen (1993) and Kumar (1987). It is reassuring that the findings of this chapter are largely consistent with many of the findings of the literature from the 1980s and 1990s, although perhaps this continuity might also indicate limited learning from global experience. This chapter makes a particular contribution through its review of more recent sub-Saharan African case studies.

The structure of this chapter is as follows: the following section reviews evidence on SEZ stimulation of employment and productivity growth based on global and sub-Saharan African experience. The third section discusses a range of policies relating to SEZs and conditions under which they are most effective. The fourth section concludes.

The character and role of special economic zones

The use of SEZs is one element of growth policies that could potentially have a net positive impact on employment, productivity and manufactured exports within the context of structural transformation. Farole (2010a, 2010b) defines SEZs as demarcated geographical areas within a country's national boundaries where government policy towards, and the regulation of, firms' activity, are differentiated from that applied to firms outside the zone. The International Labour Office has a significant information base on EPZs on its website (ILO, 2012). The aim of government policy towards SEZs is to create a policy and infrastructure environment that is exporter friendly for both domestic and foreign producers. There are various types of SEZs (for a fuller classification see Farole, 2011). Fundamentally, EPZs are a particular type of SEZ – so that all EPZs are SEZs, with SEZs being the wider category. In reviewing the substantial literature on SEZs/EPZs, one problem has been that many of the sources do not make a clear distinction between the two. However, the most common SEZs in Africa are essentially EPZs offering duty-free trade and administrative services and which range in size from very large industrial estates to single factory schemes. Some SEZs take the form of enterprise zones or technology parks aimed at fostering clusters of firms and support industries. Africa contains examples of all forms of SEZs. For example, Malawi has a number of single factory EPZ schemes designed to take advantage of US trade preferences for garments, while the Ebone tower in Mauritius is a purpose-built tower hosting a number of ICT companies.

There are basically two views on the role of SEZs and EPZs. Many have considered the creation of an EPZ to be a second best option when the first best option of free trade is not practicable (Madani, 1999; Watson, 2001). However, Stein (2008) argues that SEZs should be considered as a viable policy instrument within a more general industrial policy framework (Belloca and di Maio, 2011). In this latter view, geographical clustering through SEZ development can contribute to the raising of productivity. Companies in clusters can become more specialised, productive and innovative with externalities for the sector and for the economy as a whole (Porter, 1998; Schmitz and Nadvi, 1999).[3]

In practice, the rationale for setting up SEZs and EPZs relies on a combination of arguments based on clustering and streamlined trade policies combined with a pragmatic view of state support where an opportunity to provide help is perceived in response to pressures.

The chapter will examine the extent to which SEZs (including EPZs) can raise a country's manufactured exports and manufacturing productivity, change the economic structure and create employment in a sustained way, and whether these aims are more likely to occur within socially cohesive environment.

The effects of SEZs on job creation and structural transformation in sub-Saharan Africa

Evidence on the role of SEZs in sub-Saharan Africa is explored and categorised in three areas: (i) the levels and types of employment which are stimulated; (ii) the extent to which productivity is enhanced and innovation is encouraged; and (iii) the extent to which social cohesion is maintained.

Levels and types of employment

The incremental impact of SEZs arises when new economic activity would not have been established in the absence of SEZs. Data on the employment impact of SEZ investment globally suggests that there are approximately 3,000 zones in 135 countries, accounting for over 68 million direct jobs and over $500 billion of direct trade-related value added within the zones (FIAS, 2008). However, SEZs do not play a substantial role in overall employment in most African countries. Some 1 million SEZ jobs were found in 91 SEZs in 20 SSA countries representing only 0.2 per cent of national SSA employment (Table 14.1). Half of the EPZ employment in SSA is in South Africa, but a significant share of employment in Mauritius, Lesotho, Kenya, Nigeria and Madagascar is to be found in EPZs (ILO, 2008; and Table 14.2). Figure 14.1 provides a number of country examples showing interesting exceptions and promising examples. For example, in Ghana, employment in SEZs increased from 4,000 in 1998 to 27,798 in 2010. The share of SEZ employment in total formal employment is around 3 per cent in Tanzania and Ghana and around 1.5 per cent in Kenya (where the share of SEZs in manufacturing employment is reportedly 15 per cent).

Table 14.1 Employment in special economic zones

	Direct employment (millions)	*Percentage of national employment*
Global	68.441	0.21
Asia and the Pacific	61.089	2.30
Americas	3.084	1.15
Central/East Europe and Central Asia	1.59	0.00
Middle East and North Africa	1.458	1.59
Sub-Saharan Africa	1.04	0.20

Source: FIAS (2008) using data for 2006.

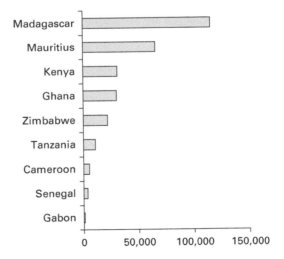

Figure 14.1 Employment in African SEZs.

Source: Based on ILO and own research (data are for 2010 or earlier).

Table 14.2 EPZ employment in selected countries, 2002–06 (ranked by 2002 employment)

Country	2002	2006	Percentage change
Global			
Mexico	1,355,000	1,212,125	−11.0
Philippines	820,960	1,128,197	37.0
Tunisia	239,800	259,842	8.0
Malaysia	200,000	369,488	85.0
Dominican Republic	170,833	154,781	−9.0
Macao, China	131,010	131,010	0.0
Bangladesh	121,000	188,394	56.0
Sri Lanka	111,033	410,851	270.0
Viet Nam	107,000	950,000	788.0
Mauritius	87,607	65,512	−25.0
Madagascar	74,000	115,000	55.0
Morocco	71,315	145,000	103.0
Costa Rica	34,000	36,000	6.0
Haiti	10,000	10,000	0.0
Sub-Saharan Africa			
Kenya	27,148	38,851	43.0
Zimbabwe	22,000	22,000	0.0
Cameroon	8,000	4,690	−41.0
Senegal	940	3,409	263.0
Gabon	790	791	0.0

Sources: ILO (2003); Boyenge (2007).

Whether employment created in SEZs adds to overall formal sector employment could be questioned, since it is difficult to construct a counterfactual. There are cases where dissatisfaction with an SEZ scheme has resulted in the loss of employment, not only for the SEZ but also for aggregate employment. For example, in Tanzania, following persistent issues with an EPZ scheme, Mount Meru Millers Limited moved its agro-processing activities to Uganda in 2011. While the firm continues to buy sunflower seeds from Tanzanian farmers, the move of the processing facilities reportedly led to the loss of hundreds of direct jobs (AllAfrica.com, 2011).

The employment impact of zones is directly linked to their overall economic performance. For example in Burundi, although some experience in marketing and selling to Europe has been gained and made available to other exporters, most benefits expected from the Zone Franche did not materialize: there was no significant attraction of FDI, and only slight employment creation in the Zone (UNCTAD, 2009). By contrast, in Mauritius the EPZ Programme was at the heart of the government's industrial development strategy in the 1970s and 1980s, and helped to attract FDI inflows in labour-intensive manufacturing, mainly from Asia, and concentrated on knitwear and garment manufacture. During this period the Mauritian EPZ hosted a significant amount of additional employment, and contributed more value added and more export revenue than sugar, which had been the primary engine of growth until then (UNCTAD, 2001). In Madagascar, EPZ export activity grew at an average annual rate of 20.2 per cent between 1996 and 2001, textile exports expanded significantly (thanks to the preferential access of clothing items to the American market within the AGOA) and significant employment was created as a result (Mangieri, 2013; Enhanced Integrated Framework, 2003).

SEZs contribute significantly to exports of manufactures both globally and in SSA (see Tables 14.3 and 14.4). They attract significant amounts of FDI through aligning with the international economy. The competitive strengths of SEZs can be accounted for in at least two differing ways: building on comparative advantage or utilising trade preferences. Ghana's experience is notable in that it used a zone to bring together cocoa- and timber-based trade, exploiting its comparative advantage and promoting exports. However, many jobs in African SEZs are linked to trade preferences for garment assembly operations. The ILO, WB and local data sources reviewed in this chapter show that a significant amount of SEZ employment

Table 14.3 EPZ share of manufactured exports and change between 2002 and 2006 for selected economies

Country	2002	2006	Percentage change
Global			
Philippines	87.0	60.0	−31.0
Malaysia	83.0	83.0	0.0
Mexico	83.0	47.0	−43.0
Macao, China	80.0	80.0	0.0
Viet Nam	80.0	80.0	0.0
Dominican Republic	80.0	80.0	0.0
Tunisia	80.0	52.0	−35.0
Morocco	61.0	61.0	0.0
Bangladesh	60.0	75.6	26.0
Costa Rica	50.0	52.0	4.0
Haiti	50.0	50.0	0.0
Sri Lanka	33.0	38.0	15.0
Maldives	13.2	47.7	261.0
Colombia	9.3	40.0	330.0
Sub-Saharan Africa			
Zimbabwe	80.0	80.0	0.0
Gabon	80.0	80.0	0.0
Kenya	80.0	86.9	9.0
Senegal	80.0	n.a.	n.a.
Mauritius	77.0	42.0	−45.0
Madagascar	38.0	80.0	111.0
Cameroon	32.0	33.0	3.0

Sources: ILO (2003); Boyenge (2007).

Table 14.4 Exports by special economic zones in 2006

	SEZ exports (US$ millions)	SEZ exports as percentage of manufactured exports
Global	851,032	41
Asia and the Pacific	510,666	41
Americas	72,636	39
Central and East Europe and Central Asia	89,666	39
Middle East and North Africa	169	36
Sub-Saharan Africa	8,605	49

Source: FIAS (2008).

in Africa is in the textiles and garments sectors (90 per cent in Mauritius and Madagascar, 33 per cent in Kenya, 11 per cent in Tanzania and Zimbabwe) and in agro-processing (60 per cent in Ghana, 50 per cent in Zimbabwe, 18 per cent in Kenya), with the remainder being accounted for by other light manufacturing and services.

Productivity and innovation effects

SEZs can be associated with productivity and innovation effects throughout the economy in a number of different ways. These include technological linkages (e.g. through technological 'spill-over' effects), skill linkages (e.g. when former SEZ staff set up companies elsewhere), export linkages (e.g. SEZ firms helping exports by non-SEZ firms) and regulatory linkages (when SEZ-type regulations are extended economy-wide). The relevance of intellectual property rights to technological development is the subject of close attention by Lall (2001), and EPZs have also been regarded as having a role within international trade in services (UNCTAD, 2004). Skill transfer through FDI is a significant issue in this context (te Velde and Xenogiani, 2007).

The evidence suggests that a number of countries have used SEZs successfully in 'upgrading' their economies, but these examples are mainly non-African (including Malaysia, Singapore, Costa Rica and Dominican Republic). Johansson and Nilsson (1997) show that in the case of Malaysia the export-generating effect of the Malaysian EPZs extends beyond the EPZs into the wider economy. Successful cases in Asia have encompassed the raising of the innovation potential of SEZs through the establishment of conditions making it cost-effective to use local suppliers, to upgrade domestic capabilities, to encourage labour circulation and to enhance the investment climate.[4]

There is a large literature on the transformational impact of SEZs in China which is referred to in Yeung *et al.* (2009). Zhihua Zeng (2011) suggests that SEZs and industrial clusters have made crucial contributions to China's economic success, playing important roles in bringing new technologies to China and in adopting modern management practices. The Chinese experience suggests that clustering and an impetus for further reform are co-benefits from SEZs (Graham, 2004), as well as favourable effects on exports and jobs. Zhihua Zeng (2010) argues that factors within the Chinese model include a strong commitment to reform and pragmatism from top leadership.

The success of EPZs in Mauritius has been due to multiplier impacts on the economy, creating demands for services in packaging, consultancy, water, electricity, transport and mechanical workshops for example, and leading to some backward linkages for the assembly sector. Domestic firms have been able to learn from foreign firms. While Mauritian EPZ exports in the 1980s were mainly from foreign firms, by 2000 these exports were often from national firms (UNECA, 2011), examples coming especially from the footloose garment industry. Mauritian firms have also been successful in raising the quality of garment products and in acquiring design and marketing capabilities (UNCTAD, 2001). Annex A to this chapter provides evidence that EPZs have helped to raise labour productivity in Kenyan manufacturing by some 20 per cent in the decade to 2006 as well as increasing employment by 40,000.

There have been significant employment increases in SEZs in Ghana, although granting free zone status to individual firms located outside designated zones may have reduced clustering effects and opportunities for spill-overs (UNCTAD, 2003). The spill-over effects in Madagascar are likely to have been limited as the Zone Franche companies have primarily relied on imported material inputs and the workforce predominantly consists of low-skilled female workers with a high rate of labour-turnover (Cling *et al.*, 2005).

The literature reviewed in this chapter suggests that SEZs can have long-lasting innovation, productivity and transformational effects but this has mainly been in evidence in Asian countries, which have put in place deliberate actions which enhance positive spill-overs, rather than in African countries.

Social cohesion

The link between SEZs and social cohesion centres around three issues. (i) How do the social conditions in SEZs compare with the rest of the economy? (ii) Are SEZs simply a tool for attracting FDI and generating exports or are they seen as a broader social development tool stimulating economic activity in backward regions? (iii) Are SEZs static enclaves or are they fully linked dynamically into the rest of the economy (and do they benefit all groups in society)?

On the first issue an ILO report sets out the main issues very clearly (ILO, 1998), and in more recent empirical work Farole (2011) suggests that SEZs tend to pay higher wages than the national minimum wage and have a predominantly female workforce. They are also less unionised and some 'unsuccessful' zones are segregated from the rest of the labour market. Based on global evidence, Amengual and Milberg (2008) find that wages tend to be higher among EPZ workers than in other sectors of the economy (with specific reference to Bangladesh, Costa Rica, Honduras, Madagascar and Sri Lanka). Workers in EPZs tend to work more hours (including excessive, and often illegal, overtime) when compared with other sectors of the economy (evidence from Bangladesh, Madagascar and Sri Lanka). There are reported violations of freedom of association in EPZs throughout the world. Most studies find very few labour unions active both inside and outside of EPZs. An ITUC report (2008), and a number of ICTFU (2003, 2004) reports, found that the ILO's core labour standards are violated in Madagascar, with Cling *et al.* (2007) arguing that the situation within the Zone Franche is not notably different than elsewhere in the country. So whilst it is widely perceived as important to improve labour market institutions (including unions) in low income countries, the evidence on whether SEZs help or hinder this process is inconclusive.

On the second issue, McCallum (2011) asks how the 'success' of the EPZ model as an engine of FDI can be reconciled with 'success' as instrument of social development. The cases of China and South Africa suggest these are contrasting objectives. In China, EPZs have grown in popularity across the economy, have attracted many investors and have turned the government further toward 'global' capitalist development, whilst at the same time restricting workers' rights. In South Africa, by contrast, unions have retained influence over government and have succeeded in holding EPZ employers accountable to workers, but the strategy has failed to produce noticeable socio-economic gains or to attract significant numbers of investors. While SEZs in China and maquilas in Honduras were set up primarily in ports, which had the highest levels of existing industrialisation, South Africa tried to develop new SEZs in order to catalyse social development in locations with low levels of industrialisation where FDI would not otherwise have been attracted. Glick and Roubaud (2006) find that in Madagascar, growth within the Zone Franche contributes substantially to improved overall gender equity in earnings in the urban economy.

Finally, with respect to the third issue, whilst SEZs are not important in quantitative terms in most African countries with respect to employment, they have been criticised for poor labour standards, especially when they are essentially localised enclaves which have little interaction with the rest of the economy. But when they work well, and when there is significant interaction between SEZs and the local economy, SEZs can generate significant employment and lead to positive development impacts. It seems that social cohesion, employment creation and structural change go hand in hand in the case of SEZs. The experience of several Asian SEZs suggests that there is significant interaction between SEZs and the local economy in successful zones. Examples of such interaction are through transport links in China's Shenzhen SEZ (World Bank, 2009), and through supplier development programmes in Singapore, but in much of Africa where the interaction with the local economy is less or when SEZs have been located in lagging regions, dynamic effects are much less significant. This type of weak interaction also applies to Latin American countries where the maquiladoras tend to have weak linkages with the domestic economy (UNCTAD, 2011).

In Madagascar, there are strong links between EPZ firms and local suppliers and, as a result, the ratio of indirect to direct employment creation is relatively high, with an estimate of 1.4 indirect jobs having been created for each Zone Franche job in 1997 (Cling and Letilly, 2001). However, a more recent study estimates an indirect to direct job ratio of 0.7 (Cling *et al.*, 2005). Both of these estimates compare favourably to the indirect to direct job ratio in Mauritius which an ILO study put at 0.25 in 1998 (Cling and Letilly, 2001). In Mozambique there have been some inward linkages between metallurgy service firms in the Beleluane EPZ and a big aluminium smelter (the Mozal project) (Enhanced Integrated Framework, 2004).

Conclusion

This review suggests that for some countries none of the SEZ performance indicators shows any significant progress (Nigeria and Senegal are examples). Even the most successful zones in Africa – such as those in Ghana, Lesotho, Madagascar and Kenya – currently appear to be facing stagnation (Kingombe and te Velde, 2012). Whilst these countries have used their SEZs to promote employment they have mostly failed to use the zones for structural transformation despite positive evidence on the past role of EPZs in Kenya. Positive outcomes have occurred in Mauritius, the Dominican Republic and Costa Rica, while in Singapore and Malaysia (for example Jurong Penang) SEZs have stimulated significant job creation. For the successful cases it seems that social cohesion, employment creation and structural change go hand in hand.

Countries such as Singapore, Malaysia and Costa Rica have been able to get out of the low skill, low income trap and these countries also have high social cohesion scores (for example with respect to lack of political troubles). Data presented in the *African Economic Outlook* suggests that in African countries with non- or weakly-functioning zones (such as Burundi, Nigeria and Senegal) there is a much higher 'political troubles' score than in countries such as Ghana, Lesotho and Mauritius with more active zones (AfDB *et al.*, 2011).

Policies and experience related to SEZs

This section is concerned with the extent to which long-term structural transformation and short-term employment generation objectives for SEZs can co-exist. We suggest that countries need to consider three specific issues if they wish to have effective SEZs: (a) solutions which address global opportunities; (b) SEZs as a strategic policy tool; and (c) learning from global best-practices. This discussion needs to be viewed within the context of 'global competitiveness' (UNCTAD, 2008) and it will refer to both global and SSA experience.

Do SEZs respond to global developments?

SEZs can be designed to make use of trade preference systems established by G20 countries such as the US African Growth and Opportunity Act (AGOA) provisions (US Government,

2013) or the EU's Everything but Arms (EBA) initiative (EU, 2013). These preference systems tend to be time bound and developing countries need to be sufficiently flexible to respond and adapt to changes in trade preference rules. When preferential tariffs and other trade regulations are changed, the value of SEZ benefits may be reduced. Cling *et al.* (2007) suggest that EPZs focused on garment assembly alone cannot be considered as being placed at the core of development and employment policies in Africa after the end of the Multifibre Arrangement (MFA) quotas. Mauritius, Madagascar and Kenya have already suffered declines for this reason in recent years. Value added in Madagascan EPZs dropped 5 per cent in 2010, continuing the reduction experienced in 2009. The textile industry has been accounting for about 95 per cent of the firms in these zones, with ownership largely being foreign – French, Mauritian and Chinese (AfDB *et al.*, 2011).

The export-oriented apparel sector in Kenya achieved rapid growth between 2000 and 2004 due to improved access to the US market under the AGOA. Apparel exports from Kenya to the USA increased from US$44 million in 2000 to US$226 million in 2004, making Kenya the second-largest exporter of clothing to the USA from SSA after Lesotho (see Table 14.5). Most of the new clothing factories had been established within EPZs. By December 2004 the EPZ clothing sector employed 34,614 workers in 30 world-class factories with an investment of US$144 million (Ksh8.6 billion) in 2004 (Mangieri, 2006).

The third-country fabric provision element of AGOA ended on 30 September 2012. Kenya has depended on imports from developing countries such as India, Bangladesh, China and Malaysia for their fabric supply. After September 2012, Kenyan textile and apparel companies needed to source raw materials such as cotton and yarn locally to qualify for duty-free import into the USA. Textile manufacturers in Kenya had been concerned about the delay in negotiating an extension to the September 2012 deadline, which had a serious impact on business with the uncertainty potentially leading to the loss of thousands of jobs. One of the key Kenyan challenges regarding AGOA has been to ensure the continuation of AGOA after the framework expires in 2015 (Mangieri, 2006).

The USA has traditionally provided a ready market for Lesotho's exports of apparel and the provisions of the AGOA has bolstered this. In 2001 and 2002, 99 per cent of Lesotho's exports

Table 14.5 Zones and trade preferences

	Kenya	*Lesotho*
AGOA: US legislation 2000 providing duty access to USA, extended to 2015 in 2003	Kenyan textile and apparel exports were US$ 292 million in 2011, which made the country the largest African supplier to the USA under AGOA	Lesotho has emerged as one of SSA's largest garments exporters to the USA
Textile and apparel: US imports from in 2010, value (US$000s)	202,256	315,365
Textile and apparel: US imports from in 2008, value (US$000s)	247,100	278,388
Post-MFA effect on EPZ firms	12 factory closures – 22 remain open	
Post-MFA effect on EPZ employment	Loss of approx. 20,000 jobs 38,600–39,800 current employees	

Sources: Interviews conducted by the authors with Kenya's EPZ Authority and Lesotho's EPZ Authority; Mangieri (2006); and AGOA info.

fell into the 'textiles and apparel' category, of which 98 per cent were AGOA-eligible, a distinction achieved by no other AGOA-eligible country. However, as in Kenya, AGOA requires countries to source fabric locally from 2012, a condition that Lesotho is unlikely to be able to meet. Both Kenya and Lesotho need to ensure sure that their SEZs are able to attract business that is not dependent on such temporary trade preferences.

SEZs and comparative advantage

SEZs can be established and maintained either (i) conforming with comparative advantage or (ii) defying comparative advantage. In Ghana the Tema SEZ has been based on a clustering of agro-companies which conform with comparative advantage. With high commodity prices, and a relative scarcity of natural resources, countries that possess such natural resources can exploit comparative advantage by building SEZs through what has been referred to as 'comparative advantage conforming industrial policy' (Lin *et al.*, 2011).

Some successful SEZs have been based on clusters based on comparative advantage. Clusters have been defined as geographic and sectoral agglomerations of enterprises (Schmitz and Nadvi, 1999). Successful SEZ clusters identified in the literature include: (a) the Tema zone in Ghana which is based on the agri–business sector; (b) the Shenzhen zone in China; (c) Jurong Park in Singapore which is based on a petrochemical cluster; (d) Penang in Malaysia which established a skills and technology park based on electronics; and (e) the Ebone Tower in Mauritius, which is based on the offshore services market. Such clusters fit well within a view of country comparative advantage.

Other examples appear to be comparative advantage defying. Nadvi and Barrientos (2004) present evidence that clusters are particularly effective if and when there are dense interactions amongst firms and support institutions, but these interactions may not occur just because of the close geographical proximity. From this perspective it may be beneficial to convert existing clusters which are already characterised by dense relationships into an SEZ.

The potential for SEZs to 'defy' comparative advantage in the right circumstances, while at the same time addressing global opportunities, is demonstrated by the zones in Singapore and Malaysia which helped to shift economic development on to a more advanced technological path. To adopt a strategy which defies comparative advantage requires significant implementation capacity, together with strategic interventions. Singapore and Malaysia implemented a set of human development, incentive and technology-related measures in their SEZs ensuring that the zones were successful.

SEZs and labour force training

The Malaysian government introduced a number of policies during the 1990s aimed at encouraging the role of the private sector training activities and reducing the direct government role including: promoting private sector participation in human resource planning through the National Vocational Training Council; promoting the role of the private sector in the provision of training through tax deduction on training expenses in approved institutions; promoting the sharing of public and private sector training resources through the exchange of trainers or allowing the use of public training facilities.[5]

Another example of an active labour training policy focused on the private sector (including multinational enterprises) is provided by the Skills Development Fund in Singapore. The Productivity and Standards Board (PSB), responsible for the fund, imposes a 1 per cent levy (it was 4 per cent before the economic crisis in 1986) on the payroll of employers for every worker earning less than a predetermined amount. This levy is distributed to firms that send their low-earning employees to approved training courses. This has had a significant impact on skills upgrading in Singapore (an estimated 10 per cent of the workforce has been to approved training courses, which has led to notable skills upgrading).

Do SEZ policies fit in overall development strategies?

The available evidence overwhelmingly supports the view that SEZs work best if they are seen as an integral part of a country's development strategy. For example, FIAS (2008) suggests that the success of zone initiatives is largely determined by the choices made in the establishment of policy frameworks, incentive packages, and bureaucratic procedures. The experience suggests that maximising the benefits of zones depends on integration into their host economies and on the overall trade and investment reform agenda. When zones are designed to pilot legal and regulatory reform within a planned policy framework, they are more likely to reach their objectives. Further, the establishment of a successful EPZ programme does not require removing only one, two or a few obstacles, it requires removing all of them simultaneously (Aggarwal, 2005).

SEZs need to be viewed as an integral part of a country's development strategy and Virgill (2009) emphasises the complementary roles of SEZ development and reform of the financial system, overall governance and corporate governance. SEZs have tended not to emerge in the most distorted (unreformed) economies. Omar and Stoever (2008) argue that SEZs alone do not lead to the structural transformation that developing countries seek, but that they can be a significant factor in a developing country development strategy when managed effectively. They argue that investments in human resource development and technology upgrading are necessary to support the emergence of local suppliers and to stimulate SEZs.

A range of complementary policies need to be marshalled when stimulating innovation through SEZs (Farole, 2011). Policy areas such as encouragement of local content in a World Trade Organization compatible way (China, Ireland, Mozambique [Mozal]), increasing domestic capabilities (skills development in Singapore and Malaysia Penang), labour circulation (placements in Shenzhen, China; and Mauritius), national investment climate reform outside the zone and infrastructure development (building specialised infrastructure inside zones and connecting zones to the remainder of the economy). All of these areas help economic and social cohesion by building bridges amongst various groups and sectors. At the same time, a more socially cohesive society is less likely to experience economic and social disruption (including labour disputes) and is more likely to lead to productive linkages.

SEZ implementation issues

Implementation (i.e. establishing and managing) SEZs raises several issues. Baissac (2003) suggests that SEZ policy should not be developed simply to generate static economic benefits such as increased employment and foreign exchange earning within an enclave system, which would be likely to lead to net benefits being small and probably negative. Additionally, SEZ schemes should not aim to achieve regional development objectives, but should be based on economic concentration around a well-developed urban centre in order to be able to access the best sources of domestic capital and the best educated productive labour, and to provide access to established urban infrastructure and amenities for prospective foreign investors. Thus SEZ location is a significant factor.

There are issues surrounding the comparative advantages of clustering relative to single factory schemes. Clustering of firms within an SEZ stimulates agglomeration economies, whilst single factory schemes do not. In addition the nature of the SEZ management agency matters, with FIAS arguing that the private sector is more efficient in supplying many types of SEZs services (FIAS, 2008).

Farole (2011) selects the following significant conditions for SEZ success: high-level long-term active and consistent government commitments to SEZ programmes over at least 5–10 years; significant private sector participation; establishment of an effective legal and regulatory framework; effective capacity, budget and accountability of regulatory authorities; and operation of an effective monitoring and evaluation system.

SEZs and economic and social cohesion

There are clear connections between the aims and objectives of different policy areas. For example, policies that promote linkages between SEZs and local firms can also capture technology spill-overs from zones and will usually promote social cohesion. A more socially cohesive society is likely to be more supportive in fostering linkages.

Figure 14.2 illustrates this virtuous circle between social cohesion, good quality growth policies and beneficial outcomes.[6] Qureshi and Te Velde (2012) find that labour productivity is higher for members of business associations than for non-members based on a sample of over 1,000 firms in seven African countries, suggesting that better cohesion can be good for firms. In two papers (Sen and te Velde, 2009; Qureshi and te Velde, 2012), the argument is that better state–business interactions will improve the quality of policies which will in turn affect performance. It is noticeable that the scores for SBRs are greater for countries that have more

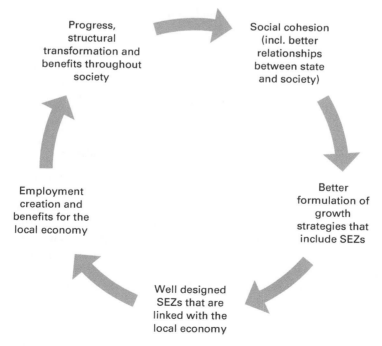

Figure 14.2   The virtuous circle of social cohesion and well performing SEZs.

Source: Authors.

Table 14.6 Factors and policies relating to SEZs as a tool for employment creation and structural transformation

Respond to global developments	*Place SEZs within growth strategies*	*Best-practice implementation*
Building on comparative advantage (e.g. agri-business, offshore services) making success more likely if state capacity is lacking	Complementary policies are required relating to linkages and building of local supply capabilities	SEZs near main markets or ports are more likely to succeed
		Zones in lagging regions are less likely to succeed
SEZs based on clustering are more likely to succeed	Active human resource development (skills and technology) is essential	An appropriate public/private mix is important in implementing zones
SEZs linked to trade preferences (e.g. garments and AGOA) are vulnerable	Specialised and effective infrastructure is essential	Leadership and strong commitment from the top is essential
	Active national labour market institutions are needed	
A flexible approach is required, with good quality institutions and effective state–business relationships	Effective state–business relationships (and social cohesion) are essential	Single factory schemes forgo clustering benefits

Source: Authors.

successful SEZs, suggesting that countries will have greater success in using SEZs when they also have better state–business relations.

Conclusions

Governments wishing to use SEZs as a tool for both employment creation and structural transformation need to attend to the following issues, which are summarised in Table 14.6: building capacity to respond appropriately to a global environment which is in constant process of evolution; establishing SEZs only when they work within a wider development strategy which has a range of complementary policies involving many stakeholders that interact continuously; and implementing SEZs with real purpose and consistency.

Overall conclusions and policy implications

Sub-Saharan countries face the twin challenge of achieving both long-term structural transformation of their economies and short-term employment creation. Addressing these challenges requires appropriate growth policies, and SEZs could play an important role as part of this process. In order for SEZs to work in sub-Saharan Africa it is necessary that they (i) respond to the latest global developments (increased demand for natural-resource-rich products, offshored services, etc.); (ii) are regarded as tools in a wider growth strategy which incorporate good quality policies and support for institutions; and (iii) follow a set of best-practices such as emphasising the clustering properties of SEZs. All of this requires significant state capacity with a consistent and coherent approach.

The evidence on SEZ development suggests that some zones (especially in Asia) have worked, whilst many others (especially in Africa) have failed. Nonetheless, some zones in SSA have attracted significant employment (for example in Madagascar, Mauritius, Ghana, Kenya, Lesotho), although the transformational aspects have been largely absent (with exceptions such as Mauritius and perhaps Kenya). Observation based on a limited sample suggests that SEZs that have emphasised clustering tend to be more successful, indicating that there is a need for SSA SEZs to focus on clustering in addition to complementary policy reforms and the encouragement of innovation.

The experience of using SEZs as a growth tool seems to indicate that social cohesion, employment generation and structural transformation go hand in hand. Significant and sustained employment generation only occurs when there is a strategy for the zone to contribute to innovation and structural transformation, because zones without such a strategy will not succeed in the long run and are vulnerable. A sustainable SEZ strategy needs to ensure that zones are not established and managed as enclaves, but involve significant linkages between zone firms and local firms, and use economic and social standards that are similar to the rest of the economy. These factors together are associated with social cohesion which in turn can lead to good growth policies and well-designed SEZs.

Notes

1 This chapter is a significantly revised version of a draft background paper prepared for the World Bank's World Development Report (WDR) 2013 by the authors on behalf of the Overseas Development Institute (ODI).

   The views presented in this chapter are those of the authors and do not necessarily represent the views of ODI or our partners. This is an adaptation of an original work by The World Bank. Views and opinions expressed in the adaptation are the sole responsibility of the authors of the adaptation and are not endorsed by The World Bank.

   We thank John Weiss and Michael Tribe for excellent editorial suggestions and comments. We would also like to thank Sylvia Tijmstra and Justin Ram for providing helpful research assistance and an anonymous referee and the WDR team for helpful comments and suggestions at an earlier stage of the chapter. While the principal focus of the chapter is on sub-Saharan African EPZ/SEZ development the literature review extends to global EPZ/SEZ development on a comparative basis.

2 Refer to the symposium in *Development Policy Review* by Lin *et al.* (2011).

3 There is a considerable literature on industrial clusters, particularly relating to SMEs, for which the Schmitz and Nadvi citation represents a good starting point.

4 There is further discussion of these 'conditions' in the third section of this chapter.

5 Further elaboration of this discussion will be found in Kingombe (2011) and Kingombe and te Velde (2012). The sources for the examples given the in text are Lall (1996) and te Velde (2002).

6 It is notoriously hard to measure social cohesion or social capital. However, Sen and te Velde (2009) argue that an effective state–business relationship (SBR) is needed for the formulation of appropriate growth policies. They measure effective SBRs on the basis of state capacity, private sector capacity, formal links between state and business, and restraints on collusive behaviour, for 20 African countries over the period 1970–2005. Using econometric techniques, they find that a better SBR score is associated with higher scores on investment climate indicators and with faster productivity growth.

References

AfDB, OECD, UNECA, and UNDP. 2011. *African Economic Outlook Report 2011*. African Economic Outlook – downloaded from http://www.africaneconomicoutlook.org/en/

Aggarwal, A., 2005. *Performance of Export Processing Zones: A Comparative Analysis of India, Sri Lanka and Bangladesh*. Mimeo, Indian Council for Research on International Economic Relations, February.

AllAfrica.com. 2011. *Tanzania: Nation's Free Economic Zones Still have Long Way*. Tanzania Daily News as reproduced in AllAfrica.com – 6 June 2011 – accessed from http://allafrica.com/stories/201106080422. html, 3 June 2013.

Alter, R. 1991. Lessons from the Export Processing Zone in Mauritius. *Finance and Development*. 28 (4) December: 7–9.

Amengual, M. and Milberg, W. 2008. *Economic Development and Working Conditions in Export Processing Zones: A Survey of Trends*. Geneva: International Labour Office. 72p – downloaded from http://ilo.org/public/french/dialogue/download/wp3englishfinal.pdf

Baissac, C. 2003. *Maximising the Developmental Impact of EPZs: A Comparative Perspective in the African Context of Needed Accelerated Growth*. A presentation at the Johannesburg EPZ Symposium. 15–16 October 2003. Danbury, CT: World Economic Processing Zones Association – downloaded from http://www.wepza.org/article7.html

Balasubramanyam, V. N. 1988. Export Processing Zones in Developing Countries: Theory and Empirical Evidence. Chapter 9 in Greenaway, D. (ed). *Economic Development and International Trade*. London: Macmillan.

Barrell, R. and te Velde D.W. 2000. Catching-Up of East German Labour Productivity in the 1990s. *German Economic Review*. 1: 271–297.

Belloca, M. and di Maio, M. 2011. *Survey of the Literature on Successful Strategies and Practices for Export Promotion by Developing Countries*. International Growth Centre Working Paper 11/0248 June 2011. London: London School of Economics.

Boyenge, J-P Singa. 2007. *ILO Database on Export Processing Zones (Revised)*. Geneva: International Labour Office.

Chen, J. 1993. Social Cost–Benefit Analysis of China's Shenzhen Special Economic Zone. *Development Policy Review*. 11 (3) September: 261–271.

Cling, J. and Letilly, G. 2001. Export Processing Zones: A Threatened Instrument for Global Economy Insertion? DIAL document de travail, DT/2001/17. Paris: Développement Institutions et Mondialisation – downloadable from http://www.dial.ird.fr/

Cling, J. P., Razafindrakoto, M. and Roubaud, F. 2005. Export Processing Zones in Madagascar: A Success Story Under Threat? *World Development*. 33 (5) May: 785–803.

Cling, J. P., Razafindrakoto, M. and Roubaud, F. 2007. *Export Processing Zones in Madagascar: The Impact of the Dismantling of Clothing Quotas on Employment and Labour Standards*. Working Papers DT/2007/06. Paris: Développement Institutions et Mondialisation downloadable from http://www.dial.ird.fr/

Draper, P., Grant, C., Kingombe, C. and te Velde, D. W. 2011. *The G20 and African Development*. South African Institute for International Affairs and Overseas Development Institute: London: ODI.

Enhanced Integrated Framework. 2003. *Madagascar: Diagnostic Trade Integration Study*. Geneva: Enhanced Integrated Framework.

Enhanced Integrated Framework. 2004. *Mozambique: Diagnostic Trade Integration Study*. Geneva: Enhanced Integrated Framework.

EU. 2013. *Everything but Arms (EBA) – Who Benefits?* Brussels: European Union – http://trade.ec.europa.eu/doclib/docs/2013/april/tradoc_150983.pdf

Farole, T. 2010a. *Second Best? Investment Climate and Performance in Africa's Special Economic Zones*. World Bank Policy Research Working Paper, 5447: Washington, DC: The World Bank – http://www-wds.worldbank.org/external/default/WDSContentServer/IW3P/IB/2010/10/18/000158349_20101018102611/Rendered/PDF/WPS5447.pdf

Farole, T. 2010b. *Special Economic Zones: Performance, Policy and Practice with a Focus on Sub-Saharan Africa*. Executive Summary. Washington, DC: The World Bank.

Farole, T. 2011. *Special Economic Zones in Africa: Comparing Performance and Learning from Global Experiences*. Washington, DC: The World Bank.

Farole, T. and Akinci, G. (eds.). 2011. *Special Economic Zones: Progress, Emerging Challenges, and Future Directions*. Washington, DC: The World Bank – http://publications.worldbank.org/index.php?main_page=product_info&products_id=24138

FIAS, 2008. *Special Economic Zones: Performance, Lessons Learned and Implication for Zone Development*. Facility for Investment Climate Advisory Service of the World Bank. Washington, DC: The World Bank – https://www.wbginvestmentclimate.org

Glick, P. and Roubaud, F., 2006. Export Processing Zone Expansion in Madagascar: What are the Labour Market and Gender Impacts? *Journal of African Economies*.15(4): 722–756.

Graham, E., 2004. Do Export Processing Zones Attract FDI and Its Benefits: The Experience from China. *International Economics and Economic Policy*. I: 87–103.

ICTFU. 2003. *Export Processing Zones: Symbols of Exploitation and a Development Dead End*. Brussels: International Confederation of Free Trade Unions.

ICFTU. 2004. *Behind the Brand Names. Working Conditions and Labour Rights in Export Processing Zones*. Brussels: International Confederation of Free Trade Unions.

ILO. 1998. *Labour and Social Issues Relating to Export Processing Zones: Report for Discussion at the Tripartite Meeting of Export Processing Zones-Operating Countries*. Geneva: International Labour Office.

ILO. 2003. *Employment and Social Policy in Respect of Export Processing Zones (EPZs)*. Geneva: International Labour Office. GB.285/ESP/5.

ILO. 2008. *Report of the InFocus INITIATIVE on Export Processing Zones (EPZs): Latest Trends and Policy Developments in EPZs*. Geneva: International Labour Office.

ILO. 2012. *Resource Guide on Export Processing Zones (EPZs)*. Geneva: International Labour Office – http://www.ilo.org/public/english/support/lib/resource/subject/epz.htm

ITUC. 2008. *Annual Survey of Violations of Trade Union Rights*. Brussels: International Trade Union Confederation.

Johansson, H. and Nilsson, L. 1997. Export Processing Zones as Catalysts. *World Development*. 25(12): 2115–2128.

Kingombe, C. 2011. *Lessons for Developing Countries from Experience with Technical and Vocational Education and Training*. IGC-SL Working Paper, http://www.theigc.org/sites/default/files/christian_kingombe_paper.pdf

Kingombe, C. and te Velde, D.W. 2012. *Structural Transformation and Employment Creation: The Role of Growth Facilitation Policies in Sub-Saharan Africa*. Draft Background Paper for the World Development Report 2013. Washington, DC: The World Bank – downloadable from http://siteresources.worldbank.org/EXTNWDR2013/Resources/

Kumar, R. 1987. Performance of Foreign and Domestic Firms in Export Processing Zones. *World Development*. 15 (10/11) October/November: 1309–1320.

Lall, S. 1996. Foreign Direct Investment Policies in the Asian NIEs. In *Learning from the Asian Tigers: Studies in Technology and Industrial Policy*. Basingstoke: Palgrave Macmillan.

Lall, S. 2001. *Indicators of the Relative Importance of IPRs in Developing Countries*. Geneva: UNCTAD and the International Centre for Trade and Sustainable Development.

Lin, J., Monga, C., te Velde, D. W., Tendulkar, S., Amsden, A., Amoako, K. Y., Pack, H. and Lim. W. 2011. Growth Identification and Facilitation: The Role of the State in Dynamics of Structural Change. *Development Policy Review*. 29(3) May: 259–310.

Madani, D. 1999. *A Review of the Role and Impact of Export Processing Zones*. Policy Research Working Paper 2238. Washington, DC: World Bank.

Mangieri, T. 2006. *African Cloth, Export Production, and Secondhand Clothing in Kenya*. Discussion Paper. Chapel Hill: Department of Geography, University of North Carolina at Chapel Hill.

Mangieri, T. 2013. Fashion, Transnationality and Swahili Men. In Soyini Madison, D. and Tranberg Hansen, K. (eds.). *African Dress: Fashion, Agency, Performance*. London: Bloomsbury.

McCallum, J. K. 2011. *Export Processing Zones: Comparative Data from China, Honduras, Nicaragua and South Africa*. Working Paper No. 21 Industrial and Employment Relations Department. Geneva: International Labour Office.

Nadvi, K. and Barrientos, S. 2004. *Industrial Clusters and Poverty Reduction: Towards a Methodology for Poverty and Social Impact Assessment of Cluster Development Initiatives*. Vienna: United Nations Industrial Development Organisation.

Omar, K. and Stoever, W. A. 2008. The Role of Technology and Human Capital in the EPZ Life-Cycle. *Transnational Corporations*. 17 (1): 135–159 – http://unctad.org/en/docs/iteiit20081a6_en.pdf

Porter, M. E. 1998. *The Competitive Advantage: Creating and Sustaining Superior Performance*. New York: The Free Press.

Qureshi, M. and te Velde, D. W. 2012. State–Business Relations, Investment Climate Reform and Firm Productivity in Sub-Saharan Africa. *Journal of International Development*. 25 (7): 912–935.

Schmitz, H. and Nadvi, K. 1999. Clustering and Industrialisation: Introduction. *World Development*. 27 (9): 1503–1514.

Sen, K. and te Velde, D. W. 2009. State Business Relations and Economic Growth in Sub-Saharan Africa. *Journal of Development Studies*. 45 (8): 1267–1283.

Spinanger, D. 1984. Objectives and Impact of Economic Activity Zones: Some Evidence from Asia. *Weltwirtschaftliches Archiv*. X (120): 64–89.

Stein, H. 2008. Africa, Industrial Policy and Export Processing Zones: Lessons from Asia. paper prepared for a UN ECA Africa Task Force Meeting, Addis Ababa, Ethiopia 10–11 July – http://policydialogue.org/files/events/Stein_africa_ind_policy__export_processing_zones.pdf

te Velde, D. W. 2002. *Government Policies for Inward Foreign Direct Investment in Developing Countries: Implications for Human Capital Formation and Income Inequality*. OECD Development Centre Technical Paper No. 193. Paris: Organisation for Economic Cooperation and Development.

te Velde, D.W. and Xenogiani, T. 2007. Foreign Direct Investment and International Skill Inequality. *Oxford Development Studies.* 35 (1): 83–104.

Tsuchiya, T. 1987. Free Trade Zones in South East Asia. In R. Peet (ed.). *International Capitalism and Industrial Restructuring: A Critical Analysis.* London: Allen & Unwin.

UNCTAD. 2001. *Investment Policy Review Mauritius.* New York and Geneva: United Nations.

UNCTAD. 2003. *Export Processing Zones at Risk? The WTO Rules on Subsidies: What Options for the Future?* Press release – http://www.unctad.org/templates/webflyer.asp?docid=3154&intItemID=226 1&lang=1

UNCTAD. 2004. *FDI in Services – A Growing Business for EPZs.* UNCTAD Investment Brief Number 2 – http://www.unctad.org/en/docs/webiteiia200417_en.pdf

UNCTAD, 2008. *Export Competitiveness and Development in LDCs: Policies, Issues and Priorities for Least Developed Countries for Action During and Beyond UNCTAD XII.* Geneva: United Nations Conference on Trade and Development.

UNCTAD. 2009. *Burundi Investment Policy Review.* Geneva: United Nations – http://unctad.org/en/ Docs/diaepcb200917ch4_en.pdf

UNCTAD. 2011. *World Investment Report 2011.* Geneva: United Nations Conference on Trade and Development.

UNECA. 2011. *Industrial Policies for the Structural Transformation of African Economies: Options and Best Practices.* Addis Ababa: United Nations Economic Commission for Africa.

US Government. 2013. *African Growth and Opportunity Act (AGOA).* Washington, DC: Office of the US Trade Representative, Office of the President – http://www.ustr.gov/trade-topics/trade-development/ preference-programs/african-growth-and-opportunity-act-agoa

Virgill, N. A. V. 2009. *Export Processing Zones: Tools of Development or Reform Delay?* A dissertation submitted in partial fulfilment of the requirements for the degree of Doctor of Philosophy at George Mason University – http://digilib.gmu.edu/dspace/bitstream/1920/4509/1/Virgill_Nicola.pdf

Wade, R. 1990. *Governing the Market.* Princeton, NJ: Princeton University Press.

Wall, D. 1976. Export Processing Zones. *Journal of World Trade Law.* 10 (5): 478–489.

Warr, P. G.. 1987a. Export Promotion via Industrial Enclaves: The Philippines Bataan Export Processing Zone. *Journal of Development Studies.* 23 (2) January: 220–241.

Warr, P. G. 1987b. Malaysia's Industrial Enclaves: Benefits and Costs. *Developing Economies.* 25 (1) March: 30–55.

Warr, P. G. 1989. Export Processing Zones: The Economics of Enclave Manufacturing. *World Bank Research Observer.* 4 (1) January: 65–88.

Warr, P. G. 1990. Export Processing Zones. Chapter 8 in Milner, C. (ed.). *Export Promotion Strategies.* Hemel Hempstead: Harvester Wheatsheaf: 130–161.

Watson, P. 2001. *Export Processing Zones: Has Africa Missed the Boat? Not Yet.* World Bank Africa Region Working Paper 17. Washington, DC: The World Bank.

World Bank. 2009. *World Development Report 2009: Reshaping Economic Geography.* Washington, DC: The World Bank.

Yeung, Y., Lee, J. and Kee, G. 2009. China's Special Economic Zones at 30. *Eurasian Geography and Economics.* 50 (2): 222–240.

Zeng, D. Z. 2010. *Building Engines for Growth and Competitiveness in China: Experience with Special Economic Zones and Industrial Clusters.* World Bank News December 10 2010 – http://www.worldbank.org/ en/news/feature/2010/12/19/building-engines-growth-competitiveness-china-experience-special-economic-zones-industrial-clusters

Zeng, D. Z. 2011. *How do Special Economic Zones and Industrial Clusters Drive China's Rapid Development?* World Bank Policy Research Working Paper 5583 – http://www-wds.worldbank.org/external/ default/WDSContentServer/WDSP/IB/2011/03/01/000158349_20110301083120/Rendered/PDF/ WPS5583.pdf

Annex A: The effects of special economic zones on labour productivity in Kenyan manufacturing

We follow Barrell and te Velde (2000), who use a two-factor CES production function with employment (L) and capital (K):

$$f(L_t, K_t) = \left\{ \lambda(\psi_{Lt} L_t)^\rho + (1 - \lambda)(K_t)^\rho \right\}^{\frac{1}{\rho}} \tag{1}$$

where $\varphi_{Lt} \equiv \ln \psi_{Lt}$ is a function of labour efficiency units, and the parameter $\rho < 1$. The labour efficiency index can be interpreted as accumulated human capital or as the skill-specific technology level. The elasticity of substitution between L and K is $\sigma = 1/(1 - \rho)$. In neo-classical theory, the technology level changes exogenously. However, it is perfectly possible to have shifts in the pattern of technical change (endogenous technical change), dependent on factors such as EPZ. For example, EPZs may attract high productivity firms that can act as a pool of knowledge for other firms leading to greater labour productivity through spill-overs and aggregation. We model the effects of EPZs on the market for skills as follows:

$$\varphi_{Lt} \equiv \ln \psi_{Lt}; \varphi_{Lt} = \gamma_{1L} + \gamma_{2L} EPZ_t \tag{2}$$

Using the first-order condition that factor productivity equals the real factor price we can derive a formula for labour demand (and also capital demand, which we not show):

$$\ln \left(\frac{L_t}{Y_t} \right) = \sigma \ln(\lambda) - \sigma \ln \left(\frac{w}{P} \right)_t + \gamma_{1L}(\sigma - 1)t + \gamma_{2L}(\sigma - 1)EPZ_t + \varepsilon_i \tag{3}$$

We use data from UNIDO for manufacturing employment, wages and value added and the WDI GDP price deflator. Kenya's EPZA publications provide data on employment in EPZs for 1993 and 1998–2007, with extrapolated data for 1994–97 (and zero before 1993) to estimate the share of employment in EPZs. The data are plotted in Figure 14.A1 and show there has been a considerable increase in the share since the start in 1993.

The estimations use data for 1990–2007 so we need to treat the results with extreme caution. The estimate in first column for the elasticity of substitution is not far from unity (so it is close to a Cobb Douglas production function). The productivity variable is not significant for this period and is negative. The EPZ variable is highly significant suggesting that EPZs have led to

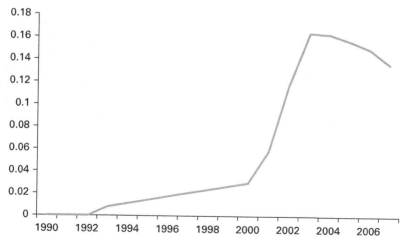

Figure 14.A1   EPZ and labour productivity in Kenyan manufacturing.

Sources: Kenya EPZA and UNIDO.

Table 14.A1 EPZ and labour productivity in Kenyan manufacturing

	Estimating (3), no EPZ	*Estimating (3) with EPZ*	*Estimating dynamic (3) with EPZ, and $\Delta \ln\left(\frac{L_t}{Y_t}\right)$ as dependent variable*
$(L/Y)_{-1}$			−0.50
			(−1.97)★
(w/P): −σ	−1.15	−1.05	
	(−8.96)★★★	(−8.68)★★★	
$(w/P)_{-1}$: $\Delta (w/P)$			−0.87
			(−5.96)★★★
Time: $\gamma_1(\sigma - 1)$	−0.01	0.02	
	(−0.83)	(1.27)	
EPZ: $\gamma_2(\sigma - 1)$		−2.41	
		(−2.62)★★	
EPZ_{-1}			−1.33
			(−2.01)★
Constant: $\sigma \ln (\lambda)$	−0.62	−0.97	−0.12
	(−1.25)	(−1.96)★	(−0.37)
Observations	18	18	17
	(1990–2007)	(1990–2007)	(1991–2007)
R-squared	0.87	0.90	0.83

Notes: Uses robust standard errors. ★, ★★, ★★★ = significant at 10%, 5% or 1% level.

higher labour productivity in Kenyan manufacturing. The time variable is not significant. The final column (3) of Table 14.A1 estimates an error term using a lagged dependent variable as an explanatory variable, a change term as a dependent variable and a change term in real wages. The EPZ variable has been lagged and is significant and positively correlated with higher labour productivity.

The extent to which EPZs have increased manufacturing productivity over the decade to 2007 has been estimated. The EPZ share variable increased by around 0.12 over the decade to 2007 and if this is multiplied by −2.41 the implication is that labour intensity (productivity) has decreased (increased) by some 29 per cent over the decade or around an annual 2.5 per cent increase in manufacturing labour productivity accountable to EPZs. If the lagged variable is used then the effects are 16 and 1.5 per cent respectively. Figure 14.A1 shows the results for this quantitative analysis of labour productivity in Kenyan manufacturing.

15

INTERNATIONAL COMPETITIVENESS IN MANUFACTURING AND THE CHINA EFFECT

Rhys Jenkins

Introduction

Over the past three decades, economic globalisation has been associated with a growing emphasis on issues of international competitiveness around the world. In 1979 the World Economic Forum published its first *Global Competitiveness Report* and during the 1980s several developed country governments created commissions and published reports on competitiveness.[1] This trend intensified in the 1990s with reports by the US Department of Commerce, the UK Cabinet Office, the UK Department of Trade and Industry and the European Commission (Lall, 2001a: fn2).

By coincidence, 1979 was also the year when China began to implement the process of economic reform which led to re-engagement with the global economy and spectacular economic growth. This resulted in a particular concern over the impact of Chinese competition in other parts of the world, especially with its accession to the World Trade Organization (WTO) in 2001. Despite the growing significance of China as a driver of global growth, its superior competitiveness has been a challenge for many countries which face the incursion of Chinese products into their domestic markets and increased competition in their major export markets. This has led to accusations of unfair competition being levelled at Chinese production with a significant part of its competitiveness being attributed to the manipulation of the exchange rate and government subsidies of various kinds.[2]

This chapter begins by revisiting the debate on 'national competitiveness' to clarify the relevance of the concept and to establish a meaningful definition in the context of globalisation. It considers the different measures of competitiveness which have been applied in the literature, including the widely used international indices that are used to rank countries according to their competitiveness.

The third section briefly documents the growth of the Chinese economy since the beginning of its integration with the global economy at the end of the 1970s. It describes the increased global competitiveness of China and locates China's growth in the broader East Asian context as part of a regional production system.

The remainder of the chapter examines the impact of China on other developing countries focusing on four key aspects which are critical in terms of industrial development: the penetration of domestic markets by Chinese goods; competition from Chinese exports in third markets; Chinese foreign direct investment (FDI) in developing countries; and diversion of FDI from other countries to China.

The rise of China and international competitiveness

The concept of 'national competitiveness'

There are sharply contrasting views amongst economists regarding 'national competitiveness'. Mainstream economists are critical of the idea that countries compete against each other in the same way as firms, arguing that this implies a zero-sum view of the international economy which is contrary to the insights from the Ricardian theory of comparative advantage. This has been expressed most forcefully by Paul Krugman (1994, 1996), who questioned the relevance of the notion of 'national competitiveness' and warned that it could be used by protectionists to undermine the liberal world trading system. The emphasis on national competitiveness according to Krugman is essentially mercantilist and inconsistent with the theory of comparative advantage which shows that all countries benefit from expanded trade. In so far as orthodox theory does address problems of competitiveness between countries, this is seen as an exchange rate problem (Boltho, 1996): countries may be uncompetitive as a result of having an overvalued exchange rate. Lall (2001b) describes this as an issue of *macroeconomic* competitiveness.

Whereas neo-classical economics has a problem with the idea of national competitiveness, there is a long heterodox tradition which addresses this issue (Reinert, 1994; Green *et al.*, 2010). Heterodox economists have challenged Krugman's argument pointing out that comparative advantage assumes perfect competition, constant returns to scale, full factor mobility within countries, equal access to technology and no externalities (Lall 2001a). In practice, market failures are pervasive so that free trade is not necessarily optimal from a dynamic point of view, which does raise issues of competitiveness. Crucial to the heterodox perspective is the view that not all economic activities are the same and that some are more dynamic than others.[3] Traditionally, in development economics, the manufacturing sector has been regarded as the key sector. In practice therefore when heterodox economists refer to national competitiveness they are usually concerned about the competitiveness of the manufacturing sector (Lall, 2001b; Wingarajan, 2003). Concerns about competitiveness are therefore often linked to fears of "premature deindustrialization" (Palma, 2008). Lall (2001b) describes this as *structural* competitiveness.

The period since 1980 has seen intensification of globalisation,[4] characterised by the fragmentation of production across a range of countries and an increased international mobility of capital. A further assumption of Ricardian comparative advantage is that factors of production are immobile between countries and, as several authors have argued, where capital is mobile, trade flows are determined (or at least affected) by absolute advantage (Shaikh, 1979; Daly and Cobb, 1989: Ch. 11; Jones, 2000: Ch. 2). Another way in which countries compete in today's increasingly globalised world is to attract internationally mobile capital. This is reflected by the incentives which governments offer to foreign investors. Indeed, in many ways various indices of competitiveness are really designed largely to reflect the attractiveness of a country as a location for international capital.

Measuring competitiveness

The two best known indices, the World Economic Forum's *Global Competitiveness Index* and the Institute of Management and Development's *World Competitiveness Scoreboard* both provide country rankings of international competitiveness. A significant input in to these indices is provided by executive surveys which provide information on corporate perspectives on the business environment in a country and cover aspects such as the efficiency of government, the sophistication of local supplier networks and the nature of competitive practices. Much of the hard data used to construct these indices also reflects a particular view of what makes countries attractive for international capital with low trade barriers, liberalisation of capital movements and flexible labour markets regarded as positive features (Lall, 2001a; Wingarajan, 2003: Ch. 3).

In terms of analysing competitiveness, one of the criticisms that has been levelled against these indices is that they mix indicators that may be regarded as determinants of competitiveness (such as government policies) with those that measure competitive performance (such as productivity growth or export growth). This is consistent with a view of the indices as measuring the attractiveness of different countries for global business, since studies of the determinants of FDI show the importance of a range of factors, with performance being particularly important.[5]

As was argued above, the heterodox view is based on a more sectoral approach, and in this chapter the emphasis is on industrial competitiveness.[6] Looking at manufacturing, competitiveness can be identified in a number of ways. First there is the performance of the country's manufactured goods in the international market which can be best indicated by changes in world market share. Given that the aggregate change in a country's share of the world market is affected by the country and product composition of its exports, a better measure of competitiveness can be derived through constant market share (CMS) analysis of exports which separates out the effect of changes at the product level from compositional effects (Fagerberg and Sollie, 1987).

Competitiveness can also be linked to the composition of exports and in particular to a notion of technological upgrading. Thus a country's manufacturing sector can be considered competitive if over time the products that it exports become increasingly sophisticated. This may also lead to shifts in the structure of production towards more technology–intensive industries, although this on its own is not a good indicator of competitiveness (Lall, 2000).[7] In terms of sustainability, it is also important for increased competitiveness to be associated with productivity growth. A temporary increase in world market share based on wage repression would not be a good indicator of growing competitiveness.

In the narrower sense of locational competition, an initial indicator of competitiveness would be inflows of FDI or more specifically a country's share of global FDI inflows. Again, taken on its own, this may be an inadequate indicator, since the adoption of a very liberal investment code might temporarily increase inflows, but this would not necessarily be sustainable in the longer term. Since investment in extractive industries may be a result of new resource discoveries, it is manufacturing FDI that is most relevant here.

The China effect and competitiveness

The literature on the effects of China's global growth on other developing countries is often discussed in terms of the competitive threat posed by China. There are several ways in which this threat manifests itself. Most attention has been given to the threat posed to other developing countries' exports of manufactures by China's growing international competitiveness and accession to the WTO. A second concern is that increased imports from China displace local producers in the domestic market, contributing to a process of 'deindustrialisation.' There is also a worry that Chinese competition will prevent countries either from establishing a foothold on the ladder of industrialisation, or moving up it into more technologically advanced activities.

Another way in which China can be seen as a competitive threat is if it diverts FDI away from other developing countries. Here China competes with other countries for a limited global supply of internationally mobile capital and makes it more difficult for other countries to attract FDI.

It is of course also possible that the 'China effect' leads to increased competitiveness of firms or sectors in other countries. This could occur as a result of Chinese inward investment which brings with it better technology or management techniques or through imports of low-cost Chinese inputs or capital equipment. There could also be an indirect impact where competition from Chinese imports forces local manufacturers to become more competitive.

China's growth and integration with the global economy

The spectacular economic performance of China over the past three decades has been largely the result of the growing competitiveness of its manufacturing sector.[8] China's share of global manufacturing value added rose from 1.4 per cent in 1980 to an estimated 17.4 per cent in 2012 (UNIDO, various years). If one takes the ability to increase a country's share of world exports of manufactures as an indicator of competitiveness, China's share increased from 0.8 per cent in 1980 to 5.2 per cent at the time of its accession to the WTO in 2001 and to 16.5 per cent by 2012 (UNCTAD, 2014). A constant market share analysis of China's export growth shows that this is largely attributable to increased competitiveness at the product level. Between 1995 and 2010, China increased its share of world exports of manufactures by 12.9 percentage points (90 per cent of which was the result of increased market share at the product level (Husted and Nishioka, 2012: 4)).

It is also the case that the composition of China's exports has shifted considerably over time from low-tech, labour-intensive products to more skill and capital-intensive manufactures (Wang and Wei, 2010; Xu, 2010: Table 1). It is true that the extent of this upgrading may be exaggerated because of the significance of processing trade which means that often it is the lower skilled, more labour-intensive parts of a particular value chain that are located in China (Amiti and Freund, 2010). However, the domestic content of Chinese manufactured exports has been increasing over time, particularly for processing exports (Koopman *et al.*, 2008), so that the extent to which this distorts the sophistication of Chinese exports is diminishing. It is clear therefore that increased Chinese competitiveness is reflected not just in the growth of China's market share but also in an upgrading of exports.

A further indication of China's growing competitiveness is the growth of productivity in the manufacturing sector. Labour productivity in manufacturing has been estimated to have increased twelve-fold between 1979 and 2009 with most of the growth coming after 1990 (Yang, 2013). Until the mid-2000s the rate of growth of wages lagged behind productivity so that unit labour costs fell by 43 per cent between 1995 and 2004 (Economist, 2010). Since then, however, wage increases have outstripped productivity and unit labour costs have increased (Ceglowski and Golub, 2011).

China's growing competitiveness is also illustrated by its ability to attract inward investment. In 1980 its share of the global stock of FDI was negligible but by 2011 this had risen to 3.5 per cent (UNCTAD, 2012, Annex Table 1.2). While initially this increase could be attributed to the removal of controls on inward investment which kept inflows artificially low, the continued increase reflects growing competitiveness as a location for global investment.

Inward investment has played a significant role in the growth of Chinese exports. Foreign firms have accounted for more than half of China's total exports since 2001 (Duan *et al.*, 2012). China constitutes part of an Asian regional production network in which firms from Japan, South Korea and Taiwan have located labour-intensive segments of their production to take advantage of lower labour costs (Gaulier *et al.*, 2007; Tong and Zheng, 2008).

China has also improved its ranking in the two main indices of country competitiveness. It rose from 27th in 1997 to 21st in 2013 in the International Institute for Management Development's (IMD) Global Competitiveness Scoreboard and is one of a small group of countries which improved their rank by at least five places over the period (IMD, 2013). Since 2000 it has improved its position in the World Economic Forum's Global Competitiveness Index from 41st to 29th in 2012/13. The fact that China is not in the top 20 in either index reflects the bias in their concept of competitiveness which leads to most of the top positions being occupied by developed countries.

Bilateral trade between China and developing countries

One of the most widespread concerns over China in both developed and developing countries has been the impact of increased Chinese imports on domestic production and jobs. This is reflected in the complaints of domestic manufacturers about 'unfair' competition from China and anti-dumping actions taken by governments against Chinese imports. China has consistently been the principal target of anti-dumping actions by WTO members since it joined the organisation (International Bar Association, 2010: Chart 1).

Before jumping to the conclusion that Chinese competition is a major problem contributing to a displacement of local producers, deindustrialisation and job losses in other developing countries, a number of factors need to be taken into account. First, as was pointed out in the previous section, part of China's export expansion has been the result of the relocation of production from other East Asian countries, particularly Japan, South Korea and Taiwan, to China. This implies that part of the increase in a country's imports from China may reflect a diversion of imports from other countries, rather than a displacement of domestic production.[9] Even where Chinese exports have not been a result of 'offshoring' by other countries, it is still possible that the growth of Chinese exports come at the expense of exports from other countries, as will be discussed in more detail in the next section.

How justified then are the claims that Chinese products are displacing domestic manufacturers in developing countries and contributing to a process of deindustrialisation? One approach to estimating the impact of increased Chinese competition at a global level is through computable general equilibrium (CGE) modelling. One such exercise by Dimaranan *et al.* (2007) showed significant losses of output in manufacturing in developing countries as a result of China's growth.[10] A limitation of this approach is that the results very much depend on the assumptions that are built in to the model and are projections of likely outcomes rather than an analysis of the actual effects that China has had on countries' manufacturing output.

An alternative approach adopted by Wood and Mayer (2009) used a Heckscher–Ohlin framework to estimate *ex post* the impact of China's entry into the global economy on the ratio of labour-intensive manufactures to primary products in the output structure of other developing countries. They found that the ratio fell in the 1990s compared to the 1980s in Latin America and East Asia, but were less clear in Sub-Saharan Africa and South Asia. They conclude that on average the impact of China's opening was to lower the share of labour-intensive manufacturing in the total of labour-intensive manufacturing plus primary production in developing countries by between 1 and 3.5 percentage points. However, they point out that this was a relatively small overall effect on the broad structure of output in other developing economies. One limitation of the study is that it only covers the period up to 2000, whereas China's penetration of other developing country markets, particularly in Latin America and Sub-Saharan Africa remained relatively low in 2000 and rose significantly over the following decade.

Detailed studies of the impact of increased Chinese imports in particular markets are surprisingly few and far between. Although there are numerous claims of the devastating effect that such competition has had on local producers, the evidence presented is often anecdotal. For example, scoping studies by the African Economic Research Consortium (AERC) claimed that Chinese competition led to local producers being displaced in Cameroon, Kenya, Ghana and South Africa (Ademola *et al.*, 2009: 498) but the evidence base in the AERC studies for this claim is sketchy. The one African country for which there is more rigorous empirical evidence of displacement of local producers by Chinese imports, particularly in the textile and garments industries, is South Africa (Morris and Einhorn, 2008; Edwards and Jenkins, 2014).

Several Latin American countries have been studied in more depth and these provide some evidence of a negative impact from Chinese competition. Only one of these studies, on Brazil, explicitly attempted to estimate the extent to which Chinese imports displaced imports from other countries, concluding that more than half of the increase in Chinese import penetration between 2001 and 2007 was associated with a reduction in the share of imports coming from other countries (Jenkins and Barbosa, 2012: 73). Nevertheless there was still a negative impact of Chinese imports on domestic production and employment, although not surprisingly this tended to be concentrated in certain industries, so that the aggregate impact on manufacturing was relatively small.

Studies of Argentina (López and Ramos, 2009; Castro *et al.*, 2009) and Chile (Alvarez and Claro, 2009) also found some evidence of a negative impact of Chinese imports on domestic manufacturing, although again this tends to be concentrated in certain industries, such as footwear, leather products, pottery, electrical and electronic products and other manufactures.[11] It should also be noted that these studies only covered the 1990s and early 2000s and that Chinese import penetration has increased even further and affected more industries since then.

As the framework outlined earlier indicated, there are also potential positive impacts of growing bilateral trade with China on the manufacturing sectors of developing countries. The rapid growth of the Chinese economy is a source of demand for other exporters. For most developing countries, particularly in Sub-Saharan Africa and Latin America, it is commodity exporters who have been the primary beneficiaries from this growth and exports from the manufacturing sector have been minimal. The main exceptions to this generalisation have been some of China's East Asian neighbours who have been integrated with China into regional production networks.

A second potential positive impact of bilateral trade arises if imports of lower priced Chinese intermediate inputs and capital goods lead to increased productivity in host countries. There is virtually no empirical research on this effect in developing countries. Alvarez and Claro (2009) tested the impact of Chinese competition on upgrading and productivity in Chilean manufacturing firms but found no evidence of such an impact. The fact that imports are classified by the type of product, and not according to the industry in which they are used, makes it difficult to identify the impacts of Chinese imports of inputs and capital goods on local productivity, except where firm level data is available. The claims of positive impacts therefore are no more than hypotheses which require further testing at present.

Chinese imports may also lead to increased productivity or upgrading by local firms, either because the least efficient firms exit an industry or because surviving firms move out of the more labour-intensive products or processes in an industry. This occurred in the South African textile industry, which was unable to compete with Chinese imports of 'commodity' textiles and began to specialise in niche markets such as material for bulletproof vests, parachutes and industrial textiles (Roberts and Thoburn, 2003). More research is needed at the firm level to see how widespread such responses have been.

Indirect trade impacts and developing country competitiveness

The impact of China on manufactured exports from other developing countries has received far more attention in the literature than competition in the domestic market. The fear in many countries, from the time that China was negotiating to join the WTO, was that once granted most favoured nation (MFN) status, Chinese goods would massively displace exports by other countries, particularly those countries which had already achieved success in developing exports of labour-intensive manufactures. This led to a spate of studies in the early 2000s which estimated the effects of China's WTO accession on global trade flows and attempted to identify which countries would be most affected by Chinese competition (Shafaeddin, 2004; Yang, 2003; Ianchonichiva and Martin, 2004; Schott, 2004; Lall and Albaladejo, 2004; Lall and Weiss, 2005).

These studies used a variety of different approaches to analyse the likely impact of China on other countries' exports. Some involved using a CGE model to simulate the impact of Chinese accession on global trade flows at fairly high levels of sectoral aggregation. Others carried out much more detailed product level analysis of the similarity between China's export structure and those of other countries using Finger and Kreinin's (1979) Export Similarity Index (ESI) or correlations between the product structures of exports.[12] These early studies were relatively optimistic that any negative impacts from Chinese competition would be limited to a few countries and to specific products, so that most developing countries would not be negatively affected by Chinese accession.

Over time, however, exporters in many countries complained of increased competition from Chinese products. With the ending of the Multi-Fibre Arrangement on 1 January 2005, textile and garment producers in countries as far apart as Bangladesh, El Salvador and Lesotho were forced to close down.[13] Nor were the impacts of Chinese competition confined to traditional labour-intensive products with more capital and skill-intensive exports being affected in countries such as Mexico and Malaysia.

Whereas the earlier research involved simulating future trade changes and identifying countries which were likely to be particularly affected by Chinese competition, with time more studies were produced looking at the actual effects of China on other countries' exports in recent years. Some of these studies used gravity models of trade with Chinese exports included as an additional independent variable (Hanson and Robertson, 2009, 2010; Athukorola, 2009; Eichengreen et al., 2007; Greenaway et al., 2008; Edwards and Jenkins, 2014). Others used an extension of Constant Market Share analysis which identified those changes in a country's share of an export market which could be attributed to Chinese competition (Batista, 2008; Jenkins, 2010). While debate continues over the extent to which other countries have lost export markets to China and how countries should respond to the Chinese challenge, it is now clear that this is a real issue for many developing countries.

Although initially the focus was on Chinese competition in developed country markets, it has also become evident that this is an issue within regional markets in both Latin America

(Gallagher and Porzecanski, 2010: 51–56; Jenkins, 2014) and Africa (Giovannetti and Sanfilippo, 2009; Edwards and Jenkins, 2014). Since intra-regional exports tend to have a higher technological content than those to developed country markets, Chinese competition in these markets is likely to make it more difficult for other countries to upgrade their manufactured exports.

Were it the case that other exporters facing competition from China could move up the technological ladder and offset losses of market share to China in low-tech or labour-intensive products by increasing their exports of high-tech products, then the loss of market share to China would not be a problem. For sub-Saharan African countries which had only recently started to export labour-intensive manufactures at the time that China joined the WTO, Chinese competition can be seen as stopping them from getting a foothold on the ladder of industrialisation (Kaplinsky and Morris, 2008). Even for countries with well-established manufacturing sectors in Latin America, the rapid upgrading of Chinese exports is making it more difficult for countries to compete in high-tech products (Gallagher and Porzecanski, 2010: Ch. 4).

While the displacement of exports by Chinese products can be interpreted as a negative impact for most developing countries, in East Asia it is more likely to be associated with an increase in exports of parts and components to China as a result of the relocation of final assembly operations to China. While it might appear from gross export figures that China has displaced exports by other East Asian countries such as South Korea or Taiwan, in fact a large share of these 'Chinese' exports may originate from those countries. If trade was measured in value added terms, the displacement would be much smaller. Indeed, where carrying out assembly in China makes products more competitive, then there might well be a positive impact on South Korean or Taiwanese exports of intermediates. The finding by Eichengreen *et al.* (2007) that in Asia lower technology exporters are being displaced by China, while more advanced countries in the region which export capital goods and intermediate products have benefited from growing Chinese demand, supports this view.[14]

Chinese FDI in developing countries

In 2000, China launched its 'Going Out' strategy to encourage Chinese companies to invest overseas and although the level of Chinese FDI remained relatively low during the first half of the decade, it has grown rapidly since then (Rosen and Hanemann, 2011: 17). In 2010 China was ranked fifth in the world in terms of outward investment flows and with falling FDI from the developed world in the aftermath of the global financial crisis, its share of global FDI increased sharply from 1 per cent in 2007 to 4.7 per cent in 2010 (UNCTAD, 2012: Annex Table 1.1).[15]

China has become a significant investor in Asia, Africa and Latin America in recent years. However, much of this investment, particularly outside of East Asia, has been in oil, mining and infrastructure rather than in manufacturing. While there have been numerous studies of the impacts of Chinese investment in the extractive industries, there are relatively few which have looked in detail at the manufacturing sector.

In Africa the main type of Chinese FDI in manufacturing has been market seeking, although this represents a fairly minor part of total Chinese investment in the region (Kaplinsky and Morris, 2009). Some smaller Chinese companies have moved from exporting from China to local assembly of Chinese parts and components for national markets (Gu, 2009). There are also examples of Chinese textile and garment producers which have invested in Africa in order to take advantage of tariff preferences in the USA and the EU, but these too are motivated mainly by market rather than efficiency considerations (Henley *et al.*, 2008: 13).

In Latin America, as in Africa, the bulk of Chinese FDI has been in the extractive industries and infrastructure (Dussel Peters, 2012). Investment in manufacturing in the region has been relatively limited and is primarily an extension of an export strategy adding relatively little value locally and supplying only the local market (CEPAL, 2011: 173). Chinese firms have not been involved in efficiency-seeking investment in Latin America up to now (Rosales and Kuwayama, 2012: 117).

The motivations of Chinese manufacturers investing in Asia, particularly in South East Asia, are somewhat different from other developing regions. Here efficiency-seeking investment has been more prominent, particularly in Vietnam, Cambodia and Laos where lower wages have made it attractive to carry out some labour-intensive activities in the face of rising wages in China's southern coastal regions where most export production is located (Zhao, 2013).

As far as manufacturing is concerned, the nature of Chinese FDI, whether of the market-seeking or the efficiency-seeking type, has tended to be associated with high levels of import dependence, so that local linkages are limited, which reduces the likely positive spillovers to local producers. On the other hand, the fact that market-seeking investment is often local assembly of imported Chinese parts, replacing imports of finished products from China, means that the displacement of local producers by FDI is not a major problem. Similarly, efficiency-seeking investment by Chinese firms relocating labour-intensive activities is unlikely to have an effect on local producers.

Diversion of FDI to China

One of the senses in which countries clearly can be seen as competing with each other is in terms of attracting foreign capital. Because, as was seen above, China went from being virtually closed to FDI before 1979 to being the largest host country in the developing world by 1992 (Moran, 1998: 15), there are good grounds for asking whether FDI has been diverted from other countries to China. At the time of China's accession to the WTO several political leaders in the ASEAN countries voiced concerns that their countries would lose investment to China.[16]

A number of studies have tried to answer this question with varying results. In Asia, studies have generally failed to find evidence of diversion of FDI to China, and some have even found a positive relationship between FDI flows to China and to some of its neighbours (Eichengreen and Tong, 2005; Chantasasawat *et al.*, 2005: Zhou and Lall, 2005; Wang *et al.*, 2007). This is generally interpreted as reflecting a complementarity between China and other Asian economies arising from their integration into regional or global production networks.

In Latin America, some studies have found that FDI in China has had a negative effect on inward investment in the region, particularly in Mexico, while others find no discernable effect (García Herrero and Santabárbara, 2007; Gallegos *et al.*, 2008; Chantasasawat *et al.*, 2004; Eichengreen and Tong, 2005). Only one study in Latin America (Cravino *et al.*, 2006) found a positive relationship between FDI in China and Latin America but this only held for aggregate FDI flows and there was no positive relationship when the link was tested using data for US manufacturing FDI. This is not surprising since the Latin American countries are not linked to China through global production networks in the same way as some Asian countries.

A limitation of all these studies is their reliance on highly aggregated data. There is scope for more work on this issue through detailed case studies of sectors and countries where diversion of FDI may have taken place.

Conclusion

This chapter has sought to locate the impact of China on industrial development in the Global South in the context of globalisation and concerns over international competitiveness. Although China has been an important source of growth in the global economy, particularly since the start of the global financial crisis, it has also been a major competitive challenge for manufacturers everywhere.

The empirical evidence reviewed here shows that the impact of China's growth has not been uniform across all countries or all industries. For many resource-rich countries, the growth of demand from China has contributed to an improvement in their terms of trade as a result of the commodity boom and an increase in direct exports to supply the growing Chinese market. In these countries, however, the manufacturing sector has come under competitive pressure from Chinese imports, which has been intensified by the appreciation of the real exchange rate associated with the boom in exports.

Countries which have developed significant exports of manufactures have faced increased Chinese competition in their export markets both in the North and in regional markets in the South. These countries are also those which are most likely to have lost out as a result of the diversion of FDI to China, although the evidence on this effect is rather limited.

Since China's export growth has been based to an important extent on final-assembly industries often involving foreign firms, this growth has also expanded the market for imported capital goods and parts and components. This has mainly benefited developed countries but it has also led to the growth of intra-regional trade in Asia with South Korea and Taiwan, and to a lesser extent Thailand and Malaysia, supplying intermediate products to Chinese industries. Moreover, with wages increasing in China, some labour-intensive production has recently been relocated to lower wage countries in South East Asia, especially Vietnam and Cambodia.

Although some commentators have suggested that this last tendency will expand in the future, so that other countries will become more competitive as locations for export-oriented manufacturing,[17] the continuing existence of large reserves of labour in rural China makes this less likely. The slowdown of growth in the North since the onset in 2008 of the global financial and economic crisis has made other developing countries more important as markets for Chinese firms, so that competition from Chinese imports is likely to intensify while, over time, there may also be a growth of market-seeking FDI to avoid the growing trade barriers that are likely to be imposed.

Acknowledgement

I am grateful to the editors and John Thoburn for comments on an earlier draft.

Notes

1 For example US President's Commission (1985), House of Lords (1985).
2 A recent example is the US Congressional-Executive Commission on China report (Sen, 2012).
3 Reinert (2007, Appendix VI) has developed this idea in terms of a 'Quality Index of Economic Activity'.
4 The World Bank for example describes the post-1980 period as the Third Wave of Globalization (World Bank, 2002).
5 Another index used to rank countries in terms of their business environment is the World Bank's *Ease of Doing Business*. This is based on executives' perceptions of different countries' investment climates and is therefore quite explicitly designed to measure attractiveness for international capital. Interestingly the Chinese and other developing country governments have objected to this index and called for the Bank to cease publishing it (Weisbrot, 2013).

6   This is the approach adopted for the UNIDO Competitive Industrial Performance Index (see UNIDO, 2013).
7   For example, a protectionist import substitution strategy might lead to a large share of production coming from more technology-intensive industries, but these would not necessarily be internationally competitive and the competitiveness of the sector would not have increased.
8   Chinese competitiveness has been attributed to a number of factors including low labour costs, an undervalued currency, government subsidies, efficient industrial clusters, reduced costs of communication and transport, the large domestic market and inflows of FDI (Adams *et al.*, 2006; Navarro, 2006). This chapter does not attempt to evaluate the relative importance of these factors but simply to establish the growing competitiveness of Chinese production in order to analyse the impacts on other developing countries.
9   If it is only the final assembly of products that is relocated to China, while parts and components continue to be sourced from other East Asian economies, focusing on the gross value of imports from China rather than the Chinese value added will tend to exaggerate the extent to which the sources of imports have really changed.
10 In fact the study was of the impact of China and India but the authors report that running the model for China on its own did not alter the results in a major way.
11 In Chile there was also a high level of import penetration in clothing but this was not the case in Argentina where the industry was much more protected.
12 For a detailed discussion of these studies and the limitations of their methodologies, see Jenkins (2008).
13 See McGhie *et al.* (2004) on Bangladesh, Thompson (2005) on Central America and Peta (2005) on Lesotho.
14 Coxhead (2007), looking at the impact of China on the South East Asian countries, comes to a similar conclusion that Chinese competition will have a negative effect on manufacturing, particularly in the less developed countries of the region.
15 While it is clear that Chinese FDI has grown rapidly in recent years, it is difficult to get accurate data on the extent and distribution of such investment. See Rosen and Hanemann (2009: 4) for a discussion of some of the data problems.
16 See for example the statements by Mahatir Mohamad, former prime minister of Malaysia and Supachi Panitchpakadi, former deputy prime minister of Thailand, quoted in Mercerau (2005).
17 Justin Lin, former chief economist at the World Bank recently suggested that "China should shift part of its labor-intensive industries to Africa to upgrade the country's economy to an advanced level and help trigger the continent's economic growth" (Jing and Xiaokun, 2013). The opportunity that rising costs in China provides for Africa to expand light manufacturing is also a central theme of a recent World Bank report (Dinh *et al.*, 2012).

References

Adams, G., Gangnes, B. and Shachmurove, Y. 2006. Why is China so Competitive? Measuring and Explaining China's Competitiveness. *World Economy*. 29 (2): 95–122.
Ademola, O., Bankole, O. and Adewuyi, A. 2009. China–Africa Trade Relations: Insights from AERC Scoping Studies. *European Journal of Development Research*. 21 (4): 485–505.
Alvarez, R. and Claro, S. 2009. David *versus* Goliath: The Impact of Chinese Competition on Developing Countries. *World Development*. 37 (3): 560–571.
Amiti, M. and Freund, C. 2010. The Anatomy of China's Export Growth. In Feenstra, R. and Wei, S-J. (eds.). *China's Growing Role in World Trade*. Chicago: University of Chicago Press: 35–61.
Athukorola, P. 2009. The Rise of China and East Asian Export Performance: Is the Crowding-Out Fear Warranted? *World Economy*. 32 (2): 234–266.
Batista, J. C. 2008. Competition Between Brazil and Other Exporting Countries in the US Import Market: A New Extension of Constant-Market-Shares Analysis. *Applied Economics*. 40 (19): 2477–2487.
Boltho, A. 1996. The Assessment: International Competitiveness. *Oxford Review of Economic Policy*. 12 (3): 1–16.
Castro, L., Olarreaga, M. and Saslavsky, D. 2009. The Impact of Trade with China and India on Argentina's Manufacturing Employment. In Lederman, D., Olarreaga, M. and Perry, G. (eds.). *China's and India's Challenge to Latin America: Opportunity or Threat?* Washington, DC: The World Bank.
Ceglowski, J. and Golub, S. 2011. *Does China Still have a Labour Cost Advantage?* CESIFO Working Paper No. 3579. Munich: Centre for Economic Studies IFO Institute – accessible from http://www.cesifo-group.de/ifoHome/publications/working-papers/

CEPAL. 2011. *La inversion extranjera en América Latin y el Caribe, 2010*. Santiago: Economic Commission for Latin America and the Caribbean.

Chantasasawat, B., Fung, K. C., Iizaka, H. and Siu, A. 2004. *Foreign Direct Investment in East Asia and Latin America: Is There a People's Republic of China Effect?* ADB Institute Discussion Paper No. 17. Tokyo: Asian Development Bank Institute.

Chantasasawat, B., Fung, K. C., Lizaka, H. and Siu, A. 2005. The Giant Sucking Sound: Is China Diverting Foreign Direct Investment from Other Asian Economies? *Asian Economic Papers*. 3 (3): 122–140.

Coxhead, I. 2007. A New Resource Curse? Impacts of China's Boom on Comparative Advantage and Resource Dependence in Southeast Asia. *World Development*. 35 (7): 1099–1119.

Cravino, J., Lederman, D. and Olarreaga, M. 2006. *Substitution Between Foreign Capital in China, India and the Rest of the World: Much Ado About Nothing*. Policy Research Working Paper 4361. Washington, DC: World Bank.

Daly, H. and Cobb, J. 1989. *For the Common Good: Redirecting the Economy Toward Community, the Environment, and a Sustainable Future*. Boston, MA: Beacon Pres.

Dimaranan, B., Ianchovichina, E. and Martin, W. 2007. Competing with Giants: Who Wins, Who Loses? In Winters, L. A. and Yusuf, S. (eds). *Dancing with Giants: China, India and the Global Economy*. Washington, DC: World Bank: 67–100.

Dinh, T., Palmade, V., Chandra, V. and Cossar, F. 2012. *Light Manufacturing in Africa, 2012: Targeted Policies to Enhance Investment and Create Jobs*. Washington, DC: World Bank.

Duan, Y., Yang, C., Zhu, K. and Chen, X. 2012. Does the Domestic Value Added Induced by China's Exports Really Belong to China? *China and World Economy*. 20 (5): 83–102.

Dussel Peters, E. 2012. *Chinese FDI in Latin America: Does Ownership Matter?* Working Group on Development and the Environment in the Americas, Discussion Paper No. 33. Medford MA: Tufts University – accessible at http://ase.tufts.edu/gdae/WorkingGroupPapers

Economist. 2010. The Next China. *The Economist*. 29 July.

Edwards, L. and Jenkins, R. 2014. The Margins of Export Competition: A New Approach to Evaluating the Impact of China on South African Exports to Sub-Saharan Africa. *Journal of Policy Modelling*. 36 (Supplement 1): S132–S150.

Eichengreen, B. and Tong, H. 2005. *Is FDI to China Coming at the Expense of other Countries?* Working Paper No. 11335. Cambridge, MA: National Bureau of Economic Research.

Eichengreen, B., Rhee, Y. and Tong, H. 2007. China and the Export of Other Asian Countries. *Review of World Economics*. 143 (2): 201–226.

Fagerberg, J. and Sollie, G. 1987. The Method of Constant Market Shares Analysis Reconsidered. *Applied Economics*. 19 (12): 1571–1583.

Finger, J. and Kreinin, M. 1979. A Measure of 'Export Similarity' and Its Possible Uses. *Economic Journal*. 89 (356): 905–912.

Gallagher, K. and Porzecanski, R. 2010. *The Dragon in the Room: China and the Future of Latin American Industrialization*. Redwood City, CA: Stanford University Press.

Gallegos, J. L., de la Cruz, Luis, J., Boncheva, A. I. and Ruiz-Porras, A. 2008. Competition Between Latin America and China for US Direct Investment. *Global Economy Journal*. 8 (2).

García–Herrero, A. and Santabárbara, D. 2007. Does China Have an Impact on Foreign Direct Investment to Latin America. In Santiso, J. (ed.). *The Visible Hand of China in Latin America*. Paris: OECD Development Centre: 133–152.

Gaulier, G., Lemoine, F. and Unal-Kesenci, D. 2007. China's Integration in East Asia: Production Sharing, FDI and High-Tech Trade. *Economic Change*. 40 (1–2): 27–63.

Giovannetti, G. and Sanfilippo, M. 2009. Do Chinese Exports Crowd-Out African Goods? An Econometric Analysis by Country and Sector. *European Journal of Development Research*. 21 (4): 506–530.

Green, A., Mostafa, T. and Preston, J. 2010. *The Chimera of Competitiveness: Varieties of Capitalism and the Economic Crisis*. Centre for Learning and Life Chances in Knowledge Economies and Societies LLAKES Research Paper (8). London: Institute of Education, University of London – http://www.llakes.org.uk (accessed 24/7/13).

Greenaway, D., Mahabir, A. and Milner, C. 2008. Has China Displaced Other Asian Countries' Exports? *China Economic Review*. 19 (2): 152–169.

Gu, J. 2009. China's Private Enterprises in Africa and the Implications for African Development. *European Journal of Development Research*. 21 (4): 570–587.

Hanson, G. and Robertson, R. 2009. China and the Recent Evolution of Latin America's Manufacturing Exports. In Lederman, D., Olarreaga, M. and Perry, G. (eds.). *China's and India's Challenge to Latin America: Opportunity or Threat?* Washington, DC: World Bank: 145–178.

Hanson, G. and Robertson, R. 2010. China and the Manufacturing Exports of Other Developing Countries. In Feenstra, R. and Wei, S-J. (eds.). *China's Growing Role in World Trade.* Chicago: University of Chicago Press: 35–61.

Henley, J., Kratzsch, S., Kulur, M. and Tandogan, T. 2008. *Foreign Direct Investment from China, India and South Africa in Sub-Saharan Africa: A New or Old Phenomenon?* UNU-WIDER Research Paper No. 2008/24. Helsinki: United Nations University.

House of Lords. 1985. *Report of the Select Committee of the House of Lords on Overseas Trade.* London: Her Majesty's Stationery Office.

Husted, S. and Nishioka, S. 2012. *China's Fare Share? The Growth of Chinese Exports in World Trade.* Available at: http://www.ewi-ssl.pitt.edu/econ/files/faculty/wp/120316_wp_HustedSteven_Chinaexports_March%2015%202012%20final_shu.pdf (accessed 1/7/13).

Ianchovichina, E. and Martin, W. 2004. Economic Impacts of China's Accession to the World Trade Organization. *World Bank Economic Review.* 18 (1): 3–28.

IMD. 2013. *IMD Releases Its 25th Anniversary World Competitiveness Rankings.* Lausanne: IMD World Competitiveness Center – available at: http://www.imd.org/news/World-Competitiveness-2013.cfm (accessed 26/6/13).

International Bar Association. 2010. *Anti-Dumping Investigations Against China in Latin America.* London: International Bar Association – available at http://www.ibanet.org/ENews_Archive/IBA_Jan_2010_ENews_AntiDumping_investigations_against_China.aspx

Jenkins, R. 2008. Measuring the Competitive Threat from China for other Southern Exporters. *The World Economy.* 31 (10): 1351–1366.

Jenkins, R. 2010. China's Global Growth and Latin American Exports. In Santos Paulino, A. and Wan, G. (eds.). *The Rise of China and India.* Basingstoke: Palgrave Macmillan: 220–240.

Jenkins, R. 2014. Chinese Competition and Brazilian Exports of Manufactures. *Oxford Development Studies.* 42 (3): 395–418.

Jenkins, R. and Barbosa, A. F. 2012. Fear for Manufacturing? China and the Future of Industry in Brazil and Latin America. *The China Quarterly.* 209 (1) March: 59–81.

Jing, F. and Xiaokun, L. 2013. Double Benefit in Manufacturing. *China Daily Africa.* 19 April – accessible at http://africa.chinadaily.com.cn/weekly/2013-04/19/content_16422840.htm (accessed 26/6/13).

Jones, R. 2000. *Globalization and the Theory of Input Trade.* Cambridge, MA: MIT Press.

Kaplinsky, R. and Morris, M. 2008. Do Asian Drivers Undermine Export-Oriented Industrialization in SSA? *World Development.* 36 (2): 254–273.

Kaplinsky, R. and Morris, M. 2009. Chinese FDI in Sub-Saharan Africa: Engaging with Large Dragons. *European Journal of Development Research.* 21 (4): 551–569.

Koopman, R., Wang, Z. and Wei, S-J. 2008. *How Much of China's Exports is Really Made in China? Assessing Domestic Value-Added When Processing Trade is Pervasive,* NBER Working Paper No. 14109. Cambridge MA: National Bureau of Economic Research.

Krugman, P. 1994. Competitiveness: A Dangerous Obsession. *Foreign Affairs.* 73 (2): 28–44.

Krugman, P. 1996. Making Sense of the Competitiveness Debate. *Oxford Review of Economic Policy.* 12 (3): 17–25.

Lall, S. 2000. The Technological Structure and Performance of Developing Country Manufactured Exports 1985–98. *Oxford Development Studies.* 28 (3): 337–369.

Lall, S. 2001a. Competitiveness Indices and Developing Countries: An Economic Evaluation of the Global Competitiveness Report. *World Development* 29 (9): 1501–1525.

Lall, S. 2001b. *Competitiveness, Technology and Skills.* Cheltenham: Edward Elgar.

Lall, S. and Albaladejo, N. 2004. China's Competitive Performance: A Threat to East Asian Manufactured Exports. *World Development.* 32 (9): 1441–1466.

Lall, S. and Weiss, J. 2005. China's Competitive Threat to Latin America: An Analysis for 1990–2002. *Oxford Development Studies.* 33 (2): 163–194.

López, A. and Ramos, D. 2009. The Argentine Case. In Jenkins, R. and Dussel Peters, E. (eds.). *China and Latin America: Economic Relations in the Twenty-First Century.* Bonn: German Development Institute: 65–157.

McGhie, J., Kwatra, A. and Davison, J. 2004. *Rags to Riches to Rags.* London: Christian Aid.

271

Mercereau, B. 2005. *FDI Flows to China: Did the Dragon Crowd Out the Tigers?* IMF Working Paper WP/05/189. Washington, DC: International Monetary Fund.

Moran, T. 1998. *Foreign Direct Investment and Development: The New Policy Agenda for Developing Countries and Economies in Transition.* Washington, DC; Institute for International Economics.

Morris, M. and Einhorn, G. 2008. Globalisation, Welfare and Competitiveness: The Impacts of Chinese Imports on the South African Clothing and Textile Industry. *Competition and Change.* 12 (4): 355–376.

Navarro, P. 2006. The Economics of the 'China Price'. *China Perspectives.* 68 (Nov–Dec): 13–27 – available at http://chinaperspectives.revues.org/3063 (accessed 24/8/12).

Palma, G., 2008. De-Industrialization, 'Premature' De-Industrialization and the Dutch Disease. In Durlauf, S. and Blume, L. (eds.). *The New Palgrave: A Dictionary of Economics* (2nd ed.). Basingstoke: Palgrave Macmillan.

Peta, B. 2005. The 'Chinese Tsunami' that Threatens to Swamp Africa. *The Independent.* 25 April.

Reinert, E. 1994. *Competitiveness and Its Predecessors – a 500-Year Cross-National Perspective.* STEP Report 03/94. Oslo: The STEP Group.

Reinert, E. 2007. *How Rich Countries Got Rich ... and Why Poor Countries Stay Poor.* London: Constable.

Roberts, S. and Thoburn, J. 2003. Adjusting to Trade Liberalisation: The Case of Firms in the South African Textile Sector. *Journal of African Economies.* 12 (1): 74–103.

Rosales, O. and Kuwayama, M. 2012. *China y América Latina y el Caribe: Hacia una relación económica y commercial estratégica.* Santiago: Comisión Económica para América Latina y el Caribe (UNECLAC).

Rosen, D. and Hanemann, T. 2009. *China's Changing Outbound Foreign Direct Investment Profile: Drivers and Policy Implications.* Policy Brief PB09–14. Washington, DC: Peterson Institute for International Economics.

Rosen, D. and Hanemann, T. 2011. *An American Open Door? Maximizing the Benefits of Chinese Foreign Direct Investment.* Special Report. Washington, DC: Centre on US–China Relations, Asia Society and Kissinger Institute on China and the United States, Woodrow Wilson International Center for Scholars.

Schott, P. K. 2004. *The Relative Competitiveness of China's Exports to the United States Vis á Vis Other Countries in Asia, the Caribbean, Latin America and the OECD.* New Haven, CT: Yale School of Management.

Sen, A. K. 2012. Congressional Report Hits Chinese Trade Practices. *Washington Times.* 11 October.

Shafaeddin, S. M. 2004. Is China's Accession to WTO Threatening Exports of Developing Countries? *China Economic Review.* 15 (2): 109–144.

Shaikh, A. 1979. Foreign Trade and the Law of Value: Parts 1 and 2. *Science and Society.* 43 (3) and 44 (1): 281–302 and 27–57.

Thompson, G. 2005. Mill Closings Hit Hard in Central America. *New York Times.* 25 March.

Tong, S. and Zheng, Y. 2008. China's Trade Acceleration and the Deepening of an East Asian Regional Production Network. *China and World Economy.* 16 (1): 66–81.

UNCTAD. 2012. *World Investment Report 2012.* Geneva: United Nations Conference on Trade and Development.

UNCTAD. 2014. UNCTADSTAT Data Center – accessible at http://unctadstat.unctad.org/wds/ReportFolders/reportFolders.aspx

UNIDO. Various years. *Yearbook of Industrial Statistics.* Vienna: United Nations Industrial Development Organization.

UNIDO. 2013. *The Industrial Competitiveness of Nations, Looking Back, Forging Ahead: Competitive Industrial Performance Report 2012/13.* Vienna: United Nations Industrial Development Organization.

US President's Commission. 1985. *The Report of the President's Commission on Industrial Competitiveness, Vol. II: Global Competition: The New Reality.* Washington, DC: US Government Printing Office.

Wang, C., Wei, Y. and Liu, X. 2007. Does China Rival Its Neighbouring Economies for Inward FDI? *Transnational Corporations.* 16 (3): 35–60.

Wang, Z. and Wei, S-J. 2010. What Accounts for the Rising Sophistication of China's Exports. In Feenstra, R. and Wei, S-J. (eds.). *China's Growing Role in World Trade.* Chicago: University of Chicago Press: 63–107.

Weisbrot, M. 2013. IMF and World Bank are Losing Clout in Developing Countries. *The Guardian.* 31 May.

Wingarajan, G. (ed.). 2003. *Competitiveness Strategy in Developing Countries: A Manual for Policy Analysis.* London: Routledge.

Wood, A. and Mayer, J. 2009. *Has China De-Industrialised Other Developing Countries?* Queen Elizabeth House Working Paper No.175. Oxford: University of Oxford.

World Bank. 2002. *Globalization, Growth and Poverty: Building an Inclusive World Economy*. World Bank Research Report 23591. Washington, DC: World Bank.

Xu, B. 2010. The Sophistication of Exports: Is China Special? *China Economic Review*. 21 (3): 482–493.

Yang, Y. 2003. *China's Integration into the World Economy; Implications for Developing Countries*. IMF Working Paper 03/245. Washington, DC: International Monetary Fund.

Yang, Y. 2013. *The Chinese Growth Miracle*. China Center for Economic Growth, National School of Development. Beijing: Peking University.

Zhao, H. 2013. China's FDI into Southeast Asia. *ISEAS Perspective*. 8. Singapore: Institute of Southeast Asian Studies.

Zhou, Y. and Lall, S. 2005. The Impact of China's FDI Surge on FDI in South-East Asia: Panel Data Analysis for 1986–2001. *Transnational Corporations*. 14 (1): 41–65.

16

IS THE CHOICE
OF TECHNIQUE DEBATE
STILL RELEVANT?[1]

Mozammel Huq

The main objective of this chapter is to explore the debate over the choice of techniques in some detail and, in the process, investigate whether it is still relevant. This debate, which has been a long one, has reached a stage where policy makers in the developing world can now see the issue in a much wider context, thus helping them to move from the pure theoretical aspect of technical choice to the practical need of technology development.

Viewing the 'choice of technique' in a wider context implies going much beyond the traditional technical choice analysis based solely on rational choice within given factor endowments. This broadening of the topic links it with more recent developments focusing on technology transfer and absorption. However, as will be apparent, we strongly believe that encompassing issues relating to technological capability considerably helps a comprehensive view of the practice of technical choice, especially in developing countries.

The order of discussion is as follows. The first section deals with the issue of optimal factor use in the context of classical and neoclassical perspectives, while in the second section the issue of technical choice is discussed, focusing on 'intermediate technology' as advanced by the 'Appropriate Technology' movement. The third section discusses the use of social prices in evaluating alternative technologies especially in the context of some pioneering studies conducted by the David Livingstone Institute of Strathclyde University. Attempts to incorporate the dynamic elements are taken up in the fourth section, while the fifth section focuses on technical choice in the context of technological capability building relating to the need for developing countries to compete in this age of globalisation. In the final section, some brief concluding remarks are made.

Optimal technical choice: Classical versus neoclassical perspectives[2]

Adam Smith (1776) sought to explain the differences that existed between countries in terms of productive capability and, taking a long-term view, he envisaged the economic growth of a country as an on-going process occurring over time as the increasing division of labour, technological progress and capital accumulation give rise to progressively rising productivity and real per capita income. Latter day classical economists including Karl Marx (1867) were also keen to understand the process of economic growth, although their industrial world was very different from that of the second half of the eighteenth century that had existed during Smith's days. Thus, the classical economists were keen to unravel the mystery of output growth and, in particular, how the use of tools and machinery helped to increase productivity per worker. As observed by Clunies-Ross *et al.* (2009: 512): "The essential message that emerged was clear: economic growth was the result of continuous improvements in the 'productive powers of labour' (progressively increasing productivity), obtained through technological progress."

In the latter part of the nineteenth century, a new school of thought called the neoclassical, or the marginalist, school emerged. Its distinguishing characteristic was to attempt to explain economic behaviour in terms of a theory of optimal choice – via substitution at the margin. The tools used for the maximisation of utility (with individuals acting in a rational manner) were extended to analyse production behaviour, thus modelling the optimum input combination. Given resources and technology, the technique which will maximise output will emerge as the optimum choice. The main consideration in such an optimum input combination is relative factor prices as dictated by the relative availability of factors.

Relative factor prices thus emerge as the central element of the model, as may be seen from Figure 16.1, which shows optimum input choice in two countries, one developed and the other developing, with two different sets of factor availabilities. In the former, capital is relatively cheaper, so it will use relatively more capital and less labour (as is shown by the steeper slope of the isocost line EF) than in the latter. Thus, in the developing country (LDC), the growth of output facing a lower capital/labour ratio will follow the ray LDC, while the developed country will follow the ray DC with a higher capital/labour ratio.

The above theoretical formulation of technical choice which emerges from the neoclassical representation has, however, faced some serious criticisms. In particular, the neoclassical assumption of a competitive market is considered as highly unrealistic. Indeed, because of market failures the prevailing market prices often fail to reflect the true relative availability of factors of production.[3] Thus, as observed by Clunies-Ross *et al.* (2009: 514),

> in many situations, the actual choice of techniques in developing countries often hardly differs from that found in developed countries.[4] It is true that there are many other factors that have contributed to such technical choices, but the failure of factor prices to reflect factor availability has often featured prominently.

Another major criticism of the neoclassical model of technical choice is its static approach, especially as the effect of time remains ignored. There is also the unrealistic assumption of the

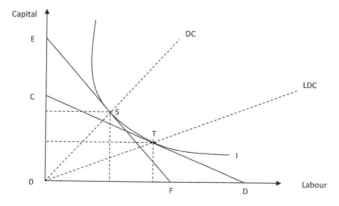

Figure 16.1 Optimum technical choice in developed (DC) and developing (LDC) countries.

existence of an infinite range of techniques, with the possibility of choosing any input combination to minimise output cost. Furthermore there is a failure to consider the fact that, depending on the kinds of output and the scales of production required, one will see the emergence of different techniques at different periods, so that, as argued by Grieve (2003: 27), the hypothetical techniques "do not necessarily represent practicable alternatives for producing a particular volume of a specific product at a particular point in time."

Thus, the thinking of the neoclassical economists differed significantly from that of the classical economists who viewed the growth process as a major outcome of the continuous improvements of labour productivity arising from the advancement of technology and with the increase in productivity taking place cumulatively. Indeed, what Smith envisaged was a dynamic sequence in which productivity improvement in one sector of the economy would help in widening markets via lowering costs of output and raising customers' real incomes, and other sectors of the economy would then exploit increased market opportunities through improvements of products and production methods thus stimulating the cumulative growth process.[5]

In contrast to the thinking of the classical economists who sought an understanding of technological improvements and the resultant productivity enhancement, based on actual innovations taking place over time, the neoclassical model tended to treat technology choice as merely a matter of factor substitution. As observed by Rosenberg (1982, 1994), the neoclassical model attempted to view technology as a sort of 'black box' which, in some mysterious ways, was helping labour productivity and the process of production.[6] Given these serious flaws many economists would prefer not to use the neoclassical analysis of technical choice. As observed by Egea (1990: 1451),

> the choice of technique paradigm should be abandoned. It not only lacks realism, as most of its critics have observed, but also the theoretical construct in which it is embedded (e.g. the price formation mechanism) is not as solid as some researchers pretend. ... It does not emanate from a theory directly concerned with the issues of technical change, growth, or technological development. Applied research on the problem of technological change has gained very little from continued use of this frame of analysis.

Appropriate Technology movement:
A radical view of technology choice

The teaching following from the neoclassical school faced a challenge especially in the developing world, which was witnessing very varied economic growth experiences. This was particularly felt during the 1950s and the 1960s when a number of thinkers including Ragnar Nurkse (1952), Raul Prebisch (1950) and Hans Singer (1950) openly challenged the neoclassical thinking of economic growth. They were particularly critical of the neoclassical belief in the efficacy of the market mechanism, enabling an efficient resource allocation.

In the early part of the second half of the twentieth century, many developing countries were taking a keen interest in industrialisation often with large-scale capital-intensive technology. The use of such imported technologies was strongly questioned, among others, by Ernst Schumacher (1973) who helped to pioneer a 'radical type' of thinking for technical choice known as the 'Appropriate Technology' movement that actively propagated the adoption of small-scale labour-intensive technology:

> Because the techniques envisaged were neither standard 'modern' nor simple unimproved traditional, they were described as representing *intermediate technology*. In his ground-breaking book, *Small is Beautiful* (1973), which became a worldwide

best seller, Schumacher argued for avoiding the current practice of adopting modern large-scale, capital-intensive and labour-saving plants which, according to him, were not doing any good to the vast majority of people in developing countries, who were living in rural areas. Schumacher argued that, given the limited investible resources, developing countries would fail to create enough jobs by concentrating on the modern capital-intensive industries with high capital requirement per job. Such a focus, to Schumacher, would give rise to a situation of dualism, with a small, relatively high-income, modern sector as an island in the midst of a vast traditional economy with very low productive activities; so Schumacher advocated the use of intermediate technologies.

(Clunies-Ross *et al.*, 2009: 515–516)

In a report prepared for the Indian Planning Commission, Schumacher argued that

a technology must be evolved which is cheap enough to be accessible to a larger sector of the community than the very rich and can be applied on a mass scale without making altogether excessive demands on the savings and foreign exchange resources of the country.

(quoted in McRobie, 1981: 19)

A close associate of Schumacher was George McRobie, who argued that for a technology to be appropriate it

should be capable of local operation and maintenance, and local or at least indigenous manufacture; it should be owned and operated by its users, and result in a significant increase in their net (real or money) income; it should utilise to the maximum extent local and renewable raw materials and energy; and it should lend itself to widespread reproduction using indigenous resources and through the medium of local markets.

(McRobie, 1991: 169)

The 'intermediate technologies', as advocated by Schumacher and his colleagues, were appealing to developing countries especially because of the various characteristics which are associated with such technologies (Stewart, 1985): more labour-using (high labour/output ratio, L/O); less capital-using (low capital/labour ratio, K/L); less skill-using; making more use of local material resources; being smaller scale; and producing more appropriate products (i.e. a simpler product designed for lower-income groups, or more intensive in the use of local material resources). The lower labour productivity of these 'intermediate technologies' by comparison with 'modern' technologies has to be compared with the productivity levels for 'traditional technologies', and with the options of labour being unemployed or underemployed. If this comparison is made then the labour productivity of intermediate technologies may look considerably more attractive. In addition, methodologically, labour productivity is only a partial efficiency measure, so that total factor productivity or broader efficiency measures (including economic profitability) also need to be brought to bear on this debate.[7]

Until recently, the Intermediate Technology Development Group (ITDG), established in 1965 in London (and later on shifted to Rugby), had been playing a major part in popularising this radical approach, often termed, as already mentioned, the 'Appropriate Technology' movement.[8] In various other parts of the world, similar organisations were also established including Volunteers in Technical Assistance (VITA) in the USA and the Brace Research

Institute in Canada. Others have also joined including AT International (USA), TOOL (Canada) and the Appropriate Technology Development Association (India). A number of international agencies such as UNICEF, the ILO, UNIFEM and IFAD have also come forward to help the various organisations which remained active in introducing intermediate technologies to developing countries (see, e.g., Kaplinsky, 1990; McRobie, 1991; Grieve, 2003).

Considering the existence of high unemployment and a serious shortage of capital in developing economies, it is not difficult to see the wide appeal of the type of technologies whose equipment is easy to produce locally at much lower cost per unit than that of their 'modern' counterparts. Through catalogues and other publications (produced by ITDG and various similar other organisations), these technologies have been actively promoted "by providing designs and instructions for manufacturing machinery and equipment for use in agriculture and transport, construction, textile manufacturing, food processing, energy supply (biomass, biogas, micro-hydro, solar and wind), provision of safe water and health care" (Clunies-Ross *et al.*, 2009: 517).

Schumacher and his associates strongly believed that the 'intermediate technologies', which they were advocating, were capable of providing the poor people in developing countries with a sustainable path of economic development. It may be mentioned that the labour-using and capital-saving bias of these technologies had strong similarities with the Minimum Capital/ Output Ratio Investment Criterion as advanced, for example, by Polak and Buchanan for evaluating investment in developing countries (Sen, 1960).

However, although appealing, the approach suffers from a number of limitations:

(a) The limited number of technologies that could be found, obviously, creates a constraint.
(b) From the point of view of efficient resource allocation, what is important is the maximisation of profit (or cost minimisation), so the labour-using or capital-saving bias of the approach might fail to pass this critical test. [9]
(c) The emphasis on the immediate increase in employment and income fails to take into account the objective that a country can have for generating higher savings (rather than maximising current employment), thus maximising the present value of output and employment over a relevant future (Sen, 1960).

Use of social prices

Morawetz (1974: 517) defined 'appropriate technology' from an economic viewpoint as "the set of techniques which makes optimum use of available resources in a given environment. For each process or project, it is the technology which maximises social welfare if factors and products are shadow priced." This test requires a profit-maximising or cost-minimising technology from the social point of view, and it is necessary to apply the DCF (discounted-cash-flow) method together with shadow pricing of inputs and outputs in order to identify such a technology.

A major attempt in identifying least-cost technology using social cost-efficiency analysis was conducted during the 1970s and the early 1980s at the David Livingstone Institute (of Strathclyde University), known as the DLI studies.[10] This was an early application of the social cost–benefit methodology advocated by Little and Mirrlees (1968),[11] followed soon afterwards by UNIDO (1972), articulating the use of accounting or shadow prices for a systematic appraisal of investment decisions. The DLI approach was an attempt to adopt cost–benefit methodology for the extensive analysis of technical choice with primary data collected from the suppliers and users of technology. The approach involved an extensive appraisal of alternative techniques through calculating the Present Value of Costs (PVCs) for each and every sub-process, thus helping to identify the least-cost techniques for each sub-process and, at the end, identifying the combined least-cost technology for the entire production process.[12] At a second stage shadow pricing methodology was used, appraising, among others, the two key inputs (labour and capital) using shadow prices or social opportunity costs. This involved the estimation of social rates of return as well as market rates of return as a basis for the identification of the economic efficiency of the identified technologies (see, e.g., Pickett, 1975; Rahim, 1979.)

This detailed analysis was very revealing. The suitability of identified techniques was tested at small, medium and large scales of production. In addition, different discount rates (principally 10 and 20 per cent) and wage levels (low and high) were used to test the sensitivity of the identified techniques to alternative social prices. These appraisals were also extended to include the sensitivity to alternative levels of capacity utilisation, and the impact of risk and uncertainty was assessed (through the use of probability values).

In these empirical studies there was a serious attempt to rigorously investigate the range of technical choices which were available and, in this process, the DLI research questioned the notion that technology importers in developing countries were faced with a highly limited technology choice – a view which was often found to prevail. The demonstration that a technology could be disaggregated through the identification of alternatives at the sub-process level also turned out to be an eye opener, showing that the developing-country investors were not in reality faced by a single technology package, so that they did not have to import an entire technology from a single source in the developed world. Rather they could identify a range of technology sources and procure the various machinery and equipment as required. They could even obtain machinery and equipment from domestic sources or from other developing countries.[13] Thus, the DLI approach adopted a systematic methodology which demonstrated that 'technology unpackaging' could be a practical process. The DLI studies also exposed the exceptionally heavy costs incurred through the use of the turn-key packaging of technology purchase, particularly associated with financing through supplier's credit.[14] In addition, investors could also consider alternative products, thus widening the range of technology types and sources even further.[15] In brief, the DLI research showed that developing countries could often have selected better technological alternatives than those adopted (see, e.g., Huq and Aragaw 1981; Khan and Rahim 1985). As observed by Pickett (1977: 776), the DLI studies "provide a basis for moving toward a more 'rational' technology policy in developing countries".

However, the DLI approach failed to consider the dynamic elements such as the costs and benefits of technology learning and the significance of externalities generated.[16] Indeed, as will be discussed later, in this age of globalisation many of the developing countries which are struggling to compete internationally a pressing issue is how 'borrowed' technologies could best be successfully introduced.

Thus the mere identification of a least-cost technology, even taking into account social costs and benefits, is not sufficient. As observed by the United Nations (1987), for a successful transfer of technology the two further conditions also needed to be satisfied: the assimilation and diffusion of those technologies in the host economy, and the development of indigenous capacities for innovation.

Attempts to incorporate dynamic elements[17]

Amartya Sen is one of the early contributors who seriously challenged the neoclassical formulation. His *Choice of Techniques* (1960) is considered a major turning point, especially as it stimulated a serious debate about whether the maximisation of savings or of employment should be the principal criterion for the choice of techniques in developing countries facing a serious shortage of investment funds and an abundance of unskilled labour. Thus, it was possible to challenge the simplistic neoclassical view of the static choice between labour and capital intensity, ignoring the growth considerations of a developing country.

Subsequently a rich debate took place, especially covering the conflict between output and employment objectives (see, e.g., Stewart and Streeten, 1972; Stewart, 1977; Tribe and Alpine, 1987). In particular, the question was posed whether maximisation of employment was compatible with maximisation of output. Then, the debate over the choice of technique took a highly meaningful turn, especially during the 1980s, with the introduction of dynamic elements involving, in particular, technology learning. A main consideration was the inability of developing countries to compete effectively internationally, as success in this regard was thought to largely determine whether it was able to move up the ladder of comparative advantage, through product and process improvements (innovations, even minor ones). The literature since the mid-1980s has been of great help in clarifying our understanding in this area. Amsden (1989), Dahlman *et al.* (1987), Enos (1991), Enos and Park (1988) and Lall (1987, 1992) can perhaps be considered as the leading contributors to this radical thinking. A number of others have advocated emphasis on the 'technological learning approach' including Amsden and Hikino (1993), Bell and Pavitt (1997), Bhalla (1996), Clunies-Ross *et al.* (2009), Grieve (2003, 2004), Hikino and Amsden (1994), Huq (2003a, 2003b) and Huq *et al.* (1993).

A common feature of the attack on the traditional view of technology choice is a challenge to the strong ideological approach of leaving the choice of technique to the free play of market forces, thus ignoring the serious constraints likely to be faced by developing countries in successfully adopting imported technologies. A key issue here is how developing countries should develop industrial competitiveness based on borrowed technologies: "Being borrowers (or say imitators) of technology rather than innovators leaves the developing countries at a distinct disadvantage since they are unable to derive monopoly profit from their production activities" (Huq, 2014a: 232). Thus, an important feature of this new approach to technology appraisal is that it takes into account the development of technological capability (viewed as a process of learning) which involves two key components, namely the development of human capital and the undertaking of research and development activities.

The importance of human capital development for technology adaptation can hardly be over-emphasised. The process enables the labour force to select, install, maintain, assimilate, design, manufacture and even create the technology. The producers do not need to be the inventors, but must have the ability to absorb borrowed technologies successfully:

> The mass educational development which took place, for example, in South Korea (and also in Singapore, Taiwan and Hong Kong) preceding their success in industrialisation is often cited as a model of appropriate preparation. Equally important is education imparted by various formal training schemes and also by in-firm training as these are very helpful in improving the technical competence of an industrial workforce. Based on an extensive search, Lall (1992, 176–178) found that in the mid-1980s the East Asian NICs (South Korea, Singapore, Taiwan and Hong Kong) were ahead of other NICs (Brazil, Mexico, India and Thailand).
>
> (Huq, 2014a: 234)

In the case of China, investment in education has been considered as a key development factor and, according to Holz (2008: 1683) the country has made so much improvement based on the agglomeration of talent that it is "in an excellent position to innovate and grow".

A study conducted for the World Bank (Tilak, 2002) extensively evaluated the case of human capital development in East Asia (covering China, Hong Kong, Japan, Singapore, South Korea, and Taiwan), aiming to draw some key lessons. An important message from Tilak's report is that the "East Asian economies have firmly believed in the importance of education for economic growth and accordingly made huge allocations to this sector" (Tilak, 2002: 19). Table 16.1 shows that during 1980–90 all four selected countries showed remarkable growth rates in their GDP, while also maintaining a high growth in education expenditure. It is true that the causal relationship between education expenditure and GDP growth could run in the opposite direction as well (i.e. high growth in GDP could have enabled these countries to maintain a growth in education expenditure). While recognising the need for further analysis, Tilak states that "investment in human capital has been regarded as the cornerstone of nation-building and the key factor of economic development in East Asia. This realisation is critically important" (Tilak, 2002: 38). The core lesson is strongly emphasised by Tilak (2002: 42): "Economic miracles do not happen out of the blue; they are based on education miracles. There are no shortcuts."

The close relationship between low per capita income and low human capital development is seen clearly in Table 16.2. Human capital development as represented by the average years of schooling is lowest in South Asia and Sub-Saharan Africa, the two regions which have the lowest per capita income in the world. Compared to industrialised regions, both males and females in these regions (South Asia and Sub-Saharan Africa) have significantly lower average years of schooling and the disadvantage is worse in the case of the females, reflecting a significant gender disparity.

Table 16.1 Growth in GDP and in education expenditure in four selected East Asian countries, 1980–90 (average annual growth rate)

Country	GDP	Expenditure on education
Singapore	6.4	7.1
Hong Kong	7.1	7.6
China	9.5	8.4
South Korea	9.7	9.5

Source: Tilak (2002: 19), based on data from World Bank and UNESCO sources.

Table 16.2 Average years of schooling and gender disparity, 2010

Region	Male	Female	Total	Gender disparity
Central Asia	9.35	9.99	9.69	1.07
East Asia and the Pacific	8.47	8.01	8.24	0.95
Eastern Europe	10.24	9.95	10.09	0.97
Industrialised countries	10.92	10.71	10.81	0.98
Latin America and the Caribbean	8.63	8.33	8.48	0.97
Middle East and North Africa	8.05	7.28	7.65	0.90
South Asia	6.41	4.79	5.62	0.75
Sub-Saharan Africa	5.98	4.89	5.43	0.82
World	8.41	7.84	8.12	0.93

Source: Son (2010: 3).

A cautionary note needs to be added: in the above discussion no attempt has been made to draw a rigorous causal relationship between education and economic growth. The non-availability of crucial data does not allow a demonstration of the case for a strong link between human capital development and technology development.

Research and development (R&D) is equally important, "considered to be the core of technology-capability building" (Clunies-Ross *et al.* 2009: 519). It extends and elaborates the skills that are there to be mastered. R&D is also an educative process for those engaged in it, and may be considered as an element in human-capital investment. Major contributors to the literature on technological development (a good example being Freeman, 1987) have identified R&D as the decisive factor in innovation and technology development. The ease of absorbing new technologies in agriculture, thanks largely to the successful R&D carried out in Asian and Latin American countries, has contributed greatly to the success of the Green Revolution. There is a very high social rate of return from R&D in agriculture, typically exceeding 20 per cent and often being higher than 40 per cent (Khan and Akbari, 1986). However, in low-income developing countries, R&D investment in the manufacturing sector is negligible and "total R&D expenditure may be less relevant a measure of *industrial* technical effort than R&D performed or financed by productive enterprises" (Lall 1992: 178).

In the past, data on R&D were often not readily available, but in recent years the World Bank (2014a) has assembled data relating to R&D for a large number of countries. Although the R&D data, as available, do not permit identification of expenditures by sectors, the data included in Table 16.3 are illuminating for a significant number of developed and developing countries. There is a wide divergence in the R&D to GDP ratio between the countries included in the table, the extremes of the range being from 0.22 per cent for Nigeria to 4.04 per cent for South Korea. It is also remarkable that some of the lower income countries, such as China (with a GNP per capita of $5,720), have a higher ratio (1.98 per cent) than that for a high income country such as the UK (1.72 per cent of GDP compared to a GNP per capita of $38,300).

Table 16.3 Investment in R&D and the availability of researchers and technicians in R&D in selected developed and developing countries, 2012

Country	GNP per capita (US$)	R&D (% of GDP)	Number of researchers and technicians in R&D (per million people)	
			Researchers	Technicians
	(1)	(2)	(3)	(4)
Brazil	11,640	1.21	710	656
Canada	50,650	1.73	4,563	1,481
China	5,720	1.98	1,020	NA
Egypt	2,980	0.43	524	277
Ethiopia	410	0.25	42	17
France	41,860	2.26	3,918	1,868
Germany	45,170	2.92	4,139	1,683
Ghana	1,580	0.38	39	30
Hong Kong	36,280	NA	NA	NA
India	1,550	0.81	160	103
Indonesia	3,420	0.08	90	NA
Israel	32,030	3.93	6,602	1,737

Italy	34,810	1.27	1,820	NA
Japan	47,690	3.39	5,158	564
Kenya	870	0.98	227	645
Korea (South)	24,640	4.04	5,928	1,065
Malaysia	9,820	1.07	1,643	158
Mexico	9,720	0.43	386	172
Nigeria	2,460	0.22	39	13
Norway	98,880	1.65	5,588	NA
Pakistan	1,250	0.33	149	58
Singapore	51,090	2.10	6,438	462
South Africa	7,460	0.76	364	105
Sri Lanka	2,910	0.16	103	89
Sweden	50,870	3.41	5,181	2,005
Tanzania	570	0.52	38	10
Thailand	5,250	0.25	332	227
Turkey	10,810	0.86	987	173
Uganda	480	0.56	37	13
UK	38,300	1.72	4,024	1,169
USA	52,350	2.79	3,979	NA

Sources: (1) World Bank (2014c); (2) World Bank (2014d); (3) World Bank (2014e); (4) World Bank (2014f).

Three simple regressions are reported in Table 16.4 based on these data.[18] As expected, R&D as a percentage of GDP is found to be positively connected with GNP per capita; the lower the GNP per capita, the lower the R&D as a percentage of GDP, as may be seen from Model 1 (the coefficient is 3.16386e-05, $N = 30$). Similar positive relationships were also observed in the cases of the number of researchers and technicians (both measured as per million people), as may be seen from Models 2 and 3 respectively (0.0822533, $N = 30$ and 0.0276792, $N = 25$). In all the three cases, the regression coefficients are highly significant (Figures 16.A1–16.A3 in the Appendix show the charts for these three cases).

Table 16.4 Regression results

	Model 1		*Model 2*		*Model 3*	
	Coefficient (standard error)	*p-value*	*Coefficient (standard error)*	*p-value*	*Coefficient (standard error)*	*p-value*
GNP per capita (US$)	3.16386e-05★ (7.09505e-06)	0.00012	0.0822533★ (0.00963469)	<0.00001	0.0276792★ (0.0042145)	<0.00001
Constant	0.73374 (0.229036)	0.00337	366.347 (311.018)	0.24875	90.6934 (111.467)	0.42420

Notes

★ Significant at the level of 1%.

Model 1: R&D regressed against GNP per capita ($N = 30$; dependent variable: R&D as % of GDP). *R*-squared = 0.425265.

Model 2: No. of researchers regressed against GNP per capita ($N = 30$; dependent variable: no. of researchers per million people). *R*-squared = 0.722453.

Model 3: No. of technicians regressed against GNP per capita ($N = 25$; dependent variable: number of technicians per million people). *R*-squared = 0.652219.

The role of scientists and technologists in the promotion of R&D has been considered so vital that under the leadership of Abdul Salam (who won the Nobel Prize for Physics in 1979) the Third World Academy of Sciences (TWAS) has been strongly emphasising the importance of the science and technology (S&T) infrastructure. Based in Trieste, the TWAS (subsequently renamed as The World Academy of Sciences) has remained a key player in promoting R&D involving local scientists and technologists as it is believed that herein lies the key to economic development in general and sustained manufacturing growth in particular in developing countries (Salam, 1987).[19] Indeed, the role of the scientific community in technology development comes out clearly from the success achieved, for example, by India in sectors such as defence and atomic energy (see, e.g., Kalam, 1999; Sandhya and Jain, 2003).

The importance of the S&T infrastructure in technological innovation is also apparent from the core focus of National Innovation Systems (NIS), a concept which emerged in the late 1980s and the early 1990s. Freeman (1987, 1995), Lundvall (1992) and Nelson (1987, 1993) are credited with developing this concept. It emphasises institution building, as will be apparent from observation of Freeman (1987: 1), who described the NIS as "the network of institutions in the public and private sectors whose activities and interactions initiate, import, modify and diffuse new technologies".[20] The concept of the NIS has strong similarities with 'technological capability building' which, as will be seen later, is almost synonymous with 'technological learning' that is considered so vital in the context of economic growth in developing countries. However, the large majority of studies on NIS are primarily focused on scientific and technical dimensions of activities aimed at R&D-based innovations. Some view this as a narrow understanding of NIS, although even under the broad NIS approach "the current use of *innovation* as almost synonymous [with] technical change ends up hindering any productive use [of such a broad approach] ... for the study of industrializing economies" (Viotti, 2001: 3). As further observed by Viotti, such an approach, encompassing "the frequent use of R&D statistics as a proxy for a wider range of S&T activities is acknowledged to be unsatisfactory (Winter, 1987; Bell, 1991; and Freeman, 1994)". The concept of NIS has been thought to be more relevant to advanced industrial countries, where innovation is "at the core of the process of technical change", in contrast to developing countries where such innovation has "a secondary role, possibly, no role at all, in the process of technical change." (Viotti, 2001: 4).

However, there is less controversy in situations where innovation is closely linked with the application and adaptation of existing techniques, which is often firm-driven. Thus considered, it is "the process by which firms master and implement the design and production of goods and services which are new to them, irrespective of whether they are new to their competitors – domestic or foreign" (Ernst *et al.*, 1998, as quoted in Siyanbola *et al.*, 2012: 4). Indeed, as far as low income developing countries are concerned,

> technological change occurs primarily through learning – that is, the acquisition, diffusion and upgrading of technologies that already exist in more technologically advanced countries – and not by pushing the global knowledge frontier further. In short, the key to technological progress in the LDCs is technological catch-up through learning rather than undertaking R&D to invent products and processes which are totally new to the world.
>
> (UNCTAD, 2007: 6)

Level of technology adoption

The distinction between different levels of activity in the process of adopting technologies within production processes was first advanced by Enos and Park (1988: 6–12) while investigating a number of South Korean large-scale firms covering three main industry sectors (petro-chemicals; synthetic fibres; machinery; and iron and steel). Their investigation involved examining the incorporation of foreign technology into production systems by looking into a transfer process involving three distinct stages:

Stage 1   Selection/purchase
Stage 2   Absorption
Stage 3   Diffusion.

Stage 1 can be regarded as careful least-cost identification. Stages 2 and 3 involve some important dynamic elements associated with technological learning. In Stage 2, the technology importer will need to master, learn, adapt and improve the technology.

A recent study conducted on behalf of the World Bank by Goldberg *et al.* (2008: xi) considers absorption as a learning activity that

> a firm can employ to integrate and commercialise knowledge and technology that is new to the firm, but not new to the world. ... Examples of absorption include: adopting new products and manufacturing processes developed elsewhere, upgrading old products and processes, licensing technology, improving organizational efficiency, and achieving quality certification.

Diffusion is the final stage of technology adoption, with the original technology recipient being able to help others to receive the technology. A good example of absorption and diffusion is perhaps provided by the technology-transfer deal between the then British car manufacturing firm Rover and the Japanese firm Honda, with the latter successfully absorbing the technology (thus reaching Stage 2) and subsequently selling technological improvements to others including Rover itself (i.e. reaching Stage 3 – see Huq, 2003b: 106).

Various capabilities

In a successful technology transfer the learning process will involve the recipient acquiring various technological capabilities. Three such capabilities (production, investment and innovation) were originally suggested by Dahlman *et al.* (1987), while subsequently Lall (1992) added a fourth (linkages). *Production capability* is needed in order to operate productive facilities: it is reflected in productive efficiency and in the ability to adapt operations to changing market circumstances. *Investment capability* is required in order to establish new productive facilities and expand existing facilities: it is reflected in project costs and in the ability to tailor project designs to suit the circumstances of the investment. *Innovation capability* is needed in order to create new technology: it is reflected in the ability to improve technology or to develop new products or services that better meet specific needs. *Linkages capability* represents the

> skills needed to transmit information, skills and technology to, and receive them from, component or raw-material suppliers, subcontractors, consultants, service firms, and technology institutions. Such linkages affect not only the productive efficiency of the enterprise (allowing it to specialise more fully) but also the diffusion of technology through the economy and the deepening of the industrial structure, both essential to industrial development.

(Lall, 1992: 168)

It is necessary to bear in mind the difficulties involved in quantifying the levels of absorption and diffusion, or to measure the various capabilities. Huq *et al.* (1993: 110–114) attempt to measure technology absorption by various engineering firms in Bangladesh. Kaplinsky has observed that "development of technological capability is expensive; it takes time; and the greater the scientific content in production, the greater the cost, and the longer the wait" (1990: 25). Also, it needs to be appreciated that the

> effective use of a new technology will depend on a number of factors including development of new skills, and improvement of managerial and administrative capability. Capability for selecting and installing new machinery and equipment, though important, is only an initial stage of technological-capability building. The recipient will also need to develop the required human skills for operating the plant and also for achieving product and process improvements so as to remain competitive in the market.
>
> (Clunies-Ross *et al.*, 2009: 522)

While recognising the difficulties, it is also necessary to emphasise the enormous benefits that the learning process can bring to developing countries struggling to compete in the world market. As observed by Hikino and Amsden (1994: 292), developing countries wanting to compete effectively with advanced countries will have to "sharpen their own managerial and organisational skills, shorten their learning period and . . . make incremental improvement in the cost, quality, and performance of their process and product." They also emphasise the key point that no technology is 'perfectly transferable' and any technology which is going to be imported will need to go through the adaptation process. Hence the urgency to develop the various capabilities listed above.

The experience of the successful East Asian industrialisation provides us with some good lessons. Kim (1990) studied Korean industrialisation extensively and found that it followed a dynamic strategy for industrialisation, with progressive technological upgrading, starting with relatively labour-intensive light industries such as textiles, garments, footwear and simple electronics, and then moving into more capital-intensive industries, such as steel and petrochemicals, and further on technologically complex sectors such as shipbuilding, car manufacturing and advanced electronics (Kim, 1990: 94).[21] In the case of Taiwan, a three-stage shift is observed, acquiring relatively simple technologies, gradually adopting them and then moving to higher levels of skill and knowledge. A similar approach to technology upgrading was observed in the case of the Chinese Mobile Communication sector by Shan and Jolly (2011: 153), with two different catching-up patterns:

> One is 'path-following' catching-up in global system for mobile communication driven by using new technology in low-end market. The other is 'leapfrogging' catching-up in the development of phone digital switches and China's own 3G standard (time division – synchronous code division multiple access).

The debate in the age of globalisation[22]

Whether the debate about the choice of industrial production techniques is still relevant demands particular care and attention in this age of globalisation. Many developing countries face serious difficulties in competing effectively at an international level, and this requires a focus on the development of technological capability. As already mentioned, investors in developing countries are technology borrowers (or imitators) and so suffer from a serious disadvantage compared to many of their counterparts in developed countries who, as inventors, enjoy monopoly profits as technology owners. Hence the need for process and product improvements in developing countries associated with the building of technological capability.

As technological development faces various types of market failure, developing country governments need to consider potential policy interventions in order to mitigate their effects and to promote technology deepening and diversification (Lall, 1996: 103). In part, this involves addressing the rent-seeking issue which was prominent during the import substituting industrialisation (ISI) phase of development during the 1960s and the 1970s in many developing countries. The 'balancing role' played by the South Korean government is particularly noteworthy: while it helped in building the training and skill base and in establishing some significant S&T institutions (e.g. the South Korean Ministry of Science and Technology and the Korean Institute of Science and Technology) and also provided its support funds for R&D, it also focused on the growth of the private sector, in particular strongly encouraging private firms to undertake R&D. As has been observed by Dahlman *et al.* (1987: 764): "Acquiring this [technological capability] experience is not automatic …. Nor is it rapid and effortless. It takes conscious effort over a long period of time." The four capabilities discussed in the previous section need to be acquired. It is a catching-up process which, as mentioned by UNIDO (2005: 10) "requires a lot of effort and institution building". In this regard, as observed by Dahlman *et al.* (1987: 775) "because of market failures and externalities in the choice, creation, and diffusion of technology, there is a more direct role for government policy".

As already emphasised, technological learning remains the key requirement because the firms need to absorb borrowed technologies successfully, involving selection, installation, maintenance, assimilation, design and manufacturing of the imported technologies. A recommendation from the report of a conference in which the author took part is perhaps worth emphasising:

As Research and Development (R&D) is an integral part of the learning process involved in the successful transfer of technology, this needs to be addressed in the development strategies of LDCs especially as R&D expenditures (as a percentage of GDP) are extremely low (or even negligible) in these countries.

(TUBITAK-UNIDO, 2011: 13)

The development of a domestic S&T infrastructure is particularly crucial because of the important role it can play in product and process improvements. For this to happen, the domestic development of R&D needs to be emphasised, as occurred in South Korea where high R&D investment is now to be found (Table 16.3). In the case of China it is clear with the growth of its R&D expenditure, it is now "firmly engaged in its S&T take off. This rapid expansion of R&D spending has established an important channel though which China's industrial enterprises are able to imitate, adapt, and improve on foreign technologies" (Jefferson *et al.*, 2006: 38).

The uncoordinated and fragmented nature of technology research that is found to exist in developing countries also needs to be addressed (Huq and Islam, 2003). Also, the commitment from national governments to ensuring the efficient absorption and adaptation of imported technology could be vital, as found in the case of South Korea. That government commitment could be essential is also demonstrated in the Indian case of producing high quality scientists in adequate numbers and also of securing the benefits derived by acquiring and applying scientific knowledge (Sandhya and Jain, 2003).

Developing countries need to mobilise their own investment funds and investment goods production in order to counterbalance the bias towards the import of foreign machinery and equipment; heavy dependence on imported equipment is unhelpful for the growth of the domestic capital goods sector as was found in the case of investment in fertilizer manufacturing in Bangladesh (Huq and Islam, 2003).[23] Tied aid and turn-key projects funded through supplier's credits are likely to have a particularly negative impact on the domestic capital goods and engineering sectors in developing countries. The stimulation of the domestic capital goods sector is considered to be very important in the promotion of technological capability (see, e.g., Amsden, 1985; Fransman, 1986; Huq and Prendergast, 1983; Lall, 1984, 1987; Pack, 1981; Westphal *et al.*, 1985). In this respect, there is recognition of the significance of technology policy which cuts across "various other policy areas including industrial policy, credit policy, education policy, export and import policy and tariff policy" (Huq, 2001: 218). A commitment in this regard necessitates careful attention to types and sources of technology, including the use of the locally produced equipment as has been the case in India.[24]

Concluding remarks

This debate over the choice of techniques is, indeed, a long-drawn one. The conventional approach suggesting the optimum technical choice follows from the thinking which emerged in the latter part of the nineteenth century, advanced by the 'neoclassical' school (also called the 'marginalist' school) of economic theorists focusing on the optimisation of utility, and the tools developed were extended to model the optimisation of the input combination. Given resources, the technique that maximises output will be the preferred technique, relative factor prices emerging as a key element of the model. Neoclassical thinking was in sharp contrast to the classical approach that provided a vision of the growth process with technology advancing and productivity increasing in a cumulative manner. Thus, the stylised neoclassical model stands in sharp contrast to the thinking of the classical economists such as Smith and Marx who were keen to understand technological improvements and the resultant productivity enhancement. Sen (1960) is one of the early contributors who seriously challenged the neoclassical formulation of optimum technical choice, questioning whether developing countries should use labour-intensive techniques found as the optimal choice based on the ruling factor prices as advocated by the neoclassical school.

In the early part of the second half of the twentieth century, there was a keen interest in industrialisation in many developing countries, following which large-scale capital-intensive technologies were being extensively imported. Such development was strongly questioned, among others, by Ernst Schumacher who helped to pioneer a 'radical type' of thinking for technical choice known as the 'Appropriate Technology' movement that actively propagated the adoption of small-scale labour-intensive technology. However, this approach, although appealing, suffers from a number of limitations.

A major attempt to examine technology choice using social cost-efficiency analysis was conducted during the 1970s and the early 1980s at the David Livingstone Institute (of Strathclyde University), known as the DLI studies. This was an early application of the social cost–benefit methodology advocated by Little and Mirrlees (1968) and UNIDO (1972), articulating the use of accounting or shadow prices for a systematic appraisal of investment decisions. The DLI approach was an attempt to adopt cost–benefit methodology for the extensive analysis of technical choice with primary data collected from the suppliers and users of technology. This involved the estimation of social rates of return as well as market rates of return as a basis for the identification of the economic efficiency of the identified technologies. The approach demonstrated that by careful selection, a developing country could easily go for a better technological alternative than those which were being adopted. However, while the DLI studies greatly helped to expose our understanding of appraising the technology alternatives (not only at the sub-process level but also from a variety of sources including machinery and equipment made in developing countries), it did not take into account the dynamic aspects of technology assimilation, diffusion and innovation.

Indeed, in the context of developing countries, the debate on technology choice took a special meaning with the introduction of the dynamic elements involving technological learning. The literature which has now emerged is very helpful in guiding policy makers in developing countries, since it embodies a deep understanding of the key issues. An important feature of the dynamic approach which has formed the basis of studies published since the mid-1980s is that the choice of technique needs to be viewed in a much wider context, involving the dynamic elements of technology learning, the two key elements of which are the development of human capital and R&D.

It is vital that policy makers in developing countries carefully appraise the dynamic aspects involved in the learning process which are essential in the building of technological capability. This is not an automatic process, and governments need to ensure that this learning takes place, even though this should not necessarily imply direct state participation in a big way; what is required is a serious commitment from the state, ensuring that the essential technology learning takes place. In South Korea, there was a serious commitment on the part of the government ensuring that imported technologies were effectively absorbed into the economy (Enos and Park, 1988). Similarly, in India the commitment from the government was critical in the success achieved in sectors such as space, defence and atomic energy as well as in manufacturing itself (Sandhya and Jain, 2003). However, in many developing countries, the absence of a serious national commitment has hindered the development of technological capability building (see, e.g., Huq and Islam, 2003).

Notes

1 This chapter complements a number of published and unpublished materials with which the author has been closely connected. He would like to thank, in particular, Anthony Clunies-Ross and David Forsyth with whom he shares the authorship of *Development Economics* (2009) in which Chapter 18 on "Building Technological Capability" especially focuses on dynamic aspects. As the chapter developed, comments and suggestions from Roy Grieve greatly helped to sharpen a number of key points. The author is also grateful to Eric Rahim, Michael Tribe, John Weiss and Girma Zawdie for their comments on an earlier version of this chapter, and also to Shaopeng Huang for his kind help in data analysis. However, none of the above is responsible for any errors or omissions.
2 This and the next section have benefited greatly from Grieve (2003, 2004).
3 While the extreme factor price distortions, and other rigidities and biases in the economic systems of developing countries found in the detailed OECD studies reported in Little *et al.*'s (1970) study have undoubtedly been reduced over the last four or five decades, not least by the process of liberalisation adopted in many countries, there must still be an argument for using a 'shadow price' adjustment in serious economic research relating to investment appraisal and choice of technique. The arguments for this approach can be based on the incidence of market failures and on the existence of tax systems which are not neutral with respect to resource allocation.
4 See, e.g., Huq and Aragaw (1981) and Huq and Prendergast (1983).
5 Some close discussions which the author had with Roy Grieve proved particularly helpful for gaining a deeper insight into Smith's view of the cumulative growth process (see also Grieve, 2003, 2004).
6 Later writers (of the neoclassical persuasion) were less inclined to engage in close consideration of technological matters; Rosenberg (1982: vi) observes that

> [these later writers] have long treated technological phenomena as events transpiring inside a black box . . . the economics profession has adhered rather strictly to a self-imposed ordinance not to inquire too seriously into what transpires inside that box.

Similarly, Rostow (1990: 454) observes that "the formulation of marginal analysis round about 1870 . . . broke the rather easy, unembarrassed linkage of technological and economic analysis that had existed for over a century".

7   Tribe (2005) discusses efficiency measures for small scale industries.

8   The UK Intermediate Technology Development Group has been renamed as "Practical Action" and its website can be found at http://practicalaction.org/

9   For example, Huq and Islam (1992) found that, in the manufacture of fertilizer from natural gas, the labour-using small-scale-technology variant (which had significantly lower capital per unit of labour than the modern large-scale capital-intensive variant) was an inferior technology in almost all areas of cost (using more of almost every input); in particular, the use of natural gas, the principal raw material, was found to be significantly higher per tonne of fertilizer produced. Both of these technology variants involved large investments costing millions of dollars and employing hundreds of people, so that even the capital-saving technology variant was a small-scale technology in the ITDG context.

10   There were in total eleven studies. Nine of these were published between 1979 and 1985 under 'the DLI Series on Choice of Technique in Developing Countries' (edited by Eric Rahim) and two earlier studies by McBain (1977) and Forsyth (1979) were published by HMSO. These studies covered a diverse range of industries including the following industries: footwear, sugar, brewing, maize milling, leather, machine tools, iron founding, bolt and nut manufacturing, cotton cloth, brick manufacturing and corrugated board manufacturing. For a description of the methodology see, e.g., Huq and Aragaw (1981), Pickett and Robson (1981), Khan and Rahim (1985) and Rahim (2003).

11   This OECD publication was revised as Little and Mirrlees (1974), which is perhaps more readily accessible.

12   By 'technology' we refer to the whole production process consisting of individual 'techniques' for each of the sub-processes or work stations.

13   The Bangladesh Machine Tools Factory was visited by the author during the course of one of the DLI studies (Huq and Prendergast, 1983) and was also subsequently covered in a separate technology study (Huq *et al.*, 1993). This was a very good example of a large-scale capital intensive plant which failed to operate effectively. Low capacity utilisation, along with poor management and non-availability of skilled labour and know-how, turned out to be major factors which made it extremely difficult for the plant to compete in the market (Huq *et al.*, 1993: 53–56).

14   The Mwanza Leather Factory, from which primary data were collected in Tanzania, is an example of technology obtained on supplier's credit. It was provided by an East European supplier; the 'package' included some second-hand machinery for a number of key operations and the management had serious reservations about the quality of most of the second-hand equipment supplied (Huq and Aragaw, 1981). The Bangladesh Leather Factory at Savar is another example covered in a subsequent industry study (Huq and Islam, 1990). As feared, both factories turned out to be cases of bad investment decisions. Later on, in the case of Ghana, it was observed that the country has been importing machinery and equipment using suppliers' credit associated with "exceptionally high investment costs and more capital intensive techniques than required" (Huq, 1989: 275).

15   The study of corrugated board and box production by Khan and Rahim (1985) provided insights on technology choices influenced by economies of scale and the character and quality of the product.

16   See, for example, Curry and Weiss (1993) who strongly emphasise the point that in appraising a project one also needs to consider "the dynamic effects arising from learning and technical change."

17   This section is based on Clunies-Ross *et al.* (2009) and Huq (2014b).

18   The main source (World Bank, various years) provides data for GNP per capita although ideally GDP per capita should have been used, especially because GDP data has been used for other variables. However, this should not create any significant discrepancy.

19   For the last three decades, the author has been associated with TWAS, taking part in some of the early Conferences organised by TWAS including two in Beijing (1987 and 2003) and one in New Delhi (2004), and also in a roundtable meeting held in Trieste (in the early 1990s) on technology promotion in developing countries.

20   As observed by Soete *et al.* (2009: 7), the approach

spells out quite explicitly the importance of the 'systematic' interactions between the various components of inventions, research, technical change, learning and innovation; the national systems of innovation brings to the forefront the central role of the state as a coordinating agent. Its particular attractiveness to policy makers lays in the explicit recognition of the need for complimentary policies, drawing attention to the weaknesses in the system, while highlighting the national setting of most of those institutions.

21 Kim has been associated with a number of other publications following this 1990 study (Kim, 1995; Westphal, Kim and Dahlman, 1985; Kim and Dahlman, 1992; Kim and Nelson, 2000).

22 This section is based on Huq (2004, 2011, 2014b).

23 A study prepared by the Bangladesh Steel and Engineering Corporation showed that as much as 37 percent of the local project cost of a large scale fertilizer plant could be completed locally, i.e. by using the local machinery manufacturing sector. Unfortunately, the heavy dependence on aid deprived Bangladesh of the opportunity of utilising its local machinery manufacturing sector. (Huq and Islam, 2003: 243).

24 Given the serious government failures found in many developing countries, any suggestion for a major state role in R&D needs to be viewed with caution. Indeed, there is a strong case for emphasising the role of the private sector in pushing R&D as was observed, for example, in South Korea. Hence the need for a finely balanced role played by the public and the private sectors in R&D. See, for example, Clunies-Ross *et al.* (2009: 525–528).

Bibliography

Amsden, A. 1985. *Insights from South Korea and Taiwan on the Engineering Sector in Bangladesh.* Planning and Project Identification Unit, Trade and Industrial Policy (TIP) Reform Programme. Dhaka, March 1985.

Amsden, A. 1989. *Asia's Next Giant: South Korea and Late Industrialisation.* Oxford: Oxford University Press.

Amsden, A. and Hikino, T. 1993. Borrowing Technology or Innovating: An Exploration of the Two Paths to Industrial Development. In Thompson, R. (ed.). *Learning and Technological Change.* London: Macmillan: 243–266.

Bell, M. 1991. *Science and Technology Policy Research in the 1990s: Key Issues for Developing Countries.* Science Policy Research Unit. Brighton: University of Sussex.

Bell, M. and Pavitt, K. 1992. *Accumulating Technological Capability in Developing Countries.* Proceedings of the World Bank Annual Conference on Development Economics. Washington, DC: World Bank: 257–281.

Bhalla, A. S. 1996. *Facing the Technological Challenge.* London: Macmillan.

Clunies-Ross, A., Forsyth, D. and Huq, M. 2009. *Development Economics.* London: McGraw-Hill.

Curry, S. and Weiss, J. 1993. *Project Analysis in Developing Countries.* London: Macmillan.

Dahlman, C. J., Ross-Larson, B. and Westphal, L. E. 1987. Managing Technological Development: Lessons from the Newly Industrializing Countries. *World Development.* 15 (6): 759–775.

Egea, A. N. 1990. Choice of Technique Revisited: A Critical Review of the Theoretical Underpinnings. *World Development.* 18 (11): 1445–1456.

Enos, J. L. 1991. *The Creation of Technological Capability in Developing Countries.* London: Pinter.

Enos, J. L. and Park, W-H. 1988. *The Adoption and Diffusion of Imported Technology: The Case of Korea.* London: Croom Helm.

Ernst, D., Siyanbola, W. O. and Ganiatsos, T. 1998. Technological Capabilities in the Context of Export-Led Growth: A Conceptual Framework. In Ernst, D., Ganiatsos, T. and Mytelka, L. K. (eds.). *Technological Capabilities and Export Success: Lessons from East Asia.* London: Routledge.

Forsyth, D. 1979. *The Choice of Manufacturing Technology in Sugar Production in Less Developed Countries.* London: HMSO.

Fransman, M. (ed.). 1986. *Machinery and Economic Development.* London: Macmillan.

Freeman, C. 1987. *Technology Policy and Economic Performance: Lessons from Japan.* London: Pinter.

Freeman, C. 1994. The Economics of Technical Change. *Cambridge Journal of Economics.* 18 (5): 463–514.

Freeman, C. 1995. The 'National System of Innovation' in Historical Perspective. *Cambridge Journal of Economics.* 19 (1): 5–24.

Goldberg, I., Branstetter, L., Goddard, J. G. and Kuriakose, S. 2008. *Globalization and Technology Absorption: Role of Trade, FDI and Cross-Border Knowledge Flows.* Washington, DC: World Bank.

Grieve, R. H. 2003. Perspectives on Technology and Development. In Huq, M. (ed.). *Building Technological Capability: Issues and Prospects – Nepal, Bangladesh and India.* Dhaka: University Press.

Grieve, R. H. 2004. Appropriate Technology in a Globalizing World. *International Journal of Technology Management and Sustainable Development.* 3 (3): 173–187.

Hikino, T. and Amsden, A. H. 1994. Staying Behind, Stumbling Back, Sneaking Up, Soaring Ahead: Late Industrialisation in Historical Perspective. In Baumol, W., Nelson, R. R. and Wolff, E. N. (eds.). *Convergence of Productivity.* New York: Oxford University Press: 286–315.

Holz C. A. 2008. China's Economic Growth 1978–2025: What We Know Today About China's Economic Growth Tomorrow. *World Development.* 36 (10): 1665–1691.

Huq, M. 1989. *The Economy of Ghana: The First 25 Years since Independence.* London: Macmillan.

Huq, M. 2001. Technology Policy for Industrialisation in a Developing Country: The Case of Bangladesh. In Huq, M. and Love, J. (eds.). *Strategies for Industrialisation: The Case of Bangladesh.* Dhaka: University Press: 195–223.

Huq, M. 2003a. Should Low-Income Countries Adopt a Technology Policy? In Azhar, A., Huq, M., Khan, M. A., Lewis, C., Shibli, A., Siddiqui, A. and Zaidi, S. H.. (eds.). *Technology and Development in the New Millennium.* Karachi: Karachi University: 37–52.

Huq, M. (ed.). 2003b. *Building Technological Capability: Issues and Prospects – Nepal, Bangladesh and India.* Dhaka: University Press.

Huq, M. 2004. Building Technological Capability in the Context of Globalization: Opportunities and Challenges Facing Developing Countries. *International Journal of Technology Management and Sustainable Development.* 3 (3): 155–172.

Huq, M. 2011. Technological Capability Building: Some Lessons of Technology Transfer for Less Developed Countries. Paper presented at the TUBITAK-UNIDO Conference in Istanbul (Pre-Conference Event for the 4th UN Conference on the Least Developed Countries), Istanbul, 7–8 February, 2011.

Huq, M. 2014a. Technological Capability Building in Developing Countries with Special Focus on Bangladesh. In Mujeri, M. (ed.), *Development: Constraints and Realisations.* Dhaka: University Press: 229–263.

Huq, M. 2014b. Building Technological Capability: Lessons of Technology Transfer for Sub-Saharan Africa and Challenges for the Future. Public Lecture delivered at the University of Cape Coast, 3 September.

Huq, M. and Aragaw, H. 1981. *Choice of Technique in Leather Manufacture.* Edinburgh: Scottish Academic Press.

Huq, M. and Prendergast, C. C. 1983. *Machine Tool Production in Developing Countries.* Edinburgh: Scottish Academic Press.

Huq, M. and Islam, K. M. N. 1990. *Choice of Technology: Leather Manufacture in Bangladesh.* Dhaka: University Press.

Huq, M. and Islam, K. M. N. 1992. *Choice of Technology: Fertilizer Manufacture in Bangladesh.* Dhaka: University Press.

Huq, M. and Islam, K. M. N. 2003. Failure to Absorb Technology: A Case Study of Fertiliser Manufacturing in Bangladesh. In Huq, M. (ed.). *Building Technological Capability: Issues and Prospects.* Dhaka: University Press.

Huq, M., Islam, K. M. N. and Islam, N. 1993. *Machinery Manufacturing in Bangladesh: An Industry Study with Particular Reference to Technological Capability.* Dhaka: University Press.

Jefferson, G. H., Albert, G. H. and Su, J. 2006. The Sources and Sustainability of China's Economic Growth. *Brookings Papers on Economic Activity.* 37 (2): 1–60.

Kalam, A. P. J. Abdul (jointly written with Tiwari, A.). 1999. *Wings of Fire: An Autobiography.* Hyderabad: Universities Press (India).

Kaplinsky, R. 1990. *The Economies of Small: Appropriate Technology in a Changing World.* London: Intermediate Technology Publications and Intermediate Technology International.

Khan, H. M. and Akbari, A. H. 1986. Impact of Agricultural Research and Extension of Crop Productivity in Pakistan: A Production Function Approach. *World Development.* 14 (6): 757–762.

Khan, R. and Rahim, E. 1985. *Corrugated Board and Box Production.* Edinburgh: Scottish Academic Press.

Kim, K. S. 1995. The Korean Miracle (1962–80) Revisited: Myths and Realities in Strategies and Development. In Stein, H. (ed.). *Asian Industrialization and Africa: Study in Policy Alternatives to Structural Adjustment.* London: Macmillan: 87–143.

Kim, L. 1990. Korea: The Acquisition of Technology. In Soesastro, H. and Pangestu, M. (eds.). *Technological Change in the Asia Pacific Economy.* Sydney: Allen & Unwin.

Kim, L. and Dahlman, C. J. 1992. Technology Policy for Industrialisation: An Integrative Framework and Korea's Experience. *Research Policy.* 21 (5): 437–52.

Kim, L. and Nelson, R. R. 2000. *Technology, Learning, & Innovation: Experiences of Newly Industrializing Economies.* Cambridge: Cambridge University Press.

Lall, S. 1984. Exports of Technology by Newly-Industrializing Countries. *World Development.* 12 (5–6): 471–480.

Lall, S. 1987. *Learning to Industrialize: The Acquisition of Technological Capability by India.* London: Macmillan.

Lall, S. 1992. Technological Capabilities and Industrialization. *World Development.* 20 (2): 165–186.

Lall, S. 1996. *Learning from the Asian Tigers: Studies in Technology and Industrial Policy.* London: Macmillan.

Little, I. M. D. and Mirrlees, J. 1968. *Manual of Industrial Project Analysis for Developing Countries,* Vol. 2. Paris: Organisation for Economic Cooperation and Development.

Little, I. M. D. and Mirrlees, J. 1974. *Project Appraisal and Planning for Developing Countries.* London: Heinemann.

Little, I. M. D., Scitovsky, T. and Scott, M. 1970. *Industry and Trade in Developing Countries.* New York: Oxford University Press.

Lundvall, B. A. (ed.). 1992. *National Innovation Systems: Towards a Theory of Innovation and Interactive Learning.* London: Pinter.

Marx, K. 1867. *Capital,* Volume I. Harmondsworth/London: Penguin Books/New Left Review. (Penguin edition published in 1990.)

McBain, N. 1977. *The Choice of Technique in Footwear Manufacture for Developing Countries.* London: HMSO.

McRobie, G. 1981. *Small is Possible.* London: Jonathan Cape.

McRobie, G. 1991. Technology Transfer from North to South. In Huq, M., Bhatt, P., Lewis, C. and Shibli, A. (eds.). *Science, Technology and Development: North South Co-Operation.* London: Frank Cass: 163–75.

Morawetz, D. 1974. Employment Implications of Industrialization in Developing Countries – A Survey. *Economic Journal.* 84 (335): 491–542.

Nelson, R. R. 1987. Innovation and Economic Developments: Theoretical Retrospect and Prospect. In Katz, J. M. (ed.). *Technology Generation in Latin American Manufacturing Industries: Theory and Case Studies Concerning Its Nature, Magnitude and Consequences.* London: Macmillan.

Nelson, R. R. (ed.) 1993. *National Innovation Systems: A Comparative Analysis.* Oxford: Oxford University Press.

Nurkse, R. 1952. *Problems of Capital Formation in Underdeveloped Countries.* Oxford: Basil Blackwell.

Pack, H. 1981. Fostering the Capital Goods Sector in LDCs. *World Development.* 9 (9): 227–250.

Pickett, J. 1975. *A Report of a Pilot Investigation of the Choice of Technology in Developing Countries.* David Livingstone Institute. Glasgow: University of Strathclyde.

Pickett, J. 1977. The Work of the Livingstone Institute on 'Appropriate Technology' – Editor's Introduction. *World Development.* 5 (9/10): 773–776.

Pickett, J. and Robson, R. 1981. *The Choice of Technology in the Production of Cotton Cloth.* Edinburgh: Scottish Academic Press.

Prebisch, R. 1950. *The Economic Development of Latin America and Its Principal Problems.* New York: UN Department of Economic Affairs – Economic Commission for Latin America (ECLA).

Rahim, E. 1979. Livingstone Institute Series on Choice of Technique: Editorial Introduction. In Keddie, J. and Cleghorn, W. (eds). *Brewing in Developing Countries.* Edinburgh: Scottish Academic Press.

Rahim, E. 2003. Choice of Technique and Technology Policy in Developing Countries. In Huq, M. (ed.). *Building Technological Capability: Issues and Prospects.* Dhaka: University Press.

Rosenberg, N. 1982. *Inside the Black Box: Technology and Economics.* Cambridge: Cambridge University Press.

Rosenberg, N. 1994. *Exploring the Black Box: Technology, Economics and History.* Cambridge: Cambridge University Press.

Rostow, W. W. 1990. *Theorists of Economic Growth from David Hume to the Present.* Oxford: Oxford University Press.

Salam, A. 1987. *Ideals and Realities.* Singapore: World Scientific Publishing.

Sandhya, G. D. and Jain, A. 2003. Science and Technology Policies for Industrial Development in India. In Huq, M. (ed.). *Building Technological Capability: Issues and Prospects.* Dhaka: University Press.

Schumacher, E. F. 1973. *Small is Beautiful: A Study of Economics as if People Mattered.* London: Vintage Books (New Edition 1973).

Schumacher, E. F. 1981. On Technology for Development Society. In McRobie, G. (ed.). *Small is Possible.* London: Jonathan Cape.

Sen, A. K. 1960. *Choice of Techniques: An Aspect of the Theory of Planned Economic Development.* Oxford: Basil Blackwell. (2nd edition 1968.)

Shan, J. and Jolly, D. R. 2011. Patterns of Technological Learning and Catch-Up Strategies in Latecomer Firms: Case Study in China's Telecom-Equipment Industry. *Journal of Technology Management in China.* 6 (2): 153–170.

Singer, H. W. 1950. The Distribution of Gains Between Investing and Borrowing Countries. *American Economic Review.* 40 (2): 473–485.

Siyanbola, W., Egbetokun, A., Adebowale, B. A. and Olamade, O. (eds.). 2012. *Innovation Systems and Capabilities in Developing Countries: Concepts, Issues and Cases.* London: Gower – accessible from www.ashgate.com – accessed on 19 September 2012.

Smith, A. 1776. *An Inquiry into the Nature and Causes of the Wealth of Nations.* Harmondsworth: Penguin Books (edition published 1982).

Soete, L., Verspagen, B. and ter Weel, B. 2009. *Systems of Innovation.* UNU-MERIT Working Paper Series No. 2009–062. Maastricht: United Nations University.

Son, H. H. 2010. *Human Capital Development.* ADB Economics Working Paper Series No. 225. Manila: Asian Development Bank.

Stewart, F. 1977. *Technology and Underdevelopment.* London: Macmillan.

Stewart, F. 1985. Macro Policies for Appropriate Technology: An Introductory Classification. In James, J. and Watanabe, S. (eds.). *Technology, Institutions and Government Policies.* London: Macmillan: 19–48.

Stewart, F. and Streeten, P. 1972. Conflicts Between Output and Employment Objectives. In Robinson, R. and Johnson, P. (eds.). *Prospects for Employment Opportunities in the 1970s.* London: HMSO.

Tilak, B. G. 2002. *Building Human Capital in East Asia: What Others Can Learn.* Washington, DC: World Bank.

Tribe, M. 2005. Economic Efficiency Measures for Small–Scale Enterprises in Developing Countries. In Tribe, M., Thoburn, J. and Palmer-Jones, R. (eds.). *Development Economics and Social Justice: Essays in Honour of Ian Livingstone.* Aldershot: Ashgate: 219–232.

Tribe, M. A. and Alpine, R. L. W. 1987. Sources of Scale Economies: Sugar Production in Less Developed Countries. *Oxford Bulletin of Economics and Statistics.* 49 (2): 209–226.

TUBITAK-UNIDO. 2011. *Report on the TUBITAK-UNIDO on Science, Technology and Innovation for LDCs* (Pre-Conference Event for the 4th UN Conference on LDCs), Istanbul, 7–8 February.

UNCTAD. 2007. *The Least Developed Countries Report 2007: Technological Learning and Innovation for Development.* New York: United Nations.

UNIDO. 1972. *Guidelines for Project Evaluation.* New York: United Nations.

UNIDO. 2005. *Industrial Development Report 2005 – Capability Building for Catching-Up: Historical, Empirical and Policy Dimensions.* Vienna: United Nations Industrial Development Organization.

United Nations. 1987. *Transnational Corporations and Technology Transfer: Effects and Policy Issues.* New York: UN Centre on Transnational Corporations.

Viotti, E. B. 2001. *National Learning Systems: A New Approach on Technical Change in Late Industrializing Economies and Evidences from the Cases of Brazil and South Korea.* Science, Technology and Innovation Discussion Paper No. 12, Centre for International Development. Cambridge, MA. Harvard University – accessible from www.cid.harvard.edu – accessed on 20 September 2012.

Westphal, L. E., Kim, L. and Dahlman, C. J. 1985. Reflections on the Republic of Korea's Acquisition of Technological Capability. In Rosenberg, N. and Frischtak, C. (eds.). *International Technology Transfer: Concepts, Measures, and Comparisons.* New York: Praeger: 167–221.

Winter, S. G. 1987. Knowledge and Competence as Strategic Assets. In Teece, D. J. (ed.). *The Competitive Challenge: Strategies for Industrial Innovation and Renewal.* Cambridge, MA: Ballinger: 159–184.

World Bank. 2014a. *World Development Indicators 2014.* Washington, DC: World Bank.

World Bank. 2014b. *GDP (Current US$).* The World Bank. Online – accessible from http://data.worldbank.org/indicator/NY.GDP.MKTP.CD – accessed 13 November 2014.

World Bank. 2014c. *GNI per Capita, Atlas Method (Current US$).* The World Bank. Online – accessible from http://data.worldbank.org/indicator/NY.GDP.MKTP.CD – accessed 13 November 2014.

World Bank. 2014d. *Research and Development Expenditure (% of GDP).* The World Bank. Online – accessible from http://data.worldbank.org/indicator/NY.GDP.MKTP.CD – accessed 13 November 2014.

World Bank. 2014e. *Researchers in R&D (per Million People).* The World Bank. Online. Online – accessible from http://data.worldbank.org/indicator/NY.GDP.MKTP.CD – accessed 13 November 2014.

World Bank. 2014f. *Technicians in R&D (per Million People).* The World Bank. Online. Online – accessible from http://data.worldbank.org/indicator/NY.GDP.MKTP.CD – accessed 13 November 2014.

Appendix: Charts plotted with the regression findings

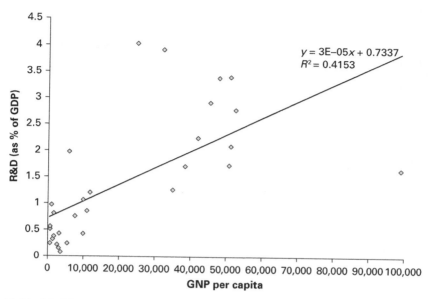

Figure 16.A1   Model 1: R&D (as percent of GDP) regressed against GNP per capita.

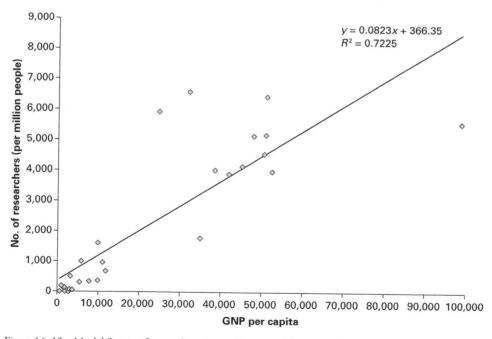

Figure 16.A2   Model 2: no. of researchers (per million people) regressed against GNP per capita.

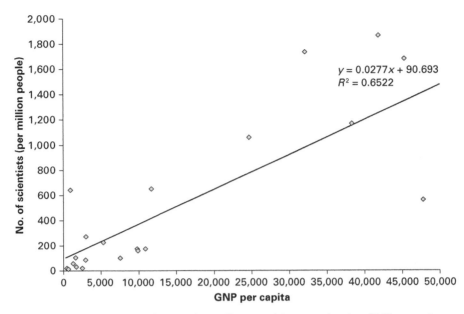

Figure 16.A3   Model 3: no. of technicians (per million people) regressed against GNP per capita.

17

TECHNOLOGICAL LEARNING IN DEVELOPING COUNTRIES

Renee Prendergast

Introduction

A dictionary definition of learning encompasses the getting of new knowledge by means of study, experience or experimentation. Thus, in principle, learning encompasses both innovation and the assimilation of existing knowledge. Technological learning refers to the learning processes involved in improving the productive capabilities of an enterprise, sector or economy to enable it to produce higher value goods and services with increasing levels of efficiency. Technological learning therefore covers all forms of learning, from standardised production activities to research and development activities close to the technological frontier. However, there may be a need to distinguish between the ability to compete at a certain level and the ability to maintain competitiveness by means of innovation. A number of different frameworks and taxonomies have been proposed for this purpose (Bell and Pavitt, 1993; Lall, 1992; Bell, 2009; Andreoni, 2012). None of these is entirely successful as it is seldom possible to classify activities as belonging exclusively to the dynamic or static sphere (Andreoni, 2012). Moreover, as Carlotta Perez has pointed out, the opportunities for development are themselves a moving target (Perez, 2001).

Technological change is central to industrialisation and this review will start with a brief overview of the relationship between macro-economic growth and technological change. It will then examine the treatment of technological learning when first applied to developing-country manufacturing firms in the 1970s (generally within state-directed import substitution models). The main body of the review will seek to draw lessons from the experience of technological learning and innovation during the subsequent period of market liberalisation and it will conclude by examining some of the indices developed to map countries' progress in the technological learning and the knowledge economy.

Economic growth and technological change

It is generally recognised that economic progress and technological change are intimately related although the ways in which this relationship has been conceptualised by economists and others has varied over time. The earliest explanations of progress were based on the accumulation of knowledge in all its forms – tacit, codified and embodied. However, with the development of a theory of capital by Turgot and Smith, this point of view was subsumed within a theory linking the accumulation of capital and growth (Prendergast, 2010). As a result, the accumulation of capital became the main focus of attention and remained so for roughly two centuries. Perhaps somewhat surprisingly, a renewed interest in technical progress as the main source of growth emerged with the development of formal growth modelling in the second half of the twentieth century. In what is now known as the Solow model, the steady state growth rate of aggregate output was found to be the sum of the growth rate of employment and the exogenously determined rate of labour augmenting technical progress. Given that technical progress was not explained within the growth models, despite being the main determinant of growth, it could be argued that "growth theory left one key number, . . . the rate of growth, unexplained" (Solow, 2000: 98). New growth theories pioneered by Romer (1986, 1990) in the late twentieth century sought to improve existing models by endogenising technological change. Whereas the earlier models tended to treat technology as a pure public good (i.e. non-excludable and non-rivalrous), in the new theories, the benefits of investment in knowledge and innovation could be partly appropriated by private firms. In addition, such investments generated externalities which were sufficient to outweigh diminishing marginal returns to capital. While there was initial optimism about the explanatory potential of the new growth theory, the promise has turned out to be somewhat illusory (Fagerberg, 1994; Pack, 1994; Solow 2000). Despite being more consistent with realities such as firm investment in R&D and non-convergence of growth rates internationally, the new growth theory has been difficult to implement empirically and has been characterised as "making assumptions about how unmeasurable things affected other unmeasurable things" (Krugman, 2013).[1]

Although the treatment of technological change in the growth theory literature remains far from satisfactory, this does not mean that the understanding of technological change has stood still. Case studies at firm, sector and country level continue to accumulate and these have facilitated the construction of a rather different view of technological change. While many of these studies have drawn inspiration from Schumpeter's work on development and innovation or from the evolutionary theories of Nelson and Winter, they do not all share the same theoretical approach (Schumpeter, 1947, 1961; Nelson and Winter, 1982). However, what these 'appreciative' theories have in common is that they view technology as organisationally embedded, active, tacit, cumulative, geographically localised and influenced by interactions between the firm and its environment.

The study of technological learning or innovation studies was first confined to the advanced industrial economies. However, issues relating to technology transfer, the appropriateness of technology and R&D in developing countries began to be explored during the 1970s.[2] This work gradually morphed into wider studies of technological capability at firm level, at sector level and at country level. Rather than focusing on innovation per se, the study of technological capability in developing countries concentrated its attention on the efforts of enterprises to absorb and extend the knowledge required for their production activities (Katz, 1976a; Lall et al., 1994). Much of the relevant technological knowledge is acquired from elsewhere. Some of it is embodied in machinery and equipment, operating manuals, patents, designs and so on. However, as has long been recognised, not all elements of 'know-how' are codifiable. Some know-how requires the engagement of experienced personnel and extensive use of training programmes. In addition, in most cases, technology has to be adapted to suit local conditions including customers, market size, raw materials, suppliers, skill sets, networks and infrastructures. Even if the goal is to achieve existing standards of quality and productivity in a given time period, considerable adaptive and innovative effort is required and in the case of complex technologies may take place over long time periods.

While much technological learning takes place at firm level, firms do not exist in isolation. They routinely draw on the skills inculcated in the workforce by the educational and training institutions of the society and by other firms, both domestic and foreign. Their capability also depends on their access to sources of technological knowledge, complementary inputs and supporting institutions, e.g. universities and research institutes, marketing support, facilities for foreign trade, information and communications technology (ICT) and general infrastructure. The options available at enterprise level are also influenced by the broad thrust of economic policy, by the policy on foreign direct investment (FDI), by the trade regime, by competition, by access to investment, credit and foreign exchange and by industrial policy more generally.

Early work on technological learning in the 1970s: East Asian experience

As noted above, research on the development of technological capability in developing countries first emerged in the 1970s, particularly in the work of Jorge Katz (1976b) who found that productivity increases in Argentinian firms could only partly be explained by learning by doing, as suggested in Arrow (1962). The other major source of productivity increases was R&D and problem solving activities carried out within firms. Such activities were not substitutes for 'imported' technological knowledge but were complementary and necessary in order to adapt newly acquired technologies to fit local conditions. Much of this activity was carried out within the subsidiaries of multinational companies (MNCs) and Katz found that it tended to be retained within the MNC rather than disseminated throughout the wider national economy. Katz's pioneering work which drew on the Latin American structuralist paradigm was soon to be marginalised as the Import Substitution Industrialization (ISI) strategies employed by most Latin American countries came under intense scrutiny. Drawing on the experience of seven countries,[3] Little *et al.* (1970) published an influential critique of ISI in which they argued that, when pushed too far, ISI became harmful to economic development. They argued for export promotion as an alternative to ISI but recognised the problems associated with the transition from an ISI policy regime to an export-oriented one. Later contributions went much further in advocating market-based approaches. Countries were encouraged to retreat from interventionist industrial policy, to dismantle various forms of protectionism, to promote foreign direct investment and to rely more heavily on market forces (Williamson, 1990). Gradually, however, a considerable body of evidence was emerging which pointed in a different direction. Amsden's (1989) study of development in South Korea indicated that far from obeying market prices, Korea deliberately got prices 'wrong'. In new industries, domestic producers benefited from tariff protection but they also were provided with incentives to export, with subsidies on inputs and with government investment to promote technical change and to provide social overhead capital such as education and infrastructure. The key difference between successful countries such as Korea and less successful developers in Latin American countries was not that Korea was outward looking and Latin America inward looking but rather that Korea disciplined all support recipients by imposing standards on them. Similarly, Wade's (1990) study of Taiwan emphasised that government deliberately got some prices 'wrong' and also used non-price policy instruments to alter the behaviour of key agents to produce a level and composition of investment which was different from those that purely market-based policies would have produced.

The role of government in the development of technological capability had already been highlighted in Enos and Park's study of the adoption and diffusion of imported technology in four industries in South Korea over a period of twenty years ending in 1985 (1988). They concluded that the Korean government had intervened with considerable success in the process of incorporating foreign technology. Early on, a policy decision had been made that the most advanced proven technology would be used in all new ventures. This had implications for the adopted scales of manufacturing plants and meant that growing demand was necessary in order to allow plants to reach full capacity. It also meant that technology selection was based on selecting the supplier rather than the technology type. Government's heavy involvement in supplier selection enabled bargaining experience to accumulate and hard bargains were driven both in terms of costs and the amount of support to be given. Foreign suppliers who fully fulfilled their original contracts were generally rewarded with repeat contracts when further expansion was required. Growing demand was important in providing incentives for improvements that would raise capacity. Expansion also allowed firms to use investment experience previously acquired, and Enos and Park found evidence that local supplier involvement increased with each new installation. At the time of their survey, Enos and Park found no evidence of significant domestic innovation, although South Korean firms did have research and development groups which while not engaged in fundamental research were involved in process improvement and in novel extensions of existing product lines.

A decade later, a study by Linsu Kim confirmed Enos and Park's findings about the importance of the government's role in technology assimilation. Kim put forward a framework for the analysis based on two technological trajectories, one for developed and one for developing countries (Kim, 1997). The trajectory for advanced countries was based on a sequence consisting of three stages proposed by Utterback and Abernathy (1975).[4] In the first *fluid (emergence)* stage, the rate of product innovation is high and process innovation low. In the second *transition (consolidation)* stage, a degree of product standardisation is achieved and there is considerable process innovation. In the third *specific (mature)* stage, there is incremental innovation with a focus on product improvement and cost reduction. Lee *et al.* (1988) had proposed a trajectory for developing countries which is the reverse of this. During the early stages of industrial development, firms acquire mature foreign technologies which they assimilate and adapt. In the second stage, the sequence of acquisition, assimilation and improvement is repeated for technologies in the transition stage. In the third stage, firms are at or near the technological frontier and invest in R&D to develop new products. Kim was of the view that government support and guidance on the process of technological assimilation was most effective in the earlier stages of development when the technologies involved were mature. Once developing country firms had advanced to the stage where they were capable of product and process innovations, government was less well positioned than the private sector to understand and respond to the dynamics of market and technological change. The same applied to the role of government research institutes (GRIs). In the early stages of industrialisation, the GRIs had an important role in facilitating technology transfer and adaptation but in the later stages, the Korean chaebol were better placed to carry out their own R&D.[5] However, there was continuing need for GRI activity in areas of national importance neglected by the chaebol. It was also the case that in the expansion of their own R&D departments, the chaebol were greatly assisted by their ability to draw on the trained scientific labour force available in the GRIs.

While the trajectories proposed by Lee *et al.* (1988) and Kim (1997) reflect the course of technological learning in a range of industries and developing countries, it is important to note that there is no automatic progression along such trajectories. It is also the case that other trajectories are possible, as will be shown by the examples of the pulp and paper and aircraft industries in Brazil. Indeed, Perez (2001) argues that although mature technologies can serve to provide growth for a certain length of time, they are not capable of driving a process of catching up because their innovation potential is exhausted. She maintains that windows of opportunity for developing countries are present not just in mature technologies but also in new technologies that are opening up. Against this, it can be argued that while it is plausible to suggest that developed countries would have fewer accumulated advantages in new industries, it is also the case that those in the best position to take advantage of the new opportunities are firms that already have built up their knowledge and competencies (Malerba and Nelson, 2011).

One aspect of Korean technological learning highlighted by Kim was that of reverse engineering.[6] In Korea (and more recently in, for example, India and China), this was used extensively in the early stages of industrialisation when it was applied primarily to standardised goods. Although such imitation results in limited technological learning, it may allow price competitiveness to be achieved where the imitator's wage cost is low. As technological mastery is achieved, more creative imitation becomes possible. Creative imitation aims to generate improved products with new performance features. It requires a willingness to learn from outside sources but also risk taking, experimentation and R&D (Bolton, 1993; Kim and Nelson, 2000). While reverse engineering is commonly associated with the early stages of industrialisation, it also found a role – not always successfully – in later stages of development. This arose when Korean firms were attempting to assimilate technologies belonging to earlier stages of developed countries' technological trajectories and the foreign firms possessing property rights in these were unwilling to provide the necessary licences (Kim, 1997; Mody, 1990). Experience in these circumstances suggests that, in the event of legal action being taken against the firm engaging in reverse engineering by the firm possessing the property rights, a licensing agreement would be reached as part of the settlement. Where the technology being sought belonged to the early, fluid stages of the developed country technological trajectory, Korean firms established R&D branches in the innovating countries to enable them to monitor ongoing developments more effectively. In some cases, they took equity stakes in innovating firms to gain access to their technology. They also entered into strategic alliances with other firms to jointly innovate technology. Although equity stakes in foreign firms provided a means of gaining access to the most advanced technologies, joint ventures where foreign firms locate in the developing country did not provide the best means for technological learning in the catch-up phase. According to Kim, a joint venture could lead to rapid initial learning but conflicts of interest would restrict learning in the longer run compared with what might be achieved by independent firms (Kim, 1997: 225–7).

In addition to various mechanisms listed above, mention should also be made of the role of buyers as an important source of foreign technology, particularly in industries such as clothing, electronics and plastics. As an alternative to direct investment, foreign buyers seeking access to lower costs developed subcontracting relationships with East Asian firms. In the course of doing so, they supplied subcontractors with product designs, and advice on production techniques and quality procedures. They also contributed to the training of personnel and facilitated visits to developed company plants. Their large forward export orders were of assistance to firms in obtaining loan finance and enabled firms to expand production facilities and avail of economies of scale (Hobday, 1995). The form of contracting known as 'original equipment manufacturer' (OEM) was particularly important in the electronics industry. Under the OEM system, the local firm produces a finished product to a precise specification. The product is then marketed by the foreign firm under its own brand name using its own distribution channels. It is in the interests of the buyer to provide the subcontractor with sufficient support to ensure that its own requirements in terms of quality, delivery and price can be met.

As the capabilities of the subcontractors grow, the OEM system may evolve into an own design and manufacture system (ODM). This involves a higher level of technological capability and in certain circumstances may allow the firm to develop sales of own brand products alongside subcontracting activities (Hobday, 1995). Using a global value chains (GVCs) conceptual framework, Humphrey and Schmitz (2002), Pietrobelli and Rabellotti (2011) and Gereffi (2013) point to mechanisms such as learning by doing, production reorganisation, acquisition of new, superior functions in the chain, and 'organisational succession' (i.e. producing for more sophisticated buyers as capability increases) as means by which learning innovation and upgrading can take place. However, these authors are at pains to point out that while integration into GVCs may facilitate trade and rapid enhancement of product and process capabilities, it is by no means a panacea. Firms may be tied into relationships that prevent functional upgrading and leave them dependent on a small number of powerful customers who impose restrictions on sales to other firms. There is also evidence that greater profits accrue to lead firms that control branding and product conception to firms supplying core technologies with contract manufacturers and call centres earning slim returns. This, in turn, means that they may lack resources to upgrade their capabilities and achieve greater autonomy (Gereffi, 2013). In these circumstances, industrial policy has an important role in selecting targets for entry into global supply chains and ensuring that domestic competition policy is sufficiently robust to prevent a crowding-out of the upgrading opportunities of domestic firms (UNCTAD, 2011, 2013). Policy has to recognise that the entire value chain may not be captured and that being the lead player in a particular industry no longer requires full blown integration.

While the Korean model of technological development achieved great success, so also did the somewhat different model pursued in Taiwan.[7] One major contrast between the two countries lies in the firm structure. In South Korea, the government helped to create and support giant firms (the chaebol), whereas in Taiwan the strategy concentrated on supporting small and medium firms. Among the advantages offered by the chaebol were: their ability to capture and internalise economies of scale and scope, their development of the organisational and technical resources to negotiate effectively with foreign suppliers and customers, rapid diffusion of capability from one field of business to another, the ability to take risks on new areas of business and the capacity to spearhead the expansion of R&D (Kim, 1997; Lall, 1992; Mody, 1990). Hence during the 1980s when expansion of the semiconductor industry emerged as a major priority, the chaebol were in a position to acquire technology and within a short timescale to begin mass production of random access memory chips and large scale integrated circuits with limited government support (Chen and Sewell, 1996; Lall, 1992; Mody, 1990). However, the concentration of economic power in the chaebol was not without its downside. It offered scope for collusion, misallocation of resources and predatory practices which retarded the growth of specialist activity in small and medium firms. By contrast with the Korean situation, Taiwanese strategy involved support for small and medium firms. This approach encouraged competition and firms had the flexibility to respond quickly to new opportunities. However, firms were also constrained in the opportunities that they could pursue, since they lacked the resources required to overcome barriers to entry, to embark on risky new projects and to conduct research and development on a substantial scale (Mody, 1990). Because of this, the Taiwanese government had to adopt a more interventionist policy. Taiwan's random access memory production was initiated by a public sector firm (Lall, 1992; Mody, 1990). Government supported a wide array of institutes to undertake applied research and to provide technological services and contract work for private industry. These organisations helped to compensate for the lack of R&D in the private sector. Government also promoted industrial parks to attract foreign and domestic investment in high technology and to promote linkages with local firms (Chen and Sewell, 1996).

While the Korea and Taiwan cases are indubitably success stories in terms of both growth and technological learning, it would be a mistake to conclude that technological learning was absent in less successful economies. Katz's studies of technological learning in Latin America indicated that considerable technological learning took place during the import substitution regime and indeed, turn-key plants and licensing contracts were carried out by Argentinian, Brazilian and Mexican metalworking firms during the 1970s and early 1980s (Katz, 2007). *A fortiori*, the same applies to India, which until the mid-1980s pursued a policy of self-sufficiency involving the restriction of foreign direct investment, import substitution and pervasive state intervention. According to Lall (1987), the particular forms of intervention pursued led to much inefficiency and underinvestment. However, it also had the effect of stimulating technological learning which, in turn, allowed India to become a successful exporter of technology to other third world countries. Lall (1987) suggested that India's success as an exporter of technology reflected its access to cheap technical manpower and its ability to adapt technology to third world conditions, but he raised the question of whether India's science and technology effort would have produced more economic benefits had a different set of policies allowed the same talents to be deployed towards different ends.

Technological learning under liberalisation

Latin America

The 1980s saw a number of major changes in policy in the developing world. Reforms involving the opening of the economies to foreign direct investment and the relaxation of various controls were initiated in India and China. Large parts of Latin America and sub-Saharan Africa experienced debt crises and were subjected to stabilisation and structural adjustment packages imposed by the International Monetary Fund, the content of which can be summarised as prudent macroeconomic policy, outward orientation and market liberalisation. These policies led to profound structural change. As Katz (2007) shows, between 1970 and 2002, Argentina, Brazil, Chile and Colombia underwent a major restructuring process in favour of natural resource processing and food production activities. Except in the case of Brazil, the engineering industries suffered a decline while the automobile industry lost ground in Argentina and Chile. In Mexico and Central America, the pattern of specialisation is different. Assembly industries producing final goods for the US market using low cost, unskilled labour predominate. While these firms use state-of-the-art just-in-time technologies and logistics, they involve very little domestic engineering content (Cimoli and Katz, 2002; Cimoli *et al.*, 2009).

Katz argues that the strong bias in the direction of natural resources exhibited by the South American economies shows that the reallocation of resources triggered by free market reforms was strongly oriented towards activities reflecting countries' natural comparative advantages. This in turn raises questions about the extent to which existing comparative advantage provides a sustainable trajectory for future development. The concern here is not with the general question of whether industrial policy in developing countries should, or should not, conform to comparative advantage as recently debated by Lin and Chang (2009). It is with the concrete evidence of technological development in specific industries. Based on studies of genetically modified soybeans and vegetable oil production in Argentina, salmon farming in Chile and fresh flowers in Colombia, Katz notes that, while firms involved in these industries engage in adaptive knowledge generating activities aimed at improving production processes, they have not shown much interest in developing proprietary technologies. He also suggests that the links between universities and industry that would be necessary for such development remain very much in their infancy, although the initial building blocks may be present (Katz, 2007).

The special problems attached to natural resource industries were highlighted by Rosenberg (1976). Because these industries are much more closely enmeshed with the natural environment,

Rosenberg speculated that innovations in them must draw on scientific disciplines which were not necessarily strong in developing countries. The experience of the pulp and paper sector in Brazil is interesting in this context. According to Toivanen and Lima Toivanen (2011), Brazil now ranks as one of the leading countries in production and technology in this industry. This international competitive advantage appears to have depended on a sustained national effort in silviculture and biotechnology as well as in new chemical and pulp processes. Firms in this industry could not simply follow the 'imitation to innovation path' described by Kim and others because they were using quite different raw materials and these, in turn, required different downstream processes (Figueiredo, 2014). The sectoral innovation system involves several actors including federal and state governments, universities and research institutes, industry associations, domestic firms and foreign equipment suppliers. Basic research and innovation is focused primarily on ways to exploit the advantages of Brazilian eucalyptus, while other aspects of R&D are focused on adopting and making use of global best-practice technologies (Toivanen and Lima Toivanen, 2011; Figueiredo, 2014).

There have been concerns that liberalisation led to the loss of output and exports in technology-intensive sectors in the main South American economies and that foreign direct investment in the form of acquisitions has led to reductions in R&D. However, there are indications that businesses such as Embrear, Brazil's aircraft producer, actually benefited from a more commercial approach. The company was founded in 1969 but the foundations for the firm had been laid much earlier through the creation of aeronautical institutes at the instigation of the Brazilian armed forces (Cassiolato *et al*,, 2002; Goldstein, 2002). Early production was in co-operation with foreign partners and a strategic decision was made to focus on design, fuselages and assembling of the final product. High value, high technology components were bought in. From the outset, there was a strong focus on exports because of the need to limit development costs. Losses, and a worsening economic situation in Brazil in the early 1990s, led to the privatisation of the firm in 1994 with the government assuming responsibility for existing losses. This was followed by large scale restructuring. Yet, as Cassiolato *et al.* and Goldstein point out, there are important elements of continuity as the later success was based on competence already built up in the design and integration of production systems. The main changes included a greater focus on the identification and fulfilment of client requirements, reduction in the number of external suppliers with the main suppliers being responsible for technological packages involving the aggregation of a group of sub-systems, and a focus on globalisation of production with a view to risk sharing. These changes involved a loss of business and even closure of firms which had previously been nurtured by Embrear. At the same time, the company expected to attract partner companies to locate near its plant as it moved to just-in-time systems. Embrear's experience reminds us that technological capability may involve the ability to participate strategically in the international division of labour and source and integrate appropriate inputs globally in a manner which contributes to overall competitive advantage. This requires not just deep technical knowledge but also the organisational and logistical knowledge needed to manage a global supply chain.[8]

While Cassiolato *et al.* regard Embrear's success as bucking the trend towards specialisation in areas of low dynamism, a study of 46 firms, mainly in the electro-electronics and bicycle and motorcycle industries in Northern Brazil, presents a more optimistic view (Figueiredo, 2008). Figueiredo found that there was substantial development of new technological capabilities following the reforms in the 1990s. However, he argues that these developments could not be attributed to the reforms alone but to a combination of government policy, foreign competition and intra-firm capability-building efforts. Likewise, Franco *et al.*'s (2011) study of the innovation practices of multinational affiliates indicates that Brazilian affiliates rely more on local than foreign innovation inputs with knowledge embodied in locally produced capital equipment being particularly important.

India

Like Latin America, India began its liberalisation process in the mid–1980s and intensified it further during the 1990s. Nonetheless, its tariffs remained higher and its import and FDI penetration lower than was the case in Latin America. Deregulation led to accelerated growth and restructuring of the Indian economy away from agriculture and towards services. As is well known the stand out performer in the Indian economy has been IT services, which grew at an annual rate of 30 per cent in the twenty years prior to the 2008 recession. With the recovery of developed market demand, exports were expected to reach US$99 billion in 2014. The foundations of this industry were laid in the 1960s with the entry of the Tata conglomerate into IT consulting and the setting up of institutes of technology and management by the Indian government. India's production of more engineers than it could absorb domestically and shortages elsewhere meant that well-educated Indian engineers obtained positions of some responsibility in the nascent US IT sector. This provided a cadre of trained professionals and entrepreneurs with a deep knowledge of the industry on which the developing Indian industry could draw (Saxenian, 2006).[9] They also provided the contacts that were necessary first to bring Indian programmers to the USA on short term contracts and later to arrange the subcontracting of work to Indian IT firms (Bhatnagor, 2006). Although entry into the industry was facilitated by low up-front costs, the sector is dominated by a small number of indigenous firms. While R&D by indigenous firms is limited, the industry has risen up the value chain with an initial focus on programming and data processing being replaced by the provision of more comprehensive packages involving the delivery of outsourced information systems and information solutions for clients. The latter is more skill intensive as it requires an understanding of client business as well as competence in information systems. Apart from English language skills and the excellent reputation of Indian software providers, the main sources of competitive advantage remain access to low cost technical labour. Bhatnagor (2006) cites annual wages of US$5,000–12,000 in India against US$25,000–35,000 in Ireland.

Until the 1980s, India's automobile industry consisted of two firms producing obsolete car models. The modern industry, which is now the sixth largest producer in the world, dates effectively from the setting up of Maruti, a joint venture between the Indian government and the Japanese small car producer Suzuki. The model produced was small and comparatively inexpensive and captured (and continues to hold) a large proportion of the Indian market. Suzuki introduced efficient manufacturing methods based on Japanese systems and launched a vigorous programme to develop local suppliers and improve their ability to deliver components of suitable quality on time (Venkatramani, 1990). These, in turn, made entry easier for other foreign manufacturers who were required by the Indian government to engage in production of vehicles, and not just in assembly of knocked-down and semi-knocked-down kits (Sagar and Chandra, 2004). It also assisted local firms adding car manufacturing to their existing activities (Kale, 2012). The entry of foreign producers helped to create intense competition in the market and this, in turn, made cost reduction an imperative. The largest of the domestic passenger car producers is Tata Motors. Initially a commercial vehicles manufacturer, Tata Motors entered the passenger car industry in the 1990s. Although Tata's commercial vehicle arm had been highly vertically integrated, on entry into the passenger car sector it sought to make greater use of outside suppliers' expertise. Towards this end it set up TACO (Tata AutoComp Systems Limited) in 1996. TACO created five subsidiaries and set up fifteen specialist joint ventures with major international component manufacturers to supply it with components and sub-assemblies. Tata Motors is unusual in developing countries in developing its cars in-house. This has the advantage of enabling it to design a car aimed specifically at the Indian market. Dubbed the Model T of the twenty-first century, the Tata Nano is a radical redesign intended to bring car ownership within the reach of a much larger market (Marukawa, 2011). Although the government is now prevented from imposing domestic content requirements under World Trade Organization (WTO) rules, localisation has come to be regarded as economically necessary given that car firms outsource about 80 per cent of their components (Sagar and Chandra, 2004). Sutton (2004) found that quality levels amongst first tier component suppliers in India (and in China) were at or near world class. However, there was greater variability amongst second tier suppliers. India is now emerging as a major production base with firms such as Hyundai designating India as its production base for small cars. Output exceeded 3.2 million units in 2012 (OICA) and both exports and the domestic market for vehicles and auto components are expected to continue to grow. Such growth requires complementary expansion of the road network which is currently poor. It also raises new innovation challenges in terms of actions required to reduce pollution control (Sagar and Chandra, 2004; Kale, 2012).

China

China's automotive industry dates back to the 1950s when Soviet technology was transferred to produce trucks in vertically integrated plants. The industry, which was expanded in the 1960s, successfully built up a self-reliant truck industry which was able to withstand foreign competition following the opening of Chinese markets (Chu, 2011). The modern industry dates from 1980s. From the outset, joint ventures were seen as the best route for achieving technology transfer and the firms were required to meet stringent localisation targets. The number of entrants was limited in order to encourage mass production and specialisation. This, coupled with a high level of protection, limited competition and resulted in high profits and inadequate incentives for upgrading. The policy of restricting entry changed as preparations for entry into the WTO began in the late 1990s. Additional foreign investment was encouraged – joint ventures in assembly but up to 100 per cent foreign ownership in auto parts. Competition was intensified, car models were updated and technology transfer improved. New indigenous auto producers also began to emerge in this period. Car production grew rapidly and China is now the world's leading car producer as well as the largest market for cars.

Although government policy pursued joint ventures with foreign producers, new domestic producers successfully entered the market with the assistance of state governments. Chery was established as a local state-owned enterprise by engineers from the oldest and largest of China's state-owned automobile manufacturers. It started out with second hand assembly plant purchased from Seat in Spain and second hand engine plant purchased from Ford in England (Marukawa, 2011). Its product technology was copied from Seat and Daewoo, as a result of which it was sued by Daewoo for infringement of its intellectual property rights (Zhengzheng, 2004). Other designs were contracted out to Japanese, Italian and Austrian design houses, as was the installation, fine-tuning and testing of production facilities. The company appointed experienced engineers who had previously worked for European and Japanese companies to senior production and design positions. It also made extensive use of outsourcing both internationally and locally to acquire key components such as engines and transmissions. In some cases, these suppliers provided technical assistance to facilitate the matching and integration of their sub-system into the vehicle design (Chu, 2011; Marukawa, 2011). Chery and other new entrants competed vigorously on price and were able to achieve prices that were one third lower than their joint venture competitors. At the end of a ten year period, Chery was producing a half a million units per annum in fourteen different models and exporting to other developing countries.

Geely, the other important domestic entrant into automobile production, was a private firm which had been engaged in motorcycle production. This firm entered the market in the late 1990s. It used the same methods as Chery to acquire product and process technology and attracted experienced engineers from foreign and domestic firms as a means of obtaining relevant know-how. In 2010, the company acquired Volvo cars from Ford motors with a view to obtaining the hybrid-car technology which Volvo had been developing. According to Chu (2011) the success of indigenous producers called into question the joint venture/trade market access for technology pursued initially by the central Chinese government. However, China's decentralisation allowed experiments by provincial governments and the success of these led to the adjustment of central government policy to one favouring indigenous producers.

The PC producer Lenovo is another major domestic Chinese success story. As with other developing country firms, it used strategic takeovers – in this case IBM's personal computer business – as well as joint ventures to acquire and consolidate the technology, marketing channels and innovation capacity that enabled it to become a leading global player in its business. Although it began as a spin-off from a government funded Institute of Computing Technology, its initial specialisation was in distribution and installation of PCs produced by foreign manufacturers.[10] This contrasts with the more usual OEM-based strategy which starts with manufacture before gradually moving into marketing and distribution (Hobday, 1995; Lee and Lim, 2001). Lenovo, initially known as Legend, first launched its own PC production in 1991 and by 1997 had overtaken IBM and Compaq as the leading computer supplier in China (Xie and White, 2004). In 2012, Lenovo's global shipments of PCs exceeded that of its global competitors, though its profit margins remained considerably lower. Lenovo's initial strategy of focusing on distribution and installation was dictated both by its lack of business experience and its lack of capital. It had the advantage of familiarising Lenovo with the needs of its customers and enabled it to build capability in the organisation of sales and marketing of PCs. The company also began production of add-on cards for Chinese word-processing. These activities enabled Lenovo to accumulate some of the capital needed to begin the manufacture of PCs. From the outset, it made use of its understanding of its Chinese customer's needs. It also sought to supply them with the fastest chips available and to do so at a price point of roughly two thirds of that of its international competitors. The latter was achieved my means of lower management costs, entry of foreign component manufactures and the benefits of its own distribution network which contributed geographic coverage as well as cost competitiveness. Lenovo's close contact with its customers provided it with a basis for identifying areas in which to focus R&D effort as competition became more intense following entry into the WTO. While customer-focused innovation was important for competitiveness in the Chinese market, Lenovo also began to invest in the development of future key technologies (Xie and White, 2004). As well as investing in R&D, Lenovo improved its technological capability through a series of joint ventures and strategic takeovers including its 2005 acquisition of IBM's personal computer business, including its ThinkPad laptop and tablet lines. This provided Lenovo with the ThinkPad brand, with advanced manufacturing technology and global sales channels. This was followed by joint ventures with manufacturing and software companies in Japan, Germany, Brazil and the United States, enabling it to become a major competitor in the global personal computer market. Lenovo's development path underlines the importance of managerial competence in facilitating the development of technological capability which was noted earlier in the case of Embrear, Brazil.

Indices and indicators of technological learning

Sectors and countries

The discussion so far highlights differences across sectors, between countries and over time in terms of the success of learning and the factors that may have contributed to it. Hobday *et al.* (2004) show that, within individual firms in Korea, capability varies substantially with some of the technologies employed being close to the innovation frontier and others being considerably behind it. The innovation strategies of firms varied from product to product and although the strategic goal of large firms was to increase the proportion of leadership products, this had to be balanced against the risks and costs of doing so. As long as markets were expanding, not being on the frontier had advantages for firms with strong process strengths in that they could avoid the risk and cost of new market creation, R&D and radical new product development. In a study of six industries across several countries, Malerba and Nelson (2011) found that different countries had been successful in different sectors and that it was not unusual for countries to do well in some sectors and not in others. India had been successful in pharmaceuticals, whereas Brazil had not. Korea had successfully caught up in automobiles and China and Brazil were in the process of doing so. In software, India, Ireland and Israel had successfully caught up, followed by China and the Philippines and later by Russia, Eastern Europe, Brazil, Argentina and Mexico. China and Korea had successfully caught up in telecommunications equipment, while India and Brazil had not. In agro-food Costa Rica had been successful in coffee, Brazil in soyabean, China in vegetables and Nigeria in cassava. In semiconductors, Korea and Taiwan had successfully caught up, while China and Malaysia were in the process of doing so. Malerba and Nelson found that a small number of factors were important to success in all countries and sectors. These were learning and capability building by firms; access to know-how; skilled human capital; and active government policy. Other factors important to success varied across sectors. In pharmaceuticals, these were access to university research (international or national); support for targeted R&D; and policy towards intellectual property rights (IPR). While IPR is considered necessary to provide firms with incentives to invest in R&D, there is evidence that, in the 1970s and 1980s, lax property rights were helpful in allowing Indian firms to acquire and deepen their capability in the pharmaceutical industry by means of reverse engineering (Gehl Sampath, 2006). Brazil also adopted a policy of lax property rights to promote the domestic pharmaceutical industry – though not successfully. This was a result of different economic incentives which caused Brazilian firms to renounce production of active pharmaceutical ingredients and concentrate instead on the production of finished products using imported raw material (Guennif and Ramani, 2012).[11] In the automobile industry, the key factor was the existence of quality suppliers, while skilled labour and venture capital were the important factors in the software industry. In telecommunications, public research organisations and policies to support R&D were vital. In agro-food, agricultural research organisations and market institutions were required for success while policies supporting targeted R&D were important in semiconductors. Malerba and Nelson (2011) point out that the learning policies adopted by particular countries evolve over time but are generally built on what has proved successful in the past and may fail when applied to sectors where different factors and different policies are required for success.

Export sophistication and capability

Malerba and Nelson (2011) have been careful to point out that their answer to the question of why, within any country, certain sectors perform better than others is dynamic rather than static and hence quite different from the answer given by traditional trade theory. But while static comparative advantage may not provide the answer to why a country progresses technologically in one sector and not in another, examination of a country's revealed comparative advantage (RCA) may provide a convenient way of evaluating the degree of technological capability which a country has achieved. As Lall (2000) notes, the assumption here is that patterns of comparative advantage between developing countries vary according to national policies for technological learning and technology import even if they have similar 'endowments' of labour, capital or skills. Consequently, by looking at a country's exports, we can infer information about the technological intensity of the country's output. The value of using trade statistics is that they are much more widely available than other measures of output and technological development.

Technological intensity

A number of taxonomies have been adopted for the purpose of classifying industries according to their technology intensity. While different classification schemes produce slightly different results, aerospace, pharmaceuticals and electronics are typically considered as science-based high technology sectors. The bulk of developing countries do not have an RCA in high tech products (i.e. the share of these products in their exports is below the share of the same products in world exports) but a small number do, particularly in electronics (Srholec, 2007). Can we conclude that the countries which have an RCA in high tech products have achieved a high level of technological capability? The answer is not necessarily. The reason for this is that the increasing fragmentation of value chains in many cases leads to certain lower technology parts of the overall production process of high tech products being carried out in the developing countries. The fact that the RCA in high tech may prove to be something of a mirage highlights the need for industrial policies focused not so much on attracting high tech industry to developing counties but on attracting activities that are skill intensive and contribute to technological catch-up (Srholec, 2007).

Instead of classifying goods according to industry characteristics, Lall *et al.* (2006) proposed a way of estimating the sophistication of traded products based on the assumption that an export is more sophisticated the higher the average income of its exporter. At the product level, the sophistication score is calculated by taking the weighted average of the exporting countries' incomes, the weights being each country's share of world exports for the particular product. This provides a unique value for each product. Each value is then standardised to range between 0 and 100, the product with the highest value being set at 100 and that with the lowest value at 0. Although the sophistication index is a useful analytical tool which is relatively easy to measure, Lall *et al.* emphasise that it is not a measure of market prospects and correlates relatively poorly with technology. Some products such as cigarettes, perfumes and chocolate have high sophistication scores, although they employ relatively low technologies. Other products such as electronics which are R&D intensive have seen their sophistication scores fall over time as a result of production fragmentation and the shifting of parts of the production process to lower income countries.

Hausmann *et al.* (2007) constructed an index that ranks traded goods in terms of their implied productivity. For a given product this measure, termed PRODY, is constructed as a weighted average of the per capita GDP of the countries exporting the product where the weights reflect the RCA of each country in that product. The income/productivity level corresponding to each country's export basket, termed EXPY, is then calculated as the export weighted PRODY for that country where the weights are the value share of each product in the country's total exports. It will be higher the more the country's export basket resembles that of rich countries and lower to the extent that it resembles the export basket of countries with a low per capita GDP. Based on data for the period 1994 to 2003, Hausmann *et al.* argue that countries that export goods with higher PRODY levels grow more rapidly even when other factors are controlled for. They argue that this shows that growth results from increasing technological capability: i.e. transferring resources from lower productivity to higher productivity goods.

While export sophistication was generally a good predictor of per capita income, Hausmann *et al.* (2007) found that in the case of India and China, per capita income was low relative to the sophistication of their exports. Focusing on the case of China, Xu (2010) argues that the discrepancy is simply a reflection of measurement biases and disappears once corrections are made for the quality of Chinese exports and the fact that most exports come from the developed coastal provinces where incomes are many times higher than in poorer regions. On the other hand, Filipe *et al.* (2013) accept that the discrepancy is real and argue that this augurs well for future growth. In their view, high measured levels of export sophistication are a sign that China is accumulating new and more complex capabilities which will eventually be reflected in higher overall GDP per capita. Against this, Marvasi, (2011) shows that China's imports are more sophisticated than its exports, although the gap between them is narrowing. This means that the sophistication of China's exports is explained mainly by the fact that it is involved in the processing and assembly of sophisticated inputs to produce sophisticated outputs which are then exported. However, Marvasi also found that export sophistication in the case of intermediate goods was not explained by imports and relied on local production capabilities including high levels of skill. Xing (2012) also argues that China's leading position as an exporter of high tech products is a myth based on outdated systems of trade statistics which are not consistent with trade based on global supply chains. Current trade statistics credit the entire value of assembled high tech products, such as iPhones, to China, thereby greatly inflating its exports and giving a false picture of their sophistication. A more accurate measure of high tech exports would be based on value added and would also take into account the fact that much of the activity taking place in China is labour-intensive assembly.

Filipe *et al.* (2013) accept that the China's high tech exports are import dependent and that the activities located in China are largely concerned with assembly and packaging. Nonetheless, they argue that these activities add to China's capabilities and improve the probability of successfully upgrading into adjacent activities. In this context, they draw on the notion of product space developed by Hidalgo *et al.* (2007). This begins with the intuitive idea that a country's ability to produce a product depends on its ability to produce other products which resemble that product in some way. This proximity between products can be measured as the conditional probability of exporting good *i* given that you export good *j*. Using international trade data disaggregated according to the Standardized International Code at four digit level (SITC-4), Hidalgo *et al.* found that products vary considerably in the degree to which they are connected to other products in this way and hence also in terms of their potential as carriers of economic development. Natural resource-based commodities and goods such as textiles and garments were found to offer less potential for development than 'core' products such as metals, machinery and chemicals. While Filipe *et al.* acknowledge that China continues to have an RCA in a large number of labour intensive products, they point out that it has continued to increase the number of core products in which it displays RCA. It has been suggested that its ability to expand the range of core products exhibiting RCA is at least partly based on capabilities accumulated during the pre-liberalisation period when comparative advantage was being defied (Filipe *et al.* 2013; Bardhan, 2010).

Innovation inputs

Studies of changing patterns of international trade may be thought of as providing an indirect means of assessing the extent of technological learning. An alternative approach involves the use of simple or composite indicators of innovation or competitiveness. An example of a simple indicator is R&D expenditure as a percentage of GDP. Composite indicators aggregate information from a variety of statistical sources with a view to capturing the multidimensional nature of technological change. Archibugi *et al.* (2009) provide an overview of the composition of some of the main composite indicators. They represent each composite indicator as being composed of four main synthetic indicators or pillars: (a) creation of new scientific and technological knowledge; (b) infrastructures and diffusion of the new ICT; (c) human capital; and (d) competitiveness. Each of these synthetic indicators is in turn composed of a number of sub-indicators, the details of which vary according to the particular index. Depending on the availability of data which tends to vary with the level of development, indicators for the creation of new science and technology knowledge may include such items as public R&D expenditures as proportion of GDP; business R&D expenditures as a proportion of GDP; patents per million population and scientific articles per million population. Sub-indicators for infrastructure include ICT expenditure as a proportion of GDP, measures of broadband, landline and mobile penetration, access to venture capital and survey-based information on quality of institutions. As far as human capital is concerned, the indicators used involve some subset of the following: the literacy rate, the proportion with secondary and/or tertiary education, the proportion of science and engineering graduates or the number of researchers per million population. The competitiveness pillar is composed variously of indicators such as the share of sales that are new to market or new to firm, the share of employment in high tech industry or services, the share of exports in high tech industries, the share of value added in high tech industry or based on survey data (as in the case of the World Economic Forum's technology index).

In constructing the composite indicators, the values attached to each indicator are normalised so that the measure indicates performance relative to other countries. Although different weights can be assigned to the different indicators, the composite index is often calculated as the arithmetic mean of the normalised values. Having conducted a comparison of a number of the main composite indices for 45 countries for which a number of indicators were available, Archibugi *et al.* (2009) found that the different composite indicators gave a reasonably uniform picture of national relative positions in innovative activities. Of the newly industrialised or developing counties covered by Archibugi *et al.*, Korea ranked highest with a mean rank of 13. South Africa had a mean rank of 33.88, Brazil 36.75, Argentina 39.25, China 39.38 and India 39.38.

The World Bank Knowledge for Development (K4D)[12] website provides an accessible interactive benchmarking tool that allows countries to "identify the problems and opportunities they face in making the transition to the knowledge economy" (World Bank, 2012). The Knowledge Assessment Methodology (KAM) makes comparisons based on 148 structural and qualitative variables. Variables are normalised on a scale from 0 (weakest) to 10 (strongest). The variables serve as proxies for the knowledge economy pillars: economic and institutional regime; education and skills; ICT and innovation systems. Some 146 countries can be compared using KAM. The options available include visual representations that reveal strengths, weaknesses, similarities and differences across countries. KAM also allows the construction of several indices, the best known of which is the Knowledge Economy Index (KEI). The 'over time comparison mode' facilitates comparisons of the performance of counties and regions on the KEI for two points in time and allows for their visual representation (Chen and Dahlman, 2005; World Bank, 2012).

Figure 17.1 KEI scorecard for China (solid plot) and India (dashed plot), 2012.

As an indication of some of the output formats available, consider the cases of China and India, both of which are acknowledged to have made gigantic strides in terms of development over the last twenty years. In the latest available KEI (for 2012), China is ranked 84th and India 109th. By comparison, in 1995, China was ranked 100th and India 106th. The basic scorecard for 2012 shows that China performs better than India by most indicators excluding the rule of law and regulatory quality (Figure 17.1). The scorecard can also be used to provide a picture of changes over time for each country. Other outputs include cross country comparisons in the form of bar charts, custom scorecards and a world map in which countries are colour coded according to their performance on a selected index or pillar.

As Archibugi *et al.* (2009) acknowledge, the World Bank's Knowledge for Development website has greatly reduced the time, effort and costs associated with knowledge economy measurement exercises. However, they suggest that while the availability of data and the ease of its manipulation brings undoubted benefits it also opens up dangers in the form of measurement without theory and of manipulating figures without having reflected sufficiently on the nature of technological change. Production and innovation capabilities are not simply some function of a set of indicators but are the product of the interaction between the resources measured by these indicators and the learning processes that take place at firm level and which, in turn, are influenced by a variety factors both internal and external to the firm. Hence, while aggregate indicators provide useful preliminary information, it is of vital importance that the focus of public policy should be not on increasing the value of the indicators but the more difficult problem of improving the economic and social conditions that the indicators attempt to capture (Archibugi *et al.*, 2009).

Technological learning and the consumer

So far, we have been concerned with technological learning by economic actors in their capacity as wealth producers but it is also worth noting that economic progress also requires technological learning by consumers. Not only that, but consumers – whether they are individuals, communities or firms – are themselves sources of innovation (von Hippel, 2005). Mobile telephones have been one of the most rapidly diffusing innovations of all time with the number of global subscriptions now approaching global population figures. While mobile telephony has important economic uses particularly amongst small business and the self-employed in countries with low penetration of landlines, research indicates that the main use is social communication. As long as access costs are not prohibitive and perceived benefits are high, consumers can quickly learn to use new technologies and integrate them into their lives often in ways that were not anticipated by the original designers (Dey *et al.*, 2011; Donner 2007). Given the high penetration rates of mobile telephony even in the poorest countries, various efforts have been made to make use of this in the delivery of public health, education and banking services. So far, with the partial exception of mobile banking, the success of these efforts has been limited and will probably have to await cost reductions in the provision of the mobile internet. China, as noted earlier, is now the world's largest market for cars as well as the largest producer. This means that large numbers have learnt how to drive and there are no reports of there being any difficulty doing so. The point here is that consumers in all parts of the world appear able to learn to use new technologies when there are benefits from doing so, and when the technologies are accessible given their budget constraints.

Conclusion

This brings us to a question posed by Mokyr (2003) which will be discussed by way of a conclusion to this chapter. The question is this: Does the fact that useful knowledge is not shared equally amongst all the countries of the world matter for economic performance? As Mokyr notes, the agent carrying out a technique does not have to understand why the technique works in the way it does.[13] The consequences of this are twofold. First, it is possible "for techniques to become increasingly sophisticated, relying on increasingly wide and diverse epistemic bases, and yet to require less and less competence because they are more and more standardised and user friendly" (Mokyr, 2003: 17). Second, much of the knowledge that drives continuous economic growth may be concentrated in the minds of a relatively small number of better trained people. As Mokyr puts it, nobody expects Luxembourg to develop their own 'knowledge of airplane construction', for them that of Boeing is quite sufficient. The point here is that in order to benefit from the fruits of useful social knowledge, it is not necessary to devote resources to acquiring that knowledge in person. This is not in dispute but, the question is, what determines the extent to which people or countries get access to fruits of social knowledge? As Adam Smith long ago pointed out, we get access to the fruits of others' labour or knowledge only by having something to offer in return and if what developing countries have to offer in exchange is less 'valued' than what rich countries offer, their ability to participate in the benefits of social knowledge will be less. This means that while it is necessary to exploit existing comparative advantage, developing countries have an imperative to insert themselves into the international division of labour in ways that offer opportunities to increase their capabilities and enhance their access to the benefits of social knowledge.[14] This requires that they identify markets in which they can compete and that they have access to the scientific and practical knowledge to allow them to do so.[15] Access to this knowledge is often costly. Some of it is controlled by international firms through ownership of intellectual property rights. Some of it has a tacit element which makes it difficult to transfer. In addition, technology designed to function in one environment usually requires modification to enable it to be used effectively in a different environment, often using different inputs and facing different input prices. All this means that the ability to absorb new technology depends on and is shaped by existing capabilities.

The fact that much of our social knowledge is owned or controlled by international firms has long been a matter of concern to students of technological capability. In the early 1970s, the issue of technological dependency was widely discussed with the development of an independent capital goods sector in developing countries seen as a necessary step to overcome this dependency (Fransman, 1986; Stewart, 1977). This period also saw the setting up of the UN Commission on Transnational Corporations with the objective of securing a Code of Conduct to promote the positive contribution of TNCs to national development goals while controlling or eliminating negative effects.[16] With the development of the Latin American debt crisis and the ideological turn towards neo-liberalism in the 1980s, the emphasis on dependency was set aside and MNCs came to be seen as the main vehicle for technology transfer. While MNCs contribute to technological transfer and learning through their direct investment and procurement activities, their technological transfer activities are necessarily subordinated to their wider global interests. There is also the problem of the imbalance of bargaining power between MNCs and developing country firms. In countries with large domestic markets, governments can improve the bargaining position of domestic firms *vis à vis* multinational firms by trading market access for access to technology. However, the freedom of action available to them is increasingly constrained by WTO rules. As a consequence, the sorts of policies pursued by the likes of Japan, South Korea and Taiwan to develop the capacity of indigenous firms are no longer a realistic option (Kim, 2001; Wade, 2014). However, some argue that despite the new constraints, there remains scope for new forms of industrial policy so that WTO rules have affected the composition of industrial policy instruments rather than their quantum (Wade, 2014; Cimoli *et al.*, 2009).

While changes in the international environment require new approaches to the development of technological capability, there are also some important constants. Domestic technological capability is a substitute for foreign capability but it is also a complement to it and necessary for adaption of foreign technology to local circumstances. Domestic capability is also necessary to reduce the transactions costs associated with the acquisition of foreign technology.

Finally, technological learning does not exist in vacuum. Its purpose is to change the basis on which countries participate in and benefit from the international division of labour. It is intimately linked to trade policy, educational policy and wider industrial and economic policies and the incentives they create. Like all learning, technological learning builds upon and is shaped by what is already known. To move forward requires time, space and resources, all of which are in short supply. A rebalancing of the international order would help to create the necessary space for development, but meanwhile countries have to make the best use of the available strategy space. (Rodrik, 2004; Wade, 2014; Cimoli *et al.*, 2009).

Notes

1 In his review of the treatment of knowledge in the growth literature, Olsson (2001) found that most growth theorists implicitly assumed that the level of technology was cardinally measurable, which is unlikely to be the case. Steedman (2003) is even more critical describing the approach of new growth theorists to the question of whether or not the stock of technological knowledge is cardinally measurable as cavalier.

2 See, for example, Cooper (1973) and Stewart (1977), the special issue of the *IDS Bulletin* on the transfer of industrial technology to underdeveloped countries edited by Charles Cooper (1970), and the special issue of *World Development* on the work of the Livingstone Institute on appropriate technology edited by James Pickett (1977).

3 The countries were: Argentina, Brazil, Mexico, India, Pakistan, The Philippines and Taiwan. Little *et al.* (1970) estimated that India and Pakistan had effective protection rates of 200 per cent; Argentina and Brazil, 100 per cent; The Philippines, 50 per cent; Taiwan, 33 per cent; and Mexico 25 per cent.

4 The focus of Utterback and Abernathy's Industry Life Cycle Model (ILC) is the relationship between the pattern of innovation, the stage of development of the production process and the basis for competition. It has points in common with Vernon's Product Life Cycle (PLC) which focused on explaining

shifts of comparative advantage in the production of manufactured goods from rich countries to developing countries. In Vernon's theory, new products are created in rich countries to serve rich country markets. As designs become standardised, the focus shifts from product to process innovation. Internationalisation takes place first though exports and then through foreign direct investment (Vernon, 1966).

5 The chaebol are large family-owned conglomerates with strong links to government. Prominent chaebol include Samsung, Hyundai, Daewoo and LG. The chaebol have features in common with the Japanese zaibatsu but, unlike the zaibutsu, they are not involved in banking operations.

6 Reverse engineering is an old and common practice which is widely used as a means of obtaining information about a rival's hardware or software. It was used extensively during the in the cold war as a means of uncovering the other side's military secrets. Of itself, it is not illegal but it may be if it involves counterfeits or clones of patented goods. Reverse engineering may be considered as a subset of a larger category of imitative practices and strategies. In the post–World War II period, these have had an important role in the industrialisation process in countries such as Japan (Bolton, 1993).

7 As has been noted by Kuznets (1988), the development policies pursued first in Japan and later in Korea and Taiwan have a number of important features in common which allow us to think in terms of an East Asian model of economic development. While government intervention in the industrialisation process has been important in all three countries, the form taken by this intervention varied depending on factors such as the level of development and the industrial structure.

8 The importance of managerial skills was emphasised by Rosenberg (2002) in his Amilcar Herrera lecture. Reflecting on the success of Reliance, India in purchasing the expertise necessary to set up an oil refining operation, Rosenberg posed the question of the extent to which core competence in large project management expertise could serve as a substitute for limited technological skills in facilitating technological transfer.

9 This reverse 'brain drain' is by no means unique to India. Kim (2000) argues that in the final decades of the twentieth century, Korean firms boosted their own capabilities through recruitment of highly trained Korean-American engineers and scientists. According to Kim, the brain drain was a serious problem for Korea in the 1970s when the bulk of Korean engineers and scientists trained abroad remained there. However, as in the Indian case, they became an important source of cutting edge skills and access to overseas technical networks when they began to be lured back to Korea from the 1980s onwards.

10 The Chinese Information and Telecommunications firm Huawei began its operations as a sales agent for a Hong Kong firm in private branch exchange (PBX) switches. After a few years it began independent commercialisation of PBX technologies aiming at hotels and small enterprises. It initially focused on rural less profitable markets which were neglected by the state supported joint ventures before expanding into Chinese metropolitan areas. In 1999, it set up an R&D centre in Bangalore in India, followed by centres in Sweden and the USA. Since 2000, it has expanded its global operations and engaged in a number of joint ventures with European and North American firms. It is now recognised as a major global ICT solutions supplier and carries out contractual work for other major telecommunications firms (Zhang and Vialle, 2014).

11 As indicated by Guennif and Ramani (2012), subsequent developments in the pharmaceutical industry in India and Brazil were influenced by the opportunities and threats resulting from liberalisation and the introduction of TRIPS (Trade Related Aspects of Intellectual Property Rights). From the point of view of technological capability, the broader intellectual property regime (IPR) under TRIPS closes some of the opportunities for second innovators to commercialise branded products without entering into formal licensing agreements. This has the effect of reducing though not eliminating the rents from second innovation. Guennif and Ramani suggest that the best option for domestic firms is to focus on generics. While the purpose of IPR is to promote innovation through investment in R&D, this presents major challenges for developing country firms because they cannot match the deep pockets of the multinational players. Collaboration with foreign firms may offer a partial solution though is unlikely to provide sufficient opportunities to climb the technological ladder.

12 The World Bank's Knowledge for Development website can be found at info.worldbank.org/etools/kam2/KAM

13 This is well understood in the literature on technological learning. For example, commenting on the earlier stages of South Korea's industrialisation, Westphal *et al.* (1981) suggested that the know-how to operate production processes efficiently was to a large degree independent of the ability to use the underlying engineering principles in investment activity. See also Lall (1987) and Kim (1997).

14 See Lin and Chang (2009) for a discussion of the issues relating to how far countries should follow or defy comparative advantage.
15 In the context of technological learning, the issue of markets is extremely important. While countries such as Korea were able to use a combination of protection and export promotion as a means of creating the space for learning while gaining access to economies of scale, such combinations are now likely to fall foul of WTO anti-dumping rules.
16 Efforts to secure a Code of Conduct on TNCs were eventually abandoned following a twenty year effort because of irreconcilable differences between the parties concerned (Fredriksson, 2003).

References

Amsden, A. H. 1989. *Asia's Next Giant*. Oxford: Oxford University Press.

Andreoni, A. 2012. *Productive Capabilities Indicators for Industrial Policy Design*. Vienna: UNIDO.

Archibugi, D., Denni, M. and Filippetti, A. 2009. The Technological Capabilities of Nations: The State of the Art of Synthetic Indicators. *Technological Forecasting and Social Change*. 76: 917–931.

Arrow, K. 1962. The Economic Implications of Learning by Doing. *Review of Economic Studies*. 29: 155–173.

Bardhan, P. 2010. *Awakening Giants, Feet of Clay: Assessing the Rise of India and China*. Princeton, NJ: Princeton University Press.

Bell, M. 2009. Innovation Capability and Directions of Development. STEPS Working Paper 33, Brighton: STEPS Centre.

Bell, M. and Pavitt, K. 1993. Technological Accumulation and Industrial Growth: Contrasts Between Developed and Developing Countries. *Industrial and Corporate Change*. 2 (2): 157–210.

Bhatnagor, S. 2006. India's Software Industry. In V. Chandra (ed.). *Technology, Adaptation and Exports*. Washington, DC: The World Bank.

Bolton, M. K. 1993. Imitation versus Innovation: Lessons to be Learned from the Japanese. *Organisational Dynamics*. 21 (3): 30–45.

Cassiolato, J. E., Bernardes, R. and Lastres, H. 2002. *Transfer of Technology for Successful Integration into the Global Economy: A Case Study of Embraer in Brazil*. New York and Geneva: UNCTAD.

Chen, C. F. and Sewell, G. 1996. Strategies for Technological Development in South Korea and Taiwan: The Case of Semiconductors. *Research Policy*. 25: 759–783.

Chen, D. H. C. and Dahlman, C. J. 2005. *The Knowledge Economy, the KAM Methodology and World Bank Operations*. Washington, DC: The World Bank, http://siteresources.worldbank.org/KFDLP/Resources/KAM_Paper_WP.pdf

Chu, W. W. 2011. How the Chinese Government Promoted a Global Automobile Industry. *Industrial and Corporate Change*. 20 (5): 1135–1276.

Cimoli, M. and Katz, J. 2002. *Structural Reforms, Technological Gaps and Economics Development: A Latin American Perspective*. Santiago: UN CEPAL.

Cimoli, M., Dosi, G. and Stiglitz, J. E. eds. 2009. *Industrial Policy and Development: The Political Economy of Capabilities Accumulation*. Oxford: Oxford University Press.

Cooper, C. ed. 1970. *The Transfer of Industrial Technology to Underdeveloped Countries*. Special Issue of *IDS Bulletin*. 3.1.

Cooper, C. 1973. *Science, Technology and Development*. London: Frank Cass.

Dey, B., Newman, D. and Prendergast, R. 2011. Analysing Appropriation and Usability in Social and Occupational Lives: An Investigation of Bangladeshi Farmers' Use of Mobile Telephony. *Information Technology and People*. 24 (1): 45–63.

Donner, J. 2007. Research Approaches to Mobile Phone Use in Developing World: A Review of Literature. *Working Paper: Mobile Use in Developing World*. Downloadable from http://74.125.155.132/scholar?q=cache:dH8xUSscd2wJ:scholar.google.com/+Donner+J+2007+mobile+telephony+literature+review&hl=en&as_sdt=2000

Enos, J. L. and Park, W. H. 1988. *The Adoption and Diffusion of Imported Technology: The Case of Korea*. Beckenham: Croom Helm.

Fagerberg, J. 1994. Technology and International Differences in Growth Rates. *Journal of Economic Literature*. 32 (3): 1147–1175.

Figueiredo, P. N. 2008. Industrial Policy Changes and Firm-Level Technological Capability Development: Evidence from Northern Brazil. *World Development*. 36 (1): 55–88.

Figueiredo, P. N. 2014. Beyond Technological Catch-Up: An Empirical Investigation of Further Innovative Capability Accumulation Outcomes in Latecomer Firms with Evidence from Brazil. *Journal of Engineering Technology Management.* 31: 73–102.

Filipe, J., Kumar, U., Usui, N. and Abdon, A. 2013. Why has China Succeeded? And Why It Will Continue to do So. *Cambridge Journal of Economics.* 37 (4): 791–818.

Franco, E., Ray, S. and Ray, P. K. 2011. Patterns of Innovation Practices of Multinational-Affiliates in Emerging Economies: Evidences from Brazil and India. *World Development.* 39 (7): 1249–1260.

Fransman, M. 1986. *Technology and Economic Development.* Brighton: Harvester Wheatsheaf.

Fredriksson, T. 2003. Forty Years of UNCTAD Research on FDI. *Transnational Corporations.* 12 (3): 1–40.

Gehl Sampath, P. 2006. *Indian Pharma within Global Reach.* UNU-MERIT, Working Paper 2006–031. Maastricht: United Nations University – Maastricht Economic and Social Research and Training Centre on Innovation and Technology.

Gereffi, G. 2013. *A Global Value Chain Perspective on Investment and Infrastructure Development in Emerging Markets.* Centre on Globalization, Governance and Competitiveness – Conference Paper. Durham NC: Duke University.

Goldstein, A. 2002. Embraer: From National Champion to Global Player. *CEPAL Review.* 77 August: 97–115.

Guennif, S. and Ramani, S. V. 2012. Explaining Divergence in Catching-up in Pharma Between India and Brazil using the NSI Framework. *Research Policy.* 41 (2): 430–441.

Hausman, R., Huang, J. and Rodrik, D. 2007. What You Export Matters. *Journal of Economic Growth.* 12 (1): 1–15.

Hidalgo, C. A., Klinger, B., Barabasi, A. L. and Hausman, R. 2007. The Product Space Conditions the Development of Nations. *Science.* 317 (5837): 482–487.

Hippel, E. von, 2005. *Democratising Innovation.* Cambridge, MA: MIT Press.

Hobday, M. 1995. East Asian Latecomer Firms: Learning the Technology of Electronics. *World Development.* 23 (7): 1171–1193.

Hobday, M., Rush, H. and Bessant, J. 2004. Approaching the Innovation Frontier in Korea: The Transition Phase to Leadership. *Research Policy.* 33 (10): 1433–1457.

Humphrey, J. and Schmitz, H. 2002. How Does Insertion in Global Value Chains Affect Upgrading in Industrial Clusters? *Regional Studies.* 36 (9): 1017–1027.

Kale, D. 2012. Sources of Innovation and Technological Capability Development in the Indian Automobile Industry. *Institutions and Economies.* 4 (2): 121–150.

Katz, J. 1976a. *Importation de Technologia, Aprendizaje Industrialization Dependiente.* México D.F.: Fondo de Cultura Económica,

Katz, J. 1976b. *Creation de Technologia en el Sector Manufacturero Argentino.* Investigation en Temas de Ciencia y Technologia – Monografia de Trabajo, No.1. Santiago: CEPAL (UN Economic Commission for Latin America).

Katz, J. 2007. *Cycles of Creation and Destruction of 'Social Capabilities' in Latin America?* Department of International Development, SLPTMD Working Paper Series No. 006. Oxford: University of Oxford. Paper presented at meeting of experts on FDI, Technology and Competitiveness. Geneva: UNCTAD. Downloadable from http://www.tmd-oxford.org/sites/www.tmd-oxford.org/files/SLPTMD-WP-006.pdf

Kim, L. 1997. *Imitation to Innovation: The Dynamics of Korea's Technological Learning.* Boston: Harvard Business Press.

Kim, L. 2000. The Dynamics of Technology Development: Lessons from the Korea Experience. Paper presented at the conference on Technology Development in East-Asia organised by the World Bank Institute in Bali, Indonesia, 14–16 December.

Kim, L. 2001. The Dynamics of Technological Learning in Industrialisation. *International Social Science Journal.* 53: 297–308.

Kim, L. and Nelson, R. R. eds. 2000. *Technology, Learning and Innovation : Experiences of Newly Industrializing Economies.* Cambridge: Cambridge University Press.

Krugman, P. 2013. The New Growth Fizzle. *New York Times,* 18 August.

Kuznets, P. W. 1988. An East Asian Model of Economic Development: Japan, Taiwan and South Korea. *Economic Development and Cultural Change.* 36 (3): S11–S43.

Lall, S. 1987. *Learning to Industrialize.* Basingstoke: Macmillan.

Lall, S. 1992. Technological Capabilities and Industrialization. *World Development.* 20(2): 165–186.

Lall, S. 2000. *The Technological Structure and Performance of Developing Country Manufactured Exports, 1985–1998.* Working Paper No. 44. Oxford: Queen Elizabeth House.

Lall, S., Navaretti, G., Teitel, S. and Wignaraja, G. 1994. *Technology and Enterprise Development*. Basingstoke: Macmillan.

Lall, S., Weiss, J. and Zhang, J. 2006. The 'Sophistication' of Exports: A New Trade Measure. *World Development*. 34 (2): 222–237.

Lee, J., Bae, Z. T. and Choi, D. K. 1988. Technology Development Processes: A Model for a Developing Country with a Global Perspective. *R&D Management*. 18 (3): 235–250.

Lee, K. and Lim, C. 2001. Technological Regimes, Catching-Up and Leapfrogging: Findings from the Korean Industries. *Research Policy*. 30 (1): 459–483.

Lin, J. and Chang, H-J, 2009. Should Industrial Policy in Developing Countries Conform to Comparative Advantage or Defy It? *Development Policy Review*. 27 (5): 483–502.

Little, I., Scitovsky, T. and Scott, M. 1970. *Industry and Trade in Some Developing Countries*. Oxford: Oxford University Press.

Malerba, F. and Nelson, R. 2011. Learning and Catching Systems: Evidence from Six Industries. *Industrial and Corporate Change*. 20 (6): 1645–1675.

Marukawa, T. 2011. Technology Acquisition by Indigenous Firms: The Case of the Chinese and Indian Automobile Industries. In Ohara, M., Vijayabaskar, M. and Lin, H. (eds.). *Industrial Dynamics in China and India*. Basingstoke: Palgrave Macmillan.

Marvasi, E. 2011. *China's Exports: What Products are Sophisticated?* Fondazione Manlio Masi Working Paper 7. Rome: Fondazione Manlio Masi.

Mody, A. 1990. Institutions and Dynamic Comparative Advantage: The Electronics Industry in South Korea and Taiwan. *Cambridge Journal of Economics*. 14 (3): 291–314.

Mokyr J. 2003. *The Knowledge Society: Theoretical and Historical Underpinnings*. Paper presented to the Ad Hoc Expert Group on Knowledge Systems, United Nations: New York, 4–5 September. Downloadable from faculty.wcas.northwestern.edu/~jmokyr/Unitednations.PDF

Nelson, R. R. and Winter, S. G. 1982. *An Evolutionary Theory of Economic Change*. Cambridge, MA: The Belknap Press of Harvard University Press.

Olsson, O. 2001. The Appearance of Knowledge in Growth Theory. *Economic Issues*. 6 (1): 1–20.

Pack, H. 1994. Endogenous Growth Theory: Intellectual Appeal and Empirical Shortcomings. *Journal of Economic Perspectives*. 8 (1): 55–72.

Perez, C. 2001. Technological Change and Opportunities for Development as a Moving Target. *CEPAL Review*. 75 December: 109–130.

Pickett, J. 1977. The work of the Livingstone Institute on 'appropriate' technology: Editor's introduction. *World Development*. 5 (9/10): 773–776.

Pietrobelli, C. and Rabellotti, R. 2011. Global Value Chains Meet Innovation Systems: Are There Learning Opportunities for Developing Countries? *World Development*. 39 (7): 1261–1269.

Prendergast, R. 2010. Accumulation of Knowledge and Accumulation of Capital in Early Theories of Growth and Development. *Cambridge Journal of Economics*. 34 (3): 413–431.

Rodrik, D. 2004. *Industrial Policy for the Twenty-First Century*. KSG Working Paper No. RWP04–047. Available at SSRN: http://ssrn.com/abstract=617544 or http://dx.doi.org/10.2139/ssrn.617544

Romer, P. 1986. Increasing Returns and Long-Run Growth. *Journal of Political Economy*. 94(5): 1002–1037.

Romer, P. 1990. Endogenous Technological Change. *Journal of Political Economy*. 98(5): S71–S102.

Rosenberg, N. 1976. *Perspectives on Technology*. Cambridge: Cambridge University Press.

Rosenberg, N. 2002. Sources of Innovation in Developing Economies: Reflections on the Asian Experience. Accessible at http://www.intech.unu.edu/events/herrera_lectures/herrera_lectures/2002_rosenberg.pdf

Sagar, A. D. and Chandra, P. 2004. *Technological Change in the Indian Passenger Car Industry*. Energy Technology Innovation Policy Discussion Paper 2004–05. John F. Kennedy School of Government. Cambridge, MA: University of Harvard.

Saxenian, A. 2006. *The New Argonauts: Regional Advantage in a Global Economy*. Cambridge, MA: Harvard University Press.

Schumpeter, J. A. 1947. *Capitalism, Socialism and Democracy*. 2nd revised edition. London: George Allen & Unwin.

Schumpeter, J. A. 1961. *The Theory of Economic Development*. Translated by R. Opie. Oxford: Oxford University Press (first published 1934 by the Department of Economics of Harvard University).

Solow, R. M. 2000. *Growth Theory: An Exposition* 2nd ed. Oxford: Oxford University Press.

Srholec, M. 2007. High-Tech Exports from Developing Countries: A Symptom of Technology Spurts or Statistical Illusion? *Review of World Economics*. 143 (2): 227–255.

Steedman, I. 2003. On 'Measuring' Knowledge in New (Endogenous) Growth Theory. In N. Salvadori (ed.). *Old and New Growth Theories: An Assessment.* Cheltenham: Edward Elgar: 127–133.

Stewart, F. 1977. *Technology and Underdevelopment.* London: Macmillan.

Sutton, J. 2004. *The Auto-Component Supply Chain in China and India: A Benchmark Study.* Discussion Paper, The Toyota Centre, Suntory and Toyota International Centres for Economics and Related Disciplines, EI/34 February. London: London School of Economics.

Toivanen, H. and Lima Toivanen, M. B. 2011. Innovation and the Emergence of the Brazilian Pulp and Paper Sector. *O Papel,* April. Espoo: VTT – Technical Research Center of Finland.

UNCTAD. 2011. *World Investment Report 2011: Non- Equity Modes of International Production and Development.* New York and Geneva: United Nations.

UNCTAD. 2013. *World Investment Report 2013: Global Value Chains: Investment and Trade for Development.* New York and Geneva: United Nations.

Utterback, J. and Abernathy, W. 1975. A Dynamic Model of Product and Process Innovation. *Omega.* 3 (6): 639–656.

Venkatramani, R. 1990. *Japan enters Indian Industry: The Maruti Suzuki Joint Venture.* Kothi, Hyderabad: Radiant Publishing House.

Vernon, R. 1966. International Investment and International Trade in the Product Cycle. *Quarterly Journal of Economics.* 80: 190–207.

Wade, R. 1990. *Governing the Market.* Princeton, NJ: Princeton University Press.

Wade, R. 2014. 'Market versus State' or 'Market with State': How to Impart Directional Thrust, Review Essay. *Development and Change* 45(4): 1–22. http://onlinelibrary.wiley.com/doi/10.1111/dech.12099/pdf

Westphal, L. E., Rhee, Y. W. and Pursell, G. 1981. *Korean Industrial Competence: Where It Came From.* Washington, DC: World Bank, Staff Working Paper No. 469.

Williamson, J. 1990. What Washington Means by Policy Reform. In Williamson, J. (ed.). *Latin American Adjustment: How Much has Happened?* Washington, DC: Institute for International Economics.

World Bank. 2012. *Measuring Knowledge in the World's Economies.* World Bank Institute Development Studies. Washington, DC: World Bank Institute. Accessible at http://siteresources.worldbank.org/INTUNIKAM/Resources/KAMbooklet.pdf

World Bank. 2014. *Knowledge for Development Website.* Accessible at info.worldbank.org/etools/kam2/KAM

Xie, W. and White, S. 2004. Sequential Learning in a Chinese Spin-off: The Case of Lenovo Group Limited. *R&D Management.* 34 (4) September: 407–422.

Xing, Y. 2012. *The People's Republic of China's High-Tech Exports: Myth and Reality.* ADBI Working Paper 357. Tokyo: Asian Development Bank Institute.

Xu, B. 2010. The Sophistication of Exports: Is China Special? *China Economic Review.* 21: 482–493.

Zhang, J. and Vialle, P. 2014. Patterns of Innovation of a Successful Latecomer Firm: A Longitudinal Analysis of the Case of Huawei. Paper presented at International Conference on Management of Innovation and Technology, Singapore; 09/2014. Accessible at http://www.researchgate.net/publication/263113184_Patterns_of_innovation_of_a_successful_latecomer_firm_a_longitudinal_analysis_of_the_case_of_Huawei

Zhengzheng, G. 2004. CM Charges Chery for Alleged Mini Car Piracy. *China Daily,* 18 December. Accessible at http://www.chinadaily.com.cn/english/doc/2004-12/18/content_401235.htm

18

MEXICO'S NEW INDUSTRIAL ORGANISATION SINCE THE 1980s

Glocal challenges from export-orientation and polarisation

Enrique Dussel Peters

In the last 20 years Mexico was first a symbol of successful socioeconomic openness and development in the context of globalisation and the North American Free Trade Agreement (NAFTA); since the beginning of the twenty-first century, however, it became a symbol for not being able to compete with Asia and China. What are the current conditions of Mexico's manufacturing sector and which were the main influences on this sector in Mexico since the 1990s?

Having these questions in mind, the chapter will be divided into three sections. The first examines a group of theoretical and methodological propositions to understand industrial development in the current historical context of globalisation based on systemic competitiveness, global commodity chains and 'territorial endogeneity'. As we shall see, this conceptual framework allows for an understanding of Mexico's manufacturing evolution since the 1990s and a dialogue between macro and micro-economists. The second section focuses on the main structural conditions and challenges for Mexico's manufacturing sector since the 1990s and particularly for the period 2000–12. This section highlights both short-term and structural conditions and changes in Mexico's manufacturing sector to understand its main challenges. Based on the former sections, the third presents the main conclusions based on Mexico's case study. As we shall see, the Mexican case is of relevance for the development of industrial organisations and manufacturing sectors in other nations.

Conceptual frameworks to understand industrial development in the twenty-first century

In development economics there has been a long development and macroeconomic tradition for understanding and justifying industrial analysis and policies. Proponents of import-substituting industrialisation (ISI) emphasised various forms of market imperfection – including low-level or underdeveloped economic equilibrium (Nurkse, 1955; Rosenstein-Rodan, 1961), domestic constraints or bottlenecks on economic development (in (skilled) labour and capital markets, in foreign exchange and in domestic savings and investment). They stressed the importance of direct state intervention, as well as industrial and trade policies, in order to achieve a balanced growth strategy which would increase capital accumulation and enhance investment in the modern sectors of developing economies. Dual economic and population structures, as well as the relationship between the agricultural and industrial sectors, played a critical role in this discourse (Lewis, 1954).[1]

At least four issues are significant in these debates:

1   Much of this debate was rooted in the initial findings and discussion of Raúl Prebisch since the 1950s and his later work at ECLAC (Economic Commission for Latin America and the Caribbean) that highlighted the limitations of development under a core–periphery model in which the latter specialised in primary goods with a low income elasticity of demand *vis à vis* manufactured goods, with higher income elasticities so trade specialisation for Latin America and the Caribbean (LAC) in primary goods resulted in a continuous loss of terms of trade (Prebisch, 1950, 1964), Structural heterogeneity within the periphery, from this perspective, resulted in differences in productivity, high levels of inequality and, thus, in underdevelopment. Intra-Latin American trade and intraregional integration, from this perspective, was an option for a different kind of development that went beyond the core–periphery model.

2   At least as relevant for this discussion were the arguments of Hirschman (1958) stating the importance of specialisation in manufacturing as a result of higher income elasticities with manufacturing activities accounting for more backward and forward linkages – with the suppliers of their inputs and users of their products – than other economic activities. Thus, a shift towards manufacturing production would have a positive effect on growth and development in general.[2]

3   In the context of ISI, and based on these arguments, a battery of instruments to support modern or 'strategic' sectors emerged: from tariffs and subsidies to non-tariff mechanisms to protect infant industries in addition to the creation of state-owned enterprises to produce imported intermediate and capital goods.

4   Parallel to these debates in the late 1960s a group of authors discussed the issue of unequal trade and dependency (Cardoso and Faleto, 1969) *vis à vis* Marxian arguments stressing that trade and any kind of exchange in capitalism *ex ante* includes exploitation and thus inequality.[3]

Since then, several of these arguments have been discussed by different groups of authors and schools of thought. Of particular interest are, on the one side, issues regarding imperfect markets: from knowledge and information (von Hayek, 1992; Stiglitz, 1989) to different forms of dynamic economies of scale, product differentiation and entry-barriers (Krugman, 1981). In several of these cases, the respective authors highlighted issues such as the under-development of labour markets, balance of payments and current-account constraints and bottlenecks, financing, innovation and production, among others, as well as different kinds of 'gap models' related to trade and the current-account (Dussel Peters, 2000; Ros, 2000). With the exception of von Hayek, all of the above-mentioned authors conclude that there is a justification for public and industrial policies. Export-oriented industrialisation (EOI) was another central response to ISI and, as we shall see below, critical for understanding Mexico's current manufacturing structure.

Export-oriented industrialisation (EOI)
and liberalisation strategy in Mexico

Over the course of the 1980s, the new orthodoxy of export-oriented industrialisation (EOI) was widely adopted by policy-makers in Latin America. The lessons of the East Asian miracle, famously summarised by the World Bank in its 1993 report (World Bank, 1993), combined with influential analyses of the 'rent-seeking' behaviour associated with earlier ISI regimes in Latin America (Krueger, 1978, 1997), led to a categorical rejection of development strategies throughout much of the region and an embrace of export-oriented policies as the key to growth and development. Convinced that creating a market-friendly environment was the best way to generate foreign direct investment (FDI), policy-makers eschewed targeted industrial policy in favour of a neutral or horizontal approach (that is, policies that attempt to affect firms, sectors and regions, for example, without any particular distinction) and macroeconomic stabilisation became the highest priority of governments that attached great importance to the task of getting the macroeconomic fundamentals right.

The argument in favour of EOI builds on the positive association between exports and economic growth or development. Contrary to ISI, EOI stresses that the global economy, through exports, is the point of reference for any economic unit (firm, region, nation, group of nations). Exports, in general, reflect efficiency; that is, non-exporting economic units are not efficient from this perspective. It emphasises neutral or export-oriented production of manufactures to maximise the efficient allocation of factors of production and a specialisation among nations according to their respective comparative cost advantages (Balassa, 1981). Moreover, it underlines the central role of manufacturing in economies of the periphery based on the transfer of industries to the periphery as a result of comparatively cheap and unskilled labour. Contrary to structural restrictions or bottlenecks imposed by industrialisation – as stressed by some ISI-authors – this "intuitive Darwinian rationale for free trade" (Bhagwati, 1991: 17) argues that the degree and the structure of protection in the periphery under ISI had a significant negative impact on the allocation of resources, and subsequently on exports and overall economic structure.

Probably the strongest argument of EOI supporters against ISI's infant industry protection and overall policy of state interventions is the rent-seeking behaviour it generates. As a result of market intervention under ISI – such as import licenses, tariffs, but in general any form of market intervention – economic units in general, including firms and countries, generate perverse (or nonmarket conforming) results in this environment: excess capacity to obtain rents provided by the state, over-utilisation of promotional instruments, and, in general, an economic structure aimed towards reaping the incentives provided by the state. In parallel, these mechanisms generate perverse social incentives and structures, as, in most of the cases, incentives are not taken by the initially expected groups (potential modern/industrial groups), but rather by rent-seeking and corrupt groups, which do not have an incentive to modernise/industrialise. The ubiquity of rent-seeking from this perspective is one of the most significant obstacles to development (Krueger, 1997).

The proposed alternative to interventionist economic management, from this perspective, is for the government to place the appropriate macroeconomic conditions for development – or the generation of a market-friendly environment – at the centre of economic policy. Opening the economy by abolishing tariff and non-tariff barriers to trade and investment, and combating inflation by means of restrictive monetary and fiscal policies, are the main macroeconomic goals of EOI. The state is minimalist, in this approach, while the private sector is conceived as the motor for future development and industrialisation.

It is in this international and national economic context that the major pillars and guidelines of the export-oriented liberalisation strategy in Mexico, since the 1980s, have developed (Aspe Armella, 1993; Dussel Peters, 2000; Salinas de Gortari, 2000, 2004; Sojo Garza-Aldape, 2005). The key features are:

1 Macroeconomic stabilisation is to 'induce' the process of microeconomic and sectoral growth and development, so all sectoral subsidies and specific policies were to be abolished in favour of neutral or horizontal policies.

2 The main priority of the government was to stabilise the macro economy. Since 1988, the government has prioritised controlling inflation, relative prices and the fiscal deficit, as well as attracting foreign investments as the main financing sources of the new strategy, since oil revenues and massive foreign credits were either not available or were insufficient. The macroeconomic priorities of the liberalisation strategy were backed by restrictive money and credit policies of the Central Bank.

3 The nominal exchange rate was used as an anti-inflationary anchor. Thus since the control of the inflation rate was the macroeconomic priority of the liberalisation strategy, the government did not allow devaluation, which would result in increasing inflation due to the higher domestic prices of imported inputs (Ibarra, 1999). Additionally, a stable and overvalued real exchange rate was seen as an incentive for foreign direct investments and particularly for investment in the financial sector.

4 Supported by the re-privatisation of the banking system beginning in the mid-1980s and the massive privatisation of state-owned industries, the Mexican private sector was to lead the economy out of the 'lost decade' of the 1980s through exports. The massive import liberalisation process, initiated at the end of 1985, was supposed to support the private manufacturing sector in order to orient it towards exports, as a result of cheaper international inputs.

5 Finally, government policies towards labour unions were of utmost significance. As reflected in the respective *Pactos Económicos* (or economic pacts between the public and private sectors, as well as with trade unions) since 1987, only a few (government-friendly) labour unions were deemed acceptable to negotiate inside firms and with the government, while the rest were declared illegal. This process, which has included violent disruptions of independent labour unions, has made national wage negotiations possible in Mexico within the framework of the respective economic pacts and with the objective to control real wage growth.

Up to the time of writing (2013) the Mexican government has continued, with few exceptions, with a consistent liberalisation strategy (PEF, 2013). NAFTA's implementation in 1994 is of fundamental relevance for the liberalisation strategy.[4] In a best case scenario, and allowing for a significant structural shift towards exports, the Mexican economy required an outlet and welcoming market for the commodities resulting from the structural change. This outlet was to be Mexico's main trading partner, the United States.

These issues are relevant for understanding the macroeconomic and policy perspective as of 2013. In the last semester of 2013 the government was attempting to allow the privatisation of the oil and electricity public companies. Additionally, and to understand the coherence and dogmatism of macroeconomic policies today, at least two policies stand out. On the one hand, and even in the international and domestic crisis since 2008, the government has explicitly rejected any kind of anti-cyclical policy, contrary to massive fiscal and sectoral programmes in countries such as China, Japan, United States and the European Union (Banxico, 2010).

On the other hand, the Secretary of Economy continued even in December of 2008 in the middle of the worst crisis since the 1990s with its unilateral liberalisation of import tariffs for manufactured goods.[5] The goal of macroeconomic stabilisation is still the main focus of macro and micro policy in Mexico in 2013.[6]

Alternative conceptual frameworks

As discussed above, most of the debates on industrialisation in Mexico have resulted from a macroeconomic perspective. Important alternative discussions on industrial organisation, trade, growth and development (Rodrik, 2001, 2007; Thirlwall, 2002) are also highly influenced by and come from a macroeconomic perspective. At least three concepts and methodological issues are relevant, from this alternative perspective, to enrich the understanding of industrial organisation in the context of 'glocal' processes, and to move beyond the discussion of the 1960s and 1970s: debates on (1) global commodity chains, (2) systemic competitiveness and (3) territorial endogeneity.

1   *Global commodity chains (GCC) and their segments.* The methodological contributions of Gary Gereffi, Jennifer Bair and Miguel Korzeniewicz, among others, have highlighted the importance of firms participating in GCC and specific segments of value chains (Gereffi and Korzeniewicz, 1994; Bair and Dussel Peters, 2006). From this perspective, GCC are constituted by different segments with specific characteristics: the yarn–textile–garments (YTG) GCC, for example, are constituted by dozens of different segments, from research and development (R&D) in new fabrics and nanotechnology to the assembly of specific parts and components in the garment industry. Although they are part of the same YTG-chain, they are extremely different in terms of technology required, employment, wages, training, financing, required equipment, participation of small and medium firms, type of investment, possibilities for trade and competition with local and global producers, and so forth. This customer-driven commodity chain is substantially different to the autoparts–automobile chain, controlled by producers and fabricators.

2   *Systemic competitiveness and collective efficiency.* Understood as a critique of Michael Porter's view of competitiveness (Porter, 1990) a group of authors at least since the 1990s have noted the importance of integrating the micro, meso and macro levels of analysis (Esser *et al.*, 1994). Thus, and contrary to a view that prioritises micro or macro aspects, this school of thought emphasises that competitiveness has to be understood at the micro, meso and macro levels; the exclusive prioritisation of one of the levels is insufficient and leads to simplistic, insufficient and limited policy proposals that do not understand the complexity of socioeconomic processes in space and time. Since then a group of authors have highlighted different factors of the systemic competitiveness approach, including the meso-economic level of competitiveness – or of inter-firm and institutional relations (Mesopartner, 2008; Meyer-Stamer, 2005), the governance and control of whole chains and respective segments and the technological and detailed characteristics of each of the products and processes. Otherwise, the analysis would lack specific knowledge and could effectively fall in a 'romanticism' by which an exclusive local perspective would be able to 'determine' the full scale of the GCC and even to negotiate with transnational corporations (Messner, 2002). Based on the contributions of these authors the meso-economic level of analysis is critical (Meyer-Stamer, 2001), as well as the degree of inter-firm integration that allows for different degrees of learning, innovation and collective efficiency (Lester and Piore, 2004; Humphrey and Schmitz, 2004).

3   *Territorial endogeneity.* While the former schools of thought and respective arguments are relevant in the current policy discussions and as an alternative to the neoclassical school of thought, they lack the concept and proposals of 'territorial endogeneity', i.e. the specific form in which territories integrate with the world market in specific segments of 'glocal' commodity chains and the particularities of the form of the systemic competitiveness they achieve (Dussel Peters, 2000, 2008). Thus, it is not the firms, but territories (whether a country, a region, a municipality or a zone) which are the socioeconomic starting point of analysis (Bair and Dussel Peters, 2006; Vázquez Barquero, 2005). From this perspective, it is important to incorporate systemic aspects of competitiveness and to move beyond a primitive macro- or microeconomic exclusive perspective. Starting from the respective territories and their potential for collective efficiency in territorial terms, the segments of GCC that integrate globally from a 'glocal' perspective – i.e. both glocal and global – need to be considered. Thus trade, industrial and business policies need both a global and territorial perspective which includes the particularities of the segments of a GCC at the relevant territorial level, so that narrowly national indicators of competitiveness and policy interventions are generally insufficient. 'Territorial endogeneity' recognises the importance of GCC, but highlights a territorial perspective as against a simplistic macroeconomic perspective that, for example, establishes a general association or elasticity between textile exports and the real exchange rate. In contrast, this approach allows for a detailed differentiation between the real exchange rate and many different items in the YTG-GCC (considering that the YTG-chain accounts for more than 4,500 items in the Harmonised Tariff System). Any direct association with the real exchange rate is unlikely to be relevant for most of these. In addition, each of the segments of a GCC requires a territorial analysis in terms of the industrial organisation and structures and factors that underlie these specific products and processes. Methodologically, the analysis should start with detailed products and processes distinguishing between products (from semiconductors to bananas) and their respective production processes (from R&D, logistics, assembly, manufacturing, final configuration and transportation for example). Policy proposals regarding an upgrading process are much more relevant from this stance. The contribution of systemic competitiveness – including micro, meso and macroeconomic levels of analysis – also enriches this debate and the policy options. However, in addition 'territorial endogeneity' usefully examines and measures supplier and client relationships, backward and forward linkages, value-added shares, R&D structures – and their respective effects – in specific segments of value-added chains in their respective territories.

Mexico's manufacturing sector

Based on EOI and Mexico's liberalisation strategy up to now, what are the main effects and results in Mexico's manufacturing sector? This section will examine three general issues regarding manufacturing – first, overall growth and trade performance; second, gross capital formation (GCF) and financing by the private sector; and third, an analysis of industrial organisation in order to understand the former general trends.

Table 18.1 reflects the disappointing growth performance of the Mexican economy since the introduction of the liberalisation strategy at the end of the 1980s. In terms of GDP per capita, Mexico's average annual growth rate was only 1.2 per cent during 1990–2012, which is far below that of many Latin American and Asian countries, particularly China (with an average growth of 9.4 per cent for the same period). This performance is also low by Mexican historical standards over the period 1940–60, with per capita growth being about 3.3 per cent on

Table 18.1 GDP per capita growth rates – selected countries, 1980–2012

	1980–2012	1990–2000	1990–2012	2000–2012
Argentina	0.6	3.3	2.8	3.0
Australia	1.9	2.1	1.8	1.5
Bolivia	0.6	1.5	1.9	2.3
Brazil	1.0	1.0	1.6	2.2
Canada	1.4	1.9	1.3	0.8
Chile	3.3	4.7	3.8	2.9
China	8.9	9.3	9.4	8.9
Costa Rica	1.4	1.9	1.3	0.8
East Asia & Pacific (all income levels)	4.2	3.4	4.2	4.7
High income OECD	1.7	1.9	1.4	0.9
Latin America & Caribbean (all income levels)	1.0	1.5	1.8	2.1
Mexico	0.7	1.5	1.2	1.0
United States	1.6	2.2	1.4	0.7
World	1.7	1.5	1.9	2.2

Source: Author's calculations based on World Bank (2013).

average. For the later period, 2000–12, per capita growth was significantly lower than in Latin America as a whole and was similar to that of the high-income OECD economies.

As expected by the EOI and the liberalisation strategy, Mexican overall trade and export performance has been outstanding in historical terms as well as compared with other economies. Trade as a percentage of GDP more than tripled for the periods 1961–80 and 2001–12, accounting for 58.2 per cent in the latter period (see Table 18.2).[7] This performance is the result of the liberalisation strategy and the implementation of NAFTA in 1994. The importance of trade in GDP is far higher than in other large countries, such as Brazil and the United States.

Two other tendencies in the economy are significant in understanding the Mexican manufacturing sector under liberalisation. On the one hand, there has been a lack of dynamism of GCF as a percentage of GDP (see Table 18.3) with the ratio remaining relatively stable throughout the period. Particularly significant is that Mexico's – and Latin America & Caribbean's – GCF

Table 18.2 Trade as percentage of GDP – selected countries and regions, 1961–2012

	1961–1980	1981–1990	1991–2000	2001–2012
Argentina	12.91	15.56	19.48	40.22
Brazil	15.20	17.33	17.87	25.76
Chile	33.78	53.71	56.78	69.67
China	10.62	24.89	38.52	58.85
Costa Rica	61.48	65.65	83.54	91.57
East Asia & Pacific (all income levels)	31.66	40.51	44.63	60.57
European Union	43.84	55.02	59.90	76.07
Korea, Republic	43.47	65.82	62.49	86.76
Latin America & Caribbean (all income levels)	25.58	33.54	41.90	49.28
Mexico	18.40	30.86	51.52	58.21
United States	13.02	18.73	22.93	26.91
World	29.91	39.01	44.54	55.58

Source: Author's calculations based on World Bank (2013).

Table 18.3 Gross capital formation as a percentage of GDP – selected countries and regions, 1961–2012

	1961–1980	1981–1990	1991–2000	2001–2012
Argentina	24.24	18.81	17.99	20.00
Brazil	21.48	20.70	18.58	17.88
Chile	18.06	18.89	25.01	22.18
China	25.72	36.09	38.95	43.51
East Asia & Pacific (all income levels)	31.57	30.65	30.77	27.77
European Union	24.75	21.58	20.38	19.88
Latin America & Caribbean (all income levels)	21.87	20.70	20.64	20.99
Mexico	21.18	21.85	23.05	24.16
OECD members	24.33	22.29	21.27	19.96
United States	19.85	19.45	18.50	17.79
World	24.01	23.16	22.42	21.64

Source: Author's calculations based on World Bank (2013).

coefficient is at a level far below that of East Asia & Pacific and China. In addition, comparative international data show that Latin America & Caribbean (LAC), and particularly Mexico, have very low levels of domestic credit to the private sector as a percentage of GDP; in the case of Mexico, for example, throughout 1960–2012, levels were never above 30 per cent, while LAC has had levels above 40 per cent since 2010.[8] East Asia & Pacific as well as China, however, have a level of private sector credit of more than 100 per cent of GDP since the beginning of the twenty-first century. Both variables show that the growth process in Mexico since liberalisation has not been accompanied by shifts in financing and investment, both compared with Mexico's own historical performance but, much more importantly, compared with competitors.

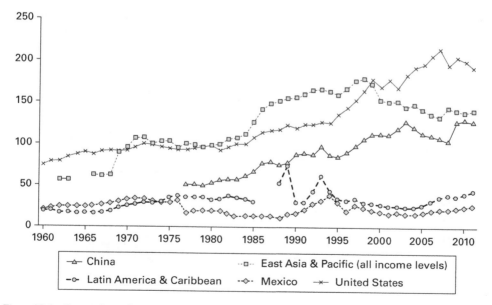

Figure 18.1 Domestic credit to private sector (percentage of GDP 1960–2012).

Source: Author's calculations based on World Bank (2013).

What are the main reasons for this disappointing performance of the economy and of manufacturing in particular? A number of points are relevant for understanding the structural change in Mexican manufacturing since the launch of the liberalisation strategy.

First, there is the surprising, and increasing, fall of manufacturing's share in GDP and employment. In spite of the initial positive expectations of NAFTA and the trade opening for manufacturing (Dussel Peters and Gallagher, 2013), the sector has witnessed a rapid fall in its share in GDP and total employment throughout the period and particularly since 2000 (see Figure 18.2). In the case of GDP, manufacturing's share fell from levels close to 24 per cent of GDP in 1988 to close to 16–17 per cent since 2005, while manufacturing's share in total employment decreased from above 35 per cent at the end of the 1980s to less than 27 per cent since 2009. In both cases there is a general downward trend over the period and particularly since the late 1990s and the beginning of the 2000s. What are the main reasons for this performance since liberalisation?

At least three issues are relevant for understanding Mexico's manufacturing structure and its decline under the liberalisation strategy. First, Mexican exports since the late 1980s increasingly have depended on 'temporary imports to be exported (TIE)'. Under EOI there have been important incentives in terms of value-added and income taxes, as well as tariffs, which encourage the import of parts and components to allow fast transformation processes in Mexico to allow their export in manufactured or semi-manufactured form (mainly to the USA).[9] Figure 18.3 shows this composition of Mexico's exports by process for 1993–2010, highlighting that exports are highly dependent on TIE and oil, accounting for almost 81.6 and 14.0 per cent of total exports during the period, respectively.[10] As a result of the former trends, EOI in Mexico's manufacturing sector has incentivised a highly dynamic and export-oriented manufacturing sector, based on TIE and ever-increasing imports with little domestic value added, also described as 'import-oriented industrialisation' (Dussel Peters, 2000). This is the main cause of the low levels of value added and 'territorial endogeneity' of Mexican exports and in manufacturing in general, given the incentives provided by the government for several decades. Thus EOI-processes in Mexico are highly dependent on imported parts and components and there is a general lack of backward and forward linkages with effects in terms of limited R&D, upgrading options, wages and employment. The issue has been

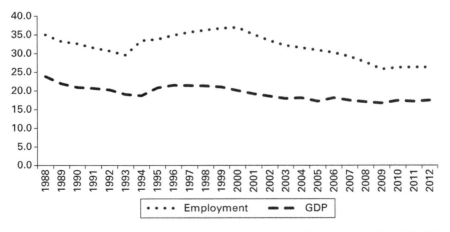

Figure 18.2 Mexico's manufacturing GDP and employment (share of respective totals), 1988–2012.

Source: Author's calculations based on World Bank (2013).

analysed and discussed in Mexico for decades. OECD-WTO TIVA (2013) examines, for example, how Mexico's domestic content in gross exports fell over 1995–2009 and shows how it is significantly lower than most OECD countries, as well as compared with Brazil, China and Russia, among others. The main reason is the low level of 'indirect' domestic content that is the indirect contribution of national suppliers. 'Indirect' domestic content in Mexico's exports is the lowest compared with other nations in the machinery and equipment category, the most significant export category since the implementation of NAFTA.

TIE often reflects primitive production processes – in some cases of highly sophisticated goods in autoparts, telecommunications and aeronautics, creating low levels of value added, R&D[11] and 'territorial endogeneity', since the higher value-added segments of global chains, as well as the production of parts and components and segments related to services, are typically located elsewhere in competitor economies. These TIE processes have become the core of Mexico's manufacturing sector, significantly affecting its value-added and employment structure.

Second, Mexico's liberalisation strategy has resulted in a massive socioeconomic polarisation process. Only a few households, firms, branches, sectors, and regions in Mexico have benefited since the late 1980s, while most have seen their economic position either remaining similar or declining. In terms of exports, for example, around 6,000 firms accounted for manufacturing exports during 2007–10 – or around 1.4 per cent of manufacturing firms in 2008 – while 1,100 manufacturing firms with more than 500 workers accounted for more than 80 per cent of total manufacturing exports (INEGI, 2013); at the branch level, only three manufacturing chapters of the Harmonised Tariff System – autoparts, automobiles and electronics – accounted for more than 71 per cent of total exports during 2001–12 (Monitor de la Manufactura Mexicana, 2013). As a result, the liberalisation strategy in Mexico has benefited a small group of big export-oriented firms with few and decreasing domestic backward linkages with subsequent relatively small effects on the domestic economy in terms of suppliers, production, wages and value added.

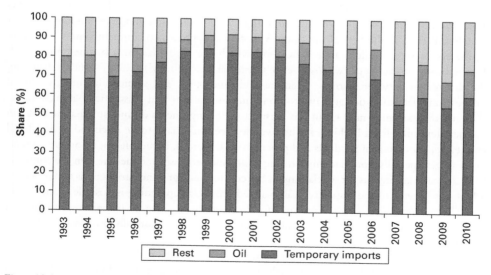

Figure 18.3 Export structure by type of programme (share of total exports), 1993–2003.

Source: Author's calculations based on SICM (2012).

Third, and even for this relatively small and 'successful' small group of capital-intensive and export-oriented firms in Mexico, since the end of the 1990s and beginning of 2000s competition from Asia and particularly from China has increased drastically and Mexico has been displaced profoundly in value-added chains such as electronics, YTG, toys and furniture. The important exception is the autoparts–automobile value-added chain where the country has a major advantage in transport costs to the USA. For the period 2000–11, for example, 95.81 per cent of Mexico's manufacturing exports to the USA in 2011 were under 'threat' of Chinese competition, while 74.45 per cent of US manufacturing exports to Mexico were under 'threat' from China (Dussel Peters and Gallagher, 2013). As this latter study shows, value-added chains such as YTG were successful in the first period of NAFTA (1994–2000), but have not been able to compete with Asia and China since then; in the case of Mexico the YTG value-added chain has lost more than 50 per cent of its employment since 2000. In aggregate terms, China is today Mexico's second trading partner, but in an import–export relationship of 10:1 in 2012, and thus China is becoming the main source of Mexico's trade balance deficit. Asia and particularly China have thus become a massive challenge for EOI in Mexico and the overall North American integration process.

Conclusions

As discussed in the first section, a dialogue between micro- and macroeconomists is still relevant for understanding industrial organisation and manufacturing under current globalisation. The theoretical debates since the 1960s in terms of dependency, imperfect markets, export-oriented industrialisation and liberalisation are critical for an overall understanding of manufacturing in most countries. In addition, however, global commodity chains, systemic competitiveness and territorial endogeneity offer methodologies and an understanding in 'space and time' of specific segments of value-added chains that is critical in the twenty-first century. From this perspective, macroeconomic elasticities and relationships are, in most of the cases, of limited help in understanding the increasing complexity of specific segments of value-added chains in particular products and processes. The Harmonised Tariff System (HTS)[12] today presents information, at the 10-digit level, for more than 17,000 products and generalisations, that is not relevant even in the best of the cases. A 'systemic' approach to competitiveness – respecting macro, meso and micro approaches – in which the particular form of integration with globalisation is fundamental (what we term 'territorial endogeneity') allows for such a dialogue. The differences between harnesses, lemons and pineapples, and semiconductors are critical and beyond 'deterministic' and macroeconomic associations and elasticities between trade, GDP and the exchange rate. From this perspective the arguments on industrialisation in Latin America stemming from Prebisch in the twentieth century, have to be discussed in detail and revisited for thousands of products and processes and, there is, by no means, a positive association between specialisation in manufacturing goods and processes and income. On the contrary, there are many arguments for specialising in agricultural and agro-industrial goods and processes in higher segments of the respective value-added chains, as upgrading is possible in any value chain. These topics are critical in terms of policy proposals, since an overall industrialisation process is by no means a necessary condition for success, as simplistically proposed in the past and currently still argued by some.

The case of Mexico's industrial organisation is strongly related to the latter conceptual discussion. Based on EOI, Mexico's liberalisation strategy strongly engaged in a specialisation in manufacturing goods. However, and as discussed above, Mexican exports have been extremely dependent on TIE and a policy stance which provides incentives to import parts, components and other processes for goods made for export. As the Mexican case shows, however, independent of the particular goods concerned this has resulted in little employment, with the use of relatively capital-intensive processes with few domestic backward linkages. Since the key inputs are imported, few innovations and R&D processes are required, resulting in a lack of competitiveness. Thus over several decades a dogmatic macroeconomic perspective has combined with perverse incentives to block an upgrading process. Mexico's manufacturing sector is thus an interesting case for understanding the limits of such an EOI strategy and its increasing unsustainability in terms of competitiveness *vis à vis* Asia and China. As discussed above, Mexico's manufacturing sector is extremely weak against Chinese competition in its main export market – the United States – and domestically has been massively displaced since 2000 in terms of its share in GDP and employment, and this is in spite of a first stage of successful integration into NAFTA.

An analysis based on territorial endogeneity suggests the need for systemic instruments to support the manufacturing sector in terms of macro-, meso- and microeconomic policies to allow for an upgrading process in specific products and processes.[13] After more than 20 years, NAFTA and market-friendly policy instruments have failed to develop Mexican manufacturing and its experience has raised profound questions about these policies and overall NAFTA integration.

Finally, while the results of EOI have been extremely limited and have caused a decline in manufacturing share in total GDP and employment, the general argument of this chapter is not a 'return' to ISI and policies and programmes of the 1970s and earlier. Such a 'back to the future' view does not make sense and is not feasible for Mexico's manufacturing sector. The argument is that considering the massive structural changes in Mexican manufacturing since the late 1980s, a new understanding is required based on the concepts and methodological approach of GCC, systemic competitiveness and territorial endogeneity – and with new policies to address the massive new challenges posed in recent decades for competitiveness in specific products and processes in particular territories. Otherwise, EOI will continue to be successful in terms of exports, productivity and other variables, but with an ever declining share of manufacturing in GDP, employment and particularly in terms of declining backward and forward linkages within the economy.

Notes

1 For a full analysis of this discussion, see: Dussel Peters (2000), Moreno-Brid and Ros (2009) and Ros (2000).
2 The approach of Kaldor (1966) and his three empirical laws or generalisations are from this perspective highly related to Hirschman's approach: first, a strong causality between economic growth and growth in manufacturing; second, a strong association between growth in a specific sector with productivity growth as a result of static and dynamic returns to scale; and third, a positive causality between growth in manufacturing and productivity beyond manufacturing (Kaldor, 1984).
3 See also the work of authors such as Samir Amin and Theotonio dos Santos, among others (Amin *et al.,* 1971; dos Santos, 1970)
4 Since the existence of statistics, the United States has been Mexico's most important trading partner, so that an export-orientation without the option of increasing exports to the United States did not make political sense (Salinas de Gortari, 2000, 2004; Weintraub, 1991).
5 By Decree the Executive sector in Mexico liberalised unilaterally more than 8,000 items on 25 December 2008 (Dussel Peters, 2009). As a result, the average tariff fell from 11.5 per cent in 2008 to 6.9 per cent in 2010 (PEF, 2010: 208).
6 While the new administration under Peña Nieto since 2013 stresses the importance of an industrial policy, it explicitly rejects the option of granting subsidies or major interventions, and highlights the goal of removing barriers and obstacles for development such as monopolies and oligopolies, so that in practice the policy stance of the current administration is very similar to EOI and the liberalisation strategy since 1988 (Moreno-Brid, 2013).

7 The change in the export-to-GDP ratio from 8.4 per cent during 1961–80 and to levels above 25 per cent on average for the periods 1991–2000 and 2001–12 illustrates an important important structural change in the economy (World Bank, 2013).

8 This is particularly true for Mexico's manufacturing sector. Financing granted by commercial banks based in Mexico to firms – as a percentage of manufacturing GDP – fell by 68 per cent during 1994–2012, while it increased by more than 380 per cent to the public sector (Monitor de la Manufactura Mexicana, 2013).

9 TIE-programmes in Mexico have been developed since the mid-1960s and are related to maquiladora and other export programmes which allow exporting firms to avoid value-added taxes, income taxes and import tariffs. Depending on the specific programme, different incentives are on offer. For a full discussion, see Dussel Peters (2003) and Katz and Dussel Peters (2006).

10 TIE, for example, typically includes processes in which parts and components – from electronics to automobiles and agriculture – are temporarily imported to be exported in a modified form; oil is not a TIE since it does not require temporary imports. While there are no specific statistics on the value added of TIE, in general, the ratio of domestic inputs to total inputs has been between 2 and 4 per cent since the beginning of these processes up to now.

11 Mexico's R&D in terms of GDP has been declining since the 1980s and accounts today for 0.4 per cent. This is directly related to the specialisation pattern of manufacturing based on TIE.

12 The HTS registers trade information at the 2-, 4-, 6-, 8- and 10-digit level, while the International Standard Industrial Classification (ISIC) includes a group of variables relevant for the manufacturing sector.

13 As discussed above, upgrading processes do not necessarily refer to highly sophisticated processes, as upgrading in apparently primitive processes can still create positive economic effects and can allow for future upgrading in new and more technologically sophisticated products.

References

Amin, S., Bettelheim, C., Arghiri, E. and Palloix, C. 1971. *Imperialismo y comercio internacional. El intercambio desigual*, Siglo XXI.

Aspe Armella, P. 1993. *El camino mexicano de la transformación económica*. Fondo de Cultura Económica.

Bair, J. and Dussel Peters, E. 2006. Global Commodity Chains and Endogenous Growth: Export Dynamism and Development in Mexico and Honduras. *World Development*. 29 (11): 203–221.

Balassa, B. 1981. *The Newly Industrializing Countries in the World Economy*. Oxford: Pergamon Press.

Banxico (Banco de México). 2010. *Informe anual 2009*. México: Banco de México.

Bhagwati, J. 1991. Is Free Trade Passé After All? In Koekkoek, A. and Mennes, L. B. M. (eds.). *International Trade and Global Development*. London: Routledge: 10–42.

Cardoso, F. and Faleto, E. 1969. *Dependencia y desarrollo en América Latina*, Siglo XXI.

Dos Santos, T. 1978. *Imperialismo y dependencia*. Mexico City: Ediciones Era.

Dussel Peters, E. 2000. *Polarizing Mexico: The Impact of Liberalization Strategy*. Boulder, CO: Lynne Rienner.

Dussel Peters, E. 2003. To be or Not to be Maquiladora. Is That the Question? *Comercio Exterior*. 53(4): 328–336.

Dussel Peters, E. 2008. GCCs and Development: A Conceptual and Empirical Review. *Competition and Change*. 12 (1): 11–27.

Dussel Peters, E. 2009. La manufactura mexicana: ¿opciones de recuperación? *Economía Informa*. 357: 41–52.

Dussel Peters, E. and Gallagher, K. 2013. NAFTA's Uninvited Guest: China and the Disintegration of North American Trade. *CEPAL Review*. 110: 83–108.

Esser, K., Hillebrand, W., Meyer-Stamer, J. and Messner, D. 1994. *Systemische Wettbewerbsfähigkeit. Internationale Wettbewerbsfähigkeit der Unternehmen und Anforderungen an die Politik*. Berlin: German Development Institute.

Gereffi, G. and Korzeniewicz, M. 1994. *Commodity Chains and Global Capitalism*. Westport, CT: Praeger.

Hirschman, A. O. 1958. *The Strategy of Economic Development*. New Haven, CT: Yale University Press.

Humphrey, J. and Schmitz, H. 2004. Governance in Global Value Chains. In Schmitz, H. (ed.). *Local Enterprises in the Global Economy*. Cheltenham: Edward Elgar: 95–109.

Ibarra, D. 1999. *Política y economía. Semblanzas y ensayos*. México City: Miguel Ángel Porrúa.

INEGI (Instituto Nacional de Estadística, Geografía e Informática). 2013. *Banco de Información Estadística*. Mexico City: INEGI.

Kaldor, N. 1966. *Causes of the Slow Rate of Economic Growth of the United Kingdom*. Cambridge: Cambridge University Press.

Kaldor, N. 1984. *Causes of Growth and Stagnation in the World Economy* (Raffaele Mattioli Lectures). Cambridge: Cambridge University Press.

Katz, J. and Dussel Peters, E. 2006. Diferentes estrategias en el Nuevo Modelo Latinoamericano: importaciones temporalis para su reexportación y transformación de materias primas. In Middlebrook, I. and Zepeda Miramontes, E. (eds.). *La industria maquiladora de exportación: ensamble, manufactura y desarrollo económico*. México, D.F.: Universidad Autónoma Metropolitana Azcapotzalco, División de Ciencias Sociales y Humanidades, Coordinación de Difusión y Publicaciones: Eón: 49–103.

Krueger, A. 1978. *Liberalization Attempts and Consequences*. Cambridge, MA: Ballinger Publishing Company.

Krueger, A 1997. Trade Policy and Economic Development: How We Learn. *The American Economic Review*. 87(1): 1–22.

Krugman, P. 1981. Trade, Accumulation, and Uneven Development. In Krugman, P. (ed.). *Rethinking International Trade*. Cambridge, MA: The MIT Press: 93–105.

Lester, R. and Piore, M. 2004. *Innovation: The Missing Dimension*. Cambridge, MA: Harvard University Press.

Lewis, W. A. 1954. Economic Development with Unlimited Supplies of Labour. *Manchester School of Economic and Social Studies*. 22: 139–191.

Mesopartner. 2008. *Milestones in a Process of Innovation, Change and Development*. Buenos Aires and Dortmund: Mesopartner.

Messner, D. 2002. The Concept of the 'World Economic Triangle': Global Governance Patterns and Options for Regions. *IDS Working Paper* 173: Brighton: Institute of Development Studies, University of Sussex: 1–99.

Meyer-Stamer, J. 2001. Was ist meso? Systemische Wettebewerbsfähigkeit: Analyseraster, Benchmarking-Tool und Handlungsrahmen. *INEF-REPORT* 55. Duisburg: Institut für Entwicklung und Frieden (Institute for Development and Peace), University of Duisburg-Essen.

Meyer-Stamer, J. 2005. *Systemic Competitiveness Revisited. Conclusions for Technical Assistance in Private Sector Development*. Duisburg: Mesopartner.

Monitor de la Manufactura Mexicana. 2013. *Monitor de la Manufactura Mexicana 10*. Mexico City: Cechimex/UNAM (Universidad Nacional Autónoma de México).

Moreno-Brid, J. C. 2013. Industrial Policy: A Missing Link in Mexico's Quest for Export-Led Growth. *Latin American Policy*. 4(2): 216–237.

Moreno-Brid, J. C. and Ros, J. 2009. *Development and Growth in the Mexican Economy*. Oxford: Oxford University Press.

Nurkse, R. 1955. *Problems of Capital Formation in Underdeveloped Countries*. Oxford: Basil Blackwell.

OECD-WTO. 2013. *Database and Analysis OECD-WTO Trade in Value Added*. Paris: Organisation for Economic Co-operation and Development–World Trade Organization – downloaded from http://www.oecd.org/industry/ind/measuringtradeinvalue-addedanoecd-wtojointinitiative.html

PEF. 2010. *Cuarto Informe Presidencial. Anexo Estadístico*. Mexico City: PEF (Poder Ejecutivo Federal).

PEF. 2013. *Plan Nacional de Desarrollo 2013–2018*. Mexico City: PEF (Poder Ejecutivo Federal).

Porter, M. 1990. *The Competitive Advantage of Nations*. New York: Free Press.

Prebisch, R. 1950. *The Economic Development of Latin America and Its Principal Problems*. New York: United Nations Department of Economic Affairs.

Prebisch, R. 1964. *Nueva política comercial para el desarrollo*. Mexico City: Fondo de Cultura Económica.

Rodrik, D. 2001. *The Global Governance of Trade as if Development Really Mattered*. New York: United Nations Development Programme.

Rodrik, D. 2007. *One Economics: Many Recipes*. Princeton, NJ: Princeton University Press.

Ros, J. 2000. *Development Theory and the Economics of Growth*. Ann Arbor: The University of Michigan Press.

Rosenstein-Rodan, P. N. 1961. Notes on the Theory of the Big Push. In Ellis, H.S. and Wallich, H. (eds.). *Economic Development for Latin America*. New York: Macmillan (St. Martin's Press): 57–67.

Salinas de Gortari, C. 2000. *México: Un paso difícil a la modernidad*. Mexico City: Plaza y Janés.

Salinas de Gortari, C. 2004. Una agenda comercial para el largo plazo. *Foreign Affairs en Español*. 4 (1): 2–16.

SICM. 2012. *Sistema de Información de Comercio de México*. México: Secretaría de Economía.

Sojo Garza-Aldape, E. 2005. *De la alternancia al desarrollo. Políticas públicas del gobierno del cambio*. Mexico City: Fondo de Cultura Económica.

Stiglitz, J. E. 1989. Imperfect Information in the Product Market. In Schmalensee, R. and Willig, R. (eds.). *Handbook of Industrial Organization*. Amsterdam: Elsevier: 769–847.

Thirlwall, A. 2002. *The Nature of Economic Growth: An Alternative Framework for Understanding the Performance of Nations*. Cheltenham: Edward Elgar.

Vázquez Barquero, A. 2005. *Las nuevas fuerzas del desarrollo*. Barcelona: Antoni Bosch.

Von Hayek, A.F. 1992. The Pretence of Knowledge (1974). In Lindbeck, A. (ed.). *Nobel Lectures: Economics 1969–1980*. Singapore: World Scientific Publishing Co. – downloaded from http://www.nobelprize.org/nobel_prizes/economic-sciences/laureates/1974/hayek-lecture.html

Weintraub, S. 1991. Regionalism and the GATT: The North American Initiative. *SAIS Review*. 11(1) Winter–Spring: 45–57. Baltimore: Project MUSE.

World Bank. 1993. *The East Asian Miracle:* Economic Growth and Public Policy. New York: Oxford University Press for the World Bank.

World Bank. 2013. *World Development Indicators*. Washington, DC: World Bank – accessed online from www.worldbank.org

19

INDUSTRIAL DEVELOPMENT IN INDIA

Uma Kambhampati

In the 1950s and 1960s the Indian Government, like the governments of many other developing countries, used industrial policy to facilitate and encourage the transition from agriculture to industry. Unlike many other developing country governments, however, it also had an active competition policy to avoid excess concentration of assets and of production. Together these policies were intended to facilitate its objective of growth with industrialisation but also with socio-economic equity. During this period, the manufacturing sector was seen as central to economic growth both by academic economists and policy makers for a number of reasons. Its processes enabled division of labour and specialisation, allowing it to benefit from increasing returns to scale, unlike the agricultural and service sectors. Manufacturing was also seen as benefiting from longer and deeper linkages (both backward and forward) and within this, the heavy industrial sector was credited with the longest and deepest linkages (a characteristic that made it the focal sector in Socialist development plans). The manufacturing sector also experienced agglomeration economies and benefits from dynamic returns to scale through learning by doing and technological improvements.

In addition to these advantages, it was felt that the shift to manufacturing was part of the 'natural' order of development because of changes on both the demand and supply sides. Thus, increasing incomes would result in an increase in the demand for manufactured products (first towards processed food and then low level consumer goods followed by higher technology consumer durables). On the supply side, increasing productivity in the agricultural sector would create an excess supply of labour in this sector which could be more productively employed in other sectors. The growth of the manufacturing sector, it was expected, would absorb this excess labour and help employ these workers provided that there was sufficient investment in the sector. Some versions of this transition formed the basis of the Lewis (1956) theory of economic development and its extensions. Rostow (1960) also argued that 'take off' into growth would require structural change towards a key sector (usually manufacturing). This transition towards manufacturing would be interrupted if there was insufficient investment in the manufacturing sector and it is to avoid this that many developing countries used industrial policies in the 1950s and 1960s. Like most developing countries becoming independent during this period, Indian planners were not convinced that industrialisation could be left to the market or that the market outcome would be appropriate for India.

In the context of its decision not to leave industrial development to the market, the Indian Government used a range of policy instruments to encourage the manufacturing sector including: (i) five year plans to target resource allocation; (ii) delineating certain industries for the public/private sectors; (iii) direct public sector involvement; and (iv) licenses and permits in order to facilitate the development of the domestic manufacturing sector. All of this was within a broad Import Substituting Industrialisation (ISI) approach which aimed at greater self-sufficiency. To allay concerns about equity, and in particular the concentration of assets in a few hands, they also used competition policy and encouraged the growth of small firms. The Indian private sector had been dominated by large industrial houses since before Independence. The existence of these industrial houses (which were family owned, family run and produced a diversified range of products and services) made control of concentration very problematic at market level. Competition policy ensured that, on the one hand, large firms did not grow larger without being subjected to regulations but on the other, that small firms also voluntarily restricted their growth for fear that they would outgrow the 'small firm' limit and lose many benefits associated with this status (Dougherty *et al.*, 2009). This resulted in a bimodal size distribution with a small number of large firms and a very large number of small firms.

In this chapter, we will discuss the growth and industrialisation strategy followed by the Indian Government from a historical perspective. We will analyse how this strategy has impacted on the structure of the Indian manufacturing sector. We will also consider the institutional changes of the 1990s and their consequences for the industrial sector.

Industrial policy

In the Indian context, the centrality of manufacturing and the role of the state in industrialising the economy found expression in the five-year plans, the first of which became operational in 1951. This plan helped to launch the industrialisation strategy, in particular the development of a mixed economy (with significant public investment and production as well as private sector involvement). This was first formalised in the Industrial Policy Resolution of 1948 which stated that "the state must play a progressively active role in the development of industries" (Government of India, nd[1]). This policy divided the economy into four sectors – those that were to be preserved as state monopolies (railways, atomic energy, defence, etc.); those that were to remain state monopolies for new units (iron and steel, mining, telecommunications, ship building, etc.); state-regulated sectors (machine tools, fertilisers, cement, etc.) and the unregulated private sector. The large industrial houses were part of the regulated private sector, while many of the small firms were part of the unregulated private sector. This classification gave way to the more formal Schedules A, B and C of the Industrial Policy Resolution of 1956 (Government of India, nd).

It was the Second Five Year plan (1956–61) (Government of India, various years (b)) which specifically targeted the industrial sector and, following the Mahalanobis Model (see Box 19.1), attempted to determine the optimal allocation of investment across sectors to maximise growth. A major aspect of the Second Five Year Plan was the central role given to the public sector in the Indian economy. A number of reasons were given for this emphasis on the public sector, including: first, that the scale of investment required in many industries was often too large for the private sector; second, that the public sector was seen to offset the economic power that concentrated in private hands; and third, that private investors often required higher risk premia for investment in some industries than was considered socially desirable. These problems were especially apparent in the heavy industrial sector that was being encouraged as part of the Mahalanobis strategy (elaborated in Box 19.1). In addition, the public sector was viewed as a policy instrument that would help the state to control the composition of economic activity, influence the wage and employment policies of the private sector and generate investible surpluses. In this context, the Industrial Development and Regulation Act (IDRA) (Government of India, various years (c); 1994; Sivadasan, 2006a) introduced at the start of the Second Plan in 1956 was the specific policy instrument that allowed the state to use industrial licenses to channel public investment and to control entry, exit, product mix, expansion and therefore the patterns of investment in the economy. This Act promoted an active role for the state in the development of infrastructure and of key sectors of the economy like defence, iron and steel, power and energy.

Box 19.1 The Mahalanobis Model

The Mahalanobis Model, which was the basis of the Second Five Year Plan in India, is also called the Feldman–Mahalanobis Model because of its similarity to the Feldman framework on which Soviet Planning in the 1930s was based. Mahalanobis built a model of an economy with two sectors – capital goods and consumer goods. While capital goods enter into the production of consumer goods and of other capital goods, consumer goods are final products. The model was that of a closed economy with no government and capital was not subject to diminishing returns. Within this model, therefore, growth could be achieved by increasing the output of the capital goods sector and this implies that, in the initial stages of development, output of the consumer goods sector is low until the industrial base has been sufficiently enlarged by investment in the capital goods sector.

In application, the Mahalanobis Model became part of the Nehru–Mahalanobis Strategy (Balakrishnan, 2010) which resulted in fast growth of the heavy goods sector. These heavy goods were described by Mahalanobis himself as "machine-building complexes with a large capacity for the manufacture of machinery to produce steel, chemicals, fertiliser, electricity, transport equipment etc." (Mahalanobis, 1955 and as quoted in Joshi, 1982). Given both the scarcity of capital goods and the foreign exchange gap, producing capital goods at home was seen as a guaranteed way to grow. The impact of this strategy can be seen on the structure of Indian industry (significant contribution of the capital goods sector) and also on a relatively large contribution made by the public sector in manufacturing.

At the same time that the public sector was being encouraged to provide investment in the large scale, heavy industrial sector, the cottage, village and small scale sector was also emphasised. This began with the Industrial Policy Resolution of 1956 and was continued in the 1977 and 1980 New Industrial Policy Statements (Government of India, nd). Given the factor endowments (inadequate access to capital, the abundant supplies of low skilled labour and the lack of standardisation that is inherent in production that is not mechanised) of the Indian economy and the extent of market imperfections (through transport barriers, for instance which limit the boundaries of the market to the purely local), it is not surprising that the small scale industrial sector continued to thrive through most of this period.

While the Third, Fourth and Fifth Plans (Government of India, various years (b)) highlighted investment in a variety of sectors including defence (in the wake of wars with both China and Pakistan), education and employment, the Sixth Plan (1980–85) began a shift away from state involvement in the industrial sector with the first moves towards liberalisation

(Government of India, 1991). As early as the New Industrial Policy Statement of 1977 (Government of India, nd), the role of the state was remarkable by its absence. The problems with the strategy being followed had become becoming increasingly obvious, though it would take almost another decade before attempts would be made to deal with the most obvious of these problems. This shift is clear from the information contained in Table 19.1, which highlights the reforms undertaken in 1985 and again in 1991.

Outcome of the industrial strategy

What was the outcome of the complex and highly structured industrial policy that had been introduced in India? Given its emphasis on manufacturing, the public sector and the heavy industrial sector, we might expect these sectors to have been at the forefront of the growth of the Indian economy. A problem with judging the success of industrial policy is the counterfactual against which the performance is to be measured. What would the contribution of the industrial sector have been in the absence of industrial policy? Surely, the Indian industrial sector would not have been as diversified as it is today, but might growth have been faster? Alternatively, might the firms in this sector have been more efficient?

In what follows, we will consider the contribution of the manufacturing sector and its diversification across sectors and segmentation by ownership as well as its productivity performance.

- *Contribution of the manufacturing sector to GDP.* As Table 19.2 shows, the manufacturing sector in India contributed only 13.7 per cent of GDP at the start of the industrial policy regime in 1960 and this rose to only about 16 per cent in the mid-1980s after the implementation of seven five-year plans. It reached a peak of 17.3 per cent in 1995 before falling back to 13.9 per cent in 2011, despite many years of relatively high growth in the economy. This contribution is low by historic BRIC standards. Brazil, for instance, saw the contribution of its manufacturing sector peak at 33 per cent of GDP (in 1980) and China saw it peak at 40 per cent of GDP in 1978. Turning to the broader industrial sector, we find that in India it grew from 19 per cent of GDP in 1960 to a peak of 28 per cent in 2005 after which it began to fall.[2] This compares to a peak of 44 per cent of GDP in Brazil (in 1980) and of 48 per cent both in China (in 1980) and in Russia (in 1990). This relatively poor performance in India was despite the elaborate industrial policy framework that was in place during this period. This poor performance has been recognised by the Government of India which set a target of 25 per cent of GDP by 2025 for the manufacturing sector (Government of India, 2011a). The table also indicates that the sectoral transition in India was away from agriculture but towards services.
- *Diversification of industrial structure and role of heavy industries.* As we have seen in Box 19.1, the Nehru–Mahalanobis strategy emphasised investment in the capital goods sector and especially in the heavy industrial sector. This was to be at the cost of the consumer goods industrial sector. Table 19.3 indicates that the top 7 sectors in manufacturing contributed about 65 per cent of total manufacturing output and 56 per cent of value added in 2010–11. More significantly, barring the food and textiles sector, the other 5 sectors all relate to relatively capital intensive production. Thus, basic metals, chemicals and machine equipment all contribute a significant proportion of total output in India. Singh (2008) argues that this diversified structure is thanks largely to India's industrial policy, its emphasis on the heavy industrial sector and on the public sector which facilitated the investment in these sectors.

Table 19.1 Timeline of industrial policy in India, 1947–1991

Policies	Main features
Industrial Policy Resolution of 1948	Government responsible for promoting, assisting and regulating the development of industry; public sector will play an active role in industry; demarcated sectors for public and private spheres; small scale industries to be encouraged because they are employment intensive and therefore inclusive
Industrial Development and Regulation Act (IDRA), 1951	First set up the industrial licensing regime in India, of which the 1956 reforms were a part
Industrial Policy Resolution of 1956	Introduced Schedules A, B and C given the Government's objective of planned and rapid development through socialist means; industries of basic and strategic importance in the public sector; reinforced the policy of encouragement of the small scale and cottage industrial sector
Monopolies and Restrictive Trade Practices Act 1969 [amended in 1980, 1982, 1984, 1986, 1988, 1991]	Prevent concentration of economic power to the common detriment; control of monopolies and prohibition of restrictive trade practices
Industrial Policy Statement, 1973 New Industrial Policy Statement, 1977	Identified priority industries where investment from large industrial houses and foreign firms would be permitted Laid emphasis on decentralisation and re-emphasised the role of small scale, tiny and cottage industries
Industrial Policy Statement, 1980	Highlighted the need for promoting competition in the domestic market; technological upgrading and modernisation; encouraged foreign investment in high technology areas; laid the foundation of a competitive export base
Rajiv Gandhi Reforms, 1985	Highlighted the need to open up domestic market to competition; free public sector from constraints and increase its autonomy; technological and managerial modernisation seen as key to increased productivity
MRTP 1985	Increase in the threshold of assets for a company to be classified as a MRTP company from Rs 25 crore to Rs 100 crore
Statement of Industrial Policy, 1991	Reduced the number of areas reserved for the public sector from 29 to 8; largely abolished industrial licensing except in a few strategic industries; emphasised efficiency and surpluses in the public sector; more managerial and entrepreneurial freedom in the private sector and for foreign investors; open access to technology and greater reliance on capital markets for funds; automatic clearance for import of capital goods in a majority of cases; broadbanding; approval for foreign investment; automatic approval for technology agreements related to high priority industries within specified parameters investment over 51% will be given
MRTP 1991	Act amended to remove threshold limits of assets in respect of MRTP companies; pre-entry scrutiny of investment by an MRTP company will be stopped; repealed all provisions relating to their expansion; brought the public sector into the scope of the Act; emphasis solely on controlling and regulating monopolistic and restrictive trade practices
National Manufacturing Policy, 2011	Objective of the policy is to enhance the share of manufacturing in GDP to 25% by 2025; increase the number of manufacturing sector jobs to 100 million by 2025; provide skill training to make rural youth employable. Increased importance given to state governments in the policy. The Central Government to provide the enabling policy framework, infrastructure to be developed through Public Private Partnerships (PPP) and State Governments to be encouraged to play an active role. Foreign investments and technologies to be welcomed, business regulations to be rationalised, competitiveness of enterprises to be prioritised

Source: Compiled by the author from various sources included in the citations and references, including (Government of India, nd; 2011a and 2011b).

Table 19.2 Contribution of the sectors to GDP in India, Brazil, China and Russia, 1960–2011 (value added as percentage of GDP)

Year	India				Brazil				China				Russia			
	Agric.	Indus.	Manuf.	Serv.	Agric.	Indus.	Manuf.	Serv.	Agric.	Indus.	Manuf.	Serv.	Agric.	Indus.	Manuf.	Serv.
1960	42.6	19.3	13.7	38.1	20.6	37.0	29.6	42.3	22.3	44.9		32.8				
1970	42.0	20.5	13.7	37.6	12.4	38.3	29.3	49.4	35.2	40.5	33.8	24.3				
1978	35.5	24.3	16.5	40.3	11.6	40.1	30.7	48.3	28.2	47.9	40.5	23.9				
1980	35.4	24.3	16.2	40.3	11.0	43.8	33.5	45.2	30.2	48.2	40.2	21.6				
1990	29.0	26.5	16.2	44.5	8.1	38.7		53.2	27.1	41.3	32.7	31.5	16.6	48.4		35.0
1995	26.3	27.4	17.3	46.3	5.8	27.5	18.6	66.7	19.0	47.2	33.7	32.9	7.2	36.0		55.9
2000	23.1	26.1	15.4	50.8	5.6	27.7	17.2	66.7	15.1	45.9	32.1	39.0	6.4	37.0		55.6
2005	18.8	28.1	15.4	53.1	5.7	29.3	18.1	65.0	12.1	47.4	32.5	40.5	4.0	38.1	18.3	57.0
2010	17.7	27.1	14.5	55.1	5.3	28.1	16.2	66.6	10.1	46.7	29.6	43.2	4.0	36.7	16.4	59.3
2011	17.2	26.4	13.9	56.4	5.5	27.5	14.6	67.0	10.0	46.6		43.4				

Source: World Bank (2012).

- *Segmented industrial structure.* Not surprisingly, given the policy emphasis on small firms and the public sector, the industrial sector that resulted was segmented by size as well as ownership. The segmentation between public and private firms is clear from Table 19.4. Towards the end of the era of directive industrial policy, in 1981, public sector firms employed one-third of all individuals employed in the formal manufacturing sector. This figure declined to approximately 25 per cent in 2005 and to 19 per cent by 2012 following the liberalisation of the economy. Despite this decline, even in 2012, almost a fifth of the employment provided in the organised sector in manufacturing was in the public sector.

In addition to this distinction, the manufacturing sector comprised a small number of formal sector firms with a relatively protected workforce and a large number of firms in the informal sector with no access to social security, employment protection, or other benefits (Sen, 2014). The formal sector, however, employs 20 per cent of workers and produces 83 per cent of manufacturing output in India (NCEUS, 2007). Not surprisingly, studies indicate that labour productivity in the formal sector was 28 times higher than that in the informal sector in 2005–6 (Mazumdar and Sarkar, 2012).

Table 19.3 Share of seven major industries in output and gross value added, 2010–11

NIC2008	Output (Rs 00,000)	% total output	GVA (Rs 00,000)	% total GVA
Total	467,621,696	100.0	82,513,336	100.0
Total of 7 industries	301,827,120	64.6	46,425,948	56.3
Coke and refined petroleum products	67,971,759	14.5	8,794,603	10.7
Basic metals	64,794,410	13.9	10,165,945	12.3
Food products	54,372,015	11.6	5,554,372	6.7
Chemicals and chemical products	35,229,032	7.5	7,213,221	8.7
Motor vehicles, trailers and semi-trailers	30,044,070	6.4	4,872,796	5.9
Textiles	27,197,382	5.8	4,803,700	5.8
Machinery and equipment n.e.c.	22,218,452	4.8	5,021,311	6.1

Source: Government of India (2010–11).

Table 19.4 Employment in the organised sector (lakh – i.e. 00,000 – persons as on 31/3)

Year	Employment in public sector manufacturing	Employment in private sector manufacturing	Total employment in manufacturing
1981	15.02	45.45	60.47
1991	18.52	44.81	63.33
1995	17.56	47.06	64.62
2000	15.31	50.85	66.16
2005	11.30	44.89	56.19
2010	10.66	51.84	62.50
2011	10.16	53.97	64.13
2012	10.71	55.26	65.97

Source: Government of India (various years (a)).

In addition to their impact on the overall structure of industry, there has been much analysis of their impact on the performance of the Indian manufacturing sector in particular. Researchers have been especially concerned with the issue of capacity utilisation within manufacturing, and the implications for productivity.

Outcome of the policies

While the growth rate of the manufacturing sector was satisfactory in the 1950s and 1960s, it began to dip in the mid-1960s and stayed low (around 3.5 per cent) until the 1980s. In the 1960s and 1970s, industrial demand was repressed through restrictive licensing of the production of consumer goods. The relatively small domestic output of consumer goods could not support the capacity created for the production of capital and intermediate goods, while at the same time the sector was not sufficiently competitive for external markets. The extent to which this sector was protected is apparent from import-weighted tariff rates of approximately 87 per cent, with effective rates of protection (ERPs) on some imports being 300 per cent (Mukherjee and Mukherjee, 2011). Effective tariff rates on imports of consumer goods were at a high of 164 per cent and in addition, the Government used non-tariff barriers on 65 per cent of all imports. This was particularly problematical because 90 per cent of these imports were inputs into the manufacturing sector and the ERPs were therefore significantly higher, a long-standing problem, which pre-occupied researchers throughout the 1970s and 1980s (see Bhagwati and Desai, 1970; Little *et al.*, 1970 for the early articulation of such concerns). Rodrik and Subramaniam (2004) calculated that the ERP for all industries between 1986 and 1990 was 125.9 per cent and it was 149.2 per cent in the intermediate goods industries. Such high ERPs unsurprisingly had an impact on the efficiency of the sector. Banga and Das (2012) calculate that average nominal tariff rates for industrial products on the eve of the reforms in 1990 was 81.69 per cent with a peak at 200 per cent. Liberalisation saw this tariff rate fall to 57.45 per cent in 1992 and then gradually to 9.43 per cent by 2009. Similar decreases could be seen in the other measures.

- *Underutilisation of capacity.* Given the closed nature of the Indian economy, the emphasis on self-sufficiency and on a domestic heavy industrial sector, it was not surprising that capacity utilisation became a problem. McCartney (2009) discusses the case of the steel plant in Durgapur which achieved a capacity utilisation of 100.6 per cent in 1964–5 but then dropped to 50 per cent in 1969 and remained around this level thereafter. This was true for many other firms in the manufacturing sector. Paul (1974) calculated that capacity utilisation in Indian industry was highest in the intermediate goods sector and lowest in the consumer goods sector in 1961–5. By 1971, only 43 per cent of capacity in the capital goods sector was being utilised. While there is considerable debate about the exact methodology used to measure capacity utilisation (Goldar, 1986; Srivastava, 1996), most studies agree that there was significant underutilisation of capacity during this period. Srivastava (1996) argued that a reduction in competitiveness and the inflexibility caused by the non-transferability of licenses from some products to others, resulted in excessive inventory holding, chronic inefficiencies and a high rate of capacity under-utilisation which was greatest in the capital goods sector. This was partly because capacity was determined by minimum efficient scale and the decision of whether to set up or not was made based on the self-sufficiency objective rather than the demand for products. Restrictions on imports and on foreign collaboration meant that technology was also widely out of date. McCartney (2009: 28) finds evidence that plants set up later tended to have lower levels of capacity utilisation and concludes that this reflected a failure of learning rather than simply lack of demand.

- *Impact on productivity and efficiency.* A number of writers (Bhagwati and Desai, 1970; Ahluwalia, 1991) argued that Indian industrial policies had a negative impact on industrial productivity and efficiency. Analysing the trends in total factor productivity (TFP) in India across two periods – 1951–65 and 1959–79 – Goldar (1986) found a positive but sluggish growth in TFP. He concluded that TFP growth was constrained by underutilisation of capacity, long gestation periods for investment projects and the ill effects of public policy. For the period 1959–79, Goldar found a significant increase in labour productivity, a significant fall in capital productivity and a positive but sluggish TFP growth in the large scale sector. Dougherty *et al.* (2009) confirm this trend concluding that the increased labour productivity was caused by capital deepening rather than improvement in TFP.

Data from this period clearly indicates that there were problems with the system which was in place. As seen above, these manifested themselves in poor performance of Indian manufacturing – in terms of capacity utilisation, efficiency and contribution to India's GDP. Writing about the pre-1991 period, Bhagwati (1993) argued that there were three main problems with the policy framework – extensive bureaucratic controls over production, investment and trade; inward looking trade and foreign investment policies and a substantial public sector which went beyond public utilities and infrastructure. Ahluwalia, a long-time critic of the Indian model, further detailed the consequences of the policies (Ahluwalia, 1991). First, the policy constrained domestic competition through barriers to the entry of firms and foreign competition through the protection of domestic industries against imports. Second, the protection offered to small scale industries and the objective of regional dispersal of growth both implied that many firms could not operate at optimal scale. Third, barriers to exit meant that firms, even when they were non–viable, could not close down and this resulted in a waste of resources and the ossification of an inefficient and inflexible industrial structure. Fourth, the system of physical controls incentivised administrative hurdles and rent–seeking activities and thereby reduced entrepreneurship. Fifth, there was little or no incentive to upgrade technology. Along similar lines, Goldar concludes that "in pursuing the policies of regional dispersal of industries, diversification and self–reliance, sufficient attention has not been paid to the question of efficiency" (Goldar, 1986: 119).

While not disagreeing that there were some problems with the industrial policy regime, Singh (2008: 12) argues that

> India today has an enviable framework for the conduct of comprehensive industrial policy in the broad sense. Many of the necessary institutions required such as the Planning Commission are in place and have broad acceptance among all the political parties and the Indian people.

In fact, Singh argues that the economic growth record of the Nehru–Mahalanobis period (1950–80), in terms of aggregate statistics, does not reflect the structural achievements of this economic model, especially in creating a scientific and technical infrastructure for a modern economy (Singh, 2008).

By 1991, the awareness of the problems in the system was heightened by the sudden onset of a currency reserves crisis which pushed India towards a liberalisation of her economy. Thus, there was some consensus that industrial policy could be more efficient but there was less agreement about how to solve the problem that it presented.

Industrial policy reforms, 1991: A change of direction?

A change of direction began in the mid-1980s and was strengthened in 1991 when India under-took liberal market reforms. These reforms (as in other parts of the developing world) were adopted in response to a foreign currency reserve crisis but very soon resulted in significant changes across the board. The consciousness that some change was required was apparent in the Industrial Policy of 1977 which was the first policy statement that did not extend public sector involvement in the economy. This was not explicitly followed up until the 1980s when Rajiv Gandhi's government once again prioritised the industrial sector in the Seventh Plan (1985–90), with the aim of increasing industrial productivity through technological progress. Under this Plan and the reforms following it (Government of India, 1991), investment deci-sions were de-licensed and the limits for firms requiring licenses were raised. As Srivastava (1996) details, during this period 25 broad industrial groups and 82 pharmaceutical products were de-licensed. Further, in 65 industries where minimum efficient scale (MES) was con-sidered important, the MES was announced and expansion to this scale was made possible without licenses. Licenses were broadbanded in some industries so that firms could produce related products without having to apply for new licenses. This was intended to improve capac-ity utilisation and increase flexibility of production. The reforms also loosened the restrictions on large industrial houses by changing the definition of monopoly from firms having Rs200 million of assets to those having more than Rs1 billion. These restrictions were further loos-ened by exempting 27 industries totally from the provisions of the Monopolies and Restrictive Trade Practices Act (MRTP) (Government of India, nd). Finally, the reforms pushed towards greater openness of the economy by increasing the number of capital goods and intermediate goods which no longer required import licenses and by providing exemptions and incentives to decrease the bias against exports. The exchange rate was made more flexible and this led to a depreciation of the Rupee (Srivastava, 1996).

A further change in direction as well as pace occurred in 1991 when the Indian economy was opened up, exposing the hitherto protected industrial sector to foreign competition, with small moves made towards privatisation and towards further modernisation of industry. The reforms in 1991 mimicked those advocated by structural adjustment packages worldwide. As in most developing countries, it was necessary to increase exports and decrease pressure on the currency. To achieve this, the government made the rupee convertible though it still remains a 'managed float' to date. Import controls were eased by dismantling some of the protective infrastructure that had been set up in the previous decades. Topalova (2007) calculated that average tariffs decreased from more than 80 per cent in 1990 to 37 per cent in 1996. Harrison *et al.* (2011) found that output tariffs in India fell from 0.96 in 1989 just before the reforms to 0.6 in 1994 and down to 0.33 in 2001. Input tariffs[3] also decreased to a third of their 1989 level from 0.60 in 1989 to 0.19 in 2001. The Government also reversed the policy of nationalisation of large numbers of foreign-owned firms that had been taken in the 1970s. There were moves to encourage exports which have borne fruit in the improved export performance of the Indian economy, especially in the services sector.

This period also saw the liberalisation of regulations controlling foreign direct investment (FDI). The pre-1990 period had relatively strict controls on shares held by foreign inves-tors, the sectors in which foreign investment was permitted, profit repatriation and foreign exchange balancing. After 1991, this was reformed to increase the limits on FDI in key sectors like telecommunications and to allow 100 per cent foreign ownership under the automatic route, without prior approval, in most sectors and activities. There remained a small list of industrial sectors in which FDI was not permitted and these include arms and ammunition, atomic energy, railway transport, coal and lignite, and mining. While annual FDI flows into India have increased significantly following these changes, they have been much smaller than FDI flows into China during this period. In 2008, FDI flows into China were $175.1 billion, while they were only $43.4billion into India. Since then, the Chinese figure has increased to $253.4 billion while the Indian figure has fallen to one-tenth of this ($25.3 billion) (OECD, 2013). In addition, the vast majority of FDI in India was acquisition of existing industrial capacity by private equity firms rather than greenfield investment, while in China most FDI has been associated with the establishment of additional industrial capacity.

While the reforms did not include large scale privatisation, the Government partially disinvested the equity of selected enterprises, exposing them to commercial objectives and opening them up to public scrutiny. State owned enterprises were encouraged to raise equity from the public rather than the government and public sector monopolies were subjected to competition from the private sector.

These reforms reflect a significant change in approach towards the manufacturing sector. Both trade liberalisation and domestic deregulation were taking place though research suggests that the former was more successful. The rate of growth of GDP increased significantly following these reforms but concern regarding the performance of the manufacturing sector remains.

Results of reforms

Following the reforms, GDP growth in India increased to 5.62 per cent per annum in 1995 and, after a dip in 2000, it increased again to 7.7 per cent in 2005 and then almost 9 per cent in 2010. While this growth brought significant optimism to the Indian economy, leading some to compare India's economic performance to that of China, the reforms have been less successful in increasing the contribution of the manufacturing sector. In fact, Banga and Das (2012) calculate that the manufacturing sector only grew by an annual average rate of 5.4 per cent in the 1990s, down from an annual average rate of 6 per cent in the 1980s. Even in the high growth period of 2000–7, manufacturing value added only grew by an annual rate of 7.4 per cent. In fact, it has been the services sector that has grown fastest since 1991 and its share has increased from 44.5 per cent of GDP in 1990 to 56.4 per cent in 2011 (see Table 19.2). This has led to concerns about premature de-industrialisation in India, the slow pace of structural change despite fast growth of the economy and jobless growth in services (Singh, 2008; Ghosh *et al.*, 2009). The extent to which this will remain an obstacle to longer term growth and development has become a matter of debate. Kochhar *et al.* (2006) looking across states in India argue that the distortions in skill intensity and scale are persistent and may allow India to bypass the more traditional manufacturing-oriented development path. However, the OECD (2007) and Dougherty *et al.* (2009) disagree with this. The latter conclude that the distortions that exist (in the labour market, scale of firms, low firm turnover, poor market integration, high concentration and persistent state ownership) represent severe restraints on the growth of productivity in manufacturing.

As discussed above, the reforms have decreased protection against imports and have led to depreciation of the currency, resulting in an increase in trade to GDP ratios from 11 per cent in 1995 to 24 per cent in 2007. Despite this, India's share of global merchandise exports decreased from 2.4 per cent in 1947 to 0.5 per cent in 1990, and from this low point increased to 1.3 per cent by 2009 (Government of India, 2011b). Even though India's exports are growing faster than the world average, manufacturing exports in India are still only 61.5 per cent of total merchandise exports as compared to 93 per cent in China. India's share of world exports exceeded

10 per cent only in primary commodities like tea, spices, leather and rice and gems and jewellery (14.8 per cent). Within the manufacturing sector, the leading exporters were pharmaceuticals and chemicals (4.9 per cent), machinery and instruments (5.1 per cent), transport equipment (6.1 per cent) and garments (4.3 per cent) (Government of India, 2013). But the sector that has seen the greatest increase in exports has been the services sector.

As we have already seen, one of the oft-discussed problems of the old industrial policy regime was the low capacity utilisation and low productivity of the manufacturing sector. Not surprisingly, a large number of studies have also analysed the response of industrial productivity to the reforms. Trivedi *et al.* (2011) contend, after a review of the literature, that TFPG (total factor productivity growth) decelerated during the 1990s compared to the 1980s. However, their conclusion remains contentious. Kathuria *et al.* (2013) argued that looking at average TFPG is meaningless because TFP varied significantly across the formal and informal sectors. Sivadasan (2006b) found increased productivity in industries that liberalised through de-licensing compared to those that did not, as well as those affected by FDI liberalisation (which saw an increase in productivity from 18 per cent to 23 per cent). The OECD (2007) found an increase in TFPG in manufacturing from less than 0.5 per cent per annum during the 1990s to 2.5 per cent per annum between 2000 and 2005. Virmani and Hashim (2011) found that TFPG decreased from 0.61 per cent per annum in the 1980s to 0.25 per cent per annum in the 1990s and then increased to 1.4 per cent per annum in the 2000s. Driffield and Kambhampati (2003), analysing the efficiency of firms in manufacturing rather than their productivity over the period 1987 to 1994, found that efficiency increased in the post-reform period in 5 out of the 6 sectors that they considered. This result was also confirmed in Kambhampati (2003) which looked specifically at the cotton textile industry in the context of the trade reforms.

Despite the reforms, Sen (2014) has found that the industrial sector remains dominated by state-owned firms and business groups and that there is limited entry by new firms. Sen argues that this is because firm exit is constrained by stringent bankruptcy rules and because incumbent firms have significant political clout that allows them to prevent entry. Chand and Sen (2002) conclude that most of the evidence suggests that the improvement in productivity has come from trade liberalisation which has increased access to imported intermediate goods rather than from domestic deregulation. Topalova (2004) too finds that domestic deregulation has been less effective than the trade liberalisation reforms undertaken since 1991.

Aghion *et al.* (2008), analysing the effects of domestic deregulation on the output of the registered manufacturing sector, found that the effects vary according to the labour market institutions in place. In particular, states with pro-employer labour regulations (like Andhra Pradesh and Tamil Nadu) saw relatively large increases in output of the manufacturing sector whereas states with pro-labour regulations (West Bengal and Maharashtra) saw declines. Testing the effects of input tariff liberalisation in the 1991 reforms, Goldberg *et al.* (2008) find that it contributed to domestic product growth both by decreasing the production costs facing domestic producers and also by relaxing the technological constraints facing these producers via access to new imported input varieties that were not available before liberalisation. Goldberg *et al.* (2010) find, on the other hand, input tariff reductions did not affect the product portfolio of multiproduct firms in India. They conclude that this is consistent with the legacy of industrial regulation in India.

The sector that was quickest in taking advantage of deregulation, however, has been the services sector. In 2006, the Indian ICT industry accounted for 5.4 per cent of GDP as against agriculture which contributed 18 per cent to GDP (UNCTAD, 2007). In fact, Goldar and Mitra (2008) find that TFP growth was faster in the services sector than in manufacturing in the post-1980 period though they conclude that, despite this, the secondary sector has provided the motor for growth. Banga and Goldar (2004) found that the contribution of services input to output growth in manufacturing was approximately 1 per cent in the 1980s and approximately 25 per cent in the 1990s.

Overall, therefore, while we can conclude that the reforms were successful in increasing the growth of the economy, they were less successful in stimulating the growth of the manufacturing sector. In a context where this sector is likely to be essential both for employment creation as well as future growth, the poor performance of the manufacturing sector is a cause for concern.

Conclusion

In this chapter, we have considered the development of the manufacturing sector in India in the context of its institutional and policy history. The complex policy structure that was used to encourage the growth of the industrial sector in the pre-1991 period was successful in creating a highly diversified industrial sector as well as a strong institutional framework. However, the policies followed resulted in significant capacity under-utilisation and low levels of competitiveness which increased inefficiency in the manufacturing sector. While the reforms of 1991 increased growth, they have not increased the contribution of this sector to GDP. Figures indicate that the manufacturing sector in India is smaller than in most other developing countries, including the BRIC countries. While economic growth has continued to take place and exports too are growing, there is concern that this growth has bypassed the manufacturing sector and therefore is unlikely to be sustainable in the long run. There are also questions about the ability of the services sector to provide the number of jobs required to employ the large working population of the country leading to a concern that growth will remain jobless with its distributional implications.

Notes

1 This document is the source for almost all of the references to government Industrial Policy Resolutions, and other Industrial Policy statements, between 1956 and 1991, but has no date associated with it. It is available from the website of the Office of the Economic Adviser, Department of Industrial Policy and Promotion (DIPP).
2 The International Standard Industrial Classification includes: (i) mining and quarrying; (ii) manufacturing; (iii) electricity, gas, steam and air conditioning supply; and (iv) water supply, sewerage, waste management and remediation activities in the Industry Sector. This is therefore much wider than manufacturing alone (United Nations, 2008: 290). It is also necessary to allow for 'margins of error' within published statistics.
3 Input tariffs have been computed by running the industry-level tariffs through India's input–output matrix for 1993/4.

Bibliography

Aghion, P., Burgess, R., Redding, S. J., and Zilibotti, F. 2008. The Unequal Effects of Liberalisation: Evidence from Dismantling the License Raj in India. *American Economic Review*. 98 (4): 1397–1412.
Ahluwalia, I. J. 1991. *Productivity and Growth in Indian Manufacturing*. New Delhi: Oxford University Press.
Balakrishnan, P., 2010. *Economic Growth in India: History and Prospect*. New Delhi: Oxford University Press.
Banga, R. and Das, A. (eds.). 2012. *Twenty Years of India's Liberalization: Experiences and Lessons*. Geneva: United Nations Conference on Trade and Development.
Banga, R. and Goldar, B. 2004. *Contribution of Services to Output Growth and Productivity in Indian Manufacturing: Pre and Post Reforms*. ICRIER Working Paper 139. Delhi: Indian Council for Research on International Economic Relations.
Bhagwati, J. 1993. *India in Transition: Freeing the Economy*. Oxford: Clarendon Press.

Bhagwati, J. and Desai, P. 1970. *India: Planning for Industrialisation.* New Delhi: Oxford University Press.

Chand, S. and Sen, K. 2002. Trade liberalization and productivity growth: evidence from Indian manufacturing. *Review of Development Economics,* 6(1): 120–132.

Dougherty, S., Herd, R. and Chalaux, T. 2009. What is Holding Back Productivity Growth in India? Recent Microevidence. *OECD Journal: Economic Studies.* 1: 1–22.

Driffield, N. and Kambhampati, U. S. 2003. Efficiency of Firms in Indian Industry: The Effect of Reforms. *Review of Development Economics.* 7 (3): 419–430.

Ghosh, J., Havlik, P., Ribeiro, M. P., and Urban, W., 2009. *Models of BRICs' Economic Development and Challenges for EU Competitiveness.* wiiw Research Report No. 359. Vienna: The Vienna Institute for International Economic Studies.

Goldar, B. 1986. *Productivity Growth in Indian Industry.* Delhi: Allied Publishers.

Goldar, B. and Mitra, A. 2008. *Productivity Increase and Changing Sectoral Composition: Contribution to Economic Growth in India.* Paper presented at the V. K. R. V. Rao Centenary Conference on "National Income and Other Macro-Economic Aggregates in a Growing Economy" organised by the Delhi School of Economics and the Institute of Economic Growth, Delhi on April 28–30, 2008.

Goldberg, P., Khandelwal, A., Pavcnik, N., and Topalova, P. 2008. *Imported Intermediate Inputs and Domestic Product Growth: Evidence from India.* NBER Working Paper 14416. Cambridge MA: National Bureau of Economic Research.

Goldberg, P., Khandelwal, A., Pavcnik, N. and Topalova, P. 2010. Multi-Product and Product Turnover in the Developing World: Evidence from India. *Review of Economics and Statistics,* 92(4): 1042–1049.

Government of India. 1991. *Statement on Industrial Policy.* New Delhi: Ministry of Industry – accessible from www. dipp.nic.in/English/Policies/Industrial_policy_statement.pdf

Government of India. 2010–11. *Annual Survey of Industries: Summary Results for Factory Sector.* Ministry of Statistics and Programme Implementation. Kolkata: Central Statistical Office – accessible from www. mospi.nic.in/mospi_new/upload/asi/ASI_main.htm?status=1&menu_id=88

Government of India. 2011a. *National Manufacturing Policy Press Note.* New Delhi: Government of India – accessible from www.commerce.nic.in/ann/National_Manfacturing_Policy2011

Government of India. 2011b. *Department of Commerce Report of the Working Group on 'Boosting India's Manufacturing Exports' Twelfth Five Year Plan (2012–17).* New Delhi: Ministry of Commerce and Industry.

Government of India. various years (a). *Economic Survey.* New Delhi: Government of India – accessible from www.indiabudget.nic.in/survey.asp

Government of India. various years (b). *Five Year Plans.* New Delhi: Planning Commission – accessible from www.planningcommission.gov.in/plans/planrel/fiveyr/index7.html

Government of India. various years (c). *Industrial Development and Regulation Act (IDRA).* New Delhi: Department of Industrial Policy and Promotion – accessible from www.business.gov.in

Government of India. nd. Office of the Economic Adviser, Department of Industrial Policy and Promotion (DIPP) – accessible from www.eaindustry.nic.in/handbk/chap001.pdf

Harrison, A. E., Martin, L. A. and Nataraj, S. 2011. "Learning vs Stealing: How Important are Market-Share Reallocations to India's Productivity Growth," mimeo.

Joshi, P.C. 1982. Dimensions of Agricultural Planning: Reflections on the Mahalanobis Approach. *Man and Development.* 4: 9–31.

Kambhampati, U. S. 2003. Trade Reforms and the Efficiency of Firms in India. *Oxford Development Studies.* 31 (2): 219–233.

Kathuria, V., Raj, R. and Sen, K. 2013. Efficiency Comparison Between Formal and Informal Firms: Evidence from Indian Manufacturing. *Journal of Industrial Statistics.* 2 (1): 1–23.

Kochhar, K., Kumar, U., Rajan, R., Subramanian, A. and Tokatlidis, I. 2006. India's Pattern of Development: What Happened, What Follows? *Journal of Monetary Economics.* 53 (5): 981–1019.

Lewis, W. A. 1956. *Theory of Economic Growth,* George Allen & Unwin, Great Britain.

Little, I. M. D., Scitovsky, T. and Scott, M. 1970. *Industry and Trade in Some Developing Countries: A Comparative Study.* Oxford: Oxford University Press.

Mahalanobis, P. C. 1955. The Operational Research to Planning in India. *Sankhya: The Indian Journal of Statistics.* 16 (1 & 2): 3–62.

Mazumdar, D. and Sarkar, S. 2012, *Manufacturing Enterprise in Asia: Size, Structure and Economic Growth.* Basingstoke: Routledge.

McCartney, M. 2009. *Political Economy, Growth and Liberalisation in India 1991–2008.* London: Routledge.

Mukherjee, S. and Mukherjee, S. 2012. *Overview of India's Export Performance: Trends and Drivers.* IIMB Research Paper 363. Bangalore: Indian Institute of Management.

NCEUS. 2007. *Report on the Conditions of Work and Promotion of Livelihoods in the Unorganised Sector. National Commission for Enterprises in the Unorganised Sector.* New Delhi: National Commission for Enterprises in the Unorganised Sector – accessible from www.nceuis.nic.in/Condition_of_workers_sep_2007.pdf

OECD. 2007. *Economic Survey of India.* Paris: Organisation for Economic Cooperation and Development – accessible from www.oecd.org/eco/surveys/india

OECD. 2013. *FDI in Figures.* Paris: Organisation for Economic Cooperation and Development – accessible from www.oecd.org/investment/FDI%20in%20figures.pdf

Paul, S. 1974. Growth and Utilisation of Industrial Capacity. *Economic and Political Weekly.* 9 (49): 2027–2032.

Rodrik, D. and Subramaniam, A. 2004. *From "Hindu Growth" to Productivity Surge: The Mystery of the Indian Growth Transition.* IMF Working Paper WP0477. Washington DC: International Monetary Fund – accessible from www.imf.org

Rostow, W. W. 1960. *The Stages of Economic Growth: A Non-Communist Manifesto.* Cambridge: Cambridge University Press.

Sen, K. 2014. The Indian Economy in the Post-Reform Period: Growth without Structural Transformation. *Proceedings of the British Academy.* 193: 47–62.

Singh, A. 2008. *The Past, Present and Future of Industrial Policy in India: Adapting to the Changing Domestic and International Environment.* Centre for Business Research, University of Cambridge Working Paper No. 376. Cambridge: University of Cambridge – accessible from www.cbr.cam.ac.uk

Sivadasan, J. 2006a. *Regulatory Regime in India: 1947 to 1998.* Ann Arbor: University of Michigan – accessible from www.webuser.bus.umich.edu/jagadees/other/indmfg_data/Reg_history_india.pdf

Sivadasan, J. 2006b. *Productivity Consequences of Product Market Liberalisation: Microevidence from Indian Manufacturing Sector Reforms.* Stephen M Ross School of Business Paper No. 1062. Ann Arbor: University of Michigan – accessible from www.webuser.bus.umich.edu/jagadees/papers/india_prod_all.pdf

Srivastava, V. 1996. *Liberalization, Productivity and Competition: A Panel Study of Indian Manufacturing.* Delhi: Oxford University Press.

Topalova, P. 2004. Trade Liberalisation and Firm Productivity: The Case of India. *IMF Working Paper No. WP/04/28* – accessible from www.imf.org/external/pubs/ft/wp/2004/wp0428.pdf

Trivedi, P., Lakshmanan, L., Jain, R. and Gupta, Y.K. 2011. *Productivity, Efficiency and Competitiveness of the Indian Manufacturing Sector.* Mumbai: Reserve Bank of India.

UNCTAD. 2007. *Information Economy Report 2007–8 – Science and Technology for Development: The New Paradigm of ICT.* New York and Geneva: United Nations Conference on Trade and Development.

United Nations. 2008. *International Standard Industrial Classification of all Economic Activities* (ISIC) Rev 4. New York: United Nations Economic and Social Affairs.

Virmani, A. and Hashim, D. A. 2011. *J-curve of Productivity and Growth: Indian Manufacturing Post-Liberalisation.* IMF Working Paper WP/11/163. Washington DC: International Monetary Fund.

World Bank. 2012. *World Development Indicators.* Washington DC: World Bank – accessible from www.data.worldbank.org/data-catalog/world-development-indicators

20

IS THERE AN
AFRICA PROBLEM?[1]

Peter Lawrence

This chapter will address the question of why African economies have not produced the kinds of structural changes that have characterised the growth of manufacturing[2] in other parts of the world. The chapter will begin with an overview of Africa's manufacturing growth performance, in comparison with other groups of developing countries. The following sections will review explanations of Africa's manufacturing performance: the adoption of import substitution strategies of industrialisation, the effects of structural adjustment policies, the high costs of 'doing business', uncompetitive wages and low skill levels, credit and investment constraints, public/private ownership and lack of export orientation, and the specific ways in which they have resulted in outcomes different from those that were expected. The chapter will conclude that while there have been variations in Africa's manufacturing performance, just as has been the case for other country groups, even the best-performing African economies have yet to develop an industrial strategy for changing the structure of manufacturing to reflect the characteristics of mature industrialisation.

Africa's industrial performance

After a promising start in the first two decades of political independence, industrial, and especially manufacturing, growth rates fell sharply and Africa's share in world manufacturing value added has remained at around 1 per cent over the last three decades. During the same period, the share of the East Asian and Pacific developing countries rose from 5 to 22 per cent.[3] Africa's share in world manufacturing exports has hovered between 0.5 and 1 per cent over the same period, while East Asia has seen its share rise from under 3 to almost 19 per cent in 2012. Over the last four decades, the share of manufactured exports in Africa's total exports rose from approximately 10 to 30 per cent, reflecting the decline in primary product export receipts, rather than a real increase in the value of manufacturing exports (calculated from World Development Indicators (World Bank, 2013)). Most African economies are still dominated by the production and export of agricultural and mineral raw materials, some increasingly so as more sources of key raw materials, especially oil and gas, are discovered across the continent.

Tables 20.1–20.4 set out the main elements of the performance of selected[4] African countries' industrial sectors since 1970 as measured by the share of industry and manufacturing in GDP, changes in manufacturing structure over time, the growth of manufacturing value added

(MVA) and the share of manufacturing in trade.[5] It is worth noting at the outset that the wide variation in performance across the selected countries emphasises the danger of treating African countries as a single and homogeneous group. In fact the data for the latest years in Table 20.1 shows that industry's share of GDP across the selected countries ranges from 13 to 70 per cent (compared with 10 to 57 per cent in the 1970s), the higher shares reflecting the domination of industrial activity by mineral extraction and its limited ancillary activities. On the other hand, shares of manufacturing in GDP range from 3 to 20 per cent, with just under half with a share of 10 per cent or less (compared with a range of 3 to 22 per cent in the 1970s, with 11 of the 25 countries on 10 per cent or below). Comparing the shares of manufacturing in GDP at the end of the period since 1970 with the beginning, 16 of the 25 countries listed showed a lower share at the end than at the beginning. While a declining share of manufacturing is a feature of developed economies as they 'mature', it is not to be expected in economies that are in the process of developing a manufacturing sector.

The manufacturing sectors of most African economies are dominated by the processing of food, beverages, tobacco, textiles, clothing, wood, metals and oil (Tribe, 2002). Over time there have been shifts in the proportions of these groups in total manufacturing. Very few countries have any MVA that derives from the durable and capital goods sector, with the exception of South Africa, whose share is well below those of all the Asian and most of the Latin American countries listed (Table 20.2). Table 20.3 details the manufacturing growth rates for the selected countries. Growth rates in the 1970s were often impressive and typical of countries starting from a low base. Growth rates dropped sharply in the 1980s and/or 1990s and in many cases have dropped further in the 2000s, though in over half the countries they have recovered, but not always to anything like their previous levels.

Although most African countries' export revenues are dominated by the export of primary products, two-thirds of these countries listed in Table 20.4 have substantially increased the share of export revenue deriving from manufacturing since the 1970s, though almost half of the group have seen very little change or even a fall in this share over the last two decades. Some of the impressive increases in share reflect the classifying of first stage processing of minerals as manufacturing, but for some countries, the production of textiles and clothing has been an important and growing source of export revenue. Imports, on the other hand, are dominated by manufactures, particularly capital goods, but also, and especially after trade liberalisation, high value consumer goods.

It might be expected that countries that have enjoyed higher rates of growth of manufacturing would also show high rates of capital formation. Unfortunately the available data does not allow a breakdown of investment to different sectors but Table 20.5 shows what has happened to gross fixed capital formation (GFCF) and foreign direct investment (FDI) overall flows as a share of GDP over this period. There is no obvious pattern that emerges between GFCF shares and manufacturing, or industrial, growth rates over the period surveyed, although it does appear that countries with a high growth rate have a minimum ratio of GFCF to GDP of around 20 per cent. The lack of a consistent pattern could be the result of different levels of productivity of investment or different allocations between sectors. Of the 26 African countries in Table 20.5, only 11 showed higher rates of GFCF in the period since 2000 compared with the beginning of the period covered. Almost all countries showed increased foreign investment relative to GDP, but once again there is no clear pattern relating relative levels of foreign investment to growth of manufacturing output, though some of the high growth countries have at some point had relatively high rates of FDI.

Tables 20.1–20.5 include data for a selection of Asian and Latin American countries. Even among this small group, there is some variation in characteristics and performance. Shares of manufacturing in GDP are considerably higher in Asia than in Latin America but both are higher than for most of the African countries. However, in the Latin American economies, there has been a sharp fall in the shares of manufacturing in GDP over the period covered, while for Asia, there have been falls in China and the Philippines, but these have been less dramatic, with shares remaining relatively high and in China's case the second highest. With the exception of Chile and Argentina, all the Asian and Latin American countries have developed substantial capital goods sectors. They have, in the main, generated consistently higher industrial and, especially, manufacturing growth rates, increased the share of trade derived from manufactures, both exports and imports, and maintained high rates of capital formation. Net flows of foreign investment have increased in relation to GDP, most notably in Chile, but they do not appear to be significantly higher in relative terms than for most African economies.

So it would appear that post-colonial Africa, even with the variability in characteristics and performance that can be observed elsewhere in the developing country group, is different. The expectation of African countries embarking on industrial growth programmes was to develop a manufacturing sector based on food and other primary product processing and then to move into the manufacture of more advanced consumption and capital goods. However, they have largely remained with much the same structure of production as at Independence. Indeed it has been argued that most African economies have been through a process of industrialisation followed by de-industrialisation, the first brought about through import substitution strategies and the second through structural adjustment policies (UNECA, 2013). There is a strongly held view that there has been some de-industrialisation generated by structural adjustment policies that encouraged import liberalisation and privatisation resulting in the decline of formerly state-owned, and subsidised, enterprises, and in a relatively poor performance when compared with other developing country groups (Mkandawire 1991; Mkandawire and Soludo, 1999: 56–9; Noorbakhsh and Paloni, 2000). One way of determining whether African economies have suffered de-industrialisation is to construct a model of the determinants of industrialisation which allows comparison of where countries are with where they 'should' be. Constructing such a model, Jalilian and Weiss (2000) find that there is evidence of de-industrialisation in almost half of the countries covered, but not in the others. As they point out, their findings do not suggest that Africa is different from elsewhere in the variability of de-industrialisation and they are consistent with the data presented in Table 20.1 for countries in their sample: Burkina Faso, Ghana and South Africa (de-industrialisation) and Cameroon, Mauritius and Senegal (no de-industrialisation). However, even where there is no evidence of de-industrialisation, there is neither evidence in Table 20.2 of any significant change in the structure of manufacturing towards a strong capital goods sector, which is a clear characteristic of the development of manufacturing in East Asia.

Import substitution industrialisation in Africa: What went wrong?

Those countries that achieved independence in the late 1950s and early 1960s adopted a basic import substitution industrialisation (ISI) strategy.[6] They set out a shopping list of manufacturing activities that they wanted to undertake and for which foreign partners were sought. These industrial activities matched the countries' consumer and intermediate import patterns and as such represented what has become known as 'easy' import substitution (Nixson, 2005). Such investment required foreign resources either in the form of hard currency, accumulated from the sale of primary products, or FDI by firms that could supply the capital goods which would produce the final output. This was attractive to foreign partners because in many cases the

Table 20.1 Industry and manufacturing shares of GDP (%): selected developing countries

	Industrial value added				Manufacturing value added			
	1971–80	1981–90	1991–2000	2001–12	1971–80	1981–90	1991–2000	2001–12
Algeria	51.9	51.2	50.7	60.3	12.8	13.0	10.5	5.8
Benin	14.0	14.0	12.9	13.2	10.5	7.8	8.0	7.8
Botswana	40.9	58.5	54.0	52.4	6.6	6.0	5.1	3.9
Burkina Faso	24.4	21.2	21.6	19.5	18.0	15.2	15.2	10.8
Cameroon	19.2	32.2	31.0	31.3	9.7	12.6	19.6	18.9
Central African Rep.	23.1	16.2	19.9	14.9	7.4	9.0	9.9	7.3
Congo, Rep.	30.5	44.5	48.5	70.6	8.4	6.9	9.9	4.3
Cote d'Ivoire	17.5	21.2	22.4	24.4	9.7	6.9	6.9	18.7
Egypt, Arab Rep.	28.6	29.7	32.2	36.7	15.2	16.5	18.5	16.2
Gabon	57.1	51.9	49.5	56.2	5.4	15.0	17.7	4.4
Gambia, The	9.6	11.6	15.8	13.9	3.5	6.3	5.0	6.0
Ghana	18.1	14.3	25.7	24.4	11.8	6.0	8.0	8.8
Kenya	20.0	19.2	17.6	18.2	12.0	8.9	10.0	11.4
Lesotho	18.6	29.4	40.6	33.8	5.9	11.9	11.5	18.6
Madagascar	16.7	13.5	12.3	15.6		13.7	16.6	13.8
Malawi	19.3	23.3	21.6	18.2	13.0	11.3	10.4	11.3
Mali	11.9	15.1	17.5	23.9	6.9	15.6	15.6	3.1
Mauritania	31.7	27.3	26.4	36.2		7.6	6.3	8.1
Mauritius	26.0	29.6	31.9	28.1	15.4	12.2	10.4	20.0
Morocco	31.0	33.4	31.6	28.8	16.9	21.2	23.5	15.7

(Continued)

Table 20.1 (Continued)

	Industrial value added				Manufacturing value added			
	1971–80	1981–90	1991–2000	2001–12	1971–80	1981–90	1991–2000	2001–12
Senegal	20.1	20.9	23.6	23.6	13.5	14.1	16.0	14.9
South Africa	41.4	42.9	34.1	31.0	21.7	23.0	20.5	17.2
Tanzania	13.8	12.7	16.6	23.6	11.9	8.6	8.3	9.2
Tunisia	28.6	35.8	31.7	30.4	11.6	17.0	19.7	17.9
Uganda	8.1	10.1	16.1	25.1	6.1	5.7	7.4	7.7
Zambia	48.5	46.4	36.6	31.1	16.9	26.9	18.7	10.6
Zimbabwe	31.7	30.7	30.3	32.3	20.1	22.2	20.8	16.0
China	45.3	43.7	45.9	46.5	37.9	35.3	32.9	32.1
India	22.7	25.7	26.1	27.3	15.5	16.0	15.7	15.2
Korea, Rep.	30.9	39.7	41.0	37.4	22.3	27.8	27.2	27.8
Malaysia	34.5	39.1	43.2	44.3	17.7	20.7	27.7	27.0
Philippines	35.6	36.4	33.0	33.2	25.8	24.9	23.6	23.2
Thailand	27.9	32.9	40.2	43.1	19.5	23.9	30.2	34.6
Argentina	45.9	39.4	29.1	32.7	35.1	29.1	19.6	21.5
Brazil	39.9	44.0	31.8	28.0	30.4	32.6	20.0	17.1
Chile	39.7	39.1	37.2	37.0	23.7	19.7	19.0	14.2
Mexico	32.3	33.5	28.0	33.7	22.7	22.9	20.5	18.5
World	37.1	34.6	30.6	27.8			20.2	17.1

Source: World Bank (2013), supplemented by World Bank (various years).

Notes: Manufacturing refers to industries belonging to ISIC divisions 15–37. Industry corresponds to ISIC divisions 10–45 and includes manufacturing (ISIC divisions 15–37). It comprises value added in mining, manufacturing (also reported as a separate subgroup), construction, electricity, water and gas.

Table 20.2 Structure of manufacturing output 1990–2009 (% of total): selected countries in Africa, Asia and Latin America

	FB&T		M&TE		T&C		Chemicals		Other manufacturing	
	1990–2000	2001–2009	1990–2000	2001–2009	1990–2000	2001–2009	1990–2000	2001–2009	1990–2000	2001–2009
Algeria	23.8	33.1	0.0	0.0	10.5	7.9	10.7	11.3	55.1	47.7
Botswana	35.5	21.9	10.8	0.0	9.1	4.5	5.4	0.0	50.0	73.6
Cameroon	41.2	35.0	0.5	0.3	9.4	9.7	5.0	6.2	44.4	48.9
Congo, Rep.	73.0	75.8	7.1	8.6	2.7	2.3	3.3	−9.1	13.9	22.3
Ethiopia	54.9	48.6	2.3	2.4	18.2	10.0	3.9	5.5	20.7	33.6
Egypt	17.0	19.5	7.9	8.1	13.2	12.0	13.7	16.7	48.2	43.7
Gambia, The	65.0	32.5	0.8	0.0	8.3	22.5	8.8	3.9	17.1	41.1
Ghana	35.6	32.5	1.7	0.6	5.1	6.4	9.7	0.0	47.9	60.5
Kenya	41.6	29.7	4.0	2.5	8.3	5.9	8.0	5.7	38.2	56.5
Madagascar	30.9	0.5	0.0	0.4	33.1	28.5	5.7	1.9	30.3	68.8
Malawi	47.8	70.8	2.1	0.6	11.8	4.8	15.5	7.6	22.9	16.2
Mauritius	26.9	28.2	1.2	1.5	48.5	41.5	4.3	0.0	20.7	28.9
Morocco	33.9	26.1	4.8	4.6	18.1	15.3	14.0	14.1	29.3	39.9
Senegal	46.6	41.4	2.7	1.7	3.7	3.4	22.2	17.9	24.8	35.6
South Africa	16.3	17.2	14.5	14.2	7.0	4.0	9.3	6.5	53.0	58.1
Tanzania	45.0	65.4	3.3	1.0	0.5	4.8	7.6	4.2	44.3	24.7
Tunisia	18.3	17.5	2.7	3.7	29.0	30.8	8.1	9.7	41.8	40.9
Uganda	53.0				7.0		8.5		31.5	
China	14.5	12.7	15.5	22.7	12.6	10.5	11.6	11.0	45.7	43.0
India	12.2	10.3	16.6	16.9	13.0	9.1	18.9	16.8	39.4	46.9
Korea, Rep.	9.4	7.0	34.3	44.4	10.8	5.7	9.7	9.0	35.9	33.9
Malaysia	9.9	9.0	12.8	32.7	5.3	2.7	9.5	11.4	62.5	44.1
Philippines	32.2	24.7	10.6	28.1	8.7	6.3	12.0	8.2	36.4	32.8
Thailand	19.0	16.4	20.2	34.5	15.5	8.3	3.6	6.1	41.8	34.7
Argentina	27.4	30.4	11.8	8.5	8.3	6.4	13.9	16.1	38.6	38.5
Brazil	17.7	18.7	18.9	19.6	8.6	6.0	16.7	11.6	38.1	44.1
Chile	29.5	15.0	3.7	1.7	6.3	1.0	11.0	17.1	49.5	78.0
Mexico	25.2	25.9	20.7	19.9	4.3	3.8	16.1	17.3	33.6	33.0

Source: World Bank (2013).

Notes: FB&T = food, beverages and tobacco; M&TE = machinery and transport equipment; T&C = textiles and clothing. 'Other manufacturing' includes wood and related products (division 33), paper and paper-related products (division 34), petroleum and related products (groups 353–56), basic metals and mineral products (divisions 36 and 37), fabricated metal products and professional goods (groups 381 and 385) and other industries (group 390) (http://data.worldbank.org/indicator/NV.MNF.OTHR.ZS.UN).

Table 20.3 Industrial and manufacturing growth rates: selected countries in Africa, Asia and Latin America (% p.a.)

	Industry, value added (annual % growth)				Manufacturing value added (annual % growth)			
	1971–80	1981–90	1991–2000	2001–12	1971–80	1981–90	1991–2000	2001–12
Algeria	5.0	2.6	1.8	3.4	9.5	4.4	-1.5	0.9
Benin	2.1	6.8	4.2	3.3	-0.6	7.4	6	2.8
Botswana	23.6	12.1	5.6	6.2	17.7	12.2	3.1	3.6
Burkina Faso	3.1	3.9	6.8	6.1	4.6	3	6.3	0.9
Cameroon	10.0	7.1	-0.7	-1.3	7.3	7.4	2.6	6.2
Central African Republic	4.4	0.8	1.2	1.3	8.2	6.5	0.4	0.7
Congo, Rep.	12.0	6.9	4.1	5.2	8.1	8.2	-2.4	10.2
Cote d'Ivoire	11.8	3.4	5.3	-0.8		2.4	4.8	-2.1
Egypt, Arab Rep.	8.9	3.9	6.0	3.7		7.1	6.3	3.4
Ethiopia		3.3	2.7	8.9		3.1	2.5	7.3
Gabon		3.3	-0.1	1.9	4.2	2.5	2.7	4.3
Gambia, The	5.8	4.4	1.8	3.3		7.5	1.4	2.8
Ghana				12.4				5.1
Kenya	9.8	4.0	0.9	4.5	12.2	4.8	1.2	3.8
Lesotho	8.9	9.3	9.0	5.7	7.2	9.6	7.4	6.7
Madagascar	0.5	-0.9	2.6	4.0		1.5	2	4.7
Malawi	6.1	3.1	1.9	7.3	1.9	4.2	0.5	2.8
Mali	1.3	4.3	6.6	1.7		5.9	-0.7	4.3
Mauritania	1.6	4.0	3.8	8.3		-1.8	4.3	4.3

Country								
Mauritius	2.0	8.9	5.6	1.6	2.8	9.8	5.3	0.9
Morocco	5.6	3.2	2.9	3.8	5.5	4.3	2.6	2.6
Senegal	3.6	3.1	3.8	4.9	-4.5	3.1	3	3
South Africa	2.7	0.8	0.8	1.3	15	3.4	5.7	3
Tanzania	4.2[a]	-1.0	2.9	9.6	5.1[a]	3.6	2.6	8.1
Tunisia	9.0	3.7	4.3	2.7	5.3	1.4	1.4	2.6
Uganda	-4.3[a]	4.6	11.1	7.9	-3.7[a]	4.2	13.2	6.1
Zambia	1.6	1.5	-3.0	7.9	3.4	4.6	1.4	4.3
Zimbabwe	2.4	3.4	1.1	0.6	4.9	3.5	-0.5	-2.1
China	11.5	9.6	13.6	11.7	9.9	9.5	12.9	10.8
India	3.7	6.2	5.6	7.7	4.1	6.2	6.1	7.2
Korea, Rep.	13.1	11.0	6.6	5.3	16.5	12	8.4	6.5
Malaysia	7.2	6.1	7.9	3.4	11.8	10	10.3	4
Philippines	7.7	0.6	2.6	3.8	6.2	1.1	2.6	4
Thailand	9.5	10.4	6.4	4.4	10.2	10	7.6	4.7
Argentina	1.9	-2.3	4.0	7.1	1.8	-1.8	2.9	4.3
Brazil	9.8	0.5	1.8	2.1			1.5	2.2
Chile	2.0	3.3	3.3	4.7	1.8	2.9	1.8	6.1
Mexico	6.7	2.0	4.1	3.5	6.3	2.3	4.5	1.9
World	2.9	2.5	2.2	2.3			3.7	3.5

Source: World Bank (2013).

Note: a 1965–80.

Table 20.4 Share of manufacturing in trade: selected countries in Africa, Asia and Latin America

	Manufacturing exports: Share of total exports (%)				Manufacturing imports: Share of total imports (%)			
	1971–80	1981–90	1991–2000	2001–12	1970–80	1981–90	1991–2000	2000–12
Algeria	2.6	1.8	3.2	2.0	75.8	67.8	64.6	74.1
Benin	9.1	46.7	6.6	14.0	69.5	68.1	55.2	47.3
Botswana			89.6	82.1			57.1	68.7
Burkina Faso	7.7	13.0	12.7	8.5	63.4	55.3	64.1	60.0
Cameroon	7.6	13.2	6.8	10.4	82.5	80.8	65.0	59.9
Central African Republic	29.6	43.5	49.0	20.2	79.3	71.2	58.4	55.0
Congo, Rep.	18.9	4.6	2.4	20.3	74.0	77.9	68.3	87.4
Cote d'Ivoire	7.6	10.0	14.1	15.7	71.7	56.3	59.8	47.2
Egypt, Arab Rep.	25.6	22.4	37.0	34.0	57.0	60.1	60.6	52.0
Ethiopia			7.5	8.4			70.1	68.8
Gabon	2.6	4.8	2.7	7.1	81.1	79.4	74.8	75.5
Gambia, The	0.1		19.0	21.0	62.4		64.2	46.0
Ghana	1.4	0.7	13.6	20.4	64.2	53.4	58.2	70.3
Kenya	12.8	13.5	26.0	32.8		60.3	62.2	62.1
Lesotho			94.9	85.8			63.1	55.5
Madagascar	7.1	9.4	26.3	48.9	69.0	62.6	63.8	65.5
Malawi	3.7	4.9	7.8	11.5	75.1	73.9	67.3	71.0
Mali	7.9	1.2	4.1	13.4	57.3	55.1	67.4	62.0
Mauritania	6.7		0.2	0.0	70.8		55.0	56.2

Mauritius	12.6	57.8	71.0	63.3	59.1	68.0	67.2	61.7
Morocco	16.7	42.3	56.6	66.4	56.6	50.4	61.7	62.6
Senegal	15.4	23.2	39.2	40.7	56.6	49.2	54.7	45.7
South Africa	31.6	18.5	47.3	51.2	83.4	69.3	75.4	66.9
Tanzania	12.3	9.2	16.6	20.4	70.1	65.6	60.3	59.8
Tunisia	25.6	52.7	76.9	75.9	63.3	64.7	76.5	72.3
Uganda			7.7	19.2	60.2	82.4	60.8	64.6
Zambia	0.6		10.7	8.7	75.6		71.9	72.3
Zimbabwe		29.9	31.7	34.4		68.0	73.7	56.7
China	54.3	52.2	83.5	92.7		70.0	75.5	69.9
India	85.4	61.3	74.9	67.2	49.2	53.2	61.4	50.6
Korea, Rep.	14.4	91.8	92.2	89.1	53.5	57.2	74.6	59.1
Malaysia	14.4	34.3	73.5	68.7	62.2	73.7	77.2	77.5
Philippines	16.4	28.8	68.3	80.9	58.4	45.1	75.3	72.1
Thailand	22.9	41.0	71.5	75.1	65.1	64.1	79.2	71.2
Argentina		25.3	31.7	31.0	70.1	75.7	79.0	85.1
Brazil	25.9	45.8	55.4	45.8	57.9	44.4	70.5	71.9
Chile	7.7	8.4	15.4	14.5	58.6	68.9	77.3	68.2
Mexico	30.1	31.2	76.5	76.1	77.2	73.0	80.6	81.8
World	61.9	65.9	73.5	70.6	57.2	64.0	74.3	69.9

Source: World Bank (2013), supplemented by World Bank (various years).

Table 20.5 Net FDI and GFCF: selected countries in Africa, Asia and Latin America

	FDI net inflows (% of GDP)				GFCF (% of GDP)			
	1970–80	1981–90	1991–2000	2000–12	1970–80	1981–90	1991–2000	2000–12
Algeria	0.9	0.0	2.0	1.5	37.6	31.2	25.6	26.1
Benin	0.5	0.8	6.3	0.9		14.6	16.1	19.9
Botswana	4.7	3.8	1.1	4.4	34.0	28.8	26.5	27.1
Burkina Faso	0.2	0.1	0.2	0.5	14.8	17.7	21.3	19.8
Cameroon	1.0	0.9	0.4	1.8	29.8	20.8	14.4	17.0
Central African Rep	1.1	0.5	1.7	3.2	9.7	10.6	11.1	11.5
Congo, Rep.	1.4	1.2	3.0	15.1	30.3	30.7	28.2	21.0
Cote d'Ivoire	1.0	0.5	3.7	1.9	23.1	14.2	11.7	11.8
Egypt, Arab Rep.	3.0	2.6	0.5	3.6	19.3	28.0	19.6	18.0
Ethiopia			4.1	2.7		15.4	17.2	22.9
Gabon	1.6	1.9	–0.8	2.2	40.7	33.3	25.5	23.9
Gambia, The	2.3	0.9	–1.0	7.2		19.3	8.8	18.9
Ghana	0.5	0.2	1.7	4.6	9.2	8.7	20.6	20.5
Kenya	0.8	0.4	0.9	0.6	20.7	19.0	17.2	19.5
Lesotho	0.3	1.7	8.4	5.1	20.6	42.1	62.3	26.3
Madagascar	0.3	0.2	4.6	5.9	9.6	10.9	12.4	27.2
Malawi	1.9	0.6	0.7	2.6	23.5	15.6	14.4	20.1
Mali	0.2	0.2	1.0	2.2	14.3	18.0	22.7	20.6
Mauritania	–0.3	0.8	1.0	9.0	17.7	27.0	19.8	31.2

Country								
Mauritius	0.3	0.7	0.9	2.0	26.4	22.0	26.2	23.1
Morocco	0.2	0.4	0.4	2.3	20.8	23.3	22.4	28.6
Senegal	0.7	0.3	1.6	2.0	13.0	17.7	20.3	27.2
South Africa	0.4	0.0	0.7	1.8	26.4	22.4	15.9	18.9
Tanzania		0.1	3.5	4.1		26.1[a]	16.8	26.0
Tunisia	1.8	1.6	2.0	3.5	25.2	27.1	25.1	22.3
Uganda	0.02	−0.14	1.6	4.4	8.9	9.2	19.5	21.9
Zambia	1.2	2.1	2.9	7.5	27.0	12.0	12.7	22.0
Zimbabwe	0.5	−0.1	2.7	1.2	16.7	16.4	18.4	9.5
China	0.0	0.7	2.5	3.7	27.2	28.9	33.6	41.4
India	0.2	0.0	0.9	1.6	15.9	21.0	23.0	30.2
Korea, Rep.	3.0	0.3	3.2	0.5	27.3	30.1	34.9	28.4
Malaysia	0.4	3.3	3.8	3.0	23.8	29.8	35.5	22.9
Philippines	0.4	0.7	6.8	1.2	22.3	21.9	22.5	20.5
Thailand		1.2	2.8	3.5	24.2	29.8	34.2	25.6
Argentina	0.3	0.7	3.0	2.1	25.8	18.8	18.0	20.2
Brazil	1.0	0.6	1.6	2.6	21.8	20.8	17.9	17.4
Chile	0.7	2.1	5.2	6.9	17.6	17.9	24.0	21.0
Mexico	0.7	1.1	4.3	2.8	20.7	19.5	19.3	20.5

Source: World Bank (2013).

Note: a 1990.

host government through its parastatal holding companies or development corporations took a majority or even 100 per cent shareholding with the foreign partner, effectively providing a loan to the value of the industrial plant it supplied, repayment of which was effectively guaranteed by the State, and the management services for which they were paid a fee. The transfer of technology, industrial skills and managerial competence was then expected to follow along with the expansion of a well-trained industrial labour force. Foreign companies were also attracted to such investments because of the protection they offered to their markets. Instead of competing with other companies for shares of African markets, they could become the sole supplier, protected against import competition by a tariff barrier. A further attraction was the possibility of offloading redundant equipment, though the use of less technologically advanced equipment did mean that employment was higher than with the latest technology and did not necessarily mean that such firms were unsuccessful.[7]

Food processing, textiles and clothing, shoes and other basic consumption goods dominated ISI. The next stage was to be the production of intermediate goods which would eventually allow a capital goods industry to grow.[8] Some countries tried to establish a regional industrial strategy in order to increase the size of the market, since the technology of plant size generated full capacity output much greater than any single country's demand. The East African Community, for example, had agreements, not always adhered to, concerning the location of specific manufacturing plants such that production was not duplicated across the Community. Exports, other than to other countries in a customs union, were precluded given the protectionist policies employed by other developing and by developed countries alike, so that domestic market size determined the level of demand.

While manufacturing output was directed to the domestic market, the material inputs of fixed and working capital were imported, even when domestic supplies of some inputs were available. The famous case of the Tanzanian Fertiliser Factory (Coulson, 1977) exemplified the outward orientation of input supply to manufacturing industries. In spite of the existence of domestic sources of phosphates, all chemical inputs were imported at a specially constructed jetty for the factory. The idea that foreign investment would generate linkages back into the domestic economy was replaced by a practice which minimised these linkages, as foreign partners found it simpler to provide a package of fixed and working capital inputs which matched the technology they supplied.

It could be argued that it was this highly dependent import substitution manufacturing strategy which was a major cause of the failure of ISI as a whole in Sub-Saharan Africa (SSA). The importing of manufacturing plant did not create less import dependence but rather more because manufacturers were dependent on supplies of foreign inputs which required foreign exchange, but were not themselves generating any foreign exchange to pay for these inputs. It was therefore hardly surprising that when, after the oil and drought shock of the 1970s, many African countries had balance of payments difficulties,[9] the first casualties were manufacturing firms heavily dependent on imported imports and spare parts. These balance of payments problems were exacerbated by what Riddell (1990: 187), in a case study of Côte d'Ivoire, calls the 'costs of foreign involvement', namely the remittances sent home by highly paid expatriate labour, and the dividend and interest payments repatriated to foreign capital. Table 20.6 tracks the current account balance of payments position of a selection of countries since 1970. Most countries have endured chronic current account deficits, with very few countries ending up in a better position at the end of the period than at the beginning. The exceptions were those richly endowed with minerals, and that especially the case after the financial crisis of 2008–9.

A further issue in early manufacturing growth was the transfer of technology which was expected to be embedded in the process of installing and operating new plant. In general, locally

Table 20.6 Current account balance of payments (% of GDP): selected years and selected African countries

	1970	1980	1981–90	1991–2000	2001–8	2008–12
Algeria	−13.9	0.6	−0.5	2.8	18.5	6.1
Benin	−6.9	−3.8	−6.8	−4.9	−6.9	−8.5
Botswana	−41.7	−12.6	5.7	8.3	10.4	−2.2
Burkina Faso	−6.3	−5.0	−1.7	−5.4	−10.1	−3.0
Cameroon	−4.1	−1.7	−4.8	−3.0	−1.8	−3.7
Central African Republic	−14.2	−5.5	−4.5	−3.9	−4.8	−8.8
Congo	−19.3	−9.8	−12.4	−13.7	−1.0	−11.4
Côte d'Ivoire	−6.4	24.8	−9.1	−3.9	1.6	4.4
Egypt	−6.9	−2.1	−3.9	0.4	1.4	−2.3
Gabon	−4.7	8.2	−3.1	5.3	15.7	7.9
Ghana	−3.4	−0.6	−2.0	−4.0	−6.5	−8.0
Kenya	−5.9	−16.4	−3.5	−9.4	−2.7	−7.1
Lesotho	−1.5	22.4	3.6	−15.7	5.7	−15.5
Madagascar	−4.2	−13.3	−7.3	−7.0	−10.8	−14.1
Malawi	−17.0	−9.8	−5.1	−6.8	−11.8	−14.1
Mali	−6.5	−7.0	−10.9	−8.3	−8.0	−9.5
Mauritania	−6.6	−23.7	−9.7	−1.8	−14.9	−9.2
Mauritius	2.7	−9.0	−2.4	−1.4	−3.5	−10.5
Morocco	−4.1	−7.9	−3.5	−1.1	0.7	−7.0
Nigeria	−3.3	3.2	−1.6	1.7	17.2	6.6
Senegal	−7.6	−14.6	−9.1	−5.6	−9.2	−5.4
South Africa	−7.7	4.7	0.6	−0.2	−4.1	−4.1
Tanzania	1.5	−0.1	−8.7	−11.6	−9.7	−14.8
Tunisia	−1.7	−12.6	−5.9	−9.7	−5.5	−10.6
Uganda	−7.1	−4.4	−0.9	−1.3	−1.2	−4.0
Zambia	6.0	−13.4	−11.2	−7.4	−7.7	3.6
Zimbabwe	−1.8	−7.0	−1.8	−4.2	−2.9	−14.2

Source: World Bank (2013), supplemented by World Bank (various years) and UNCTAD (2013b).

trained technical staff learned how to operate and maintain machinery and equipment but African countries had a dearth of engineers and technologists who could adapt and develop further the technologies embodied in the imported capital goods. The absence of a capacity to transfer technology was matched by the lack of institutional capacity to negotiate agreements with foreign investors which would secure reinvestment, rather than repatriation, of profits. In the case of joint ventures with majority state ownership, there appeared to be no mechanism for giving foreign capital incentives to ensure the profitability of the enterprises themselves. Governments were only too happy to secure foreign investment in new manufacturing and these issues seemed to be secondary to the investment itself.

Part of the reason why manufacturing investment has not generated as much employment as had been expected is that large-scale investment has been undertaken by foreign multi-national companies using capital-intensive technology requiring lower amounts of relatively skilled labour compared with technologies used by any pre-existing local firms (Langdon, 1975; Coughlin, 1988a). Neoclassical explanations of choice of technique explain this outcome in terms of overvalued exchange rates cheapening imported capital goods in relation to domestic wages, though Bagachwa (1992) implies that even if different price relativities had prevailed the choices would have been the same. A more plausible explanation is that competition in world markets demands products which are of an acceptable quality. These can usually only be guaranteed by the latest technical processes which are a product of developed country research and development. Hence choice of technique, at least in advanced manufacturing, is governed by choice of product and its quality, not relative prices of capital and labour (Stewart, 1977; Coughlin, 1988b; Wangwe, 1995). There may be choices in the case of ancillary activities which are not directly productive where more labour-intensive practices can be employed.

Although there were differences in the balance between state and private involvement, especially ownership, these patterns of manufacturing development were replicated throughout newly independent Africa (Riddell, 1990; UNECA, 2013). Yet there were potential alternatives. The use of domestic rather than foreign natural resource inputs, the creation of large- and small-scale supply industries based on local deposits of mineral inputs, and an active science and technology and research and development policy to adapt imported technologies to local needs: all were policies which would have gained maximum benefit from the imported technology (Thomas, 1974).[10] Such a strategy would have required much greater state intervention and direction which would have put a strain on the limited capacity of the State and therefore would have needed the building of institutions to make this State direction effective. In particular, the planning of manufacturing industry in an integrated, rather than 'shopping list' fashion would have required substantial organisation and the planned sequencing of production.[11] The use of foreign expertise to negotiate, where necessary, with foreign capital might also have helped to produce a more effective manufacturing investment.

A substantial body of literature examining the poor performance of manufacturing in Africa lays emphasis on these structural and institutional explanations. The begged question is why governments which pursued active development policies were unable or unwilling to develop independent and integrated manufacturing structures with strong linkages across different branches of manufacturing and also backwards and forwards to agriculture (Livingstone, 1971). So a second strand of literature concerns the class aspects of industrial development. It can be convincingly argued that the absence of both the classic indigenous industrial capitalist class to be found in European industrialisation or the 'comprador' bourgeoisie of Latin America, paved the way for the domination of foreign capital through alliances with the State and the 'bureaucratic bourgeoisie' (for example Shivji, 1975) which controlled it. The possibility for an independent industrialisation was limited by the weak bargaining position of this bureaucratic bourgeoisie resulting from the lack of technical capacity and by the fact that the interests of this class lay in consumption and rent-seeking and not in production with the purpose of accumulation, though why this should be so for SSA and not, say, for the successful East Asian or Latin American economies requires some explanation. Even if this view was presented in non-Marxist terms – for example the need to encourage entrepreneurship (see Kennedy, 1988) – there was common agreement on the importance of the State in filling the gap and taking an active role in restructuring the economy and building a manufacturing base.[12] However, in the view of Frank (1967) and the 'Dependency School' such manufacturing industrialisation as did take place would always be a dependent and limited one.

The Frankian view of dependent development was challenged by analyses which built on the work of Warren (1973, 1980) and argued for the existence of an indigenous capitalist class, borne out of trade and petty commodity production, whose primary purpose was capital accumulation (Kennedy, 1977; Swainson, 1977, 1980). Such a capitalist class was in the process of forming alliances with international capital to use its technology and other expertise (Kennedy on Ghana),[13] or of using the State to get into the position of being able to compete against foreign capital though not necessarily to become autonomous from it. (Swainson on Kenya).[14]

These studies demonstrated differences between African countries even where indigenous capitalist manufacturing classes were identified, let alone between those countries and countries such as Tanzania where the capitalist class was an 'alien' one (von Freyhold, 1977: 83). Such studies also argued against underestimating the degree to which capitalist industrialisation along with social and economic infrastructure had taken place (Sender and Smith, 1986; Sender, 1999).

However, the existence of a large number of small-scale – often one-person – manufacturing units, whether classed as 'petty commodity producers' (Le Brun and Gerry, 1975) or the urban informal sector, did raise the question of whether in strategic terms, great emphasis should be given in the early stages of manufacturing to these producers. From a Marxist point of view their chief characteristic is that they produce for their own subsistence and that they are subordinated to the capitalist mode of production. Thus typically, they produce cheap wage goods, often with scrap materials, which cheapen the means of subsistence and therefore the cost of labour. Rather than being a nascent capitalist class, these producers are more likely to join the industrial working class. Further, as Wuyts (2001) has argued, this process of cheapening labour has been sustained by imports of consumer manufactures subsidised by aid to provide incentive goods to increase agricultural and industrial productivity which itself has the effect of limiting the prospects for domestic manufacturing for both small and larger enterprises.

A different, and to some extent prevailing view, is to see these 'micro-enterprises' as forming the basis of the development of small-scale industrial workshops which could supply larger-scale domestic industry with specialist intermediate goods. Elkan (2000: 25) quotes a study by Liedholm (1990) which finds that in five African countries, which included Nigeria and Kenya, more than 50 per cent of those employed in industrial activities worked in micro-enterprises. They have also shown significant flexibility in responding to the competitive pressures following adjustment (Steel and Webster, 1992). Such enterprises are also major creators of employment – an urban labour 'sponge' in Livingstone's term (Livingstone, 1991).[15] Mead (1994) found in a survey of five countries, that over 40 per cent of all new entrants to the labour force over a decade were employed in small enterprises. Daniels and Mead (1998) found for Kenya that small enterprises contributed 12–14 per cent of GDP.[16] In Kenya in 1988 nearly 30 per cent of the manufacturing labour force worked in small enterprises employing between 0 and 49 people, of which more than half worked in micro-enterprises (Livingstone, 1991).[17] However, manufacturing only accounted for 17.6 per cent of small-scale enterprise employment, and of this 60.9 per cent was in wearing apparel and non-metal furniture production (Livingstone, 1991). In Tanzania, by comparison, 56 per cent of the urban labour force was found to be working in the informal sector[18] accounting for 32 per cent of urban income (Gaillard and Beernink, 2001), implying, as the Kenya data does, a relatively low level of productivity. As with manufacturing industry in general, linkages between the small-scale and large-scale sectors are weak, and backward linkages are particularly weak between small-scale manufacturing and agriculture (Livingstone, 1991, 2002). Conditions of work and rates of pay in these enterprises are poor, but there is some evidence that employment in such activities acts as a kind of training for workers to move on to large-scale, more formal employment (Pedersen, 2005). Mead and Liedholm (1996) in a survey of the dynamics of medium-scale enterprises (MSEs) find that they constitute both survival strategies and a basis for growth in firm size.

So part of the explanation for the poor performance of manufacturing in Africa therefore relates to the low level of development of a small-scale manufacturing sector with strong links to the large scale, often because governments have favoured large over small (Tybout, 2000), but also because large-scale enterprises have failed to create the linkages with MSEs which would inwardly orient the structure of production. Certainly it is evident from the studies of the small-scale sector that though it might be an important, though unrecognised, contributor to GDP, its role in manufacturing development has not emulated that played by its counterparts in the now developed industrial countries. The tendency towards large-scale capital-intensive manufacturing has meant that the 'missing middle' is even more missing. In class terms this means that small firms which might increase in size and diversify into other areas, thus creating a stronger local capitalist class are largely missing too. So whatever policies are pursued the absence of such a class makes it difficult to take advantage of liberalisation and offer some challenge to foreign capital. The emphasis on foreign investment is therefore not surprising given the absence of such a domestic capitalist class in most of SSA.

One recent development has been the expansion of South African investment into other parts of Africa following the demise of the Apartheid regime. The value of South African owned assets in the rest of Africa rose more than threefold between 1996 and 2001, and though only part of this was in manufacturing, other investments were in infrastructure and the financial sector, both offering complementarities to manufacturing investment, and also in the retail sector. South Africa's Industrial Development Corporation is especially active in Nigeria, where it has invested substantially in a range of activities in such branches as telecommunications, oil and gas and infrastructure (Daniel *et al.*, 2004). The major question is whether this investment expansion is likely to deepen the structure of SSA's manufacturing activity or simply replicate other foreign investment experiences. Cross African investment and trade could also become increasingly important with the renewed moves towards regional integration in all parts of Africa (UNCTAD, 2013a; Mbekeani, 2013).[19]

Structural adjustment and its effects on manufacturing

The neoclassical economic critique of African industrialisation embodied in World Bank structural adjustment policies explained the failure of import substitution strategies as stemming from state intervention and direction of the industrialisation process (World Bank, 1981). In this narrative, successful manufacturing development required an incentive structure that ensured that manufacturing enterprise was efficient and could compete in international trade. Protection had the result of creating manufacturing stagnation because it allowed firms to hide their inefficiency behind trade barriers. As many industries were state-owned or sponsored, they could also expect that governments would bail them out if they got into difficulties. High cost enterprises put prices up for everybody and contributed to low export growth or even stagnation. Alternatively, government controls on prices to prevent firms from making excessive profits simply reduced output and created parallel markets in the protected products.

Reduction of trade barriers and opening up domestic markets to competitive imports, or to foreign producers, would provide the incentive effects which would make domestic manufacturing more efficient and competitive in export markets. Firms operated below capacity because domestic markets were too small,[20] and overvalued exchange rates, resulting from pegging rates to the US dollar or the French franc, had the effect of biasing investment towards imported capital-intensive technologies, thus generating less employment than if exchange rates had been correctly aligned and precluding competitive manufacturing exports. Furthermore, overvalued exchange rates affected agricultural incomes by reducing the domestic prices of agricultural exportables, and therefore incentives to increase agricultural productivity. Low agricultural incomes resulted in inadequate effective internal market demand for manufactures with consequent under-utilisation of capacity and high unit costs of production. Manufacturing growth in Africa as everywhere was inextricably linked with export growth and with liberalisation: the removal of trade barriers, the freeing (in effect, devaluation) of exchange rates, the removal of exchange controls, the liberalisation of domestic financial markets and the privatisation of state-owned enterprises, including commercial and development banks.[21]

The implementation of liberalisation policies associated with the critique based on 'getting prices right' was expected to increase manufacturing productivity and accelerate manufacturing development. However, analysis by Lall (1995) suggested that there was little or no evidence of a sustained improvement in manufacturing performance either across Africa as a whole or across those countries that had large improvements in macroeconomic policy as judged by the World Bank (World Bank, 1994).[22] Lall showed that there was no significant difference in MVA growth between this group of countries compared with two other groups, one which had had 'small improvements' and the other with a 'deterioration' in macroeconomic policy in the data presented by the World Bank (1994). An update by Lawrence (2005) showed no clear relationship between the World Bank's categorisation of adjusting countries, and their subsequent manufacturing performance. Bennell (1998) undertook a similar exercise for both industry and manufacturing with similar conclusions. He noted the poor quality of the data and the problems associated with the methods used by World Bank (1994) to categorise countries into the three groups.[23]

There are clear difficulties in making a case for a close positive association, let alone a causative relationship, between degrees of 'structural adjustment' as measured by the World Bank, and manufacturing growth. The 'de-industrializing' view would argue that there was a negative relationship. Indeed, as Stein (1992) has cogently argued, the implementation of liberalisation policies was, at least in the short run, likely to lead to some 'de-industrialisation', as some of the macroeconomic policies associated with liberalisation and stabilisation − for example market clearing interest and exchange rates and government expenditure cuts were likely to result, as they did, in bankruptcies and depressed markets. Whatever the case, the growth data does not suggest that African manufacturing has responded to a changed macro-economic and trade environment as expected (at least by the neoclassical school) following the implementation of adjustment policies. The counterfactual is much more interesting. Had interventionist policies to rescue and rehabilitate failing enterprises been rigorously followed, rather than allowing import liberalisation to put them out of business altogether, it could be argued that SSA's manufacturing sectors would have been able to build on the previous 20 years' of accumulated learning and experience.

The cost of 'doing business' in Africa

Orthodox thinking has developed from a position of arguing that liberalising markets and fiscal and monetary stability was the basis for sustained growth to an acceptance that that changing the institutional environment is equally important. It would be difficult to disagree with the arguments of the neoclassical/new institutional school, and indeed it could be argued that the institutional problems they raise are precisely the reason for advocating a strong State which builds an effective social and economic infrastructural framework as a support for a planned and integrated industrial development. There are at least three 'institutional' factors which are cited as impeding manufacturing investment in SSA. First, investing is high risk and therefore higher returns are expected than elsewhere. There are risks associated with political stability, with crime and security and with an incompetent economic management that delivered high infla-tion. Second, communications are poor, both in terms of physical movement and telephone connections. Third, the ability to conduct business efficiently and cheaply is, according to this approach, hindered by high transactions costs, including informal payments to corrupt officials, associated with the time it takes to conclude a contract and to obtain the necessary permits. Doing business in Africa is high risk and high cost (Collier and Patillo, 2000; Eifert *et al.*, 2005). Manufacturing in particular is, as Collier observes, "a transactions-intensive activity, much more so than natural resources and agriculture" (Collier, 2000: 16), an important factor determining where Africa's comparative advantage lies, as we discuss later.

There is some evidence of an 'African factor' in countries' credit ratings but although coups, revolutions and other kinds of political upheaval do play a role in risk assessment, it appears that economic policy variables explain most of the variation in risk assessment (ul Haque *et al.*, 2000). There is some evidence that the fear that approved economic policies will not be sustained is a deterrent to investors and means that there is likely to be a substantial time lag between implementing such policies and gaining increased investment, either domestic or foreign. As Collier and Patillo (2000) observe in a comparison of Kenya, Ghana and Uganda, credit ratings take a long time to change and do not always reflect the economic fundamentals, which is hardly surprising when, as we have seen above in the case of the World Bank's assessment of structural adjustment, there is no clear relationship between the country macroeconomic policy scores and their growth rates.

Communications are another deterrent to investment. The latest reported median proportion of roads that were paved was 20 per cent (World Bank, 2013), with the highest proportion (Mauritius) 98 per cent and the lowest (Chad) 0.8 per cent. Of the continental countries, seven had more than half their roads paved, and these were mostly in North Africa. In 2012, in most mainland SSA countries, there were 10 fixed telephone lines for every 100 people, although, more positively, in two-thirds of the same set of countries there were more than 50 mobile phone subscribers to every 100 people (World Bank, 2013). Costs of telephone calls and reliability of service are also problems, and poor roads lead to high vehicle maintenance costs. Both communication problems lead firms to hold high levels of stocks of both inputs and outputs which also increase costs (Collier and Gunning, 1999a).

The new institutionalists argue that a further deterrent to manufacturing investment is the high transactions costs associated with business starts and contract enforcement. The time taken to start a business varied from 3 to 161 days (median 24) and to enforce a contract varied from 230 to 715 days (median 610) (World Bank, 2013).[24] Legal systems are not sufficiently developed to deal with cases of contract default which itself may be the result of opportunistic behaviour on the part of the defaulter, or an inability to fulfil contracts because of a shock or financial distress induced by the high costs of holding stocks, or by a shock against which the firm cannot insure either through the possession of financial reserves or through the insurance market (Collier and Gunning, 1999b).

While much of the literature identifies institutional obstacles to manufacturing and other investment, and tries to explain behaviour given these obstacles, little of it puts these deficiencies into the overall economic, political and social context of the countries concerned. The conclusion that something has to be done to reduce the costs of doing business is inescapable. But unless there is a contextual understanding of the causes, it is not clear what is to be done. One contextual element concerns the distribution of income and wealth. Detailed consideration of this is beyond the scope of this chapter. However, the highly skewed distribution of income and wealth in SSA countries means that goods markets are small, as are savings and the tax base. This has implications for levels of both private and public investment, and therefore for business costs. Highly skewed income distribution affects political stability and consequently impacts on investment risks. Improving the distribution of assets, especially land (see Griffin and Ickowitz, 2000), would affect the incomes of the large rural populations and have positive effects on the size of markets for manufactured goods.

Wages, skills and comparative advantage

Are African industrial wages 'too high' in relation to productivity and is this deterring investment? Are the low rates of educational enrolment at secondary and tertiary levels a cause of low productivity? Does SSA's abundance of unskilled labour and natural resources give the continent a comparative disadvantage in manufacturing? This section considers recent research on these issues. The research on the wages question is inconclusive; there is less ambiguity about education and skills and some scepticism about the application of static comparative advantage to a sector such as manufacturing, where dynamic scale economies can change comparative advantage over time.

Starting with wages, one effect of firms' employment of capital-intensive techniques, as the evidence above shows they do, is to create a demand for more skilled labour which in theory increases their wages. Empirical studies have indeed found that foreign firms, which are most likely to employ capital-intensive techniques, have been found to pay higher wages than local firms after controlling for age, occupation and tenure, with unskilled workers also being paid more, the average differential between foreign and local firms being between 8 and 23 per cent (te Velde and Morrissey, 2003). One explanation offered for this is that foreign firms have relatively less information about local labour markets and knowing this, local skilled workers can bargain up their wages, with a positive effect on unskilled workers' wages. This kind of evidence leads to the suggestion that wages in SSA are 'too high', certainly in relation to productivity (Teal, 2000).

There was some evidence presented in the past of labour market 'rigidities' exemplified by high public sector pay relative to the private sector, but Collier and Gunning (1999b) observe that real wages in the public sector have become lower than in the private sector throughout most of SSA. In the private sector, they argue that there is an 'implicit understanding' between governments and firms that allow firms to capture monopoly rents, part of which is paid as a wage premium (Collier and Gunning 1999b: 94). They report research showing that employees are paid at marginal product and that returns to education show the proper reward for skills. Although there is research which shows that large firms, unionisation and profitability produce wage premia, Collier and Gunning concur with Teal (1996) who shows that by allowing for the endogeneity of profits in an earnings function, size and wages are independent of each other, as is unionisation. That more profitable firms pay higher wages is likely to be the result of risk-sharing between firms and workers, a view supported by the fact that wages are found to be sensitive to changes in profit rates rather than their levels.

However, other research suggests that even when productivity is taken into account, unit labour costs are lower across SSA (except South Africa) than in the export processing zones of China (Eifert *et al.*, 2005 quoting research by Cadot and Nasir, 2001 on garment manufacturing enterprises). Bigsten *et al.* (2000), using firm-level data from five countries, found that real wages had fallen or stagnated in four of these five countries. They found that returns to labour with skills from secondary school and above were very high and consistent with a relative scarcity of such skills and therefore with the slow development of African manufacturing. They further found that returns to physical capital were very high. Taking this finding together with the known low rates of investment suggests, at least according to the neoclassical approach, that the cost of capital is high and that this might also be a reason for the failure to develop a successful manufacturing sector. Where the authors find large productivity differences between countries, as they do in the cases of Cameroon and Ghana, this is the result of differences in endowment of physical capital. Overall, the evidence on wages is very mixed and does not suggest that they are the cause of slow manufacturing growth in SSA. Indeed, there is some evidence from a recent survey that for light manufacturing, African wages are much lower than in China, for example, but that productivity is as low or even lower in some cases, thus making unit costs higher in the African countries surveyed (Dinh *et al.*, 2012) .

Raising skill levels through education and training, not least through increasing organisational and managerial efficiency (Kilby, 1961, 1962) should lead to higher wages and productivity. Enrolment ratios in primary education have risen since 1965 from an average of 52 to 94 per cent by 2000. However, enrolment ratios in secondary and tertiary education have only reached averages of 36 and 4 per cent respectively and this has to explain some of the problems of manufacturing growth. It might be expected at least that the possession of higher levels of skill by owners and/or their managers in manufacturing should lead to higher levels of productivity and greater efficiency as measured by lower costs of output. In an analysis of firms across three SSA countries, Pack and Paxson (2001) find that there is no significant effect of education levels of owner/managers on costs. Their explanation is that the lack of a competitive environment means that there is in effect no incentive to use the skills that are available to improve productivity and reduce costs by improved practices, innovations or both. Thus, in their view, in a more competitive environment such as that brought about by market liberalisation, it is likely that the skills level of managers would have a more significant impact on costs. This supports the argument of Pack (1993) that technical skills become important in a competitive environment and enable firms to take advantage of price liberalisation by increasing the responsiveness of output. Taken together with the findings of Bigsten *et al.* (2000), this set of approaches argues that raising the level of skills of the workforce through an expansion of secondary and tertiary education will increase manufacturing efficiency and growth, given a greater degree of competition. This conclusion follows from the competitive model these authors adopt, but not from the empirical work they undertake.

Africa's low level of education and its substantial endowment of natural resources relative to population, especially minerals and land, has formed the basis of the contention that the continent has a comparative advantage in natural resource exports, rather than in manufactures (Wood and Berge, 1997; Wood and Mayer, 2001). Wood and Mayer find that the shortfalls in actual as against predicted manufactured export shares can be accounted for by those factors which have been discussed above as limiting SSA's manufacturing growth – inadequate infrastructure, overvalued exchange rates, poor administration and high transactions costs. But if it is SSA's low level of education and skills and abundance of land and natural resources per capita which gives the continent a comparative disadvantage in exporting manufactures, it could be argued that policies which act on labour productivity such as higher levels of education, and transaction-cost-reducing improvements in infrastructure and administration will change these relationships (Collier, 2000). Wood and Mayer conclude that this will happen slowly in relation to SSA's competitors and that in the meantime a development strategy based on exploiting SSA's natural resource comparative advantage through increased mineral and agricultural exports is more realistic than one based on manufacturing. This may indeed be an appropriate short term strategy to accumulate resources for investment in manufacturing and associated infrastructure, but should not preclude a concurrent longer term strategy for structural shifts to manufacturing investment with consequent increases in growth (McMillan and Rodrik, 2011).

Credit and investment constrained?

The poor performance of African industrialisation, especially in the wake of two decades of structural adjustment, has led to consideration of the low level of development of financial markets which are said to constrain African firms' ability to obtain credit. Much of the neoclassical literature begs the question as to what determines the level of financial development. Bigsten *et al.* (2003: 110ff), using firm-level data from six SSA countries, report low levels of participation in formal credit markets by African manufacturing firms. Almost one-third of the 82 per cent of firms that did not apply for loans were considered to be credit constrained, either because they had inadequate collateral, found the process too difficult, or did not think they would get one if they applied. Surprisingly, only 9 per cent of the firms surveyed reported high interest rates as a reason. Very little of firms' debt was with informal lenders, even that of micro-enterprises. In an econometric analysis of the supply of and demand for credit, the authors find that on the supply side, firms which have higher expected profit-to-capital ratios,[25] are larger and already have debt are more likely to obtain credit. On the demand side, larger, more indebted and domestic firms are likely to seek more credit. It does appear that there are credit constraints for small and micro-firms that might be slowing the expansion of their numbers. To some extent this is corroborated by the evidence in Nissanke and Aryeetey (1998) that these kinds of enterprises are increasingly seeking informal sector finance as economic liberalisation expands their number. However, as Nissanke (2001) argues, while informal sources of finance as well as suppliers' credits (see Fafchamps, 1997) are an important source of finance for working capital, the expansion of MSEs requires greater investment in fixed capital and therefore access to formal sector finance. To the extent that firms find getting formal sector credit difficult, they are then limited to their own accumulated funds for any growth. Once again this is an argument for the State to provide affordable credit to help enterprises to which the formal sector may not lend.

SSA's manufacturing performance could therefore be poor because credit constraints limit levels of investment. Gross investment in SSA as a proportion of GDP averaged 15 per cent in 1965, rose to 25 per cent in 1975 and fell to 18 per cent in 2003 (see Table 20.5). One solution is to attract foreign investment. However, Moss *et al.* (2004) see continuing scepticism about foreign investment on the part of African governments as preventing rates of growth of FDI that at least match global levels. They find continuing obstacles to foreign investment, largely bureaucratic, which delay or prevent investment. They, too, cite the business climate as a barrier to such investment. However, Devarajan *et al.* (2003) analyse the relationship between investment and growth in SSA and, after excluding Botswana, which has enjoyed high investment ratios and high growth, and after controlling for endogeneity by taking initial investment ratios as instruments, discover no significant relationship between investment and growth.[26] The problem then is to explain the observed low productivity of investment. When Devarajan *et al.* look in detail at the Tanzanian case, they cannot explain the decline in productivity that they observe. It is not explained by state enterprise expansion, nor by a shift of labour from high to low productivity sectors. They find that one possible explanation is lower rates of capacity utilisation, but this can only explain part of the productivity decline.[27] They conclude that until this productivity decline can be explained, higher investment levels may yield even lower returns. However, Hoeffler (2002) shows that applying the Solow augmented growth model to 85 (including 22 SSA) countries, Africa's slow growth can be explained by low investment ratios and high population growth. It may well be the case that unless high investment ratios are accompanied by high productivity, they will not result in high rates of growth. But even if productivity had been higher. SSA will need much higher investment ratios to match East Asia's rates of manufacturing growth (see Tables 20.4 and 20.5).

Public versus private: Privatisation retarded?

A considerable increase in (especially inward) investment might have been expected as a consequence of the liberalisation policy of privatising state-owned companies, both because of the inflow of capital required to purchase and rehabilitate the enterprises and because of the improved business climate such privatisations were meant to represent. The rehabilitation of run-down state manufacturing enterprises and of the infrastructure of state-owned utilities might also be expected to improve conditions for further manufacturing investment. Nellis (2003) cites evidence from a range of sources to show that privatised firms are better run and have become more profitable, although they have considerably reduced employment, while the proportion of failures has been relatively small. Average state-owned enterprise (SOE) divestiture between 1991 and 2001 stood at 40 per cent and the largest number of privatisations in SSA has been in industry including manufacturing. However, Nellis regards this as slow progress compared with Latin America and the transition economies, although it is not clear why these are relevant comparisons, and why this should be a surprise given the context in which the SSA privatisations take place. Domestic bidders for the smaller SOEs face problems in raising funds to purchase them, especially the lack of a developed financial sector (Ariyo and Jerome, 1999).

Privatisation is also largely unpopular because the bigger potentially highly profitable enterprises end up in the hands of foreign capital with attendant fears about employment and profit repatriation (Nellis, 2003) and because politicians are seen as using privatisation for their own capital accumulation (Craig, 2000). The very political unpopularity of privatisation then becomes a brake on governments' enthusiasm for divestiture. The difficulty of attracting buyers for large SOEs is partly the consequence of the factors we have discussed above that inhibit investment in general, especially as these enterprises can only be acquired by foreign firms or by domestic capital in conjunction with foreign firms.

However, it is not clear that the conventional wisdom that the public sector performs worse than the private sector is borne out by the evidence, such as it is. Millward (1988) pointed to the difficulties of making such comparisons and the lack of evidence of a general comparative inefficiency on the part of state-owned enterprises. One study covering 70 Kenyan joint-ventures, public and private firms, did not find systematic evidence pointing to the greater technical efficiency and profitability of private as against public firms (Grosh, 1988). As Nellis notes, it has been widely observed that privatisation is likely to be successful in terms of improving enterprise performance when it is accompanied by greater market competition and active regulation (Nellis, 2003). It ought to be possible by regulatory means to improve the performance of SOEs such that either they perform better thus delivering surpluses for reinvestment and government revenue, or their better performance makes them more attractive to private sector investors.[28] This is particularly important for those public utilities on which manufacturing relies. In conclusion, the evidence for the benefits of privatisation is not clear cut and its potential contribution to manufacturing growth uncertain.

Exporting to success

The data in Tables 20.1–20.4 show some variation in manufacturing performance in SSA over the last four decades. There have been successes, at least at individual firm level, and in a few cases at country level. The research reported here on exports gives some support to an optimistic view of manufacturing exports which contests the notion of SSA's comparative advantage in non-manufactures. The availability of World Bank firm-level data for several SSA countries now allows some possibility of determining those factors which are strongly associated with manufacturing success (World Bank, 2014). However this kind of econometric work cannot explain why the determining factors are in place in some cases and not in others.

A principal theoretical argument for exporting is that it overcomes the problem of small market size faced by most African economies and therefore allows for the exploitation of increasing returns to scale.[29] A major strand running through recent research is that success of firms is strongly associated with their participation in export markets. Harding *et al.* (2004) find that older firms' growth slows, possibly because they have limited access to export markets. Large firms survive while smaller more efficient firms exit. Productivity growth is strongly associated with 'competitive pressure' as proxied by profit per employee.[30] Part of that competitive pressure can be affected by either an opening up to export markets or the entry of foreign firms which have experience in export markets. Finding evidence that successful manufacturing growth is associated with exporting could complete a virtuous circle. If size is associated with survival and with exports, then turning towards export markets enables firms to grow, especially those small efficient firms that exit because they cannot grow (Harding *et al.*, 2004). Thoburn (2005) argues that it is also possible that firms have been able to export because of the protection they have enjoyed against imports, enabling them to produce at higher capacity for a larger local market than would be the case without protection, and therefore at marginal costs that make exports competitive, following the 'exported orientated import substitution' path which has been so successful in East Asia.[31]

Other research supports the view that exports are the key to success. Söderbom and Teal (2003) find that firm size is positively associated with higher wages, higher efficiency and with exporting. They argue that Mauritius is an example of a country that has higher wages and higher manufacturing employment because of the export orientation of its relatively labour-intensive manufacturing. This can be promoted by removing the distortions in factor prices which make capital relatively cheap (one of the main purposes of financial liberalisation), thus encouraging labour-intensive production across firms of different size (Söderbom and Teal, 2004). Firms may enter into exporting, learn from exporting and become more efficient or they may become more efficient and select into exporting (Bigsten *et al.*, 2000b; 2004). Söderbom and Teal (2003) corroborate these findings and argue that for the African garment manufacturing industry, which has a potential cost advantage because of its labour intensity, success in increasing manufacturing employment and reducing poverty will require getting large firms to adopt more labour-intensive techniques, but also increase technical efficiency in order to reduce labour costs. The authors also find that exports and income growth are closely linked, but that there is no particular link between manufactured exports and income growth. However, the growth of manufacturing geared towards export markets would be one way of generating higher rates of income growth. Finally, the necessity of a favourable macroeconomic framework for exporting is emphasised by a study of six CFA (*Coopération financière en Afrique centrale*) and five non-CFA African countries which finds that managing the real exchange rate to avoid appreciation has a very positive effect on manufactured export growth (Sekkat and Varoudakis, 2000).

Conclusion: African manufacturing – back to the future?

This review of manufacturing industrialisation in SSA has shown a wide variation in country experiences within an overall picture of slow growth with elements of stagnation or decline and, sometimes, success. The original industrial policies based on ISI delivered relatively high growth rates in the early period, but these were not sustained. The research on the ISI period has not shown in any conclusive way that it was the strategy itself that was the problem but rather the unplanned implementation of ISI together with an unfortunate set of shocks during the 1970s allied with poor management of enterprises. The adoption of structural adjustment programmes has also not resulted in rapid manufacturing growth. Again, the research is ambiguous as to whether this outcome is the result of the policies themselves or because they have been poorly implemented. There have been notable, though atypical, exceptions to this story – in particular Mauritius. It is also interesting that there have been enough cases of successful firms operating throughout Africa to allow for some extensive econometric analysis of firm behaviour and characteristics and the determinants of success. Even if it is accepted that Africa has a comparative advantage in land and natural resources, most countries still have a lower share of exports from manufacturing than predicted from their other characteristics (Wood and Mayer, 2001). There is therefore room for the expansion of African manufacturing beyond its current position and it is also likely, *pace* Wood and Mayer, that changing conditions in SSA will alter the degree to which its comparative disadvantage in manufacturing is maintained.

Whether approaching the question from a structuralist or a neoclassical/institutional position, increasing Africa's manufacturing growth rate will require a number of policies pursued simultaneously. Improvements in infrastructure, especially transport and communications, in the quality of administration, in educational enrolment at secondary and tertiary levels and in reducing transactions costs, are fundamental to reducing risks and achieving the increases in investment ratios which are necessary to generate sustained growth. The improvement of infrastructure and the associated reduction of transactions costs does of course reduce the 'natural' protection (Rudaheranwa, 2000), enjoyed especially by landlocked countries and in such a case assumes that removal of this protection will accompany other policies leading to a more efficient and competitive manufacturing sector, not a likely outcome without the set of ancillary policies outlined here.

The attraction of foreign investment especially in the form of joint ventures with local private and state shareholders (still perhaps the most effective way of sharing risks) can lead to an increase in the level of management and technical skills and greater linkages with domestic manufacturers and small-scale enterprises (Moss *et al.,* 2004). The combination of policies outlined above does allow for a revival of the 'infant industry' approach as originally envisaged, where as a result of their implementation, unit costs are reduced and the new enterprises are able to compete both nationally and internationally (Tribe, 2000).

Much recent research finds that orientation towards exports is associated with successful manufacturing firms. However, some of that exporting success may be the result of prior protection against imports. Hence the wholesale adoption of the trade liberalisation package in conjunction with the improvements listed above may not be appropriate policy for some time, with protection being necessary in the short run. In this case, the trade liberalisation policies being promoted by the World Trade Organization will not help African industrialisation. It may still be the case that selective state intervention in industrial planning and pricing and improvements in the quality of that intervention is still necessary. In this context, the Africa Commission (Commission for Africa, 2005)[32] has endorsed the export-orientation approach: "manufacturing growth can become the driver of growth, if Africa breaks into the global market" (p. 218), but also recognised the importance of the role of the state in high growth countries (among which are included Mauritius and Botswana) "in attracting investment; encouraging restructuring, diversification and technological dynamism; boosting productivity, competitiveness and exports; and securing long-term growth" (p. 222). However, it is not made clear whether any part of the $550 million 'Investment Climate Facility' proposed in the report will be used to improve the quality of state intervention. As Sender (1999) observes, it is the direct intervention by the State in credit allocation to manufacturing, as well as a relatively repressive financial system, which characterised the successful East Asian economies.[33] Such a role for the State in promoting manufacturing was characteristic of industrialisation strategies in SSA in the 1960s and 1970s, and initially generated significantly high manufacturing growth rates. Whether SSA states will be assisted to perform this function effectively is another matter.

Notes

1 This chapter is an updated and heavily revised version of Lawrence (2005). Many thanks to the editors for their comments and suggestions.

2 The focus in this chapter is on manufacturing rather than industry as a whole because this sector is considered to be the most dynamic and most closely correlated with growth of GDP (see Weiss, 1988).

3 Comparisons with East Asia, rather than, say, Latin America, whose share of world manufacturing output has hardly increased over the last four decades, are appropriate here since per capita GDP for many African countries was significantly higher in 1960 than for most of the East Asian countries (see Lawrence and Thirtle, 2001).

4 The country selection for Africa was largely determined by data availability across the time periods and variables.

5 There is the usual problem of data availability, as well as reliability, and so the period covers the first year data is available after 1970 and the last year comparable data is available before 2012, as well as points in between.

6 Anyang' Nyong'o (1988: 11) points out that ISI began in a limited way under colonial rule, particularly during the Second World War.

7 See Kilby (1969) for a classic account of manufacturing development in Nigeria. See also Barker *et al.* (1986) and Coulson (2013) for a discussion of the mechanics of manufacturing industrialisation in the very different political context of Tanzania, and Riddell (1990) for a classic comparative study of manufacturing. This section of the chapter is based on these accounts as well as my own direct observations of East African manufacturing investment in the late 1960s and early 1970s.

8 See Nixson (2005) for a interesting discussion of these 'stages' of industrialisation in the African context.

9 Excluding oil-rich Nigeria and mineral-rich South Africa, SSA's gold and dollar reserves fell in real terms by 56 per cent between 1970 and 1980. By the beginning of the 1980s average import coverage by reserves was one and a half months for SSA compared with three months for East Asia and the Pacific. A third of SSA countries had less than one month's import coverage (IMF, 2013; World Bank, 2013).

10 Ironically, the UNECA study argues for the very industrialisation strategies based on Africa's rich commodity endowments, that were argued for in the years after political independence (UNECA, 2013). See also the study by Morris *et al.* (2012) which advocates a strategy of building local resource linkages to manufacturing.

11 See Luttrell (1986) for a detailed plan for an iron and steel industry for Tanzania set in the context of the industrialisation debates discussed here and heavily influenced by Thomas's theory of convergence of domestic resource use and domestic demand (Thomas, 1974). A typical catch-all industrial set of proposals for an industrialisation programme can be found in Ndam (1991).

12 Ndulu and O'Connell (1999) take a broader political economy approach to explaining general economic performance which is rooted in the early absence of political plurality and democratic constraints on what became an acquisitive political class borne of anti-imperialist one-party states.

13 Pedersen (2005: 213) in a discussion of Kenya refers to the 'alignment' of small-scale business, in an increasingly differentiated small-scale sector, with the large-scale sector in a relationship of 'mutual interdependence'.

14 For an elaboration of these issues see the articles by Kennedy (1977), Swainson (1977) and von Freyhold (1977).

15 Tribe (2005) points out that there are issues of economic efficiency and its measurement raised here.

16 Elkan (2000) points out that official statistics tend to ignore the output of micro-enterprises in estimating manufacturing GDP, though the imputation of non-marketed agricultural output has long been a part of GDP estimates.

17 See also Mensah *et al.* (2007) for Ghana.

18 See Mead and Morrisson (1996) for an informative comparison of informal sector characteristics across several developing countries.

19 As noted earlier, regional economic blocs were intended to create larger markets for domestic manufacturing. Discussion of these unions is beyond the scope of this chapter.

20 This was a major point of a prescient article based on earlier work on minimum efficient enterprise size (Brown, 1961), although Ndulu (1986), in a study of Tanzanian manufacturing, emphasises the

shortage of imported inputs and infrastructural causes of low capacity utilisation as well as the excessive growth of capacity and downplays the lack of demand as an issue.

21 See World Bank (1987) for a detailed account of its view of the relationship between industrialisation and trade and especially pp. 106–7 for its diagnosis of Africa's industrialisation problems. See also Meier and Steel (1989) for a fuller account.

22 The classifications of large and small improvements and deterioration refer to changes, between the periods 1981–6 and 1987–91, in fiscal balance (excluding grants) and total government revenue, in seignorage and inflation, and in the real effective exchange rate and the parallel market exchange rate premium (World Bank, 1994: 260–1).

23 An additional issue bearing on manufacturing performance over time is that several African countries have been through periods of political instability which affected their economic performance.

24 There appears to have been some speeding up of business start approvals, but a deterioration in time taken to enforce contracts since the numbers reported in Lawrence (2005) of medians of 61 and 295, respectively.

25 These are calculated in the way banks would be expected to do, namely making sector specific profit predictions for each firm, based on a range of observable characteristics for the sector.

26 An anonymous referee for Lawrence (2005) pointed out that trend analyses of the investment ratio and growth rate show a good relationship between the two while annualised data rarely does since the growth rate is known to be far more volatile than the investment ratio.

27 Low rates of capacity utilisation are a problem, however. UNIDO (2001) reports average rates of 30–50 per cent for SSA. These low rates are adduced to balance of payments constraints affecting the supply of imported inputs and poor management of this supply when there are no constraints (see Meier and Steel, 1989), but for a different explanation see Ndulu (1986).

28 Grenier *et al.* (2000) find that state-owned firms are more likely to export than private ones. Although these firms may have been nationalised because they exported, the fact that they are able to enter export markets suggests that they must be relatively efficient.

29 It can also overcome problems for individual supplier firms caused by the collapse of their customers (see Wangwe, 1995). See also Ndulu (1986) for other causes of low capacity utilisation and therefore failures to take advantage of scale economies.

30 Profit per employee is found to increase with firm size. Following the logic of neoclassical competition theory, large firms subjected to less competition can extract higher rents. However, an alternative explanation for high profits per employee is that large firms have more capital-intensive production techniques, more highly skilled management and better organisation, resulting in higher productivity and higher profits per employee. This latter variable may not in fact be proxying competitive pressure at all.

31 It is worth noting that the Asia experience, with which SSA's experience is usually compared, contains a variety of different development strategies and so means there is no one model from which SSA can learn (Booth, 2001).

32 Re-emphasised in its follow-up report (Commission for Africa, 2010)

33 Although Morrissey (2001) draws a less interventionist conclusion from his reading of the lessons to be learned from the highly performing Asian economies (Morrissey, 2001).

Bibliography

Anyang' Nyong'o, P. 1988. The Possibilities and Historical Limitations of Import-Substitution Industrialization in Kenya. In Coughlin, P. and Ikiara, G. K. (eds.). *Industrialization in Kenya: In Search of a Strategy*. Nairobi: Heinemann Kenya and London: James Currey: 6–50.

Ariyo, A. and Jerome, A. 1999. Privatization in Africa: An Appraisal. *World Development*. 27 (1): 201–213.

Bagachwa, M. S. D. 1992. Choice of Technology in Small and Large Firms: Grain Milling in Tanzania. *World Development*. 20 (1): 97–107.

Barker, C., Bhagavan, M. R., von Collande, P. and Wield, D. 1986. *African Industrialisation: Technology and Change in Tanzania*. Aldershot: Gower Press.

Bennell, P. 1998. Fighting for Survival: Manufacturing Industry and Adjustment in Sub-Saharan Africa. *Journal of International Development*. 10 (5): 621–637.

Bigsten, A., Collier, P., Dercon, S., Fafchamps, M., Gauthier, B., Gunning, J. W., Isaksson, A., Oduro, A., Oostendorp, R., Patillo, C., Söderbom, M., Teal, F. and Zeufack, A. 2000. Rates of Return on Physical and Human Capital in Africa's Manufacturing Sector. *Economic Development and Cultural Change*. 48 (4): 801–827.

Bigsten, A., Collier, P., Dercon, S., Fafchamps, M., Gauthier, B., Gunning, J. W., Oduro, A., Oostendorp, R., Patillo, C., Söderbom, M., Teal, F. and Zeufack, A. 2003. Credit Constraints in African Manufacturing Enterprises in Africa. *Journal of African Economies.* 12 (1): 104–125.

Bigsten, A., Collier, P., Dercon, S., Fafchamps, M., Gauthier, B., Gunning, J. W., Oduro, A., Oostendorp, R., Patillo, C., Söderbom, M., Teal, F. and Zeufack, A. 2004. Do African Manufacturing Firms Learn from Exporting? *Journal of Development Studies.* 40 (3): 115–141.

Booth, A. 2001. Why is South-East Asia Different from Taiwan and South Korea? in Lawrence, P. and Thirtle, C. (eds.). *Africa and Asia in Comparative Economic Perspective.* Basingstoke and New York: Palgrave: 35–48.

Brown, A. J. 1961. Economic Separatism Versus a Common Market in Developing Countries. *Yorkshire Bulletin.* 13 (1 and 2) May: 33–40 and November: 80–96.

Cadot, O. and Nasir, J. 2001. *Incentives and Obstacles to Growth: Lessons from Manufacturing Case Studies in Madagascar.* Regional Programme on Enterprise Development (RPED) Paper No 117. Washington, DC: World Bank: 45 pp.

Collier, P. 2000. Africa's Comparative Advantage. In Jalilian, H., Tribe, M. and Weiss, J. (eds.). *Industrial Development and Policy in Africa.* Cheltenham: Edward Elgar: 17–158.

Collier, P. and Gunning, J. W. 1999a Why has Africa Grown Slowly? *Journal of Economic Perspectives.* 13 (3): 3–22.

Collier, P. and Gunning, J. W. 1999b. Explaining African Economic Performance. *Journal of Economic Literature.* 27 (1): 64–111.

Collier, P. and Pattillo, C. (eds.). 2000. *Investment and Risk in Africa.* Basingstoke: Macmillan; New York: St Martin's Press.

Commission for Africa. 2005. *Our Common Interest.* London: Commission for Africa – accessible from http://www.commissionforafrica.info/about

Commission for Africa. 2010. *Still Our Common Interest.* London: Commission for Africa – accessible from http://www.commissionforafrica.info/about

Coughlin, P. 1988a. Economies of Scale, Capacity Utilization and Import Substitution: A Focus on Dies, Moulds and Patterns. In Coughlin, P. and Ikiara, G. K. (eds.). *Industrialization in Kenya: In Search of a Strategy.* Nairobi: Heinemann Kenya and London: James Currey: 112–125.

Coughlin, P. 1988b. Development Policy and Inappropriate Product Technology: The Kenyan Case. In Coughlin, P. and Ikiara, G. K. (eds.). *Industrialization in Kenya: In Search of a Strategy.* Nairobi: Heinemann Kenya and London: James Currey: 143–163.

Coulson, A. 1977. Tanzania's Fertiliser Factory. *Journal of Modern African Studies.* 15 (1): 119–125.

Coulson, A. 2013. *Tanzania: A Political Economy.* Oxford: Oxfrd University Press.

Craig, J. 2000. Evaluating Privatization in Zambia: A Tale of Two Processes. *Review of African Political Economy.* 27 (85): 357–366.

Daniel, J., Lutchman, J. and Naidu, S. 2004. Post-apartheid South Africa's Corporate Expansion into Africa. *Review of African Political Economy.* 31 (100): 343–348.

Daniels, L and Mead, D. C. 1998. The Contribution of Small Enterprises to Household and National Income in Kenya. *Economic Development and Cultural Change.* 47 (1): 45–71.

Devarajan, S., Easterly, W. R. and Pack, H. 2003. Low Investment is Not the Constraint on African Development. *Economic Development and Cultural Change.* 51 (3): 547–571.

Dinh, H. T., Palmade, V., Chandra, V. and Cossar, F. 2012. *Light Manufacturing in Africa: Targeted Policies to Enhance Private Investment and Create Jobs.* Washington, DC: World Bank.

Eifert, B., Gelb, A. and Ramachandran, V. 2005. *Business Environment and Comparative Advantage in Africa: Evidence from the Investment Climate Data.* Working Paper Number 56. Washington, DC: Center for Global Development: 47 pp.

Elkan, W. 2000. Manufacturing Microenterprises as Import Substituting Industries. In Jalilian, H., Tribe, M. and Weiss, J. (eds.). *Industrial Development and Policy in Africa.* Cheltenham: Edward Elgar: 22–29.

Fafchamps, M. 1997. Trade Credit in Zimbabwean Manufacturing. *World Development.* 25 (3): 795–815.

Frank, A. G. 1967. *Capitalism and Underdevelopment in Latin America: Historical Studies of Chile and Brazil.* New York: Monthly Review Press.

Gaillard, H. and Beernink, A. 2001. The Urban Informal Manufacturing Sector in Tanzania: Neglected Opportunities for Socioeconomic Development. In Szirmai, A. and Lapperre, P. (eds.). *The Industrial Experience of Tanzania.* Basingstoke: Macmillan: 318–340.

Grenier, L., McKay, A. and Morrissey, O. 2000. Exporting, Ownership and Confidence in Tanzanian Enterprises. *World Economy.* 22 (7): 995–1012.

Griffin, K. and Ickowitz, A. 2000. The Distribution of Wealth and the Pace of Development. In Griffin, K. (ed.). *Studies in Development, Strategy and Systemic Transformation*. Basingstoke: Macmillan: 66–94.

Grosh, B. 1988. Comparing Parastatal and Private Manufacturing Firms: Would Privatization Improve Performance? In Coughlin, P. and Ikiara, G. K. (eds.). *Industrialization in Kenya: In Search of a Strategy*. Nairobi and London: Heinemann Kenya and James Currey: 251–264.

Harding, A., Söderbom, M. and Teal, F. 2004. *Survival and Success Among African Manufacturing Firms*. Centre for the Study of African Economies Working Paper 2004–05. Oxford: Oxford University: 33 pp.

Hoeffler, A. 2002. The Augmented Solow Model and the African Growth Debate. *Oxford Bulletin of Economics and Statistics*. 64 (2): 135–58.

IMF. 2013. *International Financial Statistics*. Washington, DC: International Monetary Fund – accessible from www.imf.org

Jalilian, H. and Weiss, J. 2000. De-Industrialization in Sub-Saharan Africa: Myth or Crisis? In Jalilian, H., Tribe, M. and Weiss, J. (eds.). *Industrial Development and Policy in Africa*. Cheltenham: Edward Elgar: 17–158.

Kennedy, P. 1977. Indigenous Capitalism in Ghana. *Review of African Political Economy*. 8 (January–April): 21–38.

Kennedy, P. 1988. *African Capitalism: The Struggle for Ascendancy*. Cambridge: Cambridge University Press.

Kilby, P. 1961. African Labour Productivity Reconsidered. *Economic Journal*. 71 (282): 273–291.

Kilby, P. 1962. Organization and Productivity in Backward Economies. *Quarterly Journal of Economics*. 76 (2): 303–310.

Kilby, P. 1969. *Industrialization in an Open Economy: Nigeria 1945–1966*. Cambridge: Cambridge University Press.

Lall, S. 1995. Structural Adjustment and African Industry. *World Development*. 23 (12): 2019–2031.

Langdon, S. 1975. Multinational Corporations, Taste Transfer and Underdevelopment: A Case Study from Kenya. *Review of African Political Economy*. 2: 12–35.

Lawrence, P. 2005. Explaining Sub-Saharan Africa's Manufacturing Performance. *Development and Change*. 36 (6): 1121–1141.

Lawrence, P. and Thirtle, C. (eds.). 2001. *Africa and Asia in Comparative Economic Perspective*. Basingstoke: Palgrave Macmillan.

Le Brun. O. and Gerry, C. 1975. Petty Producers and Capitalism. *Review of African Political Economy*. 2: 20–32.

Liedholm, C. 1990. *The Dynamics of Small-Scale Industry in Africa and the Role of Policy*. Working Paper. East Lansing: Michigan State University.

Livingstone, I. 1971. Agriculture versus Industry in Economic Development. In Livingstone, I. (ed.). *Economic Policy for Development*. Harmondsworth: Penguin Books: 235–249.

Livingstone, I. 1991. A Reassessment of Kenya's Rural and Urban Informal Sector. *World Development*. 19 (6): 651–670.

Livingstone, I. 2002. Prospects for Rural Labour Force Absorption Through Rural Industry. In Belshaw, D. G. R. and Livingstone, I. (eds.). *Renewing Development in Sub-Saharan Africa: Policy Performance and Prospects*. London: Routledge.

Luttrell, W. L. 1986 *Post-Capitalist Industrialization: Planning Economic Independence in Tanzania*. New York: Praeger.

Mbekeani, K. K. 2013. *Intra-Regional Trade in Southern Africa: Structure, Performance and Challenges*. Regional Integration Policy Papers No. 2, NEPAD and Regional Integration and Trade Division. Tunis: African Development Bank.

McMillan, M. and Rodrik, D. 2011. *Globalization, Structural Change, and Productivity Growth*. NBER Working Paper 17143. Cambridge, Mass: National Bureau of Economic Research.

Mead, D. C. 1994. The Contribution of Small Enterprises to Employment Growth in Southern and Eastern Africa. *World Development*. 22 (12): 1881–1894.

Mead, D. C. and Morrisson, C. 1996. The Informal Sector Elephant. *World Development*. 24 (10): 1611–1619.

Mead, D. C. and Liedholm, C. 1998. The Dynamics of Micro and Small Enterprises in Developing Countries. *World Development*. 26 (1): 61–74.

Meier, G. M. and Steel, W. F. (eds.). 1989. *Industrial Adjustment in Sub-Saharan Africa*. New York: Oxford University Press for the World Bank.

Mensah, J. V., Tribe, M. and Weiss, J. 2007. The Small-Scale Manufacturing Sector in Ghana: A Source of Dynamism or of Subsistence Income? *Journal of International Development*. 19 (2): 253–273.

Millward, R. 1988. Measured Sources of Inefficiency in the Performance of Private and Public Enterprises in LDCs. In Cook, P. and Kirkpatrick, C. (eds.). *Privatization in Less Developed Countries*. Basingstoke: Palgrave Macmillan.

Mkandawire, T. 1991. De-Industrialization in Africa. In Anyang' Nyong'o, P. (ed.). *Industrialization at Bay: African Experiences*. Nairobi: Academy Sciences Publishers: 130–52.

Mkandawire, T. and Soludo, C. 1999. *Our Continent Our Future*. Dakar, Trenton, NJ and Ottawa: CODESRIA, Africa World Press and IDRC – accessible from www.idrc.ca/EN/Resources/Publications

Morris, M., Kaplinsky, R. and Kaplan, D. 2012 *One Thing Leads to Another: Promoting Industrialization by Making the Most of the Commodity Boom in Sub-Saharan Africa*. Accessible from: http://www.prism.uct.ac.za/Downloads/

Morrissey, O. 2001. Lessons for Africa from East Asian Economic Policy. In Lawrence, P. and Thirtle, C. (eds.). *Africa and Asia in Comparative Economic Perspective*. Basingstoke: Palgrave Macmillan: 35–48.

Moss, T. J., Ramachandran, V. and Shah, M. S. 2004. *Is Africa's Skepticism of Foreign Capital Justified? Evidence from East African Firm Survey Data*. Working Paper Number 41. Washington, DC: Center for Global Development: 29 pp.

Ndam, S. N. 1991. Africa's Industrial Performance: A Review and Needs Assessment. In Anyang' Ny'ongo, P. and Coughlin, P. (eds.). *Industrialization at Bay: African Experiences*. Nairobi: African Academy of Sciences: 109–130

Ndulu, B. 1986. Investment, Output Growth and Capacity Utilization in an African Economy: The Case of the Manufacturing Sector in Tanzania. *Eastern Africa Economic Review*. 2 (1): 14–30.

Ndulu, B. and O'Connell, S. A. 1999. Governance and Growth in Sub-Saharan Africa. *Journal of Economic Perspectives*. 13 (3): 41–66.

Nellis, J. 2003. *Privatization in Africa: What has Happened? What is to be Done?* Working Paper Number 25. Washington, DC: Center for Global Development: 34 pp.

Nissanke, M. K. 2001. Financing Enterprise Development in Sub-Saharan Africa. *Cambridge Journal of Economics*. 25 (3): 343–368.

Nissanke, M. K. and Aryeetey, E. 1998. *Financial Integration and Development: Liberalization and Reform in Sub-Saharan Africa*. London: Routledge.

Nixson, F. 2005. Reflections on Industrialization Strategies and Experiences in Sub-Saharan Africa. In Tribe, M., Thoburn, J. and Palmer-Jones, R. (eds.). *Development Economics and Social Justice*. Aldershot: Ashgate: 235–249.

Noorbakhsh, F. and Paloni, A. 2000. The De-Industrialization Hypothesis, Structural Adjustment Programmes and the Sub-Saharan Dimension. In Jalilian, H., Tribe, M. and Weiss, J. (eds.). *Industrial Development and Policy in Africa*. Cheltenham: Edward Elgar: 107–36.

Pack, H. 1993. Productivity and Industrial Development in Sub-Saharan Africa. *World Development*. 21 (1): 1–16.

Pack, H. and Paxson, C. 2001. Is African Manufacturing Skill Constrained. In Szirmai, A. and Lapperre, P. (eds.). *The Industrial Experience of Tanzania*. Basingstoke: Macmillan: 50–72.

Pedersen, P. O. 2005. East African Micro-Enterprises: The Negotiation of Their Labour, Gender and Rural-Urban Relations. In Tribe, M., Thoburn, J. and Palmer-Jones, R. (eds.). *Development Economics and Social Justice*. Aldershot: Ashgate: 208–218.

Riddell, R. C. 1990. *Manufacturing Africa: Performance and Prospects of Seven Countries in Sub-Saharan Africa*. London: James Currey.

Rudaheranwa, N. 2000. Transport Costs and Protection for Ugandan Industry. In Jalilian, H., Tribe, M. and Weiss, J. (eds.). *Industrial Development and Policy in Africa*. Cheltenham: Edward Elgar: 260–279.

Sekkat, K. and Varoudakis, A. 2000. Exchange Rate Management and Manufactured Exports in Sub-Saharan Africa. *Journal of Development Economics*. 61 (1): 237–253.

Sender, J. (1999) Africa's Economic Performance: Limits of the Current Consensus. *Journal of Economic Perspectives*. 13 (3): 89–114.

Sender, J. and Smith, S. 1986. *The Development of Capitalism in Africa*. London and New York: Methuen.

Shivji, I. G. 1975. *Class Struggles in Tanzania*. London and Dar es Salaam: Heinemann Educational Books and Tanzania Publishing House.

Söderbom, M. and Teal, F. 2003. How Can Policy Towards Manufacturing in Africa Reduce Poverty? A Review of the Current Evidence from Cross-Country Firm Studies. In Wohlmuth, K., Gutowski, A., Kneduk, T., Meyn, M. and Pitamber, S. (eds.). *African Entrepreneurship and Private Sector Development*. African Development Perspectives Research Group. Bremen: University of Bremen.

Söderbom, M. and Teal, F., 2004. Size and Efficiency in African Manufacturing Firms: Evidence from Firm-Level Panel Data. *Journal of Development Economics*. 73 (2): 369–394.

Söderbom, M., Teal, F., Wambugu, A. and Kahyarara, G. 2003. *The Dynamics of Returns to Education in Kenyan and Tanzanian Manufacturing*. Centre for the Study of African Economies Working Paper 2003–17. Oxford: University of Oxford: 28 pp.

Steel, W. F. and Webster, L. M. 1992. How Small Enterprises in Ghana have Responded to Adjustment. *World Bank Economic Review*. 6 (3): 423–438.

Stein, H. 1992. Deindustrialization, Adjustment, the World Bank and the IMF in Africa. *World Development*. 20 (1): 83–95.

Stewart, F. 1977. *Technology and Underdevelopment*. Basingstoke: Macmillan.

Swainson, N. 1977. The Rise of a National Bourgeoisie in Kenya. *Review of African Political Economy*. 8 (January–April): 39–55.

Swainson, N. 1980. *The Development of Corporate Capitalism in Kenya*. London: Heinemann Educational Books.

te Velde, D. W. and Morrissey, O. 2003. Do Workers in Africa get a Wage Premium if Employed in Firms Owned by Foreigners? *Journal of African Economies*. 12 (1): 41–73.

Teal, F. 1996. The Size and Sources of Economic Rents in a Developing Country Manufacturing Labour Market. *Economic Journal*. 106 (437): 963–976.

Teal, F. 2000. Why can Mauritius Export Manufactures and Ghana Not? *World Economy*. 22 (7): 981–994.

Thoburn, J. 2005. Could Import Protection drive Manufacturing Exports in Africa? In Belshaw, D. G. R. and Livingstone, I. (eds.). *Renewing Development in Sub-Saharan Africa: Policy Performance and Prospects*. London: Routledge: 285–296.

Thomas, C. Y. 1974. *Dependence and Transformation: The Economics of the Transition to Socialism*. New York: Monthly Review Press.

Tribe, M. 2000. The Concept of 'Infant Industry' in a Sub-Saharan African Context. In Jalilian, H., Tribe, M. and Weiss, J. (eds.). *Industrial Development and Policy in Africa*. Cheltenham: Edward Elgar: 75–106.

Tribe, M. 2002. An Overview of Manufacturing Development in Sub-Saharan Africa. In Belshaw, D. G. R. and Livingstone, I. (eds.). *Renewing Development in Sub-Saharan Africa: Policy Performance and Prospects*. London: Routledge: 263–284.

Tribe, M. 2005. Economic Efficiency Measures for Small-Scale Enterprises in Developing Countries. In Tribe, M., Thoburn, J. and Palmer-Jones, R. (eds.). *Development Economics and Social Justice*. Aldershot: Ashgate: 219–232.

Tybout, J. R. 2000. Manufacturing Firms in Developing Countries: How Well do They do, and Why? *Journal of Economic Literature*. 28 (1): 11–44.

Ul Haque, N., Mark, N. and Mathieson, D. J. 2000. Rating Africa: The Economic and Political Content of Risk Indicators. In Collier, P. and Pattillo, C. (eds.). *Investment and Risk in Africa*. Basingstoke and New York: Macmillan and St Martin's Press.

UNCTAD. 2013a. *Economic Development in Africa. Intra-African Trade: Unlocking Private Sector Dynamism*. Geneva: United Nations.

UNCTAD. 2013b. UNCTADSTAT Data Center – accessible at http://unctadstat.unctad.org/wds/ReportFolders/reportFolders.aspx

UNECA. 2013. *Making the Most of Africa's Commodities: Industrializing for Growth, Jobs and Economic Transformation*. Addis Ababa: United Nations Economic Commission for Africa.

UNIDO. 2001. *The Challenges of Sustainable Industrial Development in Africa*. Nairobi: United Nations Industrial Development Organization: 42 pp.

von Freyhold, M. 1977. The Post-Colonial State and Its Tanzanian Version. *Review of African Political Economy*. 8: 75–89.

Wangwe, S. M. 1995. Main Findings of the Study: A Synthesis. In Wangwe, S. M. (ed.). *Exporting Africa: Technology, Trade and Industrialization in Sub-Saharan Africa*. London: Routledge: 83–139.

Warren, B. 1973. Imperialism and Capitalist Industrialization. *New Left Review*. 81 (October): 3–44.

Warren, B. 1980. *Imperialism: Pioneer of Capitalism*. London: Verso.

Weiss, J. 1988. *Industry in Developing Countries: Theory, Policy and Evidence*. Beckenham: Croom Helm.

Wood, A. and Berge, K. 1997. Exporting Manufactures: Human Resources, Natural Resources, and Trade Policy. *Journal of Development Studies*. 34 (1): 35–59.

Wood, A. and Mayer, J. 2001. Africa's Export Structure in a Comparative Perspective. *Cambridge Journal of Economics*. 25 (3): 369–394.

World Bank. 1981. *Accelerated Development in Sub-Saharan Africa*. Oxford: Oxford University Press for the World Bank.

World Bank. 1987. *World Development Report*. New York: Oxford University Press for the World Bank – accessible from www.worldbank.org

World Bank. 1994. *Adjustment in Africa: Reform, Results and the Road Ahead*. Oxford: Oxford University Press for the World Bank.

World Bank. 2013. *World Development Indicators 2013*. Washington, DC: World Bank – accessible from www.worldbank.org

World Bank. 2014. *Enterprise Surveys*, http://www.enterprisesurveys.org

World Bank. various years. *World Development Report*. New York: Oxford University Press for the World Bank – accessible from www.worldbank.org

Wuyts, M. 2001. Informal Economy, Wage Goods and Accumulation Under Structural Adjustment: Theoretical Reflections Based on Tanzanian Experience. *Cambridge Journal of Economics*. 25 (3): 417–438.

21

INDUSTRIAL DEVELOPMENT IN TANZANIA

Reforms, performance and issues

Oliver Morrissey and Vincent Leyaro

Introduction

Tanzanian development strategy is directed towards the expansion of the economy's productive capabilities through a structural transformation of the economy where industrialisation is envisaged to play a pivotal role. This has always been the aim but it has yet to be achieved. At independence the manufacturing sector was small; in 1965 there were fewer than 600 manufacturing establishments employing at least 10 persons, mostly primary product processing and simple consumer goods. Most of these companies were owned by members of the East African Asian community or resident Europeans, and some of the largest were state-owned or owned by multinationals. Industrial output was low, accounting for only 6.6 per cent of GDP in 1966.

The independent socialist-oriented development strategy adopted by Tanzania since the Arusha Declaration of 1967 supported some growth in manufacturing, and a relatively good performance in terms of human development indicators. Szirmai and Lapperre (2001) review the early experience of industrialisation and document the large increase in the state-owned share of industry through the 1970s. By the late 1970s, a series of external shocks (in particular oil price shocks and a debt crisis) combined with internal constraints and weaknesses created severe economic imbalances. In the 1980s, Tanzania adopted four successive programmes that could be defined as World Bank Structural Adjustment Programmes (SAPs), although the World Bank was not directly involved in the first of these. Tanzania's mixed experience with adjustment has been reviewed elsewhere (Basu and Morrissey, 1997; Morrissey, 1995) and is only peripheral to the focus of this chapter (although it is, of course, relevant to the momentum for privatisation from the 1990s). Recent analysis of the performance of the manufacturing sector (Wangwe *et al.*, 2014), concentrates on identifying the emerging manufacturing subsectors, drivers of their success and challenges for sustained competitiveness. These issues will be addressed in the chapter as they are central to prospects for industrial growth and policy.

There has been a debate about de-industrialisation in sub-Saharan Africa (SSA), and whether the effect of liberalisation and adjustment has actually been to undermine the performance of African manufacturing (Jalilian and Weiss, 2000). The issues relating to this debate are surveyed by Tregenna in Chapter 6 in this volume. The World Bank (1994) argued that the performance of manufacturing was better in those SSA countries undertaking adjustment, although Bennell (1998) critically challenges this claim; there is only weak evidence for de-industrialisation, but manufacturing in SSA has tended to perform poorly irrespective of the presence of SAPs. There are a number of ways in which adjustment can help manufacturing. Trade liberalisation can increase the incentives to exporting (but, by exposing domestic firms to increased import competition, can also be the cause of de-industrialisation). The establishment of macroeconomic stability, a result of effective adjustment, can greatly improve business confidence and performance. Grenier *et al.* (1998) show that these effects were not pronounced for Tanzania up to the mid-1990s: macroeconomic instability persisted and manufacturing exports remained negligible. Since the early 2000s macroeconomic performance has improved and there is greater stability, although manufacturing exports remain low.

A third way in which liberalisation can help manufacturing is by removing 'discipline barriers' (Bennell, 1998: 631). Firms, especially state-owned, in regulated and protected environments are not exposed to market discipline and consequently fail to invest in good practice, technology and improving the skills of workers. State enterprises tend to be granted favourable access to credit, are allowed to operate at a loss, and hence impose a burden on the economy. Privatisation, a component of liberalisation, helps to rectify this. More generally, the establishment of market prices, reducing state intervention and establishing stable macroeconomic policy should all increase incentives to private producers.

The public sector state-owned enterprises (SOEs) have traditionally been important (Szirmai and Lapperre, 2001). James (1996) demonstrates that the public sector, in terms of its share of manufacturing, tended to increase in importance during the 1970s and 1980s. SOEs accounted for 16 per cent of manufacturing employment in 1967, 46 per cent in 1971, 50 per cent by the late 1970s and 53 per cent in 1982. Their share of manufacturing value added increased from 14 per cent in 1967 to 57 per cent in 1982 (James, 1996: 388). Surprisingly, perhaps, the advent of adjustment after 1986 did not usher in a decline: SOEs accounted for 11 per cent of GDP, 25 per cent of gross domestic investment and 22 per cent of employment on average over 1978–85. The corresponding figures for 1986–91 were 14 per cent of GDP, 30 per cent of investment and 22 per cent of employment (James, 1996: 390). Manufacturing was relatively buoyant over 1985–92. James (1996) attributes this success to the ability of the bureaucrats controlling SOEs to attract aid support for investment so that they could continue to grow. Privatisation has been slow in Tanzania, perhaps because of the influence of SOEs whose role in manufacturing is central to assessing the implications of privatisation; much of what has taken place has related to primary production (especially sisal, tea and coffee, and some mining), brewing and the tourism sector.

In the early 1980s, prior to any adjustment, manufacturing value added declined at an average annual rate of about 2.7 per cent; by the late 1980s it was increasing at about 4.6 per cent per annum and this was sustained into the early 1990s, when value added increased by about 2.9 per cent per annum (Bennell, 1998: 629). However, over the 1990s as a whole performance was poor, as shown in Table 21.1: manufacturing value added (MVA) per capita and MVA as a share of GDP both declined slightly between 1990 and 2000, and MVA performance was clearly worse than GDP performance (expressing both as shares of world totals). In contrast, there was a marked improvement between 2000 and 2010, and Tanzania's rank in terms of MVA per capita for 198 countries improved from 179 to 92. Over 1990 to 2010, MVA improvement kept pace with GDP growth such that MVA and GDP shares of world totals doubled (albeit still miniscule).

The second section presents a brief overview of policy initiatives and the performance of the Tanzanian economy since independence, while the third reviews specific industrial strategies over the same period. The fourth section presents an overview of manufacturing performance

Table 21.1 Manufacturing value added, 1990–2010

	1990	2000	2010	% change 1990–2010
MVApc$	22.7	22.4	37.9	67
MVApcrank	180	179	92	
MVAshare%	7.8	7.6	8.6	10
MVA%world	0.01	0.01	0.02	100
GDP%world	0.02	0.03	0.04	100

Sources: UNIDO (2014b): p. 55 for 1990; p. 64 for 2000; p. 72 for 2010.

Notes: MVApc$, manufacturing value added (MVA) per capita (pc) in $US; *MVApcrank*, rank out of 198 countries; *MVAshare%*, MVA as share of GDP; *MVA%world, GDP%world*, MVA and GDP as shares of world totals. Note that UNIDO and URT (2012: 35) reports MVA as 9.4 per cent in 2000 and 9.6 per cent in 2010, so obviously the data are contested.

in 2000–12 and the fifth considers how Tanzania got to this point by reviewing studies of firm performance since the 1990s. The sixth section reviews current industrial policy. The final section presents conclusions.

Policy and economic performance in Tanzania

The review of economic policies, reforms and performance in Tanzania can broadly be broken into three major episodes: 1961 to 1966, the post-independence period with an open and private sector led economy; 1967 to 1985, the state-controlled economy with inward looking policies; and the structural adjustment era with a series of market economy reforms from 1986 onwards. Thus, from her independence in early 1960s to date, Tanzania has experimented with two major economic policy stances: socialist-oriented and open market-oriented development strategies. This section briefly sketches the economic policies adopted during each of the periods, the measures or instruments used to implement them and the economic and human development impact.

During the first six years after independence (1961–66), the economy was fairly open and market oriented with no specific policy instruments to allocate foreign exchange or regulate prices. There were no import duties but exports (mostly traditional agricultural crops) were taxed as a source of government revenue. The predominantly agriculture (and services) based economy performed quite well in the early years, although the manufacturing sector was very small (Table 21.2(A)).

Table 21.2 Tanzania economic performance, 1961–2013

(A) Period averages

	1961–66	1967–79	1980–85	1986–95
GDP growth rate (%)	6.0	4.0	1.4	3.2
Agriculture VA (% GDP)	53.0	41.0	50.0	49.0
Mining VA (% GDP)	2.5	1.1	1.1	1.1
Manufacturing VA (% GDP)	5.3	10	7.0	8.7
Exports (% GDP)	19.3	11.4	4.0	16.2
Gross investment (% GDP)	18.5	24.3	19.9	24.1

(B) Year values

	1995	2000	2005	2010	2013
GDP growth rate (%)	3.6	5.0	7.4	7.0	6.9
Agriculture VA (% GDP)	47.1	29.5	26.1	22.7	21.6
Mining VA (% GDP)	1.3	1.5	2.4	2.4	2.3
Manufacturing VA (% GDP)	7.2	8.8	8.9	9.6	9.9
Exports (% GDP)	20.5	13.4	20.8	27.8	28.2
Gross investment (% GDP)	21.5	17	25.2	32	34.6

Sources: Bank of Tanzania (1983, 2012); World Development Indicators (2013).

Note: VA = value added.

Tanzania started to initiate a series of development policies guided by African Socialism (*Ujamaa*) following the Arusha Declaration of 1967. Massive nationalisation followed and by the early 1970s the government had control of almost all sectors; banking and major industries became state-owned, international trade and private retail trade were controlled by state agencies, administered prices (through the National Price Commission) largely replaced market prices, and monopoly government marketing boards replaced peasant cooperatives. A foreign exchange allocation system was developed in response to the balance of payment crises, and exports, imports and foreign exchange were restricted through registration and licensing. In 1974, import substitution industrialisation (ISI) was introduced through the Basic Industries Strategy (BIS) for 1975 to 1995, Tanzania's first comprehensive long-term industrialisation strategy (discussed in the next section). The strategy was formulated in the framework of pursuing socialist development principles which included marginalisation of the role of the private sector.

Economic performance was reasonable on most indicators in the early 1970s, but worsened by the late 1970s; growth fell below 1 per cent per annum in 1977 and exports fell to only 11 per cent of GDP. The decade witnessed a series of shocks that weakened the economy: the 1973–74 drought, the 1973–74 and 1979–80 oil crises, the breakup of the East Africa Community in 1977, collapses of cash crop prices in the international markets and the costly 1978–79 Kagera war with Uganda. By the beginning of the 1980s there were huge shortages of goods (particularly food), inputs and foreign exchange, a growing black market exchange rate premium, capital flight and an emerging debt crisis. Initially the government responded to these difficulties by proposing its own policy reforms but soon adopted a series of economic recovery measures sponsored by the International Monetary Fund (IMF) and World Bank (Morrissey, 1995). Although some reforms were implemented, macroeconomic performance remained weak and investment declined. Throughout the 1980s, terms of trade continued to decline, aid dependence remained high, manufacturing output stagnated at around 8 per cent of GDP and the current account deficit continued to rise, reaching 20 per cent of GDP in 1993 (Nyoni, 1997).

Although investment increased in the 1990s, most of this was directed to infrastructure and growth of private sector investment in productive activities was limited. The early 1990s were a period of failed or stalled reforms, and negotiations with the World Bank often broke down. From 1995 onwards, following the first wave of economic reforms, growth and macro-economic performance improved, as shown in Table 21.2(B). Growth has been above 5 per cent and around 7 per cent since 2005. Investment as percentage of GDP has also increased significantly to 35 per cent in 2013 compared to 21 per cent in 1995. Exports also picked up to around 28 per cent of GDP in 2013 from around 20 per cent in 1995. Manufacturing, to a less extent has also improved, from around 7 per cent of GDP in 1995 to around 10 per cent in 2010. While the share of agriculture as a percentage of GDP has fallen significantly from around 50 per cent in the mid-1990s to 22 per cent in 2013, that of manufacturing has not grown significantly (mining has accounted for an increasing share of industrial activity) so the structural transformation is still awaited.

Manufacturing in Tanzania: Reforms and policy

Manufacturing and industrial development has been at the core of Tanzanian development strategy for structural transformation since the 1960s. Industrial policy can be characterised and discussed under four periods: from 1961 to 1966 (post-independence); 1967 to 1979 (the Basic Industry Strategy); 1980 to 1995 (crisis and adjustment); and since 1996 (sustainable Industrial Policy 1996–2020). Wangwe *et al.* (2014) provide a detailed overview on which we draw, and we focus on the period since the late 1980s.

Industrial development, 1961–1966

When Tanzania achieved independence in 1961, industrial development was at a very low level, and in the years after independence this situation did not change much. There were only about 220 firms employing 10 or more people (Skarstein and Wangwe, 1986) and most of these were small establishments: the large firms at independence were mostly involved in tobacco manufacture (cigarettes), beer and soft drinks. Many of the largest capital-intensive firms were subsidiaries of multinational corporations (MNCs) and in 1961 the six largest companies were all foreign-owned: British American Tobacco, East African Breweries, Coca-Cola, Tanganyika Packers, Metal Box and Bata Shoes (Wangwe *et al.*, 2014: 5). The main sectors were processors of primary products (mainly for export) and simple consumer goods in food processing, beverages, rubber products, chemical products, clothing and footwear, and repair of transport equipment.

The newly independent government set out policies for diversification from primary production and shifting manufacturing towards capital and intermediate goods in the Three Year Development Plan (1961–63) and the First Five Year Plan (1964–68), which assumed that foreign private capital would be attracted by favourable investment conditions. The National Development Corporation (NDC), established in 1962, was mandated to spearhead industrial development in the country. There were attempts to create favourable conditions for foreign capital by offering protective tariffs, guaranteeing security of foreign investments, publishing existing investment opportunities and designing a tax incentive structure. In this early period more than 75 per cent of industrial investment was coming from the private sector (Rweyemamu, 1973).

Basic industry strategy, 1967–1979

The Arusha Declaration heralded the start of a phase which required local control of all major means of production, manufacturing, services and commerce. This included nationalising already established private sector industries and establishing new SOEs such as the State Trading Corporation and the State Mining Corporation. This period coincides with the First (1964–68) and Second (1969–74) Five Year Plans, where steps were taken to consolidate the nationalisation programme and promote the link between industrial development and rural development through the Small Industries Development Organisation (SIDO) which was established in 1973. The aim was to promote the establishment of small industries that employed simple and labour–intensive technologies, which utilised locally available human resources and raw materials (Skarstein and Wangwe, 1986). The first three mid-term development plans were not effective and were followed by the twenty years (1975–1995) Basic Industries Strategy (BIS).

Seven national goals were identified in the BIS: industrial growth; structural change; employment generation; increased equality of income distribution and of regional development; worker participation in industry; and increased self-reliance. BIS was different from the previous industrial strategies in terms of emphasis: (a) on production of basic consumer needs for the majority of the population (food, clothes and footwear, building materials, medicines, education equipment and facilities); (b) on producer (capital) goods (iron and steel, metal working and engineering, chemical industries, etc.) that have potential in creating linkages and facilitating structural transformation; and (c) using technologies appropriate to the resource endowment of Tanzania. The target was a high rate of industrial growth of 8.8 per cent per annum over 1975–95. Structural transformation was expected, through manufacturing's increased share in the economy from 7 per cent in 1970 to 18.8 per cent in 1995. The share of the consumer goods sector was expected to decline from 68 per cent in 1970 to 39 per cent in 1995.

The ambitions of the BIS were never realised as implementation was slowed down by the lack of resources following the economic crises of late 1970s (Lall and Wangwe, 1998). The manufacturing sector had grown as a share of GDP from only 3.6 per cent in 1961 to 8.4 per cent in 1967, and then to a peak of 10 per cent in 1972, but fell back to 8.5 per cent in 1979 (see Table 21.2 above). Nevertheless, between 1966 and 1979 the average industry rate of growth was around 5.7 per cent. Industrial employment as a proportion of total wage employment increased from 9.9 per cent in 1967 to 16 per cent in 1979. Industrial investment as a share of total investment was variable, falling from 14.8 per cent in 1967 to 11 per cent in 1972 and then rising to 24 per cent in 1979. Manufactured exports remained below 10 per cent of total exports during this period.

Crisis and adjustment, 1980–1995

Government monopolisation of marketing, and high effective protection of the import-substituting industrial sector in the 1970s undercut the rewards to production for export. The coffee bonanza concealed the weaknesses of the system for a few years, but when it ended the inefficiencies of the economy became apparent (Skarstein and Wangwe, 1986). As discussed above, economic performance during this period was limited by internal policy weaknesses and external shocks, and the early 1980s was a period of crisis. The Economic Recovery Programme (ERP) I (1986–89) and ERP II (1989–92) aimed to promote industrial development by: (i) rehabilitation of existing capacities rather than new investments; (ii) directing resources towards export-oriented activities; (iii) promoting private investment; and (iv) reducing the size of the public sector to give the private sector a greater role in industrial development. A programme for public enterprise reform, including divestiture and liquidation, was launched. Along with these measures, impediments to exports were also removed, such as relaxing licensing and registration requirements, reducing the number of export items subject to permit and allowing private participation in traditional exports.

Manufacturing as a share of GDP declined from about 10 per cent in the early 1980s to about 8 per cent from the mid-1980s, with no evidence of sustained growth relative to the rest of the economy (Bennell, 1998; Grenier et al., 1998). The ratio of manufacturing investment to GDP, initially around 7 per cent, declined to 5 per cent in the mid-1980s, recovering in the late 1980s to stabilise at just over 7 per cent. This was relevant because investment is an important indicator of manufacturing prospects, symptomatic of business confidence and indicative of future performance. Many SOEs were restructured but the manufacturing sector was weak and uncompetitive (Due, 1993). The textile industry, a leading industrial sector at the time, almost collapsed with the closure of 22 out of 24 mills by 1993.

Industrial development since 1996

Privatisation during the 1990s had a significant impact and SOEs accounted for less than 10 per cent of manufacturing enterprises by the mid-2000s (URT, 2009). A sector based on small and medium enterprises (SMEs) emerged: "enterprises with fewer than ten employees account for 97 percent of all manufacturing enterprises [in 2007] and ... most are family-owned firms with less than five employees" (UNIDO and URT, 2012: 16). During the preparation of Tanzania Development Vision (TDV) 2025 between 1998 and 2000 there was a consensus on the development of a more coordinated institutional framework for the implementation of plans to have a semi-industrialised economy by 2020. A series of policy initiatives have been undertaken since 2000 which are discussed in the sixth section below.

Manufacturing performance in the 2000s

Despite improvements since 2000, the Tanzanian economy remains predominantly based on agriculture and extractive sectors with rising informality; the manufacturing sector remains small. MVA as a share of GDP only reached 10 per cent after 2010, which is still below the average for the region: in 2010, MVA as a share of GDP was lower than in Mozambique, Kenya and Malawi and of neighbouring countries was only greater than that for Uganda and Rwanda (UNIDO and URT, 2012: 35). Manufacturing in Tanzania is characterised by low-value-added, low-tech activities. The food and beverages sector accounts for about 50 per cent of total MVA, and non-metallic mineral products contribute about a tenth and textiles another 5 per cent. Manufacturing activity is heavily concentrated in Dar es Salaam, with Arusha having the only other significant concentration.

The rate of employment growth in manufacturing has been disappointing, perhaps reflecting the predominance of SMEs. "Manufacturing employment accounts for less than 5 percent of the total labour force, with the largest 40 manufacturing companies employing 36 percent of all manufacturing labour ... equivalent to the employment generated by 24,000 micro enterprises" (UNIDO and URT, 2012: 17). Manufacturing firms established in 2005 or later accounted for about a tenth of industrial employment in 2012.

Although manufacturing employment growth has not been strong, some sectors have been doing relatively well. The manufacturing sectors in Tanzania with the highest share of employment in new companies are paper and textiles (both of which have expanded production in the 2000s, see Table 21.3), electrical equipment and manufactures of fabricated metals (which have not grown in the 2000s, Table 21.3). The textiles sector has created the largest number of jobs in new companies, while the food sector accounts for the second highest number of jobs created in new companies, although older companies continue to be the largest employers. The biggest concern is the lack of a critical mass of firms in a variety of sectors.

Industrial production has shown steady growth in the 2000s, with the index of total manufacturing production rising from 56 in 2000 to 188 in 2009 (Table 21.3). Relatively strong growth can be seen in wood products, paper and paper products, food and beverages, textiles, tobacco and minerals. These are likely to be relatively low technology manufacturing with some processing of primary domestic inputs. Food processing and beverages are major sectors accounting for about half of all employment in manufacturing (Sutton and Olomi, 2012: 61) so the performance is encouraging. Furniture manufacturing dominates the wood sector as most is made from local wood (although some is imported) and furniture firms tend to have a long-term relationship with timber suppliers (Sutton and Olomi, 2012: 141–3). The larger firms in Dar es Salaam tend to be owned by members of the Indian community and African owners are more common in the rest of the country.

The sectors that are likely to be more capital and technology intensive, and for which imported inputs are more important, have not grown as strongly. Electrical machinery had high production in 2000, but this declined dramatically and only had partly recovered by 2009; fabricated metals production grew in the mid-2000s but then declined; and the vehicles sector has been declining. Sutton and Olomi (2012: 178) detail the major problems facing firms in these metal and engineering sectors: expensive imports of scrap metal; poor quality of local steel; expensive and irregular power supply; poor transport infrastructure; and corruption (this appears to be a particular problem in getting land for expansion, and also includes costs of regulation and taxes).

This pattern of sector growth, weaker for sectors with higher value added, is evident in the slow growth of MVA as a share of GDP, which remains below the average for Africa (in the lower panel of Table 21.3 the figures are the same as in UNIDO, 2014b but are lower than in UNIDO and URT, 2012). Tanzanian manufacturing remains stuck in simple technology, low-value-added sectors. In 2009, Tanzania ranked 110th out of 118 countries on UNIDO's competitiveness index, somewhat worse than Uganda and Kenya, but better than Ethiopia and Malawi (UNIDO and URT, 2012: 23). Although MVA per capita at $44 in 2010 is low, it is similar to Kenya and Mozambique and much higher than Malawi or Uganda and has grown by about 5 per cent per annum through the period from 2000 to 2010; Mozambique has grown faster, whereas Malawi and Kenya have stagnated over this period (UNIDO and URT, 2012: 25).

Table 21.3 Tanzania: index of industrial production (2005 = 100)

Sector	2000	2003	2007	2009
Food and beverages	60	88	108	214
Tobacco	60	72	163	156
Textiles	61	161	159	169
Wood products	75	60	103	464
Paper and products	12	105	157	265
Mineral (non-metal)	63	86	129	188
Fabricated metal	53	113	38	64
Electrical machinery	367	115	118	179
Vehicles	143	121	94	92
Total manufacturing	56	91	124	188

MVA/GDP (2005 prices)

	2000	2005	2008	2010
Tanzania	7.6	7.9	8.4	8.6
Africa	11.6	10.8	10.5	10

Sources: UNIDO (2013), p. 828 for index values; p. 58 for MVA/GDP (manufacturing value added as a percentage of GDP).

Table 21.4 Tanzania: mining and utilities, output and value added

	Output (%)			Value added (%)		
	2008	2010	Δ%	2008	2010	Δ%
Coal	0.56	–		0.55	–	
Natural gas	9.99	1.12	16.69	14.69	21.65	0.67
Metal ores	1.53	1.55	−0.85	1.88	1.78	0.07
Mining	19.08	43.86	11.44	30.88	36.89	0.35
Electricity	65.90	50.52	2.45	47.10	36.76	−0.12
Water supply	2.93	2.95	−0.96	4.91	2.92	−0.33
Total			33.17			0.13

Source: Derived from figures in UNIDO (2014a), p. 167.

Notes: Output and value added percentage expressed as shares of total (all mining and utilities); Δ% is change in output and value added values for sectors and total over the period 2008–10.

Recently, Tanzania has performed quite well, with MVA per capita increasing by 28 per cent between 2007 and 2012 (UNIDO, 2014b: 87).

Similarly, although the value of manufactured exports is low, the annual growth rate of 31 per cent over 2000–2010 was the highest in the region; Uganda recorded 30 per cent growth but from a much lower base (UNIDO and URT, 2012: 27). From a 20 per cent share in 2000, manufactured exports increased to over 50 per cent of total exports by 2010, a share comparable to Kenya (UNIDO and URT, 2012: 29). However, most of these manufactures are low technology with little processing value added. Manufacturing in Tanzania has grown, but remains a weak sector by global standards and even compared to middle income countries in sub-Saharan Africa.

There has been considerable growth in recent years in resource sectors, especially natural gas, where output increased by 17 per cent between 2008 and 2010 (the output share fell because of high growth in other sectors), and mining/quarrying; these two sectors now account for more than half of value added in mining and utilities (Table 21.4). However, the major utilities, in particular electricity, grew relatively slowly, implying that they are failing to keep pace with industrial demand. Furthermore, growth in value added has been very low, and even negative for utilities (Table 21.4). This is consistent with erratic electricity supply often being reported as a major constraint facing firms (Sutton and Olomi, 2012).

Manufacturing in Tanzania: Performance in context

Research on manufacturing enterprises in Africa increased during the 1990s as large-scale surveys of manufacturing in Africa became available, especially those produced by the World Bank and the bilateral donor-sponsored Regional Programme on Enterprise Development (RPED). These were analysed to investigate the determinants of productivity and effects of privatisation and trade liberalisation policies implemented as part of the adjustment pro-grammes from the 1980s. For example, Bigsten et al. (1999a) investigate the determinants of the decision to export and the share of output exported for a total of 502 firms in Cameroon, Ghana, Kenya and Zimbabwe over the period 1991–95. No factors other than size were found to consistently influence the decision to export; Grenier et al. (1998) find similar results for Tanzania. Bigsten et al. (1999b), for the same four countries, find that profit appears to be the only consistent determinant of investment, especially for small firms. Teal (1995) obtains similar results for Ghana, and Grenier *et al.* (1998) find that company earnings are the major source of investment funds in Tanzania.

The importance of SOEs in Tanzania does not appear to be a reason for poor performance because studies have found that parastatals or SOEs have performed reasonably well among manufacturing firms in Tanzania. In part this may be because SOEs face limited competition (Helsinki School of Economics, 1995). Bagachwa and Mbelle (1995) reviewed case studies of nine firms, three of which were parastatals in the textiles sector, and found that exports tended to require specific technological capacity to meet higher (or different) quality standards compared with production for the domestic market, while James (1996) argued that parastatals proved adept at attracting technology. The principal constraint on firms, especially exporters, in these studies was identified as investment capability, especially access to financing but more generally to information and capacity to adapt; SOEs had no greater capabilities in general.

Grenier *et al.* (1998, 1999) analyse a 1995 survey of 83 manufacturing enterprises, covering food, textiles, wood, paper, chemicals, metals, and covering five main cities, including Dar es Salaam. The firms selected were largely within the formal sector, with little coverage of very small (or micro) firms: 43 per cent employed more than 100 people; the mean firm size was 158, although the median size was 80, reflecting the presence of a few very large firms in the sample. A detailed discussion of the survey results is provided in Grenier *et al.* (1998), focused on exporting and investment, whereas Grenier *et al.* (1999) address how ownership and exporting relate to business confidence.

Parastatals were significantly larger than other firms with an average of 310 employees, compared to 99 employees for other firms, and accounted for 55 per cent of employment. Some 27 per cent of the firms reported some exporting, a relatively large share by African standards reflecting the sample's bias towards larger, older firms. About 40 per cent reported investment in each year from 1990 to 1993 (Grenier *et al.*, 1998). Parastatals were significantly more likely to export, contrary to the findings for other SSA countries (Bigsten *et al.*, 1999a): 55 per cent of exporters were SOEs compared to 20 per cent of non-exporters, and half of the SOEs exported. Part of this is explained by the effect of size: large firms were more likely to export and more likely to be SOEs. There was no evidence that SOEs had favourable access to investment financing, a major constraint on firms; they were not more likely to invest (controlling for the fact that sustained investment is related to exporting and size). Company earnings were by far the most commonly used source to finance investment (69 per cent), followed by personal savings and domestic bank loans (about 20 per cent each). These results are consistent with studies of other SSA countries (Teal, 1995; Bigsten *et al.*, 1999b).

Grenier *et al.* (1999) provide some evidence that firms competing on the domestic market tended to feel more exposed to, and concerned with, economic policy (especially trade taxes and the exchange rate) whereas exporters were more likely to feel insulated from policy changes. This is consistent with trade liberalisation benefiting exporters. As exporters tended to be larger firms they may have been in a better position than other firms to withstand adverse economic trends. Trade liberalisation was associated with a perceived increase in competition from imports, and firms competing with imports were constrained in their ability to increase prices, whereas exporters appeared somewhat more confident than non-exporters. Thus the trade reforms implemented through the 1990s are most likely to have benefited relatively larger exporting firms, often SOEs, but did not benefit smaller firms competing domestically or with imports.

The most recent survey available (Wangwe *et al.*, 2014) interviewed some 50 firms, representative of Tanzanian manufacturing, in 2010–12. The main determinants of good performance were found to be: producing quality products; having good management, customer services and marketing strategies; good access to technology, skilled labour and innovation; experience, reputation and networking. Interestingly, compared to the early 1990s discussed above, access to financing and credit policy and availability of raw materials were less frequently mentioned as being important (Wangwe *et al.*, 2014: 26). However, access to locally produced quality inputs seemed to be an important issue in some sectors, such as food processing (Sutton and Olomi, 2012: 61) and metals (Sutton and Olomi, 2012: 178), and in beverages high and unstable prices of raw materials were noted as a constraint (Sutton and Olomi, 2012: 78). Food processing is, of course, one of the most important sectors for linkages and for adding value to local agricultural production.

Wangwe *et al.* (2014: 43) suggest that manufacturing firms in Tanzania face five types of challenges: (i) low levels of technology, irregular electricity and lack of skilled labour; (ii) a complex legal and institutional environment where laws are not enforced; (iii) limited access to financing and high cost of capital, inputs and energy; (iv) competition from imports, especially very cheap low-quality goods; (v) official regulations, charges and taxes. Of these, the most important challenges seem to be electricity supply (expensive and irregular so that firms often need their own generators, which add to costs), difficulty in gaining access to loans (at high rates of interest) and costs associated with corruption.

Sutton and Olomi (2012) emphasise the importance of capability in the growth of exporting firms, through a series of vignettes of 50 selected large firms in 16 industrial sectors based on data for 2011. They confirm that the various constraints discussed above are reported by many firms, but point out that a neglected major constraint is easy access to land for industrial development. They also confirm the importance of large firms in their sample. Although Tanzania's commodity exports are concentrated in a relatively few large firms (22 firms account for over half of all exports for seven sectors, and one firm accounts for all gold exports, which were over a third of exports in 2011) they are quite diversified across manufacturing sectors by African standards. Medium and small firms make a significant contribution to exports in some industries, notably cashew nuts and curtains. About 40 per cent of the large firms in the sample are domestic private-owned (about half of these were 'industrial start-ups' and the others evolved from domestic trading firms), the remainder being either foreign-owned or originating as SOEs. Six industries were the major contributors to export growth in the sample: fish processing; curtains; steel; cut flowers; flour and non-ferrous metal scrap (Sutton and Olomi, 2012: 6). The central feature in these firms emerging as exporters was organisational capability (managerial experience and capacity) and access to information on markets (a particular advantage of those that began as trading firms).

Current policy proposals and issues

> History has repeatedly shown that the single most important thing that distinguishes rich countries from poor ones is basically their higher capabilities in manufacturing, where productivity is generally higher and, most importantly, where productivity tends to (although does not always) grow faster than in agriculture and services.
>
> (Chang, 2007: 213)

As discussed elsewhere in this volume (e.g. by Weiss and Jalilian in Chapter 2 and by Weiss in Chapter 8), a large body of empirical evidence suggests that manufacturing is the key for growth and job creation and this is reflected in Tanzanian policy (URT, 2009). As is evident from the discussion in the third section above, this focus is not new, but has reappeared with renewed emphasis since 2000.

The desire for structural transformation has motivated Tanzanian industrial development strategies as they evolved in the 2000s. Although Tanzania's manufacturing sector showed signs of improvement since the early 1990s, import competition (mainly from Asia) has increased and represented a major challenge to competing domestic producers (as discussed in the previous section). During the second half of the 1990s, the government developed the *Sustainable Industrial Development Policy* (SIDP) 1996–2020 (URT, 1996) to shift the economic base from the public (SOEs) to the private sector and export orientation. Private sector development was supported by the provision of fiscal incentives, simplifying the regulatory framework and macro-economic stability. The industrial sector started to grow steadily through the 2000s, although, as shown above (Table 21.3), performance varied significantly across sectors and the country continues to be dependent on agricultural and resource-based products with limited value addition.

The relevance of the manufacturing sector has been reflected in many key government policy documents and initiatives since 2000. In general, Tanzania has been good at producing strategy documents but poor at identifying and implementing policy interventions which support realisation of the strategies, so that comparatively little has been achieved. UNIDO and URT (2012: 18–19) sketch the main policy initiatives and development strategies.

The *Tanzania Development Vision (TDV) 2025* (URT, 2005a) sets out the new policy framework for the transformation of Tanzania from a least developed country to a middle income country by 2025 through inducing a shift from an agricultural base to a semi-industrialised one. In this framework there is little explicit recognition and understanding of why that basic structural transformation, a feature of industrial strategy since the 1970s, has not previously been achieved. Resources are still viewed primarily in terms of minerals, and the framework contained no specific measures to harness the agriculture resource base and to develop an agro-processing sector. The importance of agro-processing is recognised in the framework but the need for reform and increased production in the agriculture sector is not given much attention. Implementation of the TDV was itself planned. The *Long Term Perspective Plan* (covering the period from 2011/12 to 2025/26) (URT, 2010a) is a roadmap for three phased five-year plans for the realisation of the TDV 2025. The first *Five Year Development Plan* (2011/12–2015/16) (URT, 2010b) emphasised industrial development as the foundation for export-led growth but is more explicit than the TDV in proposing goals and strategic interventions with key targets to be achieved by 2015 (see Table 21.5 and the discussion below).

Various strategy documents supplemented the TDV. The Export Processing Zones (EPZ) programme was initiated by the *Export Processing Zones Act (2002)*, and was institutionalised through the Export Processing Zones Authority (EPZA) in 2006. The EPZs were expected to attract investment for export-led industrialisation in order to increase foreign exchange earnings and employment and to promote domestic processing through adding value to local raw materials. By 2012, six industrial parks were operational and 17 regions had been identified for future EPZs. Insufficient funds for the development of infrastructure remained as the main constraint. The *Tanzania Mini-Tiger Plan 2020* (URT, 2005b) was introduced in 2005 to support the implementation of TDV 2025 by replicating in Tanzania the successful development of the manufacturing sector achieved by the Asian Tigers. It complemented the EPZA by proposing Special Economic Zones (SEZs) for export-led manufacturing. The Mini-Tiger Plan failed to attract adequate financial support to realise the aims.

A number of specific policy documents supported aspects of the TDV. The *Small and Medium Enterprise Development Policy 2003* (URT, 2003a) acknowledged the special role of SMEs in the context of Tanzanian industrialisation and focused on improving infrastructure, strengthening financial and business services and establishing institutions to support SME development. However, there were no specific measures to address the major constraints on firms discussed above. The *National*

Trade Policy 2003 (URT, 2003b) drafted by the Ministry of Industry and Trade strictly followed the principles stated in the TDV by focusing on private-sector-led export growth through an emphasis on 'stimulation and encouragement of value addition' as one of its chief objectives. This was an appropriate focus but few specific mechanisms to support this were proposed (and it was not clear how domestic trade policy would be a good instrument for private sector development).

The *Integrated Industrial Development Strategy (IIDS) 2025* (URT, 2013) is the latest initiative to promote the achievement of the TDV 2025. One merit of this strategy is a focus on specific sectors. Some of these sectors are relatively labour intensive, such as textiles, agro-processing (edible oil, processed cashew nuts and fruits, milk products, leather products), light engineering and tourism. Others support domestic production of intermediate inputs using local resources, such as fertilizer, chemicals, iron and steel. UNIDO and URT (2012: 87–99) provides recommendations for policy measures to achieve the IIDS objectives but these tend to be general and aspirational rather than specific. For example, trade investment and sector policies to support industry (p. 87), strategic and aligned industrial policy interventions (p. 88) or "a serious evidence-based dialogue with the private sector" (p. 93).

UNIDO and URT (2012) do include some specific interventions, such as highlighting the potential of building a local plant to utilise natural gas to substitute for imports of urea-based fertilizer and even export to Rwanda (p. 58) or of the cement sector to export regionally (p. 59). Particular emphasis is given to the poor education and skills of workers, especially in terms of computing and engineering (p. 72), and to the lack of adequate funding for vocational education and training (p. 76). It is, however, a positive step that the skills gap experienced by firms has been investigated and highlighted.

Table 21.5 Five Year Development Plan (2011–16) targets

Goal	Strategic interventions	Key targets for 2015
Transformation of the country's production and export structure commensurate with existing demand patterns in domestic, regional and global markets	Developing activities for self-sustaining industrialisation of basic industries: metal and engineering, tyres, chemical and fertilisers, cement, construction and building materials	Average annual sector growth of 11 per cent
	Promoting development of SEZ and EPZ to encourage investment in Bagamoyo, Kigoma, Mtwara, KMTC Kilimanjaro and Tanga	Manufacturing sector share of GDP increased to 12.9 per cent
		Manufacturing share of total export to rise to 19.1 per cent
	Investment and technology to enable large-scale fertiliser production using domestic natural gas and phosphate deposits	Total manufacturing employment growth from 120,000 to over 221,000
	Promoting value-added agro-industries: essential and edible oils, starch, sugar, cereal flours, sisal fibres, instant coffee, tea bags (includes textiles and garments)	
	Promoting industries to utilise mineral resources: precious metals and gemstones grading, cutting, polishing, lapidary and jewellery	
	Improving the business environment and market access	
	Promoting local participation in industry	

Source: Derived from *Five Year Development Plan* (URT, 2010b).

As shown in Table 21.5, the first five-year plan included some specific interventions to utilise the mineral and agricultural resource base. Natural gas offers a prospect of a domestic fertilizer industry (the major challenge will be financing investment in such a relatively capital- and technology-intensive industry). Adding value by processing precious minerals may be a more viable domestic industry as it can be successful on a relatively small scale, but therefore may be of limited help in meeting ambitious employment creation targets. Agro-industry may offer the greatest potential for manufacturing growth with employment generation, but as noted by Sutton and Olomi (2012) ensuring a reliable supply of quality agricultural inputs is the major challenge.

Conclusion

The simple conclusion from this review is that Tanzania has had no shortage of industrial development plans and strategies, but that these have failed to achieve the structural transformation from an agriculture-based economy to an industrial production-based economy, generating significant employment. In the first few decades after independence there were 'home grown' policies, to a greater or lesser extent inward-looking, based on various forms of state intervention. Although state-owned enterprises performed relatively well this may have been because private manufacturing performed badly, given the absence of an enabling environment. More important, perhaps, was the neglect of agriculture and its complementarities with manufacturing; strategic perspectives did not include promotion of the agricultural contribution to structural transformation, so that Tanzania adopted a focus on industrialisation alone in order to create the transformation.

The economy hit the doldrums in the 1970s, buffeted by external shocks that further undermined weak manufacturing and agricultural sectors. The government had little choice but to turn to the World Bank and IMF and to begin a slow process of policy reform that is still continuing. Some of the successes in industrial performance can be attributed to government policy interventions, in particular trade liberalisation and privatisation (UNIDO and URT, 2012: 19). The broad success of reforms in creating a more stable macroeconomic environment has been important in creating a platform for private sector growth; although manufacturing growth remains slow, there has been progress and some sectors are performing reasonably well. The most recent strategies are more outward looking, not only trade and investment liberalisation but also seeking to learn from the experience of East Asian economies that have succeeded in structural transformation and increasing manufacturing value added as a share of the economy. It is not, however, evident that Tanzanian policy makers have appreciated the role that earlier reforms in the agriculture sector had in driving the transformation in East Asia. It should be noted, for example, that the major food processing sector remains constrained by low-quality inputs.

The relative importance of the major challenges facing manufacturing firms may have changed over the past few decades but the same issues still appear as the major constraints (Sutton and Olomi, 2102; Wangwe *et al.*, 2014). First is the poor quality of infrastructure, especially electricity supply and transport facilities and services – a combination of public investment and better regulation of privatised services is required to address these problems. Second is the perennial difficulty of access to loans for investment (one reason for low technology) and working capital (constraining the ability of business to expand), and there does not appear to be a clear strategy to address this. Many firms have been established and expanded by relying on family or business capital (often profits from one business are used to establish another) but the government needs to address the performance of the banking sector. Finally, the price and quality of inputs are important, including raw materials and skilled labour. The latter is partly addressed as education provision and attainment improves, with vocational training emerging as important for delivering skilled workers. The former is less amenable to public policy relating to the primary sectors, to managing timber resources sensibly and to promoting agriculture in order to provide the quantity and quality inputs for value-added agri-business. Tanzanian industrial policy has made recent gains but much more needs to be done.

References

Bagachwa, M. and Mbelle, A. 1995. Tanzania. In Wangwe, S. (ed.). *Exporting Africa: Technology, Trade and Industrialisation in Sub-Saharan Africa*. London and New York: Routledge.

Bank of Tanzania. 1983. *Tanzania, Twenty Years of Independence (1961–1981): A Review of Political and Economic Performance*. Dar es Salaam: Bank of Tanzania.

Bank of Tanzania. 2012. *Tanzania Fifty Years of Independence (1961–2011)*. Dar es Salaam: Bank of Tanzania.

Basu, P. and Morrissey, O. 1997. The Fiscal Impact of Adjustment in Tanzania. In Patel, C. K. (ed.). *The Fiscal Impact of Adjustment in Developing Countries*. Chichester: Edward Elgar.

Bennell, P. 1998. Fighting for Survival: Manufacturing Industry and Adjustment in Sub-Saharan Africa. *Journal of International Development*. 10 (5): 621–637.

Bigsten, A., Collier, P., Dercon, S., Fafchamps, M., Gauthier, B., Gunning, J. W., Habarurema, J., Isaksson, A., Oduro, A., Oostendorp, R., Pattillo, C., Soderbom, M., Teal, F. and Zeufack, A. 1999a. Exports of African Manufactures: Macro Policy and Firm Behaviour. *Journal of International Trade and Economic Development*. 8 (1): 53–71.

Bigsten, A., Collier, P., Dercon, S., Gauthier, B., Gunning, J. W., Isaksson, A., Oduro, A., Oostendorp, R., Pattillo, C., Söderbom, M., Sylvain, M., Teal, F. and Zeufack, A. 1999b. Investment in Africa's Manufacturing Sector: A Four Country Panel Data Analysis. *Oxford Bulletin of Economics and Statistics*. 61 (4): 489–512.

Chang, H.J. 2007. *Bad Samaritans: The Myth of Free Trade and the Secret History of Capitalism*. New York: Bloomsbury Press.

Due, J. M. 1993. Liberalisation and Privatisation in Tanzania and Zambia. *World Development*. 21 (12): 1981–1988.

Grenier, L., McKay, A. and Morrissey, O. 1998. *Determinants of Exports and Investment of Manufacturing Firms in Tanzania*. University of Nottingham, School of Economics: CREDIT Research Paper 98/5.

Grenier, L., McKay, A. and Morrissey, O. 1999. Exporting, Ownership and Confidence in Tanzanian Enterprises. *The World Economy*. 22 (7): 995–1011.

Helsinki School of Economics. 1995. *Dynamics of Enterprise Development in Tanzania*. RPED Country Study Series, Report of Round II Survey, Center for International Business: Helsinki: Helsinki School of Economics.

Jalilian, H. and Weiss, J. 2000. De-Industrialisation in Sub-Saharan Africa: Myth or Crisis. In Jalilian, H., Tribe, M. and Weiss, J. (eds.). *Industrial Development and Policy in Africa*. Cheltenham: Edward Elgar: 137–156.

James, J. 1996. Public Choice, Technology and Industrialisation in Tanzania: Some Paradoxes Resolved. *Public Choice*. 89 (3–4): 375–392.

Lall, S. and Wangwe, S. 1998. Industrial Policy and Industrialisation in Sub-Saharan Africa. *Journal of African Economies*. 7 (1): 70–107.

Morrissey, O. 1995. Political Commitment, Institutional Capacity and Tax Policy Reform in Tanzania. *World Development*. 23 (4): 637–649.

Nyoni, T. 1997. *Foreign Aid and Economic Performance in Tanzania*. AERC Research Paper 61. Nairobi: African Economic Research Consortium.

Rweyemamu, J. 1973. *Underdevelopment and Industrialization in Tanzania: A Study of Perverse Capitalist Industrial Development*. Nairobi: Oxford University Press.

Skarstein, R., and Wangwe, S. 1986. *Industrial Development in Tanzania: Some Critical Issues*. Dar es Salaam: Tanzania Publishing House.

Sutton, J. and Olomi, D. 2012. *An Enterprise Map of Tanzania*. London and Dar-es-Salaam: International Growth Centre (IGC).

Szirmai, A., and Lapperre, P. 2001. *The Industrial Experience of Tanzania*. Basingstoke: Palgrave Macmillan.

Teal, F. 1995. *Does 'Getting Prices Right' Work? Micro Evidence from Ghana*. CSAE Working Paper WPS/95–19. Oxford University: Centre for the Study of African Economies.

UNIDO. 2013. *International Yearbook of Industrial Statistics 2013*. Cheltenham: Edward Edgar for United Nations Industrial Development Organization (UNIDO).

UNIDO. 2014a. *World Statistics on Mining and Utilities 2014*. Cheltenham: Edward Edgar for UNIDO.

UNIDO. 2014b. *Growth and Distribution Pattern of World Manufacturing Output: A Statistical Profile*. Working Paper 02/2014. Vienna: United Nations Industrial Development Organization.

UNIDO and URT. 2012. *Tanzania Industrial Competitiveness Report 2012*. Dar es Salaam: Ministry of Industry and Trade and President's Office Planning Commission of the United Republic of Tanzania (URT) and Vienna: United Nations Industrial Development Organization.

URT. 1996. *Sustainable Industries Development Policy 1996–2020*. Dar es Salaam: United Republic of Tanzania.

URT. 2003a. *Small and Medium Enterprise Development Policy 2003*. Dar es Salaam: Ministry of Trade and Industry, United Republic of Tanzania.

URT. 2003b. *National Trade Policy 2003*. Dar es Salaam: Ministry of Trade and Industry, United Republic of Tanzania.

URT. 2005a. *Tanzania Development Vision 2025*. Dar es Salaam: United Republic of Tanzania.

URT. 2005b. *Tanzania Mini-Tiger Plan 2020*. Dar es Salaam: United Republic of Tanzania.

URT. 2009. *Annual Survey of Industrial Production (ASIP) Statistical Report*. Dar-es-Salaam: Ministry of Industry and Trade.

URT. 2010a. *Long Term Perspective Plan*. Dar es Salaam: United Republic of Tanzania.

URT. 2010b. *Five Year Development Plan 2011/12 to 2015/16*. Dar-es-Salaam: Ministry of Industry and Trade.

URT. 2013. *Integrated Industrial Development Strategy 2025*. Dar es Salaam: United Republic of Tanzania.

Wangwe, S., Mmari, D., Aikaeli, J., Rutatina, N., Mboghoina, T. and Kinyondo, A. 2014. *The Performance of the Manufacturing Sector in Tanzania: Challenges and the Way Forward*. WIDER Working Paper 2014/085. Helsinki: United Nations University World Institute for Development Economics Research.

World Bank. 1994. *Adjustment in Africa: Reforms, Results and the Road Ahead*. New York: Oxford University Press for the World Bank.

World Bank. 2013. *World Development Indicators (WDI)*. Washington, DC: World Bank – Available at: http://data.worldbank.org/data-catalog/world-development-indicators/wdi-2013 (accessed 24 November 2014).

22

MANUFACTURING IN POST-APARTHEID SOUTH AFRICA

Performance and policy[1]

David Kaplan

Introduction

This chapter begins with a brief description of the historical development of manufacturing in South Africa and an explanation as to why manufacturing growth and employment creation have occupied centre stage in government strategies for development post-1994. However, as the first section of the chapter shows, expectations have not been met – manufacturing output growth has been modest and employment has declined consistently. This has occurred despite the pursuit of an (increasingly) active industrial policy. South Africa's industrial policy is the subject of the fourth section of the chapter in which policy is outlined and briefly critiqued. The concluding section suggests that, albeit inadvertently, some elements of industrial policy may have constrained output and, in particular, limited the employment intensity of manufacturing growth. Further advances in manufacturing output and employment will require other policy measures – most notably labour market reform and an expansion in the supply of skills.

The historical development of manufacturing industry

South Africa's industrialisation began more than a century ago, and its history is important for understanding current dilemmas. After more than two centuries of marginal colonial agriculture, South African economic dynamics were forcibly changed by the discovery of significant deposits of diamonds (1867) and gold (1886), stimulating substantial inflows of European capital and labour. Within 35 years, British conquest created a unified state from the previous patchwork comprising two colonies, two peasant-based Afrikaner (Dutch-origin settlers) states and numerous indigenous polities. The South African state, based on racial exclusion, became independent in 1910.

Some very limited manufacturing existed – most advanced in mining explosives. The active promotion of manufacturing began soon after political independence, provoked by World War I, which disrupted trade flows and weakened British imperial power, including the influence of foreign mining interests within economic policy. Between the 1920s and the 1970s, trade protection (with tariffs and quota restrictions highest on final consumer goods) and public investment in heavy industry producing key inputs (electricity, iron and steel, chemicals, pulp and paper, petroleum) drove import-substitution industrialisation (ISI). Manufacturing growth was rapid: manufacturing's contribution to GDP rose from less than 5 per cent in 1914 to 17 per cent in 1948, to 23 per cent in 1970, and then manufacturing value added grew at 7 per cent per annum between 1948 and 1974. By the 1970s, South Africa was (in one authoritative assessment) "largely self-sufficient in consumer goods … [and] producing a considerable part" of its intermediate and capital goods (Feinstein, 2005: 188). However, imports of the latter remained substantial. Import penetration ratios (the share of the local market met by imports) in food and clothing in 1970 were 11.3 per cent and 14.6 per cent respectively, but in machinery, transport equipment and chemicals, imports still contributed 57 per cent, 25.2 per cent and 39.2 per cent respectively of total supply (Kahn, 1987: 238). Furthermore domestic markets remained small (though profitable). Manufacturing did not become internationally competitive or export-focussed, continuing to run a substantial trade deficit, dependent for foreign exchange on mining exports.

Thus ISI was successful in creating an industrial base, but one which had severe limitations. Beyond trade policy and public investment, manufacturing's trajectory was inevitably shaped by the prior presence of a large-scale, and globally significant, mining industry. Technological capabilities rested on inflows of foreign direct investment and of skilled labour (and entrepreneurs) from Britain and Europe. Like other resource rent-based economies, especially in Latin America, South Africa came down firmly on the 'buy' side of the 'make-or-buy' technology acquisition process, and manufacturing did not for the most part develop national proprietary skills or learning capabilities, at least in tradable sectors. In the few activities where this did occur, they relied on considerable state support as elsewhere, but the motivation in South Africa was generally to defend white minority power. An example was oil-from-coal technology targeting energy self-sufficiency in the face of international anti-apartheid sanctions. Unlike East Asia, sustaining the political regime was not compatible with creating dynamic manufacturing capabilities.

The corporate structure was shaped by a highly developed capital market, quickly established after gold's discovery to facilitate foreign portfolio capital inflows to finance extraction. Mineral rents rose considerably in the 1930s, as depression forced devaluation, and in the 1950s when new gold ore discoveries coincided with inelastic demand and a fixed world price under the Bretton Woods exchange rate system.

The major South African mining houses, subjected to firm exchange controls and precluded from expanding abroad, increasingly invested in other sectors of the economy – notably in manufacturing. Access to low cost capital, combined with high levels of trade protection and very limited competition from foreign firms on the domestic market, resulted in high levels of economic concentration whereby a few firms dominated the local market. The conglomerates were focused on the highly profitable domestic market and had little exposure to global competition – at home or abroad.

One of several motivations for promoting manufacturing was employment creation for newly urbanised unskilled whites. But after this group had been absorbed into labour-intensive sectors by the early 1940s, black workers entered manufacturing in large numbers, doing jobs at increasingly higher skill levels, though still formally barred from high skill jobs reserved for whites. The wage structure was unequal racially, if somewhat less so than in the mining sector, but very high wages for whites (on a par in purchasing power terms with Canada and Australia – other 'white dominions' within the British Empire) underpinned domestic market growth and high (but declining) profitability.

The limits of South African manufacturing were exposed by the mid-1970s global slowdown which ended the already-disintegrating fixed exchange rate system and stable world gold market, and also cut demand for other resource exports. This macroeconomic disruption, together with rising wages and domestic political upheaval, slowed manufacturing growth, which averaged only 1.6 per cent per annum between 1974 and 1994 (the same rate as GDP).

The centrality of manufacturing post-1994

In 1994 South Africa's first democratic government accordingly inherited a manufacturing sector that was diversified but which was growing only slowly, and was highly concentrated and inefficient. There was widespread concern that much of South African manufacturing was uncompetitive and would not survive South Africa's reintegration into the global economy. Policies designed to enhance competitiveness were seen as a necessary accompaniment to enhanced integration into the global economy. Government accordingly placed considerable emphasis on industrial policy with a strong focus on enhancing competitiveness.

Two other factors were significant in placing manufacturing at the centre of policy. The first factor was economic – the terms of trade for South Africa's mineral exports appeared to be in long term decline. In particular, the price of gold, South Africa's principal export commodity, declined significantly after 1996. Moreover, the indications were that gold production volumes would fall. Above a very moderate level, South Africa's growth rate appeared to be constrained by shortages of foreign exchange. Manufactured exports expansion appeared therefore to be essential to raising the level of economic growth and employment (Hirsch, 2005: 116).

The second factor was political – the trade union movement had played a key role in overcoming apartheid. It was highly organised and politically powerful. The core of its membership was to be found in the manufacturing sector. Moreover, even during apartheid days, as it faced the prospects of sanctions which it supported but which threatened its membership with unemployment, the trade union movement had begun to develop the seeds of a policy for manufacturing development.

The new government, composed of an alliance which included the organised union movement, accordingly sought to develop a more diversified economy – one that was less dependent on the export of raw materials. Manufacturing growth, and increased manufactured exports in particular, were seen as critical to future economic prospects and assumed central stage in government's economic policy.

Manufacturing performance post-1994

This section provides a brief review of the performance of South African manufacturing industry in the period after 1994. In order to provide some comparative perspective, South Africa's manufacturing performance is assessed against that of Brazil.

Manufacturing output

Measured in rands, manufacturing output (manufacturing value added – MVA) rose slowly after 1995 (see Table 22.1). The growth rate accelerated after 2000 and peaked in 2008. Following the global recession, there was a significant decline in MVA until 2010 after which recovery has been slow, so that in 2012 MVA was only marginally above that for 2008. The compound growth rate for the entire period was 2 per cent.

Measured in constant US dollars, the average per annum growth rate for South Africa MVA was 2.4 per cent. This compares with 1.7 per cent in Brazil. However, over the period 2000–2012, MVA per annum growth in South Africa (2.4 per cent) was somewhat less than that of Brazil (2.7 per cent).

Table 22.1 Manufacturing value added, 1995–2012

(R million – constant 2005 prices)						
1995	*2000*	*2005*	*2008*	*2010*	*2011*	*2012*
197,156	222,661	259,101	297,889	282,509	292,733	299,705
($US million – current prices)						
29,010	23,025	38,442	42,899	44,731	49,347	41,895

Source: Statistics South Africa (2014).

Note: Deflator Producer Price Index P1200002 for domestic output of South Africa industry group/manufacturing/index 2000 = 100/monthly.

Table 22.2 Manufacturing value added as a share of GDP, 1995–2012 (constant 2005 prices)

1995	*2000*	*2005*	*2008*	*2010*	*2011*	*2012*
20.2	17.3	16.5	15.1	12.9	11.5	11.1

Source: Statistics South Africa (2014).

MVA as a share of GDP

Value added output growth in manufacturing has been consistently lower than GDP growth. As a result, apart from a very slight increase in 2002 and 2003, MVA as a share of GDP declined consistently from 20 per cent in 1995 to a little over 11 per cent in 2012 (see Table 22.2).

According to World Bank data, in 2010 manufacturing's share of GDP in South Africa was approximately 15 per cent – which was similar to that of Brazil (World Bank, 2014).

Manufacturing employment

Manufacturing employment in South Africa peaked in the second quarter of 1996 at 1.456 million. With the exception of the years of strong economic growth, 2006–2008, when there was a small increase in manufacturing employment, the absolute number of employees in manufacturing has declined consistently. In the last quarter of 2012, manufacturing employment in South Africa was 1.154 million – a decline of 21 per cent from its peak level (Statistics South Africa, 2012).

In sharp contrast with South Africa, despite experiencing similar rates of growth in manufacturing output, manufacturing employment in Brazil, 1996–2009, increased significantly – by an average of 3 per cent per annum. Over the same period, manufacturing employment in South Africa declined significantly – by an average of 1 per cent per annum (Kaplan, 2015).

Manufacturing investment

After some initial uncertainty with the ending of apartheid, fixed capital formation in manufacturing increased but a slow rate. The rate of increase picked up after 2002 and then increased significantly to peak in 2008 at levels twice that of 1995. There was a steep fall thereafter (see Table 22.3). There has been some increase since 2010 but gross fixed capital formation per annum in manufacturing in 2012 was still 8 per cent lower than in 2008. Reflecting gross

Table 22.3 Gross fixed capital formation: manufacturing, 1995–2012

(R million – constant 2005 prices)						
1995	*2000*	*2005*	*2008*	*2010*	*2011*	*2012*
36,917	39,922	54,838	73,886	59,448	65,698	68,271

($US million – current prices)						
5,962	4,391	8,136	12,886	11,204	14,112	12,246

Source: South African Reserve Bank, Quarterly.

capital formation, manufacturing fixed capital stock rose slowly from 1995 to 2005, and then rose significantly until 2008, after which it declined. Manufacturing fixed capital stock in 2012 was slightly lower than in 2008.

Manufacturing exports

Expressed in current US dollars, manufacturing exports increased steadily at a generally increasing rate to 2008. This was followed by a short but sharp contraction in 2009 with manufacturing exports reviving from 2010 (Table 22.4). In current US dollars, manufacturing exports are currently approximately four and a half times larger than they were in the mid-1990s. This rate of increase was a little lower than Brazil.

Expressed in constant rands, the increase in manufacturing exports is somewhat less. In constant rands, exports in 2010 are a little more than three and a half times the value of exports in 1995. Expressed either in dollars or in rands, manufacturing export growth has been much more rapid than growth in MVA. Consequently, South African manufacturing exports as a share of manufacturing output rose steadily and consistently since 1995 (see Table 22.5). Currently the export ratio is approaching one-third – more than twice the ratio in 1995.

Export composition

High technology exports as a share of manufactured exports in South Africa are low and have been declining. In the first half of the 1990s, the share of high technology exports in manufactured exports was higher in South Africa than in Brazil. By contrast, in the period 2006–2010,

Table 22.4 Manufacturing exports, 1995–2012 (current $US millions)

1995	*2000*	*2005*	*2008*	*2010*	*2011*	*2012*
12,915	18,820	33,620	50,059	45,731	54,038	57,185

Source: South African Customs and Excise (2014).

Table 22.5 Manufacturing exports as a share of manufacturing output, 1995–2012

1995	*2000*	*2005*	*2008*	*2010*	*2011*	*2012*
15	22	23	29	26	28	31

Sources: Statistics South Africa (2014); South African Customs and Excise (2014).

high technology products constituted 5.3 per cent of South African manufactured exports compared with 12 per cent for Brazil (see Table 22.6).

At the other end of technological sophistication, ores and metals constitute almost one-third of all merchandise exports for South Africa. The share of South Africa's merchandise exports made up of ores and metals has increased significantly over the last decade – partly a reflection of rising international prices for ores and metals, but also a reflection of the slow growth of other merchandise exports. This is significantly higher than exports of ores and minerals from Brazil which have averaged about 18 per cent of the total in recent years (see Table 22.7).

The conclusion is clear. South African manufactured exports have performed poorly in terms of overall growth and in terms of the composition and the sophistication of South Africa's exports in aggregate are below those of comparator countries such as Brazil.[2]

Productivity

Declining numbers in manufacturing employment combined with a moderate increase in manufacturing output has resulted in a significant increase in labour productivity. Average labour productivity is estimated to be higher in South Africa than in Mexico, Malaysia, China, Brazil and Poland and comparable to Chile (World Bank, 2010). Growth in labour productivity in South African manufacturing has also been driven by capital deepening, as manufacturing firms have become more capital intensive and the composition of manufacturing output has more capital-intensive sectors. South Africa has one of the highest K/L ratios compared with similar middle income countries – including China and Brazil (World Bank, 2009: 10). Controlling for factor intensity, labour productivity in South Africa is lower than for most other comparator countries.

Total Factor Productivity (TFP) in South African manufacturing has been increasing but aggregate TFP growth in South Africa generally lags its competitors (Clarke *et al.*, 2007: World Bank, 2011). Indeed since as far back as the 1970s, TFP growth in South African manufacturing has generally been lower than for comparable countries (Edwards and Golub, 2004; Van Dijk, 2003). Since 'within firm' TFP in South Africa is higher than for Brazil or China, this is a result of much lower 'allocative efficiency'.[3] By implication, less productive firms in South Africa retain large market shares.

Table 22.6 High technology exports as a share of manufactured exports (percentages): South Africa and Brazil, 1994–2010

	1994	*1998*	*2002*	*2006*	*2010*
Brazil	4.6	9.41	16.52	12.08	11.21
South Africa	4.88	8.75	5.16	6.46	4.28

Source: World Bank (2014).

Table 22.7 Ores and metals exports as a percentage of merchandise exports: South Africa and Brazil, 2000–2010

	2000	*2005*	*2010*
Brazil	–	8.6	17.8
South Africa	10.8	22.4	32.7

Source: World Bank (2014).

Size composition

South African manufacturing is highly concentrated – the largest four firms accounting for more than half of output in almost half of the main product groupings. There are indications that the level of concentration is high by comparison with other countries and that concentration is associated with higher pricing and lower levels of innovation (Fedderke *et al.*, 2006). Economic concentration may have been increasing. Between 2000 and 2010 the share of employment in all firms with less than 10 employees fell by almost 12 percentage points, or approximately 25 per cent (from 46.6 per cent of employment to 35 per cent). The shares of self-employed and those working in small firms are far lower in South Africa than in Brazil – and the share of employment in large firms consequently greater (Magruder, 2012). This suggests that there are far fewer new entrants in South Africa by comparison with Brazil. The lack of small firms is an important factor contribution to low employment absorption. Moreover, the consequent low levels of competition are likely to entrench the existing structures of industry and have a negative impact on productivity.

Sectoral composition

The outstanding feature in the changing sectoral composition of the South African manufacturing industry has been the constant decline in the share of the labour-intensive textiles, clothing and footwear sectors. In 1990, these sectors accounted for 7.72 per cent of total South African manufacturing production; however, by 2012 this had dropped to only 2.5 per cent, a significantly lower share than in Brazil (see Table 22.8).

This sector has seen significant declines in output and exports and accounts for more than half of employment loss for the manufacturing sector as a whole. There has also been a lesser decline in the share of other labour-intensive sectors, notably wood and furniture. By contrast, two scale- and capital-intensive sectors have significantly increased their share of manufacturing output – petroleum, chemicals, rubber and plastics most notably, and motor vehicles.

Table 22.8 Sectoral composition: manufacturing sectors sales as a percentage of total manufacturing sales, 1990–2012

	1990	*1995*	*2000*	*2005*	*2010*	*2011*	*2012*
Food and beverage	19.06	18.91	16.41	16.73	19.6	19.9	20.4
Textiles, clothing, leather, footwear	7.72	7.52	5.64	4.2	3.1	2.7	2.5
Wood, wood products, paper, publishing, printing	9.09	10.11	9.27	8.8	8.4	7.9	7.8
Petroleum, chemicals, rubber, plastics	19.4	18.91	18.37	18.5	22.14	22.6	24.4
Glass, non-metallic mineral products	3.8	3.28	2.94	3.4	3.17	3.2	3.1
Iron and steel, non-ferrous metals, metal products and machinery	22.5	20.89	24.4	24.7	22.35	22.2	21.4
Electrical machinery	3.1	3.17	3.1	2.6	3.08	3.1	2.9
Radio, television and communication, professional equipment	1.69	1.36	1.46	1.3	1.09	1	1
Motor vehicles, parts, other transport equipment	9.07	11.73	13.25	15.3	12.75	13	12.2
Furniture and other manufacturing	4.57	4.13	5.17	4.6	4.33	4.3	4.1

Source: Statistics South Africa (2014).

The green economy

One area where manufacturing is expanding is in relation to the green economy. While this sector is currently very small, it has considerable potential for growth. A recent report provides estimates of possible future net direct job creation in the formal economy across a range of activities including manufacturing. Considerable employment gains are expected in the production of: electrical vehicles and related batteries; recycled materials; solar photovoltaic components; and biofuels. Manufacturing segments with high employment potential include suppliers of: pyrolysis/gasification plants; components for wind farms; insulation materials, lighting and windows; and solar water heaters.

In the longer term (i.e. to 2025) the estimate is that there is the potential for the creation of an additional 46,049 jobs in manufacturing (Maia *et al.*, 2011: 8). By far the largest increase in employment (and hence output) will occur in services – notably in natural resource management which will add over 250,000 jobs. While this is a significant number of new manufacturing jobs, it is not sufficient to have any substantive impact on the downward trend of manufacturing employment in the aggregate. Moreover, the report has stressed that competition from imported manufactures will be fierce. Realising the predicted employment gains in manufacturing may require infant industry support, combined with access to competitively priced inputs such as steel, strong relations with global technology partners and support for R&D (Maaia *et al.*, 2011: 9–10).

Conclusion

In the post-apartheid era, the South African manufacturing industry has been characterised by very moderate growth in output and investment. Export performance has been a little better with export orientation increasing significantly. However, export orientation is below that of comparator countries and export sophistication has not advanced as rapidly as its competitors. The outstanding feature has been the consistent decline in manufacturing employment.

The sectoral composition of South African manufacturing has been changing with a persistent decline in the share of the labour-intensive sectors. Employment loss has been concentrated in these more labour-intensive sectors, but all manufacturing sectors are characterised by growing capital intensity. As a result the number of jobs generated per additional unit of manufacturing output has been consistently declining (Black and Gerwel, 2014: 250). There will very likely be a considerable expansion of green manufacturing, but the impact on aggregate manufacturing employment and output is not likely to be significant.

Trade and industrial policy post-1994

South Africa's offer to the General Agreement on Tariffs and Trade (GATT) was negotiated by the tripartite National Economic Forum in which the African National Congress (ANC) and Congress of South African Trade Unions (COSATU) actively participated. In government, the ANC continued the process of tariff liberalisation. The number of tariff lines was substantially reduced; ad valorem tariffs were substituted for specific tariffs and the number of tariff bands was reduced. The simple average import tariff fell from 21.4 per cent (inclusive of import surcharges) in 1994 to 8 per cent in early 2000. In manufacturing, effective protection declined from 48 per cent in 1993 to 12.7 per cent in 2004 (Edwards, 2005).

Industrial policy in the new government was much influenced by the work of the Industrial Strategy Project (ISP) – a policy-oriented research activity composed of a number of progressive university-based researchers and supported by the major trade union federation (COSATU) which formulated a new industrial policy. The ISP stressed, in particular, that tariff liberalisation, while necessary, would subject manufacturing to much enhanced competition for which they were ill-equipped. A number of policies were advocated, principally supply-side measures designed to enhance efficiency and productivity. "Measures aimed at strengthening underlying supply-side capacities are vital accompaniments to trade liberalisation. Indeed, trade reform should be presented as part of a package for which supply-side measures are the core component" (Joffe *et al.*, 1995: 51).

Supply-side measures included programmes to enhance efficiency and exports in a number of sectors. Two sectors were selected for special support. The first, enjoying by far the most extensive support measures, was the automobile industry. The second was clothing and textiles. Support was in the form of a rebate on imports that could be earned by exporters. These two sectors continued to receive high levels of protection.[4]

A number of support measures were also introduced for training and R&D which could be accessed by all firms, including firms in sectors other than manufacturing. South Africa had the lowest prices globally for electricity and low electricity prices were a major support to energy-intensive manufacturing and manufacturing activities downstream of minerals, and to mineral extraction processes in particular (namely beneficiation). Finally, a number of investment subsidies were provided. For small and medium-sized firms, investment subsidies were initially directed to manufacturing, but this was later extended to other sectors in the Small and Medium Enterprise Development Programme. For larger firms, there was initially a tax holiday scheme for up to six years. The tax holiday scheme was followed by the Strategic Investment Programme (SIP) which provided an investment allowance to large firms. The Critical Infrastructure Programme provided support for firms investing in new infrastructure.

A major objective of policy was to limit the concentration of economic power. A new competition regime was introduced in 1998. Mergers above a certain size had to be pre-approved. Abuses of dominance and 'restrictive vertical practices' were subject to heavy penalties and the competition authorities were empowered to initiate investigations.

Trade liberalisation together with supply-side-oriented industrial policy did not produce the results that were hoped for. Trade liberalisation may well have produced benefits – enhancing exports (Edwards and Lawrence, 2008) and consumer welfare (Daniels and Edwards, 2007) and limiting the pricing power of large firms (Aghion *et al.*, 2008). But, as outlined previously, manufacturing output and export growth were sluggish, manufacturing declined as a share of GDP and, most importantly, manufacturing employment declined significantly and consistently. Opposition to further trade liberalisation mounted, particularly on the part of the unions who argued that it adversely impacted on employment. Effectively trade reform came to a complete halt. The prevailing supply-side industrial policy was seen to be ineffective in spurring growth or exports and, in particular, in limiting employment loss. Most telling was employment loss in the labour-intensive sectors. Clothing and textiles especially saw a major reduction in employment and was responsible for half the total employment loss in manufacturing – and this despite continued tariff protection and considerable subsidies to export (Kaplan, 2015).

The policy response: The Industrial Policy Action Plan (IPAP)

In August 2007, the Ministry of Trade and Industry launched the National Industrial Policy Framework (NIPF). This broad statement of strategy was followed by the Industrial Policy Action Plan (IPAP). Successive IPAPs – the latest IPAP is for the period 2013/14 to 2015/16 – have detailed the specific measures to be taken in order to meet the objectives set out in the NIPF.

Objectives

The original NIPF set out the following objectives:

- diversification into non-traditional tradable goods and services;
- intensification of industrialisation and movement towards a knowledge economy;
- promotion of a more labour absorbing industrial path;
- broader based industrialisation with greater participation of those historically disadvantaged and poorer regions;
- contributing to industrial development of the African continent (DTI, 2007: 2–3).

However, the objectives of industrial policy have evolved and shifted over time. For example, when announcing the next version of the IPAP in Parliament in 2010, the Minister of Trade and Industry spelt out a number of different objectives including the diversification and growth of exports, improving the trade balance, building long term industrial capability, stimulating domestic technology development, catalysing skill development and the creation of 2,447,000 indirect and direct jobs over 10 years (Politicsweb, 2014).

In addition to the usual objectives of industrial policy as applied in other countries, notably the Asian new industrialised countries, the IPAP has added employment creation. Indeed, employment creation has been treated as the single most important objective of the IPAP. This is not surprising given South Africa's massive unemployment problem and a near universal social consensus that failure to grow employment significantly will threaten the very social fabric of the society. The emphasis on employment creation runs through each of the major policies advocated in the IPAP.

Policies

While there has been some evolution in policy instruments, successive IPAPs have seen seven "sets of policies … [as] … critical to achieving a scaled-up industrial policy and a shift towards strengthening the productive side of the economy in general" (DTI, 2011: 38):

1 articulation between macro- and micro-economic policies;
2 industrial financing;
3 procurement – public and private;
4 trade and tariffs;
5 competition and regulation;
6 skills and innovation;
7 sector strategies.

Articulation between macro- and micro-economic policies

The IPAP has seen favourable macroeconomic policies as fundamental to its success. This entails competitive and stable exchange rates and competitive real interest rates (DTI, 2011: 40). However, while it is an 'open secret' that there has been conflict between the DTI on the one hand and Treasury and the South African Reserve Bank on the other as concerns the appropriate level of the exchange rate, the South African Reserve Bank has shown no signs of taking active measures to lower the nominal exchange rate.

The most recent IPAP has dropped the emphasis on macroeconomic policy. However, the latest IPAP shows that real interest rates in South Africa were *below* the average for developing and transition economies for half of the years between 2004 and 2010. In addition the nominal exchange rate has declined very significantly without there being any apparent significant export response. Indeed, there is considerable evidence that declines in the nominal exchange rate may rapidly lead to domestic price increases and have only a minor impact on the level of exports (Edwards and Lawrence, 2008).

Industrial financing

The IPAP has seen the cost of financing for industrial investment as being prohibitively high, particularly in relation to long term finance. Finance, it is argued, has been increasingly attracted into consumption-driven service sectors or 'low risk' industries.[5] To compensate for the financial sector's reluctance to lend and/or high price of lending the IPAP has included a number of incentives intended to encourage capital investment.[6] These instruments include:

- The 12i Tax incentive: announced in 2010, according to the DTI, the programme has supported 13 projects with an investment value of R21.7 billion. These projects are within the priority sectors identified in the IPAP.
- The Manufacturing Competitiveness Enhancement Programme (MCEP): introduced in 2012, R5.8 billion over three years has been allocated to fund allowances for manufacturing investment. By October 2013, more than R3 billion had been approved, supporting 436 manufacturing entities and investments of R13 billion.
- The Automotive Investment Scheme (AIS): the AIS, like the 12i Tax Incentive, was introduced in 2010. The AIS provides a cash-back subsidy of 20–30 per cent of the investment.
- Loans from the Industrial Development Corporation (IDC) at below market rates.

However, there are no empirical studies that provide support for the contention that there is a failure of the banking sector to advance funding for industry, other than for upstream ventures. Moreover, South African manufacturing firms fund by far the largest part of any expansion using internal sources – retained earnings. All the indications are that companies are currently flush with cash (Thornton, 2013). The reason that companies are not investing therefore has very little to do with (the lack of) access to capital from the financial sector. There are a host of other reasons – uncertainties and low demand both domestically and abroad, are of far more significance.

While incentives for capital investment will not significantly impact on the magnitude of their investment, incentives will affect the composition of investment. Cheaper and easier access to capital will 'bias' investment toward capital intensity and away from employment. This factor substitution of capital for labour will be intensified if, at the same time as incentives are offered on the capital side, there is a 'tightening of the labour market.' The labour market has indeed been tightened, particularly as government has sought to regulate labour brokers and temporary and part-time employment.

Government procurement

Increased local procurement, and specifically government procurement, has been a central thrust of South Africa's industrial policy. Tenders for public procurements embodying in excess of US$10 million of imported content will have up-front domestic production and local supplier development requirements (DTI, 2011: 46–47). Large 'strategic procurement fleets' have been identified, such as locomotives, railway wagons, coaches, buses, pharmaceuticals and nuclear electricity. Provisions have been made to ensure that public procurement supports the growth of local productive sectors. Projects undertaken by organisations such as the Development Bank of South Africa must similarly be aligned such that they support local production. Preferential procurement regulations came into effect on 7 December 2011. These regulations require that all public entities procure locally made products at a specified level if these have been designated and listed.[7] Eight 'sectors' have been designated: rolling stock; power pylons; bus bodies; canned/processed vegetables; textiles, clothing and leather; set-top boxes for digital TV migration; pharmaceuticals and furniture (DTI, 2014: 35).

Public procurement is aligned to the Customised Sector Programmes (CSP) – the sectors that are selected for policy support. The thrust here is to enhance demand for local firms and to limit imports. This additional source of local demand is seen as a key stimulus to enhancing local production. For example, in respect of the IPAP's first prioritised industry cluster (namely metal fabrication, capital equipment and transport equipment) the potential growth in local demand via procurement is seen as the main source of growth: "Leveraging the public infrastructure programme presents the single largest opportunity to stimulate the industry through reducing import leakage of the capital and operational expenditure programmes of State Owned Enterprises (SOE) and all spheres of government" (DTI, 2011: 36). Thus, internal demand rather than exports is seen as the basis for further development and public procurement is the key instrument designed to drive internal demand.

Significantly, state procurement is not linked to enhanced export performance on the part of those awarded procurement contracts. An International Panel, composed principally of academics from the Kennedy School at Harvard University, which was invited by the National Treasury to review South Africa's growth performance advocated procurement strategy as an instrument for the development of this sector, but only in so far as it was integrally linked to enhancing exports. The Panel stated that

> it is critical that the exercise of this discretion [to favour local firms in public procurement] not be used in an inward-looking mode in order to lower the import content of the public investment program. The idea is to subsidise the industry-level learning by doing by creating a domestic supply that can become a new export activity once the ASGI-SA investments are rolled back. Therefore, the export plans of the local suppliers should be taken into consideration when qualifying domestic suppliers.
>
> (Hausmann and Klinger, 2006: 49)

Inadequate and high cost infrastructure is a key binding constraint on business growth – and more particularly on export growth. Of particular importance here is electricity provision, but also transport, especially rail, and ports. Local procurement regulations are likely to result in delays and/or higher costs and/or reconfigurations of provision in order to accommodate local suppliers. The effect of any delays or increases in cost would be to further tighten a key constraint that confronts business in general and exporters in particular.

Trade and tariffs

Tariffs are seen as "instruments of industrial policy that have implications for employment, investment, technology and productivity growth. Tariff policy should be decided on a sector-by-sector basis dictated by the imperatives of sector strategies" (DTI, 2011: 53; DTI, 2014: 43).

The IPAP has promised selected decreases in tariffs on intermediate inputs into manufacturing and other sectors. But, there have also to be what the IPAP terms 'Developmental Trade Policies' providing for "ongoing scope for industries to apply to the International Trade Administration (ITAC) for selective tariff increases on products with scope for significant potential creation/ retention of decent jobs and import replacement and 'water' between bound and applied rates" (DTI, 2011: 56; DTI, 2014: 43). There is a clear thrust in the IPAP therefore to protectionist trade policy – attempting to secure the internal market for local firms in the interests of job creation. What is omitted in the criteria for deciding on tariff increases is the likely adverse impact on exports as a result of higher tariffs.

Moreover, setting tariffs on a case by case basis is likely to encourage industry lobbying and to add further significant complexity to South Africa's already very complex tariff structure and could thus further constrain export growth. A number of industries have recently secured higher tariffs, principally on the grounds of increasing or safeguarding jobs. But these increases are at the expense of consumer welfare, and will raise the overall cost structures, thus further constraining export growth.

Competition and regulation

South African manufacturing is characterised by high levels of economic concentration. High levels of concentration have resulted in firms having considerable pricing power and have inhibited competition, productivity growth and new firm entry and imposed costs on consumers (Aghion *et al.*, 2008; Fedderke, 2013).

The IPAP sees three areas as 'problematic': concentration in the supply of certain strategic inputs into manufacturing such as carbon, stainless steel, chemical polymers, fertilisers and aluminium; concentration in respect of wage goods, particularly food; and concentration in respect of firms tendering for the public infrastructure programme. These three areas will form the core focus for the work of the Competition Commission (DTI, 2011: 63–64).

The IPAP also sees a continued active focus of the work of the Competitions Commission combined with annual reporting on the following: intermediate industrial and energy-intensive products, such as steel, chemicals, coal, fuel and cement; food and agro-processing; banking and infrastructure and construction (DTI, 2011: 64).

A significant part of the cost pressures currently impacting South African manufacturers results from public entities that have an effective monopoly – fixed line telecommunications, electricity generation and airport services, for example. These enterprises are not subject to price reviews on the part of the competitions authorities and where there are regulators, in the face of opposition from the public entities, they have often been reluctant to lower prices or take measures to enhance competition.

Skills and innovation

The IPAP sees inadequacies in the existent supply of skills. Of particular significance has been the decline in the training of artisans. The IPAP aims for a National Artisan Development Programme (NADP), "a centralised plan for artisan development with medium-to long term targets, action and funding plans" (DTI, 2011: 70) to rapidly increase the supply of artisans for the IPAP priority sectors. There will also be delivery of specialised intermediate and high level skills for the IPAP priority sectors entailing delivery partnership agreements between the DTI, the Department of Higher Education and Training, state-owned enterprises, firms and institutions of higher education (DTI, 2011: 71). The latest IPAP has three programmes for skills development – customised artisan training programmes in support of priority IPA sectors (see below); establishment of industry skill hubs (in pilot phase) and support for industrial centres of excellence (DTI, 2014: 63–64).

South African manufacturing, and particularly export manufacturing, is increasingly skill intensive. The shortage of skills curtails further development and employment of those with lesser skills. The IPAP programmes for artisanal skills and for skilling programmes for the priority sectors will go some way to addressing this issue. However, the key clearly lies with education and training policies more broadly and hence outside the scope of the DTI and of industrial policy.

Earlier IPAPs did not have explicit policies to advance innovation and technological advance in the manufacturing sector. The most recent IPAP lays much more stress on innovation and the commercialisation of new knowledge. Further support is promised for existent programmes to support skills development in innovation; commercialisation and the extension of Technology Platforms which provide technology support across a range of products, processes and services (DTI, 2014: 65–67). Sectoral case studies cite the skills shortage as the key constraint on technological development and firm level advance – and this is confirmed by statistical data (Goldberg *et al.*, 2011: 70). As with skills in general, the DTI and industrial policy exert only a marginal impact on supply.

Sector strategies

The NIPF identified "five broad *sectoral groupings* which are seen as having considerable potential for sectoral diversification: natural-resource based sectors; medium technology sectors (including downstream mineral beneficiation); advanced manufacturing sectors; labour-intensive manufacturing sectors; tradable services sectors" (DTI, 2007: 33). These so-called sectoral groupings cover most of the manufacturing sector. The IPAPs have accordingly 'targeted' a very wide range of sectors, and each successive IPAP has added additional sectoral targets. For example, the IPAP for 2010/11–2012/13 added metal fabrication, capital and transport equipment; sectors particularly arising from large public investments; 'green' and energy-saving industries; agroprocessing, linked to food security and food pricing imperatives; nuclear; advanced materials and aerospace (DTI, 2011: 79). Further additions in the latest IPAP include: cosmetics; creative industries; boatbuilding and associated services; software and pre-payment meter manufacturing (DTI, 2014).

This clearly encompasses a very wide range of sectors with yearly additions. In effect, almost everything is included. According to data provided by the IPAP, the sectors selected represent over 83 per cent of manufacturing employment (own calculation). The danger of selecting so broad a range of sectors is that it severely stretches government resources and capacities. There are a myriad of policy initiatives and programmes, few of which command significant resources and the prospect therefore is that each of the sector programmes lacks critical mass and is therefore likely to have only a marginal impact at best.

While support has been extended to almost the entire manufacturing sector, the auto and components sectors have been the principal recipient of direct support. Treasury calculations are that support is of the order of R17 billion per annum – close to two-thirds of support given to the entire manufacturing sector. Autos and components are scale and capital intensive with relatively low employment multipliers.

Conclusion

South African manufacturing has enjoyed only a very moderate growth in output combined with a consistent decline in manufacturing employment. This is despite the fact that South Africa has an active industrial policy with the declared objectives of enhancing output and particularly employment.

Clearly a number of factors, outside of the 'reach' of policy, are at play in constraining manufacturing growth and employment creation. These currently include demand constraints, as markets for South African manufactured goods have grown only slowly – particularly the European Union, and cost constraints – especially sharp increases in the costs of electricity. However, industrial policy is not without impact. Is industrial policy misdirected? Could some aspects of South Africa's current industrial policy, even if inadvertently, be contributing to the problem rather than the solution?

The short to medium term forecasts are for very moderate economic growth in the South African economy. The domestic market is unlikely to provide a major impetus to output growth in the manufacturing sector. The key to the growth of manufacturing output and employment hence lies in improved export performance. While exports are supported by the IPAP, and a number of policies are directed explicitly at enhancing export growth, much of the policy thrust is currently directed at the domestic market. This focus on the domestic market is especially evident in respect of local procurement measures and a number of the sector support programmes. Tariff policy is particularly constraining of manufacturing exports. More policy attention could be given to enhancing manufacturing exports – tackling the constraints faced by exporters and the ways in which current policies may indeed be retarding the growth of manufactured exports.

As we have seen, the trajectory of South Africa's manufacturing growth has not been demanding of employment in regard to unskilled and semi-skilled labour. Moreover, the capital and skill intensity of manufacturing growth is increasing. A number of the policies under the IPAP serve to lower the costs of capital – concessionary finance and investment incentives, in particular. While access to some of these supports requires employment guarantees, these are extremely difficult to monitor and enforce. Direct supports are principally focused on vehicles and auto components and have recently been extended to other transport equipment – all of which have a low unskilled and semi-skilled employment multiplier. Lowering capital costs and providing the largest share of financial support to less labour demanding sectors may serve to exacerbate the capital and skill demanding trajectory of South African manufacturing growth. This is particularly the case if, as is the current situation, there are no compensating policies designed to lower unit labour costs or otherwise increase flexibility in the labour market.

Employment losses have been particularly high in labour-intensive manufacturing sectors. Improvement in output and employment in these labour-intensive sectors is likely to require modifications in wages, labour regulations and working practices. The high and growing levels of capital intensity of the South African manufacturing industry in aggregate further indicate that labour market reform may be a necessary accompaniment to government's industrial policy if that policy is to achieve its ambitious targets for employment creation.

The skills constraint has curtailed the further development of skill-intensive sectors and activities. Skilled and unskilled labour are complementary, i.e. enhancing skills allows for more activities to develop that will also employ unskilled or semi-skilled workers. In particular, skill shortages limit the entry of new firms, further curtailing employment growth. Thus, the skills shortage has also limited employment opportunities for the unskilled and semi-skilled. Moreover, the skills shortage is a major factor resulting in increasing inequality in South African manufacturing employment – the significant and rising earnings differential within the manufacturing sector as between a growing supply of unskilled and semi-skilled workers on the one hand and supply-constrained skilled, professional and managerial workers on the other.

Hence labour market reform and measures to address the skills shortages are the necessary, indeed indispensable, accompaniments to an industrial policy that seeks simultaneously to enhance manufacturing growth and the unskilled and semi-skilled employment intensity of growth and so reduce earning differentials and inequality.

Notes

1 My thanks to Krzysztof Wojciechowicz for supplying me with the data on South African manufacturing and to Stephen Gelb for earlier comments on the chapter.

2 An examination of South Africa's export performance concluded that "in terms of export volumes, value and sophistication, South Africa has been a relatively poor performer" (Hausmann and Klinger, 2006: 12).

3 The aggregate TFP is a market-share-weighted mean of the 'within-firm' TFP of individual enterprises. If 'within-firm' TFP is strongly correlated with market share, i.e. allocative efficiency is high, then the aggregate TFP is also high.

4 Currently, the following tariff duties apply: textiles (up to 22 per cent); clothing (up to 45 per cent); footwear (up to 30 per cent); autos (25 per cent); and auto components (22 per cent).

5 "The private financial sector in South Africa is not adequately aggregating savings and distributing them towards productive fixed investment in the economy. Inherent market failures exist, the most critical of which is the asset–liability mismatch. The short-term nature of the source of funding, mainly short-term deposits and short-term capital inflows manifests in impatient capital eager to fund either established relatively 'low risk' industries (e.g. upstream capital and energy-intensive industries) or industries achieving profitability within a short period of time (i.e. consumption driven services)" (DTI, 2014: 40).

6 "[T]he role of public industrial financing is to channel capital into productive investments that directly and indirectly generate sustainable jobs and value-addition" (DTI, 2011: 42).

7 "[A]ll bidders and potential suppliers in the designated sectors will have to meet set minimum local content requirements. Suppliers are required to submit both a 'declaration of local content' and proof of verification (certificate/report from an accredited verification authority)" (DTI, 2014: 37).

References

Aghion, P., Braun, M. and Fedderke, J. 2008. Competition and Productivity Growth in South Africa. *Economics of Transition*. 16: 741–768.

Black, A. and Gerwel, H. 2014. Shifting the Growth Path to Achieve Employment Intensive Growth in South Africa. *Development Southern Africa*. 31 (2): 241–256.

Clarke, G., Habyarimana, J., Ingram, M., Kaplan, D. and Ramachandran, V. 2007. *An Assessment of the Investment Climate in South Africa*. Washington, DC: World Bank.

Daniels, R. and Edwards, L. 2007. The Benefit–Incidence of Tariff Liberalisation in South Africa. *Journal for Studies in Economics and Econometrics*, 31 (2): 69–88.

DTI. 2007. *A National Industrial Policy Framework*. Pretoria: Department of Trade and Industry.

DTI. 2011. *Industrial Policy Action Plan 2010/11–2012/13 Economic Sectors and Employment Cluster* (February). Pretoria: Department of Trade and Industry.

DTI. 2014. *Industrial Policy Action Plan 2013/14–2015/16 Economic Sectors and Employment Cluster* (February). Pretoria: Department of Trade and Industry.

Edwards, L. 2005. Has South Africa Liberalized Its Trade? *South African Journal of Economics*. 73 (4): 754–775.

Edwards, L. and Golub, S. S. 2004. South Africa's International Cost Competitiveness and Exports in Manufacturing. *World Development*. 32 (8): 1323–1339.

Edwards, L. and Lawrence, R. Z. 2008. South African Trade Policy Matters: Trade Performance and Trade Policy. *Economics of Transition*. 16(4): 585–608.

Fedderke, J. 2013. *Competition, Industrial Structure and Economic Growth*. Economic Research Southern Africa Working Paper 330 (February) – accessible at www.econrsa.org/node/659

Fedderke, J., Kularatne, C. and Mariotti, M. 2006. Mark-Up Pricing in South African Industry. *Journal of African Economies*. 16 (1): 28–69.

Feinstein, C.H. 2005. *An Economic History of South Africa: Conquest, Discrimination and Development*. Cambridge: Cambridge University Press.

Goldberg, I., Kaplan, D., Kuriakose, S., Tuomi, K. and Zhang, C. 2011. *Fostering Technology Absorption in Southern African Enterprises*. Washington, DC: World Bank.

Hausmann, R. and Klinger, B. 2006. *South Africa's Export Predicament*. Working Paper No, 129 Center for International Development. Cambridge, MA: Harvard University.

Hirsch, A. 2005. *Season of Hope: Economic Reform Under Mandela and Mbeki*. Scottsville: University of Kwazulu-Natal Press.

Joffe, A., Kaplan, D., Kaplinsky, R. and Lewis, D. 1995. *Improving Manufacturing Performance in South Africa. Report of the Industrial Strategy Project.* Cape Town: University of Cape Town Press.

Kahn, S. B. 1987. Import Penetration and Import Demands in the South African Economy. *South African Journal of Economics.* 55 (3): 155–162.

Kaplan, D. 2015. The Structure and Performance of Manufacturing in South Africa. In Naude, W., Szirmai, A. and Haraguchi, N. (eds.). *Structural Change and Industrial Development in the BRICs.* Oxford: Oxford University Press.

Magruder, J., 2012. High Unemployment Yet Few Small Firms: The Role of Centralized Bargaining in South Africa. *American Economic Journal: Applied Economics.* 4 (3): 138–166.

Maia, J., Giordano, T., Kelder, N., Bardien, G., Bodibe, M., Du Plooy, P., Jafta, X., Jarvis, D., Kruger-Cloete, E., Kuhn, G., Lepelle, R., Makaulule. L., Mosoma, K., Neoh, S., Netshitomboni, N., Ngozo, T. and Swanepoel, J. 2011. *Green Jobs: An Estimate of the Direct Employment Potential of a Greening South African Economy.* Midrand: Development Bank of Southern Africa – accessible from http://www.dbsa.org/

Politicsweb. 2014. *National Assembly Statement on IPAP2 by Dr Rob Davies, Minister of Trade and Industry, February 18, 2010* – accessible at http://www.politicsweb.co.za/politicsweb/view/politicsweb/en/page71656?oid=161329&sn=Detail

South African Customs and Excise. 2014. *Trade Statistics* – accessible at http://www.sars.gov.za/ClientSegments/Customs-Excise/Trade-Statistics/Pages/default.aspx

South African Reserve Bank. Quarterly. *Quarterly Bulletins* – accessible at https://www.resbank.co.za/Publications/QuarterlyBulletins/Pages/QuarterlyBulletins-Home.aspx

Statistics South Africa. 2012. *Quarterly Employment Statistics (QES).* Statistical Release PO 277 – accessible at http://beta2.statssa.gov.za/publications/P0277/P0277December2012.pdf

Statistics South Africa. 2014. *Economic Time Series/ Social Statistics/ Mid-Year Population Estimates* – accessible at http://www.statssa.gov.za/timeseriesdata/main_timeseriesdata.asp

Thornton, G. 2013. *SA Businesses Sitting on Cash Piles as 'Wait and See' Phenomenon Impact M&A Activity* – accessed on 29/05/2014 at http://www.gt.co.za/news/2013/04

Van Dijk, M. 2003. South African Manufacturing Performance in International Perspective. *South African Journal of Economics.* 71 (1): 119–142.

World Bank. 2009. *South Africa: Second Investment Climate Assessment. Business Environment Issues in Shared Growth Volume 1: Summary Report* (May). Washington, DC: World Bank.

World Bank. 2010. *South Africa: Second Investment Climate Assessment. Business Environment Issues in Shared Growth. Volume 2: Full Report* (July). Washington, DC: World Bank.

World Bank. 2011. *Improving the Business Environment for Growth and Job Creation in South Africa: the Second Investment Climate Assessment.* (October): Washington, DC: World Bank.

World Bank, 2014. *World Development Indicators 2014* – accessed from www.worldbank.org

INDEX

Note: *Italic* page numbers indicate tables; **bold** indicate figures.

For Product Safety Concerns and Information please contact our EU
representative GPSR@taylorandfrancis.com Taylor & Francis Verlag GmbH,
Kaufingerstraße 24, 80331 München, Germany

Printed and bound by CPI Group (UK) Ltd, Croydon, CR0 4YY
08/05/2025
01864358-0009